Third Edition

Databases, Types, and the Relational Model

The Third Manifesto

A detailed study of the impact
of type theory on the relational
model of data, including
a comprehensive model
of type inheritance

C. J. Date

and

Hugh Darwen

ADDISON-WESLEY

An imprint of Addison Wesley Longman, Inc.

Reading, Massachusetts ● *Harlow, England* ● *Menlo Park, California*
Berkeley, California ● *Don Mills, Ontario* ● *Sydney*
Bonn ● *Amsterdam* ● *Tokyo* ● *Mexico City*

Databases, Types, and the Relational Model *The Third Manifesto*
Third Edition
C. J. Date *and* Hugh Darwen

Publisher   Greg Tobin
Acquisitions Editor   Matt Goldstein
Project Manager   Katherine Harutunian
Senior Manufacturing Buyer   Caroline Fell

Access the latest information about Addison-Wesley titles from our World Wide Web site:
http://www.aw-bc.com/computing

Many of the designations used by manufacturers and sellers to distinguish their products are claimed as trademarks. Where those designations appear in this book, and Addison-Wesley was aware of a trademark claim, the designations have been printed in initial caps or all caps.

The programs and applications presented in this book have been included for their instructional value. They have been tested with care but are not guaranteed for any particular purpose. The published does not offer any warranties or representations, nor does it accept any liabilities with respect to the programs or applications.

ISBN 0-321-39942-0
1 2 3 4 5 6 7 8 9 10—OPM—09 08 07 06

All logical differences are big differences

—Ludwig Wittgenstein

———— ♦ ♦ ♦ ♦ ♦ ————

Again I must remind you that
A Dog's a Dog—A CAT'S A CAT

—T. S. Eliot, demonstrating that
logical differences are not
everything, and nor is logic

———— ♦ ♦ ♦ ♦ ♦ ————

We would like to dedicate this book to
philosophers and poets everywhere

Contents

────── ◆ ◆ ◆ ◆ ◆ ──────

—— ◆ ◆ ◆ ◆ ◆ ——

PART II   FORMAL SPECIFICATIONS

——— ◆ ◆ ◆ ◆ ◆ ———

PART III   INFORMAL DISCUSSIONS AND EXPLANATIONS

Chapter 7   **RM Proscriptions   191**

Chapter 8   **OO Prescriptions   199**

Chapter 9   **OO Proscriptions   205**

—————— ◆◆◆◆◆ ——————

PART IV   SUBTYPING AND INHERITANCE

Chapter 15   **Multiple Inheritance with Scalar Types   317**

Chapter 16   **Inheritance with Tuple and Relation Types   337**

APPENDIXES

Appendix A   **A New Relational Algebra   361**

Preface

This is a textbook on database management. It is based on an earlier book by the same authors, *Foundation for Future Database Systems: The Third Manifesto* (Addison-Wesley, 2000), but it has been thoroughly revised—indeed, completely rewritten—from start to finish. Part of our reason for wanting to revise it was to make it more suitable as a textbook (the earlier book, by contrast, was quite terse and formal and not very easy to read); in particular, most chapters now include a set of exercises, solutions to which can be found in the Solutions Manual at the Web site (see later in this preface). However, we have naturally taken the opportunity to incorporate many other changes as well, including numerous clarifications, a certain amount of restructuring, many more examples, and—we regret to have to say—quite a few corrections also.

Like its predecessor, the book is organized around the ideas of *The Third Manifesto*. As Chapter 1 explains in more detail, *The Third Manifesto*—the *Manifesto* for short—is a proposal for a foundation for data and database management systems (DBMSs); it can be seen as an abstract blueprint for the design of a DBMS and the language interface to such a DBMS. In particular, it serves as a basis for a model of type inheritance, also discussed in this book. The overall structure of the book is thus as follows. First of all, it is divided into four major parts:

I.   Preliminaries
II. Formal Specifications
III. Informal Discussions and Explanations
IV. Subtyping and Inheritance

To elaborate briefly:

■   Part I (three chapters) sets the scene by explaining in general terms what the *Manifesto* is all about and why we wrote it. It also contains an informal overview of both the relational model and a theory of types. We recommend that you read these chapters fairly carefully before moving on to later parts of the book.

■   Part II (two chapters) is the most formal part. It contains the *Manifesto* proper and a grammar for a language based on *Manifesto* principles called **Tutorial D**. *Note:* This part of the book is provided mainly for reference purposes; it is not necessary, and probably not even a good idea, to study it exhaustively, at least not on a first reading. **Tutorial D** in particular is intended to be largely self-explanatory. Even though examples throughout the book are based on it, therefore, it should not be necessary to study the **Tutorial D** grammar in depth in order to understand those examples.

■   Part III is the real heart of the book. It consists of six chapters, one for each of the six sections of the *Manifesto* as defined in Part II. Each chapter discusses the relevant section of the *Manifesto* in detail, with examples, and thereby explains the motivations and rationale behind the formal proposals of Part II.

■   Finally, Part IV (five chapters) does for type inheritance what Parts I-III do for the *Manifesto* proper.

In addition to the foregoing, there are ten appendixes, including one in particular (Appendix J) that gives an annotated and consolidated list of references for the entire book. *Note:* References throughout the book take the form of numbers in square brackets. For example, the reference "[3]" refers to the third item in the list in Appendix J: viz., a paper by Malcolm P. Atkinson and O. Peter Buneman entitled "Types and Persistence in Database Programming Languages," published in *ACM*

Computing Surveys, Volume 19, No. 2, in June 1987.

 We defer discussion of exactly who the book is aimed at and what readers are expected to know to Chapter 1.

TO THE INSTRUCTOR

The Solutions Manual is available only to qualified instructors. Please visit Addison-Wesley's Instructor Resource Center (*www.aw.com/irc*) or contact your local Addison-Wesley Sales Representative to access the solutions.

THE *MANIFESTO* WEB SITE

The *Manifesto* Web site *www.thethirdmanifesto.com* (available to all readers of this book) contains a wealth of relevant additional material, including at the time of writing:

- Articles and papers by the authors

- Information about forthcoming seminars and presentations by C. J. Date and others

- Copies of handouts for various lectures given by Hugh Darwen

- A grammar, suitable for driving a mechanical parser, for the language **Tutorial D**

- Links to related Web sites, in particular those for certain projects related to implementation of the ideas of the *Manifesto*

The projects just mentioned include:

- *Rel:* A prototype implementation of **Tutorial D** by Dave Voorhis, of Armchair Airlines Computer Services Inc. in Canada and the University of Derby, England. We recommend Rel for use by teachers and students of relational theory. Rel is available as Open Source from *dbappbuilder.sourceforge.net.*

- *Duro:* A project by René Hartmann to create a relational database library based on the *Manifesto,* written in C. It supports a relational algebra and transactions, and is implemented using Berkeley DB. Duro is available as Open Source from *duro.sourceforge.net.*

- *D4:* D4 is the language used in Dataphor, a commercial product from Alphora, of Provo, Utah. Dataphor is the first known attempt at a commercial implementation of *The Third Manifesto.* It uses syntax similar to that of **Tutorial D.** *Note:* Because the product provides a front end to SQL, D4 deviates from the *Manifesto* by including support for SQL-style nulls, finding a conflict here between the *Manifesto* and the primary Dataphor design goal of automating application development. Nevertheless, the language does conform in many other respects and its authors say that the ideas of the *Manifesto* "have helped us achieve a level of automation that we never dreamed possible when we first set out to build the product." For further information visit *www.alphora.com.*

- D^b *("D flat"):* An amusingly named project undertaken by Peter Nicol in his final year as a student at the University of Manchester Institute of Science and Technology (UMIST) in the United Kingdom. A description is available at *www.thethirdmanifesto.com.*

There is also an e-mail discussion forum: E-mails to *ttm@thethirdmanifesto.com* are distributed to all registered participants. To register and receive information about this forum and how to use it, send an empty e-mail to *ttm-subscribe@thethirdmanifesto.com*.

ACKNOWLEDGMENTS

The number of people who have supported us over the years in our work on the *Manifesto* in general and this book in particular has now grown so large that it is no longer feasible to list them all here. With apologies to other supporters, therefore, we would just like to mention the following: Shai Berger, Peter Elderon, Maurice Gittens, Jonathan Leffler, David McGoveran, Åke Persson, Bryn Rhodes, and Andrew Sieber. All of these helped in one way or another to ensure that this book finally saw the light of day in its present form. We would also like to thank Doug Inkster, David McGoveran, Jeremy Peel, Sudha Ram of the University of Arizona, Greg Speegle of Baylor University, Junping Sun of Nova Southeastern University, Vassilis Tsotras of UC Riverside, and especially Jonathan Leffler again, for their careful and constructive comments on earlier versions of the manuscript. Finally, we would like once again to thank our wives, Lindy Date and Lindsay Darwen, for their support throughout this project, and to acknowledge our copyeditor, Elisabeth Beller, for her assistance and usual high standards of professionalism.

C. J. Date, *Healdsburg, California*
Hugh Darwen, *Shrewley, England*
2005

Part I:

PRELIMINARIES

This first part of the book consists of three introductory chapters. Chapter 1 contains background information, including in particular brief explanations of certain fundamental ideas—e.g., the distinction between *model* and *implementation*—that pervade and underlie the entire book; Chapter 2 consists of a review of the relational model; and Chapter 3 provides a detailed introduction to our theory of types. Everything else in the book builds on the material of these three chapters.

Chapter 1

Background and Overview

This book is about the foundations of database technology. It is meant as a basis for self-study or as a text to accompany an advanced course on databases. We should immediately explain that "advanced"! The book is advanced not because of the subject matter, which is mostly not that difficult, but rather because of the treatment, which is meant to be fairly rigorous and detailed (even definitive, so far as it goes): more rigorous and detailed, perhaps, than might be suitable for a first course in the subject. But it is our belief that anyone who is serious about database technology—in particular, anyone who claims to be a database professional—really ought to be familiar with this material. Professionals need to know the foundations of their field, whatever that field might be.

What makes this book different? We feel there are two key features that make it stand out: its strong focus on the relational model, and its thorough treatment of type theory (and together, of course, the relational model and type theory are precisely the foundations referred to in the previous paragraph). To amplify:

- **The relational model:** We must stress that what we are *not* doing is proposing some kind of "new" or "extended" relational model. Rather, we are concerned with what might be called the "classical" version of that model; we have tried to provide as careful and accurate a description of that classical model as we possibly can. It is true that we have taken the opportunity to dot a few *i*'s and cross a few *t*'s (i.e., to perform a few minor tidying activities here and there); however, the model as we describe it departs in no essential respects from Codd's original vision as documented in references [20-22]. (Indeed, we even toyed at one point with the idea of calling the book *A Relational Model of Data for Large Shared Data Banks.*)

- **Type theory:** Relations in the relational model have *attributes,* and those attributes in turn have *types* (also called *domains*). Thus, the relational model certainly assumes that types exist. However, it nowhere says just what those types must be, nor does it have much to say about what properties those types must have; in other words, the relational model and type theory are almost completely independent of each other (they are *orthogonal,* to use the jargon). In this book, we present a detailed theory of types that complements the relational model, and we explore some of its implications. In particular, we show that our type theory serves as a basis for a comprehensive model of type inheritance.

Who then is the book aimed at? Well, in at least one sense it is definitely not self-contained—it does assume you are seriously interested in database technology and are reasonably well acquainted with classical database theory and practice. However, we have tried to define and explain, as carefully as we could, any concepts that might be thought novel. Thus, we have tried to make the book suitable for both reference and tutorial purposes; moreover, we have clearly identified those portions of the book that are more formal in style and are provided primarily for reference. Thus, our intended audience is just about anyone with a serious interest in database technology, including but not limited to the following:

- Data and database administrators

- "Information modelers" and database designers

- Database application designers and implementers

- Database students, graduate and undergraduate

- Computer science professors specializing in database issues

- Database language designers and standardizers

- Database product implementers and other vendor personnel

- People responsible for database product evaluation and acquisition

For academic readers in particular, we should add that we have tried to present the material in a way that is clear, precise, correct, and uncluttered by the baggage—not to say mistakes—that often, sadly, seem to accompany commercial products. Thus, we believe the book provides an opportunity to acquire a firm understanding of database fundamentals without being distracted by irrelevancies.

THE THIRD MANIFESTO

This book is organized in large part around the ideas of *The Third Manifesto*. *The Third Manifesto*—the *Manifesto* for short—is a formal proposal by the present writers for a solid foundation for data and database management systems (DBMSs). Like Codd's original papers, therefore, it can be seen as an abstract blueprint for the design of a DBMS and the language interface to such a DBMS. Among other things, it lays the foundation for what we believe is the logically correct approach to integrating object and relational technologies, or in other words to building what are sometimes called *object/relational* DBMSs. (We will have more to say on this particular topic in the subsection "A Little History" later in this section.) However, we must immediately add that the ideas of the *Manifesto* are not limited to object/relational databases as such but are applicable to other kinds of databases also: for example, temporal databases, spatial databases, and databases used in connection with the World Wide Web. They are also applicable to the design of *rule engines,* also known as *business logic servers,* which some writers regard as the next generation of general-purpose DBMS products [66].

Now, you will not be surprised to hear that the *Manifesto* rests squarely in the classical relational tradition. In other words, the ideas of the *Manifesto* are in no way intended to supersede those of the relational model, nor do they do so; rather, they use the ideas of the relational model as a base on which to build. The relational model is still highly relevant to database theory and practice and will remain so for as far out as anyone can see. Thus, we see our *Manifesto* as being very much in the spirit of Codd's original work and continuing along the path he originally laid down. We are interested in evolution, not revolution.

Why Did We Write It?

We wrote the first version of the *Manifesto* [35] in the early 1990s because we were concerned about certain trends we observed in the database industry at that time (trends that, we should add, we continue to observe in some circles to this day). Among other things, we were concerned about certain well-publicized but ill-considered attempts to integrate object and relational technologies. Not that there is anything wrong with the idea of such integration per se, we hasten to add; the problem lay in the specific manner in which that integration was being attempted. Chapter 9 elaborates on this issue.

We were not the first writers to address these matters. In fact, one of our original aims in writing *The Third Manifesto* was to respond to two earlier ones (hence our choice of title):

- *The Object-Oriented Database System Manifesto* [2]

- *The Third-Generation Database System Manifesto* [130]

Like our own *Manifesto,* each of these documents proposed a basis on which to build DBMSs. However:

- The first essentially ignored the relational model. In our opinion, this flaw was more than enough to rule it out as a serious contender. In any case, it seemed to us that it failed to give firm direction.

- The second did correctly embrace the relational model, but failed to emphasize (or indeed even mention) the hopelessness of continuing to follow a commonly accepted perversion of that model—namely, SQL—in pursuit of relational ideals. In other words, it simply assumed that SQL, with all its faults, was (and is) an adequate realization of the relational model and hence an adequate foundation on which to build.

Regarding SQL in particular, we feel that any attempt to move forward, if it is to stand the test of time, must reject SQL unequivocally. Our reasons for taking this position are too many and varied for us to spell them out in detail here; in any case, we have described them in depth in many other places (see, e.g., references [27], [41], [44-45], [51], and [62] among others). Of course, we do realize that SQL databases and applications are going to be with us for a long time—to think otherwise would be quite unrealistic—and so we do have to pay some attention to the question of what to do about today's SQL legacy. The *Manifesto* therefore does include some specific suggestions in this regard (see Chapter 10 for a detailed discussion).

Further analysis of the proposals of references [2] and [130] can be found in the annotation to those references in Appendix J. Also, a detailed examination of how SQL measures up to the ideas of the *Manifesto* can be found in Appendix H.

What Problem Were We Trying to Solve?

We need to explain what problem we were trying to solve when we first wrote our *Manifesto*. (What follows is an edited version of what we said at that time.) It was our belief—borne out by subsequent events—that DBMSs needed to evolve to deal with much more sophisticated kinds of data than they were capable of at the time; in other words, we needed to find a way of extending, dramatically, the range of possible kinds of data we could keep in our databases. For example, we might imagine a biological database that included a BIRD relation like the one shown in Fig. 1.1 below.

BIRD	NAME	DESCR	PIC	VIDEO	SONG	MIGR
	Robin	xxxxx	...	.....	♪♪♪♪	....
	Osprey	xxxxx	...	.....	♪♪♪♪	....
	......	.....	...	.....	....	....

```
where NAME  is a bird name                      (text)
and   DESCR is a description of that bird        (XML doc)
and   PIC   is a picture of the bird             (photo)
and   VIDEO is a movie of the bird               (video)
and   SONG  is the bird's song                   (audio)
and   MIGR  is the bird's migration route        (map)
```

Fig. 1.1: The BIRD relation

Note: We follow convention in Fig. 1.1 and similar figures throughout this book in using *double underlining* to mark components of primary keys—despite the fact that (as we will see in the next chapter) the *Manifesto* does not require primary key support.

Before going any further, we should make it clear that, strictly speaking, the table in Fig. 1.1 is not really a relation at all, even though we said it was just now. Rather, it is a *picture* of a relation, as displayed on a computer screen perhaps, that contains among other things certain icons. Clicking on, say, the SONG icon ("♪♪♪♪") in the Robin row in that picture might cause the system to play a recording of a robin singing; and, loosely speaking, it is that recording, not the icon, that is the actual value of the SONG component of the Robin row within the BIRD relation.

To get back to the main thread of our discussion: Of course, we would need to be able to operate on such new kinds of data, too. In the case of the BIRD relation, for example, we might want to find information concerning birds whose migration route includes Italy:

```
SELECT  NAME, DESCR, SONG, VIDEO
FROM    BIRD
WHERE   INCLUDES ( MIGR, COUNTRY('Italy') )
```

Note: We use SQL as the basis for this example for reasons of familiarity, despite the fact that (as indicated in the previous subsection) the *Manifesto* expressly proscribes it.

So the problem we were addressing was this: How could we support new kinds of data within the classical relational framework? (Of course, we did take it as axiomatic that we wanted to stay in that framework; it would be unthinkable to walk away from what is, at the time of writing, well over 35 years of relational research and development.) And the key to the solution was, of course, *type theory:* It all boiled down to the issue of what types of data we were allowed to keep within database relations. Hence our focus on type theory in this book.

Topics Deliberately Omitted

As you know by now, this book is not about SQL (at least, not directly). Nor is it about commercial products. Rather, it is about *principles* (in this context, just another word for foundations). Why? Because principles endure;[1] principles are solid; principles are what you need to know in order to be able to understand—and analyze, and evaluate, and perhaps judge—vendor claims, commercial products, the SQL language, and numerous other developments and pronouncements in the database field.

Of course, a real DBMS will necessarily include many features over and above those that can properly be regarded as foundation features as such. Such features include:

- Recovery and concurrency controls

- Security and authorization controls

- Stored and triggered procedures (the latter more usually known, somewhat inappropriately, as just *triggers*)

- Support for the development of generic applications (e.g., some kind of *call-level interface*)

- Performance tuning and other administration controls

and many other things besides. Now, we recognize that such features can be extremely important in practice—in fact, the quality of support for them can make or break a DBMS as a commercial

---

1. By contrast, products change all the time, and so does SQL.

proposition. As already stated, however, they are not part of the foundation per se; they are therefore not addressed in the *Manifesto,* and they are not discussed in the present book (at least, not much).

We also have little to say regarding matters of implementation. As explained in more detail in the section "Some Crucial Logical Differences" later in this chapter, we draw a sharp distinction between model issues and implementation ones, and we believe it is important to get the model right first before worrying about how to implement it—though we should immediately add that we have at least thought about implementation matters enough to have reason to believe that everything we propose is indeed implementable.[1] In particular, much existing SQL implementation technology should be useful and usable in implementing the ideas of the *Manifesto,* even though we reject SQL as such. (In fact, we venture to suggest that implementing the *Manifesto* should actually be easier than implementing SQL, for reasons we hope will become clear as we proceed.)

What about Objects?

Something else we need to explain at the outset has to do with our adoption—or lack thereof, rather, for the most part—of terminology from the object world.[2] In the early to middle 1990s, there were those who argued that object technology was destined to replace relational technology. Few now subscribe to that position, but it might still be claimed that object technology does at least have some contributions to make to the database field. We do not dispute that claim; however, we prefer not to use object terminology, even when we make use of object concepts (or, at least, concepts that might have some counterpart in the object world), because we do not find that terminology appropriate to our purpose. For consider:

- First of all, the very term *object* itself does not seem to have a precise or universally agreed-upon meaning. Sometimes it seems to mean a *value;* sometimes a *variable;* sometimes even a *type;* and there might be other interpretations as well. (Sometimes an object is defined to be an *instance,* but that definition merely shifts the question of interpretation on to this latter term. In this book, therefore, we avoid the use of the term *instance* also, except in very informal contexts.)

- As a label, moreover, that same term *object* is applied to a wide variety of quite distinct endeavors. It is used among other things to describe a certain *graphic interface* style, a certain *programming* style, certain *programming languages* (not the same thing as programming style, of course), and certain *analysis* and *design* techniques—all of these in addition to a certain approach to what is after all the principal focus of this book, database management. And it is quite clear that the term does not mean the same thing in all of these different contexts (see, e.g., the annotation to reference [9] in Appendix J).

Similar comments apply to other object terms as well (*class, method,* and so on). Given this state of affairs, therefore, and given also that we are trying to be precise in this book (for the most part, at any rate), we prefer to avoid terminology that might be subject to misinterpretation.

There is another point we need to make clear in this connection, though. To repeat, we are (of course) interested throughout this book in the field of database management. We are therefore interested in—among many other things—the applicability of object concepts and technology to that field. *Please note, therefore, that all remarks made in this book concerning object concepts and technology must be*

---

1. In this respect, we might again claim to be following Codd, who wrote, possibly tongue in cheek, in his famous 1970 paper [21]: "Neither ... linguistic details nor ... implementation problems are discussed. Nevertheless, the material presented should be adequate for experienced systems programmers to visualize several approaches."

2. Throughout this book we favor the abbreviated term *object* over the longer form *object-oriented.*

understood in this light. We offer no opinion whatsoever regarding the usefulness of object ideas in any other context.

A *Little History*

Being organized as it is around *The Third Manifesto,* this book can be seen as a reincarnation of, and replacement for, two previous books (though it has been drastically revised, and in fact totally rewritten). The first of those previous books was published in 1998, under the title *Foundation for Object/Relational Databases: The Third Manifesto* [82]. We chose that title because "object/relational" DBMSs were a hot topic at the time; we were concerned in particular that certain portions of the industry were going about implementing such DBMSs in a way that seemed to us seriously flawed, and we wanted to do our best to help correct matters. In retrospect, however, we now realize the title was a little unfortunate in at least two respects:

- It got the emphasis wrong, in that it suggested that the book was concerned with object/relational databases exclusively, whereas (as already indicated) the ideas of the *Manifesto* are much wider-ranging.

- In any case, we regard "object/relational" primarily as a marketing term. Indeed, it is our contention that a true *relational* system—that is, a system that supported the relational model properly, with all that such support entails—would in fact *be* an "object/relational" system (which is why we usually set the term in quotation marks).

We went on to publish a revised version of that first book in 2000 under the somewhat better title *Foundation for Future Database Systems: The Third Manifesto* [83]. But that title too was not perfect. The problem with the future is, it never arrives!—and we would like to see the industry in general act on the ideas of the *Manifesto* as soon as possible (we take this subject seriously). Certainly there is room for improvement in the current crop of commercial products.

And so to the present book. This time we have chosen what we hope is a more appropriate title; in particular, we have tried to get away from the shortcomings of the two earlier titles. And we have, as already indicated, taken the opportunity to overhaul the text from beginning to end. Thus, although the overall message remains unchanged, what you hold in your hands is to all intents and purposes a brand new book.

BACK TO THE RELATIONAL FUTURE

It is a major thesis of both the *Manifesto* and this book that we need to move away from SQL and get back to our relational roots. In other words, we do not believe that SQL is capable of providing the kind of solid foundation we seek. Rather, we believe any such foundation must be firmly rooted in **the relational model of data,** first presented to the world in 1969 by E. F. Codd in reference [20].

Now, we have already said we acknowledge the desirability of supporting certain features that are commonly regarded as aspects of object orientation. However, we believe the features in question are orthogonal to (i.e., independent of) the relational model as such. In other words, we claim that the relational model needs no *extension,* no *correction,* no *subsumption*—and, above all, no *perversion*—in order for it to be possible to define some database language that (a) is truly relational, (b) does accommodate those desirable orthogonal features, and (c) can represent the firm foundation we seek.

Let there be such a language, and let its name be **D.** Please note immediately that no special significance attaches to this choice of name—we use it merely to refer generically to any language that conforms to the principles laid down in the *Manifesto.* There could be any number of distinct languages all qualifying as a valid **D.** We define one such language in this book; we call it **Tutorial D,** and we use it as the basis for most of our examples.

The *Manifesto* defines a variety of prescriptions and proscriptions that apply to any such **D**. Some of those prescriptions arise from the relational model, and these we call **Relational Model Prescriptions,** abbreviated **RM Prescriptions**. Prescriptions that do not arise from the relational model we call **Other Orthogonal Prescriptions,** abbreviated **OO Prescriptions**. We similarly classify the *Manifesto's* proscriptions into RM and OO categories. The various prescriptions and proscriptions are itemized and discussed in detail in Parts II and III of this book.

In addition to the prescriptions and proscriptions just mentioned, the *Manifesto* includes a series of **Very Strong Suggestions,** likewise divided into RM and OO categories; again, see Parts II and III. Also, Part IV contains the definition of a model of type inheritance, and that model is likewise formulated as a series of prescriptions—**Inheritance Model Prescriptions,** abbreviated **IM Prescriptions**. (Please note, however, that almost everything to do with that inheritance model is ignored prior to Part IV, except for the occasional remark here and there. The material of Part IV extends, but does not invalidate, the material presented in earlier parts of the book.)

For definiteness, we assume throughout the *Manifesto* and throughout this book that the language **D** is imperative in style. Like all such languages, therefore, it is based on the four core concepts **type, value, variable,** and **operator**.[1] For example, we might have a type called INTEGER; the integer 3 might be a value of that type; N might be a variable of that type, whose value at any given time is some integer value (i.e., some value of that type); and plus ("+") might be an operator that applies to integer values (i.e., to values of that type). See the section "Some Crucial Logical Differences" later in this chapter for further elaboration of these concepts.

As an aside, we remark that if it is true that the *Manifesto* can be regarded as defining a foundation for database technology, then the concepts of type, value, variable, and operator can be regarded as providing a foundation for that foundation. And since the value, variable, and operator concepts in turn all rely on the type concept, we might go further and say the type concept can be regarded as a foundation for the foundation for the foundation ... In other words, the type concept is the most fundamental of all, as we will soon see.

Back to the language **D**. We have said that **D** is imperative in style (or so we will assume). Now, some writers equate the term *imperative* with the term *procedural,* but we do not (even though they both refer to a style of programming in which the programmer explicitly directs the computer to carry out certain processes). Actually, neither term is very precisely defined; however, *procedural* usually connotes a rather low level of abstraction, while *imperative* does not (at least, not necessarily). In other words, procedural languages are imperative, but imperative languages are not necessarily procedural. In particular, the language **D**—or its relational portion, at any rate—is at a comparatively high level of abstraction and is thus imperative but not procedural.

One last point to close this section: Do not infer from our assumption of an imperative style that we discount the possibility of (e.g.) a functional style; at the time of writing, however, we have not investigated such a possibility in any depth. But we should point out that certain of the prescriptions, proscriptions, and suggestions spelled out in this book would have to be reformulated in the context of a functional **D**. For example, a functional **D** would obviously have no need of variables at all, in the usual programming sense of that term, and hence would not need any update operators either.

---

1. Note that we distinguish between operators and operations—an *operation* is the process carried out when an *operator* is invoked. That said, however, we should say too that the terms can often be used interchangeably. For example, no real harm is done if we replace "operator" by "operation" in the sentence "Plus is an operator that takes two integers as input and returns another integer as output."

SOME GUIDING PRINCIPLES

Throughout our work on the *Manifesto* (and related work), we have tried to follow certain guiding principles, of which the most important—indeed, it underpins all the rest—is this:

All logical differences are big differences.

The relevance of this maxim, which is due to Wittgenstein [91], is as follows. The relational model is at heart *a formal system:* just as a DBMS is, or an operating system (or indeed any computer program, come to that). Formal systems are what computers are, or can be made to be, good at. And, of course, the basis of any formal system is *logic*. It follows that with respect to formal systems in general, and with respect to the matters that are the concern of the *Manifesto* in particular, differences that are logical in nature are very important ones, and we need to pay very careful attention to them.

Incidentally, we might point out, slightly tongue in cheek, that Wittgenstein's maxim has an interesting corollary: namely, that *all logical mistakes are big mistakes*. Because, of course, a mistake is a difference—a difference between what is right and what is wrong. And we do unfortunately observe a number of logical mistakes that have been made, and still are being made, in the industry as a whole ...

We further conjecture that the inverse of Wittgenstein's maxim is true as well: namely, that *all nonlogical differences are small differences*—by which we mean, not that (e.g.) psychological differences are unimportant in general, but that they *are* unimportant from the point of view of formal systems in particular. In the context of the *Manifesto* specifically, therefore, we pay little attention to nonlogical considerations, such as matters of syntax. (Syntax is important from a human factors point of view, of course, and in our design of **Tutorial D** in particular we have naturally tried to favor good syntax over bad. However, we do not regard differences that are mere differences in syntax as logical differences, nor as very important ones.)

Another fundamental principle we have tried to follow is that of **conceptual integrity** (the term is due to Fred Brooks). In his classic *The Mythical Man-Month* [12], Brooks has this to say:

> [Conceptual] integrity is *the* most important consideration in system design. It is better to have a system omit certain anomalous features [and] to reflect one set of design ideas, than to have one that contains many good but independent and uncoordinated ideas [*italics in the original*].

And writing 20 years later, he adds:

> A clean, elegant programming product must present ... a coherent mental model ... [Conceptual] integrity ... is the most important factor in ease of use ... **Today I am more convinced than ever.** Conceptual integrity *is* central to product quality [*boldface and italics in the original*].

Let us elaborate briefly on this question of conceptual integrity. In order to maintain integrity of concepts, it is clearly necessary to have some concepts in the first place. Furthermore, the concepts in question had better be carefully chosen, preferably few in number, agreed upon by all parties concerned, and indeed agreeable, not disagreeable, in nature. As an obvious example, suppose the product in question is a DBMS specifically, and suppose the agreed-upon concepts are those of the relational model. Then that product must adhere rigidly to *all* aspects of that model. In particular, it must not sacrifice the conceptual integrity of that model to some vaguely defined goal such as "keeping the syntax simple" [31].

We will have occasion to refer to these guiding principles many times in the pages ahead.

SOME CRUCIAL LOGICAL DIFFERENCES

The following logical differences are worth examining right away, since they are relevant to just about everything to be discussed in this book:

- Model vs. implementation

- Value vs. variable

- Value vs. appearance

Many others will be identified in the chapters to come. See also reference [79].

Model vs. Implementation

The first logical difference we want to discuss is that between *model* and *implementation*. First some definitions:

- A **model** (sometimes referred to as a *data* model specifically) is an abstract, self-contained, logical definition of the objects, operators, and so forth, that together constitute the abstract machine with which users interact.[1] The objects allow us to model the *structure* of data. The operators allow us to model its *behavior*. *Note:* The term *objects* here is to be understood in its generic sense, not in the special sense of object orientation. Also, the term *users*, here and elsewhere throughout this book, is intended to mean end users and/or application programmers and/or transactions, as the context demands.

- An **implementation** of a given model is a physical realization on a real computer system of the components of the abstract machine that together constitute that model. *Note:* The term *implementation*, here and elsewhere throughout this book, is to be understood to mean implementation of "the system" (i.e., the DBMS itself), not implementation of some application that runs on top of the DBMS.

As you can see, the distinction between model and implementation is really just an important special case of the familiar distinction between logical and physical aspects of a system. And just in case it might not be obvious, we would like to make it clear that our primary concern throughout the *Manifesto,* and throughout this book, is with the model specifically, not the implementation (though our informal discussions and explanations do occasionally touch on matters of implementation for purposes of clarification).

Observe, incidentally, that keeping the model and its implementation rigorously separate—in particular, not cluttering up the model with implementation matters—is what enables us to achieve **data independence** [76,86]. Indeed, we fail to achieve that objective precisely to the extent that we fail to observe that separation.

---

1. The term *architecture* is sometimes used with much the same meaning. To quote Brooks once again, "the architecture of a system [is] the complete and detailed specification of the user interface" [12]. We prefer *model* to *architecture* because over the years the latter term has grown to acquire a variety of meanings, most of them not very precise. (In fairness, we should admit that the same is also of the term *model* to some extent [68]; certainly the term *data model* in particular has two very different meanings. See the annotation to reference [76] in Appendix J.)

Value vs. Variable

The second logical difference we want to elaborate on here is that between *values* and *variables* (where by *variable* we mean a variable in the usual programming sense). Following Cleaveland [19], we define these concepts as follows:

- A **value** is an "individual constant": for example, the individual constant that is the integer 3. A value has *no location in time or space*. However, values can be represented in memory by means of some encoding, and such representations, or (our preferred term in this context) *appearances*, do have locations in time and space. Indeed, any number of distinct appearances of the same value can exist at any number of distinct locations in time and space, meaning, loosely, that any number of different variables—see the bullet item immediately following—can have the same value, at the same time or different times. Note in particular that, by definition, **a value cannot be updated;** for if it could, then after such an update it would not be that value any longer (in general).

- A **variable** is a holder for an appearance of a value. A variable does have a location in time and space.[1] Also, of course, variables, unlike values, **can be updated;** that is, the current value of the variable in question can be replaced by another value, probably different from the previous one. (Of course, the variable in question is still the same variable after the update.)

Please note very carefully that it is not just simple things like the integer 3 that are legitimate values. On the contrary, values can be arbitrarily complex; for example, a value might be a geometric point, or a polygon, or an X-ray, or an XML document, or a fingerprint, or an array, or a stack, or a list, or a relation (and on and on). Analogous remarks apply to variables too, of course.

By the way, the distinction between values and variables might seem obvious, but it is not always observed in the literature; in fact, it is easy to fall into traps in this area. By way of illustration, consider the following extract from a tutorial on object databases [137] (the italicized comments in brackets are by the present authors):

> We distinguish the declared type of a variable from ... the type of the object that is the current value of the variable [*so an object is a value*] ... We distinguish objects from values [*so an object is not a value after all*] ... A **mutator** [is an operator such that it is] possible to observe its effect on some object [*so in fact an object is a variable*].

Value vs. Appearance

The third and last logical difference we want to discuss here is the one, touched on in the preceding subsection, between a value per se and an appearance of that value in some particular context (in particular, an appearance as the current value of some variable). As already explained, the very same value can appear in many different contexts simultaneously. Each of those appearances consists, internally, of some encoding or physical representation of the value in question. For example, the integer value 12 occurs exactly once in the set of integers—there is exactly one integer 12 "in the universe," as it were—but any number of variables might simultaneously contain an appearance of that integer as their current value, as in this **Tutorial D** example:

---

1. We are speaking intuitively here, not formally. The notion that variables "have location" is useful for explaining what variables are in an informal sense, but that notion is not part of our formal definition of a variable. That definition is explained later, in Chapter 14 in particular.

```
VAR X INTEGER ;
VAR Y INTEGER ;

X := 12 ;  /* assign the value 12 to the variable X */
Y := 12 ;  /* assign the value 12 to the variable Y */
```

What is more, some of those appearances might be physically represented by means of, say, a decimal encoding, and others by means of a binary encoding, of that particular integer (in the example, X might contain the "packed decimal" encoding 00010010 while Y contains the "pure binary" encoding 00001100). Thus, there is also a logical difference between an appearance of a value, on the one hand, and the internal encoding or physical representation of that appearance, on the other; in fact, there might even be a logical difference between the encodings used for different appearances of the same value.

The foregoing remarks notwithstanding, we usually find it convenient, for fairly obvious reasons, to abbreviate *encoding of an appearance of a value* to just *appearance of a value,* or (more often) to just *value,* so long as there is no risk of ambiguity in doing so. Note carefully too that *appearance of a value* is a model concept, whereas *encoding of an appearance* is an implementation concept. For example, users certainly might need to know whether variables X and Y contain appearances of the same value (i.e., whether those variables "compare equal"); however, they do not need to know whether those appearances use the same physical encoding.

CONCLUDING REMARKS

As already explained, the *Manifesto* consists of a series of prescriptions, proscriptions, and very strong suggestions. For purposes of reference, and also to give some idea of the scope of the *Manifesto,* we show overleaf a mnemonic list of those prescriptions, proscriptions, and suggestions. We remind you that OO in that list stands for **Other Orthogonal**. *Note:* An analogous list for our inheritance model appears in Chapter 12. No significance should be attached to the sequence in which items appear in either list.

RM Prescriptions

1. Scalar types
2. Scalar values are typed
3. Read-only vs. update operators
4. Physical vs. possible representations
5. Expose possible representations
6. Type generator TUPLE
7. Type generator RELATION
8. Equality
9. Tuples
10. Relations
11. Scalar variables
12. Tuple variables
13. Relation variables (relvars)
14. Kinds of relvars
15. Candidate keys
16. Databases
17. Transactions
18. Relational algebra
19. Relvar names, relation selectors, and recursion
20. User-defined tuple and relational operators
21. Assignments
22. Comparisons
23. Integrity constraints
24. Total database constraints
25. Catalog
26. Language design

RM Proscriptions

1. No attribute ordering
2. No tuple ordering
3. No duplicate tuples
4. No nulls
5. No nullological mistakes

6. No internal-level constructs
7. No tuple-level operations
8. No composite attributes
9. No domain check override
10. Not SQL

OO Prescriptions

1. Compile-time type checking
2. Type inheritance (conditional)
3. Computational completeness
4. Explicit transaction boundaries
5. Nested transactions
6. Aggregate operators and empty sets

OO Proscriptions

1. Relvars are not domains
2. No object IDs

RM Very Strong Suggestions

1. System keys
2. Foreign keys
3. Candidate key inference
4. Transition constraints
5. Quota queries
6. Generalized transitive closure
7. User-defined generic operators
8. SQL migration

OO Very Strong Suggestions

1. Type inheritance
2. Types and operators unbundled
3. Single-level store

We close this chapter by confessing that we do feel a little uncomfortable with the idea of calling what is, after all, primarily a technical document a "manifesto." According to *Chambers Twentieth Century Dictionary,* a manifesto is a written declaration of the intentions, opinions, or motives of some person or group (e.g., a political party). By contrast, *The Third Manifesto* is—we hope—a matter of science and logic, not mere "intentions, opinions, or motives." Given the historical precedents that led us to write it, however, our title was effectively chosen for us.

EXERCISES

1. Define and distinguish between the terms *database* and *DBMS* as carefully as you can. What do you regard as the foundations of database technology?

2. What do you understand by the term *orthogonality?*

3. Explain the following in your own words: architecture; conceptual integrity; data independence; implementation; logical difference; model.

4. What is *The Third Manifesto?* What problem was it originally intended to solve?

5. In the body of this chapter, we said the concepts of *type, value, variable,* and *operator* can be regarded as providing "a foundation for the foundation." Explain this remark as carefully as you can.

6. What do you understand by the term "object/relational database"?

7. Explain the logical differences between a value, an appearance of a value, and an encoding of an appearance of a value.

8. What is **D**?

9. In the body of this chapter, we said the table in Fig. 1.1 was not a relation but, rather, a *picture* of a relation (in general, in fact, there is always a logical difference between a thing and a picture of that thing). What are some of the specific points of difference between the table in Fig. 1.1 and the relation it depicts?

10. Distinguish between *imperative, procedural,* and *functional* programming languages. Give examples of each. Can you identify any other language styles?

11. Who was E. F. Codd?

12. If you are familiar with SQL, identify some of the major differences between it and the relational model. *Note:* A precise definition of the relational model appears in the next chapter.

Chapter 2

A Survey of the Relational Model

Most of this book assumes you have a reasonably good understanding of the relational model. This chapter is meant to serve as a quick refresher course on that model; in effect, it summarizes much of what you will be expected to know in later chapters. A detailed tutorial on this material, and much more, can be found in reference [76]; if you are familiar with that reference, you probably do not need to read this chapter in detail. But if your knowledge of the relational model derives from other sources—especially ones based on SQL—then you probably do need to read this chapter fairly carefully, because it emphasizes numerous important topics that other sources typically do not. Such topics include:

- Relations vs. types

- Relation values vs. relation variables

- Predicates and propositions

- Relation-valued attributes

- The crucial role of integrity constraints

- Relational assignment and comparisons

and many others.

THE RUNNING EXAMPLE

Examples in this book are based for the most part on the familiar suppliers-and-parts database (see Fig. 2.1 overleaf for a set of sample values). The semantics are as follows:

- Relvar S represents *suppliers* (more accurately, suppliers *under contract*).[1] Each supplier has one supplier number (S#), unique to that supplier; one name (SNAME), not necessarily unique (though the SNAME values in Fig. 2.1 do happen to be unique); one rating or status value (STATUS); and one location (CITY).

- Relvar P represents *parts* (more accurately, *kinds* of parts). Each kind of part has one part number (P#), which is unique; one name (PNAME); one color (COLOR); one weight (WEIGHT); and one location where parts of that kind are stored (CITY).

- Relvar SP represents *shipments* (it shows which parts are supplied by which suppliers). Each shipment has one supplier number (S#), one part number (P#), and one quantity (QTY); there is at

---

1. The term *relvar* is short for *relation variable*. It is explained in detail in the section "Relation Variables" later in this chapter. Also, note that throughout this book we favor the terms *relation, attribute,* and *tuple*—usually pronounced to rhyme with *couple*—over their less formal and less precise counterparts *table, column,* and *row* (except in SQL contexts).

most one shipment at any given time for a given supplier and a given part. Notice that the database of Fig. 2.1 includes one supplier, S5, with no shipments at all.

S

S#	SNAME	STATUS	CITY
S1	Smith	20	London
S2	Jones	10	Paris
S3	Blake	30	Paris
S4	Clark	20	London
S5	Adams	30	Athens

P

P#	PNAME	COLOR	WEIGHT	CITY
P1	Nut	Red	12.0	London
P2	Bolt	Green	17.0	Paris
P3	Screw	Blue	17.0	Oslo
P4	Screw	Red	14.0	London
P5	Cam	Blue	12.0	Paris
P6	Cog	Red	19.0	London

SP

S#	P#	QTY
S1	P1	300
S1	P2	200
S1	P3	400
S1	P4	200
S1	P5	100
S1	P6	100
S2	P1	300
S2	P2	400
S3	P2	200
S4	P2	200
S4	P4	300
S4	P5	400

Fig. 2.1: The suppliers-and-parts database—sample values

Here are **Tutorial D** definitions for these three relvars:

```
VAR S REAL RELATION
  { S# S#, SNAME NAME, STATUS INTEGER, CITY CHAR }
    KEY { S# } ;

VAR P REAL RELATION
  { P# P#, PNAME NAME, COLOR COLOR, WEIGHT WEIGHT, CITY CHAR }
    KEY { P# } ;

VAR SP REAL RELATION
  { S# S#, P# P#, QTY QTY }
    KEY { S#, P# } ;
```

Detailed discussion of the foregoing definitions can be found in Chapter 6, under RM Prescription 13. For present purposes, it is sufficient to observe that:

- Each relvar has a set of *attributes;* for example, relvar S has four attributes, called S#, SNAME, STATUS, and CITY.

- Each attribute has a *type;* for example, the types of the attributes of relvar S are called S#, NAME, INTEGER, and CHAR, respectively.

In this chapter we will mostly take types for granted—we will discuss them in detail in the next chapter—but it is at least worth stating explicitly that attributes can be of *any type whatsoever.*[1] In particular, those types can be either system defined (built in) or user defined. In our running example, we will assume, where it makes any difference, that types INTEGER (integers) and CHAR (character strings of arbitrary length) are system defined and all others are user defined.

TUPLES

Since relations are built out of tuples, it is convenient to begin by defining the term *tuple* precisely. Given a collection of types Ti ($i = 1, 2, ..., n$, where $n \geq 0$), not necessarily all distinct, a **tuple value** (*tuple* for short) over those types[2]—t, say—is a set of n ordered triples of the form $<Ai,Ti,vi>$, where Ai is an **attribute name,** Ti is a **type name,** and vi is a **value** of type Ti. Moreover:

- The value n is the **degree** (or *arity*) of t.

- The ordered triple $<Ai,Ti,vi>$ is a **component** of t.

- The ordered pair $<Ai,Ti>$ is an **attribute** of t, and it is uniquely identified by the attribute name Ai (attribute names Ai and Aj are the same only if $i = j$). The value vi is the **attribute value** for attribute Ai of t. The type Ti is the corresponding **attribute type**. *Note:* There is, of course, a logical difference between an attribute and its name; among other things, an attribute is a pair but its name is a singleton. This fact notwithstanding, we often (as we just did) use expressions such as "attribute Ai," informally, to mean the attribute whose *name* is Ai. Similar remarks apply to various other constructs, including types, variables, and operators.

- The complete set of attributes is the **heading** of t.

- The **tuple type** of t is determined by the heading of t, and the heading and that tuple type both have the same attributes (and hence the same attribute names and types) and the same degree as t does. The **tuple type name** is, precisely, TUPLE{H}, where {H} is the heading. Thus, the particular tuple type name under discussion can be expressed in **Tutorial D** as follows:

```
TUPLE { A1 T1, A2 T2, ..., An Tn }
```

The order in which the attributes are specified is immaterial, however; thus, for example,

```
TUPLE { A1 T1, A2 T2 }   and   TUPLE { A2 T2, A1 T1 }
```

both denote the same tuple type, in **Tutorial D**.

Here is a sample tuple:

---

1. This remark is true in general, but there are exceptions, of which one of the most important is this: Attributes of relations in the database—as opposed to relations that are local to the application (see RM Prescription 14)—are not allowed to be of type *pointer*. See Chapter 9 for further explanation.

2. We might also reasonably say the tuple is "over" its *attributes,* q.v.

S#	S#	SNAME	NAME	STATUS	INTEGER	CITY	CHAR
S1		Smith			20	London	

The attribute names here are S#, SNAME, STATUS, and CITY; the corresponding type names are, respectively, S#, NAME, INTEGER, and CHAR; and the corresponding values are, respectively, S#('S1'), NAME('Smith'), 20, and 'London'—though most of these expressions have been simplified somewhat in the picture (and we will make use of similar simplifications in such pictures throughout this book). The degree of this tuple is four. Its heading is:

S#	S#	SNAME	NAME	STATUS	INTEGER	CITY	CHAR

Its type in **Tutorial D** terms is:

```
TUPLE { S# S#, SNAME NAME, STATUS INTEGER, CITY CHAR }
```

Now, it is common in informal contexts to omit the type names from a heading, showing just the attribute names. Informally, therefore, we might represent the foregoing tuple thus:

S#	SNAME	STATUS	CITY
S1	Smith	20	London

In **Tutorial D,** the following expression could be used to denote this tuple:

```
TUPLE { S# S#('S1'), SNAME NAME('Smith'), STATUS 20, CITY 'London' }
```

This expression is an example of a *tuple selector invocation.* We will have more to say about such expressions in Chapter 3; here we just remark that—as you might have noticed—the keyword TUPLE does double duty in **Tutorial D,** being used in connection with both tuple selector invocations and tuple type names. An analogous remark applies to the keyword RELATION (see the next section, "Relations").

Properties of Tuples

Tuples possess a number of important properties, all of them immediate consequences of the foregoing definitions. To be specific:

- Every tuple contains exactly one value (of the appropriate type) for each of its attributes.

- Note carefully that, by definition, a tuple considered in its entirety is also a value. For emphasis, we sometimes speak of "tuple values" explicitly, but we usually abbreviate that term to just *tuples* (exactly as we usually abbreviate, e.g., "integer values" to just *integers*).

- There is no left-to-right ordering to the components of a tuple. This property follows because a tuple has a *set* of components, and sets in mathematics have no ordering to their elements. (Our reason for including the redundant qualifier "left-to-right" in the foregoing sentence is explained in the next section.)

- Every subset of a tuple is a tuple. For example, given the tuple—

S#	SNAME	STATUS	CITY
S1	Smith	20	London

—what we might call "the {S#,CITY} value in this tuple" is itself a tuple:

S#	CITY
S1	London

In like fashion, every subset of a heading is a heading.

As an aside, we note that this bullet item is the first place in the text to use the term *subset*. We therefore take the opportunity to say that, throughout this book, we take statements of the form "*b* is a subset of *a*" (equivalently, "*a* is a superset of *b*"), noncontroversially, to include the possibility that *a* and *b* might be equal; if we wish to exclude that possibility, we will talk explicitly in terms of *proper* subsets and supersets. Also, we take statements of the form "*a* is a set" (again noncontroversially) to include the possibility that *a* might be empty; if we wish to exclude *that* possibility, we will talk explicitly in terms of *nonempty* sets.

Tuple Equality

Two tuples are equal, obviously enough, if and only if they are in fact the very same tuple (just as, e.g., two integers are equal if and only if they are the very same integer). However, it is worth spelling out the semantics of tuple equality in detail, since so much in the relational model depends on it; for example, candidate keys, functional dependencies, and most of the operators of the relational algebra are all defined in terms of it. Here then is a precise definition:

- Tuples *t1* and *t2* are **equal** if and only if they have the same attributes $A1, A2, \ldots, An$ and, for all i ($i = 1, 2, \ldots, n$), the value of Ai in *t1* is equal to the value of Ai in *t2*.

Furthermore (this might seem obvious but it needs to be said), if *p1* and *p2* are appearances of tuples *t1* and *t2*, respectively, then *p1* and *p2* are **duplicates** of each other if and only if *t1* and *t2* are equal—i.e., if and only if *t1* and *t2* are the very same tuple. (See the section "Some Crucial Logical Differences" in Chapter 1 if you need to refresh your memory regarding the meaning of the term *appearance*.)

RELATIONS

Now we can define the term *relation*. A **relation value** (*relation* for short), *r* say, consists of a *heading* and a *body,* where:

- The **heading** of *r* is a heading as defined in the previous section. Relation *r* has the same attributes (and hence the same attribute names and types) and the same degree as that heading does.

■ The **body** of *r* is a set of tuples, all having that same heading (and the cardinality of that set is the **cardinality** of *r*).

The **relation type** of *r* is determined by the heading of *r*, and it has the same attributes (and hence the same attribute names and types) and degree as that heading does. The **relation type name** is, precisely, RELATION{*H*}, where {*H*} is the heading. In **Tutorial D,** therefore, we can express a relation type name as here:

```
RELATION { A1 T1, A2 T2, ..., An Tn }
```

(The order in which the attributes are specified is immaterial, however.) Here is a sample relation:

S# S#	SNAME NAME	STATUS INTEGER	CITY CHAR
S1	Smith	20	London
S2	Jones	10	Paris
S3	Blake	30	Paris
S4	Clark	20	London
S5	Adams	30	Athens

Its type in **Tutorial D** is:

```
RELATION { S# S#, SNAME NAME, STATUS INTEGER, CITY CHAR }
```

As previously noted, it is common in informal contexts to omit the type names from a heading, showing just the attribute names. Informally, therefore, we might represent the foregoing relation as follows (as we did in Fig. 2.1, in fact):

S#	SNAME	STATUS	CITY
S1	Smith	20	London
S2	Jones	10	Paris
S3	Blake	30	Paris
S4	Clark	20	London
S5	Adams	30	Athens

The following expression could be used in **Tutorial D** to denote this relation:

```
RELATION { TUPLE { S# S#('S1'), SNAME NAME('Smith'), STATUS 20, CITY 'London' } ,
           TUPLE { S# S#('S2'), SNAME NAME('Jones'), STATUS 10, CITY 'Paris' } ,
           TUPLE { S# S#('S3'), SNAME NAME('Blake'), STATUS 30, CITY 'Paris' } ,
           TUPLE { S# S#('S4'), SNAME NAME('Clark'), STATUS 20, CITY 'London' } ,
           TUPLE { S# S#('S5'), SNAME NAME('Adams'), STATUS 30, CITY 'Athens' } }
```

(This expression is a *relation selector invocation.* See Chapter 3.)

Properties of Relations

- Note that, strictly speaking, a relation does not contain tuples—it contains a body, and that body in turn contains tuples. Informally, however, it is convenient to talk as if relations contained tuples directly, and we will follow this simplifying convention throughout this book.

- Every subset of a body is a body (loosely, every subset of a relation is a relation).

- No relation ever contains two or more distinct appearances of the same tuple ("duplicate tuples"). This property follows because a body is a set of tuples, and sets in mathematics have no duplicate elements. Now, you probably know that SQL tables are allowed to contain duplicate rows, and SQL tables are thus not relations, in general. Please understand, therefore, that in this book we *always* use the term "relation" to mean a relation—without duplicate tuples, by definition—and not an SQL table. Please note further that relational operations *always* produce a result without duplicate tuples, again by definition.

- Relations have no top-to-bottom ordering to their tuples and no left-to-right ordering to their attributes, pictures like Fig. 2.1 notwithstanding. (Actually, attributes have no ordering of any kind, and it would be logically correct to drop that "left-to-right" qualifier. But to say merely that attributes have no ordering could be misconstrued to mean that attribute *values* cannot be ordered—top to bottom, as it were—and we therefore include the qualifier for emphasis. Purely for consistency, therefore, we include the qualifier "top-to-bottom" in connection with tuple ordering as well.)

- Every tuple of every relation contains exactly one value for each attribute of that relation; i.e., relations are always *normalized* or in what has historically been called *first normal form,* 1NF.[1] *Note:* In connection with this point, it needs to be said that much of the literature talks about—and SQL products support—the use of what are called *nulls* in attribute positions to indicate that some value is missing for some reason. However, since (by definition) nulls are not values, the notion of a "tuple" containing nulls is a contradiction in terms. A "tuple" that contains nulls is not a tuple, and a "relation" that contains such a "tuple" is not a relation. Thus, **relations never contain nulls**.

- Like a tuple, a relation considered in its entirety is a value. Fig. 2.1, for example, shows three such values. For emphasis, we sometimes speak of *relation values* explicitly, but we usually abbreviate that term to just *relations* (exactly as we usually abbreviate *tuple values* to just *tuples*). See the next section ("Relation Variables") for further discussion of this issue.

Relation-Valued Attributes

As noted near the end of the section "The Running Example" earlier in this chapter, attributes of relations can be of any type whatsoever (with certain exceptions that we can safely ignore here). It follows that such attributes can be of relation types in particular, since relation types are certainly types; in other words, attributes can be **relation valued,** meaning we can have relations with attributes whose values are relations in turn. An example of such a relation is shown in Fig. 2.2, overleaf (we will return to this example in our discussion of the GROUP and UNGROUP operators in the section "Relational

---

1. Our understanding of the term *first normal form* has changed somewhat over the years. See reference [74] for an exhaustive discussion of this issue.

Operators," later in this chapter).

<table>
<tr><th>S#</th><th>PQ</th></tr>
<tr><td>S1</td><td><table><tr><th>P#</th><th>QTY</th></tr><tr><td>P1</td><td>300</td></tr><tr><td>P2</td><td>200</td></tr><tr><td>P3</td><td>400</td></tr><tr><td>P4</td><td>200</td></tr><tr><td>P5</td><td>100</td></tr><tr><td>P6</td><td>100</td></tr></table></td></tr>
<tr><td>S2</td><td><table><tr><th>P#</th><th>QTY</th></tr><tr><td>P1</td><td>300</td></tr><tr><td>P2</td><td>400</td></tr></table></td></tr>
<tr><td>S3</td><td><table><tr><th>P#</th><th>QTY</th></tr><tr><td>P2</td><td>200</td></tr></table></td></tr>
<tr><td>S4</td><td><table><tr><th>P#</th><th>QTY</th></tr><tr><td>P2</td><td>200</td></tr><tr><td>P4</td><td>300</td></tr><tr><td>P5</td><td>400</td></tr></table></td></tr>
<tr><td>S5</td><td><table><tr><th>P#</th><th>QTY</th></tr><tr><td></td><td></td></tr></table></td></tr>
</table>

Fig. 2.2: A relation with a relation-valued attribute

RELATION VARIABLES

Consider Fig. 2.1 once again. As noted in the previous section (at the end of the subsection "Properties of Relations"), that figure shows three relation **values:** namely, those that happen to appear in the database at some particular time. But, of course, if we were to look at the database at some different time, we would probably see three *different* relation values appearing in their place. In other words, S, P, and SP in that database are really **variables:** *relation* variables, to be precise, meaning variables whose permitted values are relation values (and the logical difference discussed in Chapter 1 between values and variables in general thus applies to relation values and relation variables in particular). For example, suppose relation variable S currently has the value—the relation value—shown in Fig. 2.1, and suppose we delete the tuples (actually there is just one such) for suppliers in Athens:

```
DELETE S WHERE CITY = 'Athens' ;
```

(**Tutorial D** syntax again). The result is shown in Fig. 2.3.

S#	SNAME	STATUS	CITY
S1	Smith	20	London
S2	Jones	10	Paris
S3	Blake	30	Paris
S4	Clark	20	London

Fig. 2.3: Relation variable S (as shown in Fig. 2.1) after deleting suppliers in Athens

Conceptually, what has happened here is that *the old relation value of S has been replaced en bloc by a new one.* Of course, the old value (with five tuples) and the new one (with four) are somewhat similar to each other, but they certainly are different values. In fact, the DELETE just shown is logically equivalent to, and indeed shorthand for, the following **relational assignment:**

```
S := S WHERE NOT ( CITY = 'Athens' ) ;
```

As in all assignments, what is happening here is that (a) the source expression on the right side is evaluated, and then (b) the result of that evaluation is assigned to the target variable on the left side. As already stated, the net effect is thus to replace the "old" value of S by a "new" one, or in other words to update the variable S. Note that the left side of the assignment must identify a variable specifically; variables are updatable by definition, while values (also by definition) are not. In the final analysis, in fact, to say that *V* is a variable is to say, precisely, that *V* can serve as the target for an assignment operation, no more and no less.

In analogous fashion, of course, relational INSERT and UPDATE operators are also shorthand for certain relational assignments. Thus, while **Tutorial D** certainly does support the familiar INSERT, DELETE, and UPDATE operators on relation variables (as we will see in Chapters 5 and 6), it expressly recognizes that those operators are really just shorthands, albeit convenient ones, for certain relational assignments. (We follow convention throughout this book in using the generic term *update* to refer to the INSERT, DELETE, and UPDATE—and assignment—operators considered collectively; indeed, we have already been doing this, as you might have noticed. When we want to refer to the UPDATE operator specifically, we will set it in all uppercase as just shown.)

Back to relation variables. As you probably know, most of the literature in fact uses the term *relation* when what it really means is a relation *variable* (as well as when it means a relation per se—i.e., a relation value). Historically, however, this practice has certainly caused confusion. In this book, therefore, we distinguish very carefully between relation variables and relations per se. We also follow reference [35] in using the term **relvar** as a convenient shorthand for *relation variable* (as you already know). More to the point, we take care always to phrase our remarks in terms of relvars, not relations, when it really is relvars we mean, and in terms of relations, not relvars, when it really is relations we mean.

By way of example, here repeated from the section "The Running Example" is a **Tutorial D** definition for the suppliers relvar S:

```
VAR S REAL RELATION
   { S# S#, SNAME NAME, STATUS INTEGER, CITY CHAR }
     KEY { S# } ;
```

The KEY specification here defines a candidate key for the relvar (see the subsection "Keys" later in this section). The REAL specification indicates that this is a real relvar as opposed to a virtual one—real and virtual relvars being the *Manifesto* counterparts to what SQL would call base tables and views, respectively (see the section "Virtual Relvars" later in this chapter).

Any given relvar is of some relation type, and all possible values of that relvar are of that same type. For relvar S, that type is explicitly specified in the relvar definition as:

```
RELATION { S# S#, SNAME NAME, STATUS INTEGER, CITY CHAR }
```

The terms *heading, body, attribute, tuple, cardinality,* and *degree,* defined in the previous section for relation values, can all be interpreted in the obvious way to apply to relvars as well. (In the case of *body, tuple,* and *cardinality,* they must be understood as applying to the specific relation that happens to be the current value of the relvar in question.)

Some Remarks on Updating

We return for a moment to the issue of updating relvars, because there is another point to be made in connection with that issue, viz.: *Relational assignment, regardless of what syntax we use to express it, is really a set-level operator.* UPDATE, for example, updates a *set* of tuples in the target relvar (loosely speaking!—see further discussion below). Informally, we often talk of, e.g., updating some individual tuple, but it must be clearly understood that:

- Such talk really means that the set of tuples we are updating just happens to have cardinality one.

- Sometimes, moreover, updating a set of tuples of cardinality one is impossible.

Suppose, for example, that the suppliers relvar S is subject to the constraint (see the section "Integrity Constraints" later in this chapter) that suppliers S1 and S4 are always located in the same city. Then any "single-tuple" UPDATE on S that attempts to change the city for just one of those two suppliers must necessarily fail. Instead, both suppliers must be updated simultaneously, perhaps as here:

```
UPDATE S WHERE S# = S#('S1') OR S# = S#('S4') ( CITY := some value ) ;
```

We now observe that to talk as we have just been doing of "updating a tuple" (or set of tuples, rather) is really somewhat imprecise—not to say sloppy—as well. If something is subject to update, then that something must be a variable, not a value; and tuples, like relations, are *values* and cannot be updated, by definition. Furthermore, we certainly do not mean, when we talk of "updating a tuple within some relvar," that we are updating a tuple *variable* (for if we did mean that, then we would be talking about variables containing other variables, a concept to which we do not subscribe at all). Rather, what we really mean when we talk of, e.g., updating tuple *t1* to *t2* within some relvar is that we are **replacing** one tuple by another. And even that talk is still just shorthand; what we *really* mean is that we are replacing the original value of the relvar, *r1* say, by another value *r2*, and *r2* is equal to (*r1* MINUS *s1*) UNION *s2*, where *s1* and *s2* are relations containing just *t1* and *t2*, respectively.

Analogous remarks apply to phrases such as "updating attribute *A*" within some tuple. In this book, we will continue to talk from time to time in terms of updating tuples or attributes thereof—the practice is convenient—but it must be clearly understood that such talk is only shorthand, and rather sloppy shorthand at that.

Keys

Let *K* be a subset of the heading of relvar *R*. Then *K* is a **candidate key** (or just *key* for short) for *R* if and only if it possesses both of the following properties:

- *Uniqueness:* No possible value for *R* contains two distinct tuples with the same value for *K*.

- *Irreducibility* (also known as *nonredundancy* or *minimality*): No proper subset of K has the uniqueness property.

Observe that the key concept applies to relvars specifically (an analogous notion can be defined for relation values as well, but relvars are the important case). For the suppliers-and-parts database, the sole keys are {S#} for relvar S, {P#} for relvar P, and {S#,P#} for relvar SP. Note the braces, by the way: Keys are *sets* of attributes, not attributes per se, even when the set in question involves just a single attribute as it does for relvars S and P. Note too that, by definition, key values are tuples!—and so we see that, as claimed earlier, the definition of key relies on the notion of tuple equality. For such reasons, we always enclose the pertinent attribute name(s) in braces, as in the examples at hand.

Any given relvar always has at least one key (why?). If it has two or more, the relational model has historically required—at least in the case of real relvars—that one be chosen as the *primary* key, and the others are then *alternate* keys. While this discipline (i.e., choosing a primary key) might be useful in practice, we do not insist on it, because we regard the idea of making one key somehow "more equal than others" as a psychological issue merely [52]. Of course, we do not prohibit it either, and indeed we tend to adopt it in our own examples. In particular, we assume—where it makes any difference—that {S#}, {P#}, and {S#,P#} are the primary keys for relvars S, P, and SP, respectively (as the double underlining in Fig. 2.1 suggests).

We also define the notion of a *superkey*. A **superkey** is a superset of a key; equivalently, a subset of the heading of relvar R is a superkey for R if it possesses the uniqueness property but not necessarily the irreducibility property. In the case of the suppliers relvar S, for example, every set of attributes that includes S#—the full heading in particular—is a superkey. Note that if the system is told that K is a key for relvar R, it can enforce the uniqueness property for K but not the irreducibility property; in other words, it can guarantee at best only that K is a superkey. (If we wished, however, we could at least impose a syntax rule to the effect that if two distinct keys are defined for the same relvar, then neither can be a superset of the other.)

Another important concept, related to that of keys, is that of *functional dependency*. Let A and B be subsets of the heading of relvar R. Then the **functional dependency** $A \rightarrow B$ holds for R if and only if, in every possible value for R, whenever two tuples have the same value for A, they also have the same value for B.[1] For example, suppose there were an integrity constraint on relvar S to the effect that if two suppliers are located in the same city, then they must also have the same status. Then the functional dependency

```
{ CITY } → { STATUS }
```

would hold for that relvar S.

We will have little to say regarding functional dependencies in this book, but it is interesting to note in passing that they provide the basis for an alternative definition of the notion of a superkey. To be specific, let X be a subset of the heading of relvar R; then X is a superkey for R if and only if the functional dependency $X \rightarrow Y$ holds for every subset Y of the heading of R.

Foreign Keys

Let $R1$ and $R2$ be relvars, not necessarily distinct. Let K and FK be subsets of the headings of $R1$ and $R2$, respectively, such that (a) K is a key for $R1$ and (b) there exists a (very often empty) sequence of attribute renamings—see the section "Relational Operators" later in this chapter—that maps K into K'

---

1. Those A and B values are themselves tuples, so we see that the notion of functional dependency also relies on the notion of tuple equality.

(say), such that *K'* and *FK* consist of exactly the same attributes. Then *FK* is a **foreign key** if and only if, for all time, every tuple in the current value of *R2* has a value for *FK* that is equal to the value of *K'* obtained from some necessarily unique tuple in the current value of *R1*. In the case of suppliers and parts, for example, {S#} and {P#} in relvar SP are foreign keys, and they match—or **reference**—the sole candidate key (in fact, the primary key) in relvars S and P, respectively.

It follows immediately from the foregoing that *no database is ever allowed to contain any unmatched foreign key values*—where an "unmatched foreign key value" is a foreign key value in the current value of some referencing relvar *R2* for which there does not exist a tuple with the applicable candidate key value in the current value of the applicable referenced relvar *R1*. This rule is known as the **referential integrity** rule. (In case it is not obvious, by "referencing relvar" we mean the relvar that includes the foreign key, and by "referenced relvar" we mean the relvar that includes the applicable candidate key. In the case of suppliers and parts, for example, SP is a referencing relvar and S and P are both referenced relvars.)

Note: We include this brief subsection because foreign keys are of considerable pragmatic importance, and also because they were part of the relational model as originally defined (see references [20-21], also reference [70]). However, we must emphasize that foreign keys are not truly fundamental—they merely provide a convenient shorthand for certain integrity constraints that are commonly required in practice.[1] For this reason, *The Third Manifesto* merely suggests, and does not prescribe, foreign key support (see Chapter 10).

Relvars vs. Types

We close this section by pointing out that there is an obvious logical difference between relvars and types: Relvars *have* types but *are not* types. Indeed, a relvar is a variable, and variables are not types. We mention this point explicitly because many people attempt to argue to this day (albeit not usually in these terms) that relvars *are* types: a mistake that we examine in detail, along with a related one, in Chapter 9.

RELVARS, RELATIONS, AND PREDICATES

Everything we have said about relvars and relations in this chapter so far is accurate, of course, but there is another way to think about these matters—not the way (we hasten to add) in which the database community usually does think about them, but we venture to suggest it should be. To be more specific, it is common to think of a relvar as if it were just a simple abstraction of a traditional computer file; but we think the ideas discussed in this section can lead to a deeper understanding of what relational databases are really all about.

Consider the suppliers-and-parts database once again. That database contains three relvars, and of course each of those relvars is supposed to represent some portion of reality in some way. In fact, we can make this statement more precise: Each of those relvars represents some **predicate,** and each of those predicates is, in essence, a generic statement about some portion of reality. Here is an example:

Supplier S# is under contract, is named SNAME, has status STATUS, and is located in city CITY.

This predicate is the **intended interpretation**—also known as the **intension** (note the spelling)—for the suppliers relvar S.

---

1. Similar remarks apply to candidate keys, but here the practical benefits of providing a shorthand are overwhelming.

So what exactly is a predicate?[1]   In general, it is a *function;* like all functions, it takes a set of parameters and it returns a result when it is invoked.   But a predicate in particular is a *truth-valued* function, meaning the result it returns when invoked is a truth value (TRUE or FALSE).   In the case of the predicate just shown for relvar S, for example, the parameters are the attributes of the relvar heading—S#, SNAME, STATUS, and CITY—and they stand for values of the corresponding types (i.e., S#, NAME, INTEGER, and CHAR, respectively).   When we invoke the function (or *instantiate the predicate,* as the logicians say), we substitute arguments for the parameters.   Suppose we substitute the argument values S1, Smith, 20, and London, respectively.   Then we obtain the following **proposition:**

Supplier S1 is under contract, is named Smith, has status 20, and is located in city London.

Now, a proposition in logic is, in general, a statement that is unconditionally either true or false; however, the particular propositions we are interested in here are supposed to be ones that evaluate to TRUE, a point we will return to in just a moment.   In the example just shown, the proposition is indeed true—at least, so we believe—because a tuple corresponding to that proposition does currently appear in relvar S (see Fig. 2.1).

More generally, let relvar *R* represent predicate *P;* then *P* is the **relvar predicate** for relvar *R*.[2] Moreover, let the current value of *R* be *r;* then each tuple *t* in *r* can be regarded as representing a certain proposition *p*, derived by invoking, or instantiating, *P* with the attribute values from *t* being substituted for the parameters of *P*.   And (very important!) *we assume by convention that each such proposition—each proposition, that is, that is represented by some tuple in* r—*evaluates to TRUE.*   Thus, given the sample value for relvar S shown in Fig. 2.1, we assume the following propositions all evaluate to TRUE:

Supplier S1 is under contract, is named Smith, has status 20, and is located in city London.

Supplier S2 is under contract, is named Jones, has status 10, and is located in city Paris.

Supplier S3 is under contract, is named Blake, has status 30, and is located in city Paris.

And so on.   Furthermore, we subscribe, noncontroversially, to the **Closed World Assumption** [121], which says that if a given tuple plausibly could appear in the relvar at some time but in fact does not, then the corresponding proposition is understood by convention to be one that evaluates to FALSE at the time in question.   For example, the tuple

```
TUPLE { S# S#('S6'), SNAME NAME('Lopez'), STATUS 30, CITY 'Madrid' }
```

is (let us agree) a plausible supplier tuple; however, it does not appear in the current value of relvar S as shown in Fig. 2.1, and so we are entitled to assume that the corresponding proposition—

Supplier S6 is under contract, is named Lopez, has status 30, and is located in city Madrid.

—evaluates to FALSE at this time.   In other words, the relvar contains, at any given time, *all* and *only* the tuples that represent true propositions at that time.

More terminology: Again, let *P* be the relvar predicate or *intension* for relvar *R,* and let the value

---

1. Actually there is a slight lack of consensus on this question in the literature; not all logicians would agree with every detail in our definition of the term.   However, we believe they would agree with the essence of that definition.

2. In references [82,83] and elsewhere we called relvar predicates *external* predicates.

of R at some given time be r. Then r—or the body of r, to be more precise—constitutes the **extension** of P at that given time. (Observe, therefore, that the extension varies over time but the intension does not.) Another way of saying the same thing is to say that relation r is "the current manifestation" of predicate P. Yet another way is to say that r contains exactly the tuples that make P evaluate to TRUE (at the time in question).

Now, if we think of each relvar as containing the tuples that make its predicate evaluate to TRUE at the time in question, it follows that we can think in a similar way about *arbitrary relational expressions*. For example, consider the following expression:

```
S { S#, SNAME, STATUS }
```

This expression denotes a *projection*—see the section "Relational Operators" later in this chapter—of the current value of relvar S on attributes S#, SNAME, and STATUS. The result of that projection contains all tuples of the form

```
TUPLE { S# s, SNAME n, STATUS t }
```

such that a tuple of the form

```
TUPLE { S# s, SNAME n, STATUS t, CITY c }
```

currently appears in relvar S for some CITY value c. Thus, that result represents the current extension of a predicate that looks like this:

There exists some city CITY such that supplier S# is under contract, is named SNAME, has status STATUS, and is located in city CITY.

Observe that the result relation has three attributes and the corresponding predicate has three parameters; CITY is not a parameter to that predicate but a **bound variable** instead, thanks to the fact that it is **quantified** by the phrase *there exists some city*.[1] Another, perhaps clearer, way of making the same point—i.e., that the predicate has three parameters, not four—is to observe that the predicate as just stated is logically equivalent to this one:

Supplier S# is under contract, is named SNAME, has status STATUS, and is located in some city.

This version of the predicate very clearly has just three parameters.

It follows from the foregoing that virtual relvars in particular represent certain predicates (see the section "Virtual Relvars" later in this chapter). For example, let virtual relvar SST be defined as follows:

```
VAR SST VIRTUAL ( S { S#, SNAME, STATUS } ) ;
```

Then the relvar predicate for relvar SST is precisely:

Supplier S# is under contract, is named SNAME, has status STATUS, and is located in some city.

There are a few more points to be made regarding predicates and propositions. First, we have

---

1. Bound variables are not variables in the usual programming sense, they are variables in the sense of predicate logic. See reference [78] or reference [112] if you need further explanation of quantifiers, bound variables, and related matters.

said that a predicate has a set of parameters. Of course, that set can be empty—and if it is, then the predicate in question degenerates to a proposition (certainly it is unconditionally either true or false). In other words, all propositions are predicates, but most predicates are not propositions.

Second, we have said that a predicate is "a generic statement about some portion of reality." We can now see that it is precisely the fact that the statement is, in general, parameterized that makes it generic (and if the set of parameters is empty, then that "generic" statement becomes rather specific!).

Third, we have also said, in the case of a relvar predicate specifically, that the parameters correspond to the attributes of the relvar; thus, a relvar of degree *n* represents a predicate with *n* parameters, or what the logicians call an *n*-place predicate. However, no harm is done, logically speaking, if we think of that set of *n* parameters as constituting a single *tuple* parameter (and corresponding arguments, in some instantiation of the predicate, as constituting a single tuple value). Thus, we can simplify our discussions somewhat by considering relvar predicates always to be **monadic,** meaning they are defined in terms of just one (tuple) parameter. And we can then go on to think of a given tuple *t* (of the appropriate tuple type) as either *satisfying* or *violating* a given relvar predicate *P*. To be specific, tuple *t* **satisfies** predicate *P* if and only if the proposition obtained from *P* by substituting *t* for its (tuple) parameter evaluates to TRUE, and it **violates** it if and only if it does not satisfy it.

Fourth, a matter of notation: For clarity, we have deliberately used different symbols, *R* and *P*, for a relvar and its predicate. Sometimes, however, there are good reasons to conflate the two. Thus, we will occasionally write expressions of the form *R(t)*—meaning, specifically, that tuple *t* appears in relvar *R* and therefore satisfies the relvar predicate corresponding to *R*.

Relations vs. Types

It follows from everything we have said in this section so far that:

- *Types* **comprise the things we can talk about.**

- *Relations* **comprise the truths we utter about those things.**

In other words, types give us things we can talk about—in effect, they give us our vocabulary—and relations give us the ability to say things about the things we can talk about. (There is a nice analogy here that might help you remember and appreciate these important points: *Types are to relations as nouns are to sentences.*) In the case of suppliers, for example, the things we can talk about are supplier numbers, names, integers, and character strings, and the things we can say are things of the form "The supplier with the specified supplier number is under contract, has the specified name, has the status denoted by the specified integer, and is located in the city denoted by the specified character string." Note the following important corollaries! In order (as we put it earlier) to "represent some portion of reality":

1. Types and relations are both *necessary*—without types, we have nothing to talk about; without relations, we cannot say anything.

2. Types and relations are *sufficient,* as well as necessary—we do not need anything else, logically speaking. (Well, we need relvars too, in order to reflect the fact that reality changes over time, but not to reflect any *particular* portion of reality.)

3. Types and relations are *not the same thing.*

With regard to the last of these points, incidentally, we saw in the previous section that there is a logical difference between relvars and types—a relvar is a variable, and variables are not types. By the same token, we now see that there is a logical difference between relations and types as well—a relation is a value, and values are not types either.

INTEGRITY CONSTRAINTS

An integrity constraint (usually abbreviated to just *constraint*) can be thought of as a *boolean expression*—also known as a *logical, conditional,* or *truth-valued* expression—that is required to evaluate to TRUE.[1] Constraints are so called because they constrain the values that can appear in some context. They fall into two broad categories, which we call *type constraints* and *database constraints,* respectively:

- A **type constraint** defines the set of values that constitute a given type.

- A **database constraint** limits the set of values a given database is permitted to assume. *Note:* Local or private (nondatabase) data is subject to constraints too, but such matters are beyond the scope of this book.

Type Constraints

In **Tutorial D,** type constraints are specified as part of the definition of the type to which they apply. For example:

```
TYPE S# POSSREP { C CHAR CONSTRAINT SUBSTR ( C, 1, 1 ) = 'S'
                 AND CHAR_LENGTH ( C ) ≥ 2
                 AND CHAR_LENGTH ( C ) ≤ 5 } ;
```

This definition constrains supplier numbers to be such that they can "possibly be represented" by a character string C of from two to five characters, of which the first must be an "S"; we have assumed the existence of an operator called CHAR_LENGTH, which returns the length in characters of its character string argument. (In practice we might additionally want to specify that every character in C after the first is a decimal digit; we do not do so in the example for reasons of simplicity only.) *Note:* Possible representations and related matters are explained in detail in Chapter 3. Several further examples of type constraints can be found under RM Prescription 1 in Chapter 6.

Type constraints are checked during the execution of some *selector* operator for the type in question (see Chapter 3). For example, the expression S#('S1') is an invocation of a selector (also called S#) for type S#, and it returns the supplier number for supplier S1. As another example, the expression S#('X2') is also such an invocation; it fails on a type constraint violation, however, because the first character of the character string argument is not an "S". See RM Prescription 23 in Chapter 6 for further discussion.

Database Constraints

Database constraints are specified in **Tutorial D** by means of an explicit CONSTRAINT statement (or by some shorthand that is effectively equivalent to some such CONSTRAINT statement). Here are some examples (note the constraint names DBC1-DBC5 and the appeals to the self-explanatory operators IS_EMPTY and COUNT):

```
CONSTRAINT DBC1 IS_EMPTY ( S WHERE STATUS < 1 OR STATUS > 100 ) ;
```

---

1. Formally, in fact, a constraint is a proposition.

Meaning: Supplier status values must be in the range 1-100 inclusive. This constraint involves just a single attribute of a single relvar;[1] note that it can be checked for a given supplier by examining just the pertinent supplier tuple in isolation. If relvar S already contains a supplier tuple that violates this constraint when the foregoing CONSTRAINT statement is executed, that execution will fail, of course. More generally, whenever the user attempts to define a new database constraint, the system will first check to see that the constraint in question is satisfied by the database at that time; if not, the constraint is rejected, otherwise it is accepted and enforced from that point forward.

```
CONSTRAINT DBC2 IS_EMPTY ( S WHERE CITY = 'London' AND STATUS ≠ 20 ) ;
```

Meaning: Suppliers in London must have status 20. This constraint involves two distinct attributes (of the same relvar), but it is still the case that it can be checked for a given supplier by examining just the pertinent supplier tuple in isolation.

```
CONSTRAINT DBC3 COUNT ( S ) = COUNT ( S { S# } ) ;
```

Meaning: {S#} is a superkey for relvar S. Like constraints DBC1 and DBC2, this constraint still involves just one relvar; however, it clearly cannot be checked for a given supplier by examining just the pertinent supplier tuple in isolation. *Note:* The **Tutorial D** syntax KEY {S#} might be regarded as shorthand for the foregoing more longwinded expression (ignoring the fact that keys are supposed to be irreducible as well as unique, and ignoring also the fact that the KEY syntax does not include a constraint name); in other words, if K is a key for $R,$ then that fact is a database constraint. In like manner, if the functional dependency $A \rightarrow B$ holds for $R,$ then that fact also is a database constraint.

```
CONSTRAINT DBC4 IS_EMPTY ( ( S JOIN SP ) WHERE STATUS < 20 AND P# = P#('P6') ) ;
```

Meaning: No supplier with status less than 20 can supply part P6. Observe that this constraint involves—in fact, interrelates—two distinct relvars, S and SP. In general, of course, a database constraint might involve any number of distinct relvars.

```
CONSTRAINT DBC5 SP { S# } ‖≤‖ S { S# } ;
```

Meaning: Every supplier number in the shipments relvar must also exist in the suppliers relvar. Notice that this constraint involves a *relational comparison;* to be specific, it requires that the body of the relation that is the projection on S# of the current value of relvar SP be a subset of the body of the relation that is the projection on S# of the current value of relvar S.[2] Given that {S#} is a key—in fact, *the* key—for relvar S, of course, we can see that this constraint is basically just the foreign key constraint from shipments to suppliers; thus, foreign key constraints also are database constraints.

Database constraints are required to be satisfied—i.e., to evaluate to TRUE, given the values currently appearing in the database—**at statement boundaries;** in other words, such constraints are conceptually checked at the end of any statement that might cause them to be violated ("immediate checking"). If any such check fails, the effects on the database of the statement in question are undone and an exception is raised.

As an aside, we remark that since statements are delimited by semicolons in **Tutorial D,** we might

---

1. It is not, however, what references [82,83] call an *attribute constraint,* which is simply a constraint to the effect that a specified attribute is of a specified type.

2. We denote the comparison operator "is a subset of" by the special symbol " ‖≤‖ " (instead of the more usual mathematical symbol) for typographical reasons. See Chapter 5.

say, very informally, that database constraint checking is "done at semicolons." *Note:* The term *statement* here basically means relational assignment; fundamentally, relational assignment is the *only* operator that can update the database. (We ignore here relvar definitions and other statements of a definitional nature, such as the CONSTRAINT statement itself, that cause updates to be made to the database *catalog*. In fact, of course, all such statements are really just relational assignments anyway; to be specific, they are relational assignments in which the target relvars happen to be relvars in the catalog.) Observe, therefore, that statements that update nothing in the database at all—including the statements BEGIN TRANSACTION, COMMIT, and ROLLBACK in particular—do not involve any database constraint checking. See Chapter 6 for further discussion.

Now let *C1*, *C2*, ..., *Cn* be all of the database constraints defined for some given database *DB* (but ignore the constraint names, for simplicity). Then the conjunction

```
( C1 ) AND ( C2 ) AND ... AND ( Cn ) AND TRUE
```

can be regarded as the **total** constraint for database *DB*. Note that final "AND TRUE," by the way; the implication is that if no constraints are explicitly specified for a given database, then the default is just TRUE. The reason this observation is valid is that no *Ci* and *Cj* can contradict one another.[1] Why not? Because if *Ci* is declared first, then *Cj* will necessarily evaluate to FALSE when the CONSTRAINT statement that declares it is executed, and that execution will therefore certainly fail.

Let *DB* be a database, then, and let *DBC* be the total constraint for *DB*. Since we have said that all database constraint checking is immediate—i.e., "done at semicolons"—*database DB is never allowed to violate that constraint DBC:* a state of affairs that we refer to as **The Golden Rule.** Another way of saying the same thing is that no update on database *DB* can be accepted if it leads to a violation of the constraint *DBC;* thus, the constraint *DBC* constitutes the **criterion for acceptability of updates** on database *DB*.

One consequence of the foregoing is that no update on relvar *R* in database *DB* can be accepted if it leads to a violation of any portion of constraint *DBC* that involves that relvar *R:* a weaker form of **The Golden Rule.** *More terminology:* Any portion of *DBC* that involves relvar *R* is a *relvar constraint* for *R,* and the conjunction *RC* of all such portions is the **total** constraint for *R* (see Appendix E for further discussion).[2] Hence, we can say that no update on relvar *R* can be accepted if it leads to a violation of constraint *RC*.

RELATIONAL OPERATORS

The relational model includes an open-ended set of generic operators known collectively as **the relational algebra** (the operators are generic because they apply to all possible relations, loosely speaking). Each operator takes at least one relation as input and produces another as output. In this section, we define a number of such operators; we also give a few examples, but only where we think the operators in question might be unfamiliar to you. *Note:* The fact that the output is always a relation is referred to as the relational **closure** property. It is that property that, among other things, allows us to write *nested relational expressions.*

---

1. A *contradiction* in logic is an expression such as *C* AND NOT *C* that always evaluates to FALSE. (By contrast, a *tautology* is an expression such as *C* OR NOT *C* that always evaluates to TRUE.)

2. In references [82,83] and elsewhere we called total relvar constraints *internal predicates*—partly because the total relvar constraint for *R* can be characterized as an attempt to formalize what we called in those same references the *external* (i.e., relvar) predicate for *R*.

Rename

Let *a* be a relation with an attribute *X* and no attribute *Y*. Then the expression

```
a RENAME ( X AS Y )
```

yields a relation that differs from *a* only in that the name of the specified attribute is *Y* instead of *X*.

Tutorial D also supports a "multiple" form of RENAME, according to which, e.g., the expression

```
a RENAME ( X1 AS Y1 , X2 AS Y2 )
```

is shorthand for

```
( a RENAME ( X1 AS Y1 ) ) RENAME ( X2 AS Y2 )
```

In other words, the individual renamings *X1* AS *Y1* and *X2* AS *Y2* are executed in sequence as written.

Tutorial D also supports "multiple" forms of EXTEND, SUMMARIZE, WRAP/UNWRAP, and GROUP/UNGROUP (see later in this section), to all of which analogous remarks apply.

Restrict

Let *a* be a relation and let *p* be a predicate[1] that is quantifier free (see the next paragraph) and takes just one parameter, a tuple with heading equal to that of *a*. Then the **restriction** of *a* according to *p*—

```
a WHERE p
```

—is a relation with heading equal to that of *a* and with body consisting of all tuples *t* of *a* that satisfy *p*. For example, the expression

```
S WHERE STATUS > 10
```

evaluates to a relation with heading equal to that of relvar S and body consisting of all tuples from the current value of S that satisfy the predicate STATUS > 10. (Note that "STATUS > 10" can indeed be regarded as a predicate with sole parameter a tuple with the same heading as S.)

We now explain the term *quantifier free*. A given monadic predicate is **quantifier free** if we can determine whether a given tuple satisfies it by examining just that tuple in isolation. Such a predicate is also said to be a **restriction predicate** or a **restriction condition** (sometimes a **simple** restriction condition, for emphasis).

Now, Tutorial D provides no explicit support for quantifiers at all. However, it does support them implicitly (in effect), and for user convenience it allows the predicate *p* in the expression

```
a WHERE p
```

---

1. Predicate *p* here is not a relvar predicate in the sense of that term discussed earlier in this chapter; in particular, unlike those earlier predicates, it must be *computable*, meaning the system must be able to evaluate it (given an appropriate argument, of course). To elaborate: If tuple *t* appears in relvar *R*, the system can certainly "compute" the fact that *t* satisfies the relvar predicate *P* for *R*; *P* is computable in that sense. But if the user attempts to insert *t* into *R*, the system has no way to "compute" whether or not *t* satisfies *P*; all it can do is check to see whether inserting *t* into *R* will cause any integrity constraint to be violated.

not to be quantifier free (again, in effect). In other words, **Tutorial D** supports "WHERE predicates" of arbitrary complexity, loosely speaking.

Project

Let relation *a* have attributes *X*, *Y*, ..., *Z* (and possibly others). Then the **projection** of *a* on *X*, *Y*, ..., *Z*—

```
a { X, Y, ..., Z }
```

—is a relation with:

- A heading derived from the heading of *a* by removing all attributes not mentioned in the set { *X*, *Y*, ..., *Z* }

- A body consisting of all tuples { *X x*, *Y y*, ..., *Z z* } such that a tuple appears in *a* with *X* value *x*, *Y* value *y*, ..., and *Z* value *z*

   Tutorial D also allows the foregoing projection to be expressed as *a* { ALL BUT *U*, *V*, ... *W* }, where *U*, *V*, ..., *W* are all of the attributes of *a* apart from *X*, *Y*, ..., *Z*. An analogous remark applies to SUMMARIZE (BY form only), GROUP, and WRAP (see later in this section).

Join

Let relations *a* and *b* have attributes

```
X1, X2, ..., Xm, Y1, Y2, ..., Yn
```

and

```
Y1, Y2, ..., Yn, Z1, Z2, ..., Zp
```

respectively; i.e., the *Y* attributes *Y1*, *Y2*, ..., *Yn* (only) are common to the input relations *a* and *b*, the *X* attributes *X1*, *X2*, ..., *Xm* are the other attributes of *a*, and the *Z* attributes *Z1*, *Z2*, ..., *Zp* are the other attributes of *b*. Observe that:

- We can assume without loss of generality, thanks to the availability of RENAME, that no attribute Xi ($i = 1, 2, ..., m$) has the same name as any attribute Zj ($j = 1, 2, ..., p$).

- Every attribute Yk ($k = 1, 2, ..., n$) has the same type in both *a* and *b* (for otherwise it would not be a common attribute, by definition).

For brevity, let the *X* attributes all taken together be denoted just *X*, and similarly for *Y* and *Z*. Then the **join** of *a* and *b*—

```
a JOIN b
```

—is a relation with heading the (set-theoretic) union of the headings of *a* and *b* and body consisting of all tuples *t* such that *t* is the (set-theoretic) union of a tuple appearing in *a* and a tuple appearing in *b*. In other words, the heading is { *X*, *Y*, *Z* }, and the body consists of all tuples { *X x*, *Y y*, *Z z* } such that a tuple appears in *a* with *X* value *x* and *Y* value *y* and a tuple appears in *b* with *Y* value *y* and *Z* value *z*.

Some logical consequences of the foregoing definition:

- If $n = 0$, join degenerates to (relational) *cartesian product*. *Note:* This operation differs from conventional cartesian product in that it gives a result that is a relation (of degree $m+p$). Conventional cartesian product, by contrast, gives a result that is a set of ordered pairs (of tuples, one each from a and b). As a consequence, relational cartesian product, unlike its conventional counterpart, is both commutative and associative. From this point forward, we will take the term *cartesian product* (sometimes just *product*, unqualified) to refer to the relational operator specifically, barring explicit statements to the contrary.

- If $m = p = 0$, a JOIN b degenerates to a INTERSECT b—see the next subsection. (Cartesian product and intersection are thus both special cases of join. This fact notwithstanding, for psychological reasons **Tutorial D** supports INTERSECT explicitly, though not cartesian product.)

- If $p = 0$, a JOIN b degenerates to a SEMIJOIN b, which is equivalent to (a JOIN b){X,Y} (in other words, it is the join of a and b, projected back on the attributes of a). Likewise, if $m = 0$, a JOIN b degenerates to b SEMIJOIN a.

Join is both commutative and associative. **Tutorial D** therefore supports an *n*-adic form of the operator, and it allows unnecessary parentheses to be omitted from an uninterrupted sequence of dyadic joins. For example, the expressions

```
a JOIN ( b JOIN c )
```

and

```
( a JOIN b ) JOIN c
```

can both be unambiguously abbreviated to just

```
a JOIN b JOIN c
```

They can also be written as JOIN {a,b,c} (and the order in which the operands are specified here is immaterial).

Furthermore, it turns out to be desirable to define both (1) joins of just a single relation and (2) joins of no relations at all. Let s be a set of relations. Then:

1. If s contains just one relation r, then the join of all relations in s—in **Tutorial D**, JOIN {r}—is simply r.

2. If s contains no relations at all, then the join of all relations in s—in **Tutorial D**, JOIN {}—is TABLE_DEE. *Note:* TABLE_DEE is the unique relation having degree zero and cardinality one. See Chapter 6 for further explanation.

Union, Intersect, and Difference

Let a and b be relations of the same type. Then:

- The **union** of those relations, a UNION b, is a relation of the same type, with body consisting of all tuples t such that t appears in a or b or both. *Note:* **Tutorial D** also supports "disjoint union" (D_UNION), which is a version of union that requires its operands to be disjoint (i.e., to have no tuples in common). As we will see in Chapter 6, D_UNION can be useful in defining the semantics of INSERT, also in certain integrity constraints.

■   The **intersection** of those relations, *a* INTERSECT *b,* is a relation of the same type, with body consisting of all tuples *t* such that *t* appears in both *a* and *b.*

■   The **difference** between those relations, *a* MINUS *b* (in that order), is a relation of the same type, with body consisting of all tuples *t* such that *t* appears in *a* and not *b. Note:* **Tutorial D** also supports SEMIMINUS (semidifference); the expression *a* SEMIMINUS *b* is equivalent to *a* MINUS (*a* SEMIJOIN *b*). Observe in particular that if *a* and *b* are of the same type, then *a* SEMIMINUS *b* degenerates to *a* MINUS *b.* (This fact notwithstanding, **Tutorial D** supports MINUS explicitly—though this support, like that for INTERSECT, is included mainly for psychological reasons.)

Like join, union and intersection are each both commutative and associative. **Tutorial D** therefore supports an *n*-adic form of both, and it allows unnecessary parentheses to be omitted from an uninterrupted sequence of dyadic unions or intersections. For example, the expressions

```
a UNION ( b UNION c )
```

and

```
( a UNION b ) UNION c
```

can both be unambiguously abbreviated to just

```
a UNION b UNION c
```

They can also be written as UNION {*a,b,c*} (and the order in which the operands are specified here is immaterial).

Furthermore, it turns out to be desirable to define both (1) unions and intersections of just a single relation and (2) unions and intersections of no relations at all. Let *s* be a set of relations all of the same type *RT.* Then:

1.   If *s* contains just one relation *r,* then the union and intersection of all relations in *s*—in **Tutorial D,** UNION {*r*} and INTERSECT {*r*}—are both simply *r.*

2.   If *s* contains no relations at all, then:

   ■   The union of all relations in *s*—in **Tutorial D,** UNION *h* {}, where *h* is the heading of *RT*—is the empty relation of type *RT.* Note the need to specify the result heading *h* in this case, since there is no input relation from which that heading can be inferred.

   ■   The intersection of all relations in *s*—in **Tutorial D,** INTERSECT *h* {}, where *h* is the heading of *RT*—is the "universal" relation of type *RT* (i.e., that unique relation of type *RT* that contains all possible tuples of type TUPLE *h*).[1] We remark in passing that the term *universal relation* is more frequently used in the literature with a rather different meaning

---

1. You might see an apparent contradiction here: Given that INTERSECT is a special case of JOIN, you might have expected both operators to give the same result when applied to no relations at all, but they do not. See Exercise 33 at the end of the chapter.

(see, e.g., reference [101]).

Extend

Let *a* be a relation. Then the **extension**

```
EXTEND a ADD ( exp AS Z )
```

is a relation with

- A heading consisting of the heading of *a* extended with the attribute Z

- A body consisting of all tuples *t* such that *t* is a tuple of *a* extended with a value for attribute Z that is computed by evaluating *exp* on[1] that tuple of *a*

Relation *a* must not have an attribute called Z, and *exp* must not refer to Z. Observe that the result has cardinality equal to that of *a* and degree equal to one plus that of *a*. The type of Z in that result is the type of *exp*.

Here is a simple example of EXTEND:

```
EXTEND S ADD ( 3 * STATUS AS TRIPLE )
```

The result of this operation, given our usual sample data values, is shown in Fig. 2.4.

S#	SNAME	STATUS	CITY	TRIPLE
S1	Smith	20	London	60
S2	Jones	10	Paris	30
S3	Blake	30	Paris	90
S4	Clark	20	London	60
S5	Adams	30	Athens	90

Fig. 2.4: Extending S (as shown in Fig. 2.1) to add a "triple status" attribute

By the way, do not make the mistake in this example of thinking that relvar S has been changed in the database. EXTEND is not an SQL-style ALTER TABLE. Rather, the result of the EXTEND expression is simply a derived relation, just as (e.g.) the result of the expression S JOIN SP is a derived relation. Analogous remarks apply to all of the other relational algebra operators, of course: in particular, to RENAME (see earlier in this section).

---

1. To be more precise, evaluating *exp* "on" some tuple *u* of *a* means (a) substituting, for each appearance in *exp* of an attribute name *A* from *a*, the value of attribute *A* from that tuple *u* and then (b) evaluating the modified version of *exp* that results.

Summarize

Let *a* and *b* be relations. Then the **summarization**

```
SUMMARIZE a PER ( b ) ADD ( summary AS Z )
```

is a relation defined as follows:

- First, *b* must be of the same type as some projection of *a*; i.e., every attribute of *b* must be an attribute of *a*. Let the attributes of that projection (equivalently, of *b*) be *A1, A2, ..., An*.

- The heading of the result consists of the heading of *b* extended with the attribute Z.

- The body of that result consists of all tuples *t* such that *t* is a tuple of *b* extended with a value for attribute Z. That Z value is computed by evaluating *summary* over[1] all tuples of *a* that have the same value for attributes *A1, A2, ..., An* as tuple *t* does. (Of course, if no tuples of *a* have the same value for *A1, A2, ..., An* as tuple *t* does, then *summary* is evaluated over an empty set of tuples.)

Relation *b* must not have an attribute called Z, and *summary* must not refer to Z. Observe that the result has cardinality equal to that of *b* and degree equal to one plus that of *b*. The type of Z in that result is whatever the type of *summary* is.

Here is a simple example of SUMMARIZE:

```
SUMMARIZE SP PER ( S { S# } ) ADD ( COUNT ( ) AS P_COUNT )
```

The result of this operation, given our usual sample data values, is shown in Fig. 2.5. Observe in particular that the result includes a tuple for supplier S5. *Note:* If you happen to be familiar with SQL, it might help to point out that, by contrast, the SQL expression

```
SELECT S#, COUNT(*) AS P_COUNT
FROM   SP
GROUP  BY S#
```

S#	P_COUNT
S1	6
S2	2
S3	1
S4	3
S5	0

Fig. 2.5: Summarizing SP (from Fig. 2.1) to obtain "number of shipments per supplier"

---

1. Remarks analogous to those in footnote 1 on the previous page apply here also.

yields a result containing no tuple for supplier S5, because relvar SP as shown in Fig. 2.1 contains no such tuple either. In other words, it might be thought that the expression just shown is an SQL analog of the SUMMARIZE expression earlier, but in fact it is not—not quite.

Here is another example:

```
SUMMARIZE S PER ( S { CITY } ) ADD ( AVG ( STATUS ) AS AVG_STATUS )
```

In this example, "relation *b*" is not just "of the same type as" some projection of "relation *a*," it actually *is* such a projection. In such a case, **Tutorial D** allows the expression to be abbreviated slightly, thus:

```
SUMMARIZE S BY { CITY } ADD ( AVG ( STATUS ) AS AVG_STATUS )
```

Either way, the result is as shown in Fig. 2.6.

CITY	AVG_STATUS
London	20
Paris	20
Athens	30

Fig. 2.6: Summarizing S (from Fig. 2.1) to obtain "average status per city"

Tutorial D also allows the PER or BY specification in SUMMARIZE to be omitted entirely, in which case the specification PER (TABLE_DEE) is implicit. Again, see Chapter 6 for further explanation of TABLE_DEE.

We assume you are familiar with the semantics of the various kinds of "summaries" (COUNT, SUM, AVG, and so forth) and omit further details here. However, we stress the point that a summary is not the same thing as an aggregate operator invocation (see below). An aggregate operator invocation is an expression[1] and is allowed wherever a literal or, more generally, a selector invocation of the appropriate type would be allowed. A summary, by contrast, is merely an operand within a SUMMARIZE invocation; it is not an expression, it has no meaning outside the context of a SUMMARIZE invocation, and in fact it cannot appear outside that context.

So what then is an aggregate operator invocation? Well, an aggregate operator is, very loosely, an operator that derives a single value from the "aggregate" of such values appearing in some specified relation or in some specified attribute of some specified relation. As with the business of summaries earlier, we assume you are familiar with the semantics of such operators and do not give detailed definitions here. However, we do give a few examples and corresponding results (based on our usual sample data values). Note the difference between the two AVG examples in particular: The first—in which the comma and the second argument could be omitted if desired—returns the average of the three status values in the projection of S over STATUS; the second returns the average of the five status values in S.

---

1. Usually, though not always, a scalar expression specifically (see Chapter 5). For present purposes we take the term *scalar expression* to mean, simply, an expression that is neither tuple nor relation valued. The whole matter of "scalarness" is discussed in detail in Chapter 3; for now we just assume it is well understood.

```
COUNT ( S )                                                   /* result    5 */

COUNT ( S { CITY } )                                          /* result    3 */

AVG   ( S { STATUS }, STATUS )                                /* result   20 */

AVG   ( S, STATUS )                                           /* result   22 */

MAX   ( S, STATUS )                                           /* result   30 */

SUM   ( EXTEND S ADD ( ( ( 2 * STATUS ) + 1 ) AS XYZ ), XYZ )  /* result  225 */

OR    ( EXTEND S ADD ( ( STATUS > 20 ) AS TEST ), TEST )      /* result TRUE */
```

Group and Ungroup

The fact that we can have relations with attributes that are relation valued leads to the need for operators for mapping between relations that contain such attributes and relations that do not. For example:

```
SP GROUP ( { P#, QTY } AS PQ )
```

Given our usual sample data, this expression yields the result shown in Fig. 2.7 (opposite). *Explanation:* Observe first that the original expression

```
SP GROUP ( { P#, QTY } AS PQ )
```

—loosely, "group SP over P# and QTY"—might be read as "group SP *by* S#," S# being the sole attribute of SP not mentioned in the GROUP specification.[1] The result is a relation defined as follows. First, the heading looks like this:

```
{ S# S#, PQ RELATION { P# P#, QTY QTY } }
```

In other words, it consists of a relation-valued attribute PQ (where PQ values in turn have attributes P# and QTY), together with all of the other attributes of SP (of course, "all of the other attributes of SP" here just means attribute S#). Second, the body contains exactly one tuple for each distinct S# value in SP (and no other tuples). Each tuple in that body consists of the applicable S# value (*s*, say), together with a PQ value (*pq*, say) obtained as follows:

- Each SP tuple is replaced by a tuple (*x*, say) in which the P# and QTY components have been "wrapped"—see the next subsection—into a tuple-valued component (*y*, say).

- The *y* components of all such tuples *x* in which the S# value is equal to *s* are then "grouped" into a relation, *pq*, and a result tuple with S# value equal to *s* and PQ value equal to *pq* is thereby obtained.

---

1. If you happen to be familiar with SQL, it might help to point out that—*very* loosely speaking—GROUP in **Tutorial D** specifies the attributes that are to be grouped together, whereas GROUP BY in SQL specifies the *other* attributes (i.e., the attributes that control the grouping). In other words, the expression SP GROUP ({P#,QTY} AS PQ) might be read as "group SP **by** S#," S# being the sole attribute of SP not mentioned in the GROUP specification. Indeed, the "grouping" {P#,QTY} in the example can alternatively be specified as {ALL BUT S#}, in **Tutorial D**.

The overall result is thus indeed as shown in the figure. Note in particular that the result includes no tuple for supplier S5 (because relvar SP does not currently do so either).

<table>
<tr><th>S#</th><th>PQ</th></tr>
<tr><td>S1</td><td><table><tr><th>P#</th><th>QTY</th></tr><tr><td>P1</td><td>300</td></tr><tr><td>P2</td><td>200</td></tr><tr><td>P3</td><td>400</td></tr><tr><td>P4</td><td>200</td></tr><tr><td>P5</td><td>100</td></tr><tr><td>P6</td><td>100</td></tr></table></td></tr>
<tr><td>S2</td><td><table><tr><th>P#</th><th>QTY</th></tr><tr><td>P1</td><td>300</td></tr><tr><td>P2</td><td>400</td></tr></table></td></tr>
<tr><td>S3</td><td><table><tr><th>P#</th><th>QTY</th></tr><tr><td>P2</td><td>200</td></tr></table></td></tr>
<tr><td>S4</td><td><table><tr><th>P#</th><th>QTY</th></tr><tr><td>P2</td><td>200</td></tr><tr><td>P4</td><td>300</td></tr><tr><td>P5</td><td>400</td></tr></table></td></tr>
</table>

Fig. 2.7: Grouping SP over P# and QTY

Observe that the result of *r* GROUP ({ *A1*, *A2*, ..., *An* } AS *B*) has degree equal to $nr\text{-}n+1$, where *nr* is the degree of *r*.

Now we turn to UNGROUP. Let SPQ be the relation shown in Fig. 2.7. Then the expression

```
SPQ UNGROUP ( PQ )
```

(perhaps unsurprisingly) gives us back our usual SP relation. To be more precise, it yields a relation defined as follows. First, the heading looks like this:

```
{ S# S#, P# P#, QTY QTY }
```

In other words, the heading consists of attributes P# and QTY (derived from attribute PQ), together with all of the other attributes of SPQ (i.e., just attribute S#, in the example). Second, the body contains exactly one tuple for each combination of a tuple in SPQ and a tuple in the PQ value within that SPQ tuple (and no other tuples). Each tuple in that body consists of the applicable S# value (*s*, say), together with P# and QTY values (*p* and *q*, say) obtained as follows:

- Each SPQ tuple is replaced by an "ungrouped" set of tuples, one such tuple (*x*, say) for each tuple in the PQ value in that SPQ tuple.

- Each such tuple *x* contains an S# component (*s*, say) equal to the S# component from the SPQ tuple in question and a tuple-valued component (*y*, say) equal to some tuple from the PQ component from the SPQ tuple in question.

- The y components of each such tuple x in which the S# value is equal to s are then "unwrapped"—see the next subsection—into separate P# and QTY components (p and q, say), and a result tuple with S# value equal to s, P# value equal to p, and QTY value equal to q is thereby obtained.

The overall result is thus, as claimed, our usual SP relation.

Note: It follows from the definition of UNGROUP that if SPQ had included a tuple for supplier S5, with PQ value an empty relation—if SPQ had the value shown in Fig. 2.2 in particular—then the result of evaluating SPQ UNGROUP (PQ) would still include no tuple for supplier S5.

Observe that the result of r UNGROUP (B)—where the relations that are values of the relation-valued attribute B have heading { $A1, A2, \ldots, An$ }—has degree equal to $nr + n - 1$, where nr is the degree of r.

Additional Operations

Tutorial D supports a few additional operations over and above those described so far. For purposes of reference, we briefly summarize those additional operations in this subsection.

Compose: Let a and b be as for JOIN. Then a COMPOSE b is equivalent to (a JOIN b){X,Z}. *Note:* If a and b have no attributes in common, then COMPOSE degenerates to JOIN (and that JOIN in turn degenerates to cartesian product).

Semijoin and Semidifference: We have already mentioned the fact that **Tutorial D** supports these operators directly. However, it also supports more user-friendly syntax for both, according to which a SEMIJOIN b and a SEMIMINUS b can be expressed as

```
a MATCHING b    and    a NOT MATCHING b
```

(respectively). For example, the query "Get suppliers who do not supply part P1" can be formulated thus:

```
S NOT MATCHING ( SP WHERE P# = P#('P1') )
```

Substitute:[1] We do not attempt to define this operator here in full generality (such a definition appears in Chapter 5), but content ourselves with a simple example. Consider the following expression:

```
UPDATE S WHERE CITY = 'Paris' ( STATUS := 2 * STATUS , CITY := 'Nice' )
```

The first point to note about this expression is that it *is* an expression, not a statement (there is no terminating semicolon), and it has no effect on relvar S. What it does do is yield a relation containing just those tuples from relvar S for which the city is Paris—except that, in those tuples, the status is doubled and the city is set to Nice. The overall expression is thus equivalent to the following:

---

1. The name *substitute* here has nothing to do with the substitution of arguments for parameters, nor with the concept of *substitutability* as understood in the context of type inheritance (see Part IV).

```
WITH ( S WHERE CITY = 'Paris' ) AS T1 ,
     ( EXTEND T1 ADD ( 2 * STATUS AS NEW_STATUS , 'Nice' AS NEW_CITY ) ) AS T2 ,
       T2 { ALL BUT STATUS, CITY } AS T3 ,
     ( T3 RENAME ( NEW_STATUS AS STATUS , NEW_CITY AS CITY ) ) AS T4 :
  T4
```

Notice the use of WITH here to introduce names for the results of certain subexpressions. We will be making heavy use of this construct in the chapters to come. See Chapter 5 for a formal explanation.

Now, in Chapter 3 we will see that operators in general fall into two disjoint categories, read-only vs. update operators; and (at the risk of confusing you) we need to stress the fact that the substitute operator UPDATE is not an update operator!—it is a read-only operator instead. We use the keyword UPDATE because the operator does closely resemble the familiar UPDATE statement in its effect. In fact, given support for the substitute operator UPDATE as sketched above, the effect of the UPDATE statement

```
UPDATE R WHERE p ( attribute updates ) ;
```

can neatly be defined as being equivalent to that of the following assignment:

```
R := ( R WHERE NOT ( p ) ) UNION ( UPDATE R WHERE p ( attribute updates ) ) ;
```

Again, see Chapter 5 for a formal explanation. *Note:* For the remainder of this book, we will rely on context to make it clear whether the term "UPDATE operator" refers to the read-only or update operator of that name.

Wrap and Unwrap: Consider the following relation types:

```
RELATION { S# S#, P# P#, QTY QTY }

RELATION { S#, PQ TUPLE { P# P#, QTY QTY } }
```

Let us refer to these types as *SPT3* and *SPT2*, respectively, and let SP3 and SP2 be relvars of types *SPT3* and *SPT2*, respectively (where the 3 and 2 refer to the number of attributes in each case). Then:

- The expression

```
SP3 WRAP ( { P#, QTY } AS PQ )
```

  takes the relation that is the current value of SP3 and, for each tuple in that relation, "wraps" the P# and QTY components of that tuple to yield a single tuple-valued PQ component. The result of the expression is thus of type *SPT2*, and so (e.g.) the following assignment is valid:

```
SP2 := SP3 WRAP ( { P#, QTY } AS PQ ) ;
```

- The expression

```
SP2 UNWRAP ( PQ )
```

  takes the relation that is the current value of SP2 and, for each tuple in that relation, "unwraps" the (tuple-valued) PQ component of that value to yield two scalar components P# and QTY. The result of the expression is thus of type *SPT3*, and so (e.g.) the following assignment is valid:

```
SP3 := SP2 UNWRAP ( PQ ) ;
```

Divide: We defer a detailed explanation of this operator to Chapter 6 (see RM Prescription 18).

Tclose: "Tclose" stands for *transitive closure*. Let a be a binary relation with attributes X and Y, both of the same type T. Then the **transitive closure** of a, TCLOSE a, is a relation a^+ with heading the same as that of a and body a superset of that of a, defined as follows: The tuple

```
{ X x, Y y }
```

appears in a^+ if and only if it appears in a or there exists a sequence of values $z1, z2, ..., zn$, all of type T, such that the tuples

```
{ X x, Y z1 }, { X z1, Y z2 }, ..., { X zn, Y y }
```

all appear in a. See RM Prescription 19 in Chapter 6 for further explanation, also RM Very Strong Suggestion 6 in Chapter 10.

Relational Operations on Relvars

As we have seen, the operators of the relational algebra apply, by definition, to relation *values* specifically. In particular, of course, they apply to the values that happen to be the current values of relation *variables*. As a consequence, it clearly makes sense to talk about—for example—"the projection on attribute A of relvar R," meaning the relation that results from taking the projection on that attribute A of the current value r of that relvar R.

Sometimes, however, it is convenient to use expressions like "the projection on attribute A of relvar R" in a slightly different sense. By way of example, suppose we define a virtual relvar, or view, of the suppliers relvar S, called SC, that consists of just the S# and CITY attributes of that relvar (see the next section). In **Tutorial D,** that definition might look like this:

```
VAR SC VIRTUAL ( S { S#, CITY } ) ;
```

In this example, we might say, loosely but very conveniently, that relvar SC is "the projection on S# and CITY of relvar S"—meaning, more precisely, that the value of SC at all times is the projection on S# and CITY of the value of relvar S at the time in question. In a sense, therefore, we can talk in terms of projections of relvars per se, rather than just in terms of projections of current values of relvars. We hope this kind of dual usage on our part will not cause you any confusion.

VIRTUAL RELVARS

A virtual relvar or view V is a relvar whose value at time t is the result of evaluating a certain relational expression at that time t. The expression in question is specified when V is defined. To repeat an example from the previous section:

```
VAR SC VIRTUAL ( S { S#, CITY } ) ;
```

The goal is to make virtual relvars look like real ones to the user (meaning, of course, the user who uses them, as opposed to the user who actually defines them). If this goal is achieved, several advantages accrue (see reference [76] for a detailed discussion); but can it be achieved? Well, the implication is that the user must be allowed to operate on the virtual relvar exactly as if were real, and such operations must be mapped by the system into certain "equivalent" operations on the real relvars in terms of which the virtual one is—possibly via many levels of indirection—ultimately defined.

Read-only operations are straightforward. For example, the expression

```
SC WHERE CITY = 'London'
```

can be mapped very simply by the system into

```
( S { S#, CITY } ) WHERE CITY = 'London'
```

But what about update operations? As you are probably aware, the view update problem has been the subject of investigation for many years. When we wrote this book's predecessor [83], we thought that problem was solved, but we realized subsequently that there were still some unanswered questions. For that reason we choose not to discuss the issue further here; instead, we refer you to Appendix E for a detailed examination of the topic.

We close this section by emphasizing that we do *not,* in this book, reserve the term *relvar* to mean a real relvar exclusively (SQL, by contrast, very commonly uses the term *table* to mean a "base table" exclusively). If we want to say that some relvar *R* is a real relvar specifically—or a virtual relvar specifically, come to that—then we will say as much explicitly.

THE RELATIONAL MODEL

For purposes of future reference, we close this chapter with a rather abstract definition of the relational model, based on one in reference [70]. Briefly, the relational model consists of the following five components:

1. An open-ended collection of **scalar types,** including in particular type BOOLEAN (truth values)

2. A **relation type generator** and an intended interpretation for relations of types generated thereby

3. Facilities for defining **relation variables** of such generated relation types

4. A **relational assignment** operator for assigning relation values to such relation variables

5. An open-ended collection of generic **relational operators** for deriving relation values from other relation values

We offer the following additional comments on these five components:

1. The scalar types can be system or user defined, in general; thus, a means must be available for users to define their own scalar types (this requirement is implied, partly, by the fact that the set of such types is open ended). A means must therefore also be available for users to define their own scalar operators, since types without operators are useless. The only required system-defined scalar type is BOOLEAN (the most fundamental type of all), but a real system will surely support other built-in scalar types (e.g., INTEGER) as well.

2. The relation type generator allows users to specify individual relation types as desired (see Chapters 3-6 for further explanation). The intended interpretation for a given relation of a given relation type is as a set of true propositions, all of them instantiations of some common predicate.

3. Facilities for defining relation variables must be available (of course). Relation variables are the only variables allowed in a relational database. *Note:* This latter observation is in accordance

with Codd's *Information Principle*. Codd stated that principle in various forms and in various places over the years (indeed, he was known to refer to it as *the* fundamental principle underlying the relational model). One possible formulation is as follows:

The entire information content of the database is represented in one and only one way: namely, as explicit values in attribute positions in tuples in relations.

(Reference [76] remarks that this principle might better be called *The Principle of Uniform Representation*. *The Principle of Uniformity of Representation* might be better still; certainly it is more accurate, though somewhat clumsy.)

4.   Variables are updatable by definition; hence, every kind of variable is subject to *assignment*, and relation variables are no exception. INSERT, DELETE, and UPDATE shorthands are permitted and indeed useful, but strictly speaking they are only shorthands.

5.   The generic relational operators are the operators that make up the relational algebra, and they are therefore built in (though there is no inherent reason why users should not be able to define additional operators of their own, if desired). They are used for the formulation of relational expressions. Those expressions in turn serve many purposes; for example, they are used in query formulation, in virtual relvar definition, and (very important!) in the specification of constraints.

EXERCISES

1.   State *The Information Principle*.

2.   What is a relational assignment?

3.   Define the terms *attribute, body, cardinality, degree, heading, relation, relvar,* and *tuple*.

4.   State as precisely as you can what it means for two tuples to be equal.

5.   Which of the relational operators defined in this chapter have a definition that does not rely on tuple equality?

6.   What is a relation-valued attribute (RVA)? Give an example of a relation with (a) one RVA, (b) two RVAs. Also give two more relations that represent the same information as those relations but do not involve RVAs. Also give an example of a relation with an RVA such that there is no relation that represents precisely the same information but has no RVA. Finally, assuming all of your example relations are in fact values of corresponding relvars, give relvar predicates for those relvars.

7.   What is an aggregate operator?

8.   Define the operators *extend, summarize, wrap, unwrap, group,* and *ungroup*.

9.   Write **Tutorial D** tuple selector invocations for a typical tuple from (a) the parts relvar, (b) the shipments relvar.

10. Write a **Tutorial D** expression that returns TRUE if the current value of the parts relvar P is empty and FALSE otherwise. Do not use the IS_EMPTY shorthand.

11. Given the usual suppliers-and-parts database, what is the value of the expression S JOIN SP JOIN P? What is the corresponding predicate? *Warning:* There is a trap here.

12. Given sample values for the suppliers-and-parts database as shown in Fig. 2.1, what values do the following expressions denote? In each case, also give an informal interpretation of the expression in natural language.

    a.   S SEMIJOIN (SP WHERE P# = P#('P2'))

    b.   P NOT MATCHING (SP WHERE S# = S#('S2'))

    c.   S { CITY } UNION P { CITY }

    d.   S { CITY } MINUS P { CITY }

    e.   S { CITY } D_UNION P { CITY }

    f.   S { S#, CITY } COMPOSE P { P#, CITY }

    g.   JOIN { (S RENAME (CITY AS SC)) { SC } , (P RENAME (CITY AS PC)) { PC } }

    h.   WITH (S WHERE NOT (CITY = 'Athens')) AS T1 ,
             (T1 RENAME (CITY AS SC)) AS T2 ,
             (P WHERE NOT (CITY = 'London')) AS T3 ,
             (T3 RENAME (CITY AS PC)) AS T4 :
           TCLOSE (JOIN { T2 { SC } , T4 { PC } })

13. Write **Tutorial D** expressions for the following queries on the suppliers-and-parts database:

    a. Get all shipments.

    b. Get supplier numbers for suppliers who supply part P1.

    c. Get suppliers with status in the range 15-25 inclusive.

    d. Get part numbers for parts supplied by a supplier in London.

    e. Get part numbers for parts not supplied by any supplier in London.

    f. Get city names for cities in which at least two suppliers are located.

    g. Get all pairs of part numbers such that some supplier supplies both of the indicated parts.

    h. Get the total number of parts supplied by supplier S1.

    i. Get supplier numbers for suppliers with a status lower than that of supplier S1.

    j. Get supplier numbers for suppliers whose city is first in the alphabetic list of such cities.

    k. Get part numbers for parts supplied by all suppliers in London.

    l. Get supplier-number/part-number pairs such that the indicated supplier does not supply the indicated part.

m.   Get all pairs of supplier numbers, S*x* and S*y* say, such that S*x* and S*y* supply exactly the same set of parts each.

14.   Which if any of the following expressions are equivalent?

a.   `SUMMARIZE r PER ( r { } ) ADD ( COUNT ( ) AS CT )`

b.   `SUMMARIZE r ADD ( COUNT ( ) AS CT )`

c.   `SUMMARIZE r BY { } ADD ( COUNT ( ) AS CT )`

d.   `EXTEND TABLE_DEE ADD ( COUNT ( r ) AS CT )`

15.   What do you understand by the term *first normal form?*

16.   Let R be a relvar of degree n. What is the maximum number of candidate keys R might possess?

17.   What do you understand by the terms *proposition* and *predicate?* Give examples.

18.   Explain the term *relvar predicate.* Give relvar predicates for the parts and shipments relvars from the suppliers-and-parts database.

19.   Explain the Closed World Assumption.

20.   In the body of the chapter, we said any type whatsoever can be used as the basis for defining attributes, in general. That qualifier "in general" was there for a reason, however. Can you think of any exceptions to this general rule?

21.   Define the terms *functional dependency, candidate key,* and *foreign key.*

22.   Candidate keys are *sets* of attributes. What happens if the set in question is empty (i.e., contains no attributes)? Can you think of any uses for such an empty (or "nullary") candidate key?

23.   *(This is essentially a repeat of Exercise 9 from Chapter 1, but you should be able to give a more comprehensive answer now.)* There are many logical differences between a relation and a table. List as many as you can.

24.   What is the closure property of the relational algebra?

25.   Using **Tutorial D,** write integrity constraints for the suppliers-and-parts database to express the following requirements:

a.   All London suppliers must have status 20.

b.   No two suppliers can be located in the same city.

c.   At most one supplier can be located in Athens at any one time.

d.   There must exist at least one London supplier.

e.   The average supplier status must be at least 10.

f.   Every London supplier must be capable of supplying part P2.

What operations can cause these constraints to be violated?

26.   Let *r* be a relation of degree *n*. How many different projections of *r* are there?

27.   Union, intersection, cartesian product, and join are all both commutative and associative. Verify these claims. Also verify that semijoin is associative but not commutative.

28.   Consider the expression *a* JOIN *b*. If *a* and *b* have disjoint headings, this expression is equivalent to *a* TIMES *b* (where TIMES denotes cartesian product); if they have the same heading, it is equivalent to *a* INTERSECT *b*. Verify these claims. What is the expression equivalent to if the heading of *a* is a proper subset of that of *b?*

29.   Show that MINUS can be regarded as a special case of SEMIMINUS.

30.   In ordinary arithmetic there are two special numbers, 1 and 0, with the properties that

```
x * 1  =  1 * x  =  x
```

and

```
x * 0  =  0 * x  =  0
```

for all numbers *x*. What relations if any play analogous roles in the relational algebra? Investigate the effect of the algebraic operations discussed in this chapter on those relations.

31.   What do the following **Tutorial D** expressions denote?

a.   `RELATION { S# S#, P# P#, QTY QTY } { }`

b.   `RELATION { TUPLE { S# S#('S1'), P# P#('P1'), QTY QTY(300) } }`

c.   `RELATION { TUPLE { } }`

d.   `RELATION { } { TUPLE { } }`

e.   `RELATION { } { }`

32.   Closure is important in the relational model for the same kind of reason that numeric closure is important in ordinary arithmetic. In arithmetic, however, there is one situation where the closure property breaks down, in a sense—namely, division by zero. Is there any analogous situation in the relational algebra?

33.   Given that intersect is a special case of join, why do not both operators give the same result when applied to no relations at all?

34.   Let *r* be the relation denoted by the following expression:

```
SP GROUP ( { } AS X )
```

Show what *r* looks like, given our usual sample value for SP. Also show the result of

```
r UNGROUP ( X )
```

35. Let *A* and *B* be relvars. State the candidate key(s) for each of the following:

    a. `A WHERE p`

    b. `A {...}`

    c. `A UNION B`

    d. `A INTERSECT B`

    e. `A MINUS B`

    f. `A JOIN B`

    g. `EXTEND A ADD ( exp AS Z )`

    h. `SUMMARIZE A PER ( B ) ADD ( exp AS Z )`

    Assume in each case that *A* and *B* meet the requirements for the operation in question (e.g., they are of the same type, in the case of UNION).

36. Show that WRAP and UNWRAP are really just shorthand for certain combinations of other operators.

37. Consider this expression:

    ```
    SUMMARIZE SP PER ( S { S# } ) ADD ( COUNT ( ) AS NP )
    ```

    Give an expression involving EXTEND instead of SUMMARIZE that is logically equivalent to this expression.

38. Define virtual relvars for the following:

    a. Suppliers in London

    b. Supplier numbers for suppliers who supply every purple part

    c. Supplier-number/part-number pairs for suppliers and parts that are not in the same city

39. Consider the suppliers-and-parts database, but ignore the parts relvar for simplicity. Here in outline are two possible designs for suppliers and shipments:

    ```
    1.    S  { S#, SNAME, STATUS, CITY }
          SP { S#, P#, QTY }

    2.    SSP { S#, SNAME, STATUS, CITY, P#, QTY }
          XSS { S#, SNAME, STATUS, CITY }
    ```

Design 1 is as illustrated in Fig. 2.1. In Design 2, by contrast, relvar SSP contains a tuple for every shipment, giving the applicable part number and quantity and full supplier details, and relvar XSS contains supplier details for suppliers who supply no parts at all. Write virtual relvar definitions to express Design 2 in terms of Design 1 and vice versa. Also, show the applicable integrity constraints for each design. Does either design have any obvious advantages over the other? If so, what are they?

40.   It is sometimes suggested that a relvar is really just a traditional computer file, with tuples instead of records and attributes instead of fields. Discuss.

41.   We have seen that every relvar (and in fact every relation) corresponds to some predicate. Is the converse true?

Chapter 3

Toward a Theory of Types

This chapter resembles the previous one in that a detailed tutorial on the material to be discussed can be found in reference [76]; if you are familiar with that reference, therefore, you might not need to study this chapter in depth. Unfortunately, however, the material in question is, arguably, supported even less widely and less well by current products than the relational model is. As a result, most readers will probably need to read the chapter fairly carefully.

Our subject is data types (*types* for short). As we saw in Chapter 1, types are fundamental; in particular, every value is of some type, so is every attribute of every tuple and every relation, and so is every variable. So what is a type? Essentially, it is **a named, finite set of values.**[1] Examples include:

- Type INTEGER (the set of all integers)

- Type CHAR (the set of all character strings)

- Type S# (the set of all supplier numbers)

And when we say that (e.g.) some relation has an attribute STATUS of type INTEGER, what we mean is that values of that attribute are integers, and nothing but integers. Points arising:

- First, types are also called *domains,* especially in relational contexts; and in object contexts they are sometimes called *object classes,* or just *classes* for short. We remark as an aside that SQL also uses the term *domain,* but not in the relational sense. A domain in SQL might be regarded, loosely, as a kind of syntactic template that can be used as a basis for defining attributes (or columns, rather).

- Second, a caveat: We are trying to be reasonably precise in this book. Therefore, instead of saying that, e.g., type INTEGER is the set of *all* integers, we ought really to say that it is the set of *all integers that are capable of representation in the computer system under consideration;* there will always be some integers that are beyond the representational capability of any given computer system (which is why we say in our model that types are always finite). Analogous remarks apply to many subsequent statements and examples, as you might expect; we will not bother to spell the point out explicitly every time, however, letting this one caveat do duty for all.

- Third, we remind you that types are not limited to simple things like integers. Indeed, we saw in Chapter 1 that values and variables can be arbitrarily complex—and that is so precisely because the types of those values and variables can be arbitrarily complex. Thus, to paraphrase a remark from that chapter, a type might consist of geometric points, or polygons, or X-rays, or XML documents, or fingerprints, or arrays, or stacks, or lists, or relations (and on and on). Note the case of XML documents in particular! As mentioned in Chapter 1, a battle raged in the 1990s over the claim that object technology would replace relational technology. That battle is won, but we now find ourselves with another on our hands—there are now those who claim that *XML* technology will replace relational technology. We reject this claim; instead, we regard "XML

---

1. Possibly an *empty* set of values (in which case we have *an empty type*). This possibility will be touched on from time to time in the next few chapters but will not become really important until we get to Part IV.

documents" as just another data type that can be handled perfectly well in a proper relational framework. Indeed, you might have noticed in the BIRD example in Chapter 1 (Fig. 1.1) that we showed attribute DESCR as being of just such a type.

- Fourth, we have said a type is a set of values (more precisely, a *named* set of values), but it would be more correct to say it is *the set of all values that satisfy a certain* **type constraint**. In **Tutorial D,** such constraints can be defined as suggested by the following example (repeated from Chapter 2):

```
TYPE S# POSSREP ( C CHAR CONSTRAINT SUBSTR ( C, 1, 1 ) = 'S'
                                AND CHAR_LENGTH ( C ) ≥ 2
                                AND CHAR_LENGTH ( C ) ≤ 5 } ;
```

This statement constrains type S# (supplier numbers) to consist of all values that can possibly be represented by a character string C of from two to five characters, of which the first must be an "S" (for further discussion of POSSREP definitions, see the section "Possible Representations" later in this chapter). *Note:* The CONSTRAINT portion of the POSSREP definition is optional; omitting it is equivalent to specifying CONSTRAINT TRUE.

- Fifth, the fact that types are named is important. Types with different names are different types (even if they have essentially the same POSSREP definition).

As noted in Chapter 2, any given type is either **system defined** (i.e., built in) or **user defined,** and we will assume as we did in that chapter that, of the three types mentioned earlier, INTEGER and CHAR are system defined and S# is user defined. (We remark in passing that the terminology of system- vs. user-defined types is sanctioned by usage but is not very good. After all, to a user who merely makes use of some user-defined type—as opposed to the user who is actually responsible for defining that type—the type in question behaves in all major respects just like a system-defined one; indeed, that is really the whole point. In other words, the distinction being sought is not so much one of users vs. the system but, rather, one of users playing different roles in different contexts.)

Any given type has an associated set of **operators** that can be applied to values and variables of the type in question; i.e., values and variables of a given type can be operated upon solely by means of the operators defined for that type.[1] For example, in the case of the system-defined type INTEGER:

- The system provides an assignment operator ":=" for assigning integer values to integer variables.

- It also provides operators "=", "<", and so on for comparing integers.

- It also provides operators "+", "*", and so on for performing arithmetic on integers.

- It does not provide operators "||" (concatenate), SUBSTR (substring), and so on for performing string operations on integers; in other words, string operations on integers are not supported.

By contrast, in the case of the user-defined type S#, we would certainly define assignment and comparison operators (":=", "=", "≠", and so on); however, we would probably not define operators "+", "*", and so on, which would mean that arithmetic on supplier numbers would not be supported (why would we ever want to add or multiply two supplier numbers?).

---

1. Actually this observation is tautologous. See the discussion of *strong typing* in the section "Operators," later in this chapter.

We now proceed to explore the foregoing ideas, and some of their many implications, in detail.

VALUES ARE TYPED

Every **value** has, or is of, some type. In other words, if *v* is a value, then *v* can be thought of as carrying around with it a kind of flag that announces "I am an integer" or "I am a supplier number" or "I am a geometric point" (and so on). Note that, by definition, any given value always has exactly one type,[1] which never changes. It follows that distinct types are *disjoint,* meaning they have no values in common. It also follows that everything that denotes or returns a value can be thought of as having a type as well. To be specific:

- Every **variable** is explicitly declared to be of some type, meaning that every possible value of the variable in question is a value of the type in question (the *declared type* of that variable). For example:

```
VAR N INTEGER ;
```

- Every **attribute** is explicitly or implicitly declared to be of some type, meaning that every possible value of the attribute in question is a value of the type in question (the *declared type* of that attribute). Here are some examples:

```
VAR S REAL RELATION { ... STATUS INTEGER, ... } ... ;

VAR SC VIRTUAL ( S { S#, CITY } ) ;

EXTEND S ADD ( CHAR_LENGTH ( CITY ) AS CN_LENGTH )
```

In the first example, attribute STATUS is explicitly declared to be of type INTEGER; in the second example, attributes S# and CITY are implicitly declared to be of types S# and CHAR, respectively (see the discussion of *relation type inference* at the very end of the section "Selectors and THE_ Operators," later in this chapter); in the third example, attribute CN_LENGTH is implicitly declared to be of type INTEGER (since INTEGER is the declared type of the CHAR_LENGTH operator—see the bullet item immediately following).

- Every **operator** that returns a result is explicitly declared to be of some type, meaning that every possible result that can be returned by an invocation of the operator in question is a value of the type in question (the *declared type* of that operator). For example:

```
OPERATOR ABS ( I INTEGER ) RETURNS INTEGER ;
   RETURN ( IF I ≥ 0 THEN +I ELSE -I END IF ) ;
END OPERATOR ;
```

The specification RETURNS INTEGER means that operator ABS ("absolute value") is of declared type INTEGER—it returns an integer when it is invoked. *Note:* The RETURN statement in this example constitutes the *implementation code* for operator ABS. Some languages, especially ones that support type inheritance, allow that code to be omitted from the operator definition and provided "later" (i.e., separately), thereby allowing several distinct implementations

---

1. Except possibly if type inheritance is supported.

to be provided for the same operator. See Part IV for further discussion.

- Every **parameter** of every operator is explicitly declared to be of some type, meaning that every possible argument that can be substituted for the parameter in question is a value of the type in question (the *declared type* of that parameter). Operator ABS, for example, has just one parameter, I, of declared type INTEGER, and so the following expressions are valid invocations of that operator:

```
ABS ( N )

ABS ( ( 3 + N1 ) * N2 )
```

(In the first example here, we are assuming that N is a variable of type INTEGER; in the second, we are assuming that N1 and N2 are also variables of type INTEGER.)

> *Note:* Actually, the foregoing paragraph is not quite precise enough. Operators in general fall into two disjoint categories, **read-only** vs. **update** operators. When a read-only operator—ABS is an example—is invoked, it returns a result and does not update anything, except possibly for local variables. By contrast, when an update operator is invoked, it does update at least one "nonlocal" variable and it does not return a result; also, of course, anything that is to be updated must *be* a variable, not a value (and if that variable is specified as an argument, then it must be of the same type as the corresponding parameter). Here by way of example is an update version of ABS:

```
OPERATOR ABS ( I INTEGER ) UPDATES { I } ;
   I := ( IF I ≥ 0 THEN +I ELSE -I END IF ) ;
END OPERATOR ;
```

As you can see, this definition includes an UPDATES specification instead of a RETURNS specification; that UPDATES specification indicates that parameter I is *subject to update,* meaning among other things that arguments corresponding to that parameter must be variables specifically. Note that the operator itself is now not typed, since it returns no value, and an ABS invocation is thus no longer a valid expression. See the section "Operators" later in this chapter for further discussion.

- More generally, every **expression** is at least implicitly declared to be of some type (the *declared type* of that expression): namely, the type declared for the outermost operator involved, where by *outermost operator* we mean the operator executed last in evaluation of the expression in question. For example, the declared type of the expression

```
N1 * ( 3 + N2 )
```

is the declared type of the operator "*" (multiply).

Note: The reason we keep saying *declared type* when the term *type,* unqualified, might seem sufficient is that in Part IV of this book we will meet another type, called the *most specific type.* Of course, we can and do adopt the convention prior to Part IV that the unqualified term *type* means the declared type specifically, barring explicit statements to the contrary; but we still often use the explicit qualifier *declared,* for emphasis.

Polymorphic Operators

The foregoing remarks on operator and parameter types need some refinement if the operator in question is *polymorphic*. A **polymorphic** operator is one for which the arguments can be of different types on different invocations. For example, we might be able to use "||" (concatenate) on both character strings and bit strings, in which case "||" would be polymorphic. Two obvious and important examples of polymorphic operators are:

- **Equality comparison** ("="): Clearly, we can test any two values *v1* and *v2* for equality, just so long as *v1* and *v2* are of the same type. Thus, "=" is polymorphic—it applies to integers, and character strings, and supplier numbers, and in fact to values of every possible type.

- **Assignment** (":="): We can also assign any value *v* to any variable *V,* just so long as *v* and *V* are of the same type. Thus, ":=" is polymorphic also, and it applies to values and variables of every type.

While we are on the subject, there are several more important points to be made in connection with these two operators:

1. To repeat, the *Manifesto* requires both of them to apply to every type (though SQL does not). What is more, it requires them to have the obvious semantics, too (see points 2 and 6 below), though again SQL does not.

2. The "=" operator might alternatively be called *identity,* since the comparison *v1* = *v2* evaluates to TRUE if and only if *v1* and *v2* are in fact the very same value.

3. Equality comparison is of declared type BOOLEAN (it returns a truth value). Assignment, being an update operator, has no type.

4. For the benefit of readers who might be familiar with object systems, we stress the point that assigning value *v* to variable *V* really does have the effect in our model of placing (an appearance of) that value *v* in that variable *V.* In other words, we do not embrace the semantics found in some object languages according to which (a) declaring a variable to be of type *T* really means the variable contains the *address* of some object of type *T,* and (b) "assigning *v* to *V*" really means assigning the *address* of *v* to *V.* (In fact, the phrase "the address of *v*" is a contradiction in terms; *v,* being a value, has no location in time and space and thus has no address.)

5. Logically speaking, assignment is the only update operator we need—all others are just shorthand for certain assignments (we made this point explicitly in the case of relational assignment in the previous chapter, but in fact it is true for assignment in general). We have argued elsewhere, however (see reference [84]), that the assignment operator we need must be what we call a *multiple* assignment, not the more conventional "single" form. See RM Prescription 21 for further explanation.

6. The assignment operator is required to satisfy *The Assignment Principle,* which can be stated thus: Following assignment of *v* to *V,* the comparison *v* = *V* evaluates to TRUE.[1]

---

1. Note that this principle applies to relational assignment in particular, though we did not call that fact out explicitly in the previous chapter. Note too that triggered procedures (especially "INSTEAD OF triggers," which are supported by some SQL products, though not at the time of writing by the SQL standard) have the potential to violate the principle.

TYPES VS. REPRESENTATIONS

As we saw in Chapter 1, there is a logical difference between (a) a value as such, on the one hand, and (b) the physical encoding or representation of such a value inside the system, on the other. In fact, of course, this logical difference is really a consequence of a more fundamental one: namely, the difference between a type and its physical representation. Types are a model issue; physical representations are an implementation issue. For example, supplier numbers might be physically represented as character strings, but it does not follow that we can perform string operations on supplier numbers; rather, we can perform such operations only if corresponding operators have been defined for the type. And the operators we define for a given type will depend on the intended meaning of the type in question, not on the way values of that type happen to be physically represented—indeed, those physical representations should be **hidden from the user.** In other words, the distinction we draw between type and physical representation is one important aspect of data independence [76].

We note in passing that data types, especially user-defined ones, are sometimes called *abstract data types* (ADTs) in the literature, to stress the foregoing point (the point, that is, that types must be distinguished from their physical representation). We do not use this term ourselves, however, because it suggests there might be some types that are not abstract in this sense, and we believe a distinction should always be drawn between a type and its physical representation. Also, the term *abstract type* is sometimes used (though not by us) to mean something quite different: namely, a type such that every value of the type in question must also be a value of some proper subtype of that type (and a type that is not abstract in this sense is then called a *concrete* type). Such matters are discussed and explained further in Part IV of this book.

SCALAR VS. NONSCALAR TYPES

The scalar notion is well established in the languages world. Loosely, we say a type is **scalar** if it has no user-visible components, and **nonscalar** if it is not scalar. We also say that values, variables, attributes, operators, parameters, and expressions of some type *T* are scalar or nonscalar according as type *T* itself is scalar or nonscalar. For example:

- Type INTEGER is a scalar type; hence, values and variables (and so on) of type INTEGER are also all scalar, meaning they have no user-visible components. Similar remarks apply to (e.g.) the user-defined type S#.

- Tuple and relation types are nonscalar—the pertinent user-visible components being, of course, the corresponding attributes—and hence tuple and relation values and variables (and so on) are also all nonscalar.

That said, we now have to say too that these notions are quite informal. The truth is, it seems to be very difficult to come up with a definition of the term *scalar* that is both precise and useful; indeed, reference [74] shows that the concept of *atomicity*—which is just the concept of "scalarness" by another name—has no absolute meaning. For example, consider the string 'New York' (a value of type CHAR). If this string is considered to be a single value, then it seems reasonable to think of it as scalar; but if it is considered to be composite (consisting as it does of a sequence of either words or letters), then it seems reasonable to think of it as nonscalar.

For such reasons, we nowhere rely *formally* in this book on the notion of scalarness. However, we do make heavy use of the notion informally. To be more specific (and barring explicit statements to the contrary), we use the term *scalar type* to mean a type that is neither a tuple type nor a relation type, and we use the term *nonscalar type* to mean a type that is either a tuple type or a relation type. We also use the terms *scalar value, nonscalar value, scalar operator, nonscalar operator,* etc., analogously. (By *operator* here, we mean a read-only operator, of course, since update operators have no type. We might try saying an update operator is scalar if it updates a scalar argument—but then we would presumably also have to say an operator that updates both a scalar and a nonscalar argument is both scalar and nonscalar simultaneously.)

POSSIBLE REPRESENTATIONS

For simplicity, we now assume until further notice that all types are both scalar and user defined, barring explicit statements to the contrary. Let *T* be such a type. As we have seen, then, the physical representation of values of type *T* is hidden from the user; in fact, such representations can be arbitrarily complex—in particular, they can have components—but, to repeat, those components will be hidden from the user. However, we do require that values of type *T* have at least one declared **possible representation,**[1] and such possible representations are *not* hidden from the user; in particular, they do have user-visible components. Understand, however, that the components in question are *not* components of the type, they are components of the possible representation; the type as such is still scalar in the sense previously explained.

By way of example, consider the user-defined type QTY ("quantity"), whose definition in **Tutorial D** might look like this:

```
TYPE QTY POSSREP { I INTEGER } ;
```

This type definition says, in effect, that quantities can "possibly be represented" by values of the system-defined type INTEGER (for simplicity, we ignore the fact that, in practice, we would probably want to constrain those integers to be greater than zero). In this example, therefore, the possible representation (which henceforth we abbreviate to just **possrep**) certainly does have user-visible components[2]—in fact, it has exactly one such, called I, of type INTEGER—but quantities per se do not.

Here is a slightly more complex example:

```
TYPE POINT      /* geometric points in two-dimensional space */
      POSSREP CARTESIAN { X RATIONAL, Y RATIONAL }
      POSSREP POLAR { R RATIONAL, THETA RATIONAL } ;
```

This definition includes declarations of two distinct possreps, CARTESIAN and POLAR, reflecting the fact that points in two-dimensional space can indeed "possibly be represented" by either cartesian or polar coordinates. Each of those possreps in turn has two components, both of which are of

---

1. We assume here that *T* is not a *dummy* type. Dummy types have to do with our inheritance model and are discussed in Part IV of this book; we ignore them until further notice.

2. As we have had occasion to remark before (in connection with the terminology of user-defined types), the term *user* is always a little vague, and you might be wondering just what we mean when we say that possrep components are "user-visible." Essentially, what we mean is that any user who needs to invoke a selector or THE_ operator effectively needs to be aware of the corresponding possrep components, since (as we will see later, in the section "Selectors and THE_ Operators") selectors and THE_ operators are defined in terms of those components. Furthermore, in the case of selectors in particular, the user will need to be aware of the corresponding type constraint, and type constraints also are defined in terms of possrep components.

type RATIONAL[1] and both of which are user visible. Like type QTY, however, type POINT is still scalar—the type as such has no user-visible components.

Despite the message of the previous paragraph, we must now say that it is often convenient, informally, to refer to the components of a given possrep as if they were in fact components of the type. For example, we might refer, informally, to the *x* and *y* coordinates of some point (instead of what we should be doing, which is referring to the *x* and *y* coordinates of *the cartesian possible representation of that point*). Please note immediately that this usage is more than a little sloppy—but, to repeat, it is convenient, and we will adopt it from time to time in what follows.

A note on syntax: First of all, if possrep *PR* is declared as part of the definition of type *T*, we say, loosely, that "*PR* is a possrep for type *T*" (instead of, as would be more logically correct, "*PR* is a possrep for values of type *T*"). In **Tutorial D,** moreover, if type *T* has a possrep with no explicit name, then that possrep is named *T* by default. Thus, the definition already given for type QTY—

```
TYPE QTY POSSREP { I INTEGER } ;
```

—can be regarded as shorthand for the following longer one:

```
TYPE QTY POSSREP QTY { I INTEGER } ;
```

Further discussion of possreps—in particular, an explanation of our motivation for introducing the concept—can be found under RM Prescriptions 4 and 5 in Chapter 6. See also Appendix C.

SELECTORS AND THE_ OPERATORS

Let *PR* be a possrep for type *T*. Then the declaration of *PR* causes automatic definition of the following more or less self-explanatory operators:

- A **selector** operator, which allows the user to specify or *select* a value of type *T* by supplying a value for each component of *PR*

- A set of **THE_** operators (one such operator for each component of *PR*), which allow the user to access the *PR* components corresponding to a specified value of type *T*

Note: When we say declaration of *PR* causes "automatic definition" of these operators, what we mean is that whoever is responsible for defining type *T*, and therefore for declaring *PR*, is also responsible for defining the operators. Observe, therefore, that *automatic* does not necessarily mean *automated*. (To be a little more precise, we do not necessarily expect the implementation code for selectors and THE_ operators to be provided automatically; however, we do expect it to be provided automatically for certain other required operators, including "=" and ":=" in particular.)

By way of example, here are some sample selector and THE_ operator invocations for type POINT:

```
CARTESIAN ( 5.0, 2.5 )
/* selects the point with x = 5.0, y = 2.5 */
```

---

1. Throughout this book we use the more accurate RATIONAL in place of the more usual REAL (and we assume it is a built-in type).

```
CARTESIAN ( X1, Y1 )
/* selects the point with x = X1, y = Y1,        */
/* where X1 and Y1 are variables of type RATIONAL */

POLAR ( 2.7, 1.0 )
/* selects the point with r = 2.7, θ = 1.0 */

THE_X ( P )
/* denotes the x coordinate of the point in P, */
/* where P is a variable of type POINT         */

THE_R ( P )
/* denotes the r coordinate of the point in P */

THE_Y ( exp )
/* denotes the y coordinate of the point denoted by */
/* the expression exp (which is of type POINT)      */
```

Note that (a) selectors have the same name as the corresponding possrep; (b) THE_ operators have names of the form THE_C, where C is the name of the corresponding component of the corresponding possrep; (c) the syntax of selector and THE_ operator invocations is self-explanatory. Note too that selector invocations are a generalization of the familiar concept of a literal. (All literals are selector invocations, but not all selector invocations are literals; in fact, a selector invocation is a literal if and only if all of its arguments are literals in turn.)

A note regarding the term "literal": The concept might be familiar, but it seems to be very hard to find a good definition for it in the literature! Here is our own preferred definition: A **literal** is a symbol that denotes a value that is fixed and determined by the particular symbol in question (and the type of that value is therefore also fixed and determined by the symbol in question). Loosely, we can say that a literal is *self-defining.* Here are some **Tutorial D** examples:

```
4                                     /* a literal of type INTEGER  */

2.7                                   /* a literal of type RATIONAL */

'ABC'                                 /* a literal of type CHAR     */

FALSE                                 /* a literal of type BOOLEAN  */

S#('S1')                              /* a literal of type S#       */

CARTESIAN ( 5.0, 2.5 )                /* a literal of type POINT    */
```

We remark in passing that our model explicitly requires every value of every type, be it scalar or nonscalar, to be denotable by means of some literal (see RM Prescription 4).

Back to selectors and THE_ operators. To see how these ideas might work in practice, suppose the physical representation of points is in fact cartesian coordinates (though there is no need, in general, for a physical representation to be identical to any of the corresponding possreps). Then the system will provide certain highly protected operators,[1] denoted in what follows by *lowercase pseudocode,* that effectively expose that physical representation, and the *type implementer* can then use those operators to implement the necessary CARTESIAN and POLAR selectors. (Obviously the type implementer is—in fact, must be—an exception to the general rule that users are not aware of physical representations.) For example:

```
OPERATOR CARTESIAN ( X RATIONAL, Y RATIONAL ) RETURNS POINT ;
   BEGIN ;
      VAR P POINT ;  /* P is a variable of type POINT */
      X component of physical representation of P := X ;
      Y component of physical representation of P := Y ;
      RETURN ( P ) ;
   END ;
END OPERATOR ;


OPERATOR POLAR ( R RATIONAL, THETA RATIONAL ) RETURNS POINT ;
   RETURN ( CARTESIAN ( R * COS ( THETA ), R * SIN ( THETA ) ) ) ;
END OPERATOR ;
```

Observe that the POLAR definition makes use of the CARTESIAN selector, as well as the presumably built-in operators SIN and COS. Alternatively, the POLAR definition might be expressed directly in terms of the protected operators, thus:

```
OPERATOR POLAR ( R RATIONAL, THETA RATIONAL ) RETURNS POINT ;
   BEGIN ;
      VAR P POINT ;
      X component of physical representation of P := R * COS ( THETA ) ;
      Y component of physical representation of P := R * SIN ( THETA ) ;
      RETURN ( P ) ;
   END ;
END OPERATOR ;
```

The type implementer can also use those protected operators to implement the necessary THE_ operators, thus:

```
OPERATOR THE_X ( P POINT ) RETURNS RATIONAL ;
   RETURN ( X component of physical representation of P ) ;
END OPERATOR ;


OPERATOR THE_Y ( P POINT ) RETURNS RATIONAL ;
   RETURN ( Y component of physical representation of P ) ;
END OPERATOR ;


OPERATOR THE_R ( P POINT ) RETURNS RATIONAL ;
   RETURN ( SQRT ( THE_X ( P ) ** 2 + THE_Y ( P ) ** 2 ) ) ;
END OPERATOR ;
```

---

1. Just what is involved in protecting those operators, thereby making them unavailable to most users, is essentially a security matter and beyond the purview of the *Manifesto* as such. For our purposes, we simply assume that excluding them from **Tutorial D** is sufficient to provide the necessary protection.

```
OPERATOR THE_THETA ( P POINT ) RETURNS RATIONAL ;
    RETURN ( ARCTAN ( THE_Y ( P ) / THE_X ( P ) ) ) ;
END OPERATOR ;
```

Observe that the definitions of THE_R and THE_THETA make use of THE_X and THE_Y, as well as the operators SQRT and ARCTAN (which, we assume, are built in and have the obvious semantics). Alternatively, THE_R and THE_THETA might be defined directly in terms of the protected operators (details left as an exercise).

So much for the POINT example. However, it is important to understand that all of the concepts we have discussed in connection with that example apply to simpler types as well: type QTY, for example. Here are some sample selector invocations for that type:

```
QTY ( 100 )

QTY ( N )

QTY ( N1 + N2 )
```

And here are some sample THE_ operator invocations:

```
THE_I ( Q )

THE_I ( Q1 + Q2 )
```

We are assuming in these examples that (a) N, N1, and N2 are variables of type INTEGER; (b) Q, Q1, and Q2 are variables of type QTY; and (c) "+" is a polymorphic operator—it applies to both integers and quantities.

By the way, observe that since values are always typed, it is strictly incorrect to say that, e.g., "the quantity for a certain shipment is 100." A quantity is a value of type QTY, not a value of type INTEGER! In the example, therefore, we should more properly say the quantity is QTY(100), not 100 as such. In informal contexts, however, we usually do not bother to be quite so precise, thus using, e.g., 100 as a convenient shorthand for QTY(100). In particular, we typically use such shorthands when we draw pictures of relations as tables (e.g., on paper), as we saw in several examples in Chapters 1 and 2.

We give one further example of a type definition:

```
TYPE LINESEG POSSREP ( BEGIN POINT, END POINT ) ;
```

Type LINESEG denotes line segments, and it has associated THE_ operators THE_BEGIN and THE_END (each of which is type POINT). This example thus illustrates the fact that a given possrep can be declared in terms of user-defined types, not just system-defined types as in all of our previous examples (in other words, a user-defined type is indeed a type and can be used in all of the ways that types in general can be used).

For simplicity, we assume throughout this book from this point forward that all operators with names of the form THE_C (for some C) are indeed THE_ operators of the kind we have been discussing.

THE_ Pseudovariables

Consider the following example:

```
VAR P POINT ;

P := CARTESIAN ( 5.0, 2.5 ) ;
THE_X ( P ) := 2.0 ;
```

Explanation: Variable P is declared to be of type POINT, and the first assignment assigns to that variable P the point with *x* coordinate 5.0 and *y* coordinate 2.5. The second assignment then "zaps" the *x* coordinate of P, setting it to 2.0, so that P now contains the point with *x* coordinate 2.0 and *y* coordinate 2.5 (unchanged).

The expression THE_X(P) on the left side of the second assignment in the foregoing example is a **pseudovariable reference:** a THE_ pseudovariable reference, to be precise (other kinds are possible).[1] In general, a pseudovariable reference is an operational expression that appears in some target position (e.g., on the left side of an assignment); thus, a THE_ pseudovariable reference in particular is a THE_ operator invocation appearing in such a target position. Such an invocation actually *designates*—instead of just returning the value of—the specified component of its argument. (More precisely, it designates the specified component of *the applicable possible representation of* that argument.) Thus, the assignment

```
THE_X ( P ) := 2.0 ;
```

actually assigns the value 2.0 to the X component of the argument variable P.

Pseudovariable references can be nested, as in this example:

```
VAR LS LINESEG ;

THE_X ( THE_BEGIN ( LS ) ) := 6.5 ;
```

More generally, in fact, a pseudovariable reference can appear wherever a variable reference of the same type can appear. In other words: *Pseudovariables are variables* (loosely speaking).

We now observe that pseudovariables in general, including THE_ pseudovariables in particular, are in fact logically unnecessary, because any assignment in which the target is a pseudovariable is logically equivalent to another in which it is not. Consider the following example once again:

```
THE_X ( P ) := 2.0 ;
```

This assignment is logically equivalent to the following one:

```
P := CARTESIAN ( 2.0, THE_Y ( P ) ) ;
```

Similarly, the assignment

```
THE_X ( THE_BEGIN ( LS ) ) := 6.5 ;
```

is logically equivalent to this one:

```
LS := LINESEG ( CARTESIAN ( 6.5, THE_Y ( THE_BEGIN ( LS ) ) ) , THE_END ( LS ) ) ;
```

In other words, THE_ pseudovariables per se are not strictly necessary in order to support the

---

1. The term *pseudovariable* is taken from PL/I; *virtual variable* might be a little more apt.

kind of component-level updating we have been discussing. However, assignment to a THE_ pseudovariable does seem intuitively more attractive than the alternative (for which it can be regarded as a shorthand); also, using THE_ pseudovariables provides a higher degree of imperviousness to changes in the syntax of the corresponding selector. Moreover, assignment to a pseudovariable is likely to be easier to implement efficiently than the alternative for which it is a shorthand (though of course performance issues are never a primary consideration in our model, nor in the design of the language **D**).

Nonscalar Types

We now turn briefly to tuple and relation types.[1] We focus first on tuple types specifically. Here repeated from Chapter 2 is an example of such a type:

```
TUPLE { S# S#, SNAME NAME, STATUS INTEGER, CITY CHAR }
```

Now, tuple types do not have possreps as such; nor do they really need them, because the type itself can be regarded as playing a kind of "possrep" role. In other words, just as we can behave *as if* values of type QTY, say, were physically represented by integers, so in the case at hand we can behave *as if* values of the tuple type shown were physically represented by tuples of that type. For example, here is a selector invocation for that tuple type (also repeated from Chapter 2):

```
TUPLE { S# S#('S1'), SNAME NAME('Smith'), STATUS 20, CITY 'London' }
```

Observe how the syntax of this selector supports the idea that the tuple type serves as its own possrep (as it were), because it relies on the fact that the components of that type—i.e., the attributes—are indeed user visible.

As for "THE_ operators," tuple types neither have nor need them; instead, their functionality is provided by what **Tutorial D** calls *attribute extractors*. For example, if *tx* is an expression of the tuple type under discussion, then the expression

```
STATUS FROM tx
```

returns the corresponding STATUS value, just as a hypothetical "THE_STATUS" operator would. *Note:* It would be possible to use attribute extractors as pseudovariables, too, but **Tutorial D** does not; instead, it provides analogous functionality by means of statements of the form illustrated here:

```
UPDATE tv ( STATUS := 15 ) ;
```

This statement has the effect of setting the STATUS component of the tuple variable *tv* (which we assume to be of the tuple type under discussion, of course) to the value 15. It is shorthand for the following:

```
tv := TUPLE { S# S# FROM tv , SNAME SNAME FROM tv , STATUS 15 , CITY CITY FROM tv } ;
```

A note on tuple type inference: One important advantage of the tuple type naming scheme prescribed in the *Manifesto*—viz., that such names be of the form TUPLE{...}—is that it facilitates the task of determining the type of the result of an arbitrary tuple expression. For example, consider the following tuple expression (actually a tuple projection):

---

1. Such types are in fact *generated* types. See the section "Type Generators" later in this chapter for further explanation of this point.

```
tx { S#, CITY }
```

where *tx* is as above. This particular expression evaluates to a tuple that is derived from the current value of *tx* by "projecting away" attributes SNAME and STATUS, and the tuple type of that derived tuple is, precisely,

```
TUPLE { S# S#, CITY CHAR }
```

Similar remarks apply to all possible tuple expressions.

Finally, everything in this subsection regarding tuple types applies equally well to relation types also, mutatis mutandis.[1] Thus, each relation type serves as its own possrep (as it were); the corresponding selector relies on the fact that components of the type are user-visible; and operators are available that provide read-only and update access to any attribute of any tuple in any relation of the type in question (speaking rather loosely!). We omit further discussion here—except to point out that, with regard to the question of relation type inference specifically, we have already indicated what is involved in our explanation of the relational operators in Chapter 2. For example, the type of the result of the expression *a* UNION *b* is the same as that of both *a* and *b*.

SYSTEM-DEFINED TYPES

We assumed for the most part in the previous two sections that the scalar types we were dealing with were all user defined. But what about built-in types? Well, almost certainly there will be some built-in types that comply with everything we said in those sections. For example, we might have a built-in type called DATE, representing dates on the Gregorian calendar. Then:

- An obvious possrep for dates is:

  ```
  POSSREP { YEAR INTEGER, MONTH INTEGER, DAY INTEGER CONSTRAINT ... }
  ```

  (Details of the CONSTRAINT specification, which would be needed in practice to ensure that dates conform to the rules of the Gregorian calendar, are tedious but straightforward and are therefore omitted here.)

- The corresponding selector would take the form

  ```
  DATE ( y, m, d )
  ```

  where *y*, *m*, and *d* are integer expressions.

- The corresponding THE_ operators might look like this (though for historical reasons they will probably use some different syntax):

---

1. In case you are not familiar with this useful expression, we offer a brief explanation here. Essentially, it means *with all necessary changes having been made* (and it can save a good deal of writing). In the case at hand, for example, the "necessary changes" involve such things as replacing appearances of the term *tuple* by the term *relation*, replacing tuple selector invocations by relation selector invocations, replacing references to tuple variables by references to relvars, and so on.

```
THE_YEAR ( d )
THE_MONTH ( d )
THE_DAY ( d )
```

where *d* is an expression (or a variable, if the THE_ operator invocation is being used as a pseudovariable reference) of type DATE.

We remark in passing that type DATE is an example of a built-in type that might have several distinct possreps. For example, a possrep involving month names instead of numbers might be desirable from a human factors point of view. (And the physical representation is likely to be different again; it might, for example, consist of "day number since the beginning of time.")

What about a simpler built-in type such as INTEGER? Well, clearly the system has to specify a format for writing integer literals—probably as an optionally signed sequence of decimal digits, as in **Tutorial D**. By definition, then, that format can be regarded as a "possrep for integers," in a sense. However, we take the position that the possrep in question is not a *declared* one. Everything we have said about possreps in this chapter so far applies specifically to ones that are explicitly declared; in particular, our earlier remarks regarding selectors and THE_ operators apply specifically to possreps that are explicitly declared but not to ones that are not. In our example, then, type INTEGER has no declared possrep, and therefore no THE_ operators. It does have a selector, but invocations of that selector are always simple integer literals, nothing more general.

Incidentally, just as type DATE might well have several distinct possreps, so type INTEGER might have several distinct literal formats (in other words, several distinct selectors). For example, 15, X'F', and B'1111' might be distinct integer literals, all denoting the value fifteen.

From this point forward, we will take the unqualified term *possible representation,* or the abbreviated form *possrep,* to refer to a declared possrep specifically (barring explicit statements to the contrary).

OPERATORS

We have already seen several examples of operator definitions in this chapter, but it is time to take a closer look. We begin by repeating the read-only and update versions of ABS ("absolute value") from the section "Values Are Typed" earlier in the chapter. For clarity, however, we now rename them R_ABS and U_ABS, respectively:

```
OPERATOR R_ABS ( I INTEGER ) RETURNS INTEGER ;
   RETURN ( IF I ≥ 0 THEN +I ELSE -I END IF ) ;
END OPERATOR ;

OPERATOR U_ABS ( I INTEGER ) UPDATES { I } ;
   I := ( IF I ≥ 0 THEN +I ELSE -I END IF ) ;
END OPERATOR ;
```

An invocation of R_ABS—e.g., R_ABS(N1+N2)—is an expression of type INTEGER, and it can appear wherever an integer literal would be allowed; in particular, it can be nested inside other expressions. An invocation of U_ABS, by contrast, is not an expression at all (not of type INTEGER and not of any other type), and it cannot be nested inside other expressions; instead, such an invocation takes the form of an explicit CALL statement, or something logically equivalent to such a statement. For example:

```
CALL U_ABS ( N ) ;
```

N here must be a variable specifically (of type INTEGER), not some more general expression.

Why do we distinguish between read-only and update operators? Without getting into too much detail—further elaboration can be found in Chapter 6, also Chapter 14—the answer has to do with *avoiding side effects*. For example, if an expression such as N1+U_ABS(N2) were valid, it would not only return some integer value but would also have the side effect of updating the variable N2.

Here is another example, DIST ("distance between"). This read-only operator takes two parameters of one user-defined type (POINT) and returns a result of another (LENGTH):

```
OPERATOR DIST ( P1 POINT, P2 POINT ) RETURNS LENGTH ;
   RETURN ( WITH THE_X ( P1 ) AS X1 , THE_X ( P2 ) AS X2 ,
               THE_Y ( P1 ) AS Y1 , THE_Y ( P2 ) AS Y2 :
            LENGTH ( SQRT ( ( X1 - X2 ) ** 2 + ( Y1 - Y2 ) ** 2 ) ) ) ;
END OPERATOR ;
```

We are assuming that the LENGTH selector takes an argument of type RATIONAL. Also, recall from the previous chapter that the purpose of WITH is to simplify the formulation of expressions by allowing names to be introduced to refer to the results of subexpressions. See Chapter 5 for further details.

Our next example is the required "=" operator for type POINT:

```
OPERATOR EQ ( P1 POINT, P2 POINT ) RETURNS BOOLEAN ;
   RETURN ( THE_X ( P1 ) = THE_X ( P2 ) AND THE_Y ( P1 ) = THE_Y ( P2 ) ) ;
END OPERATOR ;
```

Observe that the expression in the RETURN statement here makes use of the built-in "=" operator for type RATIONAL. For simplicity, we will assume from this point forward that the usual infix notation "=" can be used for the equality operator (for all types, that is, not just type POINT); we omit consideration of how such an infix notation might be specified, since it is basically just a matter of syntax. *Note:* In practice, we would expect the code for "=" to be provided by the system (again, for all types, not just for type POINT); we show an explicit definition above for type POINT only for pedagogic reasons.

Here now is the required "<" operator for type QTY:

```
OPERATOR LT ( Q1 QTY, Q2 QTY ) RETURNS BOOLEAN ;
   RETURN ( THE_I ( Q1 ) < THE_I ( Q2 ) ) ;
END OPERATOR ;
```

We are assuming here, reasonably enough, that QTY has been defined as an **ordinal type**—an ordinal type being, precisely, a type for which the operator "<" is defined.[1] Note that the expression in the RETURN statement makes use of the built-in "<" operator for type INTEGER. Again, we will assume from this point forward that the usual infix notation can be used for this operator (for all ordinal types, that is, not just type QTY). *Note:* There is quite a lot more that would be need to be said and done in connection with ordinal types in any real implementation. In particular, an argument could be made that some types for which "<" is supported are not really usable for typical ordinal purposes (type CHAR might be a case in point). Such considerations are beyond the scope of the present book, however; see reference [85] for further discussion.

---

1. **Tutorial D** requires ordinal types to be explicitly declared as such, via the specification ORDINAL in the type definition. We omit such specifications from our examples in this chapter for simplicity. Of course, not all types are ordinal; type POINT, for example, is not, and neither are tuple or relation types.

Type Conversions

Consider the following definition for type S# (a simplified version of the definition shown earlier in the chapter):

```
TYPE S# POSSREP { C CHAR } ;
```

By default, the specified possrep has the name S#, and hence the corresponding selector operator does, too. The following is thus a valid selector invocation:

```
S#('S1')
```

(it returns a certain supplier number). Observe, therefore, that the S# selector might be regarded, loosely, as a **type conversion** operator that converts character strings to supplier numbers. Analogously, the P# selector might be regarded as a conversion operator that converts character strings to part numbers; the QTY selector might be regarded as a conversion operator that converts integers to quantities; and so on.

Incidentally, we follow convention in using the term *type conversion* here, but it is not a good term. After all, to say a character string is being "converted" to a supplier number suggests the character string is being changed somehow, but such is not the case (of course not!—the character string is a value and cannot be changed in any way, by definition). Indeed, to suggest that two values are really the same in all respects except that they happen to be of different types is to appeal to some concept that is certainly not part of our model. Rather, what is really going on with "type conversion" is that a *mapping* is being applied, a mapping from values of one type to values of another. Given a particular character string, for example, the mapping in question identifies the unique supplier number that corresponds to that string.

Back to selectors in particular. Of course, we can think, loosely, of the S# selector as being a "type conversion" operator only because the corresponding possrep happens to involve exactly one component. In that special case, however, we can also think (again loosely) of the corresponding THE_ operator as an operator that performs type conversion in the opposite direction. For example, if SID is a variable of type S#, then the expression

```
THE_C ( SID )
```

effectively converts the supplier number denoted by SID to a character string.

Now, in the section "Values Are Typed" earlier in this chapter, we said that (a) the source and target in an assignment must be of the same type, and (b) the comparands in an equality comparison must also be of the same type. In some systems, however, these rules are not directly enforced; that is, it might be possible in such a system to request, e.g., a comparison between a supplier number and a character string, perhaps as here:

```
... WHERE S# = 'S2'
```

Here the left comparand is of type S# and the right comparand is of type CHAR. On the face of it, therefore, the comparison should fail on a type error (a compile-time type error, in fact). Conceptually, however, it would be possible for the system to realize that it can use the S# "conversion operator"—i.e., the S# selector—to convert the CHAR comparand to type S#, thereby effectively rewriting the comparison as follows:

```
... WHERE S# = S#('S2')
```

Alternatively, it could use the THE_C "conversion operator" instead to rewrite the comparison thus:

```
... WHERE THE_C ( S# ) = 'S2'
```

Either way, the comparison will now be valid.

Invoking a conversion operator implicitly as in the foregoing examples is known as **coercion**. However, it is well known that coercion can lead to errors. In this book, therefore, we follow *The Principle of Cautious Design* [46] and adopt the position that coercions are not permitted—operands must always be of the appropriate types, not merely coercible to those types. Of course, we do allow explicit type conversion operators (or CAST operators, as they are usually known) to be defined and invoked when necessary. For example:

```
CAST_AS_CHAR ( 530 )
```

As we have already pointed out, selectors—at least, those that take just one argument—can also be thought of as explicit type conversion operators, of a kind, and a similar remark applies to the corresponding THE_ operators.

Now, you might have realized that what we are talking about here is what is known in language circles as **strong typing**. Different writers have slightly different definitions for this term [125]; as we use it, however, it means, among other things, that (a) every value *has* a type, and (b) whenever we try to perform an operation, the system checks—preferably at compile time, otherwise at run time—that the operands are of the right types for the operation in question.[1] For example, consider the following expressions:

```
WEIGHT + QTY  /* part weight plus shipment quantity */

WEIGHT * QTY  /* part weight times shipment quantity */
```

The first expression makes no sense, and the system should reject it. The second, on the other hand, does make sense—it denotes the total weight for all parts involved in the shipment. So the operators we would define for weights and quantities in combination would presumably include "*" but not "+".

Here are a couple more examples, involving comparison operations this time:

```
WEIGHT > QTY

EVEN > ODD
```

Again the first expression does not make sense, but the second does. (We are assuming in the second example that EVEN is of type EVEN_INTEGER and ODD is of type ODD_INTEGER, with the obvious semantics.) So the operators we would define for weights and quantities in combination presumably would not include ">", but those for even and odd integers presumably would. *Note:* In practice, EVEN_INTEGER and ODD_INTEGER might both be subtypes of type INTEGER, in which case the ">" operator would probably be *inherited* from this latter type (see Part IV).

---

1. In fact, OO Prescription 1 requires **D** to be such that all type checking can be done at compile time, except possibly if type inheritance is supported.

Some Implications

Complete support for operators along the lines sketched in the present section has a number of significant implications, which we now briefly summarize:

- First, and most important, it means the system will know (a) exactly **which expressions are valid,** and (b) the **type of the result,** for every valid expression.

- It also means that the total collection of types known to the system will be a **closed set;** that is, the type of the result of every valid expression will be a type that is known to the system. Observe in particular that this closed set of types must include the type BOOLEAN, if comparisons are to be valid expressions [77].

- In particular, the fact that the system knows the type of the result of every valid expression means it knows which **assignments** are valid, and also which **comparisons.**

TYPE GENERATORS

We turn now to types that are obtained by invoking some *type generator*. Abstractly, a **type generator** is just a special kind of operator; it is special because (a) it returns a type instead of, e.g., a scalar value, and (b) the invocation occurs at compile time instead of run time. For example, we might write

```
VAR SALES ARRAY QTY (12) ;
```

to define a variable called SALES whose permitted values are one-dimensional arrays of 12 quantities.[1] In this example, the expression ARRAY QTY (12) can be regarded as an invocation of the ARRAY type generator, and it returns a specific array type. That specific array type is a **generated type** (a nonscalar generated type, as it happens, though scalar generated types are possible too). Points arising:

1. Type generators are known by many different names in the literature: *type constructors, parameterized types, polymorphic types, type templates, generic types,* possibly others too.

2. Generated types are indeed types, and can be used wherever ordinary "nongenerated" types can be used. For example, we might define some relvar to have some attribute of type ARRAY QTY (12). By contrast, type generators as such are *not* types.

3. Like types, type generators can be either system or user defined, in general. In other words, the system might allow users to define their own type generators (though we do not require **D** to support such functionality, and **Tutorial D** in particular does not do so).

4. A generated type is system or user defined according as the corresponding type generator is system or user defined.

    In general, generated types have possreps—or, at least, can be thought of as having possreps—that are derived in a fairly obvious way from (a) a *generic* possrep that applies to the type

---

1. The examples in this section are not formulated in terms of pure **Tutorial D** because **Tutorial D** does not support general-purpose arrays—but arrays are such a familiar construct that it seemed a good idea to use them as a basis for this discussion.

generator in question and (b) the user-visible component(s) of the specific generated type in question. In the case of ARRAY QTY (12), for example:

■   There will be some generic possrep defined for one-dimensional arrays in general: probably as a sequence of *array elements* that can be identified by subscripts in the range from *lower* to *upper*, where *lower* and *upper* are the applicable bounds (1 and 12, in our example).

■   The user-visible components are precisely the 12 array elements just mentioned.

In like manner, there will be operators that provide the required selector and THE_ operator functionality. For example, the expression (actually an array literal)

```
ARRAY QTY ( QTY( 2), QTY( 5), QTY( 9), QTY( 9), QTY(15), QTY(27),
            QTY(33), QTY(32), QTY(25), QTY(19), QTY( 5), QTY( 1) )
```

might be used to specify a particular value of type ARRAY QTY (12) ("selector functionality"). Likewise, the expression

```
SALES (3)
```

might be used to access the third component (i.e., the third array element) of the array value that happens to be the current value of the array variable SALES ("THE_ operator functionality"). It might also be used as a pseudovariable reference, as here:

```
SALES (3) := QTY(17) ;
```

Assignment and equality comparison operators also apply to values and variables of the generated type. For example, here is a valid assignment:

```
SALES := ARRAY QTY ( QTY( 2), QTY( 5), QTY( 9), QTY( 9), QTY(15), QTY(27),
                     QTY(33), QTY(32), QTY(25), QTY(19), QTY( 5), QTY( 1) ) ;
```

And here is a valid equality comparison:

```
SALES = ARRAY QTY ( QTY( 2), QTY( 5), QTY( 9), QTY( 9), QTY(15), QTY(27),
                    QTY(33), QTY(32), QTY(25), QTY(19), QTY( 5), QTY( 1) )
```

Note: Any given type generator will also have a set of generic constraints and generic operators associated with it (generic in the sense that the constraints and operators in question will apply to every specific type obtained via invocation of the type generator in question). For example, in the case of the ARRAY type generator:

■   There might be a generic constraint to the effect that the lower bound must not be greater than the upper bound.

■   There might be a generic "reverse" operator that takes an arbitrary one-dimensional array as input and returns as output another such array containing the elements of the given one in reverse order.

In fact, the "selectors," "THE_ operators," and assignment and equality comparison operators already discussed are also effectively derived from certain generic operators.

Of course, the type generators that are of particular interest in this book are TUPLE and (especially) RELATION. See Chapters 4-6 for further discussion.

CONCLUDING REMARKS

As noted at the beginning of the chapter, the material of this chapter is likely to be less familiar to many readers than that of Chapter 2 was. It is therefore worth summarizing the main points we have covered.

First of all, a type is *a named, finite set of values:* namely, the set of all values that satisfy a certain *type constraint,* which is specified in **Tutorial D,** in the case of scalar types specifically, by a POSSREP definition and its subordinate CONSTRAINT specification.[1] Every type has an associated set of *read-only* and *update operators* for operating on values and variables of the type in question. Values and variables are always typed; so also are *attributes,* (read-only) *operators, parameters,* and more generally *expressions* of arbitrary complexity.

Types can be arbitrarily complex; thus, we can have types whose values are numbers, or strings, or dates, or times, or audio recordings, or maps, or video recordings, or XML documents, or geometric points (and so on). Types *constrain operations,* in that the operands to any given operation are required to be of the types defined for that operation (*strong typing*). Strong typing is a good idea because it allows certain errors to be caught (preferably at compile time, otherwise at run time).

Types can be *system-* or *user-defined;* they can also be *scalar* or *nonscalar.* A scalar type has no user-visible components. (The most important *non*scalar types in the relational model are relation types, which were discussed in Chapter 2.) We distinguish between *types* and their *physical representation* (types are a *model* issue, physical representations are an *implementation* issue). However, we do require that user-defined scalar types in particular have at least one explicitly declared *possible* representation or *possrep.* Each such possrep causes automatic definition of one *selector* operator and, for each component of that possrep, one *THE_ operator* (also a corresponding THE_ *pseudovariable*). We support explicit *type conversions* but no implicit *coercions.* We also support the definition of any number of additional operators for scalar types, and we require that *equality comparison* ("=") and *assignment* (":=") be available for every type (with prescribed semantics).

We also discussed *type generators,* which are compile-time operators that return types (ARRAY is a typical example, though not one that is supported in **Tutorial D**). Generated types have possreps (of a kind), constraints, and operators that are derived from the *generic* possreps, constraints, and operators associated with the applicable type generator.

One final point (not mentioned explicitly in the body of the chapter): Recall from Chapter 1 that values—and hence *sets* of values also—"have no location in time or space"; conceptually, those sets of values already exist, and always will exist (think of type INTEGER, for example). It follows in particular that the operation that defines a scalar type (the TYPE statement, in **Tutorial D**) does not actually create the corresponding set of values; all it does is introduce a *name* by which that set of values can be referenced. Likewise, the operation that destroys a scalar type (DROP TYPE in **Tutorial D**) does not actually destroy the corresponding set of values, it merely drops the name that was introduced by the corresponding type definition.

EXERCISES

1.   What is a type?

2.   What is a literal?

3.   State the rules regarding operand types for the assignment (":=") and equality ("=") operators.

---

1. We will encounter another method of specifying type constraints when we get to Part IV of this book.

4. Elaborate on the following logical differences:

argument	vs.	parameter
generated type	vs.	nongenerated type
physical representation	vs.	possible representation
read-only operator	vs.	update operator
scalar	vs.	nonscalar
type	vs.	representation
user-defined type	vs.	system-defined type
user-defined operator	vs.	system-defined operator

5. Why is it desirable to distinguish between read-only and update operators?

6. Explain the following in your own words: coercion; ordinal type; polymorphic operator; pseudovariable; selector; strong typing; THE_ operator; type generator.

7. Why are pseudovariables logically unnecessary?

8. Give some examples of polymorphic operators. Are the operators of the relational algebra polymorphic? What about aggregate operators such as SUM?

9. Define an operator that, given a rational number, returns the cube of that number.

10. Define a read-only operator that, given a point with cartesian coordinates x and y, returns the point with cartesian coordinates $f(x)$ and $g(y)$, where f and g are predefined operators (of type RATIONAL in each case).

11. Repeat Exercise 10 but make the operator an update operator.

12. Give a type definition for a scalar type called CIRCLE whose values are circles in two-dimensional euclidean space. What selectors and THE_ operators apply to this type? Also:

    a. Define a set of read-only operators to compute the diameter, circumference, and area of a given circle.

    b. Define an update operator to double the radius of a given circle (more precisely, to update a given variable of type CIRCLE in such a way that its circle value is unchanged except that the radius is twice what it was before).

13. Give some examples of types for which it might be useful to define two or more distinct possreps. Can you think of an example where distinct possreps have different numbers of components?

14. Give an appropriate set of scalar type definitions for the suppliers-and-parts database. Do not attempt to write the relvar definitions.

15. We pointed out in the section "Selectors and THE_ Operators" in this chapter that it is strictly incorrect to say that (e.g.) the quantity for a certain shipment is 100 ("a quantity is a value of type QTY, not a value of type INTEGER"). As a consequence, Fig. 2.1 is rather sloppy, inasmuch as it pretends that it *is* correct to think of, e.g., quantities as integers. Given your answer to Exercise 14, show the correct way of referring to the various scalar values in that figure.

16. Given your answer to Exercise 14, which of the following scalar expressions are valid? For those that are, state the type of the result; for the others, show an expression that will achieve what appears to be the desired effect.

    a.   `CITY = 'London'`

    b.   `SNAME || PNAME`

    c.   `QTY * 100`

    d.   `QTY + 100`

    e.   `STATUS + 5`

    f.   `'ABC' < CITY`

    g.   `COLOR = CITY`

    h.   `CITY || 'burg'`

17. It is sometimes suggested that types are really variables, in a sense. For example, employee numbers might grow from three digits to four as a business expands, so we might need to update "the set of all possible employee numbers." Discuss.

18. A type is a set of values, so (as noted near the beginning of the chapter) we can define an *empty* type to be a type where the set in question is empty. Can you think of any uses for such a type?

19. A possrep has a set of components, so we might define some type as having an empty possrep. What are the implications?

20. The *Manifesto* requires "=" to apply to every type; more specifically, it requires *v1* = *v2* to evaluate to TRUE if and only if *v1* and *v2* are the very same value. SQL, by contrast, does not require "=" to apply to every type, nor does it prescribe the semantics in all cases where it does apply. What are the implications of this state of affairs?

21. *(For discussion.)* As noted in the body of the chapter, there are those who would claim that XML technology is destined to replace relational technology. There is an XML data model (actually several different ones, of which the most important is probably *the semistructured data model*); there is an XML data definition language (actually at least two of them); there is an XML query language (at least three of them); and there are XML databases and XML DBMSs. What do you think is the true nature—the true technical nature, that is—of the relationship between these developments and relational technology? *Note:* A tutorial on XML from a database perspective can be found in Chapter 27 of reference [76].

Part II:

FORMAL SPECIFICATIONS

This part of the book is provided mainly for reference; **you probably should not even attempt to read it straight through**—not on a first reading, anyway. Chapter 4 is *The Third Manifesto* itself (the "no frills" version); it consists of the various prescriptions, proscriptions, and very strong suggestions that together constitute the *Manifesto* proper, with almost no explanatory material at all. To put it another way, Chapter 4 lays down a set of rules that the language **D** must abide by. (We remind you that the name **D** refers generically to any language that conforms to the principles of the *Manifesto;* in principle, any number of distinct languages could qualify as a valid **D**.) Chapter 5 then defines the language we call **Tutorial D**—i.e., a **D** defined primarily to serve as a basis for examples elsewhere in the book.

We stress the point that apart from (a) the references in OO Prescription 2 and OO Very Strong Suggestion 1 in Chapter 4 and (b) a few remarks in passing in Chapter 5, everything to do with type inheritance is ignored in these two chapters. The material of Part IV extends, but does not invalidate, the material presented in this part of the book.

Chapter 4

The Third Manifesto

RM PRESCRIPTIONS

1. A **scalar data type** (**scalar type** for short) is a named, finite set of scalar values (**scalars** for short). Given an arbitrary pair of distinct scalar types named *T1* and *T2*, respectively, with corresponding sets of scalar values *S1* and *S2*, respectively, the names *T1* and *T2* shall be distinct and the sets *S1* and *S2* shall be disjoint; in other words, two scalar types shall be equal—i.e., the same type—if and only if they have the same name (and therefore the same set of values). **D** shall provide facilities for users to define their own scalar types (*user-defined* scalar types); other scalar types shall be provided by the system (*built-in* or *system-defined* scalar types). **D** shall also provide facilities for users to destroy user-defined scalar types. The system-defined scalar types shall include type **boolean** (containing just two values, here denoted TRUE and FALSE), and **D** shall support all four monadic and 16 dyadic logical operators, directly or indirectly, for this type.

2. All scalar values shall be **typed**—i.e., such values shall always carry with them, at least conceptually, some identification of the type to which they belong.

3. A **scalar operator** is an operator that, when invoked, returns a scalar value (the **result** of that invocation). **D** shall provide facilities for users to define and destroy their own scalar operators (*user-defined* scalar operators). Other scalar operators shall be provided by the system (*built-in* or *system-defined* scalar operators). Let *Op* be a scalar operator. Then:

   a. *Op* shall be **read-only,** in the sense that invoking it shall cause no variables to be updated other than ones that are purely local to *Op*.

   b. Every invocation of *Op* shall denote a value ("produce a result") of the same type, the **result type**—also called the **declared type**—of *Op*. The definition of *Op* shall include a specification of the declared type of *Op*. That type shall be nonempty.

   c. The definition of *Op* shall include a specification of the type of each parameter to *Op*, the **declared type** of that parameter. That type shall be nonempty. If parameter *P* is of declared type *T*, then, in every invocation of *Op*, the argument *A* that corresponds to *P* in that invocation shall also be of type *T*, and that argument *A* shall be **effectively assigned** to *P*. *Note:* The prescriptions of this paragraph c. shall also apply if *Op* is an update operator instead of a read-only operator.

   It is convenient to deal with update operators here as well, despite the fact that such operators are not scalar (nor are they nonscalar—in fact, they are not typed at all). An **update operator** is an operator that, when invoked, is allowed to update at least one variable that is not purely local to that operator. Let *V* be such a variable. If the operator accesses *V* via some parameter *P*, then that parameter *P* is **subject to update.** **D** shall provide facilities for users to define and destroy their own update operators (*user-defined* update operators). Other update operators shall be provided by the system (*built-in* or *system-defined* update operators). Let *Op* be an update operator. Then:

   d. No invocation of *Op* shall denote a value ("produce a result").

e.   The definition of *Op* shall include a specification of which parameters to *Op* are subject to update. If parameter *P* is subject to update, then, in every invocation of *Op*, the argument *A* that corresponds to *P* in that invocation shall be a variable specifically, and, on completion of the execution of *Op* caused by that invocation, the final value assigned to *P* during that execution shall be **effectively assigned** to *A*.

4.   Let *T* be a nonempty scalar type, and let *v* be an appearance in some context of some value of type *T*. By definition, *v* has exactly one **physical representation** and one or more **possible representations** (at least one, because there is obviously always one that is the same as the physical representation). Physical representations for values of type *T* shall be specified by means of some kind of *storage structure definition language* and shall not be visible in **D**. As for possible representations:

a.   If *T* is user defined, then at least one possible representation for values of type *T* shall be declared and thus made visible in **D**. For each possible representation *PR* for values of type *T* that is visible in **D**, a **selector** operator *S*, of declared type *T*, shall be provided with the following properties:

1.   There shall be a one-to-one correspondence between the parameters of *S* and the components of *PR* (see RM Prescription 5). For definiteness, assume the parameters of *S* and the components of *PR* each constitute an ordered list of *n* elements ($n \geq 0$), such that the *i*th element in the list of parameters corresponds to the *i*th element in the list of components; then the declared types of the *i*th elements in the two lists shall be the same ($i = 1, 2, ..., n$).

2.   Every value of type *T* shall be produced by some invocation of *S* in which every argument is a literal.

3.   Every successful invocation of *S* shall produce some value of type *T*.

b.   If *T* is system defined, then zero or more possible representations for values of type *T* shall be declared and thus made visible in **D**. A possible representation *PR* for values of type *T* that is visible in **D** shall behave in all respects as if *T* were user defined and *PR* were a declared possible representation for values of type *T*. If no possible representation for values of type *T* is visible in **D**, then at least one **selector** operator *S*, of declared type *T*, shall be provided with the following properties:

1.   Every argument to every invocation of *S* shall be a literal.

2.   Every value of type *T* shall be produced by some invocation of *S*.

3.   Every successful invocation of *S* shall produce some value of type *T*.

5.   Let some declared possible representation *PR* for values of scalar type *T* be defined in terms of components *C1, C2, ..., Cn* ($n \geq 0$), each of which has a name and a declared type. Let *v* be a value of type *T*, and let *PR(v)* denote the possible representation corresponding to *PR* for that value *v*. Then *PR(v)* shall be **exposed**—i.e., a set of read-only and update operators shall be provided such that:

a.   For all such values *v* and for all *i* ($i = 1, 2, ..., n$), it shall be possible to "retrieve" (i.e., read the value of) the *Ci* component of *PR(v)*. The read-only operator that provides this functionality shall have declared type the same as that of *Ci*.

b.   For all variables V of declared type T and for all i ($i = 1, 2, ..., n$), it shall be possible to update V in such a way that if the values of V before and after the update are v and v' respectively, then the possible representations corresponding to PR for v and v' (i.e., $PR(v)$ and $PR(v')$, respectively) differ in their Ci components.

Such a set of operators shall be provided for each possible representation declared for values of type T.

6.   **D** shall support the **TUPLE** type generator. That is, given some heading $\{H\}$ (see RM Prescription 9), **D** shall support use of the **generated type** TUPLE$\{H\}$ as a basis for defining (or, in the case of values, selecting):

    a.   Values of that type (see RM Prescription 9)

    b.   Variables of that type (see RM Prescription 12)

    c.   Attributes of that type (see RM Prescriptions 9 and 10)

    d.   Components of that type within declared possible representations (see RM Prescription 5)

    e.   Read-only operators of that type (see RM Prescription 20)

    f.   Parameters of that type to user-defined operators (see RM Prescriptions 3 and 20)

The generated type TUPLE$\{H\}$ shall be referred to as a **tuple type,** and the name of that type shall be, precisely, TUPLE$\{H\}$. The terminology of *degree, attributes,* and *heading* introduced in RM Prescription 9 shall apply, mutatis mutandis, to that type, as well as to values and variables of that type (see RM Prescription 12). Tuple types TUPLE$\{H1\}$ and TUPLE$\{H2\}$ shall be equal if and only if $\{H1\} = \{H2\}$. The applicable operators shall include operators analogous to the RENAME, *project,* EXTEND, and JOIN operators of the relational algebra (see RM Prescription 18), together with tuple assignment (see RM Prescription 21) and tuple comparisons (see RM Prescription 22); they shall also include (a) a tuple selector operator (see RM Prescription 9), (b) an operator for extracting a specified attribute value from a specified tuple (the tuple in question might be required to be of degree one—see RM Prescription 9), and (c) operators for performing tuple "nesting" and "unnesting."

7.   **D** shall support the **RELATION** type generator. That is, given some heading $\{H\}$ (see RM Prescription 9), **D** shall support use of the **generated type** RELATION$\{H\}$ as the basis for defining (or, in the case of values, selecting):

    a.   Values of that type (see RM Prescription 10)

    b.   Variables of that type (see RM Prescription 13)

    c.   Attributes of that type (see RM Prescriptions 9 and 10)

    d.   Components of that type within declared possible representations (see RM Prescription 5)

    e.   Read-only operators of that type (see RM Prescription 20)

    f.   Parameters of that type to user-defined operators (see RM Prescriptions 3 and 20)

The generated type RELATION{*H*} shall be referred to as a **relation type,** and the name of that type shall be, precisely, RELATION{*H*}. The terminology of *degree, attributes,* and *heading* introduced in RM Prescription 9 shall apply, mutatis mutandis, to that type, as well as to values and variables of that type (see RM Prescription 13). Relation types RELATION{*H1*} and RELATION{*H2*} shall be equal if and only if {*H1*} = {*H2*}. The applicable operators shall include the usual operators of the relational algebra (see RM Prescription 18), together with relational assignment (see RM Prescription 21) and relational comparisons (see RM Prescription 22); they shall also include (a) a relation selector operator (see RM Prescription 10), (b) an operator for extracting the sole tuple from a specified relation of cardinality one (see RM Prescription 10), and (c) operators for performing relational "nesting" and "unnesting."

8. **D** shall support the **equality** comparison operator "=" for every type *T*. Let *Op* be an operator with a parameter *P*, let *P* be such that the argument corresponding to *P* in some invocation of *Op* is allowed to be of type *T*, and let *v1* and *v2* be values of type *T*. Then *v1* = *v2* shall evaluate to TRUE if and only if, for all such operators *Op*, two successful invocations of *Op* that are identical in all respects except that the argument corresponding to *P* is *v1* in one invocation and *v2* in the other are indistinguishable in their effect.

9. A **heading** {*H*} is a set of ordered pairs or **attributes** of the form <*A,T*>, where:

    a. *A* is the name of an **attribute** of {*H*}. No two distinct pairs in {*H*} shall have the same attribute name.

    b. *T* is the name of the **declared type** of attribute *A* of {*H*}.

    The number of pairs in {*H*}—equivalently, the number of attributes of {*H*}—is the **degree** of {*H*}.
      Now let *t* be a set of ordered triples <*A,T,v*>, obtained from {*H*} by extending each ordered pair <*A,T*> to include an arbitrary value *v* of type *T*, called the **attribute value** for attribute *A* of *t*. Then *t* is a **tuple value (tuple** for short) that **conforms** to heading {*H*}; equivalently, *t* is of the corresponding tuple type (see RM Prescription 6). The degree of that heading {*H*} shall be the **degree** of *t*, and the attributes and corresponding types of that heading {*H*} shall be the **attributes** and corresponding **declared attribute types** of *t*. Given a heading {*H*}, a *selector* operator, of type TUPLE{*H*}, shall be available for selecting an arbitrary tuple conforming to {*H*}; every such tuple shall be produced by some invocation of that selector in which every argument is a literal, and every successful invocation of that selector shall produce some such tuple.

10. A **relation value** *r* (**relation** for short) consists of a *heading* and a *body,* where:

    a. The **heading** of *r* shall be a heading {*H*} as defined in RM Prescription 9; *r* **conforms** to that heading (equivalently, *r* is of the corresponding relation type—see RM Prescription 7). The degree of that heading {*H*} shall be the **degree** of *r*, and the attributes and corresponding types of that heading {*H*} shall be the **attributes** and corresponding **declared attribute types** of *r*.

    b. The **body** of *r* shall be a set *B* of tuples, all having that same heading {*H*}. The cardinality of that body shall be the **cardinality** of *r*.

    Given a heading {*H*}, a *selector* operator, of type RELATION{*H*}, shall be available for selecting an arbitrary relation conforming to {*H*}; every such relation shall be produced by some invocation of that selector in which every argument is a literal, and every successful invocation of that selector shall produce some such relation.

11. **D** shall provide facilities for users to define **scalar variables**. Each scalar variable shall be named and shall have a specified nonempty (scalar) **declared type**. Let scalar variable *V* be of declared type *T;* for so long as variable *V* exists, it shall have a value that is of type *T*. Defining *V* shall have the effect of initializing *V* to some value—either a value specified explicitly as part of the operation that defines *V*, or some implementation-defined value if no such explicit value is specified.

12. **D** shall provide facilities for users to define **tuple variables**. Each tuple variable shall be named and shall have a specified nonempty **declared type** of the form TUPLE{*H*} for some heading {*H*}. Let variable *V* be of declared type TUPLE{*H*}; then the degree of that heading {*H*} shall be the **degree** of *V*, and the attributes and corresponding types of that heading {*H*} shall be the **attributes** and corresponding **declared attribute types** of *V*. For so long as variable *V* exists, it shall have a value that is of type TUPLE{*H*}. Defining *V* shall have the effect of initializing *V* to some value—either a value specified explicitly as part of the operation that defines *V*, or some implementation-defined value if no such explicit value is specified.

13. **D** shall provide facilities for users to define **relation variables** (**relvars** for short)—both database relvars (i.e., relvars that are part of some database) and application relvars (i.e., relvars that are local to some application). **D** shall also provide facilities for users to destroy database relvars. Each relvar shall be named and shall have a specified **declared type** of the form RELATION{*H*} for some heading {*H*}. Let variable *V* be of declared type RELATION{*H*}; then the degree of that heading {*H*} shall be the **degree** of *V*, and the attributes and corresponding types of that heading {*H*} shall be the **attributes** and corresponding **declared attribute types** of *V*. For so long as variable *V* exists, it shall have a value that is of type RELATION{*H*}.

14. Database relvars shall be either *real* or *virtual*. A **virtual relvar** *V* shall be a database relvar whose value at any given time is the result of evaluating a certain relational expression at that time; the relational expression in question shall be specified when *V* is defined and shall mention at least one database relvar. A **real relvar** shall be a database relvar that is not virtual. Defining a real relvar *V* shall have the effect of initializing *V* to some value—either a value specified explicitly as part of the operation that defines *V*, or an empty relation if no such explicit value is specified.

     Application relvars shall be either *public* or *private*. A **public relvar** shall be an application relvar that constitutes the perception of the application in question of some portion of some database. A **private relvar** shall be an application relvar that is completely private to the application in question and is not part of any database. Defining a private relvar *V* shall have the effect of initializing *V* to some value—either a value specified explicitly as part of the operation that defines *V*, or an empty relation if no such explicit value is specified.

15. By definition, every relvar shall have at least one **candidate key**. At least one such key shall be defined, either explicitly or implicitly, at the time the relvar in question is defined, and it shall not be possible to destroy all of the candidate keys of a given relvar (other than by destroying the relvar itself).

16. A **database** shall be a named container for relvars; the content of a given database at any given time shall be a set of database relvars. The necessary operators for defining and destroying databases shall not be part of **D** (in other words, defining and destroying databases shall be done "outside the **D** environment").

17. Each **transaction** shall interact with exactly one database. However, distinct transactions shall be

able to interact with distinct databases, and distinct databases shall not necessarily be disjoint. Also, **D** shall provide facilities for a transaction to define new relvars, or destroy existing ones, within its associated database (see RM Prescription 13).

18. **D** shall support the usual operators of the **relational algebra** (or some logical equivalent thereof). Specifically, it shall support, directly or indirectly, at least the operators RENAME, *restrict* (WHERE), *project,* JOIN, UNION, INTERSECT, MINUS, DIVIDEBY, EXTEND, SUMMARIZE, GROUP, and UNGROUP. All such operators shall be expressible without excessive circumlocution. **D** shall support **type inference** for relation types, whereby the type of the result of evaluating an arbitrary relational expression shall be well defined and known to both the system and the user.

19. **Relvar names** and **relation selector invocations** shall both be valid relational expressions. **Recursion** shall be permitted in relational expressions.

20. **D** shall provide facilities for users to define and destroy their own **tuple operators** (*user-defined* tuple operators) and **relational operators** (*user-defined* relational operators). Paragraphs a.-c. from RM Prescription 3 shall apply, mutatis mutandis.

21. **D** shall support the **assignment** operator "`:=`" for every type T. The assignment shall be referred to as a scalar, tuple, or relation (or relational) assignment according as T is a scalar, tuple, or relation type. Let V and v be a variable and a value, respectively, of the same type. After assignment of v to V, the equality comparison $V = v$ shall evaluate to TRUE (see RM Prescription 8). Furthermore, all variables other than V shall remain unchanged, apart possibly from variables defined in terms of V or variables in terms of which V is defined or both.

    D shall also support a **multiple** form of assignment, in which several individual assignments shall be performed as a single operation. Let MA be the multiple assignment

```
A1 , A2 , ... , An ;
```

(where $A1, A2, ..., An$ are individual assignments, each assigning to exactly one target variable, and the semicolon marks the overall end of the operation). Then the semantics of MA shall be defined by the following pseudocode (Steps a.-d.):

a. For $i := 1$ to n, expand any syntactic shorthands involved in Ai. After all such expansions, let MA take the form

```
V1 := X1 , V2 := X2 , ... , Vz := Xz ;
```

for some $z \geq n$, where Vi is the name of some variable not defined in terms of any others and Xi is an expression of declared type the same as that of Vi.

b. Let p and q ($1 \leq p < q \leq z$) be such that Vp and Vq are identical and there is no r ($r < p$ or $p < r < q$) such that Vp and Vr are identical. Replace Aq in MA by an assignment of the form

```
Vq := WITH Xp AS Vq : Xq
```

and remove Ap from MA. Repeat this process until no such pair p and q remains. Let MA now consist of the sequence

```
U1 := Y1 , U2 := Y2 , ... , Um := Ym ;
```

where each Ui is some Vj ($1 \leq i \leq j \leq m \leq z$).

c. For $i := 1$ to m, evaluate Yi. Let the result be yi.

d. For $i := 1$ to m, assign yi to Ui.

Note: Step b. of the foregoing pseudocode makes use of the WITH construct of **Tutorial D.** For further explanation, see Chapter 5.

22. **D** shall support certain **comparison operators,** as follows:

   a. The operators for comparing scalars shall include "=", "≠", and (for ordinal types) "<", ">", etc.

   b. The operators for comparing tuples shall include "=" and "≠" and shall not include "<", ">", etc.

   c. The operators for comparing relations shall include "=", "≠", "‖≤‖" ("is a subset of"), and "‖≥‖" ("is a superset of") and shall not include "<", ">", etc.[1]

   d. The operator "ϵ" for testing membership of a tuple in a relation shall be supported.

In every case mentioned except "ϵ" the comparands shall be of the same type; in the case of "ϵ" they shall have the same heading. *Note:* Support for "=" for every type is in fact required by RM Prescription 8.

23. **D** shall provide facilities for defining and destroying **integrity constraints (constraints** for short). Let C be a constraint; C can be thought of as a boolean expression (though it might not be explicitly formulated as such), and it shall be **satisfied** if and only if that boolean expression evaluates to TRUE. No user shall ever see a state of affairs in which C is not satisfied. There shall be two kinds of constraints:

   a. A **type** constraint shall specify the set of values that constitute a given type.

   b. A **database** constraint shall specify that values of a given set of database relvars taken in combination shall be such that a given boolean expression (which shall mention no variables other than the database relvars in question) evaluates to TRUE. Insofar as feasible, **D** shall support **constraint inference** for database constraints, whereby the constraints that apply to the result of evaluating an arbitrary relational expression shall be well defined and known to both the system and the user.

24. Let *DB* be a database; let *DBC1, DBC2, ..., DBCn* be all of the database constraints defined for *DB* (see RM Prescription 23); and let *DBC* be any boolean expression that is logically equivalent to

------

1. We denote the comparison operators "is a subset of" and "is a superset of" by the special symbols "‖≤‖" and "‖≥‖" (instead of the more usual mathematical symbols) for typographical reasons. See Chapter 5.

(DBC1) AND (DBC2) AND ... AND (DBCn) AND TRUE

Then *DBC* is **the total database constraint** for *DB*.

25.   Every database shall include a set of database relvars that constitute the **catalog** for that database. **D** shall provide facilities for assigning to relvars in the catalog.

26.   **D** shall be constructed according to well-established principles of **good language design**.

RM PROSCRIPTIONS

1.   **D** shall include no concept of a "relation" whose attributes are distinguishable by ordinal position. Instead, for every relation *r* expressible in **D**, the attributes of *r* shall be distinguishable by *name*.

2.   **D** shall include no concept of a "relation" whose tuples are distinguishable by ordinal position. Instead, for every relation *r* expressible in **D**, the tuples of *r* shall be distinguishable by *value*.

3.   **D** shall include no concept of a "relation" containing two distinct tuples *t1* and *t2* such that the comparison "*t1* = *t2*" evaluates to TRUE. It follows that (as already stated in RM Proscription 2), for every relation *r* expressible in **D**, the tuples of *r* shall be distinguishable by *value*.

4.   **D** shall include no concept of a "relation" in which some "tuple" includes some "attribute" that does not have a value.

5.   **D** shall not forget that relations with no attributes are respectable and interesting, nor that candidate keys with no components are likewise respectable and interesting.

6.   **D** shall include no constructs that relate to, or are logically affected by, the "physical" or "storage" or "internal" levels of the system.

7.   **D** shall support no tuple-at-a-time operations on relvars or relations.

8.   **D** shall not include any specific support for "composite" or "compound" attributes, since such functionality can more cleanly be achieved, if desired, through the type support already prescribed.

9.   **D** shall include no "domain check override" operators, since such operators are both ad hoc and unnecessary.

10.   **D** shall not be called SQL.

OO PRESCRIPTIONS

1.   **D** shall permit **compile-time type checking**.

2.   If **D** supports **type inheritance,** then such support shall conform to the inheritance model defined in Part IV of this book.

3.   **D** shall be **computationally complete**. That is, **D** may support, but shall not require, invocation from so-called host programs written in languages other than **D**. Similarly, **D** may support, but

shall not require, the use of other languages for implementation of user-defined operators.

4. Transaction initiation shall be performed only by means of an explicit **begin transaction** operator. Transaction termination shall be performed only by means of a **commit** or **rollback** operator; commit must always be explicit, but rollback can be implicit (if and only if the transaction fails through no fault of its own). If transaction *TX* terminates with commit ("normal termination"), changes made by *TX* to the applicable database shall be committed. If transaction *TX* terminates with rollback ("abnormal termination"), changes made by *TX* to the applicable database shall be rolled back.

5. **D** shall support **nested transactions**—i.e., it shall permit a *parent* transaction *TX* to initiate a *child* transaction *TX'* before *TX* itself has terminated, in which case:

    a. *TX* and *TX'* shall interact with the same database (as is in fact required by RM Prescription 17).

    b. Whether *TX* shall be required to suspend execution while *TX'* executes shall be implementation-defined. However, *TX* shall not be allowed to terminate before *TX'* terminates; in other words, *TX'* shall be wholly contained within *TX*.

    c. Rollback of *TX* shall include the rolling back of *TX'* even if *TX'* has terminated with commit. In other words, "commit" is always interpreted within the parent context (if such exists) and is subject to override by the parent transaction (again, if such exists).

6. Let *AggOp* be an **aggregate** operator, such as SUM. If the argument to *AggOp* happens to be empty, then:

    a. If *AggOp* is essentially just shorthand for some iterated scalar dyadic operator *Op* (the dyadic operator is "+" in the case of SUM), and if an identity value exists for *Op* (the identity value is 0 in the case of "+"), then the result of that invocation of *AggOp* shall be that identity value.

    b. Otherwise, the result of that invocation of *AggOp* shall be undefined.

OO PROSCRIPTIONS

1. Relvars are not domains.

2. No database relvar shall include an attribute of type pointer.

RM VERY STRONG SUGGESTIONS

1. **D** should provide a mechanism according to which values of some specified candidate key (or certain components thereof) for some specified relvar are **supplied by the system**. It should also provide a mechanism according to which an arbitrary relation can be extended to include an attribute whose values (a) are unique within that relation (or within certain partitions of that relation) and (b) are once again **supplied by the system**.

2. **D** should include some declarative shorthand for expressing **referential constraints** (also known as **foreign key** constraints).

3.   Let *RX* be a relational expression. By definition, *RX* can be thought of as designating a relvar, *R* say—either a user-defined relvar (if *RX* is just a relvar name) or a system-defined relvar (otherwise). It is desirable, though not always entirely feasible, for the system to be able to **infer the candidate keys** of *R*, such that (among other things):

   a.   If *RX* constitutes the defining expression for some virtual relvar *R'*, then those inferred candidate keys can be checked for consistency with the candidate keys explicitly defined for *R'* and—assuming no conflict—become candidate keys for *R'*.

   b.   Those inferred candidate keys can be included in the information about *R* that is made available (in response to a "metaquery") to a user of **D**.

   D should provide such functionality, but without any guarantee (a) that such inferred candidate keys are not proper supersets of actual candidate keys or (b) that such an inferred candidate key is discovered for every actual candidate key.

4.   **D** should support **transition constraints**—i.e., constraints on the transitions that a given database can make from one value to another.

5.   **D** should provide some shorthand for expressing **quota queries**. It should not be necessary to convert the relation concerned into (e.g.) an array in order to formulate such a query.

6.   **D** should provide some shorthand for expressing the **generalized transitive closure** operation, including the ability to specify generalized *concatenate* and *aggregate* operations.

7.   **D** should provide some means for users to define their own generic **operators,** including in particular generic **relational** operators.

8.   **SQL** should be implementable in **D**—not because such implementation is desirable in itself, but so that a painless migration route might be available for current SQL users. To this same end, existing SQL databases should be convertible to a form that **D** programs can operate on without error.

OO VERY STRONG SUGGESTIONS

1.   Some level of **type inheritance** should be supported (in which case, see OO Prescription 2).

2.   Operator definitions should be **logically distinct** from the definitions of the types of their parameters and results, not "bundled in" with those latter definitions (though the operators required by RM Prescriptions 4, 5, 8, and 21 might be exceptions in this regard).

3.   **D** should support the concept of **single-level storage.**

RECENT *MANIFESTO* CHANGES

There are a number of differences between the *Manifesto* as defined in the present chapter and the version documented in this book's predecessor (reference [83]). For the benefit of readers who might be familiar with that earlier version, we summarize the main differences here.

- RM Prescription 1 has been simplified and corrected. In particular, (a) the requirement that values and variables of type *T* be operable upon solely by means of operators defined for type *T* has been deleted, since it was tautologous; (b) the references to RM Prescriptions 4 and 5 have been deleted, since they were redundant.

- Type **truth value** has been renamed type **boolean,** and the truth values *true* and *false* have been renamed TRUE and FALSE, respectively.

- RM Prescription 3 has been restructured to make it clear that scalar operators are read-only by definition, while update operators have no type at all but can update variables (arguments in particular) of any type. Paragraph a. outlaws side effects on the part of read-only operators. Paragraph b. requires result types to be nonempty. Paragraph c. requires parameter types to be nonempty. Paragraph e. explains the semantics of parameters that are subject to update in terms of effective assignment instead of (as previously) in terms of passing by reference vs. passing by value.

- RM Prescription 4 now refers explicitly to nonempty types. It allows empty possreps. Also, "actual" representations are now called physical representations, and the requirement that declared possreps be defined as part of the pertinent type definition (instead of, possibly, elsewhere) has been deleted.

- Several omissions to do with selectors have been rectified: Result types (and in fact the complete semantics) of tuple and relation selectors are specified; scalar selector parameters are explained; and possreps and selectors for system-defined scalar types are specified. Also, result types are specified for the read-only operators that access possrep components.

- The phrase "at most only" has been deleted from paragraph b. of RM Prescription 5. (As it stood, that phrase rendered the paragraph vacuous, while deleting "at most" but keeping "only" would result in a prescription that could be awkward to satisfy.)

- RM Prescriptions 6 and 7 have been extended to include tuple and relation types as possible declared types for parameters and read-only operators.

- RM Prescription 11 now defines tuples in terms of tuple types instead of vice versa.

- Headings are now denoted $\{H\}$ instead of H.

- The fact that (except for relvars) variables must have a nonempty declared type is now stated explicitly, as is the fact that they always have a value (there is no such thing as an unitialized variable). Real relvars can now be explicitly initialized.

- RM Prescription 14 has been expanded to include details of application relvars.

- Candidate key specifications can now be implicit (for virtual relvars in particular; previously we required them always to be explicit, but that was just an oversight).

- RM Prescription 18 now mentions GROUP and UNGROUP.

- RM Prescription 20 has been generalized.

- RM Prescription 21 has been clarified (and, in the case of multiple assignment, corrected).

- RM Prescription 23 now explicitly spells out the semantics of type and database constraints (attribute and relvar constraints as such are no longer mentioned).

- RM Prescription 24 has been revised and simplified.

- RM Very Strong Suggestion 8 has been deleted (and RM Very Strong Suggestion 9 has been renumbered accordingly); very strongly suggesting the "special values" approach to missing information is (we now feel) to promote that approach more than it merits.

- OO Very Strong Suggestion 1 has been abbreviated.

- OO Very Strong Suggestions 3 and 4 have been deleted (and OO Very Strong Suggestion 5 has been renumbered accordingly); we no longer believe there are any strong arguments in favor of supporting additional "collection" type generators, over and above RELATION.

In addition to all of the foregoing, almost all of the prescriptions, proscriptions, and very strong suggestions have been reworded (in some cases extensively). However, those revisions in themselves are not intended to induce any changes in what is being described.

Chapter 5

T u t o r i a l   D

Tutorial D is a computationally complete programming language with fully integrated database functionality. It is deliberately not meant to be "industrial strength"; rather, it is a "toy" language, whose principal purpose is to serve as a teaching vehicle. As a consequence, many features that would be required in an industrial-strength language are intentionally omitted. (Extending the language to incorporate such features, thereby turning it into what might be called **Industrial D,** could be a worthwhile project.) For example, there is no support for any of the following:

- Sessions and connections

- Any form of communication with the outside world (I/O facilities, etc.)

- Exception handling and feedback information

In connection with this last point, however, we should at least say that we expressly do not want a form of exception-handling that requires the user to pass a feedback argument on each and every operator invocation (such an approach would effectively force all operators to be update operators).

For obvious reasons, there is also no support for any of the items listed in the subsection "Topics Deliberately Omitted" in Chapter 1 (security and authorization, triggered procedures, and so forth). Nor is there any support for type inheritance; however, extensions to deal with this latter topic are described in Part IV of this book.

In addition to the foregoing, many minor details, both syntactic and semantic, that would require precise specification in an industrial-strength language have also been ignored. For example, details of the following are all omitted:

- Language characters, identifiers, scope of names, etc.

- Reserved words (if any), comments,[1] delimiters and separators, etc.

- Operator precedence rules (except for a couple of important special cases)

- "Obvious" syntax rules (e.g., distinct parameters to the same operator must have distinct names)

On the other hand, the language is meant to be well designed, as far as it goes.[2] Indeed, it must be—for otherwise it would not be a valid **D,** since it would violate RM Prescription 26 (which requires every **D** to be constructed according to principles of good language design).

As already noted, **Tutorial D** is computationally complete, meaning that entire applications can be

---

1. In our examples we show comments as text strings bracketed by "/*" and "*/" delimiters.

2. Some might not agree that **Tutorial D** is well designed, because certain constructs in the language could lead to the need for unbounded lookahead on the part of the compiler. This issue would need to be addressed in an industrial-strength **D.** One possibility we are considering is to require parentheses around (a) pseudovariable references that are not nested inside other such references and (b) boolean expressions that immediately follow the keyword WHERE. Further discussion of this issue, including other possible approaches to resolving it, can be found at the website *www.thethirdmanifesto.com.*

written in the language; it is not just a "data sublanguage" that relies on some host language to provide the necessary computational capabilities. In accordance with the assumptions spelled out in Chapter 1, moreover, it is also (like most languages currently in widespread use) imperative in style—though it is worth mentioning that the "data sublanguage" portion, being based as it is on relational algebra, can in fact be regarded as a functional language if considered in isolation.[1] In practice we would hope that this portion of the language would be implemented in an interactive form as well as in the form of a programming language per se; in other words, we endorse *the dual-mode principle* as described in, e.g., reference [76].

Tutorial D is a relational language, of course, but in some respects it can be regarded as an object language as well. For one thing, it supports the concept of single-level storage (see OO Very Strong Suggestion 3). More important, it supports what is probably the most fundamental feature of object languages: namely, **it allows users to define their own types.** And since there is no reliance on a host language, there is no *impedance mismatch* between the types available inside the database and those available outside (i.e., there is no need to map between the arbitrarily complex types used in the database and the probably rather simple types provided by some conventional host language).[2] In other words, we agree with the object community's complaint that there is a serious problem in trying to build an interface between a DBMS that allows user-defined types and a programming language that does not. For example, if the database contains a value of type POLYGON, then in Tutorial D that value can be assigned to a local variable also of type POLYGON—there is no need to break it down into, say, a sequence of number pairs representing the (x,y)-coordinates of the vertices of the polygon in question. Altogether, then, it seems fair to characterize Tutorial D as a true "object/relational" language (inasmuch as that term has any objective meaning!).

Tutorial D has been designed to support all of the prescriptions and proscriptions of *The Third Manifesto* as defined in Chapter 4. It deliberately does not support all of the very strong suggestions mentioned in that chapter, though it does support some of them (possible extensions to deal with others are considered briefly in Chapter 10). The language is also deliberately not meant to be minimal in any sense—it includes numerous features that are really just shorthand for certain combinations of others. (This remark applies especially to its relational support, as should already be clear from Chapter 2.) However, it is at least true that the shorthands in question are specifically designed to be shorthands [31]; i.e., the redundancies are deliberate, and are included for usability reasons.

Most of the rest of this chapter consists of a BNF grammar for Tutorial D. The grammar is defined by means of what is essentially standard BNF notation, except for a couple of simplifying extensions that we now explain. Let $<xyz>$ denote an arbitrary syntactic category (i.e., anything appearing on the left side of some BNF production rule). Then:

- The expression $<xyz\ list>$ denotes a sequence of zero or more $<xyz>$s in which each pair of adjacent $<xyz>$s is separated by at least one space.

- The expression $<xyz\ commalist>$ denotes a sequence of zero or more $<xyz>$s in which each pair of adjacent $<xyz>$s is separated by a comma (as well as, optionally, one or more spaces before the comma or after it or both).

---

1. More precisely, the read-only features of the data sublanguage portion can be so regarded. *Note:* It is well known that a relational data sublanguage can be based on either relational algebra or relational calculus. It is also well known that an algebraic style is intuitively preferable for some tasks, a calculus style for others. As already mentioned, Tutorial D uses an algebraic style, for definiteness.

2. Actually the term *impedance mismatch* is used to mean several different things, of which the mismatch referred to here, between database and language types, is only one.

Chapter 5 / Tutorial D   95

Observe in particular that most of the various lists and commalists described in what follows are allowed to be empty. The effect of specifying an empty list or commalist is usually obvious; for example, an <*assignment*> for which the contained commalist of <*assign*>s is empty degenerates to a <*no op*> ("no operation"). Occasionally, however, there is something a little more interesting to be said about such cases (see Exercise 9 at the end of the chapter).

Finally, a few miscellaneous points:

- All syntactic categories of the form <*... name*> are defined to be <*identifier*>s, barring explicit production rules to the contrary. The category <*identifier*> in turn is terminal and is not defined here.

- A few of the production rules include an alternative on the right side that consists of an ellipsis followed by plain text. In such cases, the plain text is intended as an informal—i.e., natural language—explanation of the syntactic category being defined (or one form of that syntactic category).

- Some of the production rules are accompanied by a prose explanation of certain additional syntax rules or the corresponding semantics or both—but only where such explanations seem necessary and have not already been given in earlier chapters.[1] (For this reason among others, the grammar is not suitable for driving a mechanical parser, nor is it meant to be; instead, it is meant to serve as an understandable, albeit fairly formal, definition of the constructs that are syntactically valid in the language. As noted in the preface, a grammar suitable for mechanical parsing can be found at the website *www.thethirdmanifesto.com.*)

- Please note that braces "{" and "}" in the grammar stand for themselves; i.e., they are symbols in the language being defined, not symbols of the metalanguage as they usually are. To be more specific, we use braces to enclose commalists of items when the commalist in question is intended to denote a set of some kind, implying that (a) the order in which the items appear within that commalist is immaterial and (b) if an item appears more than once, it is treated as if it appeared just once (usually; the exceptions are EXACTLY and the *n*-adic versions of COUNT, SUM, AVG, and D_UNION, q.v., for which repeated items have significance). Note, therefore, that if for some <*xyz*> A and B are <*xyz commalist*>s enclosed in braces that differ only in the order in which the individual <*xyz*>s appear, then A and B denote the same thing and are regarded as interchangeable.

- The language defined by this grammar observes the logical difference between expressions and statements. An expression denotes a value; it can be thought of as a rule for computing or determining the value in question. A statement does not denote a value; instead, it causes some action to occur, such as assigning a value to some variable or changing the flow of control.

- As already noted, various extensions to the language as defined by this grammar are proposed later in the book (especially in Part IV). A syntactic summary of the entire language—including the inheritance extensions from Part IV, but excluding extensions motivated merely by certain of the suggestions in Chapter 10—can be found in Appendix I.

- Finally, the language defined by this grammar constitutes a significant revision of **Tutorial D** as defined in this book's predecessor [83]. For readers who might be familiar with the earlier version, the section "Recent Language Changes" (following the sections on the grammar per se)

---

1. For a formal definition of the semantics of the relational algebra operators in particular, however, see Appendix A.

summarizes the most important of those revisions.

COMMON CONSTRUCTS

```
<type>
    ::=    <scalar type> | <tuple type> | <relation type>

<scalar type>
    ::=    <scalar type name> | SAME_TYPE_AS ( <scalar exp> )

<tuple type>
    ::=    <tuple type name> | SAME_TYPE_AS ( <tuple exp> )
         | TUPLE SAME_HEADING_AS ( <nonscalar exp> )

<relation type>
    ::=    <relation type name> | SAME_TYPE_AS ( <relation exp> )
         | RELATION SAME_HEADING_AS ( <nonscalar exp> )

<user op def>
    ::=    <user update op def> | <user read-only op def>

<user update op def>
    ::=    OPERATOR <user op name> ( <parameter def commalist> )
             UPDATES { [ ALL BUT ] <parameter name commalist> } ;
           <statement>
         END OPERATOR
```

The *<parameter def commalist>* is enclosed in parentheses instead of braces, as is the corresponding *<argument commalist>* in an invocation of the operator in question (see *<user op inv>*, later), because we follow convention in relying on ordinal position for argument/parameter matching.[1] The *<parameter name commalist>* identifies parameters that are subject to update.

In practice, it might be desirable to support an external form of *<user update op def>* as well. Syntactically, such a *<user update op def>* would include, not a *<statement>* as above, but rather a reference to an external file that contains the code that implements the operator (possibly written in some different language). It might also be desirable to support a form of *<user update op def>* that includes neither a *<statement>* nor such an external reference; such a *<user update op def>* would define merely what is called a *specification signature* for the operator in question, and the implementation code would then have to be defined elsewhere. Splitting operator definitions into separate pieces in this way is likely to prove particularly useful if type inheritance is supported (see Part IV). Analogous remarks apply to *<user read-only op def>*s as well, q.v.

```
<parameter def>
    ::=    <parameter name> <type>
```

---

1. Observe that this remark is true of read-only as well as update operators. In particular, it is true of scalar selector operators—that is, the arguments to a *<scalar selector inv>* are specified as a commalist in parentheses, even though the corresponding parameters are specified as a commalist in braces (see *<possrep def>*, later; see also the section "A Remark on Syntax" at the end of the chapter).

```
<user read-only op def>
    ::=    OPERATOR <user op name> ( <parameter def commalist> ) RETURNS <type> ;
              <statement>
          END OPERATOR
```

The *<user op name>* denotes a scalar, tuple, or relational operator, depending on the specified *<type>*.

```
<user op inv>
    ::=    <user op name> ( <argument commalist> )

<argument>
    ::=    <exp>

<exp>
    ::=    <scalar exp> | <nonscalar exp>

<scalar exp>
    ::=    <scalar with exp> | <scalar nonwith exp>

<nonscalar exp>
    ::=    <tuple exp> | <relation exp>

<tuple exp>
    ::=    <tuple with exp> | <tuple nonwith exp>

<relation exp>
    ::=    <relation with exp> | <relation nonwith exp>

<scalar with exp>
    ::=    WITH <name intro commalist> : <scalar exp>
```

Let *SWE* be a *<scalar with exp>*, and let *NIC* and *SE* be the *<name intro commalist>* and the *<scalar exp>*, respectively, in *SWE*. The individual *<name intro>*s in *NIC* are executed in sequence as written. As the next production rule shows, each such *<name intro>* includes an *<exp>* and an *<introduced name>*. Let *NI* be one of those *<name intro>*s, and let the *<exp>* and the *<introduced name>* in *NI* be *X* and *N*, respectively. Then *N* denotes the value obtained by evaluating *X*, and it can appear subsequently in *SWE* wherever the expression (*X*)—i.e., *X* in parentheses—would be allowed. Analogous remarks apply to *<tuple with exp>*s and *<relation with exp>*s, q.v.

```
<name intro>
    ::=    <exp> AS <introduced name>

<tuple with exp>
    ::=    WITH <name intro commalist> : <tuple exp>

<relation with exp>
    ::=    WITH <name intro commalist> : <relation exp>

<user op drop>
    ::=    DROP OPERATOR <user op name>
```

```
<selector inv>
    ::=   <scalar selector inv> | <tuple selector inv> | <relation selector inv>

<scalar var ref>
    ::=   <scalar var name>

<tuple var ref>
    ::=   <tuple var name>

<relation var ref>
    ::=   <relation var name>

<attribute ref>
    ::=   <attribute name>

<possrep component ref>
    ::=   <possrep component name>

<assignment>
    ::=   <assign commalist>
```

The semantics of *< assignment >* are those of *multiple* assignment, as required and specified by RM Prescription 21.

```
<assign>
    ::=   <scalar assign> | <tuple assign> | <relation assign>
```

SCALAR DEFINITIONS

```
<scalar type name>
    ::=   <user scalar type name> | <built-in scalar type name>

<built-in scalar type name>
    ::=   INTEGER | RATIONAL | CHARACTER | CHAR | BOOLEAN
```

As indicated, **Tutorial D** supports the following built-in scalar types:

- INTEGER (signed integers): literals expressed as an optionally signed decimal integer; usual arithmetic and comparison operators, with usual notation.

- RATIONAL (signed rational numbers): literals expressed as an optionally signed decimal mantissa (including a decimal point), optionally followed by the letter E and an optionally signed decimal integer exponent (examples: 5., 5.0, 17.5, -5.3E+2); usual arithmetic and comparison operators, with usual notation.

- CHARACTER or CHAR (varying-length character strings): literals expressed as a sequence, enclosed in single quotes, of zero or more characters; usual string manipulation and comparison operators, with usual notation—"||" (concatenate), SUBSTR (substring), etc. By the way, if you are familiar with SQL, do not be misled here; the SQL data type CHAR corresponds to *fixed*-length character strings (the varying-length analog is called VARCHAR), and an associated length—default one—must be specified as in (e.g.) CHAR(25). **Tutorial D** does not support a fixed-length character string type.

- BOOLEAN (truth values): literals TRUE and FALSE; usual comparison operators (= and ≠) and boolean operators (AND, OR, NOT, etc.), with usual notation. Note that **Tutorial D**'s support for type BOOLEAN goes beyond that found in many languages in at least three ways:

  1. It includes explicit support for the XOR operator (exclusive OR). The expression *a* XOR *b* (where *a* and *b* are <*bool exp*>s) is semantically identical to the expression *a* ≠ *b*.

  2. It supports *n*-adic versions of the operators AND, OR, and XOR. The syntax is:

     ```
     <n-adic bool op name> { <bool exp commalist> }
     ```

     The <*n-adic bool op name*> is AND, OR, or XOR. AND returns TRUE if and only if all specified <*bool exp*>s evaluate to TRUE. OR returns FALSE if and only if all specified <*bool exp*>s evaluate to FALSE. XOR returns TRUE if and only if the number of specified <*bool exp*>s that evaluate to TRUE is odd.

  3. It supports an *n*-adic operator of the form

     ```
     EXACTLY ( <integer exp>, { <bool exp commalist> } )
     ```

     Let the <*integer exp*> evaluate to N.[1] Then the overall expression evaluates to TRUE if and only if the number of specified <*bool exp*>s that evaluate to TRUE is N. *Note:* If the number of specified <*bool exp*>s is zero—i.e., if the <*bool exp commalist*> is empty—the comma following the <*integer exp*> must be omitted.

In practice we would expect a variety of other built-in scalar types to be supported in addition to the foregoing: DATE, TIME, perhaps BIT (varying-length bit strings), and so forth. We omit such types here as irrelevant to our main purpose.

```
<user scalar type def>
    ::=   <user scalar root type def>
```

The syntactic category <*user scalar root type def*> is introduced merely to pave the way for the inheritance support to be discussed in Part IV. All types are root types in the absence of inheritance support.

```
<user scalar root type def>
    ::=   TYPE <user scalar type name> [ ORDINAL ] <possrep def list>

<possrep def>
    ::=   POSSREP [ <possrep name> ]
              { <possrep component def commalist> [ <possrep constraint def> ] }

<possrep component def>
    ::=   <possrep component name> <type>
```

---

1. The detailed syntax of <*integer exp*>s is not specified in this chapter; however, we note that an <*integer exp*> is of course a numeric expression and hence a <*scalar exp*> also.

No two distinct *<possrep def>*s within the same ** can include a component with the same *<possrep component name>*.

```
<possrep constraint def>
    ::=   CONSTRAINT <bool exp>
```

The *<bool exp>* must not mention any variables, but *<possrep component ref>*s can be used to denote the corresponding components of the applicable possible representation ("possrep") of an arbitrary value of the scalar type in question.

```
<user scalar type drop>
    ::=   DROP TYPE <user scalar type name>

<scalar var def>
    ::=   VAR <scalar var name> <scalar type or init value>

<scalar type or init value>
    ::=   <scalar type> | INIT ( <scalar exp> ) | <scalar type> INIT ( <scalar exp> )
```

If *<scalar type>* and the INIT specification both appear, *<scalar exp>* must be of type *<scalar type>*. If *<scalar type>* appears, the scalar variable is of that type; otherwise it is of the same type as *<scalar exp>*. If the INIT specification appears, the scalar variable is initialized to the value of *<scalar exp>*; otherwise it is initialized to an implementation-defined value.

TUPLE DEFINITIONS

```
<tuple type name>
    ::=   TUPLE <heading>

<heading>
    ::=   { <attribute commalist> }

<attribute>
    ::=   <attribute name> <type>

<tuple var def>
    ::=   VAR <tuple var name> <tuple type or init value>

<tuple type or init value>
    ::=   <tuple type> | INIT ( <tuple exp> ) | <tuple type> INIT ( <tuple exp> )
```

If *<tuple type>* and the INIT specification both appear, *<tuple exp>* must be of type *<tuple type>*. If *<tuple type>* appears, the tuple variable is of that type; otherwise it is of the same type as *<tuple exp>*. If the INIT specification appears, the tuple variable is initialized to the value of *<tuple exp>*; otherwise it is initialized to an implementation-defined value.

RELATIONAL DEFINITIONS

```
<relation type name>
    ::=    RELATION <heading>

<relation var def>
    ::=    <database relation var def> | <application relation var def>
```

A *< relation var def >* defines a relation variable (i.e., a relvar). In practice it might be desirable to provide a way of defining relation constants or *relcons* also (see RM Prescription 14 in Chapter 6 for further discussion). Note that **Tutorial D** already supports two built-in relcons called TABLE_DEE and TABLE_DUM (see the section "Relational Operations" later in this chapter).

```
<database relation var def>
    ::=    <real relation var def> | <virtual relation var def>
```

A *< database relation var def >* defines a database relvar—i.e., a relvar that is part of the database. In particular, therefore, it causes an entry to be made in the catalog. Note, however, that neither databases nor catalogs are explicitly mentioned anywhere in the syntax of **Tutorial D**.

```
<real relation var def>
    ::=    VAR <relation var name> REAL <relation type or init value>
           <candidate key def list>
```

The keyword REAL can alternatively be spelled BASE. An empty *< candidate key def list >* is permitted, though not required, only if (a) the *< relation type or init value >* specifies or includes INIT (*< relation exp >*) or (b) *< relation type >* is of the form SAME_TYPE_AS (*< relation exp >*); it is equivalent to a *< candidate key def list >* that contains exactly one *< candidate key def >* for each key that can be inferred by the system from the *< relation exp >* in that INIT or SAME_TYPE_AS specification (see RM Very Strong Suggestion 3 in Chapter 10).

```
<relation type or init value>
    ::=    <relation type> | INIT ( <relation exp> ) | <relation type> INIT ( <relation exp> )
```

An INIT specification can appear only if either REAL (or BASE) or PRIVATE is specified for the relvar in question (see *< application relation var def >*, later, for an explanation of PRIVATE). If *< relation type >* and the INIT specification both appear, *< relation exp >* must be of type *< relation type >*. If *< relation type >* appears, the relvar is of that type; otherwise it is of the same type as *< relation exp >*. If and only if the relvar is either real or private, then (a) if the INIT specification appears, the relvar is initialized to the value of *< relation exp >*; (b) otherwise it is initialized to the empty relation of the appropriate type.

```
<candidate key def>
    ::=    KEY { [ ALL BUT ] <attribute ref commalist> }
```

In accordance with the discussions in Chapter 2, we use the unqualified keyword KEY to mean a candidate key specifically. **Tutorial D** does not explicitly support primary keys as such.

```
<virtual relation var def>
    ::=    VAR <relation var name> VIRTUAL ( <relation exp> ) <candidate key def list>
```

The *< relation exp >* must mention at least one database relvar and no other variables. An empty

< candidate key def list > is equivalent to a *< candidate key def list >* that contains exactly one *< candidate key def >* for each key that can be inferred by the system from *< relation exp >* (see RM Very Strong Suggestion 3 in Chapter 10).

```
<application relation var def>
    ::=   VAR <relation var name> <private or public> <relation type or init value>
              <candidate key def list>
```

An empty *< candidate key def list >* is permitted, though not required, only if (a) the *< relation type or init value >* specifies or includes INIT (*< relation exp >*) or (b) *< relation type >* is of the form SAME_TYPE_AS (*< relation exp >*); it is equivalent to a *< candidate key def list >* that contains exactly one *< candidate key def >* for each key that can be inferred by the system from the *< relation exp >* in that INIT or SAME_TYPE_AS specification (see RM Very Strong Suggestion 3 in Chapter 10).

```
<private or public>
    ::=   PRIVATE | PUBLIC


<relation var drop>
    ::=   DROP VAR <relation var ref>
```

The *< relation var ref >* must denote a database relvar, not an application one.

```
<constraint def>
    ::=   CONSTRAINT <constraint name> <bool exp>
```

A *< constraint def >* defines a database constraint. The *< bool exp >* must not mention any variable that is not a database relvar. (**Tutorial D** does not support the definition of constraints on scalar variables or tuple variables or application relvars, though there is no logical reason why it should not do so.)

```
<constraint drop>
    ::=   DROP CONSTRAINT <constraint name>
```

SCALAR OPERATIONS

```
<scalar nonwith exp>
    ::=   <scalar var ref> | <scalar op inv> | ( <scalar exp> )


<scalar op inv>
    ::=   <user op inv> | <built-in scalar op inv>


<built-in scalar op inv>
    ::=   <scalar selector inv> | <THE_ op inv> | <attribute extractor inv> | <agg op inv>
            | ... plus the usual possibilities
```

It is convenient to get "the usual possibilities" out of the way first. By this term, we mean the usual numeric operators ("+", "*", etc.), character string operators ("||", SUBSTR, etc.), and boolean operators, all of which we have already said are built-in operators in **Tutorial D**. It follows that numeric expressions, character string expressions, and in particular boolean expressions—i.e., *< bool exp >* s—are all *< scalar exp >* s (and we assume the usual syntax in each case). The following are also *< scalar exp >* s:

- A special form of *<bool exp>*, IS_EMPTY (*<relation exp>*), which returns TRUE if and only if the relation denoted by *<relation exp>* is empty. (In practice, it might be useful to support an IS_NOT_EMPTY operator as well.)

- CAST expressions of the form CAST_AS_*T* (*<scalar exp>*), where *T* is a scalar type and *<scalar exp>* denotes a scalar value to be converted ("cast") to that type. *Note:* We use syntax of the form CAST_AS_*T* (...), rather than CAST (... AS *T*), because this latter form raises "type TYPE" issues—e.g., what is the type of operand *T*?—that we prefer to avoid.

- IF-THEN-ELSE and CASE expressions of the usual form (and we assume without going into details that tuple and relation analogs of these expressions are available also).

The syntax of *<scalar selector inv>* has already been explained (see Chapter 3 for several examples). *Note:* Whether scalar selectors are regarded as built in or user defined could be a matter of some debate, but the point is unimportant for present purposes. Analogous remarks apply to THE_ operators and attribute extractors also (see the next two production rules).

```
<THE_ op inv>
    ::=    <THE_ op name> ( <scalar exp> )
```

We include this production rule in this section because in practice we expect most *<THE_ op inv>*s to denote scalar values. In fact, however, a *<THE_ op inv>* will be a *<scalar exp>*, a *<tuple exp>*, or a *<relation exp>*, depending on the type of the *<possrep component>* corresponding to *<THE_ op name>*.

```
<attribute extractor inv>
    ::=    <attribute ref> FROM <tuple exp>
```

We include this production rule in this section because in practice we expect most attributes to be scalar. In fact, however, an *<attribute extractor inv>* will be a *<scalar exp>*, a *<tuple exp>*, or a *<relation exp>*, depending on the type of *<attribute ref>*.

```
<agg op inv>
    ::=    <agg op name> ( [ <integer exp>, ] <relation exp> [, <attribute ref> ] )
```

The *<integer exp>* and following comma must be specified if and only if the *<agg op name>* is EXACTLY. The *<attribute ref>* must be omitted if the *<agg op name>* is COUNT; otherwise, it can be omitted if and only if the *<relation exp>* denotes a relation of degree one, in which case the sole attribute of that relation is assumed by default. For SUM and AVG, the attribute denoted by *<attribute ref>* must be of some type for which the operator "+" is defined; for MAX and MIN, it must be of some ordinal type; for AND, OR, XOR, and EXACTLY, it must be of type BOOLEAN; for UNION, D_UNION, and INTERSECT, it must be of some relation type. *Note:* We include this production rule in this section because in practice we expect most *<agg op inv>*s to denote scalar values. In fact, however, an *<agg op inv>* will be a *<scalar exp>*, a *<tuple exp>* (potentially), or a *<relation exp>* depending on the type of the operator denoted by *<agg op name>*. (Given the aggregate operators currently defined, for UNION, D_UNION, and INTERSECT it is a *<relation exp>*, otherwise it is a *<scalar exp>*.)

```
<agg op name>
    ::=    COUNT | SUM | AVG | MAX | MIN
       | AND | OR | XOR | EXACTLY | UNION | D_UNION | INTERSECT
```

104 Part II / Formal Specifications

COUNT returns a result of type INTEGER; SUM, AVG, MAX, MIN, UNION, D_UNION, and INTERSECT return a result of the same type as the attribute denoted by the applicable < *attribute ref* >;[1] AND, OR, XOR, and EXACTLY return a result of type BOOLEAN. The < *agg op name* >s AND and OR can alternatively be spelled ALL and ANY, respectively. *Note:* **Tutorial D** includes support for *n*-adic versions of (a) AND, OR, XOR, and EXACTLY (see the section "Scalar Definitions" earlier in this chapter) and (b) UNION, D_UNION, INTERSECT, and JOIN (see the section "Relational Operations," later). It also includes support for *n*-adic versions of COUNT, SUM, AVG, MAX, and MIN; for example, SUM {1,2,5,2} is a valid < *scalar exp* >, and it evaluates to 10.

```
<scalar assign>
    ::=   <scalar target> := <scalar exp> | <scalar update>

<scalar target>
    ::=   <scalar var ref> | <scalar THE_ pv ref>
```

The abbreviation *pv* stands for *pseudovariable.* Pseudovariables are regarded as variables in **Tutorial D,** implying among other things that a pseudovariable reference can appear wherever the grammar requires a variable reference. *Note:* As mentioned in Chapter 3, it would be possible, if desired, to include support for other kinds of pseudovariables in addition to the THE_ pseudovariables mentioned in this grammar. In particular, it would be possible to support pseudovariables patterned after **Tutorial D**'s existing attribute extractors.

```
<scalar THE_ pv ref>
    ::=   <THE_ pv name> ( <scalar target> )
```

The < *possrep component* > corresponding to < *THE_ pv name* > must be of some scalar type.

```
<scalar update>
    ::=   UPDATE <scalar target> ( <possrep component assign commalist> )
```

Let the < *scalar target* >, *ST* say, be of type *T*. Every < *possrep component assign* >, *PCA* say, in the < *possrep component assign commalist* > is syntactically identical to an < *assign* >, except that:

- The target of *PCA* must be a < *possrep component target* >, *PCT* say.

- *PCT* must identify, directly or indirectly,[2] some *Ci* (*i* = 1, 2, ..., *n*), where *C1, C2, ..., Cn* are the components of some possrep *PR* for type *T* (the same possrep *PR* in every case).

- *PCA* is allowed to contain a < *possrep component ref* >, *PCR* say, wherever a < *selector inv* > would be allowed, where *PCR* is some *Ci* (*i* = 1, 2, ..., *n*) and denotes the corresponding possrep

---

1. It might be preferable in practice to define AVG in such a way that, e.g., taking the average of a collection of integers returns a rational number. We do not do so here merely for reasons of simplicity.

2. The phrase *directly or indirectly* appears several times in this chapter in contexts like this one. In terms of the present context, we can explain it as follows: Again, let < *possrep component assign* > *PCA* specify < *possrep component target* > *PCT*. Then *PCA* **directly** identifies *Ci* as its target if *PCT* is *Ci;* it **indirectly** identifies *Ci* as its target if *PCT* takes the form of a < *possrep THE_ pv ref* > *PTPR*, where the argument at the innermost level of nesting within *PTPR* is *Ci*. The meaning of the phrase *directly or indirectly* in other similar contexts is analogous.

component value from *ST.*

Steps a. and b. of the definition given for multiple assignment under RM Prescription 21 in Chapter 4 are applied to the *<possrep component assign commalist>*. The result of that application is a *<possrep component assign commalist>* in which each *<possrep component assign>* is of the form

```
Ci := exp
```

for some *Ci,* and no two distinct *<possrep component assign>*s identify the same target *Ci.* Then the original *<scalar update>* is equivalent to the *<scalar assign>*

```
ST := PR ( X1, X2, ..., Xn )
```

(*PR* here is the selector operator corresponding to the possrep with the same name.) The arguments *Xi* are defined as follows:

- If a *<possrep component assign>*, *PCA* say, exists for *Ci,* then let the *<exp>* from *PCA* be *X*. For all *j* ($j = 1, 2, ..., n$), replace references in *X* to *Cj* by (THE_*Cj(ST)*). The version of *X* that results is *Xi*.

- Otherwise, *Xi* is THE_*Ci(ST)*.

```
<possrep component target>
    ::=    <possrep component ref> | <possrep THE_ pv ref>

<possrep THE_ pv ref>
    ::=    <THE_ pv name> ( <possrep component target> )

<scalar comp>
    ::=    <scalar exp> <scalar comp op> <scalar exp>
```

Scalar comparisons are a special case of the syntactic category *<bool exp>*.

```
<scalar comp op>
    ::=    = | ≠ | < | ≤ | > | ≥
```

The operators "=" and "≠" apply to all scalar types; the operators "<", "≤", ">", and "≥" apply to ordinal types only.

TUPLE OPERATIONS

```
<tuple nonwith exp>
    ::=    <tuple var ref> | <tuple op inv> | ( <tuple exp> )

<tuple op inv>
    ::=    <user op inv> | <built-in tuple op inv>

<built-in tuple op inv>
    ::=    <tuple selector inv> | <THE_ op inv> | <attribute extractor inv>
           | <tuple extractor inv> | <tuple project> | <n-adic other built-in tuple op inv>
           | <monadic or dyadic other built-in tuple op inv>
```

Although we generally have little to say regarding operator precedence, we find it convenient to give high precedence to tuple projection in particular. An analogous remark applies to relational projection also (see the next section).

```
<tuple selector inv>
     ::=   TUPLE { <tuple component commalist> }

<tuple component>
     ::=   <attribute ref> <exp>

<tuple extractor inv>
     ::=   TUPLE FROM <relation exp>
```

The *< relation exp >* must denote a relation of cardinality one.

```
<tuple project>
     ::=   <tuple exp> { [ ALL BUT ] <attribute ref commalist> }
```

The *< tuple exp >* must not be a *< monadic or dyadic other built-in tuple op inv >*.

```
<n-adic other built-in tuple op inv>
     ::=   <n-adic tuple union>

<n-adic tuple union>
     ::=   UNION { <tuple exp commalist> }
```

The *< tuple exp >* s must be such that if the tuples denoted by any two of those *< tuple exp >* s have any attributes in common, then the corresponding attribute values are the same.

```
<monadic or dyadic other built-in tuple op inv>
     ::=   <monadic other built-in tuple op inv> | <dyadic other built-in tuple op inv>

<monadic other built-in tuple op inv>
     ::=   <tuple rename> | <tuple extend> | <tuple wrap> | <tuple unwrap>
         | <tuple substitute>

<tuple rename>
     ::=   <tuple exp> RENAME ( <renaming commalist> )
```

The *< tuple exp >* must not be a *< monadic or dyadic other built-in tuple op inv >*. The individual *< renaming >* s are executed in sequence as written.

```
<renaming>
     ::=   <attribute ref> AS <introduced name>
         | PREFIX <character string literal> AS <character string literal>
         | SUFFIX <character string literal> AS <character string literal>
```

For the syntax of *< character string literal >*, see *< built-in scalar type name >*. The *< renaming >* PREFIX *a* AS *b* causes all attributes of the applicable tuple or relation whose name begins with the characters of *a* to be renamed such that their name begins with the characters of *b* instead. The *< renaming >* SUFFIX *a* AS *b* is defined analogously.

```
<tuple extend>
    ::=   EXTEND <tuple exp> ADD ( <extend add commalist> )
```

The *<tuple exp>* must not be a *<monadic or dyadic other built-in tuple op inv>*. The individual *<extend add>*s are executed in sequence as written.

```
<extend add>
    ::=   <exp> AS <introduced name>
```

Both *<tuple extend>* and *<extend>* make use of *<extend add>*. We explain both cases here, but it is convenient to treat them separately:

- In the *<tuple extend>* case, the *<exp>* is allowed to include an *<attribute ref>*, *AR* say, wherever a *<selector inv>* would be allowed. If the *<attribute name>* of *AR* is that of an attribute of the tuple denoted by the *<tuple exp>* in that *<tuple extend>*, then it denotes the corresponding attribute value; otherwise the *<tuple extend>* must be contained in some expression in which the meaning of *AR* is defined.

- In the *<extend>* case, the *<exp>* is again allowed to include an *<attribute ref>*, *AR* say, wherever a *<selector inv>* would be allowed. Let *r* be the relation denoted by the *<relation exp>* in that *<extend>*. The *<exp>* can be thought of as being evaluated for each tuple of *r* in turn. If the *<attribute name>* of *AR* is that of an attribute of *r*, then (for each such evaluation) *AR* denotes the corresponding attribute value from the corresponding tuple; otherwise the *<extend>* must be contained in some expression in which the meaning of *AR* is defined.

```
<tuple wrap>
    ::=   <tuple exp> WRAP ( <wrapping commalist> )
```

The *<tuple exp>* must not be a *<monadic or dyadic other built-in tuple op inv>*. The individual *<wrapping>*s are executed in sequence as written.

```
<wrapping>
    ::=   { [ ALL BUT ] <attribute ref commalist> } AS <introduced name>
```

```
<tuple unwrap>
    ::=   <tuple exp> UNWRAP ( <unwrapping commalist> )
```

The *<tuple exp>* must not be a *<monadic or dyadic other built-in tuple op inv>*. The individual *<unwrapping>*s are executed in sequence as written.

```
<unwrapping>
    ::=   <attribute ref>
```

The specified attribute must be of some tuple type.

```
<tuple substitute>
    ::=   UPDATE <tuple exp> ( <attribute assign commalist> )
```

Syntactically, a *<tuple substitute>* is identical to a *<tuple update>*, except that it contains a *<tuple exp>* in place of the *<tuple target>* required in a *<tuple update>*. Let *t* be the tuple denoted by the *<tuple exp>*, and let *A1, A2, ..., An* be the attributes of *t*. Every *<attribute assign>*, *AA* say, in the < *attribute assign commalist* > is syntactically identical to an < *assign* > , except that:

- The target of *AA* must be an < *attribute target* > , *AT* say.

- *AT* must identify, directly or indirectly, some *Ai* (i = 1, 2, ..., n).

- *AA* is allowed to contain an < *attribute ref* > , *AR* say, wherever a < *selector inv* > would be allowed. If the < *attribute name* > of *AR* is that of some *Ai* (i = 1, 2, ..., n), then *AR* denotes the corresponding attribute value from *t;* otherwise the < *tuple substitute* > must be contained in some expression in which the meaning of *AR* is defined.

Steps a. and b. of the definition given for multiple assignment under RM Prescription 21 in Chapter 4 are applied to the < *attribute assign commalist* > . The result of that application is an < *attribute assign commalist* > in which each < *attribute assign* > is of the form

```
Ai := exp
```

for some *Ai,* and no two distinct < *attribute assign* > s identify the same target *Ai.* Now consider the expression

```
UPDATE t ( Ai := X, Aj := Y )
```

where $i \neq j$. (For definiteness, we consider the case where there are exactly two < *attribute assign* > s; the revisions needed to deal with other cases are straightforward.) This expression is equivalent to the following:

```
( ( EXTEND t ADD ( X AS Bi, Y AS Bj ) ) { ALL BUT Ai, Aj } )
                         RENAME ( Bi AS Bk, Bj AS Aj, Bk AS Ai )
```

Here *Bi, Bj,* and *Bk* are arbitrary distinct names that are different from all existing attribute names in *t.*

```
<attribute target>
    ::=    <attribute ref> | <attribute THE_ pv ref>

<attribute THE_ pv ref>
    ::=    <THE_ pv name> ( <attribute target> )

<dyadic other built-in tuple op inv>
    ::=    <dyadic tuple union> | <tuple compose>

<dyadic tuple union>
    ::=    <tuple exp> UNION <tuple exp>
```

The < *dyadic tuple union* > *r* UNION *s* is equivalent to the < *n-adic tuple union* > UNION {*r,s*}.

```
<tuple compose>
    ::=    <tuple exp> COMPOSE <tuple exp>
```

The < *tuple exp* > s must not be < *monadic or dyadic other built-in tuple op inv* > s. They must be such that if the tuples they denote have any attributes in common, then the corresponding attribute values are the same.

```
<tuple assign>
    ::=   <tuple target> := <tuple exp> | <tuple update>

<tuple target>
    ::=   <tuple var ref> | <tuple THE_ pv ref>

<tuple THE_ pv ref>
    ::=   <THE_ pv name> ( <scalar target> )
```

The *< possrep component >* corresponding to *< THE_ pv name >* must be of some tuple type.

```
<tuple update>
    ::=   UPDATE <tuple target> ( <attribute assign commalist> )
```

Let *TT* be the *< tuple target >*, and let *A1, A2, ..., An* be the attributes of *TT*. Every *< attribute assign >*, *AA* say, in the *< attribute assign commalist >* is syntactically identical to an *< assign >*, except that:

- The target of *AA* must be an *< attribute target >*, *AT* say.

- *AT* must identify, directly or indirectly, some *Ai* ($i = 1, 2, ..., n$).

- *AA* is allowed to contain an *< attribute ref >*, *AR* say, wherever a *< selector inv >* would be allowed. If the *< attribute name >* of *AR* is that of some *Ai* ($i = 1, 2, ..., n$), then *AR* denotes the corresponding attribute value from *TT;* otherwise the *< tuple update >* must be contained in some expression in which the meaning of *AR* is defined.

Steps a. and b. of the definition given for multiple assignment under RM Prescription 21 in Chapter 4 are applied to the *< attribute assign commalist >*. The result of that application is an *< attribute assign commalist >* in which each *< attribute assign >* is of the form

```
    Ai := exp
```

for some *Ai,* and no two distinct *< attribute assign >*s identify the same target *Ai*. Now consider the *< tuple update >*

```
    UPDATE TT ( Ai := X, Aj := Y )
```

where $i \neq j$. (For definiteness, we consider the case where there are exactly two *< attribute assign >*s; the revisions needed to deal with other cases are straightforward.) This *< tuple update >* is equivalent to the following *< tuple assign >*:

```
    TT := UPDATE TT ( Ai := X, Aj := Y )
```

(The expression on the right side here is a *< tuple substitute >* invocation.)

```
<tuple comp>
    ::=   <tuple exp> <tuple comp op> <tuple exp>
        | <tuple exp> ε <relation exp> | <tuple exp> ∉ <relation exp>
```

Tuple comparisons are a special case of the syntactic category *< bool exp >*. The symbol "ε" ("epsilon") denotes the set membership operator; it can be read as *belongs to* or *is a member of* or just *is* *in* or *in*. The expression *t ∉ r* is defined to be semantically equivalent to the expression NOT (*t ∈ r*).

```
<tuple comp op>
    ::=   = | ≠
```

RELATIONAL OPERATIONS

```
<relation nonwith exp>
    ::=   <relation var ref> | <relation op inv> | ( <relation exp> )

<relation op inv>
    ::=   <user op inv> | <built-in relation op inv>

<built-in relation op inv>
    ::=   <relation selector inv> | <THE_ op inv> | <attribute extractor inv> | <project>
        | <n-adic other built-in relation op inv>
        | <monadic or dyadic other built-in relation op inv>

<relation selector inv>
    ::=   RELATION [ <heading> ] { <tuple exp commalist> } | TABLE_DEE | TABLE_DUM
```

If the keyword RELATION is specified explicitly, (a) *< heading >* must be specified if *< tuple exp commalist >* is empty; (b) every *< tuple exp >* in *< tuple exp commalist >* must have the same heading; (c) that heading must be exactly as defined by *< heading >* if *< heading >* is specified. TABLE_DEE and TABLE_DUM are shorthand for the *< relation selector inv >*s RELATION{}{TUPLE{}} and RELATION{}{}, respectively (see RM Prescription 10 in Chapter 6 for further explanation).

```
<project>
    ::=   <relation exp> { [ ALL BUT ] <attribute ref commalist> }
```

The *< relation exp >* must not be a *< monadic or dyadic other built-in relation op inv >*.

```
<n-adic other built-in relation op inv>
    ::=   <n-adic union> | <n-adic disjoint union> | <n-adic intersect> | <n-adic join>

<n-adic union>
    ::=   UNION [ <heading> ] { <relation exp commalist> }
```

Here (a) *< heading >* must be specified if *< relation exp commalist >* is empty; (b) every *< relation exp >* in *< relation exp commalist >* must have the same heading; (c) that heading must be exactly as defined by *< heading >* if *< heading >* is specified. The same remarks apply to *< n-adic disjoint union >* and *< n-adic intersect >*, q.v.

```
<n-adic disjoint union>
    ::=   D_UNION [ <heading> ] { <relation exp commalist> }
```

The relations denoted by the *< relation exp >*s must be pairwise disjoint.

```
<n-adic intersect>
    ::=   INTERSECT [ <heading> ] { <relation exp commalist> }
```

If the *<relation exp commalist>* is empty, the *<n-adic intersect>* evaluates to the "universal" relation of the applicable type: i.e., the unique relation of that type that contains all possible tuples with the applicable *<heading>*. In practice, the implementation might want to outlaw, or at least flag, any expression that requires such a value to be materialized.

```
<n-adic join>
     ::=   JOIN { <relation exp commalist> }

<monadic or dyadic other built-in relation op inv>
     ::=   <monadic other built-in relation op inv> | <dyadic other built-in relation op inv>

<monadic other built-in relation op inv>
     ::=   <rename> | <where> | <extend> | <wrap> | <unwrap> | <group> | <ungroup>
         | <substitute> | <tclose>

<rename>
     ::=   <relation exp> RENAME ( <renaming commalist> )
```

The *<relation exp>* must not be a *<monadic or dyadic other built-in relation op inv>*. The individual *<renaming>*s are executed in sequence as written.

```
<where>
     ::=   <relation exp> WHERE <bool exp>
```

The *<relation exp>* must not be a *<monadic or dyadic other built-in relation op inv>*. Let *r* be the relation denoted by *<relation exp>*. The *<bool exp>* is allowed to contain an *<attribute ref>*, *AR* say, wherever a *<selector inv>* would be allowed. The *<bool exp>* can be thought of as being evaluated for each tuple of *r* in turn. If the *<attribute name>* of *AR* is that of an attribute of *r*, then (for each such evaluation) *AR* denotes the corresponding attribute value from the corresponding tuple; otherwise the *<where>* must be contained in some expression in which *AR* is defined. *Note:* The *<where>* operator of **Tutorial D** includes the *restrict* operator of relational algebra as a special case.

```
<extend>
     ::=   EXTEND <relation exp> ADD ( <extend add commalist> )
```

The *<relation exp>* must not be a *<monadic or dyadic other built-in relation op inv>*. The individual *<extend add>*s are executed in sequence as written.

```
<wrap>
     ::=   <relation exp> WRAP ( <wrapping commalist> )
```

The *<relation exp>* must not be a *<monadic or dyadic other built-in relation op inv>*. The individual *<wrapping>*s are executed in sequence as written.

```
<unwrap>
     ::=   <relation exp> UNWRAP ( <unwrapping commalist> )
```

The *<relation exp>* must not be a *<monadic or dyadic other built-in relation op inv>*. The individual *<unwrapping>*s are executed in sequence as written.

```
<group>
    ::=    <relation exp> GROUP ( <grouping commalist> )
```

The *<relation exp>* must not be a *<monadic or dyadic other built-in relation op inv>*. The individual *<grouping>*s are executed in sequence as written.

```
<grouping>
    ::=    { [ ALL BUT ] <attribute ref commalist> } AS <introduced name>
```

```
<ungroup>
    ::=    <relation exp> UNGROUP ( <ungrouping commalist> )
```

The *<relation exp>* must not be a *<monadic or dyadic other built-in relation op inv>*. The individual *<ungrouping>*s are executed in sequence as written.

```
<ungrouping>
    ::=    <attribute ref>
```

The specified attribute must be of some relation type.

```
<substitute>
    ::=    UPDATE <relation exp> ( <attribute assign commalist> )
```

Syntactically, a *<substitute>* is identical to a *<relation update>*, except that it contains a *<relation exp>* in place of the *<relation target>* (and optional WHERE *<bool exp>*) required in a *<relation update>*. Let *r* be the relation denoted by the *<relation exp>*, and let *A1, A2, ..., An* be the attributes of *r*. Every *<attribute assign>*, *AA* say, in the *<attribute assign commalist>* is syntactically identical to an *<assign>*, except that:

- The target of *AA* must be an *<attribute target>*, *AT* say.

- *AT* must identify, directly or indirectly, some *Ai* (*i* = 1, 2, ..., *n*).

- *AA* is allowed to contain an *<attribute ref>*, *AR* say, wherever a *<selector inv>* would be allowed. *AA* can be thought of as being applied to each tuple of *r* in turn. If the *<attribute name>* of *AR* is that of some *Ai* (*i* = 1, 2, ..., *n*), then (for each such application) *AR* denotes the corresponding attribute value from the corresponding tuple; otherwise the *<substitute>* must be contained in some expression in which the meaning of *AR* is defined.

Steps a. and b. of the definition given for multiple assignment under RM Prescription 21 in Chapter 4 are applied to the *<attribute assign commalist>*. The result of that application is an *<attribute assign commalist>* in which each *<attribute assign>* is of the form

```
Ai := exp
```

for some *Ai*, and no two distinct *<attribute assign>*s identify the same target *Ai*. Now consider the expression

```
UPDATE r ( Ai := X, Aj := Y )
```

where $i \neq j$. (For definiteness, we consider the case where there are exactly two *<attribute assign>*s; the revisions needed to deal with other cases are straightforward.) This expression is equivalent to the following:

```
( ( EXTEND r ADD ( X AS Bi, Y AS Bj ) ) { ALL BUT Ai, Aj } )
                        RENAME ( Bi AS Bk, Bj AS Aj, Bk AS Ai )
```

Here *Bi, Bj,* and *Bk* are arbitrary distinct names that are different from all existing attribute names in *r*.

```
<tclose>
    ::=    TCLOSE <relation exp>
```

The *<relation exp>* must not be a *<monadic or dyadic other built-in relation op inv>*. Furthermore, it must denote a relation of degree two, and the attributes of that relation must both be of the same type.

```
<dyadic other built-in relation op inv>
    ::=    <dyadic union> | <dyadic disjoint union> | <dyadic intersect> | <minus>
         | <dyadic join> | <compose> | <semijoin> | <semiminus> | <divide> | <summarize>
```

```
<dyadic union>
    ::=    <relation exp> UNION <relation exp>
```

The *<relation exp>*s must not be *<monadic or dyadic other built-in relation op inv>*s, except that either or both can be another *<dyadic union>*.

```
<dyadic disjoint union>
    ::=    <relation exp> D_UNION <relation exp>
```

The *<relation exp>*s must not be *<monadic or dyadic other built-in relation op inv>*s, except that either or both can be another *<dyadic disjoint union>*. The relations denoted by the *<relation exp>*s must be disjoint.

```
<dyadic intersect>
    ::=    <relation exp> INTERSECT <relation exp>
```

The *<relation exp>*s must not be *<monadic or dyadic other built-in relation op inv>*s, except that either or both can be another *<dyadic intersect>*.

```
<minus>
    ::=    <relation exp> MINUS <relation exp>
```

The *<relation exp>*s must not be *<monadic or dyadic other built-in relation op inv>*s.

```
<dyadic join>
    ::=    <relation exp> JOIN <relation exp>
```

The *<relation exp>*s must not be *<monadic or dyadic other built-in relation op inv>*s, except that either or both can be another *<dyadic join>*.

```
<compose>
    ::=    <relation exp> COMPOSE <relation exp>
```

The *<relation exp>*s must not be *<monadic or dyadic other built-in relation op inv>*s.

```
<semijoin>
    ::=    <relation exp> SEMIJOIN <relation exp>
```

The *<relation exp>*s must not be *<monadic or dyadic other built-in relation op inv>*s. The keyword SEMIJOIN can alternatively be spelled MATCHING.

```
<semiminus>
    ::=    <relation exp> SEMIMINUS <relation exp>
```

The *<relation exp>*s must not be *<monadic or dyadic other built-in relation op inv>*s. The keyword SEMIMINUS can alternatively be spelled NOT MATCHING.

```
<divide>
    ::=    <relation exp> DIVIDEBY <relation exp> <per>
```

The *<relation exp>*s must not be *<monadic or dyadic other built-in relation op inv>*s.

```
<per>
    ::=    PER ( <relation exp> [, <relation exp> ] )
```

Reference [34] defines two distinct "divide" operators that it calls the Small Divide and the Great Divide, respectively. In **Tutorial D**, a *<divide>* in which the *<per>* contains just one *<relation exp>* is a Small Divide, a *<divide>* in which it contains two is a Great Divide. See RM Prescription 18 in Chapter 6 for further explanation.

```
<summarize>
    ::=    SUMMARIZE <relation exp> [ <per or by> ] ADD ( <summarize add commalist> )
```

The *<relation exp>* must not be a *<monadic or dyadic other built-in relation op inv>*. Omitting *<per or by>* is equivalent to specifying PER (TABLE_DEE). The individual *<summarize add>*s are executed in sequence as written.

```
<per or by>
    ::=    <per> | BY { [ ALL BUT ] <attribute ref commalist> }
```

Let *r* be the relation to be summarized. If *<per>* is specified, it must contain exactly one *<relation exp>*. Let *pr* be the relation denoted by that *<relation exp>*. Then every attribute of *pr* must be an attribute of *r*. Specifying BY $\{A1,A2,\ldots,An\}$ is equivalent to specifying PER $(r\{A1,A2,\ldots,An\})$.

```
<summarize add>
    ::=    <summary> AS <introduced name>
```

```
<summary>
    ::=    <summary spec> ( [ <integer exp>, ] [ <scalar exp> ] )
```

Let *r* and *pr* be as defined under the production rule for *<per or by>*. Then:

- The *<integer exp>* and following comma must be specified if and only if the *<summary spec>* is EXACTLY or EXACTLYD. The *<integer exp>* is allowed to include an *<attribute ref>*, *IAR* say, wherever a *<selector inv>* would be allowed. If the *<attribute name>* of *IAR* is that of an attribute of *pr,* then *IAR* denotes the corresponding attribute value from some tuple of *pr;* otherwise the *<summary>* must be contained in some expression in which *IAR* is defined.

- The *<scalar exp>* must be specified if and only if the *<summary spec>* is not COUNT. The *<scalar exp>* is allowed to include an *<attribute ref>*, *SAR* say, wherever a *<selector inv>* would be allowed. If the *<attribute name>* of *SAR* is that of an attribute of *r,* then *SAR* denotes the corresponding attribute value from some tuple of *r;* otherwise the *<summary>* must be contained in some expression in which *SAR* is defined.

For SUM, SUMD, AVG, and AVGD, the value denoted by *<scalar exp>* must be of some type for which the operator "+" is defined; for MAX and MIN, it must be of some ordinal type; for AND, OR, XOR, EXACTLY, and EXACTLYD, it must be of type BOOLEAN; for UNION, D_UNION, and INTERSECT, it must be of some relation type. Observe that *<summary>* and *<agg op inv>* are not the same thing, although the type of any given *<summary>* is the same as that of its *<agg op inv>* counterpart.

```
<summary spec>
    ::=    COUNT | COUNTD | SUM | SUMD | AVG | AVGD | MAX | MIN
         | AND | OR | XOR | EXACTLY | EXACTLYD | UNION | D_UNION | INTERSECT
```

The suffix "D" ("distinct") in COUNTD, SUMD, AVGD, and EXACTLYD means "eliminate redundant duplicate values before performing the summarization." COUNT and COUNTD return a result of type INTEGER; SUM, SUMD, AVG, AVGD, MAX, MIN, UNION, D_UNION, and INTERSECT return a result of the same type as the value denoted by the applicable *<scalar exp>*;[1] AND, OR, XOR, EXACTLY, and EXACTLYD return a result of type BOOLEAN. The *<summary spec>*s AND and OR can alternatively be spelled ALL and ANY, respectively.

```
<relation assign>
    ::=    <relation target> := <relation exp>
         | <relation insert> | <relation delete> | <relation update>

<relation target>
    ::=    <relation var ref> | <relation THE_ pv ref>

<relation THE_ pv ref>
    ::=    <THE_ pv name> ( <scalar target> )
```

The *<possrep component>* corresponding to *<THE_ pv name>* must be of some relation type. *Note:* Let *rx* be the *<relation exp>* appearing in the *<virtual relation var def>* that defines some virtual relvar *V*. Then it would be possible, assuming *V* is updatable (see Appendix E), to allow *rx* to serve as a relation pseudovariable also. However, this possibility is not reflected in the grammar defined in this chapter.

```
<relation insert>
    ::=    INSERT <relation target> <relation exp>
```

---

1. It might be preferable in practice to define the *<summary spec>*s AVG and AVGD in such a way that, e.g., taking the average of a collection of integers returns a rational number. We do not do so here merely for reasons of simplicity.

```
<relation delete>
    ::=   DELETE <relation target> [ WHERE <bool exp> ]
```

Let the *<relation target>* be *RT*. The *<bool exp>* is allowed to contain an *<attribute ref>*, *AR* say, wherever a *<selector inv>* would be allowed. The *<bool exp>* can be thought of as being evaluated for each tuple of *RT* in turn. If the *<attribute name>* of *AR* is that of an attribute of *RT*, then (for each such evaluation) *AR* denotes the corresponding attribute value from the corresponding tuple; otherwise the *<relation delete>* must be contained in some expression in which the meaning of *AR* is defined.

```
<relation update>
    ::=   UPDATE <relation target> [ WHERE <bool exp> ] ( <attribute assign commalist> )
```

Let *RT* be the *<relation target>*, and let *A1, A2, ..., An* be the attributes of *RT*. The *<bool exp>* is allowed to contain an *<attribute ref>*, *AR* say, wherever a *<selector inv>* would be allowed. The *<bool exp>* can be thought of as being evaluated for each tuple of *RT* in turn. If the *<attribute name>* of *AR* is that of some *Ai* ($i = 1, 2, ..., n$), then (for each such evaluation) *AR* denotes the corresponding attribute value from the corresponding tuple; otherwise the *<relation update>* must be contained in some expression in which the meaning of *AR* is defined. Every *<attribute assign>*, *AA* say, in the *<attribute assign commalist>* is syntactically identical to an *<assign>*, except that:

- The target of *AA* must be an *<attribute target>*, *AT* say.

- *AT* must identify, directly or indirectly, some *Ai* ($i = 1, 2, ..., n$).

- *AA* is allowed to contain an *<attribute ref>*, *AR* say, wherever a *<selector inv>* would be allowed. *AA* can be thought of as being applied to each tuple of *r* in turn. If the *<attribute name>* of *AR* is that of some *Ai* ($i = 1, 2, ..., n$), then (for each such application) *AR* denotes the corresponding attribute value from the corresponding tuple; otherwise the *<relation update>* must be contained in some expression in which the meaning of *AR* is defined.

Steps a. and b. of the definition given for multiple assignment under RM Prescription 21 in Chapter 4 are applied to the *<attribute assign commalist>*. The result of that application is an *<attribute assign commalist>* in which each *<attribute assign>* is of the form

```
Ai := exp
```

for some *Ai*, and no two distinct *<attribute assign>*s identify the same target *Ai*. Now consider the *<relation update>*

```
UPDATE RT WHERE b ( Ai := X, Aj := Y )
```

where $i \neq j$. (For definiteness, we consider the case where there are exactly two *<attribute assign>*s; the revisions needed to deal with other cases are straightforward.) This *<relation update>* is equivalent to the following *<relation assign>*:

```
RT := ( RT WHERE NOT ( b ) ) UNION ( UPDATE RT WHERE b ( Ai := X, Aj := Y ) )
```

Note: The expression following UNION here is a *<substitute>* invocation in parentheses.

```
<relation comp>
    ::=   <relation exp> <relation comp op> <relation exp>
```

Relation comparisons are a special case of the syntactic category *<bool exp>*.

```
<relation comp op>
    ::=   = | ≠ | |<| | |≤| | |>| | |≥|
```

Note: The symbols "|≤|" and "|<|" denote "subset of" and "proper subset of," respectively; the symbols "|≥|" and "|>|" denote "superset of" and "proper superset of," respectively. We use these special symbols (instead of the more usual mathematical symbols) for typographical reasons.

RELATIONS AND ARRAYS

The Third Manifesto prohibits tuple-at-a-time retrieval from a relation as supported by, e.g., FETCH via a cursor in SQL. But **Tutorial D** does allow a relation to be mapped to a one-dimensional *array* (of tuples), so an effect somewhat analogous to such tuple-at-a-time retrieval can be obtained, if desired, by first performing such a mapping and then iterating over the resulting array.[1] But we deliberately adopt a very conservative approach to this part of the language. A fully orthogonal language would support arrays as "first-class citizens"—implying support for a general ARRAY type generator, and arrays of any number of dimensions, and array expressions, and array assignment, and array comparisons, and so on. However, to include such extensive support in **Tutorial D** would complicate the language unduly and might well obscure more important points. For simplicity, therefore, we include only as much array support here as seems absolutely necessary; moreover, most of what we do include is deliberately "special cased." Note in particular that we do not define a syntactic category called *<array type>*.

```
<array var def>
    ::=   VAR <array var name> ARRAY <tuple type>
```

Let *A* be a **Tutorial D** array variable; then the value of *A* at any given time is a one-dimensional array containing zero or more tuples all of the same type. If it contains at least one, the lower bound is one; otherwise it and the upper bound are both zero. Let the values of *A* at times *t1* and *t2* be *a1* and *a2*, respectively. Then *a1* and *a2* need not necessarily contain the same number of tuples, and *A*'s upper bound thus varies with time. Note that the only way *A* can acquire a new value is by means of a *<relation get>* (see below); in practice, of course, additional mechanisms will be desirable, but we do not specify any such mechanisms here.

```
<relation get>
    ::=   LOAD <array target> FROM <relation exp> ORDER ( <order item commalist> )

<array target>
    ::=   <array var ref>

<array var ref>
    ::=   <array var name>
```

Points arising:

---

1. In accordance with RM Proscription 7, **Tutorial D** supports nothing at all analogous to SQL's tuple-at-a-time *update* operators (i.e., UPDATE or DELETE "WHERE CURRENT OF *cursor*").

■ Tuples from the relation denoted by <*relation exp*> are loaded into the array variable designated by <*array target*> in the order defined by the ORDER specification. If <*order item commalist*> is empty, tuples are loaded in an implementation-defined order.

■ The headings associated with <*array target*> and <*relation exp*> would normally have to be the same. But it would be possible, and perhaps desirable, to allow the former to be a proper subset of the latter. Such a feature could allow the sequence in which tuples were loaded into the array variable to be defined in terms of attributes whose values were not themselves to be retrieved—thereby allowing, e.g., retrieval of employee numbers and names in salary order without at the same time actually retrieving those salaries.

■ LOAD is really *assignment,* of a kind (in particular, it has the effect of replacing whatever value the target previously had). However, we deliberately do not use assignment syntax for it because it effectively involves an implicit type conversion (i.e., a *coercion*) between a relation and an array. We have already given our reasons in Chapter 3 for not wishing to support coercions; in the case at hand, therefore, we prefer to define a new operation (LOAD), with operands that are explicitly defined to be of different types, instead of relying on conventional assignment plus coercion.

```
<order item>
    ::=    <direction> <attribute ref>
```

A useful extension in practice might be to allow <*scalar exp*> in place of <*attribute ref*> here.

```
<direction>
    ::=    ASC | DESC
```

```
<relation set>
    ::=    LOAD <relation target> FROM <array var ref>
```

The array identified by <*array var ref*> must not include any duplicate tuples.

We also need a new kind of <*tuple exp*> and an <*array cardinality*> operator (a special case of <*integer exp*>):

```
<tuple exp>
    ::=    ... all previous possibilities, together with:
         | <array var ref> ( <subscript> )
```

```
<subscript>
    ::=    <integer exp>
```

```
<array cardinality>
    ::=    COUNT ( <array var ref> )
```

STATEMENTS

```
<statement>
    ::=    <statement body> ;
```

```
<statement body>
    ::=   <previously defined statement body>  |  <begin transaction>  |  <commit>  |  <rollback>
          |  <call>  |  <return>  |  <case>  |  <if>  |  <do>  |  <while>  |  <leave>  |  <no op>
          |  <compound statement body>

<previously defined statement body>
    ::=   <assignment>
          |  <user op def>  |  <user op drop>  |  <user scalar type def>  |  <user scalar type drop>
          |  <scalar var def>  |  <tuple var def>  |  <relation var def>  |  <relation var drop>
          |  <constraint def>  |  <constraint drop>
          |  <array var def>  |  <relation get>  |  <relation set>

<begin transaction>
    ::=   BEGIN TRANSACTION
```

BEGIN TRANSACTION can be issued when a transaction is in progress. The effect is to suspend execution of the current transaction and to begin a new child transaction (see OO Prescription 5 in Chapter 8 for further explanation). COMMIT or ROLLBACK terminates execution of the transaction most recently begun, thereby reinstating as current—and continuing execution of—the suspended parent transaction, if any. *Note:* An industrial-strength **D** might usefully allow BEGIN TRANSACTION to assign a name to the transaction in question and then require COMMIT and ROLLBACK to reference that name explicitly. However, we choose not to specify any such facilities here.

```
<commit>
    ::=   COMMIT

<rollback>
    ::=   ROLLBACK

<call>
    ::=   CALL <user op inv>
```

The user-defined operator being invoked must be an update operator specifically. Arguments corresponding to parameters that are subject to update must be specified as *<scalar target>*s, *<tuple target>*s, or *<relation target>*s, as applicable.

```
<return>
    ::=   RETURN [ <exp> ]
```

The *<exp>* is required for a read-only operator and prohibited for an update operator. *Note:* An update operator need not contain a *<return>* at all, in which case an implicit *<return>* is executed when the END OPERATOR is reached.

```
<case>
    ::=   CASE ; <when def list> [ ELSE <statement> ] END CASE

<when def>
    ::=   WHEN <bool exp> THEN <statement>

<if>
    ::=   IF <bool exp> THEN <statement> [ ELSE <statement> ] END IF
```

```
<do>
    ::=    [ <statement name> : ] DO <scalar var ref> := <integer exp> TO <integer exp> ;
           <statement> END DO


<while>
    ::=    [ <statement name> : ] WHILE <bool exp> ; <statement> END WHILE


<leave>
    ::=    LEAVE <statement name>
```

A variant of *<leave>* that merely terminates the current iteration of the loop and begins the next might be useful in practice.

```
<no op>
    ::=    ... an empty string


<compound statement body>
    ::=    BEGIN ; <statement list> END
```

One final point to close this section: Elsewhere in this book, we often make use of *end of statement, statement boundary,* and similar expressions to refer to the time when integrity checking is done, among other things. In such contexts, *statement* is to be understood, in **Tutorial D** terms, to mean a *<statement>* that contains no other *<statement>*s nested inside itself; i.e., it is not a *<case>*, *<if>*, *<do>*, *<while>*, or compound statement.

RECENT LANGUAGE CHANGES

There are a number of differences between **Tutorial D** as described in the present chapter and the version of the language defined in this book's predecessor [83]. For the benefit of readers who might be familiar with that earlier version, we summarize the main differences here.

- The previous version allowed certain braces or parentheses to be omitted if what was contained within those braces or parentheses consisted of just one item (or sometimes no item at all). The present version does not.

- In many places the previous version required some list or commalist to be nonempty where the present version does not.

- The previous version allowed possrep component names to be omitted, but the present version does not.

- The ability has been added (a) to define a tuple variable to have the same heading as a specified relation expression and (b) to define a relvar to have the same heading as a specified tuple expression.

- Support for the boolean operators XOR and EXACTLY has been added. For AND, OR, and XOR, both infix (dyadic) and prefix (*n*-adic) syntax are supported (of course, EXACTLY is intrinsically *n*-adic).

- Ordinal types are now explicitly declared as such.

- Update operators are no longer regarded as (or limited to being) scalar; thus, scalar, tuple, and relation parameters can all be subject to update and identified as such in the UPDATES specification. Update operators, but not read-only operators, can also directly update variables that are not local to the operator in question.

- An ALL BUT option has been added to the UPDATES and KEY specifications.

- The commalist of <*assign*>s in UPDATE (various forms) is now enclosed in parentheses instead of braces.

- BASE has been introduced as an alternative spelling for REAL.

- The keywords LOCAL and GLOBAL on <*application relation var def*>s have been replaced by PRIVATE and PUBLIC, respectively.

- An INIT specification is now supported for REAL (or BASE) and PRIVATE relvars.

- INIT specifications can now be used to determine the type of the variable being declared.

- The initializing expression in INIT is now enclosed in parentheses, as is the defining expression in a virtual relvar definition.

- A new form of <*scalar assign*> has been added, using the keyword UPDATE.

- For syntactic reasons, tuple join has been replaced by tuple union (semantically, of course, the operators are equivalent).

- Support for disjoint union (D_UNION) has been added.

- Prefix (*n*-adic) versions of union (including tuple union), disjoint union, intersect, and join are now supported.

- MATCHING and NOT MATCHING have been introduced as alternative spellings for SEMIJOIN and SEMIMINUS, respectively.

- The operators <*substitute*>, <*tuple substitute*>, and <*tuple compose*> have been introduced.

- A BY form of SUMMARIZE has been added.

- AND and OR have been introduced as preferred spellings for ALL and ANY, respectively. COUNT is now written COUNT (). Aggregate operators XOR, EXACTLY, UNION, D_UNION, and INTERSECT have been introduced. All of the aggregate operators have both (a) *n*-adic forms and (b) summary analogs in SUMMARIZE. Also, the aggregate operators COUNT, SUM, AVG, and EXACTLY have additional summary analogs COUNTD, SUMD, AVGD, and EXACTLYD, for which redundant duplicate values are eliminated before the summarization is done.

- The IN operator is now written ϵ.

- GROUP and UNGROUP now support multiple grouping and ungrouping.

- The syntax of the ordering specification on <*relation get*> has changed.

- The <*with*> statement has been dropped and WITH expressions have been clarified.

- A number of minor corrections have been made.

In addition to all of the foregoing, many syntactic category names and production rules have been revised (in some cases extensively). However, those revisions in themselves are not intended to induce any changes in the language being defined.

A REMARK ON SYNTAX

You might have noticed that the syntax of operator invocations in **Tutorial D** is not very consistent. To be specific:

- User-defined operators use a prefix style, with positional argument/parameter matching.

- Built-in operators, by contrast, sometimes use an infix style ("+", "=", MINUS, etc.) and sometimes a prefix style (MAX, EXACTLY, *n*-adic JOIN, etc.).

- Some of those built-in operators rely on positional argument/parameter matching ("+", MINUS, MAX, EXACTLY, etc.), while others do not[1] ("=", *n*-adic JOIN, etc.). Also, those that rely on positional matching use parentheses to enclose their arguments, while others use braces.

- Some operators seem to use a mixture of prefix and infix styles (SUMMARIZE, DIVIDEBY, etc.), or even a wholly private style of their own (project, THE_ operators, CASE, CAST, etc.).

- Finally, it could be argued that reliance on ordinal position for argument/parameter matching violates the spirit, if not the letter, of RM Proscription 1 (which prohibits the use of ordinal position to distinguish the attributes of a relation)—especially in the case of scalar selectors, where the sequence of defining parameters (in the corresponding possrep definition) should not matter but does.

Given all of the above, the possibility of adopting a more uniform style seems worth exploring. Now, we deliberately did no such thing in earlier sections of this chapter because we did not want **Tutorial D** to look even more outlandish than it might do already. Now, however, we can at least offer some thoughts on the subject. The obvious approach would be to do both of the following:

- Permit (if not mandate) a prefix style for everything

- Perform argument/parameter matching on the basis of names instead of position

  In the case of scalar selectors, for example, we might propose

  ```
  CARTESIAN { Y 2.5, X 5.0 }
  ```

as a possible replacement for

---

1. Or, at least, the order in which the arguments are specified in such cases is immaterial.

```
CARTESIAN ( 5.0, 2.5 )
```

(note in particular that the parentheses have been replaced by braces). In other words, the suggestion is that a general *< op inv>* ("operator invocation") should take the form

```
<op name> { <argument spec commalist> }
```

where *< op name>* identifies the operator in question and *< argument spec>* takes the form

```
<parameter name> <exp>
```

There are some difficulties, however. For one thing, this new prefix style seems clumsier than the old in the common special case in which the operator takes just one parameter, as with (e.g.) SIN, COS, and sometimes COUNT. For another, some common operators (e.g., "+", "=", ":=" have names that do not abide by the usual rules for forming identifiers. For a third, built-in operators, at least as currently defined, have no user-known parameter names. Now, we could perhaps fix this last problem by introducing a convention according to which those names are simply defined to be P1, P2, P3, etc., thus making (e.g.) expressions like this one valid:

```
JOIN { P1 r1 , P2 r2 , P3 r3 , ... , P49 r49 }
```

Again, however, the new syntax in this particular case seems clumsier than the old, since JOIN is associative and the order in which the arguments are specified makes no difference.

Another difficulty arises in connection with examples like this one:

```
MINUS { P1 r1 , P2 r2 }
```

Here it becomes important to know which is the P1 parameter and which the P2 (*r1* MINUS *r2* and *r2* MINUS *r1* are not equivalent, in general). Some additional apparatus would be required to communicate such information to the user.

EXERCISES

1. Write a set of **Tutorial D** data definitions for the suppliers-and-parts database (relvar definitions only; Exercise 14 in Chapter 3 already asked for the type definitions).

2. Define virtual relvars for (a) suppliers with status greater than ten; (b) shipments of red parts; (c) parts not available from any London supplier.

3. Distinguish between database and application relvars.

4. Is the boolean operator XOR associative?

5. Consider the prefix (*n*-adic) versions of AND, OR, and XOR. What happens if the specified *< bool exp commalist>* contains just one *< bool exp>*? What if it contains none at all?

6. The expression XOR {*< bool exp commalist>*} is defined to evaluate to TRUE if and only if an odd number of the specified *< bool exp>*s evaluate to TRUE. Justify this definition.

7. What does the expression EXACTLY (0,{*< bool exp commalist>*}) return? What if the *< bool exp commalist>* is empty?

8. Give **Tutorial D** formulations for the following updates to the suppliers-and-parts database:

    a. Insert a new shipment with supplier number S1, part number P1, quantity 500.

    b. Insert a new supplier S10 (name and city Smith and New York, respectively; status not yet known).

    c. Delete all blue parts.

    d. Delete all parts for which there are no shipments.

    e. Change the color of all red parts to orange.

    f. Replace all appearances of supplier number S1 by appearances of supplier number S9 instead.

    In each case, give two formulations, one using INSERT, DELETE, or UPDATE (as applicable) and one using a pure relational assignment.

9. The **Tutorial D** grammar presented in this chapter involves numerous lists and commalists. In every case, what happens if the list or commalist is empty?

10. The LOAD statement involves an ORDER specification. Considered as an operator in its own right, however, ORDER is rather unusual. In what respects?

11. Consider the following type definition:

    ```
    TYPE ELLIPSE POSSREP { A RATIONAL, B RATIONAL, CTR POINT
                           CONSTRAINT A ≥ B } ;
    ```

    (This is a simplified version of an example we will be using extensively in later chapters.) Now let E be a variable of type ELLIPSE, and consider the following two statements:

    a.   `THE_A ( E ) := 7.0 , THE_B ( E ) := 5.0 ;`

    b.   `UPDATE E ( A := 7.0 , B := 5.0 ) ;`

    Is there any logical difference between these statements? If so, what is it?

12. Data definition operations (for objects in the database, at least) cause updates to be made to the catalog. But the catalog is only a collection of relvars, just like the rest of the database; so could we not just use the familiar update operations INSERT, DELETE, and UPDATE to update the catalog appropriately? Discuss.

13. Design an extension to the syntax of the **Tutorial D** SUMMARIZE operator that would make, e.g., an expression of the form

    ```
    ( MAX ( X ) - MIN ( Y ) ) / 2
    ```

    a valid *<summary>*.

14. Suppose we are given the following definitions:

```
TYPE POINT POSSREP { X RATIONAL, Y RATIONAL } ;
TYPE CIRCLE POSSREP { R RATIONAL, CTR POINT } ;
TYPE COLORED_CIRCLE POSSREP { CIR CIRCLE, COL COLOR } ;

VAR CC COLORED_CIRCLE ;
```

The following is a valid assignment statement with variable CC as target:

```
UPDATE CC ( UPDATE CIR ( UPDATE CTR ( X := 2 * X ) ) ) ;
```

Show a completely expanded version of this statement that makes no use of the UPDATE shorthand.

Part III:

INFORMAL DISCUSSIONS AND

EXPLANATIONS

In many ways, the chapters that follow are really the heart of the book. There are six of them, one for each of the six sections of the *Manifesto* itself:

6.   RM Prescriptions

7.   RM Proscriptions

8.   OO Prescriptions

9.   OO Proscriptions

10.   RM Very Strong Suggestions

11.   OO Very Strong Suggestions

We remind you that the abbreviation OO here stands for **Other Orthogonal**.

Each chapter contains one section for each prescription, proscription, or suggestion, as applicable. (As a consequence, the chapters vary in length considerably. Chapter 6 in particular is very long.) Each section begins by repeating the formal statement from Chapter 4 of the relevant prescription or proscription or suggestion, in italics to order to set it off from the discussions and examples that follow. The examples are expressed in **Tutorial D,** of course, but for the most part they should be fairly self-explanatory—you should not need to study Chapter 5 in depth in order to understand them.

With respect to Chapter 7, incidentally ("RM Proscriptions"), you might notice that most if not all of the proscriptions in question are in fact logical consequences of the *prescriptions* described in Chapter 6. In view of the many unfortunate mistakes we observe in the design of the language SQL, however, we felt it necessary to spell out some of those consequences explicitly, by way of clarification.

As with Part II, everything to do with type inheritance is ignored in this part of the book, apart from (a) the unavoidable references in OO Prescription 2 and OO Very Strong Suggestion 1 (in Chapters 8 and 11, respectively) and (b) a few remarks in passing here and there in other chapters. Again, the material of Part IV extends but does not invalidate the material presented in this part of the book.

One last point: In general, the *Manifesto* is intended to be open ended. That is, anything not explicitly prescribed or proscribed is permitted, unless of course it leads to a violation of some explicit prescription or proscription. For example, a language could include support for "temporal data" [85] and still be a valid **D,** even though no such support is prescribed in the *Manifesto* as such.

Chapter 6

RM Prescriptions

RM PRESCRIPTION 1: SCALAR TYPES

*A **scalar data type** (**scalar type** for short) is a named, finite set of scalar values (**scalars** for short). Given an arbitrary pair of distinct scalar types named T1 and T2, respectively, with corresponding sets of scalar values S1 and S2, respectively, the names T1 and T2 shall be distinct and the sets S1 and S2 shall be disjoint; in other words, two scalar types shall be equal—i.e., the same type—if and only if they have the same name (and therefore the same set of values). **D** shall provide facilities for users to define their own scalar types (user-defined scalar types); other scalar types shall be provided by the system (built-in or system-defined scalar types). **D** shall also provide facilities for users to destroy user-defined scalar types. The system-defined scalar types shall include type **boolean** (containing just two values, here denoted TRUE and FALSE), and **D** shall support all four monadic and 16 dyadic logical operators, directly or indirectly, for this type.*

We begin by reminding you from Chapter 3 that the terms *domain* and *class*—short for *object class*—are sometimes used as synonyms for *type* (in relational and object contexts, respectively), and we occasionally use these latter terms ourselves if the context demands. However, we prefer *type*. We remind you too that, in general, we take the unqualified term *type* to refer to types of all kinds: scalar or otherwise, built in or otherwise, generated or otherwise. In this section, however, we focus on scalar types in particular, and the term *type* should thus be taken to refer to such a type specifically, barring explicit statements to the contrary.

We refer generically to values of some scalar type as *scalar values* (*scalars* for short, or just *values* if there is no risk of ambiguity). Likewise, we refer generically to variables whose values are constrained to be scalars as *scalar variables* (or just *variables* if there is no risk of ambiguity). Note, however, that the physical representation of such scalar values and variables can be arbitrarily complex. For example, a given scalar value might have a physical representation consisting of an array of stacks of lists of character strings. But, of course, such physical representations are always hidden from the user; they are part of the implementation, not part of the model. (Do not be misled by the fact that scalar types usually[1] have "possible" representations—*possreps* for short—that, unlike physical representations, are definitely not hidden from the user. In other words, if type *T* has a possrep *PR* and *PR* has a component *C*, then *C* is visible to the user. However, *C* is, specifically, a component of *PR,* not a component of *T* as such. See RM Prescription 4 for further elaboration.)

Scalar types can be user or system defined (i.e., built in). We require that at least one built-in scalar type be supported: namely, type **boolean** (BOOLEAN in **Tutorial D**).[2] Following reference [77], we justify this requirement as follows:

---

1. The exceptions are dummy types and empty types. Dummy types are part of our inheritance model and are ignored in this chapter. As for empty types, they are of little significance unless inheritance is supported, but it is necessary to say something about them in this chapter nevertheless.

2. As we saw in Chapter 5, **Tutorial D** also supports INTEGER, RATIONAL, and CHARACTER (CHAR for short) as built-in scalar types.

■ If we can write an expression *X* that evaluates to a value *v* of type *T,* we must surely also be able to declare a variable *V* of that same type *T*—for otherwise the system would violate several well-known principles of language design (see RM Prescription 26). In other words, *T* must be a type that is "known to the system," and every expression must evaluate to a value that is of some type that is known to the system.

■ One kind of expression we definitely need to be able to write is an expression of the form *v1* = *v2* (i.e., an expression that tests two values for equality—see RM Prescription 8). And, of course, such expressions return a value of type BOOLEAN. It follows that BOOLEAN needs to be a type that is known to the system.

Now we turn to user-defined scalar types. Here are some examples. First we consider the suppliers-and-parts database from Chapter 2 (and again we assume that attributes STATUS and CITY are of built-in types INTEGER and CHAR, respectively). Here are possible definitions for the types needed for the remaining attributes:

```
TYPE S# ORDINAL POSSREP { C CHAR } ;

TYPE P# ORDINAL POSSREP { C CHAR } ;

TYPE NAME ORDINAL POSSREP { N CHAR } ;

TYPE COLOR POSSREP { C CHAR } ;

TYPE WEIGHT ORDINAL POSSREP { WT RATIONAL CONSTRAINT WT > 0.0 } ;

TYPE QTY ORDINAL POSSREP { I INTEGER CONSTRAINT I > 0 } ;
```

Examples similar to these were discussed in Chapter 3, and we refer you to that chapter for the basics. Here we just draw your attention to a few additional points:

■ All of these types except COLOR are ordinal types, and we now explicitly show—as we did not in Chapter 3—the necessary ORDINAL specification for such types. (Recall that an ordinal type is one for which the operator "<" is supported.)

■ Note that, e.g., types S# and P# are different types, even though they have essentially the same possrep (in particular, of course, they have different names). Thus, an S# value *s* and a P# value *p* are different values, even if they can both "possibly be represented" by the same character string *c.*

■ Types WEIGHT and QTY both involve an explicit CONSTRAINT specification. Thus, whereas the only constraint on (for example) type COLOR is that it must be representable as a character string—meaning every possible string apparently corresponds to some valid color!—weights and quantities are both constrained to be greater than zero. (More precisely, they are constrained to be such that they can be represented by a numeric value that is greater than zero. Notice how the CONSTRAINT specifications rely on using possrep component names to refer to the corresponding possrep components for an arbitrary value of the type in question. For example, the CONSTRAINT specification I > 0 for type QTY means: "Every value of type QTY is such that its integer possible representation I is greater than zero.")

■ Type WEIGHT in particular raises the question of *units* (e.g., pounds vs. grams). We choose to ignore this question for now; in effect, we simply assume—partly reasonably and partly not—that it makes sense to talk about a given weight without any mention of the corresponding units. Analogous remarks apply to several other types that we use as examples, both here and in later chapters. The whole question of types vs. units is discussed in detail in Appendix C.

Here are some more examples (note carefully that they are still all examples of scalar types specifically, even the last one, because they have no user-visible components):

```
TYPE LENGTH ORDINAL POSSREP { M RATIONAL CONSTRAINT M ≥ 0.0 } ;

TYPE ANGLE ORDINAL
     POSSREP { RHO RATIONAL CONSTRAINT RHO ≥ 0.0 AND RHO < 2 * 3.14159 } ;

TYPE POINT       /* geometric points in two-dimensional space */
     POSSREP POINT { X RATIONAL, Y RATIONAL }
     POSSREP POLAR { R LENGTH, THETA ANGLE } ;

TYPE ELLIPSE POSSREP { A LENGTH, B LENGTH, CTR POINT CONSTRAINT A ≥ B } ;

TYPE POLYGON POSSREP { VERTICES RELATION { V# INTEGER, VERTEX POINT } } ;
```

Explanation:

- Type LENGTH is similar to the ones we have already shown in connection with the suppliers-and-parts database.

- Type ANGLE is also similar. In this case, the constraint says that angles must be greater than or equal to zero and less than 2π; we are assuming that angles are measured in radians (2π radians = 360°), which is why we call the possrep component RHO. Again, however, see Appendix C for further discussion of types and units.

- Type POINT is a variation on type POINT as already discussed in Chapter 3; note in particular that (a) it is not an ordinal type and (b) it involves two distinct possreps, one cartesian and one polar. The definition differs from that given in Chapter 3 in two ways. First, the cartesian possrep has been renamed POINT—the same as the type itself—for simplicity (and we will adopt this simplification throughout the rest of this book). Second, the polar possrep components are now of some user-defined type instead of, as previously, the system-defined type RATIONAL—R is of type LENGTH and THETA is of type ANGLE. *Note:* Possible CONSTRAINT specifications for type POINT are discussed later in this chapter, under RM Prescriptions 8 and 23.

- Type ELLIPSE (not ordinal) also has a possrep defined in terms of user-defined types; components A, B, and CTR of that possrep correspond to the major semiaxis *a,* the minor semiaxis *b,* and the center *ctr,* respectively, of the ellipse in question. (We are assuming for simplicity that ellipses are always oriented such that their major axis is horizontal and their minor axis vertical, so that *a, b,* and *ctr* together do indeed constitute a valid possrep. The CONSTRAINT specification constrains the major axis *a* to be greater than or equal to the minor semiaxis *b*—in other words, ellipses are always "short and fat," not "tall and thin.")

- Finally, type POLYGON (also not ordinal) differs from the previous examples in that the sole component, VERTICES, of its declared possrep (which is named POLYGON by default) is relation valued. To be specific, a given polygon might possibly be represented by a relation containing one tuple for each vertex of the polygon in question; that tuple would contain a vertex number (a value of type INTEGER), together with the corresponding vertex itself (a value of type POINT). To repeat, however, polygons are still scalar values, even though they have a possrep with a nonscalar component. *Note:* Possible CONSTRAINT specifications for type POLYGON are discussed later in this chapter, under RM Prescription 23.

We remind you from Chapter 3 that it is possible for a scalar type to be empty (meaning there are no values of the type in question). As noted in footnote 1 on page 129, the real significance of this fact will not manifest itself until we get to type inheritance, but it is at least necessary to state explicitly in the *Manifesto* from time to time that some type must not be empty. To be specific:

- RM Prescription 3 requires result types for scalar operators to be nonempty and parameter types for scalar and update operators to be nonempty.

- RM Prescription 20 requires result types for tuple-valued operators and parameter types for tuple- and relation-valued operators to be nonempty.

- RM Prescription 11 requires types of scalar variables to be nonempty.

- RM Prescription 12 requires types of tuple variables to be nonempty.

Note that there is no such thing as an empty relation type—why not?—and the question of prohibiting such a type in certain contexts (e.g., as the result type for a relation-valued operator) thus does not arise.

Here is an example of destroying a user-defined scalar type:

```
DROP TYPE ELLIPSE ;
```

Note finally that although we do not prescribe such a thing, we do not mean to preclude the possibility that **D** might usefully include some kind of "alter type" operator as a shorthand.

RM PRESCRIPTION 2: SCALAR VALUES ARE TYPED

*All scalar values shall be **typed**—i.e., such values shall always carry with them, at least conceptually, some identification of the type to which they belong.*

This prescription merely insists that there be no such thing as a "typeless" scalar value—every such value must be a value of some scalar type. As we put it in Chapter 3, if *v* is a scalar value, then *v* can be thought of as carrying around with it a kind of flag that announces "I am an integer" or "I am a supplier number" or "I am a geometric point" (and so on). Observe that, by definition, any given value (a) will always be of exactly one type (except possibly if type inheritance is supported), and (b) can never change its type. Observe also that it follows from the first of these points that—as required by RM Prescription 1, in fact—distinct types are *disjoint*, meaning they have no values in common (again, except possibly if type inheritance is supported).

Note: All of the foregoing points concerning scalar values apply, mutatis mutandis, to tuple and relation values also, since tuple and relation values are ultimately made out of scalar values. See RM Prescriptions 6 and 7.

RM PRESCRIPTION 3: READ-ONLY VS. UPDATE OPERATORS

A ***scalar operator*** *is an operator that, when invoked, returns a scalar value (the* ***result*** *of that invocation). D shall provide facilities for users to define and destroy their own scalar operators (user-defined scalar operators). Other scalar operators shall be provided by the system (built-in or system-defined scalar operators). Let Op be a scalar operator. Then:*

a.   Op *shall be* **read-only**, *in the sense that invoking it shall cause no variables to be updated other than ones that are purely local to* Op.

b.   *Every invocation of* Op *shall denote a value ("produce a result") of the same type, the* **result type**—*also called the* **declared type**—*of* Op. *The definition of* Op *shall include a specification of the declared type of* Op. *That type shall be nonempty.*

c.   *The definition of* Op *shall include a specification of the type of each parameter to* Op, *the* **declared type** *of that parameter. That type shall be nonempty. If parameter* P *is of declared type* T, *then, in every invocation of* Op, *the argument* A *that corresponds to* P *in that invocation shall also be of type* T, *and that argument* A *shall be* **effectively assigned** *to* P. *Note: The prescriptions of this paragraph c. shall also apply if* Op *is an update operator instead of a read-only operator.*

   It is convenient to deal with update operators here as well, despite the fact that such operators are not scalar (nor are they nonscalar—in fact, they are not typed at all). An **update operator** *is an operator that, when invoked, is allowed to update at least one variable that is not purely local to that operator. Let* V *be such a variable. If the operator accesses* V *via some parameter* P, *then that parameter* P *is* **subject to update**. *D shall provide facilities for users to define and destroy their own update operators (user-defined update operators). Other update operators shall be provided by the system (built-in or system-defined update operators). Let* Op *be an update operator. Then:*

d.   *No invocation of* Op *shall denote a value ("produce a result").*

e.   *The definition of* Op *shall include a specification of which parameters to* Op *are subject to update. If parameter* P *is subject to update, then, in every invocation of* Op, *the argument* A *that corresponds to* P *in that invocation shall be a variable specifically, and, on completion of the execution of* Op *caused by that invocation, the final value assigned to* P *during that execution shall be* **effectively assigned** *to* A.

The discussion that follows is split into three subsections, one for scalar operators, one for update operators, and one with some observations that apply to both.

Scalar Operators

A scalar operator *Op* is an operator that returns a scalar value—meaning, more precisely, that any given invocation of *Op* denotes some scalar value and can therefore appear wherever a literal representation of that value could appear. For example, recall the scalar operator ABS ("absolute value") from Chapter 3, which returns the absolute value of its integer argument. That operator is of declared type INTEGER; thus, if N is a variable of declared type INTEGER, then, e.g., the expression

```
ABS ( N - 1 ) * 3
```

is valid and is also of declared type INTEGER. (We are relying here on the fact that the operators "-" and "*", when applied to integer arguments, both return an integer result.)

Like scalar types, scalar operators can be either user or system defined (built in). **Built-in** scalar operators are defined, necessarily, only in connection with built-in types. For the built-in types supported by **Tutorial D** (BOOLEAN, INTEGER, RATIONAL, and CHAR), we assume built-in scalar operators as follows:

- For all four types, the equality operator "=" (required for every type by RM Prescription 8)

- For BOOLEAN, the logical operators NOT, AND, OR, XOR, etc. (required by RM Prescription 1)

- For INTEGER, RATIONAL, and CHAR, the comparison operators "<", "≤", etc. (see RM Prescription 22)

- For INTEGER and RATIONAL, the arithmetic operators "+", "*", etc.

- For CHAR, the string operators "||" (concatenate), SUBSTR (substring), etc.

and so on. (*Exercise:* What are the declared types of these operators?) **User-defined** operators, by contrast, can be defined in connection with either built-in types or user-defined ones (or a mixture, of course). Several examples—ABS, DIST, and others—were given in Chapter 3, and we refer you to that chapter if you need to refresh your memory regarding the basics; however, we give a few more examples here in order to make some additional points.

First, here is the required "=" operator for type LENGTH:

```
OPERATOR EQ ( L1 LENGTH, L2 LENGTH ) RETURNS BOOLEAN ;
   RETURN ( THE_M ( L1 ) = THE_M ( L2 ) ) ;
END OPERATOR ;
```

(This example is very similar to one we gave in Chapter 3.) Points arising:

- The operator is defined in terms of two parameters, both of declared type LENGTH. When it is invoked, therefore, the corresponding arguments must both be of type LENGTH also.

- The operator is of declared type BOOLEAN. Observe that it is precisely because its declared type is scalar that we regard the operator as scalar also. Observe too that parameters and arguments to a scalar operator do not necessarily have to be scalar themselves, though they are in the case at hand.

- The expression in the RETURN statement makes use of THE_ operators to access possrep components of its arguments (see RM Prescription 5). It also makes use of the built-in operator "=" for type RATIONAL. In fact, we will assume from this point forward that the equality operator for *every* type uses the familiar "=" notation; we omit consideration of how that notation might be specified, since (as noted in Chapter 3) it is basically just a matter of syntax.

- As also noted in Chapter 3, it should never be necessary in practice to spell out the definition of "=" for any type at all (despite the foregoing example). Instead, that definition can and should be provided by the system when the type in question is defined.

- LENGTH also happens to be an ordinal type, implying that the operators "≠", "<", "≤", ">", and "≥" all apply and need to be defined, in one way or another. (Actually, several additional operators are also required for ordinal types: *first, last, next, prior,* and possibly others. We omit the details here, referring you to reference [85] for further discussion.)

Now, the foregoing example is perhaps not very good, precisely because in practice we would expect the "=" definition to be provided by the system, as already noted. Here by contrast is a more realistic example:

```
OPERATOR REFLECT ( P POINT ) RETURNS POINT ;
   BEGIN ;
      VAR Q POINT ;
         Q := POINT ( - THE_X ( P ) , - THE_Y ( P ) ) ;
      RETURN ( Q ) ;
   END ;
END OPERATOR ;
```

Given a point P, with cartesian coordinates (x,y), this operator returns the "reflected" or "inverse" point with cartesian coordinates $(-x,-y)$. Note the use of a local variable, Q. Points arising:

- Like all scalar operators, REFLECT is *read-only:* It does not update anything apart from the purely local variable Q (in fact, an exception should be raised if it tries to do so). We require scalar operators to be read-only—equivalently, we require update operators not to return a value—in order to prevent side effects.[1] For suppose, contrariwise, that we were able to define REFLECT in such a way as not only to return the inverse point as before, but also (say) to update its argument to set it to that inverse point. Then, e.g., the assignment

```
V := REFLECT ( Z ) ;
```

  would have the side effect of updating the variable Z. We might even imagine a database retrieval operation having the side effect of updating the database! *Note:* Despite all we have just said, we often use the qualifier *read-only* explicitly for emphasis, even though scalar operators are read-only by definition.

- Paragraph c. of RM Prescription 3 says that arguments are *effectively assigned* to parameters. In the invocation REFLECT(Z), for example, the value of the argument Z is effectively assigned to the parameter P before the operator is executed. But we are defining a model here, of course; in practice, the implementation is free to perform the passing of arguments any way it chooses, just so long as the effect is logically indistinguishable from that of effective assignment.

- Since scalar operators have a declared type (meaning every invocation of the operator in question denotes a value of that type), it follows that scalar expressions in general have a declared type. To be specific, let X be such an expression. By definition, X specifies an invocation of some scalar operator Op (where the arguments, if any, to that invocation of Op are specified as expressions in turn). Then the declared type of X is, precisely, the declared type of Op. For example, any expression of the form REFLECT(z) has declared type POINT, regardless of how complex the expression z happens to be.

We close this subsection with a couple more examples. First, here is a simpler definition of REFLECT:

---

1. We require tuple- and relation-valued operators to be read-only as well for the same reason.

```
OPERATOR REFLECT ( P POINT ) RETURNS POINT ;
    RETURN ( POINT ( - THE_X ( P ) , - THE_Y ( P ) ) ) ;
END OPERATOR ;
```

This definition is simpler than the previous one in that it avoids the need for the local variable Q and the concomitant need to use a compound statement ("BEGIN; ... END;" in **Tutorial D**).

Second, here is an admittedly rather contrived example of a scalar operator with a nonscalar—actually relational—parameter:

```
OPERATOR CITY_COUNT ( R RELATION { CITY CHAR }, C CHAR ) RETURNS INTEGER ;
    RETURN ( COUNT ( R WHERE CITY ≥ C ) ) ;
END OPERATOR ;
```

Two sample invocations:

```
CITY_COUNT ( P { CITY }, 'London' )
```

```
CITY_COUNT ( S { CITY }, 'New York' )
```

Given our usual sample values, these two invocations return 3 and 1, respectively.

Update Operators

An update operator is an operator that updates something other than a purely local variable and does not return a result. Here by way of example is an update version of REFLECT:

```
OPERATOR REFLECT ( P POINT ) UPDATES { P } ;
    BEGIN ;
        P := POINT ( - THE_X ( P ) , - THE_Y ( P ) ) ;
        RETURN ;
    END ;
END OPERATOR ;
```

This operator is defined in terms of a single parameter P, of declared type POINT, and, when invoked, it updates the argument corresponding to that parameter appropriately. That argument must be of the same type as that parameter; moreover, it must be a variable specifically, since in the final analysis it is only variables that can be updated. (Recall from Chapter 5, however, that **Tutorial D** allows a *pseudovariable* to appear wherever a variable is required; in other words, pseudovariables are variables, loosely speaking.)

To avoid confusion, let us change the names of the read-only and update versions of REFLECT to R_REFLECT and U_REFLECT, respectively. Then there are several logical differences between the two, which we now explain:

- R_REFLECT has a declared type but U_REFLECT does not.

- R_REFLECT returns a result; an R_REFLECT invocation has a value and is an expression and can be nested inside other expressions. U_REFLECT, by contrast, does not return a result; it has an UPDATES specification instead of a RETURNS specification, and there is no result expression in the RETURN statement.[1] (In the particular example under discussion, omitting the RETURN would mean we could omit the BEGIN and END as well—the compound statement would reduce to a single assignment statement.)   Hence, a U_REFLECT invocation does not have a value and is not an expression and cannot be nested inside other expressions.   It follows that U_REFLECT must be invoked by means of an explicit CALL statement (or something logically equivalent to such a statement)—for example:

```
CALL U_REFLECT ( Z ) ;
```

- Like scalar operators, update operators can be either user or system defined (built in). However, the only built-in update operator—in fact, the only update operator logically required—is assignment (":="), which is prescribed for every type by RM Prescription 21; any update operator is logically equivalent to some sequence of one or more assignments (any of them possibly a multiple assignment). For pragmatic reasons, however, we do permit user-defined update operators of arbitrary complexity. *Note:* The assignment operator per se (":=") resembles the equality operator ("=") in that it should never be necessary in practice to spell out its definition for any type at all. Instead, that definition can and should be provided by the system when the type in question is defined.

- We already know that, for an update operator as for a read-only operator, arguments must be of the same type as the corresponding parameters, and they are effectively assigned to those parameters when the operator is invoked. After the operator has completed execution, moreover, those parameters that are subject to update (i.e., those mentioned in the UPDATES specification) are effectively assigned back to the corresponding arguments, thereby achieving the intended update result. Again, however, we are defining a model here; in practice, the implementation is free to achieve the intended update result any way it chooses, just so long as the effect is logically indistinguishable from that of effective assignment. In particular, it might choose to use *pass by reference* for the arguments in question, in which case an assignment to a parameter that is subject to update will really be an assignment direct to the corresponding argument.

We close this subsection with another example:

```
OPERATOR CHANGE_SCITY ( R RELATION ( S# S#, SNAME NAME, STATUS INTEGER, CITY CHAR },
                        X S#, C CHAR ) UPDATES { R } ;
    UPDATE R WHERE S# = X ( CITY := C ) ;
END OPERATOR ;
```

Two sample invocations:

```
CALL CHANGE_SCITY ( S, S#('S1'), 'Oslo' ) ;

CALL CHANGE_SCITY ( S, S#('S8'), 'Oslo' ) ;
```

Given our usual sample values, these two invocations move supplier S1 to Oslo and have no effect, respectively.

---

1. In fact, the RETURN statement could be omitted entirely in **Tutorial D,** in which case an implicit RETURN will be executed when the END OPERATOR is reached. (In the particular example under discussion, omitting the RETURN would mean we could omit the BEGIN and END as well—the compound statement would reduce to a single assignment statement.)

Miscellaneous Issues

Tutorial D allows user-defined operators of all kinds to be destroyed by means of the DROP OPERATOR statement. For example:

```
DROP OPERATOR CHANGE_SCITY ;
```

Observe now that many of the operators we have been discussing—many of the built-in ones, at any rate—are *overloaded*. An operator is **overloaded** if another operator exists with the same name. To take the most obvious example, "=" is overloaded; there is an "=" operator that works for integers, and another that works for character strings, and another that works for supplier numbers, and in fact one for every type. Other examples include ":=" (which, like "=", is defined for every type); "+" (which is defined for both integers and rational numbers, as well as—probably—lengths, quantities, weights, and so on);[1] "<" (which is defined for integers, rational numbers, character strings, and in fact all ordinal types); and so on. *Note:* We are assuming here that type inheritance is not in effect, for otherwise the operators under discussion might be inherited from some common supertype instead of being overloaded as such. See Part IV of this book for further explanation.

The *Manifesto* permits the overloading of user-defined operators as well. That is, the fact that a user-defined operator *Op* exists does not preclude the possibility of defining another operator with the same name *Op* but a different number of parameters or different parameter declared types (and hence different, though preferably similar, semantics). Moreover, if two distinct operators do exist with the same name, those operators might have different result declared types.

To pursue the point a little further, it might even be possible not just to overload but to **override** an existing operator—i.e., replace it entirely—by defining another operator with the same name, same number of parameters, and same parameter and result declared types but different semantics. For example, it might be possible to override a built-in LOG operator, which returns natural logarithms, say, by one that returns logarithms to base 10 instead. For obvious reasons, we recommend that this feature be used with all due caution.

We conclude this subsection, and this section, with a few remarks on terminology:

- *Parameters:* Parameters that are subject to update are sometimes called *read/write* parameters, on the grounds that they are both "read" and "written" during execution of the pertinent operator. By the same token, parameters that are not subject to update are sometimes called *read-only* parameters. *Note:* We neither prescribe nor proscribe what might be called *write-only* parameters.

- *Operators:* In object systems, read-only and update operators are called *observers* and *mutators*, respectively, and operators in general are called *methods*. Read-only operators in particular are also called *functions*, both in object systems and elsewhere. We have several reasons for not wanting to use this latter term, however. First of all, a function is, strictly speaking, a many-to-one mapping from argument values to result values; thus, a read-only operator is indeed a function. However, the term *function* is often used, loosely, as a synonym for *operator*, and thus taken to include update operators in particular. But an update operator is not a function, because (a) there is no result value and (b) typically, at least one of its arguments must be, very specifically, a variable instead of a value. Moreover, read-only operators might not be functions

---

1. Some languages even use "+" to denote string concatenation. Overloading "+" in this way does not seem very wise, however, because it has the consequence that the expressions $a+b$ and $b+a$ are not necessarily equivalent (concatenation is not commutative).

either, if they were allowed to return more than one result (see Appendix A) or to be what the SQL standard [99] calls "possibly nondeterministic" (meaning distinct invocations with the same arguments might give different results, a possibility we do not allow).

■ *Overloading:* We spoke earlier of "overloaded operators," and that term is indeed the one conventionally used in this context. But it should be clear that it is really operator *names* that are overloaded, not operators as such. In the case of "+", for example, the situation is that the same name "+" is being used to refer to several different operators, and thus it is that name "+" that is really being overloaded.

■ *Polymorphism:* In Chapter 3, we said an operator is *polymorphic* if its arguments can be of different types on different invocations, and we gave "=" and ":=" as examples. Now we are saying that "=" and ":=" are *overloaded,* and you might be forgiven for wondering just what is going on here: Are these operators overloaded, or are they polymorphic? In fact, they are both; overloading is simply one kind of polymorphism (it is sometimes explicitly called "ad hoc polymorphism" [15]). Other kinds include *inclusion* polymorphism, to be discussed in Part IV of this book, and *generic* polymorphism, which is the kind that arises in connection with a type generator (it is the kind of polymorphism exhibited by, among other things, the operators of the relational algebra).

RM PRESCRIPTION 4: PHYSICAL VS. POSSIBLE REPRESENTATIONS

Let T *be a nonempty scalar type, and let* v *be an appearance in some context of some value of type* T. *By definition,* v *has exactly one* **physical representation** *and one or more* **possible representations** *(at least one, because there is obviously always one that is the same as the physical representation). Physical representations for values of type* T *shall be specified by means of some kind of* storage structure definition language *and shall not be visible in* **D**. *As for possible representations:*

a.   *If* T *is user defined, then at least one possible representation for values of type* T *shall be declared and thus made visible in* **D**. *For each possible representation* PR *for values of type* T *that is visible in* **D**, *a* **selector** *operator* S, *of declared type* T, *shall be provided with the following properties:*

1.   *There shall be a one-to-one correspondence between the parameters of* S *and the components of* PR *(see RM Prescription 5). For definiteness, assume the parameters of* S *and the components of* PR *each constitute an ordered list of* n *elements (*n ≥ 0*), such that the* ith *element in the list of parameters corresponds to the* ith *element in the list of components; then the declared types of the* ith *elements in the two lists shall be the same (*i = 1, 2, ..., n*).*

2.   *Every value of type* T *shall be produced by some invocation of* S *in which every argument is a literal.*

3.   *Every successful invocation of* S *shall produce some value of type* T.

b.   *If* T *is system defined, then zero or more possible representations for values of type* T *shall be declared and thus made visible in* **D**. *A possible representation* PR *for values of type* T *that is visible in* **D** *shall behave in all respects as if* T *were user defined and* PR *were a declared possible representation for values of type* T. *If no possible representation for values of type* T *is visible in* **D**, *then at least one* **selector** *operator* S, *of declared type* T, *shall be provided with the following properties:*

1.   *Every argument to every invocation of S shall be a literal.*

2.   *Every value of type T shall be produced by some invocation of S.*

3.   *Every successful invocation of S shall produce some value of type T.*

The discussion that follows is split into three subsections, one each for user-defined and system-defined types and one with a few miscellaneous observations. For simplicity we assume all types are scalar, barring explicit statements to the contrary; we also assume all types are both user defined and nonempty, again barring explicit statements to the contrary.

User-Defined Types

It is convenient to begin our discussion by taking a brief look at object systems. Now, it is well known that such systems had difficulty when they first appeared over ad hoc query and related matters. The reason was that objects could be accessed only by means of whatever predefined methods (i.e., operators) had been provided for the class in question; ad hoc query and access via predefined methods are conflicting concepts, almost by definition.[1] For example, suppose objects of class POINT have an associated GET_X method to "get" (i.e., read) their *x* coordinate, but no analogous GET_Y method. Then even simple queries like the following—

■   Get the *y* coordinate of point P

■   Given some set *S* of points, get all points in *S* that lie on the *x* axis

■   Given some set *S* of points, get all points in *S* whose *y* coordinate lies within some range

(and many others like them)—obviously cannot be handled; in fact, they cannot even be formulated.

We note, however, that one method that must be provided for every class is what the *Manifesto* calls a **selector,** in order to allow for the "selection" or specification of an arbitrary value of the class in question. Consider the following code fragment:

```
VAR X RATIONAL ;
VAR Y RATIONAL ;
VAR P POINT ;

X := + 4.0 ;
Y := - 2.5 ;
P := POINT ( X, Y ) ;
```

Variable P now contains a certain POINT value: namely, the point with cartesian coordinates (+4.0,-2.5). And as we know from Chapter 3 and elsewhere, the expressions 4.0 and -2.5 are RATIONAL selector invocations and the expression POINT(X,Y) is a POINT selector invocation. Observe, therefore, that:

---

1. We deliberately use the terminology of *objects, methods,* and *classes* throughout this discussion of object systems.

- *The parameters to a given selector* S *together constitute, necessarily, a possible representation for objects of the pertinent class* C. For example, it is clearly possible for points to be represented by means of cartesian coordinates. Given a class *C,* therefore, together with a selector *S* for that class, we can say there exists a possible representation or *possrep, PR* say, for that class *C* that corresponds to that selector *S.*

- If a method analogous to the GET_X method discussed above were to be provided for *every component* of possrep *PR,* then objects of class *C* could be accessed for retrieval purposes just as if *PR* were the *physical* representation and that physical representation were exposed to the user. In other words, ad hoc queries and the like involving objects of class *C* could now be performed after all. (In the example, if GET_X and GET_Y methods were both available for points, then ad hoc queries and the like involving points could be performed after all.)

- It is usual in contexts such as the one at hand to speak not of GET_ methods alone, but rather of GET_ *and SET_* methods. SET_ methods are the update analogs of GET_ methods. In the case of points, for example, SET_X and SET_Y methods might be provided to update the *x* and *y* coordinates, respectively, of a specified POINT variable. And just as the provision of GET_ methods for all components of some possrep effectively makes arbitrary queries possible, so the provision of SET_ methods for all components of some possrep effectively makes arbitrary updates possible too. (More precisely, it is the fact that GET_ and SET_ methods—or analogs of those methods, rather—are available for all components of some possrep *together with the fact that invocations of those methods can be arbitrarily nested* that effectively makes arbitrary queries and updates possible. See RM Prescription 5.)

In view of the foregoing, we decided in the *Manifesto* to insist on some appropriate discipline. To be more specific (and reverting now to our more usual terminology), RM Prescription 4 requires that:

- Every (nonempty, user-defined, scalar) type *T* must have at least one declared possrep that is capable of representing every value of type *T. Note:* The *Manifesto* does not use the abbreviation *possrep,* though we do in this book in our informal explanations. More important, recall from Chapter 3 that a (nonempty, user-defined, scalar) type can have any number of distinct possreps, just so long as it has at least one. A type can also have a possrep that is not declared (such would be the case with points, for example, if we omitted to declare the polar possrep). Clearly, however, an undeclared possrep is of little interest; in fact, we adopt the obvious convention that from this point forward the unqualified term *possible representation* and its abbreviated form *possrep* always mean a declared possrep specifically, barring explicit statements to the contrary.

- Declaring a possrep causes "automatic" definition of a corresponding selector (and selectors cannot be defined in any other way).[1] Possreps and selectors are thus in one-to-one correspondence with each other; for every possrep there is a unique corresponding selector and vice versa. (In fact, possrep components and selector parameters are in one-to-one correspondence, too.) In **Tutorial D,** therefore, we adopt the obvious convention of giving the selector and the corresponding possrep the same name, to underscore their hand-in-glove relationship (though they are logically distinct concepts).

And RM Prescription 5, q.v., goes on to insist that GET_ and SET_ operators, or something logically equivalent to such operators, be "automatically" provided for every component of every

---

1. As noted in Chapter 3, "automatic" here probably does not mean *automated* (at least in the case of a user-defined type). An analogous remark applies to THE_ operators also (see RM Prescription 5).

possrep. *Note:* As we know, **Tutorial D** actually supports *THE_ operators* instead of GET_ and SET_ operators as such, for reasons to be explained under RM Prescription 5. Observe too that—in contrast to the situation found in some object systems—the semantics of those operators are *prescribed by the model* and cannot be overridden. What is more, analogous remarks apply to all of the operators that are prescribed by the model, including "=", ":=", and selector operators in particular.

System-Defined Types

The situation regarding possreps and selectors for system-defined scalar types was discussed in Chapter 3. Here we just remind you that:

- It is likely that some system-defined types will have possreps and selectors just as user-defined types do. Type DATE (Gregorian dates) might be an example; type COMPLEX (complex numbers) might be another.

- Others will have no declared possrep at all (type INTEGER might be an example). For such a type, however, the system will at least support a limited form of selector that permits literals of the type in question to be specified.

Miscellaneous Issues

We close this section with a number of miscellaneous points having to do with physical vs. possible representations and the associated notion of selectors:

- In accordance with RM Proscription 6 (see Chapter 7), physical representations are not visible in **D**. Rather (as RM Prescription 4 in fact requires), they are specified by means of some logically distinct *storage structure definition language,* details of which are beyond the scope of both the *Manifesto* and this book.

- Despite the previous point, it might help to stress the fact (already mentioned in Chapter 1) that if *v1* and *v2* are distinct appearances of values of type *T,* there is no requirement that the physical representations of *v1* and *v2* be of the same form. For instance, one appearance of a certain integer might have a packed decimal physical representation and another—possibly of the very same integer—a pure binary physical representation. We observe, however, that in such a situation the system would have to know how to convert between the physical representations in question, in order to be able to implement assignments and comparisons correctly.

- We remark that the relational model effectively requires *relations*—and, implicitly, tuples also—to have "possreps" that are visible to the user (we discussed this notion in Chapter 3; the user-visible components are the corresponding attributes, of course). In effect, therefore, what RM Prescriptions 4 and 5 do is prescribe facilities for scalars that are analogous to certain facilities already prescribed for tuples and relations by the relational model.

- It is an open question as to whether any scalar type *T* can have a possrep that is defined, directly or indirectly, in terms of *T* itself. More precisely, let *T* be a scalar type, and let $S(1)$, $S(2)$, ... be a sequence of sets defined as follows:

  $S(1) = \{\ t : t$ is the declared type of some scalar component,
  or the declared type of some attribute of some tuple- or relation-valued component,
  of some possrep for $T\ \}$

$S(i) = \{\ t : t$ is the declared type of some scalar component,
　　or the declared type of some attribute of some tuple- or relation-valued component,
　　of some possrep for some type in $S(i\text{-}1)\ \}$
　　$(i > 1)$

If there exists some n ($n > 0$) such that T is a member of $S(n)$, then T is *recursively defined*.[1] Thus, the open question is whether recursively defined scalar types should be permitted. We do not feel obliged to legislate on this question so far as our model is concerned; for the purposes of the present book, however, we follow *The Principle of Cautious Design* [46] and assume (where it makes any difference) that such types are not permitted. We remark that if T is not recursively defined, then there will exist some n ($n > 0$) such that every type in $S(n)$ is system defined.

- Turning now to selectors: Observe first that selector operators are read-only, by definition. Further, RM Prescription 4 requires, reasonably enough, that if S is a selector for type T, then:

  - S is of declared type T (thus, no invocation of S ever yields a value not of type T).

  - Every value of type T is obtainable by some invocation of S in which the arguments are all literals specifically, meaning the invocation in question is a literal (of type T) in turn. In other words, there must be a means of specifying an arbitrary literal of type T.

- Note that it is possible for two distinct invocations of a given selector to return the same value; for example, the expressions 3.0 and 3.00 both denote the same rational number. See RM Prescription 8 for further discussion of this point.

We close this section with a brief examination of the logical difference between selectors as we have defined them and the *constructors* typically found in place of such selectors in object languages:

- What a selector does is select some value (what the object world calls *an immutable object*) from some specific set of values. For example, the expression 3 can be regarded as a selector invocation that selects the value three from the set of integers (i.e., from type INTEGER).

- By contrast, what a constructor does is allocate storage for some variable (what the object world calls *a mutable object*).[2] We do not prohibit such operators. Within a database, however, the only variables we permit are, very specifically, *relation* variables (see RM Prescriptions 13 and 16). In the case of variables in databases, therefore:

  - The only "constructor" we permit is, specifically, the operator that defines a real database relvar (see RM Prescription 13). That operator causes any necessary storage allocation to be done and initializes the relvar in question.

  - Importantly, those relvars, unlike "mutable objects," are always named. ("Mutable objects" typically have no names, in the usual sense of that term; they must therefore be referenced by address instead of by name. See OO Proscription 2 in Chapter 9 for further

---

1. This definition requires a slight extension if type inheritance is supported (see Chapter 12).

2. In some object languages, constructors initialize variables instead of or as well as allocating storage for them. We note in passing that SQL also supports something it calls constructors, but SQL's constructors are not constructors in the object sense at all. See Chapter 10 (RM Very Strong Suggestion 8) or Appendix H for further explanation.

discussion of this point.)

■   In order to avoid confusion, therefore, we prefer not to use the "constructor" terminology at all. *Note:* For the same reason (i.e., to avoid confusion), we also prefer our *type generator* terminology over the possibly more usual *type constructor* terminology. See RM Prescriptions 6 and 7.

RM PRESCRIPTION 5: EXPOSE POSSIBLE REPRESENTATIONS

Let some declared possible representation PR *for values of scalar type* T *be defined in terms of components* C1, C2, ..., Cn *(n ≥ 0), each of which has a name and a declared type. Let* v *be a value of type* T, *and let* PR*(v) denote the possible representation corresponding to* PR *for that value* v. *Then* PR*(v) shall be* **exposed**—*i.e., a set of read-only and update operators shall be provided such that:*

a.   *For all such values* v *and for all* i *(i = 1, 2, ..., n), it shall be possible to "retrieve" (i.e., read the value of) the* Ci *component of* PR*(v). The read-only operator that provides this functionality shall have declared type the same as that of* Ci.

b.   *For all variables* V *of declared type* T *and for all* i *(i = 1, 2, ..., n), it shall be possible to update* V *in such a way that if the values of* V *before and after the update are* v *and* v' *respectively, then the possible representations corresponding to* PR *for* v *and* v' *(i.e.,* PR*(v) and* PR*(v'), respectively) differ in their* Ci *components.*

Such a set of operators shall be provided for each possible representation declared for values of type T.

Once again we split our discussion into three subsections, one each for user-defined and system-defined types and one with a few miscellaneous observations, and we assume for simplicity that all types are scalar and nonempty.

User-Defined Types

We explained the basic motivation behind RM Prescription 5 in the previous section; here we focus on the specific syntax used in **Tutorial D** in this connection, since that syntax has been designed to serve as a good realization of exactly the semantics we desire, no more and no less. Let *PR* be a possrep for type *T,* and let *PR* have components *C1, C2, ..., Cn.* Define THE_*C1,* THE_*C2,* ..., THE_*Cn* to be a family of operators such that, for each *i* (*i* = 1, 2, ..., *n*), THE_*Ci* has the following properties:

■   Its sole parameter is of declared type *T.*

■   If the invocation THE_*Ci*(*v*) appears in a source position—e.g., on the right side of an assignment—then it returns the *Ci* component of the value *v.* (More precisely, it returns the value of the *Ci* component of the possible representation *PR*(*v*) of the value of its argument expression *v.*)

■   If the invocation THE_*Ci*(*V*) appears in a target position—e.g., on the left side of an assignment—then:

■   First, the argument expression *V* must consist of a variable reference specifically. (Recall that we regard pseudovariables as variables, however.)

- Second, the expression serves as a **pseudovariable reference,** which means that it actually *designates*—instead of just returning the value of—the *Ci* component of that variable. (More precisely, it designates the *Ci* component of the possible representation *PR(V)* of that variable; here we are extending our "*PR(v)*" notation in a slight and obvious way.)

We gave several examples of the use of THE_ operators and pseudovariables in Chapter 3. Here we just remind you of the following:

- Any assignment that involves a pseudovariable is logically equivalent to another that does not (i.e., pseudovariables are just shorthand, loosely speaking). For example, if P and Z are a variable of type POINT and an expression of type RATIONAL, respectively, then the assignment

```
THE_X ( P ) := Z ;
```

is shorthand for this one:

```
P := POINT ( Z, THE_Y ( P ) ) ;
```

By the way, it follows from this point (no pun intended) that we could satisfy part b. of RM Prescription 5 with assignment alone, just so long as the *read-only* THE_ operators were available.

- THE_ operator invocations can be nested, in both source and target positions.[1] For example, let type LINESEG have a possrep with components BEGIN and END, both of type POINT, and let Z and LS be variables of types RATIONAL and LINESEG, respectively. Then both of the following assignments are valid:

```
Z := THE_X ( THE_BEGIN ( LS ) ) ;
```

```
THE_X ( THE_BEGIN ( LS ) ) := Z ;
```

Incidentally, we can use this LINESEG example to show why we prefer our THE_ operators over the more traditional GET_ and SET_ operators. The basic point is precisely that THE_ pseudovariable references can be nested, whereas SET_ operator invocations cannot (recall that SET_ operators are update operators, meaning among other things that—in our model, at any rate, but for good reasons!—invoking such an operator does not return a value). Thus, for example, a "SET_ operator" analog of the second of the foregoing assignments would have to look something like this:

```
VAR Q POINT ;

Q := GET_BEGIN ( LS ) ;
CALL SET_X ( Q, Z ) ;        /* set X component of Q      = Z */
CALL SET_BEGIN ( LS, Q ) ;   /* set BEGIN component of LS = Q */
```

This example shows why we prefer THE_ *pseudovariables* to SET_ operators. For symmetry,

---

1. As noted in Chapter 3, the term *pseudovariable* is taken from PL/I; observe, however, that we allow pseudovariable references to be nested, whereas PL/I does not. Observe too that we use the terms *invocation* and *reference* interchangeably in connection with pseudovariables.

therefore, we also prefer THE_ *operators* (read-only operators, that is) to GET_ operators—though here we are really talking about a purely syntactic issue, not a logical difference, since GET_ operators are read-only and invocations of read-only operators can be nested as deep as we like.

A few further syntactic points:

- As noted in Chapter 3, we assume for simplicity that all operators with names of the form THE_*C* are indeed THE_ operators of the kind we have been discussing.

- In practice, a more user-friendly way of meeting the requirements of the present prescription might use some kind of dot-qualification syntax. For example, the two assignments shown earlier involving variables Z and LS might better be expressed as follows:

```
Z := LS.BEGIN.X ;

LS.BEGIN.X := Z ;
```

  In this book, however, we will stay with our THE_ notation.

- Note that it is a logical consequence of the **Tutorial D** approach to RM Prescription 5 that if *PR1* and *PR2* are distinct possreps for the same type *T*, then *PR1* and *PR2* cannot have any component names in common; for if *PR1* and *PR2* both had a component called *C,* and if *x* were an expression of type *T*, then the expression THE_*C*(*x*) would be ambiguous.

System-Defined Types

The situation regarding THE_ operators for system-defined types, like that regarding possreps and selectors, was discussed in Chapter 3. Just to remind you briefly:

- It is likely that some system-defined types will have possreps, and hence THE_ operators, just as user-defined types do. For example, type COMPLEX (complex numbers) might have a possrep with components REAL and IMAG, and corresponding THE_ operators THE_REAL and THE_IMAG.

- Others will have no declared possrep at all; type INTEGER might be an example. Such a type has no THE_ operators (and no need for them, either).

Miscellaneous Issues

We close this section with a number of miscellaneous points having to do with THE_ operators and related matters.

- Let type *T* have a possrep *PR* with just one component *C*. Then there is not much point, though nothing logically wrong, in using THE_*C* as a pseudovariable, because it saves little (it is no simpler than its longhand counterpart in this particular case). By way of example, recall that type LENGTH has a possrep with just one component, M. Let variable L be of type LENGTH, then, and consider the following logically equivalent assignments:

```
THE_M ( L ) := 5.0 ;     /* "shorthand" */

L := LENGTH ( 5.0 ) ;    /* "longhand"  */
```

- Once again, let type *T* have a possrep *PR* with components *C1, C2, ..., Cn.* Observe now that it is desirable that those components be mutually independent (i.e., *orthogonal*)—for otherwise, if V is a variable of type T, then updating THE_$Ci(V)$ might affect THE_$Cj(V)$ for some j ($j \neq i$). Here is a somewhat contrived example. Consider type POINT, whose cartesian possrep has two components X and Y, both of type RATIONAL. Suppose we replace that possrep by one involving two rational numbers X and Z, where X is as before and $Z = X + Y$ (i.e., the z value for any given point is the sum of the x and y values for that point). Using an obvious shorthand notation, then, updating x to 4 for the point with $x = 2$ and $z = 3$, say, will actually yield the point with $x = 4$ and $z = 5$, thereby causing z to be updated as a side effect.

- It follows as a special case of the foregoing bullet item that it is desirable that no component Ci of PR be logically redundant—where, by the phrase "Ci is logically redundant," we mean that, for all values v of type T, THE_$Ci(v)$ is some function of THE_$Cj(v)$, ..., THE_$Ck(v)$ for some j, ..., k all distinct from i.

- Note finally that, logically speaking, declaring a possrep PR for type T is really just shorthand for specifying that certain operators are available for values and variables of type T: namely, a certain selector and certain THE_ operators. In the case of type POINT, for example, declaring the cartesian possrep (with the same name POINT and with components X and Y, both of type RATIONAL) really means that:

    - There exists a read-only operator (a selector) called POINT that takes two arguments, both of type RATIONAL, and returns a result of type POINT.

    - A given value is of type POINT if and only if it is returned by some invocation of that POINT operator.

    - There exist two read-only operators called THE_X and THE_Y, respectively, each of which takes just one parameter (of type POINT) and returns a result of type RATIONAL. Let p be a value of type POINT, and let POINT(x,y) be the POINT invocation that returns p. Then THE_X(p) returns x and THE_Y(p) returns y.

    - THE_X and THE_Y pseudovariables are also available.

RM PRESCRIPTION 6: TYPE GENERATOR *TUPLE*

D shall support the **TUPLE** *type generator. That is, given some heading {H} (see RM Prescription 9), D shall support use of the* **generated type** *TUPLE{H} as a basis for defining (or, in the case of values, selecting):*

a.   Values of that type (see RM Prescription 9)

b.   Variables of that type (see RM Prescription 12)

c.   Attributes of that type (see RM Prescriptions 9 and 10)

d.   Components of that type within declared possible representations (see RM Prescription 5)

e.   Read-only operators of that type (see RM Prescription 20)

f.   Parameters of that type to user-defined operators (see RM Prescriptions 3 and 20)

*The generated type TUPLE{H} shall be referred to as a **tuple type,** and the name of that type shall be, precisely, TUPLE{H}. The terminology of degree, attributes, and heading introduced in RM Prescription 9 shall apply, mutatis mutandis, to that type, as well as to values and variables of that type (see RM Prescription 12). Tuple types TUPLE{H1} and TUPLE{H2} shall be equal if and only if {H1} = {H2}. The applicable operators shall include operators analogous to the RENAME, project, EXTEND, and JOIN operators of the relational algebra (see RM Prescription 18), together with tuple assignment (see RM Prescription 21) and tuple comparisons (see RM Prescription 22); they shall also include (a) a tuple selector operator (see RM Prescription 9), (b) an operator for extracting a specified attribute value from a specified tuple (the tuple in question might be required to be of degree one—see RM Prescription 9), and (c) operators for performing tuple "nesting" and "unnesting."*

The main reason the *Manifesto* talks about tuples at all is because it obviously has to talk about both relations and scalars, and tuples are the logical middle ground—relations are made out of tuples, and tuples are made out of scalars, loosely speaking. And since we clearly need to support both relation values and variables and scalar values and variables, it would seem artificial not to support tuple values and variables as well. That said, however, we should say too that we do not expect tuple values and variables to play much of a part in any real application of **D** except in that "logical middle ground" kind of way. In particular, we remind you that we do not permit tuple variables—or scalar variables, come to that—within a database (see RM Prescription 16).

RM Prescription 6 depends heavily on RM Prescription 9, where the concept of a tuple is precisely defined. But the basic ideas were covered in earlier chapters; in particular, Chapter 2 explained the terminology of *degree, attributes,* and *heading,* and Chapter 3 discussed *tuple type inference,* the *attribute extractor* operator, and the general notion of *type generators* (of which the TUPLE type generator is an important special case). We therefore concentrate here on aspects of RM Prescription 6 that were not covered in those earlier chapters. We begin with an example:

```
VAR ADDR TUPLE { STREET CHAR, CITY CHAR, STATE CHAR, ZIP CHAR } ;
```

The expression TUPLE{...} here is an invocation of the TUPLE type generator; the statement overall defines a tuple variable called ADDR, of type

```
TUPLE { STREET CHAR, CITY CHAR, STATE CHAR, ZIP CHAR }
```

—an example of a generated (tuple) type. Just to remind you:

- Each of the four name/type pairs is an attribute (and the set of all four attributes is the heading) of that tuple type, and the degree of that tuple type is four.

- Since the attributes within the braces constitute a set, the order in which they are specified is immaterial. Thus, the tuple type under discussion could equally well be represented as, e.g.,

```
TUPLE { ZIP CHAR, STREET CHAR, STATE CHAR, CITY CHAR }
```

  Note: An analogous observation applies to all constructs in **Tutorial D** that denote sets; from this point forward we will not bother to say so explicitly every time we encounter such a construct but will let this one paragraph do duty for all.

- Variable ADDR has the same attributes, heading, and degree as the type does, and so do all possible values of that variable.

Note, incidentally, that the attributes in the example all happen to have the same type (CHAR), but of course different attributes can have different types, in general. (They must have different names, of course, as we know from Chapter 2. See also RM Prescription 9.) Note too that **Tutorial D** deliberately does not provide a separate "define tuple type" operator. One reason (not the only one) for this omission is that such an operator would presumably involve the introduction of a name for the tuple type in question—i.e., a name over and above the name TUPLE{...} that it already has—and such names would complicate other aspects of our proposal: the question of when two tuple types are equal, for example. For such reasons, we simply permit tuple types to be *used* inline, as it were (as in the example), without requiring, or indeed permitting, them to be separately defined.

Here now is an example of a tuple assignment:

```
ADDR := TUPLE { STREET '1600 Pennsylvania Ave.', CITY 'Washington', STATE 'DC', ZIP '20500' } ;
```

The expression on the right side of this assignment is a tuple selector invocation (in fact, it is a tuple literal). In general, the tuple variable on the left of a tuple assignment and the tuple expression on the right must be of the same type—i.e., they must have the same attribute names, and corresponding attributes must be of the same type in turn.

Tutorial D also supports a shorthand form of tuple assignment, as illustrated by this example:

```
UPDATE ADDR ( ZIP := '20501' ) ;
```

This statement is shorthand for the following:

```
ADDR := UPDATE ADDR ( ZIP := '20501' ) ;
```

(The expression on the right side here is a "tuple substitute" invocation.) Expanding the expression on the right side, this statement in turn is shorthand for the following:

```
ADDR := ( ( EXTEND ADDR ADD ( '20501' AS NEWZIP ) ) { ALL BUT ZIP } )
                                       RENAME ( NEWZIP AS ZIP ) ;
```

And *this* statement is clearly equivalent to:

```
ADDR := TUPLE { STREET FROM ADDR, CITY FROM ADDR, STATE FROM ADDR, ZIP '20501' } ;
```

Note the use of *attribute extractor* operations in this last assignment. We discussed attribute extractors in Chapter 3; here we just remark that it might be more user friendly in practice to support some kind of dot-qualification syntax for them, thereby writing, e.g., ADDR.STATE instead of STATE FROM ADDR. It might even be desirable to extend that syntax to allow, e.g., expressions of the form A.B.C.D, where A denotes some tuple with a tuple-valued component B—see later in this section—and B has a tuple-valued component C and C has a component D (which might or might not itself be tuple valued). In this book, however, we will stay with our FROM notation.

Here now is an example of a tuple equality comparison:

```
ADDR = TUPLE { STREET '1600 Pennsylvania Ave.', CITY 'Washington', STATE 'DC', ZIP '20500' }
```

The comparands must be of the same type.

RM Prescription 6 also requires support for "operators analogous to the RENAME, *project*, EXTEND, and JOIN operators of the relational algebra." Here are some examples (we assume that ADDR has the same White House address as its initial value in every case). Note that, by virtue of the tuple type inference mechanism described in Chapter 3, the type of the result in every case is self-evident.

```
ADDR RENAME ( ZIP AS POSTCODE )                          /* tuple attribute renaming */

Result:  TUPLE { STREET '1600 Pennsylvania Ave.',
                 CITY 'Washington', STATE 'DC', POSTCODE '20500' }


ADDR RENAME ( PREFIX 'ST' AS 'G')                        /* ditto, prefix variant */

Result:  TUPLE { GREET '1600 Pennsylvania Ave.',
                 CITY 'Washington', GATE 'DC', ZIP '20500' }


ADDR { STATE, ZIP }                                      /* tuple project */

Result:  TUPLE { STATE 'DC', ZIP '20500' }


ADDR { ALL BUT CITY, STREET }                            /* ditto, "ALL BUT" variant */

Result:  Same as previous example.

EXTEND ADDR ADD ( NAME('Clark Kent') AS NAME )           /* tuple extend */

Result:  TUPLE { NAME NAME('Clark Kent'), STREET '1600 Pennsylvania Ave.',
                 CITY 'Washington', STATE 'DC', ZIP '20500' }



ADDR UNION TUPLE { NAME NAME('Clark Kent'), COUNTRY 'USA' }    /* tuple union or join */

Result:  TUPLE { NAME NAME('Clark Kent'), STREET '1600 Pennsylvania Ave.',
                 CITY 'Washington', STATE 'DC', ZIP '20500', COUNTRY 'USA' }
```

Several points arise in connection with tuple union in particular:

- First, if the operands have any attributes in common, then each such attribute must have the same value in both.

- Second, as the comment in the example suggests, the operator might equally well be called tuple *join* (tuple union and tuple join being the same operator, logically speaking).

- Third, **Tutorial D** also supports an *n*-adic form of the operator (see Chapter 5).

- Fourth, we are overloading the name UNION, since of course we support such an operator for relations as well as tuples. *Note:* A similar remark applies to the operators RENAME, *project,* and EXTEND among others.

- Finally, observe that tuple union and tuple extend can each be expressed in terms of the other.

Actually, **Tutorial D** goes beyond RM Prescription 6 in that it supports tuple analogs of certain other relational operators also: COMPOSE, WRAP/UNWRAP, and *substitute* or UPDATE. We omit the details here, except to say that WRAP and UNWRAP together provide the required tuple "nest" and "unnest" capabilities. (RM Prescription 6 refers to those capabilities as nesting and unnesting rather than wrapping and unwrapping because nesting and unnesting are the terms most commonly used in the literature. We prefer our wrap/unwrap terminology, however, because the nest/unnest terminology carries too much baggage with it. See in particular the remark concerning "NF² relations" under RM Prescription 7 later in this chapter.)

Next, note that (as indicated in the discussion of attribute extractors earlier) the *Manifesto* requires support for tuples—and relations also—with tuple-valued attributes (and all **D** operators that apply to tuples in general are available for values of the attributes in question). For example, the following **Tutorial D** statement defines a variable of a tuple type for which one of the attributes is of another such type:

```
VAR NADDR2 TUPLE { NAME NAME, ADDR TUPLE { STREET CHAR, CITY CHAR, STATE CHAR, ZIP CHAR } } ;
```

Notice the logical difference between this variable and the following one:

```
VAR NADDR5 TUPLE { NAME NAME, STREET CHAR, CITY CHAR, STATE CHAR, ZIP CHAR } ;
```

NADDR5 has five attributes; NADDR2, by contrast, has just two.

Finally, it is an open question as to whether any heading can be defined, directly or indirectly, in terms of itself (and hence whether any tuple type can be defined in terms of itself). More precisely, let $\{H\}$ be a heading, and let $S(1)$, $S(2)$, ... be a sequence of sets defined as follows:

$S(1) = \{\, t : t$ is the declared type of some attribute in $\{H\}\, \}$

$S(i) = \{\, t : t$ is the declared type of some component of some possrep for some scalar type, or the declared type of some attribute of some tuple or relation type, in $S(i\text{-}1)\, \}$
    $(i > 1)$

If there exists some n $(n > 0)$ such that TUPLE$\{H\}$ or RELATION$\{H\}$ is a member of $S(n)$, then the heading $\{H\}$ is *recursively defined*.[1] Thus, the open question is whether recursively defined headings should be permitted. We do not feel obliged to legislate on this question so far as our model is concerned; for the purposes of the present book, however, we follow *The Principle of Cautious Design* [46] and assume (where it makes any difference) that such headings are not permitted. We remark that if $\{H\}$ is not recursively defined, then there will exist some n $(n > 0)$ such that every type in $S(n)$ is system defined.

Tuple Types vs. Possreps

You might have noticed a certain similarity between **Tutorial D**'s *tuple type* syntax (in a TUPLE type generator invocation) and its *possrep definition* syntax (in a scalar type definition): Both basically involve a commalist of components, each consisting of a name and a type, and you might be wondering whether there are two concepts here or only one. In fact there are two (and the syntactic similarity is unimportant). For example, if *A* and *B* are tuple types, then we might very well want to join values of those types together; but if they are possreps, then there is no question of wanting to join values of those possreps—or values of the scalar types corresponding to those possreps—together.

There is more to be said, however. Consider the following tuple type (let us call it *TT*):

```
TUPLE { NAME NAME, STREET CHAR, CITY CHAR, STATE CHAR, ZIP CHAR }
```

Consider also the following scalar type definition:

---

1. As with recursively defined scalar types, this definition requires a slight extension if type inheritance is supported (see Chapter 12).

```
TYPE ST POSSREP { NAME NAME, STREET CHAR, CITY CHAR, STATE CHAR, ZIP CHAR } ;
```

Now, clearly there is *some* relationship between tuple type *TT* and scalar type ST. In order to see what that relationship is, let *t* be a tuple variable of type *TT*. Then the following expression (actually a scalar selector invocation)—

```
ST ( NAME FROM t , STREET FROM t , CITY FROM t , STATE  FROM t , ZIP  FROM t )
```

—will return a scalar value of type ST. Likewise, if *s* is a scalar variable of type ST, then the tuple selector invocation—

```
TUPLE { NAME THE_NAME ( s ) , STREET THE_STREET ( s ) , CITY THE_CITY ( s ) ,
                 STATE THE_STATE ( s ) , ZIP THE_ZIP ( s ) }
```

—will return a tuple value of type *TT*. In other words, there is a one-to-one correspondence between tuple values *t* of type *TT* and scalar values *s* of type ST. And it might be desirable in practice to provide some kind of syntactic shorthand for converting from type *TT* to type ST and vice versa (perhaps along the lines of the WRAP and UNWRAP operators mentioned earlier).

RM PRESCRIPTION 7: TYPE GENERATOR *RELATION*

*D shall support the **RELATION** type generator. That is, given some heading {H} (see RM Prescription 9), D shall support use of the **generated type** RELATION{H} as the basis for defining (or, in the case of values, selecting):*

a.   Values of that type (see RM Prescription 10)

b.   Variables of that type (see RM Prescription 13)

c.   Attributes of that type (see RM Prescriptions 9 and 10)

d.   Components of that type within declared possible representations (see RM Prescription 5)

e.   Read-only operators of that type (see RM Prescription 20)

f.   Parameters of that type to user-defined operators (see RM Prescriptions 3 and 20)

*The generated type RELATION{H} shall be referred to as a **relation type,** and the name of that type shall be, precisely, RELATION{H}. The terminology of degree, attributes, and heading introduced in RM Prescription 9 shall apply, mutatis mutandis, to that type, as well as to values and variables of that type (see RM Prescription 13). Relation types RELATION{H1} and RELATION{H2} shall be equal if and only if {H1} = {H2}. The applicable operators shall include the usual operators of the relational algebra (see RM Prescription 18), together with relational assignment (see RM Prescription 21) and relational comparisons (see RM Prescription 22); they shall also include (a) a relation selector operator (see RM Prescription 10), (b) an operator for extracting the sole tuple from a specified relation of cardinality one (see RM Prescription 10), and (c) operators for performing relational "nesting" and "unnesting."*

———— ♦ ♦ ♦ ♦ ♦ ————

This prescription has the same general pattern as RM Prescription 6, and the discussions that follow therefore parallel those in the previous section, somewhat. Again we begin with an example:

```
VAR PQ ... RELATION { P# P#, QTY QTY } ... ;
```

(We have omitted portions of the definition that are irrelevant to our main purpose.) The expression RELATION{...} is an invocation of the RELATION type generator; the statement overall defines a relation variable (or relvar) called PQ, of type

```
RELATION { P# P#, QTY QTY }
```

—an example of a generated (relation) type. Each of the name/type pairs is an attribute (and the set containing both of them is the heading) of that relation type, and the degree of that type is two; moreover, relvar PQ has the same attributes, heading, and degree as the type does, and so do all possible values of that variable.

Note that **Tutorial D** deliberately does not provide a separate "define relation type" operator, for much the same reasons that it does not provide an explicit "define tuple type" operator. Instead, we simply permit relation types to be *used* inline, as it were (as in the example), without requiring, or indeed permitting, them to be separately defined.

Here now is an example of a relation assignment:

```
PQ := RELATION { TUPLE { P# P#('P1'), QTY QTY( 600) } ,
                 TUPLE { P# P#('P5'), QTY QTY( 500) } ,
                 TUPLE { QTY QTY(1000), P# P#('P2') } ,
                 TUPLE { P# P#('P4'), QTY QTY( 500) } ,
                 TUPLE { QTY QTY( 400), P# P#('P3') } ,
                 TUPLE { P# P#('P6'), QTY QTY( 100) } } ;
```

The expression on the right side of this assignment is a relation selector invocation (in fact, it is a relation literal). In general, the relvar on the left of a relation assignment and the relational expression on the right must be of the same type—i.e., they must have the same attribute names, and corresponding attributes must be of the same type in turn. Here is another example:

```
PQ := SUMMARIZE SP PER ( P { P# } ) ADD ( SUM ( QTY ) AS QTY ) ;
```

This statement assigns to relvar PQ a relation consisting of part numbers from relvar P and corresponding total quantities from relvar SP (speaking a trifle loosely).

The next example illustrates the required **tuple extractor** operator, which extracts the sole tuple from a relation of cardinality one:

```
VAR PQX TUPLE { P# P#, QTY QTY } ;

PQX := TUPLE FROM ( PQ WHERE P# = P#('P1') ) ;
```

(The tuple extractor invocation here is the expression on the right side of the assignment.) A runtime error will occur if the expression following TUPLE FROM in a tuple extractor invocation returns a relation of cardinality anything other than one.

Tutorial D also supports the usual INSERT, DELETE, and UPDATE shorthand forms of relation assignment. Here are some examples. First, INSERT:

```
INSERT PQ ( SUMMARIZE SP PER ( P { P# } ) ADD ( SUM ( QTY ) AS QTY ) ) ;
```

Expanded form:

```
PQ := PQ UNION ( SUMMARIZE SP PER ( P { P# } ) ADD ( SUM ( QTY ) AS QTY ) ) ;
```

This expansion implies that an attempt to insert a tuple that is already present is not an error; however, we would not object if the implementation did so regard it. If it did, the UNION in the expansion would have to be replaced by D_UNION (see Chapter 2).[1]

Next, a DELETE example:

```
DELETE SP WHERE S# = S#('S4') OR S# = S#('S5') ;
```

Expanded form:

```
SP := SP WHERE NOT ( S# = S#('S4') OR S# = S#('S5') ) ;
```

We do not legislate on the question of whether it is an error if the DELETE has no effect (i.e., if the relation denoted by the expression following the DELETE keyword is empty), but the foregoing expansion assumes it is not.

Finally, an UPDATE example:

```
UPDATE S WHERE CITY = 'Paris' ( STATUS := 2 * STATUS , CITY := 'Nice' ) ;
```

Expanded form:

```
S := ( S WHERE NOT ( CITY = 'Paris' ) )
       UNION
     ( UPDATE S WHERE CITY = 'Paris' ( STATUS := 2 * STATUS , CITY := 'Nice' ) ) ;
```

We do not legislate on the question of whether it is an error if the UPDATE has no effect (i.e., if the relation denoted by the expression between the UPDATE keyword and the opening parenthesis is empty), but the foregoing expansion assumes it is not. *Note:* The expression denoting the second UNION operand in that expansion is an invocation of the *substitute* operator. As explained in Chapters 2 and 5, it is shorthand for an expression that might look like this:

```
WITH ( S WHERE CITY = 'Paris' ) AS T1 ,
     ( EXTEND T1 ADD ( 2 * STATUS AS NEW_STATUS , 'Nice' AS NEW_CITY ) ) AS T2 ,
     T2 { ALL BUT STATUS, CITY } AS T3 ,
     ( T3 RENAME ( NEW_STATUS AS STATUS , NEW_CITY AS CITY ) ) AS T4 :
T4
```

Now we turn our attention to relation comparisons. Here is an example:

```
PQ ‖≥‖ ( SUMMARIZE SP PER ( P { P# } ) ADD ( SUM ( QTY ) AS QTY ) )
```

As explained under RM Prescription 22, the comparands must be of the same type.[2]

---

1. Alternatively, we might consider providing two different shorthands: INSERT, which does not regard an attempt to insert an existing tuple as an error, and D_INSERT, which does (thanks to Jonathan Leffler for this suggestion).

2. Recall from Chapter 5 that the symbol "‖≥‖" denotes the comparison operator "is a superset of."

RM Prescription 7 also requires support for "the usual operators of the relational algebra." However, we defer discussion of this requirement to the section on RM Prescription 18, later (except to say that the required relational "nest" and "unnest" capabilities are provided by GROUP and UNGROUP, which were discussed in Chapter 2).

Next, recall from Chapter 2 that the *Manifesto* requires support for relations (and tuples) with relation-valued attributes, and all **D** operators that apply to relations in general are available for values of the attributes in question. (However, we explicitly do not espouse NF²—"NF squared"—relations as described in, e.g., reference [122], because they involve significant extensions to the classical relational algebra, extensions that we find unnecessary.) By way of example, the following **Tutorial D** statement defines a variable of a relation type for which one of the attributes is of another such type:

```
VAR SPQ ... RELATION { S# S#, PQ RELATION { P# P#, QTY QTY } } ... ;
```

Notice the logical difference between this relvar and our usual shipments relvar SP—SP has three attributes; SPQ, by contrast, has just two.

We remark in passing that operations on relations and relvars with relation-valued attributes can become quite complex. Here by way of example are a couple of UPDATEs involving relvar SPQ:

```
UPDATE SPQ WHERE S# = S#('S2')
  ( UPDATE PQ WHERE P# = P#('P3') ( QTY := QTY * 2 ) ) ;

UPDATE SPQ WHERE S# = S#('S2')
  ( INSERT PQ RELATION { TUPLE { P# P#('P5'), QTY QTY(500) } } ) ;
```

Exercise: Give relational assignments that are equivalent to these two UPDATE statements.

Finally, we remind you from our discussion of RM Prescription 6 that it is an open question as to whether any heading can be defined, directly or indirectly, in terms of itself; it is therefore also an open question as to whether any relation type can be defined in terms of itself. However, we assume for the purposes of this book (where it makes any difference) that such headings and relation types are not permitted.

RM PRESCRIPTION 8: EQUALITY

*D shall support the **equality** comparison operator "=" for every type T. Let Op be an operator with a parameter P, let P be such that the argument corresponding to P in some invocation of Op is allowed to be of type T, and let v1 and v2 be values of type T. Then v1 = v2 shall evaluate to TRUE if and only if, for all such operators Op, two successful invocations of Op that are identical in all respects except that the argument corresponding to P is v1 in one invocation and v2 in the other are indistinguishable in their effect.*

—————— ♦♦♦♦♦ ——————

We discussed the equality operator in some detail in Chapter 3. The definition given above is essentially standard (see, e.g., reference [10]). By way of example, let CH2 and CH3 denote the CHAR values 'AB' and 'AB ', respectively (note the trailing space in CH3). Suppose further that—as is not the case in **Tutorial D**—type CHAR were defined in such a way that the comparison CH2 = CH3 gave TRUE. Then the operator CHAR_LENGTH (see Chapter 2) would have to be defined in such a way that the comparison CHAR_LENGTH (CH2) = CHAR_LENGTH (CH3) gave TRUE also.[1] Conversely, if CHAR_LENGTH, or any other operator on character strings, gives a different result depending on whether it is invoked on CH2 or CH3, then by definition the comparison CH2 = CH3 must give FALSE.

Next, observe that the phrase "for all such operators *Op*" in RM Prescription 8 applies to THE_ operators in particular, a fact that has some important consequences. To elaborate, let type *T* have a possrep *PR* that involves a component *C*. Let expressions *X1* and *X2* denote values of type *T*. If THE_C(*X1*) ≠ THE_C(*X2*), then *X1* ≠ *X2* as explained above (i.e., *X1* and *X2* denote distinct values). It follows that no value of type *T* can possibly be represented in two different ways using the same possrep *PR*. By way of example, suppose type RATIONAL is not built in and we wish to define such a type for ourselves. One possrep we might consider is pairs of integers, representing the numerator and denominator of the rational value in question:

```
TYPE RATIONAL ORDINAL
    POSSREP { N INTEGER, D INTEGER CONSTRAINT D > 0 } ;
```

However, this definition is inadequate as it stands, because it would allow, e.g., (3,2), (6,4), (9,6), ... all as equally valid representations for the rational number 1.5. We therefore need to extend the CONSTRAINT specification appropriately, perhaps as follows:

```
TYPE RATIONAL ORDINAL
    POSSREP { N INTEGER, D INTEGER CONSTRAINT D > 0 AND COPRIME ( N, D ) } ;
```

Here we assume the existence of an operator COPRIME that returns TRUE if its two integer arguments have no common factors other than unity and FALSE otherwise. The effect is that the only valid representation for (e.g.) the rational number 1.5 is the *canonical form* (3,2). Thus, the selector invocation

```
RATIONAL ( 3, 2 )
```

will succeed, but the selector invocations

```
RATIONAL (  6, 4 )
RATIONAL (  9, 6 )
RATIONAL ( 12, 8 )
```

(and many others like them) will fail, because they violate the applicable type constraint.[2]

By way of another example, consider the polar possrep for type POINT. Clearly, if THE_R(*p*) = LENGTH(0.0) for some point *p*, then *p* is the origin, no matter what the value of THE_THETA(*p*) might be. In order to comply with RM Prescription 8, therefore, we need to tighten up our definition of that possrep, perhaps as follows:

---

1. SQL violates RM Prescription 8 on precisely this example, among others. Moreover, if CH2 = CH3 gives TRUE, then CH3||CH2 = CH2||CH3 (i.e., 'AB AB' = 'ABAB ') should surely give TRUE also, implying that embedded as well as trailing spaces are meaningless for this particular type; yet this latter comparison in fact gives FALSE in SQL.

2. We remark in passing that an analogous argument does not apply to the built-in type RATIONAL—or more generally to any built-in type with no declared possrep—because such types have no THE_ operators anyway (thus, e.g., 5.3E1 and .53E2 might both be valid ways of selecting, or specifying, the rational number 53).

```
TYPE POINT ...
     POSSREP POLAR ( R LENGTH, THETA ANGLE
                CONSTRAINT IF R = LENGTH ( 0.0 ) THEN THETA = ANGLE ( 0.0 ) END IF ) ;
```

Now the only valid POLAR invocation for the origin is:

```
POLAR ( LENGTH ( 0.0 ), ANGLE ( 0.0 ) )
```

Recall now that "=" is *overloaded,* in the sense that the comparison *v1* = *v2*, where *v1* and *v2* are of the same type *T,* is valid for all types *T*. What is more, we do not preclude the possibility of allowing *v1* and *v2* to be of different types (thereby supporting comparisons between, e.g., integers and rational numbers, or U.S. dollar values and U.K. sterling values); in other words, we do not preclude the possibility of overloading "=" still further. **Tutorial D,** however, assumes that the operator is not further overloaded in this way, but instead requires its operands always to be of the same type.

RM PRESCRIPTION 9: TUPLES

*A **heading** {H} is a set of ordered pairs or **attributes** of the form* <A,T>, *where:*

a.   A *is the name of an **attribute** of {H}. No two distinct pairs in {H} shall have the same attribute name.*

b.   T *is the name of the **declared type** of attribute* A *of {H}.*

*The number of pairs in {H}—equivalently, the number of attributes of {H}—is the **degree** of {H}.*
     Now let t *be a set of ordered triples* <A,T,v>, *obtained from {H} by extending each ordered pair* <A,T> *to include an arbitrary value* v *of type* T, *called the **attribute value** for attribute* A *of* t. *Then* t *is a **tuple value (tuple** for short) that **conforms** to heading {H}; equivalently,* t *is of the corresponding tuple type (see RM Prescription 6). The degree of that heading {H} shall be the **degree** of* t, *and the attributes and corresponding types of that heading {H} shall be the **attributes** and corresponding **declared attribute types** of* t. *Given a heading {H}, a selector operator, of type* TUPLE{H}, *shall be available for selecting an arbitrary tuple conforming to {H}; every such tuple shall be produced by some invocation of that selector in which every argument is a literal, and every successful invocation of that selector shall produce some such tuple.*

————— ♦ ♦ ♦ ♦ —————

The purpose of this prescription is simply to pin down the notions of *heading* and *tuple* precisely. Little elaboration should be necessary, since we have already discussed these topics in detail under RM Prescription 6 and in Chapter 2. However, there are a few points, all of them direct consequences of the definition, that are worth calling out explicitly:

- No tuple contains anything over and above the prescribed <*A,T,v*> triples. In particular, there are no "hidden" components (a) that can be accessed only by invocation of some special operator instead of by means of a simple attribute reference, or (b) that cause invocations of the usual operators on tuples—or on relations—to have irregular effects. For example, there are no hidden timestamps as are proposed in, e.g., reference [126].

- Note that within any given <*A,T,v*> triple, *T* is in fact implied by *v*, thanks to RM Prescription 2. This fact is recognized in the syntax of **Tutorial D,** which in effect represents such triples (within tuple selector invocations) by means of <*A,v*> *pairs.*

- Tuples and headings of degree zero are valid (indeed, they are required by virtue of RM Proscription 5, which is discussed in the next chapter). Let *t1* and *t2* be two such tuples. Then it follows from the definition of tuple equality in Chapter 2 that *t1* and *t2* are equal; in fact, they are the very same tuple. Thus, there is exactly one tuple of degree zero, and we refer to it as **the 0-tuple** or, equivalently, **the empty tuple.**

- Let attribute $<A,T>$ within heading $\{H\}$ be such that type T is empty. Then the tuple type TUPLE$\{H\}$ is empty as well (meaning there are no tuples of that type).

RM PRESCRIPTION 10: RELATIONS

*A **relation value** r (**relation** for short) consists of a* heading *and a* body, *where:*

a.   *The **heading** of r shall be a heading $\{H\}$ as defined in RM Prescription 9; r **conforms** to that heading (equivalently, r is of the corresponding relation type—see RM Prescription 7). The degree of that heading $\{H\}$ shall be the **degree** of r, and the attributes and corresponding types of that heading $\{H\}$ shall be the **attributes** and corresponding **declared attribute types** of r.*

b.   *The **body** of r shall be a set B of tuples, all having that same heading $\{H\}$. The cardinality of that body shall be the **cardinality** of r.*

Given a heading $\{H\}$, a selector *operator, of type RELATION$\{H\}$, shall be available for selecting an arbitrary relation conforming to $\{H\}$; every such relation shall be produced by some invocation of that selector in which every argument is a literal, and every successful invocation of that selector shall produce some such relation.*

This prescription requires little elaboration, since we have already discussed the topic in detail under RM Prescription 7 and in Chapter 2. There is just one point that is worth discussing further, as follows. As we saw under RM Prescription 9, tuples of degree zero are valid; thus, relations of degree zero are necessarily valid as well. In fact, there are exactly two such: one whose body contains just one tuple—the 0-tuple, of course—and one whose body contains no tuples at all. Following reference [29], we call these two relations, informally, TABLE_DEE and TABLE_DUM, respectively (DEE and DUM for short). What makes them so special is the fact that they can be interpreted as TRUE and FALSE, respectively, as we now explain.

Consider the projection of the suppliers relvar S on S#:

```
S { S# }
```

Let us refer to the result of this projection as *r;* given our usual sample data values, *r* contains five tuples. Now consider the projection of that relation *r* on the empty set of attributes:

```
r { }
```

Clearly, projecting any *tuple* on no attributes at all yields an empty tuple; thus, every tuple in the relation *r* produces an empty tuple when *r* is projected on no attributes. But all empty tuples are duplicates of one another; thus, projecting the 5-tuple relation *r* on no attributes yields a relation with no attributes and one (empty) tuple, or in other words TABLE_DEE.

Now recall from Chapter 2 that every relvar has an associated predicate. For relvar S, that predicate looks something like this:

> *Supplier S# is under contract, is named SNAME, has status STATUS, and is located in city CITY.*

For the projection *r* = S{S#}, it looks like this:

> *There exists some name SNAME and some status STATUS and some city CITY such that supplier S# is under contract, is named SNAME, has status STATUS, and is located in city CITY.*

And for the projection *r*{}, it looks like this:

> *There exists some supplier number S# and some name SNAME and some status STATUS and some city CITY such that supplier S# is under contract, is named SNAME, has status STATUS, and is located in city CITY.*

Observe now that this last predicate is in fact a proposition:[1] It evaluates to TRUE or FALSE, unconditionally. In the case at hand, *r*{} is TABLE_DEE and the predicate (proposition) clearly evaluates to TRUE. But suppose no suppliers at all were represented in the database at this time. Then S{S#} would yield an empty relation *r*, *r*{} would be TABLE_DUM, and the predicate (proposition) in question would evaluate to FALSE.

Now, it is well known that, in logic, TRUE is *the identity with respect to AND;* that is, if *p* is an arbitrary proposition, then the expressions *p* AND TRUE and TRUE AND *p* both reduce to simply *p*. Analogously, in ordinary arithmetic, 0 is the identity with respect to "+" and 1 is the identity with respect to "*"; that is, for all numbers *x*, the expressions $x + 0$, $0 + x$, $x * 1$, and $1 * x$ all reduce to simply *x*. In the same kind of way, in the relational algebra, **TABLE_DEE is the identity with respect to JOIN;** that is, the join of any relation *r* with TABLE_DEE is simply *r*.[2] In particular, therefore, just as the AND of no propositions is TRUE, the sum of no numbers is zero, and the product of no numbers is one, so **the join of no relations is TABLE_DEE.** (In Chapter 2 we simply stated this fact without any justification; now, however, we have justified it.)

RM PRESCRIPTION 11: SCALAR VARIABLES

*D shall provide facilities for users to define **scalar variables**. Each scalar variable shall be named and shall have a specified nonempty (scalar) **declared type**. Let scalar variable V be of declared type T; for so long as variable V exists, it shall have a value that is of type T. Defining V shall have the effect of initializing V to some value—either a value specified explicitly as part of the operation that defines V, or some implementation-defined value if no such explicit value is specified.*

This prescription does not seem to require much in the way of further explanation, except perhaps for the part concerning initialization. (The remarks that follow apply to all kinds of variables, mutatis mutandis, not just to scalar variables specifically.)

---

1. Recall from Chapter 2 that any predicate for which the corresponding set of parameters is empty is in fact a proposition.

2. As explained in Chapter 2, join degenerates to (relational) cartesian product if the operands have no attributes in common. It follows that join always degenerates to cartesian product if either operand is DEE or DUM; thus, the join we are talking about here ("the join of any relation *r* with TABLE_DEE") is in fact a cartesian product.

It is our position that a variable that has no value is a contradiction in terms; in particular, therefore, variables in **D** are always initialized, at least implicitly. (Of course, this fact does not prohibit an implementation from flagging any attempt to reference a variable that has not yet been explicitly assigned a value.) Here by way of example are a few **Tutorial D** scalar variable definitions with explicit INIT specifications (note how—as the comments indicate—the type of the variable is inferred from the type of the INIT expression in each of these examples):

```
VAR N INIT ( 0 ) ;                                          /* type INTEGER */

VAR X INIT ( LENGTH ( 6.5 ) ) ;                             /* type LENGTH  */

VAR P INIT ( POLAR ( LENGTH ( 1.0 ) , ANGLE ( 3.14159 / 4 ) ) ) ;   /* type POINT   */

VAR LS INIT ( LINESEG ( POINT ( 0.0, 0.0 ) , POINT ( 1.0, 1.0 ) ) ) ;   /* type LINESEG */
```

These examples notwithstanding, **Tutorial D** does permit a variable definition to include both an explicit type declaration and an INIT specification, as in this example:

```
VAR M INTEGER INIT ( 0 ) ;
```

In such a case, of course, the INIT expression must be of the type specified (INTEGER, in the example).

RM PRESCRIPTION 12: TUPLE VARIABLES

*D shall provide facilities for users to define **tuple variables**. Each tuple variable shall be named and shall have a specified nonempty **declared type** of the form TUPLE{H} for some heading {H}. Let variable V be of declared type TUPLE{H}; then the degree of that heading {H} shall be the **degree** of V, and the attributes and corresponding types of that heading {H} shall be the **attributes** and corresponding **declared attribute types** of V. For so long as variable V exists, it shall have a value that is of type TUPLE{H}. Defining V shall have the effect of initializing V to some value—either a value specified explicitly as part of the operation that defines V, or some implementation-defined value if no such explicit value is specified.*

Again little further explanation seems to be needed, and we content ourselves with a few examples (note the INIT specifications and inferred types in each case after the first):

```
VAR PQ TUPLE { P# P#, QTY QTY } ;

VAR PQX INIT ( TUPLE { P# P#('P1'), QTY QTY(600) } ) ;
/* type TUPLE { P# P#, QTY QTY } */

VAR ADDR INIT ( TUPLE { STREET '', CITY '', STATE '', ZIP '' } ) ;
/* type TUPLE { STREET CHAR, CITY CHAR, STATE CHAR, ZIP CHAR } */

VAR NADDR2 INIT ( TUPLE { NAME NAME(''),
                    ADDR TUPLE { STREET '', CITY '', STATE '', ZIP '' } } ) ;
/* type TUPLE { NAME NAME,                                          */
/*              ADDR TUPLE { STREET CHAR, CITY CHAR, STATE CHAR, ZIP CHAR } } */
```

```
VAR NADDRS2
     INIT ( TUPLE { NAME NAME(''),
                      ADDRS RELATION { STREET CHAR, CITY CHAR, STATE CHAR, ZIP CHAR } { } } ) ;
/* type TUPLE { NAME NAME,                                                            */
/*                 ADDRS RELATION { STREET CHAR, CITY CHAR, STATE CHAR, ZIP CHAR } } */
```

RM PRESCRIPTION 13: RELATION VARIABLES (RELVARS)

*D shall provide facilities for users to define **relation variables (relvars** for short)—both database relvars (i.e., relvars that are part of some database) and application relvars (i.e., relvars that are local to some application). D shall also provide facilities for users to destroy database relvars. Each relvar shall be named and shall have a specified **declared type** of the form RELATION{H} for some heading {H}. Let variable V be of declared type RELATION{H}; then the degree of that heading {H} shall be the **degree** of V, and the attributes and corresponding types of that heading {H} shall be the **attributes** and corresponding **declared attribute types** of V. For so long as variable V exists, it shall have a value that is of type RELATION{H}.*

———— ♦ ♦ ♦ ♦ ————

Here by way of example are **Tutorial D** definitions (repeated from Chapter 2) for relvars S, P, and SP from the suppliers-and-parts database:

```
VAR S REAL RELATION
  { S# S#, SNAME NAME, STATUS INTEGER, CITY CHAR }
    KEY { S# } ;

VAR P REAL RELATION
  { P# P#, PNAME NAME, COLOR COLOR, WEIGHT WEIGHT, CITY CHAR }
    KEY { P# } ;

VAR SP REAL RELATION
  { S# S#, P# P#, QTY QTY }
    KEY { S#, P# } ;
```

These definitions are more or less self-explanatory, except perhaps for (a) the REAL specifications, which mean the relvars are real as opposed to virtual (see the paragraph immediately following), and (b) the KEY specifications, which specify candidate keys (see RM Prescription 15). Relvars S, P, and SP are now part of the database—i.e., the database catalog has been updated to include entries describing them. In accordance with RM Prescription 14, moreover, each of those relvars has as its initial value an empty relation (of the applicable type), since no other initial value has been explicitly specified.

Note: **D** supports both database and application relvars, but we defer detailed discussion of the latter to the next section. Further, database relvars can be either real or virtual, but again we defer detailed discussion of the latter to the next section—except to remind you that (as noted in Chapter 2) real and virtual relvars are the *Manifesto* counterparts to what are commonly called base tables and views, respectively.

Here now is an example of destroying a relvar:

```
DROP VAR SP ;
```

The specified relvar must be a database relvar (in **Tutorial D** terms, its definition must have specified either REAL or VIRTUAL, not PRIVATE or PUBLIC).

Although we do not prescribe such a thing, we do not mean to preclude the possibility that **D** might usefully include some kind of "alter relvar" operator as a shorthand (analogous to ALTER TABLE in SQL).

One last point to close this section (and it applies to relvars of all kinds, not just real ones): Do not make the mistake of thinking that a relation variable is a set of tuple variables. A relation variable is a variable whose permitted values are relation values; updating a relation variable replaces the current relation value of that variable by another such value. There is no notion, nor can there be any notion, that "updating a relation variable" really means updating some tuple variable(s) within the relation variable in question. As explained in Chapter 2, we do sometimes talk, very loosely, of "updating some tuple within some relvar" (from t to t', say), but all we mean by such talk is that the "old" and "new" values of the relvar in question differ only inasmuch as the old one includes t and the new one includes t' instead.

RM PRESCRIPTION 14: KINDS OF RELVARS

Database relvars shall be either real *or* virtual. *A **virtual relvar** V shall be a database relvar whose value at any given time is the result of evaluating a certain relational expression at that time; the relational expression in question shall be specified when V is defined and shall mention at least one database relvar. A **real relvar** shall be a database relvar that is not virtual. Defining a real relvar V shall have the effect of initializing V to some value—either a value specified explicitly as part of the operation that defines V, or an empty relation if no such explicit value is specified.*

Application relvars shall be either public *or* private. *A **public relvar** shall be an application relvar that constitutes the perception of the application in question of some portion of some database. A **private relvar** shall be an application relvar that is completely private to the application in question and is not part of any database. Defining a private relvar V shall have the effect of initializing V to some value—either a value specified explicitly as part of the operation that defines V, or an empty relation if no such explicit value is specified.*

———— ♦ ♦ ♦ ♦ ————

Virtual Relvars

Database relvars are either real or virtual ("base tables or views"). Real relvars were discussed under RM Prescription 13. Here by contrast are a couple of examples of virtual relvars:

```
VAR PART_CITIES VIRTUAL ( P { P#, CITY } )      /* projection of parts on P# and CITY */
    KEY { P# } ;

VAR COLOCATED VIRTUAL ( S JOIN P )              /* join of suppliers and parts on CITY */
    KEY { S#, P# } ;
```

Relvars PART_CITIES and COLOCATED are now part of the database, in the sense that—like the relvars S and P in terms of which they are defined[1]—they are now described by entries in the database catalog. The value of each of these virtual relvars at time t is the value at time t of the relational expression in terms of which it is defined. *Note:* If the KEY specifications were omitted, the

---

1. We do not preclude the possibility of defining views of application relvars as well as database ones. For simplicity, however, we assume throughout this book that all virtual relvars are database relvars specifically.

relvars would be considered to have whatever candidate keys could be inferred by the system for their defining expressions (see RM Very Strong Suggestion 3 in Chapter 10).

Now, it is well known (but still worth mentioning explicitly) that virtual relvars serve two rather different purposes:

1. A user who actually *defines* a virtual relvar *V* is, obviously, aware of the expression *X* in terms of which *V* is defined. Such a user can use the name *V* wherever the expression *X* is intended, but such uses are basically just shorthand.

2. By contrast, a user who is merely informed that relvar *V* exists and is available for use is typically *not* aware of the defining expression *X*. To such a user, in fact, relvar *V* should ideally look and behave just like a real relvar. Of course, it is also well known that there are difficulties over updating virtual relvars; thus, it is unclear at the time of writing to what extent this objective can be achieved. We observe, however, that if any relvar turns out to be intrinsically nonupdatable, then we would not be justified in calling it a relvar—i.e., a *variable*—in the first place. See Appendix E for further discussion.

We distinguish between these two cases when necessary by referring to them explicitly as Case 1 and Case 2, respectively. Note in particular, however, that we do not make any distinctions in this regard regarding updatability in particular—we intend Case 1 and Case 2 virtual relvars to be exactly as updatable as each other.

We observe further that, at least for Case 2, the decision as to which relvars should be considered real and which virtual is to some degree arbitrary (we say "to some degree" because database design theory sometimes has something to say on such matters). For example, let the values of relvars *A*, *B*, and *C* at time *t* be *a*, *b*, and *c*, respectively. If it is true for all such times *t* that *a* and *b* are projections of *c* and *c* is the join of *a* and *b*, then either (a) *A* and *B* could be real and *C* virtual, or (b) *C* could be real and *A* and *B* virtual. It follows that there should be no arbitrary and unnecessary distinctions between real and virtual relvars. We refer to this fact—or perhaps *objective* would be a better word, given the uncertainties over updatability already mentioned—as *The Principle of Interchangeability* (of real and virtual relvars).

Private Relvars

A private relvar is simply a local variable that happens to be a relvar; it is not part of the database and has no entry in the catalog. For example:

```
VAR PQ PRIVATE RELATION { P# P#, QTY QTY } KEY { P# } ;
```

Relvar PQ is initialized to the following empty relation:

```
RELATION { P# P#, QTY QTY } { }
```

Public Relvars

Suppose application *A* accesses database relvar *V* directly by name (note that we do not prohibit such a possibility, though we would not object if the implementation did so). Clearly, then, application *A* is vulnerable to changes in the definition of *V*. In the interests of logical data independence, therefore [86], we prescribe support for *public relvars*. A public relvar represents the application's perception of some portion of the database. For example:

```
VAR ZS PUBLIC RELATION { S# S#, SNAME NAME, CITY CHAR }
   KEY { S# } ;
```

This definition effectively asserts that "the application believes" there is a relvar in the database called ZS, with attributes and key as specified. Such is not the case, of course—but there is a database relvar called S (with attributes and key as specified for ZS but with one additional attribute), and we can clearly define a mapping between them, thus:

```
ZS  ≡  S { S#, SNAME, CITY }
```

The right side of this mapping denotes the projection of S on S#, SNAME, and CITY. The mapping is performed outside the application.[1] Now if it ever becomes necessary to change the definition of relvar S in any way, logical data independence can be preserved by changing the mapping and not the application.

The concept of public relvars allows us to draw a sharp distinction between the database as it is known (a) to the system and (b) to the application. In other words, we maintain two sets of definitions, one in the application and one in the catalog; the former represent the application's perception of the database and the latter represent the database "as it really is," and maintaining the mapping between the two is what enables us to achieve logical data independence.

We close this subsection by pointing out that (as you might have realized already) public relvars amount to little more than a slight variation on Case 2 virtual relvars. That is, a public relvar can be thought of as a Case 2 virtual relvar, *R* say, except that:

a.   The mapping of *R* to the relvar(s) in terms of which *R* is defined is specified not as part of the definition of *R* itself but, rather, somewhere external to that definition.

b.   The structure of *R* is explicitly specified as part of the definition of *R* itself, instead of being inferred from that mapping.

In fact, Case 2 virtual relvars were always intended, like public relvars, to serve as a mechanism for achieving logical data independence; unfortunately, however, the manner of their commercial realization undermined that objective, at least in SQL. The problem with SQL views in this regard is that an SQL view definition explicitly reveals the mapping information and so makes it difficult to hide that information from the user—despite the fact that hiding that information is exactly what needs to be done. (Indeed, the structural information, which the user does need to know about, is not defined explicitly but is inferred from the mapping.) Thus, it would be possible to dispense with the public relvar concept if the Case 2 virtual relvar concept were revised appropriately. We do not propose any such revision here, however, for fear of introducing confusion—and so the criticisms just articulated apply to our virtual relvars almost but not quite as much as they do to SQL views. (We say "not quite" because we do at least allow integrity constraints to refer to virtual relvars.)

Relation Constants

Let *V* be a virtual relvar, and let *X* be the defining expression for *V*. As noted in Chapter 5, *X* must not mention any variables other than database relvars (but it must mention at least one of those, for otherwise it would have a constant value and *V* would not be a variable at all). As also noted in Chapter 5, however, the ability to define *relation constants* or "relcons" might well be useful in practice. For example (to invent some syntax on the fly):

---

1. We leave details of the mapping process to implementers, though we observe that the language **D** might be used for the purpose.

```
CONST PQ6 RELATION { TUPLE { P# P#('P1'), QTY QTY( 600) } ,
                     TUPLE { P# P#('P2'), QTY QTY(1000) } ,
                     TUPLE { P# P#('P3'), QTY QTY( 400) } ,
                     TUPLE { P# P#('P4'), QTY QTY( 500) } ,
                     TUPLE { P# P#('P5'), QTY QTY( 500) } ,
                     TUPLE { P# P#('P6'), QTY QTY( 100) } } ;
```

Now, it might be objected that a virtual relvar *V* can have a constant value even if its defining expression does mention at least one database relvar and no other variables. For example:

```
VAR NO_SUPPLIERS VIRTUAL ( S WHERE FALSE ) ;
```

This relvar is always empty (INSERTs will always fail unless the set of tuples to be inserted is empty), and thus it certainly has a constant value. But this state of affairs is not really different in kind from one in which the relvar is real but subject to a certain constraint:

```
VAR R REAL ... ;
```

```
CONSTRAINT R_IS_EMPTY ( IS_EMPTY ( R ) ) ;
```

Like R in this example, NO_SUPPLIERS is not *intrinsically* nonupdatable—in both cases, it is just that the existence of a certain constraint implies that certain updates (not all) will fail.[1] To be more specific, both relvars are subject to the constraint "for all tuples in the relvar, FALSE," which evaluates to TRUE if and only if the relvar is empty. See Appendix E for further explanation.

It might also be objected that a virtual relvar *V* can have different values at different times even if its defining expression fails to mention any database relvars at all. For example:

```
VAR TODAY VIRTUAL ( RELATION { TUPLE { D CURRENT_DATE ( ) } } ) ;
```

We are assuming here that CURRENT_DATE is a niladic built-in operator that returns "the date today"; in effect, it is a kind of system variable (and the defining expression for TODAY thus does mention a variable, albeit not a database relvar). While it might be useful to support some such functionality, we feel that such considerations are secondary to our main purpose. We also feel that to use the terminology of virtual relvars in connection with such functionality is to muddy an otherwise clear picture (virtual relvars were always intended to provide views of the database specifically). Note in particular that it makes little sense to attempt to apply explicit updates to a "relvar" like TODAY.

RM PRESCRIPTION 15: CANDIDATE KEYS

*By definition, every relvar shall have at least one **candidate key**. At least one such key shall be defined, either explicitly or implicitly, at the time the relvar in question is defined, and it shall not be possible to destroy all of the candidate keys of a given relvar (other than by destroying the relvar itself).*

We discussed candidate keys (keys for short) and gave a precise definition of the concept in Chapter 2.

---

1. In fact, the virtual relvar NO_SUPPLIERS seems to be logically indistinguishable from a *real* relvar defined to be SAME_TYPE_AS(S) and subject to the constraint that it must be empty.

Here we just give a few self-explanatory examples of relvars with two or more keys (we have already seen several examples of relvars with just one):

```
VAR TAX_BRACKET REAL RELATION { LOW MONEY, HIGH MONEY, PERCENTAGE RATIONAL }
   KEY { LOW }
   KEY { HIGH }
   KEY { PERCENTAGE } ;

VAR ROSTER REAL RELATION { DAY DAY, HOUR HOUR, GATE GATE, PILOT NAME }
   KEY { DAY, HOUR, GATE }
   KEY { DAY, HOUR, PILOT } ;

VAR MARRIAGE REAL RELATION { SPOUSE_A NAME, SPOUSE_B NAME, DATE_OF_MARRIAGE DATE }
   /* assume no polygamy and no couple marrying each other more than once ... */
   KEY { SPOUSE_A, DATE_OF_MARRIAGE }
   KEY { DATE_OF_MARRIAGE, SPOUSE_B }
   KEY { SPOUSE_B, SPOUSE_A } ;
```

Note: As we know, every relvar has at least one key. In the case of a virtual relvar, explicit specification of such keys is optional, because (as mentioned under RM Prescription 14) the system should be able to infer them for itself. In other cases, at least one key must be specified explicitly at the time the relvar is defined—unless, again, the system is able to infer such keys for itself, as it can in **Tutorial D,** for example, if SAME_TYPE_AS is used in the relvar definition (see Chapter 5).

RM PRESCRIPTION 16: DATABASES

*A **database** shall be a named container for relvars; the content of a given database at any given time shall be a set of database relvars. The necessary operators for defining and destroying databases shall not be part of **D** (in other words, defining and destroying databases shall be done "outside the **D** environment").*

A database as we use the term is a purely logical concept; how it maps to physical storage is implementation-defined. In the extreme case, a single **D** database could be physically distributed across any number of disparate computers, running any number of disparate DBMSs, at any number of mutually remote sites. We have two major reasons for wanting to include such a concept in the *Manifesto:*

- To draw a boundary between data that is *persistent* and data that is not

- To draw a boundary between data that is accessible to a given transaction and data that is not

First, regarding persistence: Databases (and nothing else) are persistent, meaning, loosely, that their lifetime is greater than that of a typical transaction or application execution. More precisely, once an update has been applied to a database and committed, that update is guaranteed never to be rolled back (except possibly as noted under OO Prescription 5 in Chapter 8). Note carefully, therefore, that since the only kind of variable we permit within a database is, very specifically, the database relvar, the only kind of variable that might possess the property of persistence is such a relvar. Thus, we do not subscribe to the object-world dictum "persistence orthogonal to type"—see, e.g., references [2], [3], and [130]—for reasons explained in detail in references [57] and [65]. (It might help to point out that "persistence orthogonal to type" is effectively the direct opposite of *The Information Principle.*)

Second, regarding accessibility: Any given transaction is defined to interact with exactly one database, meaning that (a) every database relvar accessed by that transaction belongs to the same database, and therefore that (b) every database relvar mentioned within a given relational expression belongs to the same database (see RM Prescriptions 17 and 18). Thus, if database *DB* is the database associated with transaction *TX,* then *TX* must not mention any relvar *R* that belongs to some distinct database *DB'* and not to database *DB*.

Incidentally, it follows from the foregoing that database relvar names must be unique within their containing database. This is one reason why we insist that defining and destroying databases be done "outside the **D** environment"—for if not, we would need a scope within which *database* names were unique, which would simply push the issue of name uniqueness out to another level. In practice, of course, defining and destroying databases will presumably be done by means of some kind of system-provided utilities (and the user might even think of those utilities, harmlessly, as being part of the overall "**D** environment").

We do not prescribe a mechanism for making and breaking the necessary connections between transactions and databases. In practice, such operations will presumably be performed by means of some kind of CONNECT and DISCONNECT statements. The reason we do not prescribe any such mechanism is simply that, in practice, such mechanisms involve far too many concepts—clients, servers, processes, sessions, "DBMS instances," and many other things—that are beyond the purview of the *Manifesto* as such.

RM PRESCRIPTION 17: TRANSACTIONS

*Each **transaction** shall interact with exactly one database. However, distinct transactions shall be able to interact with distinct databases, and distinct databases shall not necessarily be disjoint. Also, **D** shall provide facilities for a transaction to define new relvars, or destroy existing ones, within its associated database (see RM Prescription 13).*

———— ♦ ♦ ♦ ♦ ♦ ————

This prescription needs no elaboration here.

RM PRESCRIPTION 18: RELATIONAL ALGEBRA

*D shall support the usual operators of the **relational algebra** (or some logical equivalent thereof). Specifically, it shall support, directly or indirectly, at least the operators RENAME, restrict (WHERE), project, JOIN, UNION, INTERSECT, MINUS, DIVIDEBY, EXTEND, SUMMARIZE, GROUP, and UNGROUP. All such operators shall be expressible without excessive circumlocution. D shall support **type inference** for relation types, whereby the type of the result of evaluating an arbitrary relational expression shall be well defined and known to both the system and the user.*

———— ♦ ♦ ♦ ♦ ♦ ————

All of the operators mentioned in this prescription were defined in Chapter 2, with the sole exception of DIVIDEBY. We will explain that operator in detail in just a moment; first, however, we offer a few comments on certain other aspects of this prescription.

■   As noted in Chapter 2, the operators of the relational algebra are generic, in the sense that they work for all relations, loosely speaking. They are generic precisely because they are associated with a certain type generator—viz., RELATION—and not with some specific type: neither a specific scalar type such as INTEGER or ELLIPSE, nor a specific nonscalar type such as some particular tuple or relation type. Contrast the situation with user-defined operators, relational or otherwise, in **Tutorial D,** where parameters are defined to be of certain specific types and corresponding arguments are required to be of those exact same types.

- The prescription requires that the operators "be expressible without excessive circumlocution." Now, we realize this requirement is not very precise as it stands, but it is difficult to make it more so. We mean it to imply among other things that:

  - Existential and universal quantification (loosely, EXISTS and FORALL) should be equally easy to express. By way of a trivial example, consider the natural language queries "Get suppliers who supply part P1" and "Get suppliers who do not supply part P1." Note that these two queries do conceptually involve EXISTS and FORALL, respectively—the first effectively means "Get suppliers such that there exists a corresponding shipment where the part number is P1" and the second "Get suppliers such that for all corresponding shipments the part number is not P1." Here are possible **Tutorial D** formulations of these queries:

    ```
    S MATCHING ( SP WHERE P# = P#('P1') )
    ```

    ```
    S NOT MATCHING ( SP WHERE P# = P#('P1') )
    ```

    Loosely speaking, these two expressions return suppliers S1 and S2 and suppliers S3, S4, and S5, respectively, given our usual sample data.

  - Projection over specified attributes and projection over all but specified attributes should be equally easy to express. Here by way of example are **Tutorial D** formulations of the queries "Get supplier number for all suppliers" and "Get all but supplier number for all suppliers":

    ```
    S { S# }
    ```

    ```
    S { ALL BUT S# }
    ```

- Of course, RM Prescription 18 does not prohibit support for additional relational operators. **Tutorial D** in particular includes support for SEMIJOIN (or MATCHING), SEMIMINUS (or NOT MATCHING), D_UNION, COMPOSE, WRAP/UNWRAP, *substitute* (UPDATE), TCLOSE (see RM Prescription 19), and *n*-adic (prefix) versions of UNION, D_UNION, INTERSECT, and JOIN.

- The prescribed support for relation type inference was discussed in Chapters 2 and 3.

DIVIDEBY

DIVIDEBY is a generalized version of Codd's original divide operator [22]. Codd's divide required the divisor and dividend to be such that the heading of the divisor was a proper subset of that of the dividend. Subsequently, Todd [133] introduced an extended form of divide that applied to any pair of relations whatsoever.[1] Unfortunately, both of these operators suffered from certain problems over empty relations; moreover, it turned out that Todd's divide was in fact not exactly an extended form of Codd's—they were really two different operators. In reference [34], therefore, the present writers proposed (a) a generalized version of Codd's divide ("the Small Divide") and (b) a generalized version of

---

1. Except that, as in (e.g.) join, attributes with the same name in the two relations had to be of the same type.

Todd's divide ("the Great Divide") that overcame the difficulties with empty relations. We now explain these operators, with examples, starting with the Small Divide.

Consider the query "Get suppliers who supply every purple part" (the point of the example being that, given our usual sample data, the set of purple parts is empty). Using Codd's divide, then, we might write:

```
SP { S#, P# } DIVIDEBY ( P WHERE COLOR = COLOR('Purple') ) { P# }
```

This expression is shorthand for the following:

```
WITH ( P WHERE COLOR = COLOR('Purple') ) AS PP ,
     ( SP { S# } JOIN PP { P# } ) AS QQ ,
     ( QQ MINUS SP { S#, P# } ) AS RR :
SP { S# } MINUS RR { S# }
```

But this expression misses suppliers who supply no parts at all—even though (logically speaking) such a supplier does supply every purple part, because, as is well known, "FORALL *x* (*exp*)" always evaluates to TRUE if there are no *x*'s, regardless of what the boolean expression *exp* happens to be. By contrast, the following expression (which involves a Small Divide) is guaranteed to give the right answer in all cases:

```
WITH ( P WHERE COLOR = COLOR('Purple') ) AS PP :
S { S# } DIVIDEBY PP { P# } PER ( SP { S#, P# } )
```

This expression is defined to be shorthand for the following:

```
WITH ( P WHERE COLOR = COLOR('Purple') ) AS PP ,
     ( S { S# } JOIN PP { P# } ) AS QQ ,
     ( QQ MINUS SP { S#, P# } ) AS RR :
S { S# } MINUS RR { S# }
```

This latter expression differs from the Codd expansion in that the second line refers to S instead of SP; it therefore extracts supplier numbers from S, not SP, and in particular it does return supplier numbers for suppliers who supply no parts at all.

Now, we made a tacit assumption in the foregoing Small Divide that the dividend and the divisor have disjoint headings—*dend* and *dor,* say—and the PER relation has a heading—*per,* say—that is the union of *dend* and *dor.* But it is a simple matter to extend the definition to allow *dend, dor,* and *per* to be any headings whatsoever, thereby permitting the example to be simplified to just:

```
WITH ( P WHERE COLOR = COLOR('Purple') ) AS PP :
S DIVIDEBY PP PER ( SP )
```

Since (a) the only common attribute for S and SP is S# and (b) the only common attribute for SP and PP is P#, this expression can easily be defined in such a way as to be semantically equivalent to the earlier version.

We turn now to the Great Divide. Suppose we are given an extended version of the suppliers-and-parts database that looks like this (in outline):

```
S    { S#, ... }
SP   { S#, P# }                    /* ignore QTY for simplicity */
P    { P#, ..., COLOR, ... }
PJ   { P#, J# }
J    { J#, ... }
```

"J" here stands for "projects," and relvar PJ indicates which parts are used in which projects. Now consider the query "Get S#/J# pairs such that supplier S# supplies all red parts used in project J#." Let RPJ stand for the expression:

```
( PJ JOIN ( P WHERE COLOR = COLOR('Red') ) )
```

Using Todd's divide, then, we might write

```
SP { S#, P# } DIVIDEBY RPJ { P#, J# }
```

This expression is defined to yield a relation with heading {S#,J#} and with body consisting of all tuples $<s,j>$ such that a tuple $<s,p>$ appears in SP for *all* tuples $<p,j>$ appearing in PJ. *Note:* We deliberately depart from our formal notation for tuples here, for simplicity.

It should not be necessary to go into great detail to persuade you that, like Codd's divide, Todd's divide suffers from problems—worse problems, in fact—over empty relations. For example, the expression shown above misses $<s,j>$ tuples where (a) project *j* uses no red parts or (b) supplier *s* supplies no parts and there happen to be no red parts. By contrast, the following expression is guaranteed to give the right answer in all cases:

```
S { S# } DIVIDEBY J { J# } PER ( SP { S#, P# }, RPJ { P#, J# } )
```

This expression is defined to be shorthand for the following:

```
( S { S# } JOIN J { J# } )
    MINUS ( ( S { S# } JOIN RPJ { P#, J# } )
              MINUS ( SP { S#, P# }
                        JOIN RPJ { P#, J# } ) ) { S#, J# }
```

Converting this expression into an equivalent step-at-a-time version using WITH and introduced names is left as an exercise for the reader. Note, however, that again we have made a tacit assumption—this time to the effect that the dividend and the divisor have disjoint headings *dend* and *dor*, say, and the PER relations have headings *per1* and *per2*, say, such that *dend* is the difference between *per1* and *per2* (in that order) and *dor* is the difference between *per2* and *per1* (in that order). Again, however, it is a simple matter to extend the definition to allow *dend, dor, per1,* and *per2* to be any headings whatsover, thereby permitting the foregoing example to be simplified to just:

```
S DIVIDEBY J PER ( SP, RPJ )
```

Since (a) the only common attribute for S and SP is S#, (b) the only common attribute for SP and RPJ is P#, and (c) the only common attribute for RPJ and J is J#, this expression can easily be defined in such a way as to be semantically equivalent to the earlier version.

Incidentally, observe the effect if the operand ordering is altered thus:

```
J DIVIDEBY S PER ( RPJ, SP )
```

This expression yields $<j,s>$ tuples such that project *j* uses all red parts supplied by supplier *s*.

We now observe that expressions involving DIVIDEBY (either version) can always be replaced by logically simpler—though sometimes lengthier—expressions involving relation comparisons instead (see RM Prescription 22). For example, here is another formulation of the query "Get suppliers who supply every purple part":

```
S WHERE ( ( SP RENAME ( S# AS X ) ) WHERE X = S# ) { P# } ‖≥‖
                      ( P WHERE COLOR = COLOR('Purple') ) { P# }
```

Explanation: For a given supplier, identified by the S# value from some tuple *t* in relvar S, the expression

```
( ( SP RENAME ( S# AS X ) ) WHERE X = S# ) { P# }
```

yields the set of part numbers for parts shown in relvar SP as currently being supplied by that supplier. That set of part numbers is then compared with the set of part numbers currently appearing in relvar P for purple parts. If and only if the two sets are equal, then that tuple *t* from relvar S is included in the result. (We have omitted the final projection over supplier numbers for simplicity, since it would probably not be wanted in practice anyway.)

We also show an alternative formulation of the same query (still involving a relational comparison, but avoiding the use of RENAME) in order to illustrate another point:

```
S WHERE ( ( SP JOIN RELATION { TUPLE { S# S# } } ) { P# } ‖≥‖
                    ( P WHERE COLOR = COLOR('Purple') ) { P# }
```

Explanation: For a given supplier, identified by the S# value from some tuple *t* in relvar S, the expression

```
SP JOIN RELATION { TUPLE { S# S# } }
```

yields the set of shipments currently appearing in relvar SP for that supplier (the second S# in the expression as written is a reference to the S# attribute of relvar S). The rest of the explanation is as before.

We close this section with a somewhat embarrassing admission. The fact is, we have belatedly realized that our own language **Tutorial D** fails to satisfy one of our declared principles of good language design! The principle in question is known as *similarity* [6] or *syntactic consistency* [31] (see RM Prescription 26), and the failure concerns the syntax for <*divide*> and <*summarize*>. These constructs both make use of a construct called <*per*>, and they do so for similar purposes. But a certain cognitive dissonance between them can be observed, which we now explain.

Consider first the use of <*per*> in <*summarize*>, as in the following example ("For each supplier, get a count of the number of parts supplied by that supplier"):

```
SUMMARIZE SP PER ( S { S# } ) ADD ( COUNT ( ) AS NO_OF_PARTS )
```

Compare this expression with our earlier example of a Small Divide ("Get suppliers who supply every purple part"):

```
WITH ( P WHERE COLOR = COLOR('Purple') ) AS PP :
S { S# } DIVIDEBY PP { P# } PER ( SP { S#, P# } )
```

In the <*summarize*> example, the "PER relation" gives the supplier numbers of the suppliers we are interested in, while what we might call the primary operand, SP, gives the information we seek regarding those suppliers. In the <*divide*> example, by contrast, one of the primary operands—the dividend, S{S#}—gives supplier numbers of the suppliers we are interested in, while the divisor, PP{P#}, gives part numbers of the parts we are interested in and the "PER relation" gives the information we seek regarding those suppliers and those parts.

The *<summarize>* syntax looks right: The relation to be summarized is indeed (the current value of) SP and not S{S#}. It seems, therefore, that our mistake is in the syntax of *<divide>*. To be consistent with *<summarize>*, our Small Divide example should look like this:

```
WITH ( P WHERE COLOR = COLOR('Purple') ) AS PP :
SP { S#, P# } DIVIDEBY PP { P# } PER ( S { S# } )
```

Here the dividend and the "PER relation" have been interchanged; in other words, the "PER relation" gives the suppliers we are interested in, the divisor gives the parts we are interested in, and the dividend gives the information we need about those suppliers and parts.

Similarly, our example of a Great Divide—

```
S { S# } DIVIDEBY J { J# } PER ( SP { S#, P# }, RPJ { P#, J# } )
```

—would look better like this:

```
SP { S#, P# } DIVIDEBY RPJ { P#, J# } PER ( S { S# } , J { J# } )
```

Here the *two* "PER relations" give the suppliers and projects we are interested in, and the dividend and divisor give the shipment and usage information we need about those suppliers and projects.

This change to our syntax for *<divide>*, if implemented, would have the following satisfactory effect: For both the Small Divide and the Great Divide, the heading of the result would be the union of the headings of the dividend and divisor, minus the common attributes. It is not so easy to determine an analogous rule with reference to the actual **Tutorial D** syntax.

We offer this lamentable failure on our part as an object lesson to language designers everywhere. We spare you the details of how it happened ... Suffice it to say that language design is hard.

RM PRESCRIPTION 19: RELVAR NAMES, RELATION SELECTORS, AND RECURSION

***Relvar names** and **relation selector invocations** shall both be valid relational expressions.* ***Recursion** shall be permitted in relational expressions.*

In **Tutorial D,** relvar names and relation selector invocations are indeed both valid relational expressions. First, the expression *R,* where *R* is a relvar name, serves as a (relation) *variable reference;* it denotes the value of relvar *R* at the time in question. Second, relation selector invocations were discussed under RM Prescriptions 7 and 10; we have seen several examples already, both in this chapter and in Chapter 2, but here are a couple more:

```
RELATION { S# S#, P# P#, QTY QTY } { TUPLE { S# SX, P# PX, QTY QX * 3 } ,
                                     TUPLE { S# SY, P# PY, QTY QY * 7 } }
```

This expression takes the overall form:

```
RELATION <heading> <body>
```

The *<heading>* is { S# S#, P# P#, QTY QTY }, while the body in turn takes the form:

```
{ <tuple exp commalist> }
```

In the example, the commalist contains two *<tuple exp>* s, each of which is in fact a tuple selector invocation. *Note:* Actually, the *<heading>* in the foregoing example could safely be omitted because it is implied by the declared type of the two tuple selector invocations. The example could thus be simplified to just:

```
RELATION { TUPLE { S# SX, P# PX, QTY QX * 3 } ,
           TUPLE { S# SY, P# PY, QTY QY * 7 } }
```

By way of another example, recall from Chapter 5 that **Tutorial D** supports the two built-in "relcons" TABLE_DEE and TABLE_DUM. These names stand for the relation selector invocations

```
RELATION { } { TUPLE { } }
```

and

```
RELATION { } { }
```

(respectively). In each case, the first pair of braces denotes an empty heading; it can be omitted from the TABLE_DEE expansion, but not from the TABLE_DUM expansion (why not?). See the discussion of RM Prescription 10 for further explanation.

Turning now to recursion: First of all, **Tutorial D** includes direct support for the transitive closure operator TCLOSE, whose definition is inherently recursive. Consider the bill-of-materials relation MM shown in Fig. 6.1. That relation is an example of what is sometimes called a *digraph relation,* because it can be represented as a graph of nodes and directed arcs (see Fig. 6.2). *Note:* It is sometimes more convenient from an intuitive point of view to convert a digraph such as that of Fig. 6.2 into a pure hierarchy with possibly repeated nodes. Fig. 6.3 shows a hierarchic version of the digraph of Fig. 6.2.

MM	MAJOR_P# : P#	MINOR_P# : P#
	P1	P2
	P1	P3
	P2	P3
	P2	P4
	P3	P5
	P4	P6

Fig. 6.1: Relation MM

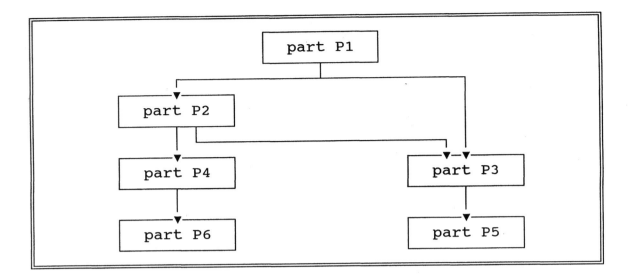

Fig. 6.2: Graph of relation MM

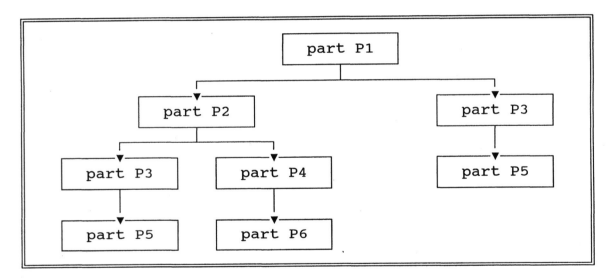

Fig. 6.3: Graph of relation MM as a hierarchy

Now, since MM has exactly two attributes both of the same type, we can apply the transitive closure operation to it. Here is a definition of that operation (an alternative to the one already given in Chapter 2). Let r be a binary relation with attributes X and Y, both of the same type T. Then the **transitive closure** of r, TCLOSE r, is a relation r^+ with heading the same as that of r and body a superset of that of r, defined as follows: The tuple $\{<X,T,x>,<Y,T,y>\}$ appears in r^+ if and only if it appears in r or there exists a value z of type T such that the tuple $\{<X,T,x>,<Y,T,z>\}$ appears in r and the tuple $\{<X,T,z>,<Y,T,y>\}$ appears in r^+. (In other words, the "$<x,y>$" tuple appears in r^+ only if there is a path in the graph from node x to node y, loosely speaking.) Fig. 6.4 opposite shows the transitive closure of relation MM.

TCLOSE is important in connection with the *part explosion* problem—i.e., the problem of finding all components, at all levels, of some specified part—and similar "recursive query" applications.

MAJOR_P# : P#	MINOR_P# : P#
P1	P2
P1	P3
P2	P3
P2	P4
P3	P5
P4	P6
P1	P4
P1	P5
P1	P6
P2	P5
P2	P6

Fig. 6.4: Transitive closure of MM

Tutorial D also includes the ability for users to define recursive operators of their own. Here is an example:

```
OPERATOR TRANCLO ( XY RELATION { X P#, Y P# } ) RETURNS RELATION { X P#, Y P# } ;
   RETURN ( WITH ( XY UNION ( ( XY COMPOSE ( XY RENAME ( Y AS Z, X AS Y ) ) )
                                                  RENAME ( Z AS Y ) ) ) AS TTT :
           IF TTT = XY THEN TTT          /* unwind recursion    */
              ELSE TRANCLO ( TTT )        /* recursive invocation */
           END IF ) ;
END OPERATOR ;
```

Operator TRANCLO takes a relational parameter and returns a relational result. Now let relation MM be as shown in Fig. 6.1. Then the expression

```
( TRANCLO ( MM RENAME ( MAJOR_P# AS X , MINOR_P# AS Y ) ) )
                          RENAME ( X AS MAJOR_P# , Y AS MINOR_P# )
```

returns the result shown in Fig. 6.4 *without* using the built-in operator TCLOSE. (We make no claim that TRANCLO is very efficient, but it can surely be improved in this regard.)

We close this discussion of recursion by pointing out that we could if we wanted define the transitive closure of MM as a virtual relvar, using either TCLOSE—

```
VAR MMTC VIRTUAL ( TCLOSE ( MM ) ) ;
```

—or TRANCLO:

```
VAR MMTC VIRTUAL ( ( TRANCLO ( MM RENAME ( MAJOR_P# AS X , MINOR_P# AS Y ) ) )
                          RENAME ( X AS MAJOR_P# , Y AS MINOR_P# ) ) ;
```

RM PRESCRIPTION 20: USER-DEFINED TUPLE AND RELATIONAL OPERATORS

*D shall provide facilities for users to define and destroy their own **tuple operators** (user-defined tuple operators) and **relational operators** (user-defined relational operators). Paragraphs a.-c. from RM Prescription 3 shall apply, mutatis mutandis.*

For simplicity we concentrate in what follows on relational operators specifically, but many of the points apply to tuple operators equally well, mutatis mutandis.

A relational operator is an operator that, when invoked, returns a relation value. RM Prescription 18 requires support for certain built-in relational operators; the present prescription additionally requires users to be able to define their own. Note, however, that the built-in operators are generic while user-defined ones are not (but see RM Very Strong Suggestion 7 in Chapter 10).

One example of a user-defined relational operator, TRANCLO, was discussed in the previous section. Here is another (and simpler) example:

```
OPERATOR PQO () RETURNS RELATION { P# P#, TOTQ QTY } ;
    RETURN ( SUMMARIZE SP PER ( P { P# } ) ADD ( SUM ( QTY ) AS TOTQ ) ) ;
END OPERATOR ;
```

This operator has no parameters, so an invocation looks like this:

```
PQO ()
```

Here is a moderately complicated example of a relational expression involving two PQO invocations ("Get pairs of part numbers, *px* and *py* say, such that the total quantity for *px* is greater than that for *py*"):

```
( ( ( PQO () RENAME ( P# AS PX, TOTQ AS TQX ) )
       JOIN
     ( PQO () RENAME ( P# AS PY, TOTQ AS TQY ) ) )
       WHERE TQX > TQY ) { PX, PY }
```

Here now is an example of a *parameterized* user-defined relational operator:

```
OPERATOR TQP ( PZ P# ) RETURNS RELATION { TOTQ QTY } ;
    RETURN ( ( PQO () WHERE P# = PZ ) { TOTQ } ) ;
END OPERATOR ;
```

Observe that operator TQP invokes the previously defined operator PQO. Here is an example of its use:

```
VAR P1_TOTQ QTY ;

P1_TOTQ := TOTQ FROM ( TUPLE FROM ( TQP ( P#('P1') ) ) ) ;
```

A run-time error will occur if the expression following TUPLE FROM returns a relation of cardinality anything other than one.

We remark in passing that operator PQO, since it involves no parameters, could logically be replaced by a virtual relvar, thus:

```
VAR PQO VIRTUAL ( SUMMARIZE SP PER ( P { P# } ) ADD ( SUM ( QTY ) AS TOTQ ) ) ;
```

(We do not mean to suggest by these remarks that the expression PQO() should be allowed to appear in a relational target position, however.) By contrast, operator TQP is not equivalent to any virtual relvar.

Finally, here is an example of destroying a user-defined relational operator:

```
DROP OPERATOR TQP ;
```

RM PRESCRIPTION 21: ASSIGNMENTS

*D shall support the **assignment** operator* ":=" *for every type* T. *The assignment shall be referred to as a scalar, tuple, or relation (or relational) assignment according as* T *is a scalar, tuple, or relation type. Let* V *and* v *be a variable and a value, respectively, of the same type. After assignment of* v *to* V, *the equality comparison* V = v *shall evaluate to TRUE (see RM Prescription 8). Furthermore, all variables other than* V *shall remain unchanged, apart possibly from variables defined in terms of* V *or variables in terms of which* V *is defined or both.*

*D shall also support a **multiple** form of assignment, in which several individual assignments shall be performed as a single operation. Let* MA *be the multiple assignment*

```
A1 , A2 , ... , An ;
```

(where A1, A2, …, An *are individual assignments, each assigning to exactly one target variable, and the semicolon marks the overall end of the operation). Then the semantics of* MA *shall be defined by the following pseudocode (Steps a.-d.):*

a. *For* i := 1 *to* n, *expand any syntactic shorthands involved in* Ai. *After all such expansions, let* MA *take the form*

```
V1 := X1 , V2 := X2 , ... , Vz := Xz ;
```

for some z ≥ n, *where* Vi *is the name of some variable not defined in terms of any others and* Xi *is an expression of declared type the same as that of* Vi.

b. *Let* p *and* q *(1 ≤ p < q ≤ z) be such that* Vp *and* Vq *are identical and there is no* r *(r < p or p < r < q) such that* Vp *and* Vr *are identical. Replace* Aq *in* MA *by an assignment of the form*

```
Vq := WITH Xp AS Vq : Xq
```

and remove Ap *from* MA. *Repeat this process until no such pair* p *and* q *remains. Let* MA *now consist of the sequence*

```
U1 := Y1 , U2 := Y2 , ... , Um := Ym ;
```

where each Ui *is some* Vj *(1 ≤ i ≤ j ≤ m ≤ z).*

c. *For* i := 1 *to* m, *evaluate* Yi. *Let the result be* yi.

d. *For* i := 1 *to* m, *assign* yi *to* Ui.

Note: *Step b. of the foregoing pseudocode makes use of the WITH construct of **Tutorial D**. For further explanation, see Chapter 5.*

——— ◆ ◆ ◆ ◆ ———

Of course, we have seen many examples of assignment in this book already. However, there is quite a lot more to be said on the subject:

- First of all, we remind you yet again that assignment is the only update operator we need, logically speaking. For this reason, assignment is the only update operator actually prescribed by the *Manifesto*. But additional update operators, either system or user defined, are of course not precluded. (We remind you too that assignment itself is required only because of our assumption, discussed in Chapter 1, that **D** is imperative in style.)

- RM Prescription 21 requires that after assignment of the value v to the variable V, the comparison $V = v$ must give TRUE. Of course, this requirement is effectively just a definition of what it *means* to assign v to V; as mentioned in Chapter 3, we refer to it as *The Assignment Principle*. Note that the principle applies to views (i.e., virtual relvars) in particular. For example, let LS be "suppliers in London":

```
VAR LS VIRTUAL ( S WHERE CITY = 'London' ) ;
```

Then the following INSERT on LS will fail:

```
INSERT LS RELATION
        { TUPLE { S# S#('S6'), SNAME NAME('Lopez'), STATUS 30, CITY 'Madrid' } } ;
```

Observe that the INSERT fails, and the database remains unchanged, even though it would clearly be possible "to insert the new tuple" into the underlying real relvar S. The trouble is, that new tuple would not appear in the target relvar LS, and we would be faced with a violation of *The Assignment Principle*. *Note:* In fact, an SQL version of the example might "succeed" by doing exactly that—i.e., violating *The Assignment Principle* [41,99].

- Recall from RM Prescription 3 that assignment (":=") is overloaded, in the sense that assigning v to V, where v and V are of the same type T, is supported for all types T. In fact, we do not preclude the possibility of allowing v and V to be of different types (thereby supporting assignment of, e.g., an integer value to a rational variable, or a U.S. dollar value to a U.K. sterling variable); in other words, we do not preclude the possibility of overloading ":=" still further. **Tutorial D,** however, assumes that the operator is not further overloaded in this way, but instead requires its operands always to be of the same type.

- Recall from RM Prescriptions 7 and 6, respectively, that **Tutorial D** supports the familiar INSERT, DELETE, and UPDATE operators as shorthand for certain relational assignments, and a tuple UPDATE operator as shorthand for a certain tuple assignment. In fact, it also supports a scalar UPDATE operator as shorthand for a certain scalar assignment. Here is an example:

```
TYPE ELLIPSE POSSREP { A LENGTH, B LENGTH, CTR POINT CONSTRAINT A ≥ B } ;

VAR E ELLIPSE ;

UPDATE E ( B := LENGTH ( 3.0 ) ) ;
```

The UPDATE statement here is shorthand for the following scalar assignment:

```
E := ELLIPSE ( THE_A ( E ), LENGTH ( 3.0 ), THE_CTR ( E ) ) ;
```

We will have more to say regarding this scalar UPDATE operator under RM Prescription 23.

Multiple Assignment

RM **Prescription** 21 also requires support for **multiple** assignment (and we occasionally refer to the conventional assignment operator as *single* assignment, for emphasis). In effect, multiple assignment allows us to carry out several presumably interrelated single assignments as an atomic operation, without any integrity checking being done until all of the assignments in question have been executed. For example, suppose that—for some strange reason—relvar S is subject to the constraint that suppliers S2 and S3 must have total status 40. Given our usual sample data values, then, each of the following single assignments will fail (we use the UPDATE shorthand for convenience):

```
UPDATE S WHERE S# = S#('S2') ( STATUS := 15 ) ;

UPDATE S WHERE S# = S#('S3') ( STATUS := 25 ) ;
```

But the following *multiple* assignment will succeed (again we use the UPDATE shorthand; note that the two component assignments are separated by a comma, not a semicolon, and are thereby bundled into a single operation):

```
UPDATE S WHERE S# = S#('S2') ( STATUS := 15 ) ,
UPDATE S WHERE S# = S#('S3') ( STATUS := 25 ) ;
```

The foregoing example shows multiple assignment on a single target relvar. Here by contrast is an example with two distinct targets (and this time we use the DELETE shorthand):

```
DELETE SP WHERE S# = S#('S1') ,
DELETE S  WHERE S# = S#('S1') ;
```

RM Prescription 21 includes a precise definition of the semantics of multiple assignment.[1] The basic idea is that, first, all of the source expressions are evaluated; second, the constituent single assignments are executed in sequence. Now, the reason all of the source expressions are evaluated first is basically to ensure that the constituent assignments are all independent of one another, in the sense that none of them depends on the result of any of the others. However, a complication arises if two or more of those constituent assignments involve the same target variable (a state of affairs that is not an error, please note; sometimes we do explicitly want the same target variable to appear more than once). Indeed, the "double UPDATE" example already discussed—

```
UPDATE S WHERE S# = S#('S2') ( STATUS := 15 ) ,
UPDATE S WHERE S# = S#('S3') ( STATUS := 25 ) ;
```

—is a case in point. Let us examine this example more closely.

First of all, the double UPDATE shown is shorthand for the following double assignment (this expansion corresponds to Step a. of the definition):

---

1. The semantics are not entirely straightforward; indeed, we got them wrong on at least three previous occasions [84].

```
S := ( S WHERE NOT ( S# = S#('S2') ) )
       UNION
     ( UPDATE S WHERE S# = S#('S2') ( STATUS := 15 ) ) ,
S := ( S WHERE NOT ( S# = S#('S3') ) )
       UNION
     ( UPDATE S WHERE S# = S#('S3') ( STATUS := 25 ) ) ;
```

It should be clear now that if we simply evaluate the two source expressions and then perform the two constituent assignments, the first of those assignments will have no lasting effect. The purpose of Step b. of the definition is to take care of such problems. Applying that step, we replace the foregoing double assignment by the following single one:

```
S := WITH
   ( S WHERE NOT ( S# = S#('S2') ) )
     UNION
   ( UPDATE S WHERE S# = S#('S2') ( STATUS := 15 ) ) AS S :
   ( S WHERE NOT ( S# = S#('S3') ) )
     UNION
   ( UPDATE S WHERE S# = S#('S3') ( STATUS := 25 ) ) ;
```

The net effect is that, loosely speaking, the second of the two constituent assignments is performed on *the result of* the first.

RM PRESCRIPTION 22: COMPARISONS

*D shall support certain **comparison operators**, as follows:*

a.   *The operators for comparing scalars shall include "=",   "≠", and (for ordinal types) "<", ">", etc.*

b.   *The operators for comparing tuples shall include "=" and "≠" and shall not include "<", ">", etc.*

c.   *The operators for comparing relations shall include "=", "≠", "‖≤‖" ("is a subset of"), and "‖≥‖" ("is a superset of") and shall not include "<", ">", etc.*

d.   *The operator "ε" for testing membership of a tuple in a relation shall be supported.*

In every case mentioned except "ε" the comparands shall be of the same type; in the case of "ε" they shall have the same heading. Note: *Support for "=" for every type is in fact required by RM Prescription 8.*

This prescription requires comparands to be of the same type (or, in the case of "ε", to have the same heading). Once again it might be possible to relax this requirement in practice; in **Tutorial D,** however, we adopt the same conservative position as we did with regard to assignment and require comparands to be of exactly the same type. (Except for "ε", which is a special case. Of course, the comparison *t ε r* is logically equivalent to *rt ‖≤‖ r,* where *rt* is a relation containing just tuple *t,* from which fact the type requirements for such a comparison can immediately be inferred.)

Several examples involving relation comparisons specifically have been given earlier in the chapter, under RM Prescriptions 7 and 18.

RM PRESCRIPTION 23: INTEGRITY CONSTRAINTS

*D shall provide facilities for defining and destroying **integrity constraints** (**constraints** for short). Let C be a constraint; C can be thought of as a boolean expression (though it might not be explicitly formulated as such), and it shall be **satisfied** if and only if that boolean expression evaluates to TRUE. No user shall ever see a state of affairs in which C is not satisfied. There shall be two kinds of constraints:*

a. *A **type** constraint shall specify the set of values that constitute a given type.*

b. *A **database** constraint shall specify that values of a given set of database relvars taken in combination shall be such that a given boolean expression (which shall mention no variables other than the database relvars in question) evaluates to TRUE. Insofar as feasible, D shall support **constraint inference** for database constraints, whereby the constraints that apply to the result of evaluating an arbitrary relational expression shall be well defined and known to both the system and the user.*

———— ♦ ♦ ♦ ♦ ————

Chapter 2 gave an overview of the general subject of integrity constraints—in particular, it discussed the two kinds of constraints mentioned in the prescription—but there is quite a lot more to be said on the subject.

Type Constraints

Note: We use the term type *throughout this subsection to mean a scalar type specifically. Tuple and relation types are subject to type constraints as well, but we defer discussion of this issue to the final subsection ("Miscellaneous Issues") in this section.*

A type constraint is, precisely, a definition of the set of values constituting a given type. Several examples were given under RM Prescription 1; we repeat one of those examples here to serve as a basis for further discussion.

```
TYPE ANGLE ORDINAL POSSREP { RHO RATIONAL CONSTRAINT RHO ≥ 0.0
                                      AND RHO < 2 * 3.14159 } ;
```

Explanation: We concentrate on the boolean expression within the CONSTRAINT specification:

```
RHO ≥ 0.0 AND RHO < 2 * 3.14159
```

The two appearances of RHO here denote the RHO possrep component for an arbitrary value of type ANGLE. Values of that type are thereby constrained to be such that they can be represented by a rational number greater than or equal to zero and less than 2π. Any expression that is supposed to evaluate to an angle but does not yield a value in this range will fail.

Now let us generalize from this example. It should be clear that, ultimately, the only way any expression can yield a value of type *T* is by means of some invocation of some selector for type *T*. Hence, the only way any expression can violate the type constraint for type *T* is if the selector invocation in question does so. It follows that *type constraints can always be thought of, at least conceptually, as being checked during the execution of some selector invocation;* that is, we can never tolerate an expression that is supposed to denote a value of type *T* but in fact fails to do so (indeed, "a value of type *T*" that is not a value of type *T* is simply a contradiction in terms). As a consequence, no variable—in particular, no relvar—can ever be assigned a value that is not of the appropriate type.

Incidentally, it might help here to spell out the logical difference between a *type* error and a type *constraint* error:

■ A *type* error occurs if some operator is invoked with an argument not of the type of the corresponding parameter.

■ A type *constraint* error occurs if some selector is invoked with arguments that violate the applicable type constraint.

Type errors should be detectable at compile time—except possibly as noted under OO Prescription 1 in Chapter 8—while type constraint errors will not be detectable until run time, in general.

Anyway, as you can see from the ANGLE example, a type constraint is (as previously stated) basically just a specification of the values that constitute the type in question. In **Tutorial D,** therefore, we bundle such constraints with the definition of a possrep for the type in question, and we identify them by means of the applicable possrep name. It follows that such a constraint can be destroyed only by destroying the corresponding possrep, which in practice might mean destroying the type itself.

Note: Even if it includes no explicit CONSTRAINT specification, a declared possrep represents an *a priori* constraint on the type, of course. For example, the type definition

```
TYPE NAME ORDINAL POSSREP { N CHAR } ;
```

constrains names to be such that they can be represented by a character string. In other words, omitting the CONSTRAINT specification from a given possrep definition is equivalent to specifying CONSTRAINT TRUE.

We now present some further examples in order to illustrate a number of additional points. Here first is the ELLIPSE example once again:

```
TYPE ELLIPSE POSSREP { A LENGTH, B LENGTH, CTR POINT CONSTRAINT A ≥ B } ;
```

Suppose variable E is of type ELLIPSE and its current value has a major semiaxis *a* of length five and a minor semiaxis *b* of length four. Now consider the assignment:

```
THE_B ( E ) := LENGTH ( 6.0 ) ;
```

This assignment will fail (why?), but it is not the assignment per se that is in error. Instead, the error is inside a selector invocation once again—even though no such invocation is directly visible in the example—because the assignment shown is really shorthand for this longer one:

```
E := ELLIPSE ( THE_A ( E ), LENGTH ( 6.0 ), THE_CTR ( E ) ) ;
```

And it is the selector invocation on the right side here that fails (at run time, too, be it noted).

Next consider type POINT, which has two possreps, POINT (cartesian coordinates) and POLAR (polar coordinates). Suppose for the sake of the example that the only points we are interested in are those that lie within a circle with center the origin and radius 100:

```
TYPE POINT POSSREP POINT { X RATIONAL, Y RATIONAL
                           CONSTRAINT SQRT ( X ** 2 + Y ** 2 ) ≤ 100.0 }
            POSSREP POLAR { R LENGTH, THETA ANGLE
                           CONSTRAINT R ≤ LENGTH ( 100.0 )
                               AND IF R = LENGTH ( 0.0 )
                                   THEN THETA = ANGLE ( 0.0 ) END IF } ;
```

The constraint checking here is done, conceptually, during execution of invocations of the POINT and POLAR selectors. Note carefully that the two possreps are logically equivalent, in the sense that every value of the type can possibly be represented either way; indeed, it would be an error if they were not equivalent in this sense. Given this state of affairs, therefore, we can talk unambiguously in terms of "the" type constraint for type POINT; in general, in fact, we can regard any given type as being subject to exactly one type constraint.

Now we turn to a fairly complicated example (an extended form of one previously discussed under RM Prescription 1):

```
TYPE POLYGON POSSREP { VERTICES RELATION { V# INTEGER, VERTEX POINT }
                CONSTRAINT
                    WITH COUNT ( VERTICES ) AS N :
                        COUNT ( VERTICES { V# } ) = N AND
                        COUNT ( VERTICES { VERTEX } ) = N AND
                        IS_EMPTY ( VERTICES WHERE V# < 1 OR V# > N ) } ;
```

Explanation: Note first that, as explained under RM Prescription 1, type POLYGON is still a scalar type, despite the fact that it has a possrep that involves a relational component. The CONSTRAINT specification involves three separate constraints all ANDed together. The first constrains values of type POLYGON to be such that no two tuples in the VERTICES relation have the same vertex number (V#); the second constrains values of type POLYGON to be such that no two tuples in the VERTICES relation have the same vertex (VERTEX). The third (together with the first) ensures that if polygon *p* has *n* vertices, then the *n* tuples in the VERTICES relation for *p* contain exactly the V# values 1, 2, ..., *n*.

Finally, we return to type ELLIPSE in order to make another point. Suppose as before that variable E is of type ELLIPSE and its current value has major and minor semiaxes of length five and four, respectively, and consider the following assignment:

```
THE_A ( E ) := LENGTH ( 3.0 ) , THE_B ( E ) := LENGTH ( 2.0 ) ;
```

Applying the definition of multiple assignment from RM Prescription 21, we discover that this statement is shorthand for this one:

```
E := WITH ELLIPSE ( LENGTH ( 3.0 ), THE_B ( E ), THE_CTR ( E ) ) AS E :
    ELLIPSE ( THE_B ( E ), LENGTH ( 2.0 ), THE_CTR ( E ) ) ;
```

Given the stated initial values (*a* five and *b* four), however, the ellipse selector invocation immediately following WITH will raise a type constraint error at run time; to be specific, it will attempt to produce an ellipse with *a* three and *b* four, thereby violating the constraint $a \geq b$. In order to avoid this problem, we can replace the original multiple assignment to THE_A(E) and THE_B(E) by the following:

```
UPDATE E ( A := LENGTH ( 3.0 ), B := LENGTH ( 2.0 ) ) ;
```

Here we are using the scalar UPDATE operator (see RM Prescription 21), which is defined in the case at hand to be shorthand for the following:

```
E := ELLIPSE ( LENGTH ( 3.0 ), LENGTH ( 2.0 ), THE_CTR ( E ) ) ;
```

Now no type constraint error will occur.

Database Constraints

Note: *We use the term* relvar *throughout this subsection to mean a database relvar specifically.*

A database constraint is a constraint on the values a given database is permitted to assume. Such a constraint must not mention any variables apart from database relvars, but otherwise can be arbitrarily complex. Several examples of such constraints (DBC1-DBC5) were shown in Chapter 2, but we give a few more here.

```
CONSTRAINT DBC6 IS_EMPTY ( P ) OR COUNT ( P WHERE COLOR = COLOR('Red') ) > 0 ;
```

Meaning: If there are any parts at all, at least one of them must be red.

For our next example, we return to the relvar SPQ first discussed under RM Prescription 7:

```
VAR SPQ ... RELATION { S# S#, PQ RELATION { P# P#, QTY QTY } } ... ;

CONSTRAINT DBC7 COUNT    ( SPQ UNGROUP ( PQ ) ) =
                  COUNT ( ( SPQ UNGROUP ( PQ ) ) { S#, P# } ) ;
```

Meaning: Within any SPQ tuple, no two distinct tuples in the PQ value have the same part number; equivalently, {S#,P#} is a superkey—see Chapter 2—for the result of SPQ UNGROUP (PQ) (we are relying here on the fact that {S#} is a candidate key for SPQ). Now, you might be surprised to learn that **Tutorial D** deliberately does not allow attribute PQ of relvar SPQ to be defined thus:

```
PQ RELATION { P# P#, QTY QTY } KEY { P# }
```

One reason for this state of affairs—not the only one—is that such syntax would apparently imply that the *key* constraint for relation-valued attribute PQ (to speak very loosely!) is part of the relation *type* definition for relvar SPQ, which is not the case.

One more example:

```
CONSTRAINT DBC8 SP { P# } = P { P# } ;
```

Meaning: There must be at least one shipment for every part. (Of course, it is also the case that there must be exactly one part for every shipment, by virtue of the fact that {P#} is a candidate key for parts and a matching foreign key for shipments, but we have not bothered to show this latter constraint here.)

Database constraints are conceptually checked at the end of any statement that might cause them to be violated ("immediate checking"). Thus, any statement that attempts to assign a value to a given relvar or combination of relvars that violates any database constraint will effectively just be rejected. *Note:* Conventional wisdom has it that database constraints need not be checked until end-of-transaction or COMMIT time ("deferred checking"). As is shown in reference [84], however, deferred checking opens the door to numerous problems; moreover, given the availability of multiple assignment, which allows us to perform any number of updates as a single operation, it is logically unnecessary, and we therefore prohibit it. In other words (quoting RM Prescription 23, but with added emphasis): *No user shall ever see a state of affairs in which [any constraint] is not satisfied.*

Here is an example of destroying a database constraint:

```
DROP CONSTRAINT DBC3 ;
```

Of course, database constraints can apply to any combination of real and virtual relvars, in general:

- A given real relvar *R* considered in isolation can be regarded as being subject to just those database constraints that mention that relvar *R* (as briefly discussed in Chapter 2).

■ A given virtual relvar *V* considered in isolation can be regarded as being subject to constraints that are derived in the obvious way from the expression that defines *V*. For example, consider the following virtual relvar XS:

```
VAR XS VIRTUAL ( EXTEND S ADD ( 3 * STATUS AS TRIPLE ) ) ;
```

Relvar XS is subject to all of the constraints that apply to relvar S, together with the additional constraint that, within any XS tuple, the TRIPLE value must be three times the STATUS value.

■ For a final example, suppose we define two virtual relvars as follows:

```
VAR LS  VIRTUAL ( S WHERE CITY = 'London' ) ;

VAR NLS VIRTUAL ( S WHERE NOT ( CITY = 'London' ) ) ;
```

Then relvars S, LS, and NLS taken in combination are subject to the following constraint:

```
CONSTRAINT DBC9 D_UNION { LS { S# }, NLS { S# } } = S { S# } ;
```

Constraint Inference

In the past, integrity constraints have typically been thought of as applying to "real" data only, but we regard them as applying to "virtual" data as well, as already indicated. **Constraint inference** is the process of inferring the constraints that apply to such virtual data from those that apply to the real data in terms of which that virtual data is defined.

We have already seen a couple of examples of constraint inference in action (see the examples involving virtual relvar XS in the previous subsection and virtual relvar LS under RM Prescription 21). For more specifics, see Appendix E, also reference [28] and the discussion of RM Very Strong Suggestion 3 in Chapter 10. *Note:* There are known to be certain limits on the degree to which constraint inference might be feasible in practice (see, e.g., reference [5]). This fact accounts for the slightly hesitant tone of the final portion of RM Prescription 23, which requires only that **D** shall support constraint inference "insofar as feasible."

Miscellaneous Issues

We close this section with a few miscellaneous points having to do with integrity constraints in general.

First we consider the question of type constraints for tuple and relation types. Such types are certainly subject to such constraints, but the constraints in question are essentially just a logical consequence of those that apply to the types in terms of which those tuple and relation types are defined. For example, consider the following tuple type once again:

```
TUPLE { NAME NAME, ADDR TUPLE { STREET CHAR, CITY CHAR, STATE CHAR, ZIP CHAR } }
```

Values of this type are constrained to be tuples with two components, NAME and ADDR. Values of the NAME component are constrained to be values of type NAME. Values of the ADDR component are constrained to be tuples with four components, STREET, CITY, STATE, and ZIP ... and so on.

Now, it might be desirable to impose more restrictive type constraints on tuple and relation types (more restrictive, that is, than those just mentioned—viz., the ones implied by the types in terms of which those tuple and relation types are defined). In the case of the tuple type just discussed, for example, we might want to impose the additional constraint that STATE values are valid U.S. state names. Now, we can achieve this particular effect easily enough by specifying attribute STATE to be of type STATE_NAME, say (instead of CHAR), where STATE_NAME is defined as follows:

```
TYPE STATE_NAME POSSREP { SN CHAR CONSTRAINT SN = 'Alabama'
                                      OR SN = 'Alaska'
                                      . . . . . . . . . . . .
                                      OR SN = 'Wyoming' } ;
```

What we cannot do, however, is say that STATE is of type STATE_NAME as just defined *and* that STATE values are limited to (say) Alaska, California, and Hawaii.[1] In order to be able to do such a thing, we would need to be able to express an appropriate type constraint as part of the operation that defines the tuple type in question. And we saw under RM Prescription 6 that **Tutorial D,** at least, currently (and deliberately) supports no such operation.

The second of our miscellaneous issues has to do with constraints on application-local or nondatabase data. RM Prescription 23 concentrates on database data specifically[2] because database data is the principal focus of the *Manifesto.* However, constraints analogous to those we have been discussing could well apply to local or private data also; to be specific, such constraints could apply to scalar and tuple variables and to private relvars. (Public relvars are a special case; the constraints that apply to those are derived, in accordance with the constraint inference mechanism already discussed, from the constraints that apply to their counterparts in the database.) We choose not to discuss such matters any further in this book.

The last of our miscellaneous issues has to do with *business rules.* Now, this term is not very precisely defined, but one interpretation is that a business rule is simply an integrity constraint (albeit one that is, usually, expressed in natural language instead of a formal language like **Tutorial D**). Thus, a DBMS that supports integrity constraints in accordance with RM Prescription 23 might be seen as what some writers would refer to as a *rule engine* [66].

RM PRESCRIPTION 24: TOTAL DATABASE CONSTRAINTS

Let DB be a database; let DBC1, DBC2, ..., DBCn be all of the database constraints defined for DB (see RM Prescription 23); and let DBC be any boolean expression that is logically equivalent to

```
( DBC1 ) AND ( DBC2 ) AND ... AND ( DBCn ) AND TRUE
```

*Then DB is **the total database constraint** for DB.*

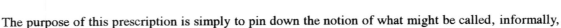

The purpose of this prescription is simply to pin down the notion of what might be called, informally, "the" constraint for a given database. Loosely speaking, the *total* constraint for a given database is the logical AND of all of the individual constraints specified for that database.

Note: RM Prescription 23 requires that no user shall ever see a state of affairs in which any individual database constraint is violated, and hence necessarily that no user shall ever see a state of affairs in which the total database constraint is violated. Thus, no assignment statement can ever leave

---

1. We could use the facilities defined in Part IV of this book to achieve something similar—though not identical—to the desired effect, but the details are beyond the scope of the present discussion.

2. And on types, of course, which are relevant to both database and nondatabase data.

the database in a state that violates its own total constraint: a state of affairs that we refer to as **The Golden Rule**.

RM PRESCRIPTION 25: CATALOG

*Every database shall include a set of database relvars that constitute the **catalog** for that database. **D** shall provide facilities for assigning to relvars in the catalog.*

Note that—as is in fact required by RM Prescriptions 16 and 17—we regard the catalog as part of the database it describes, not as a separate database in its own right. It follows that the catalog must be self-describing. This point aside, we deliberately make no attempt to prescribe the structure of the catalog in detail.

As for **D** providing "facilities for assigning to relvars in the catalog": All this means is that it must be possible for suitably authorized users to update the catalog appropriately. In practice, of course, such assignments will normally be performed by means of data definition operators: "define type," "define relvar," "define constraint," "drop type," and so on. (Note, therefore, that "define type" and the rest are all update operators, in the last analysis.)

RM PRESCRIPTION 26: LANGUAGE DESIGN

*D shall be constructed according to well-established principles of **good language design**.*

As with RM Prescription 18 (where we required the operators of the relational algebra to be "expressible without excessive circumlocution"), we recognize that this prescription is not very precise as it stands, but it is difficult to make it more so. However, the general intent is just that **D** should avoid the many design errors we observe in SQL in particular (see, for example, references [41], [44-45], and [62], among others). To quote reference [43]:

> There are well-established principles for the design of languages, but little evidence that SQL has been designed in accordance with any of them [*slightly reworded*].

Examples of such principles include *generality, parsimony, completeness, similarity, extensibility, openness,* and especially *orthogonality*. (This list is taken from reference [6]; a somewhat similar list can be found in reference [31]. See also the remarks on *conceptual integrity* in Chapter 1.) In connection with the principle of *orthogonality* in particular [54], we would like to say that we agree strongly with the following remarks from reference [119]:

> Most languages are too big and intellectually unmanageable. The problems arise in part because the language is too restrictive; the number of rules needed to define a language increases when a general rule has additional rules attached to constrain its use in certain cases. (Ironically, these additional rules usually make the language *less* powerful.) ... *Power through simplicity, simplicity through generality, should be the guiding principle* [*italics in the original*].

EXERCISES

1.   RM Prescription 1 requires support for "all four monadic and 16 dyadic logical operators." Give truth tables for all of these operators.

2.   The dyadic logical operator NOR (also known as the *Peirce arrow* and usually written as a down arrow, "↓") is defined to return TRUE if and only if both of its operands are FALSE. In other words, the expression $p \downarrow q$ is equivalent to NOT p AND NOT q (it can be thought of as *neither nor*—neither the first nor the second operand is TRUE). Show that all 20 monadic and dyadic logical operators can be formulated in terms of this operator alone. Is the same true of the operator OR? (OR, of course, can be thought of as the negation of NOR.)

3.   Define a virtual relvar ("view") consisting of supplier numbers and part numbers for suppliers and parts that are not colocated.

4.   **Tutorial D** goes beyond RM Prescription 6 in that it supports tuple analogs of certain additional relational operators: *compose, wrap/unwrap*, and *substitute* (see Chapter 5). Provide definitions for these tuple operators.

5.   Show that the relational operators GROUP and UNGROUP are really just shorthand for certain combinations of other operators.

6.   Reference [85] defines another relational operator of a grouping nature called PACK (as well as a corresponding UNPACK operator). If you are familiar with these operators, are GROUP and UNGROUP just special cases? Justify your answer.

7.   SQL includes a "relational" update operator called MERGE that can be described, informally, as a combination of INSERT and UPDATE; very loosely speaking, each source tuple is used to update the matching target tuple, if such a matching tuple exists, or is inserted otherwise. Design an analogous operator for **Tutorial D**.

8.   Why are there only two relations of degree zero?

9.   The following SQL query is not valid but should be:

```
SELECT DISTINCT
FROM    S, SP
WHERE   S.S# = SP.S#
AND     S.CITY = 'Athens'
```

What do you think it should return? Give a natural language interpretation of the query. What do you think the interpretation should be if DISTINCT were omitted?

10.   TABLE_DEE and TABLE_DUM can be interpreted as TRUE and FALSE, respectively. So can we dispense with type BOOLEAN after all?

11.   Investigate the effect of the algebraic operations discussed under RM Prescription 18 on TABLE_DEE and TABLE_DUM.

12.   Let R be defined as TCLOSE A. What is the predicate for R?

13.   In the body of the chapter, we gave one reason why **Tutorial D** does not provide a separate

"define tuple type" or "define relation type" operator. Can you think of any other advantages of the **Tutorial D** approach?

14. Loosely, we might say that two databases *DB1* and *DB2* are *information equivalent* if and only if every relation that can be derived from *DB1* can also be derived from *DB2* and vice versa. What is involved in making this definition more precise?

15. Show that any expression involving SUMMARIZE can always be replaced by one involving EXTEND instead.

16. Let E be a variable of declared type ELLIPSE (see, e.g., RM Prescription 1 for a definition of this type). What is the logical difference, if any, between the following statements?

```
UPDATE E ( B := LENGTH ( 2.0 ) ) ;

THE_B ( E ) := LENGTH ( 2.0 ) ;
```

17. With E as in the previous exercise, show the expanded form of the following statement:

```
UPDATE E ( A := LENGTH ( 3.0 ), THE_X ( CTR ) := 5.0 ) ;
```

18. Let that same variable E denote an ellipse with *a* five and *b* four. Then the following statement will give rise to a type error; why?

```
THE_A ( E ) := LENGTH ( 3.0 ) , THE_B ( E ) := LENGTH ( 2.0 ) ;
```

The following, by contrast, will not; why not?

```
UPDATE E ( A := LENGTH ( 3.0 ), B := LENGTH ( 2.0 ) ) ;
```

19. Let operator INTEGERS be as follows: The expression INTEGERS(a,b)—where we assume for simplicity that $a \leq b$—yields a relation with just one attribute (also of type INTEGER) called N. The body of that relation contains one tuple for each integer from a to b inclusive (each such tuple containing just the integer in question) and no other tuples. Write a **Tutorial D** definition of this operator.

20. Consider relvar SPQ, discussed under RM Prescription 7 and elsewhere:

```
VAR SPQ REAL RELATION { S# S#, PQ RELATION { P# P#, QTY QTY } } KEY { S# } ;
```

What is the predicate for this relvar?

21. Let *T* be an **ordered tree,** defined as follows. *T* consists of *N* nodes ($N \geq 0$). Every node has a sequence of *M* **child** nodes ($M \geq 0$); if $M = 0$, the node is a **leaf** node. Every child node has exactly one **parent** node. If $N > 0$, exactly one node (the **root**) is not a child node. Devise a relational representation for *T*. Define and write implementation code for operators to traverse *T* in preorder, postorder, and inorder (see, e.g., Knuth [105] if you are not familiar with these terms).

22. Several commercial products support the concept of *tuple IDs* in some shape or form. If you are familiar with such a product, do you think its support for tuple IDs constitutes a violation of *The Information Principle*? Justify your answer.

23. Does it make sense for a possrep to have a component whose type is empty?

24. Why is the phrase "an empty relation type" a contradiction in terms?

25. Can you think of an example of a type that might sensibly be recursively defined? Can you give a **Tutorial D** definition for such a type?

26. Does **Tutorial D** as defined in Chapter 5 prohibit recursively defined tuple and relation types? If not, do you think it should?

27. Evaluate **Tutorial D** against RM Prescription 26.

Chapter 7

RM Proscriptions

RM PROSCRIPTION 1: NO ATTRIBUTE ORDERING

*D shall include no concept of a "relation" whose attributes are distinguishable by ordinal position.
Instead, for every relation* r *expressible in* **D**, *the attributes of* r *shall be distinguishable by* name.

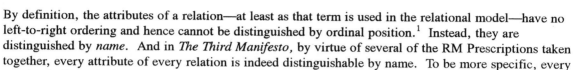

By definition, the attributes of a relation—at least as that term is used in the relational model—have no left-to-right ordering and hence cannot be distinguished by ordinal position.[1] Instead, they are distinguished by *name*. And in *The Third Manifesto,* by virtue of several of the RM Prescriptions taken together, every attribute of every relation is indeed distinguishable by name. To be more specific, every relation in **D** is obtained by evaluating some relational expression, and (at least in **Tutorial D**) the rules for such expressions are such as to guarantee that the desired property is satisfied. For let *rx* be such an expression. Then:

- If *rx* consists of a relational expression enclosed in parentheses, then its semantics are the same as if those parentheses were removed.

- If *rx* consists of a relation selector invocation, then the attribute names are specified, implicitly or explicitly, as part of that invocation.

- If *rx* consists of a relvar reference (in other words, a relvar name), then the attribute names are specified, implicitly or explicitly, as part of the definition of the relvar in question.

- If *rx* consists of a THE_ operator invocation in which the possrep component being accessed is relation valued, then the attribute names are specified, implicitly or explicitly, as part of the definition of the relation-valued component in question.

- If *rx* consists of an attribute extractor invocation in which the attribute being accessed is relation valued, then the attribute names are specified, implicitly or explicitly, as part of the definition of the attribute in question.

- If *rx* consists of an invocation of a user-defined relational operator, then the attribute names are specified, implicitly or explicitly, as part of the definition of the operator in question.

- If *rx* consists of an invocation of some built-in relational operator, then the attribute names are inferred by means of the prescribed relation type inference mechanism.

- If *rx* consists of an <*introduced name*> or a <*relation with expression*>, then *rx* is basically shorthand for one of the cases already considered.

---

1. For reasons that need not concern us here, relations in mathematics, unlike their counterparts in the relational model, do have a left-to-right order to their attributes (and likewise for tuples, of course).

Despite all of the foregoing, we still feel it worthwhile to state RM Proscription 1 explicitly, owing to the mistakes we observe in SQL in this connection (mistakes, in fact, that show—or, rather, are among those that show—that SQL tables are not true relations). Among other things, the proscription implies:

- No anonymous attributes, as in SQL's SELECT A+B FROM T and its VALUES construct (the latter of which is effectively SQL's counterpart to the *Manifesto*'s relation selector)

- No duplicate attribute names, as in SQL's SELECT A, A FROM T and SELECT T1.A, T2.A FROM T1, T2

- No shorthands that rely on attribute ordering, as in SQL's SELECT * INTO ... FROM T and INSERT INTO T VALUES (...)[1]

- No hidden "tuple ID" or timestamp attributes, as in some of today's SQL implementations

The problems caused by a failure to abide by RM Proscription 1 are discussed in detail in references [32] and [75].

A note on SQL: The experienced SQL user might observe that SQL applications can sometimes safely use what might be called "pseudorelational" expressions such as SELECT A+B FROM T by providing the required column names in the context (the context, that is, in which those expressions are embedded). For example, the expression

```
SELECT * FROM ( SELECT A + B FROM T ) AS X ( C )
```

returns a table with a single column named C, despite the anonymous column in the table returned by the subquery SELECT A+B FROM T. Similarly, the expression

```
VALUES ( 1, 2 )
```

returns a table with one row and two anonymous columns; however, in the expression

```
SELECT A FROM ( VALUES ( 1, 2 ) ) AS T ( A, B )
```

the column names A and B are specified in the context. Analogous remarks apply to examples like this one:

```
INSERT INTO T ( A, B ) VALUES ( 1, 2 ) ;
```

Clearly, applications that use such "pseudorelational" expressions only in safe contexts are immune to external changes in column order. Thus, it might be argued that the syntax SQL provides for "pseudorelational" expressions can conveniently be used in place of relational expressions in certain safe contexts. But admitting "pseudorelations" into the language at all gives rise to all sorts of needless complication for everybody concerned: end users, administrators, application developers, teachers, students, standardizers, DBMS implementers, and so on. Hence this proscription, and hence **Tutorial D**'s required attribute names in the syntax for its EXTEND, SUMMARIZE, and relation selector

---

1. The problem with these SQL constructs is that they rely on the left-to-right attribute ordering as defined in the corresponding CREATE or ALTER TABLE statement(s), instead of on a left-to-right ordering specified within the SELECT or INSERT statement itself.

operators.

RM PROSCRIPTION 2: NO TUPLE ORDERING

D shall include no concept of a "relation" whose tuples are distinguishable by ordinal position. Instead, for every relation r expressible in D, the tuples of r shall be distinguishable by value.

By definition, the tuples of a relation have no top-to-bottom ordering and hence cannot be distinguished by ordinal position. Of course, this fact does not mean that such an ordering cannot be imposed for, e.g., presentation purposes; however, it does mean that the effect of imposing such an ordering is to convert the relation into something that is not a relation (typically a one-dimensional array of tuples—see the discussion of RM Proscription 7 later in this chapter). It also means that:

- The operator that imposes the ordering is not a relational operator, precisely because the result is not a relation.

- The operator in question therefore cannot appear in a relational expression; in particular, it cannot appear in the definition of a virtual relvar.

RM PROSCRIPTION 3: NO DUPLICATE TUPLES

D shall include no concept of a "relation" containing two distinct tuples t1 and t2 such that the comparison "t1 = t2" evaluates to TRUE. It follows that (as already stated in RM Proscription 2), for every relation r expressible in D, the tuples of r shall be distinguishable by value.

By definition, relations do not contain duplicate tuples. Yet SQL does permit duplicate "tuples" in its tables[1]—another of the many reasons why SQL tables are not true relations [72]. In the *Manifesto,* by contrast, duplicate tuples are absolutely, categorically, and unequivocally outlawed. What we tell you three times is true.

RM PROSCRIPTION 4: NO NULLS

D shall include no concept of a "relation" in which some "tuple" includes some "attribute" that does not have a value.

By definition, tuples, and therefore relations, do not contain nulls (nulls are not values!). SQL, however, does permit nulls in its tables—yet another reason why SQL tables are not true relations. In the

---

1. Possibly because the SQL designers thought duplicate removal would be expensive, especially if the table in question in fact had no duplicates in the first place. However, reference [28] shows that it is often possible to prove that duplicates cannot occur, in which case the duplicate removal process can be "optimized away."

Manifesto, by contrast, nulls are absolutely, categorically, and unequivocally outlawed (and so too therefore is *n*-valued logic for any $n > 2$).

RM PROSCRIPTION 5: NO NULLOLOGICAL MISTAKES

D shall not forget that relations with no attributes are respectable and interesting, nor that candidate keys with no components are likewise respectable and interesting.

Nullology is the study of the empty set [29] (it has nothing to with nulls!). Now, sets in general are ubiquitous in the relational world; for example, a relation has both a set of attributes and a set of tuples. And, since the empty set is certainly a set, it follows that wherever **D** permits sets in general to appear, it should permit empty sets in particular to appear as well. Two important special cases are those mentioned in this proscription: relations with no attributes and candidate keys with no components. We discussed the first of these under RM Prescription 10 in Chapter 6; now we offer a few words on the second.

Since relations and relvars with no attributes are permitted, candidate keys with no components ("empty keys") must certainly be permitted too. Indeed, such a key is the only candidate key—the only possible candidate key!—for a relvar with no attributes; but other relvars (i.e., relvars with at least one attribute) can have empty keys, too. In fact, to say that relvar *R* has an empty key is to say, precisely and possibly usefully, that *R* never contains more than one tuple [29]. Incidentally, if relvar *R* has an empty key, then that empty key is the only key for *R* (why?).

At the time of writing, SQL does not support either relations with no attributes or keys with no components. *Note:* These omissions are not the only nullological mistakes in SQL, but they are among the most egregious. Others include incorrect treatment, in a variety of ways, of relations with no tuples (see, e.g., references [49-50] and [62]), and inconsistent treatment, again in a variety of ways, of dyadic relational operators when the relations involved have no common attributes (see, e.g., reference [41]). See also the discussion of OO Prescription 6 in Chapter 8.

RM PROSCRIPTION 6: NO INTERNAL-LEVEL CONSTRUCTS

D shall include no constructs that relate to, or are logically affected by, the "physical" or "storage" or "internal" levels of the system.

This proscription is a logical consequence of the strong separation we insist on between model and implementation (it should be obvious that allowing implementation considerations to show through at the model level undermines physical data independence, and it can adversely affect portability and intersystem operability, too). Here are some specific corollaries of this proscription:

- The mapping between public application relvars and database relvars (discussed under RM Prescription 14 in Chapter 6) is defined by means of some logically distinct mapping language and is not visible to the application.

- Like the relational model, the *Manifesto* deliberately does not say which database relvars if any are physically stored and which not; in particular, it expressly does not say that real ones are physically stored and virtual ones not, nor does it say anything about the storage structures to be used for those relvars that are physically stored. To do otherwise would be quite inappropriate.

However, we remark that many SQL implementations use storage structures that bear a close resemblance to the perceived structure of a relation, thereby encouraging bad practice such as "denormalization" and the use of nulls. For better approaches, see references [81] and [134].

- RM Prescription 4 refers to "some kind of *storage structure definition language.*" RM Proscription 6 implies that the statements of that language—in particular, the mappings of databases to physical storage—must be cleanly separable from everything in **D**.

- As discussed at several points in Chapter 6, the storage structure definition language mentioned in RM Prescription 4 is used to define (among other things) physical representations of scalar values and variables. Those physical representations are thus hidden from the user—i.e., they are not visible in **D**. Analogous remarks apply to tuple and relation values and variables, of course, as well as to scalar ones.

Note: RM Proscription 6 does not prohibit support for operators that expose certain aspects of the implementation for, e.g., debugging purposes (EXPLAIN, which is supported by several of today's SQL products, is an example of such an operator). However, we do not regard such operators as part of **D**.

RM PROSCRIPTION 7: NO TUPLE-LEVEL OPERATIONS

D shall support no tuple-at-a-time operations on relvars or relations.

——— ◆ ◆ ◆ ◆ ———

The operators of the relational algebra—which are, by definition, all read-only operators—are *set-at-a-time,* in the sense that their operands and results are whole relations (i.e., sets of tuples, loosely speaking) rather than individual tuples per se. As a consequence, there is never any need for applications to access some relation a tuple at a time in order to compute some desired result, and **D** is therefore expressly prohibited from supporting such operations. If the application does need to process some relation tuple by tuple for some reason (perhaps for display or printing purposes), it should not have to access that relation piecemeal as SQL does with its operation of "fetching via a cursor." In **Tutorial D,** we prefer the approach of simply "loading" the tuples of the relation in question, in some specified order, into a local array variable, after which the application can iterate over the array elements in the familiar fashion. Here is an example:

```
VAR I INTEGER ;
VAR SX S# ;
VAR QX QTY ;
VAR SQA ARRAY TUPLE { S# S#, QTY QTY } ;

LOAD SQA FROM ( SP WHERE P# = P#('P1') ) { S#, QTY } ORDER ( ASC S# ) ;

DO I := 1 TO COUNT ( SQA ) ;
   BEGIN ;
      SX := S#  FROM SQA (I) ,        /* "fetch" ith S# */
      QX := QTY FROM SQA (I) ;        /* and QTY values */
      /* now process SX and QX */
   END ;
END DO ;
```

Note that this approach does not imply that the array variable need be accommodated entirely in main memory (i.e., it can "spill" out on to the disk if necessary). Note also that the load operation does not necessarily need to behave like a "breakpoint" (meaning the last tuple must be loaded before the instruction immediately following the LOAD can be executed). Thus, we see no reason why all of the requirements satisfied by SQL's "FETCH via a cursor" cannot be satisfied at least equally well by our approach.

As for update operators, the intent of the proscription is to prohibit **D** from supporting, e.g., an operation that inserts just a single tuple into a relvar, if that operation is the *only* means of inserting tuples into relvars (as was the case in some early SQL implementations). Multi-tuple INSERTs are effectively mandated by our required support for relational assignment. If a single-tuple INSERT is supported, it must be definable as shorthand for inserting a relation of cardinality one. Similar remarks apply to DELETE and UPDATE operators, if supported.

RM PROSCRIPTION 8: NO COMPOSITE ATTRIBUTES

D shall not include any specific support for "composite" or "compound" attributes, since such functionality can more cleanly be achieved, if desired, through the type support already prescribed.

It is sometimes suggested—see, for example, reference [23]—that it should be possible somehow to combine, say, attributes S# and P# from the shipments relvar SP into a single *composite* attribute, S#_P# say. Reference [53] argues against this idea, strongly. It does not seem appropriate, or necessary, to repeat all of the arguments of reference [53] here; suffice it to say that the kind of "composite attribute" support typically proposed mixes together all kinds of notions that would be better kept separate. As RM Proscription 8 suggests, the functionality in question can effectively be achieved anyway, if desired, by means of the type support prescribed elsewhere in the *Manifesto*.

RM PROSCRIPTION 9: NO DOMAIN CHECK OVERRIDE

D shall include no "domain check override" operators, since such operators are both ad hoc and unnecessary.

Recall that *domain* is just another term for *type,* and "domain check override" [23] thus means, in essence, overriding the system's type checking mechanism: on the face of it, not a very desirable goal! Space precludes a detailed explanation here, but basically the objective is to allow, e.g., joins to be done even when the join attributes are defined on different domains (i.e., are of different types). However, closer analysis reveals that the whole idea is based on a failure to make a clear distinction between types and representations. Not only is it ad hoc and unnecessary, therefore (as RM Proscription 9 states), but it simply does not stand up at all, logically speaking, under proper scrutiny, and we therefore reject it.

RM PROSCRIPTION 10: NOT SQL

D shall not be called SQL.

Little seems necessary by way of elaboration here; we are merely trying to "head off at the pass" certain marketing tricks—not without precedent—that we suspect might be tried if some version of **D** were ever to become a commercial reality.

EXERCISES

1. Why is the prohibition against top-to-bottom tuple ordering (RM Proscription 2) a good idea?

2. Suppose that, RM Prescription 1 notwithstanding, there were a left-to-right ordering to the attributes of a relation. Define as precisely as you can a UNION operator for such "relations."

3. Which of the RM Proscriptions does SQL violate? Which of those violations constitute violations of *The Information Principle?*

4. *(Repeated from the body of the chapter.)* If relvar *R* has an empty key *K*, then that key *K* is the *only* candidate key for *R*. Why?

5. Why are tuple-at-a-time operators prohibited (RM Proscription 7)?

6. Why are composite attributes prohibited (RM Proscription 8)?

7. What exactly is wrong with "domain check override" (RM Proscription 9)?

8. What in a nutshell is the objection to nulls and many-valued logic (RM Proscription 4)? What is the argument in favor of these constructs?

9. In the suppliers-and-parts database, suppose some parts have no color and some have an unknown weight. Modify the design of Fig. 2.1—see Chapter 2—accordingly. (This exercise might be suitable as a basis for group discussion.)

10. Consider any SQL product that might be available to you. Does that product involve any violations of RM Proscription 6? Identify as many such violations as you can. If possible, perform this exercise for at least two different SQL products and compare the results.

Chapter 8

O O P r e s c r i p t i o n s

OO PRESCRIPTION 1: COMPILE-TIME TYPE CHECKING

*D shall permit **compile-time type checking**.*

By this prescription, we mean merely that, insofar as feasible, it shall be possible to check at compile time that no type errors can occur at run time; in other words, type errors shall be detectable by inspection of the program source text alone (again, insofar as feasible). Of course, this requirement does not preclude the possibility of "compile and go" or interpretive implementations.

Compile-time type checking is also known as *static* type checking. It is widely regarded as a desirable objective [135]. We remark, however, that it cannot be fully achieved if (but only if) type inheritance is supported; that is, there will be certain situations with inheritance in which type checking cannot be completed until run time—hence the "insofar as feasible" qualifications above. See OO Prescription 2 (also the discussion of the TREAT operator in Chapter 14) for further discussion.

Incidentally, it has been suggested that OO Prescription 1 is in conflict with RM Prescription 25 (which requires the catalog to be updatable), because updating the catalog at run time could invalidate the type checking that was done at compile time. But all that is needed to avoid this problem is a mechanism for repeating the type checking at run time—perhaps by recompiling the source code—if such updates occur. Some DBMS products behave in exactly this manner today.

OO PRESCRIPTION 2: TYPE INHERITANCE (CONDITIONAL)

*If D supports **type inheritance**, then such support shall conform to the inheritance model defined in Part IV of this book.*

Despite the fact that languages and products that support some kind of type inheritance do exist (and indeed have done so for some time), and despite the fact that type inheritance has been discussed for many years in books and articles and presentations, there is still no consensus in the data management community on a formal, rigorous, and abstract type inheritance model. To quote reference [131]:

> The basic idea of inheritance is quite simple ... [and yet, despite] its central role in current object systems, inheritance is still quite a controversial mechanism ... [A] comprehensive view of inheritance is still missing.

Part IV of this book describes an inheritance model that (we believe) could serve to fill this gap. The model in question is one that has been developed and refined over the past several years by the present authors, and we offer it as a serious candidate for consideration by the community at large. We do not include it as a mandatory component of the *Manifesto,* however—we merely insist that **if** type inheritance is supported at all, **then** that support shall be based on the model described in Part IV.

As an aside, we speculate that one reason for the aforementioned lack of consensus is that inheritance was first introduced in the context of software engineering; i.e., it was more of an implementation idea than a theoretical one, intended primarily to simplify certain aspects of software development and maintenance (see, e.g., references [9] and [100]). Its application to, and attempted incorporation into, an abstract theory of data came later. If this speculation is correct, then there is a parallel that can usefully be drawn with the development of database systems in general. To spell that parallel out:

- The early (hierarchic and network) database systems can be seen as attempts to impose a thin layer of abstraction over certain implementation techniques that were in wide use at the time.

- However, those systems never really succeeded in making the clear distinction between model and implementation that we now regard as so important.

- Indeed, that distinction was not properly made until 1969, when the relational model—a true, abstract, implementation-independent model (or theory) of data—was first defined.

Analogously, we see at least some of the current inheritance "models" not as true models per se, but merely as attempts to abstract just a little from certain current implementation techniques (and again we observe a failure to make a clear distinction between model and implementation).

We should also say something about the distinction between single and multiple inheritance. Briefly (and somewhat loosely), single inheritance means each subtype has a single supertype, and hence inherits properties from just that one type; multiple inheritance means a subtype can have two or more supertypes, and hence can inherit properties from two or more types. (Of course, these ideas are elaborated, considerably, in Part IV of this book.) Now, it has often been argued that it might be possible to support single inheritance only, without worrying about the additional complexities (if any) of multiple inheritance. Our position, by contrast, is rather different: We believe that single inheritance *logically implies* multiple inheritance, and hence that support for single inheritance by itself makes little sense. If **D** supports inheritance at all, therefore, we require that it support multiple inheritance in particular. (This latter requirement does not imply that an implementation that supports inheritance needs to support every last detail of our model, however; for example, it might be possible to omit support for what we call *dummy types*.)

We observe finally that support for inheritance implies certain extensions to—among other things—the definitions in Chapters 4 and 6 of scalar, tuple, and relation values and scalar, tuple, and relation variables. As indicated under OO Prescription 1 above, it also implies a need to relax the static type checking requirement slightly. See Part IV for further discussion (especially Chapter 14).

OO PRESCRIPTION 3: COMPUTATIONAL COMPLETENESS

*D shall be **computationally complete**. That is, **D** may support, but shall not require, invocation from so-called host programs written in languages other than **D**. Similarly, **D** may support, but shall not require, the use of other languages for implementation of user-defined operators.*

The general intent of this prescription is twofold:

- It must be possible to write entire applications in **D**, instead of having to use one language for database access and another for general computation. In other words, we do not endorse the "embedded data sublanguage" approach adopted in SQL (we do not prohibit it, either, but we do insist that users should have the option of not having to use it). *Note:* Over the years, the idea that users should not have to use an embedded data sublanguage in order to access the database has been proposed by many people, including one of the present authors [42]. As noted in Chapter 5, one important consequence of that idea is that we can avoid the problem of *impedance* *mismatch* between the types available inside the database and those available outside; i.e., there is no need to map between the (arbitrarily complex) types used inside the database and the (possibly rather simple, and almost certainly different) types provided by some host language.

- It must be possible to use **D** to write the code that implements user-defined operators, instead of having to resort to using some other language for this purpose. *Note:* Several examples of **Tutorial D** operator definitions were given in Chapters 3 and 6. However, we did note in those chapters that certain operators—specifically, those selectors and THE_ operators that make use of the highly protected operators that expose physical representations—could not be defined entirely in **D**, since those protected operators are themselves not part of **D**. Further, we note that the ability to define operators in some other language leads to the possibility of writing programs in **D** that invoke operators provided by some third party (e.g., operators included in an off-the-shelf library package).

We should add that we do not intend this prescription to undermine such matters as **D**'s optimizability unduly. Nor do we intend it to be a recipe for the use of procedural constructs such as loops to subvert the system's support for declarative queries and the like. Rather, the point is that computational completeness will be needed (in general) for the implementation of user-defined operators anyway, and to be able to implement such operators in **D** itself might well be more convenient than having to make excursions into some other language—excursions that in any case are likely to cause problems for optimizers. We do recognize that it might prove necessary in practice to prohibit the use of certain **D** features outside the code that implements such operators, so long as such prohibitions do not too severely restrict what can be done by a free-standing application (i.e., one that does not require invocation from some program written in some other language).

OO PRESCRIPTION 4: EXPLICIT TRANSACTION BOUNDARIES

*Transaction initiation shall be performed only by means of an explicit **begin transaction** operator. Transaction termination shall be performed only by means of a **commit** or **rollback** operator; commit must always be explicit, but rollback can be implicit (if and only if the transaction fails through no fault of its own). If transaction TX terminates with commit ("normal termination"), changes made by TX to the applicable database shall be committed. If transaction TX terminates with rollback ("abnormal termination"), changes made by TX to the applicable database shall be rolled back.*

We require, noncontroversially, that all database operations be performed within the context of some transaction; here we are simply trying once again to avoid certain mistakes we observe in the design of SQL. To be specific:

- Prior to 1999, the SQL standard had no explicit "begin transaction" operator; instead, a transaction was started implicitly whenever the application executed a "transaction-initiating" statement while no transaction was currently in progress.[1] One consequence of this omission was that there was no obvious way to provide "transaction-wide" information—for example, isolation level [96]—that was specific to just one transaction. Of course, the *Manifesto* does not directly address isolation level or similar matters at all, but it does at least provide the explicit "begin

---

1. An explicit START—not BEGIN—TRANSACTION operator was added in 1999, but its use is optional (it has to be, because it still has to be possible for compatibility reasons to begin transactions implicitly as well).

transaction" operator that is needed as a basis for addressing them. (Perhaps we should add that, regarding isolation level specifically, the only level we would want to support—i.e., the only one we would regard as logically correct—would be whatever level is defined to provide total isolation; all others have the potential for causing logical mistakes.)

- SQL allows transactions to terminate implicitly as well, in which case—to quote reference [41]—"the system ... automatically executes either a ROLLBACK or a COMMIT ... it is implementation-dependent which" (!). *Note:* The term *implementation-dependent* is defined by the SQL standard to mean "possibly differing between SQL-implementations, but not specified by this International Standard and not required to be specified ... for any particular SQL-implementation." So whether the system executes a COMMIT or a ROLLBACK might not even be documented! It could even change from release to release.

As for the explanations in this prescription of normal vs. abnormal termination: The objective here is simply to spell out the fact that databases, and therefore relvars contained within databases, possess the property of *persistence*. In fact, as indicated in our discussion of RM Prescription 16 in Chapter 6, database relvars are the *only* variables to possess this property.

OO PRESCRIPTION 5: NESTED TRANSACTIONS

*D shall support **nested transactions**—i.e., it shall permit a* parent *transaction TX to initiate a* child *transaction TX' before TX itself has terminated, in which case:*

a. TX *and* TX' *shall interact with the same database (as is in fact required by RM Prescription 17).*

b. *Whether* TX *shall be required to suspend execution while* TX' *executes shall be implementation-defined. However,* TX *shall not be allowed to terminate before* TX' *terminates; in other words,* TX' *shall be wholly contained within* TX.

c. *Rollback of* TX *shall include the rolling back of* TX' *even if* TX' *has terminated with commit. In other words, "commit" is always interpreted within the parent context (if such exists) and is subject to override by the parent transaction (again, if such exists).*

The idea of nested transactions can be thought of as a generalization of the familiar notion of *savepoints* [96]. Savepoints allow a transaction to be organized as a *sequence* of actions that can be rolled back individually (loosely speaking); nesting, by contrast, allows a transaction to be organized, recursively, as a *hierarchy* of such actions. In other words:

- BEGIN TRANSACTION is extended to support subtransactions (i.e., if BEGIN TRANSACTION is issued when a transaction is already running, it starts a *child* transaction).

- COMMIT "commits" but only within the relevant *parent scope* (if this transaction is a child).

- ROLLBACK undoes work back to the start of this particular subtransaction (including children, grandchildren, etc., of this subtransaction, even if these latter transactions terminated with commit).

Note that nested transactions will be awkward to implement—from a purely syntactic point of view!—in a language that lacks an explicit BEGIN TRANSACTION statement (see the previous prescription): There has to be some explicit way of indicating that an inner transaction is to be started, and marking the point to roll back to if that inner transaction fails. Note further that (as our earlier remarks indicate) we do explicitly require the syntax for beginning and ending an inner transaction to be the same as that for beginning and ending an outermost transaction. This requirement is in the interest of modular programming—an application should be able to begin a transaction without having to know whether that transaction will be part of some outer transaction.

OO PRESCRIPTION 6: AGGREGATE OPERATORS AND EMPTY SETS

Let AggOp *be an **aggregate** operator, such as SUM. If the argument to* AggOp *happens to be empty, then:*

a.   *If* AggOp *is essentially just shorthand for some iterated scalar dyadic operator* Op *(the dyadic operator is "+" in the case of SUM), and if an identity value exists for* Op *(the identity value is 0 in the case of "+"), then the result of that invocation of* AggOp *shall be that identity value.*

b.   *Otherwise, the result of that invocation of* AggOp *shall be undefined.*

The general concept of identity values was discussed under RM Prescription 10 in Chapter 6. Identity values corresponding to the aggregate operators supported in **Tutorial D** are as follows:

- AVG: *None*

- COUNT, SUM: Zero

- MAX, MIN: "Negative infinity" and "positive infinity," respectively (where *negative infinity* and *positive infinity* refer to the lowest and highest value of the applicable—necessarily ordinal—type, respectively)[1]

- AND: TRUE

- OR and XOR: FALSE

- EXACTLY: *See below*

- UNION and D_UNION: An empty relation

- INTERSECT: A universal relation

EXACTLY is a special case, because it takes an additional argument (viz., a nonnegative integer). Let that argument have value n. Then, if the aggregate argument is empty, the operator returns TRUE if n is zero and FALSE otherwise.

Incidentally, it is worth pointing out that COUNT can be regarded as a special case of SUM. For example, the expression

---

1. For certain data types (e.g., CHAR) where "positive infinity" is very large, the implementation might want to outlaw, or at least flag, invocations of MIN on an empty set (if those invocations really need the result to be materialized).

```
COUNT ( S )
```

is logically equivalent to this one:

```
SUM ( EXTEND S ADD ( 1 AS ONE ), ONE )
```

We remark that SQL satisfies OO Prescription 6 for COUNT but fails for everything else. To be specific, for all of the aggregate operators it supports apart from COUNT, it defines the result of applying the operator in question to an empty set to be null. In particular, it defines both the SUM and the AVG of an empty set to be null.

EXERCISES

1.   Why is compile-time type checking a good idea?

2.   What do you understand by the term *computational completeness?*

3.   What is a data sublanguage?

4.   What do you understand by the term *impedance mismatch?*

5.   OO Prescription 6 explains the effect of the aggregate operators on an empty set. What should the effect be in each case if the argument is a singleton set instead (i.e., a set of cardinality one)?

6.   At least one commercially available product violates OO Prescription 5 by supporting *autonomous* subtransactions, meaning that a given child transaction can issue a "global commit" whose effects persist even if the corresponding parent transaction subsequently terminates with rollback. One purpose of such a feature is to allow an audit trail to be maintained that includes a record of failed transactions as well as successful ones. Discuss.

Chapter 9

O O   P r o s c r i p t i o n s

OO PROSCRIPTION 1: RELVARS ARE NOT DOMAINS

Relvars are not domains.

We first made this point in Chapter 2, in the subsection "Relvars vs. Types" at the end of the section on relation variables. Briefly, a relvar is a variable; a domain is a type; variables are not types (and types are not variables). In other words, we categorically reject the equation "relvar = class" advocated in, e.g., references [102-103] (recall that types are often called *classes* in object systems). But why might anyone advocate such an equation, anyway? It is instructive to consider this question in detail. (The discussion that follows is based on one that previously appeared in reference [76].)

Consider the following simple "class" definition, expressed in a hypothetical object language:

```
CREATE OBJECT CLASS EMP
    ( EMP#      CHAR(5),
      SAL       NUMERIC,
      HOBBY     CHAR(20),
      WORKS_FOR CHAR(20) ) ;
```

And now consider the following SQL "base table" definition:

```
CREATE TABLE EMP
    ( EMP#      CHAR(5),
      SAL       NUMERIC,
      HOBBY     CHAR(20),
      WORKS_FOR CHAR(20) ) ;
```

These two definitions certainly look very similar, and the idea of equating them thus looks very tempting. And indeed some of the "object/relational" systems that appeared in the 1990s, including some commercial products, effectively did just that. So let us take a closer look. More precisely, let us take the CREATE TABLE statement just shown and consider a series of possible extensions to it that, some have argued, serve to make it more "object-like." (The discussion that follows is based on a specific product; in fact, it is based on an example in the vendor's own product documentation. We do not identify that product here, however, since it is not our intent in this book to criticize or praise specific products. Rather, the criticisms we will be making apply, mutatis mutandis, to *any* system that espouses the "relvar = class" equation.)

The first extension is to permit *composite attributes* (i.e., attributes that are *tuple valued*). More specifically, we allow attribute values within a given relvar to be tuples from some other relvar, or possibly from the same relvar (?). This first extension is thus roughly analogous to allowing objects to contain other objects, thereby supporting the *containment hierarchy* concept [76]. In the example, we might replace the original CREATE TABLE statement by the following collection of statements (refer to Fig. 9.1):

```
CREATE TABLE EMP
      ( EMP#       CHAR(5),
        SAL        NUMERIC,
        HOBBY      ACTIVITY,
        WORKS_FOR COMPANY ) ;

CREATE TABLE ACTIVITY
        ( NAME      CHAR(20),
          TEAM      INTEGER ) ;

CREATE TABLE COMPANY
        ( NAME      CHAR(20),
          LOCATION  CITYSTATE ) ;

CREATE TABLE CITYSTATE
        ( CITY      CHAR(20),
          STATE     CHAR(2) ) ;
```

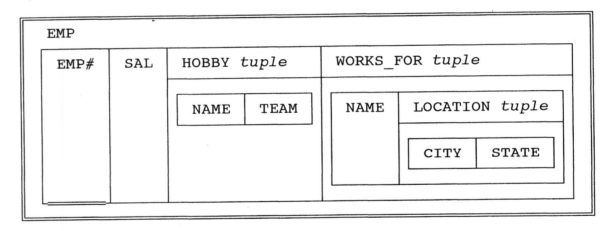

Fig. 9.1: Attributes containing (pointers to) tuples—deprecated

Explanation: Attribute HOBBY in relvar EMP is declared to be of type ACTIVITY. ACTIVITY in turn is a relvar of two attributes, NAME and TEAM, where TEAM gives the number of players in a team corresponding to NAME (e.g., if NAME = 'Soccer' then TEAM = 11). Each HOBBY value is thus actually a tuple with two components, a NAME component and a TEAM component (more precisely, it is a tuple that currently appears in relvar ACTIVITY). Observe, therefore, that we have already violated OO Proscription 1—the "domain" for attribute HOBBY is defined to be the *relvar* ACTIVITY. We will come back to this point later.

Similarly, attribute WORKS_FOR in relvar EMP is declared to be of type COMPANY, and COMPANY is also a relvar of two attributes, one of which is defined to be of type CITYSTATE, which is another two-attribute relvar, and so on. In other words, relvars ACTIVITY, COMPANY, and CITYSTATE are all considered to be types (domains) as well as relvars. The same is true for relvar EMP itself, of course.

As an aside, we remark that we have characterized this first extension as *attributes containing tuples* because that is the way advocates of the "relvar = class" equation themselves characterize it. It would be more accurate, however, to characterize it as "attributes containing *pointers to* tuples"—an issue we will examine more closely in a few moments, and more closely still in the next section. (In Fig. 9.1, therefore, we should really replace each of the three occurrences of the term *tuple* by the term *pointer to tuple.*)

Remarks analogous to those of the previous paragraph apply to the second extension also, which is to allow *relation-valued attributes;* that is, attribute values within a given relvar are allowed to be, not just single tuples, but sets of tuples from some other relvar, or possibly from the same relvar (?). This second extension is thus roughly analogous to allowing objects to contain "collection" objects [76]—a more complex version of the containment hierarchy. (We remark in passing that in the particular product on which our example is based, those collection objects can be sequences or bags[1] as well as sets per se.) For example, suppose employees can have an arbitrary number of hobbies, instead of just one (refer to Fig. 9.2):

```
CREATE TABLE EMP
     ( EMP#      CHAR(5),
       SAL       NUMERIC,
       HOBBIES   SET OF ( ACTIVITY ),
       WORKS_FOR COMPANY ) ;
```

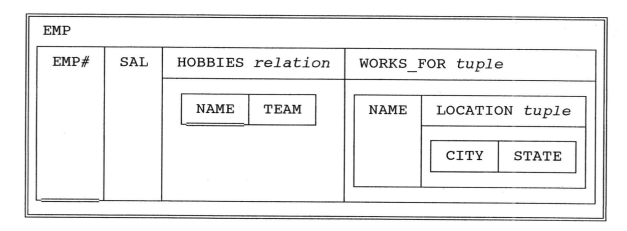

Fig. 9.2: Attributes containing sets of (pointers to) tuples—deprecated

Explanation: The HOBBIES value within any given tuple of relvar EMP is now, conceptually, a set of zero or more tuples from relvar ACTIVITY.

The third extension is to permit relvars to have associated *methods* (i.e., operators). For example:

```
CREATE TABLE EMP
     ( EMP#      CHAR(5),
       SAL       NUMERIC,
       HOBBIES   SET OF ( ACTIVITY ),
       WORKS_FOR COMPANY )
METHOD RETIREMENT_BENEFITS ( ) : NUMERIC ;
```

Explanation: RETIREMENT_BENEFITS is a method that takes a given EMP tuple as its argument and produces a result of type NUMERIC.

So much for a quick overview of how the "relvar = class" equation might be realized in

---

1. A *bag* (also known as a *multiset*) is like a set, except that it permits duplicates.

practice.[1] So what is wrong with it? Well, observe immediately that, as noted earlier, a relvar is a variable and a class is a type; so how can they possibly be the same? This first observation should be logically sufficient to stop the "relvar = class" idea dead in its tracks. However, there is more that can usefully be said, so let us continue for a while.

Observe next, then, that there is a difference in kind—a logical difference, in fact—between the attribute definitions (e.g.) SAL NUMERIC and WORKS_FOR COMPANY. NUMERIC is a true data type; it places a time-independent constraint on the values that can legally appear in attribute SAL. By contrast, COMPANY is not a true data type; the constraint it places on the values that can appear in attribute WORKS_FOR is *time dependent* (it depends, obviously, on the current value of relvar COMPANY). In fact, as pointed out earlier, the relvar vs. domain distinction has been muddied here.

Next, we have seen that tuple "objects" are apparently allowed to contain other such "objects"; for example, EMP "objects" apparently contain COMPANY "objects." But they do not—not really; instead, they contain *pointers* to those "contained objects," and users must be absolutely clear on this fact. For example, suppose the user updates some particular COMPANY tuple in some way (refer back to Fig. 9.1). Then that update will immediately be visible in all EMP tuples that "contain" that COMPANY tuple. (Please understand that we are not saying this effect is undesirable, only that it has to be explained to the user. But explaining it to the user amounts to telling the user that the "model" shown in Fig. 9.1 is incorrect—EMP tuples do not contain COMPANY tuples, they contain *pointers to* COMPANY tuples instead, as already stated.)

Here are some further implications and questions arising from this same point:

- Can we insert an EMP tuple and specify a value for the "contained" COMPANY tuple that does not currently exist in the COMPANY relvar? If the answer is *yes*, the fact that attribute WORKS_FOR is defined as being of type COMPANY does not mean very much, since it does not significantly constrain the INSERT operation in any way. If the answer is *no*, the INSERT operation becomes unnecessarily complex—the user has to specify, not just an existing company name (i.e., a foreign key value) as would be required in the analogous relational situation, but an entire existing COMPANY tuple. Moreover, specifying an entire COMPANY tuple means, at best, telling the system something it already knows; at worst, it means that if the user makes a mistake, the INSERT will fail when it could perfectly well have succeeded.

- Suppose we want an ON DELETE RESTRICT rule for companies (i.e., an attempt to delete a company must fail if the company has any employees). Presumably this rule must be enforced by procedural code, say by some method *M* (note that relvar EMP has no foreign key to which a declarative version of the rule might be attached). Furthermore, regular DELETE operations must now not be performed on relvar COMPANY other than within the code that implements that method *M*. How is this requirement enforced? Analogous remarks and questions apply to other foreign key rules, of course, such as ON DELETE CASCADE.

- Note too that deleting an EMP tuple presumably will not cascade to delete the corresponding COMPANY tuple, despite the pretense that the EMP tuple contains that COMPANY tuple.

Next, suppose we define view V to be the projection of EMP over (say) just the attribute HOBBIES. V is a relvar too, of course, but a virtual relvar instead of a real one. So if "relvar = class" is a correct equation, V is also a class. *What class is it?* Also, classes have methods; *what methods apply to V?*

---

1. The product on which our example is based goes a lot further than we have suggested—for example, it also supports "subtables and supertables" (see Appendix G)—but the extensions we have discussed so far are sufficient for present purposes.

Well, "class" EMP has just one method, RETIREMENT_BENEFITS, and that method clearly does not apply to "class" V. In fact, it hardly seems reasonable that *any* methods that apply to "class" EMP would apply to "class" V—and there certainly are no others. So it looks as if (in general) *no methods at all* apply to the result of a projection; i.e., the result, whatever it is, is not really a class after all. In fact, it is clear that when people equate relvars and classes, it is specifically real relvars they have in mind—they are forgetting about the virtual ones. (Certainly the pointers discussed above are pointers to tuples in real relvars, not derived ones.) But to distinguish between real and virtual relvars in this way is a serious mistake, because the question as to which relvars are real and which virtual is (as we have explained elsewhere) to some considerable degree arbitrary.

Finally, *what domains are supported?* Those who advocate the "relvar = class" equation never seem to have much to say about domains, presumably because they cannot see how domains as such fit into their overall scheme—and yet domains are essential, as we know. What is more, the "relvar = class" equation merely gives us an alternative way of doing things we can already do with regular relvars; it does not provide support for user-defined types in general (consider, for example, how the scheme sketched above might be used to implement QTY, POINT, and all of the other examples of user-defined types discussed in Chapter 6 under RM Prescription 1).

You might also like to consider the following question: If the tuples of a certain relvar represent "objects" of some "class"—meaning in particular that the content of that "class" varies over time—what term is used for the set of *all possible* "objects" that might ever appear in that "class" (i.e., at any time)?

It follows from all of the above that we are not talking about the relational model any more. In particular, the fundamental data construct is no longer a relation containing values, it is a "relation"—actually not a proper relation at all, so far as the relational model is concerned—containing values *and pointers*. In other words, **we have undermined the conceptual integrity of the relational model** (see Chapter 1).

As a kind of footnote to the foregoing discussion, it is interesting to speculate on what would have happened if Codd had not originally used the term *domain* instead of *data type,* and the object community had not then introduced the term *object class* for the same concept. When the requirement arose for users to be able to define their own data types, the only possible term that could have been used to refer to those types would surely have been *user-defined data types*—and any proposal to support such things in a manner that suggested they were not data types would thus surely have been open to well-founded criticism.

OO PROSCRIPTION 2: NO OBJECT IDS

No database relvar shall include an attribute of type pointer.

As we saw in the previous section, a system that violates OO Proscription 1 will almost certainly violate OO Proscription 2 as well. However, it is possible—and, sadly, not at all unusual in practice—to violate OO Prescription 2 without violating OO Proscription 1, so it is worth discussing OO Proscription 2 in its own right.

We begin by taking an informal look at the idea, mentioned a couple of times in the previous section, that some relvar *R2* might have an attribute whose values are pointers to tuples in some relvar *R1.* Why might anyone want to do such a thing? The answer seems to be bound up with performance; the argument, such as it is, is that it is quicker to follow a pointer than to do a join. Of course, to argue thus is to confuse model and implementation issues once again; nevertheless, it is an argument that is frequently heard.

Observe now, however, that—by definition!—pointers point to *variables,* not *values* (because variables have addresses and values do not). By definition, therefore, if some relvar is allowed to have an attribute whose values are "pointers to tuples," then those pointers point to tuple *variables,* not to tuple *values*.   **But there is no notion of a tuple variable in the relational model.**   The relational model deals with relation values, which are (loosely speaking) sets of tuple values, which are in turn (again loosely speaking) sets of scalar values.   It also deals with relation variables, which are variables whose values are relations.   However, it does *not* deal with tuple variables (which are variables whose values are tuples) or scalar variables (which are variables whose values are scalars).[1]   The *only* kind of variable included in the relational model—and the only kind of variable permitted in a relational database—is, very specifically, the *relation* variable.   *It follows that a violation of OO Proscription 2 constitutes a major departure from the relational model, introducing as it does an entirely new kind of variable* (thereby violating *The Information Principle,* in fact).   As noted in the previous section, in fact, we would argue that it seriously undermines the conceptual integrity of the relational model.

The foregoing argument has many implications, far too many to elaborate on here; more detail can be found in reference [59] if you are interested.   We content ourselves in the remainder of this section with a slightly more formal look at OO Proscription 2 per se.

First of all, then, we need to be clear about the distinction between pointers and *names.* Following reference [125], we can distinguish these concepts as follows:

- A **name** is a character string.[2]   Names are *labels* or *identifiers* that are attached to program objects (typically variables) and are used to identify those objects symbolically.

- A **pointer** is an address.   Like names, pointers are used to identify program objects (typically variables), but they do so not symbolically, as names do, but by the *location* of those objects.

So we see that names and pointers are both used to *refer to* or *reference* variables (among other things); the intuitive difference between them is that names are externally visible, while pointers are not—the latter are, to repeat, addresses.   Of course, we are speaking here purely from a conceptual point of view—the addresses in question are not necessarily direct hardware addresses; the point is, however, they can always be thought of as direct hardware addresses.

Now, the source of the pointer notion is, of course, the fact that the concept of a variable is really an abstraction of the concept of *an area of storage,* implying that variables do indeed have addresses. Programming languages thus often support address or pointer values and variables (in other words, they support an address or pointer type).   Hence, to repeat, a pointer value is an address, and a pointer variable is a variable whose permitted values are addresses.

The address or pointer type has two fundamental operations associated with it, usually called *referencing* and *dereferencing,* respectively:[3]

- **Referencing:** Given a variable *V*, the referencing operator applied to *V* returns the address of *V*. Note that—even though the operator is read-only!—the argument *V* must be specified as a *variable reference* specifically, not as a literal or more general expression (probably not even as a pseudovariable reference).   The reason is, of course, that values do not have addresses, variables do (recall from Chapter 1 that values have no location in time or space, while variables do).

---

1. And it certainly does not deal with tuple variables that are somehow "contained in" some relation variable, since (as noted at the end of the section on RM Prescription 13 in Chapter 6) this latter is a notion that makes no sense.

2. We do not mean to suggest that a name is a value of type CHAR; more particularly, we do not mean to suggest that a name can be denoted by some expression of type CHAR in the language **D.**

3. SQL is unusual in that it has a dereferencing operator—it might even be said to have two different dereferencing operators—but no referencing operator.   Furthermore, those dereferencing operators are unusual too, in that they return values, not variables.   See references [59] and [76] for further explanation.

- **Dereferencing:** Given a variable *A* of type address, the dereferencing operator applied to *A* returns the variable whose address is currently contained in *A*. **Note carefully that the operator returns a variable, not a value.** The reason is, again, that values do not have addresses, variables do. (Of course, if the dereferencing operator invocation occurs in a source position instead of a target position—in particular, if it occurs on the right side of an assignment—it can be regarded, harmlessly, as returning the value of the variable in question instead of returning that variable per se.)

Now, object systems rely heavily on the concept of **object IDs,** and object IDs are essentially pointers as just described. OO Proscription 2 thus means that we reject the notion of object IDs, at least insofar as such IDs might be permitted within databases.[1] As a consequence, we also reject both:

- The notion that certain database objects might make use of such IDs in order to reference—and, in particular, to *share*—other such objects

- The notion that users might have to dereference such IDs, either explicitly or implicitly, in order to access such objects

In fact, we reject the notion of objects (in the special sense in which that term is understood in object systems, as opposed to its normal natural language sense) entirely.

Perhaps we should stress the point that OO Proscription 2 does not prohibit support for pointers in the nondatabase portions of **D**. We do note, however, that pointers, even if limited to the nondatabase portions of **D**, can lead to a serious problem if type inheritance is also supported (see Appendix F).

We should also stress the fact that OO Proscription 2 does not prevent database relvars from having attributes whose values are names (in particular, names of variables) instead of addresses. For example, a database relvar might reasonably have an attribute whose values are (say) "operating system file names" or "database relvar names." Indeed, relvars with attributes whose values are database relvar names will certainly be needed in the catalog. To what extent **D** should provide any corresponding dereferencing operators is a question that requires further study, however; in **Tutorial D** we adopt the conservative position that no such operators are provided at all. The following observations are pertinent:

- First of all, a type whose values are names of variables does logically resemble, somewhat, a type whose values are pointers. If we permit such types, therefore, we run the risk of backsliding into the kind of pointer free-for-all found in prerelational systems—with its attendant looping, and pointer chasing, and lack of proper end user access, and so on and so forth—and that state of affairs is definitely something we want to avoid.

- On the other hand, we cannot prevent users from defining a type whose values are variable names. And perhaps there is no need to. For consider:

  - The only variables **D** allows *within the database* are, very specifically, database relvars. Hence, the only "pointers" to database data that might be allowed in **D** are, very specifically, *database relvar names.*

  - As far as data in the database is concerned, therefore, the only kind of dereferencing **D**

---

1. As noted under RM Proscription 1 in Chapter 7, we also reject the concept of hidden "tuple IDs" (some writers seem to equate that concept with object IDs—see, e.g., the annotation to reference [130]).

might possibly need is an operation that would allow a database relvar to be specified, not directly by means of its name, but indirectly by means of a variable whose value is that name. In SQL terms, for example, such a facility might mean that, in place of the familiar SELECT * FROM T, the user would be able to say SELECT * FROM V, where V is a program variable whose *value* is the required name T.

- ▪ As far as data in the database is concerned, therefore, support in **D** for "pointers" and dereferencing would not constitute a return to the kind of pointer free-for-all mentioned (and objected to) above.

- ▪ The foregoing remarks notwithstanding, we do not (to repeat) prescribe any such explicit dereferencing operator for **D**. Indeed, we observe that if **D** were to support a mechanism akin to the PREPARE and EXECUTE capabilities of "dynamic SQL" or (perhaps better) the analogous **Prepare** and **Execute** capabilities of the SQL Call-Level Interface [41,99], explicit dereferencing as such would be unnecessary anyway. (For the benefit of readers who might not be familiar with these SQL features, we should explain that PREPARE or **Prepare** allows a source language statement—possibly a dynamically constructed source language statement—to be compiled at run time, and EXECUTE or **Execute** then allows the compiled version of such a statement to be executed. We remark that, as hinted in Chapter 1, an industrial strength **D** would certainly require some such mechanism in order to allow the construction of applications that support ad hoc interactions on the part of the end user.)

We observe in conclusion that the heavy reliance of object systems on object IDs lends weight to our belief that such systems are designed primarily *by* programmers *for* programmers. The relational model, by contrast, explicitly recognizes that the primary purpose of databases is to serve end users rather than application programmers (though this objective does not rule out the possibility of their serving application programmers too, of course). For this very reason, Codd deliberately excluded pointers from the relational model when he first defined it. Here is his stated rationale for doing so [23]:

It is safe to assume that all kinds of users [including end users in particular] understand the act of comparing values, but that relatively few understand the complexities of pointers [including the complexities of referencing and dereferencing in particular]. The relational model is based on this fundamental principle ... [The] manipulation of pointers is more bug-prone than is the act of comparing values, even if the user happens to understand the complexities of pointers.

It is thus sad to see that the SQL standard now permits—in fact, encourages—the use of pointers within "relations" ("relations" in quotes because those "relations" are in fact not relations at all, in the sense of the relational model). And the pointers in question are, of course, not mere database relvar names as above but genuine "object ID"-style pointers. This is backsliding with a vengeance.

EXERCISES

1. Distinguish as carefully as you can between names and pointers.

2. Explain the referencing and dereferencing operators. In what respects are these operators rather unusual?

3. If you are familiar with SQL, repeat Exercise 2 for the SQL versions of the operators in question.

4. Explain the concept of *object IDs* in your own words. Compare and contrast them with (a) the concept of *surrogate keys,* (b) the concept of "row IDs" or "tuple IDs."

5.   What are the reasons typically given in practice for violating OO Proscription 1? What about OO Proscription 2?

6.   Why does a violation of OO Proscription 1 seem to lead inevitably to a violation of OO Proscription 2?

7.   What do you understand by the term "containment hierarchy"? What if anything is the analog of that concept in the relational world?

8.   What do you understand by the term "collection object"? What if anything is the analog of that concept in the relational world?

9.   Why does a violation of OO Proscription 2 constitute a violation of *The Information Principle?* What are the consequences of such violation?

10.   What do you understand by the SQL terms **Prepare** and **Execute?** Why are such features desirable?

11.   Why do you think OO Proscriptions 1 and 2 are not included in Chapter 7? Are they not both logical consequences of the relational model and thus in fact *RM* Proscriptions?

12.   Attempt to implement user-defined types POINT and ELLIPSE (from Chapter 6) in the style of the "data types" ACTIVITY and COMPANY of the HOBBY and WORKS_FOR attributes shown in Fig. 9.1. Given that implementation, describe how you think the effect of the following **Tutorial D** assignment might be obtained:

```
THE_X ( THE_CTR ( E ) ) := 5.0 ;
```

(where E is a variable of declared type ELLIPSE).

13.   The term *data type* was in widespread use in the computer programming world of 1970. Why do you think Codd chose the term "domain" for that concept in his relational model of data? What, if any, adverse consequences have arisen from that choice of term? Why are object classes called object classes and not (data) types? What, if any, adverse consequences have arisen from that choice of term?

14.   "Types are to nouns as relations are to ...": Complete this sentence.

Chapter 10

RM Very Strong Suggestions

RM VERY STRONG SUGGESTION 1: SYSTEM KEYS

*D should provide a mechanism according to which values of some specified candidate key (or certain components thereof) for some specified relvar are **supplied by the system**. It should also provide a mechanism according to which an arbitrary relation can be extended to include an attribute whose values (a) are unique within that relation (or within certain partitions of that relation) and (b) are once again supplied by the system.*

Caveat: We should make it clear at the outset here that RM Very Strong Suggestion 1 raises a number of issues (including but not limited to language design issues) that are not yet fully resolved. The discussion that follows should therefore be regarded not as a definitive statement, but rather just as notes toward the kind of functionality we feel is desirable. Note that the functionality in question is not currently included in **Tutorial D,** though we do believe it would be useful in an industrial-strength language.

With that caveat out of the way, we now observe that (as the text of the suggestion indicates) we are really talking about two separate but related ideas here. We begin with the familiar notion of **default values,** which we explain as follows. Let R be a relvar, and let R have an attribute A of declared type T. If attribute A is defined to have default value d (a value of type T, of course), then it is at least syntactically valid to specify tuples—more precisely, relations containing tuples—for insertion into R that do not include an explicit A component; such tuples are conceptually extended with an $<A,T,d>$ triple before the actual insertion is done. For example, suppose attribute STATUS of the suppliers relvar S is defined to have default value 10, perhaps as follows (hypothetical syntax):

```
VAR S REAL RELATION { S# S#, SNAME NAME, STATUS INTEGER, CITY CHAR }
    KEY { S# }
    DEFAULT { STATUS 10 } ;
```

Then the following INSERT might be syntactically valid:

```
INSERT S RELATION { TUPLE { S# S#('S6'), SNAME NAME('Lopez'), CITY 'Madrid' } } ;
```

The relation that is actually inserted looks like this:

```
RELATION { TUPLE { S# S#('S6'), SNAME NAME('Lopez'), STATUS 10, CITY 'Madrid' } }
```

An assignment analog of the foregoing INSERT might look as follows:

```
S := S UNION RELATION { TUPLE { S# S#('S6'), SNAME NAME('Lopez'),
                        STATUS DEFAULT ( S, STATUS ), CITY 'Madrid' } } ;
```

We are assuming here that the operator invocation DEFAULT (R,a) returns the default value of the specified attribute a (STATUS in the example) of the relvar denoted by the specified relvar reference R (S in the example).

Next, we suggest an extension to the foregoing mechanism according to which default values are provided by invoking some system-defined operator, instead of being defined explicitly as part of the attribute definition. For example, let relvar READING contain a set of instrument readings taken during the course of some experiment. Further, let that relvar include an attribute called READING#, defined as follows:

```
READING# INTEGER
   ...
DEFAULT { READING# SERIAL () }
```

SERIAL here is the name of a system-defined operator, with semantics as follows:

- Let the very first INSERT into the READING relvar insert *n* tuples. Then those tuples will be given READING# values 1, 2, ..., *n* (in some unspecified order).

- Let some subsequent INSERT into the READING relvar insert *p* tuples. Then those tuples will be given READING# values $N+1$, $N+2$, ..., $N+p$ (in some unspecified order), where N is the highest READING# value previously assigned.[1]

For simplicity, we assume—though the assumption is perhaps not 100 percent necessary—that if SERIAL or other such operator is specified, then the attribute in question *must* obtain its values via the default mechanism; i.e., "the attribute is nonupdatable" (again, speaking somewhat loosely). We also assume that a means exists for a suitably skilled and authorized user (perhaps the database administrator) to define such operators. Observe that those operators will probably not be conventional scalar operators in the sense of RM Prescription 3. For one thing, they might require access to certain "environment variables" (e.g., the system clock) that might not be directly available to a conventional user of **D**. For another, they will typically involve, and might even update, certain "hidden arguments" (i.e., arguments not mentioned explicitly when the operator is invoked); for example, one hidden argument to SERIAL is the highest value previously assigned.

Here now are some examples of further operators that could be useful in appropriate circumstances:

- *SERIAL within some scope:* For example, the relvar ORDER_LINE might include an ORDER# attribute whose values are provided by some business process, together with a LINE# attribute of type INTEGER with a default value defined thus:

```
DEFAULT { LINE# SERIAL () WITHIN ORDER# }
```

- *NOW:* This operator provides "the time now" (perhaps as a time or timestamp value, perhaps as an integer, perhaps as a character string, depending on the type of the attribute in question).

- *USERID:* This operator provides the user ID of the user inserting the tuples in question.

To get back to RM Very Strong Suggestion 1 specifically, the relevance of all of the above to candidate keys should be obvious. For example, the complete definition of the ORDER_LINE relvar might look like this:

---

1. We remark that these READING# values might be thought of as *tuple IDs;* note, however, that those tuple IDs are not hidden from the user, as they are in certain SQL systems. We point out too that there is an element of unpredictability involved in using the SERIAL operator. For example, if we insert (a relation containing) three tuples into an empty relvar, all in a single operation, we cannot say which tuple gets which ID—we know only that they get IDs 1, 2, and 3 in some unspecified order.

```
VAR ORDER_LINE REAL RELATION { ORDER# CHAR, LINE# INTEGER, ITEM# CHAR, QTY QTY }
    KEY { ORDER#, LINE# }
    DEFAULT { LINE# SERIAL () WITHIN ORDER# } ;
```

We turn now to the second principal part of RM Very Strong Suggestion 1. The basic idea is as follows: We would like to be able to tag the tuples of the result of an arbitrary relational expression in such a way that the tuples remain distinct from one another, even if we "project away" the attribute(s) that would otherwise have made them so. Such a feature would be useful in our proposed support for SQL migration (see the discussion of RM Very Strong Suggestion 8 later in this chapter).

Now, you can probably see right away that we might be able to achieve the foregoing effect if we were allowed to invoke operators like SERIAL just as if they were ordinary scalar operators—in EXTEND, for example. The trouble is, however, that (as already noted) they are not ordinary scalar operators, because they typically involve certain hidden arguments. Instead, therefore, we suggest the introduction of a new relational operator, TAG. Here is an example of its use:

```
( SP TAG WITHIN { S# } AS P#_SERIAL ) { ALL BUT P# }
```

Given our usual sample data, one possible result of evaluating this expression is shown in Fig. 10.1. (The result is not unique, in general, because TAG, like SERIAL, involves some degree of unpredictability. However, we do require that such results be *repeatable;* that is, if *x* is an expression, we require that *x* always return the same output given the same input, even if it involves an invocation of TAG.)

S#	QTY	P#_SERIAL
S1	300	1
S1	200	5
S1	400	3
S1	200	4
S1	100	6
S1	100	2
S2	300	1
S2	400	2
S3	200	1
S4	200	3
S4	300	1
S4	400	2

Fig. 10.1: TAG example: one possible result

Explanation: The TAG operation tags tuples of the relation resulting from evaluation of a specified relational expression (the relational expression in the example is just SP, and so the resulting relation is simply the current value of relvar SP, of course). The specification WITHIN {S#} means those tags are to be unique within distinct S# values (and we assume for simplicity that they start from one for each such S# value; of course, we could extend the definition of the TAG operator to allow the user to specify a different starting value). Thus, the overall result of the TAG operation in the example has attributes S#, P#, QTY, and P#_SERIAL (this last one due to the AS P#_SERIAL specification).

We then "project away" the P# attribute to obtain a result such as that shown in Fig. 10.1. Note that the cardinality of the projection is necessarily the same as that of SP, whereas the same would not be true, in general, if we did not retain the P#_SERIAL attribute.

We remark finally that TAG could be useful in situations in which sensitive information needs to be concealed from certain users. For example, suppose we are given an employees relvar EMP, with attributes EMP# and SALARY. Then the expression

```
( EMP TAG AS EMP_TAG ) { EMP_TAG, SALARY }
```

could be used as the basis for defining a virtual relvar that would permit statistical analysis to be done on employee salaries without revealing exactly who earns what (in effect, the expression replaces employee numbers by tags).

RM VERY STRONG SUGGESTION 2: FOREIGN KEYS

*D should include some declarative shorthand for expressing **referential constraints** (also known as **foreign key** constraints).*

——————— ♦ ♦ ♦ ♦ ———————

RM Prescription 23 requires support for the definition (and of course enforcement) of database constraints of potentially arbitrary complexity. And since a referential constraint is really just a special case of such a constraint, it must of course be capable of formulation in terms of the support provided under RM Prescription 23. Here, for example, is a **Tutorial D** formulation (repeated from Chapter 2) of the referential constraint from shipments to suppliers:

```
CONSTRAINT DBC5 SP { S# } ‖≤‖ S { S# } ;
```

RM Very Strong Suggestion 2 simply recognizes that it might be desirable to provide some more user-friendly special-case syntax for such constraints. For example:

```
VAR S  REAL RELATION { S# S#, ... } KEY { S# } ;

VAR SP REAL RELATION { S# S#, ... } KEY { S#, P# }
    FOREIGN KEY { S# } REFERENCES S ;
```

By way of a second example, consider the following:

```
VAR EMP REAL RELATION { EMP# EMP#, ..., MGR# EMP#, ... } KEY { EMP# }
    FOREIGN KEY { MGR# } REFERENCES EMP { EMP# } ;
```

Here attribute MGR# represents the employee number of the manager of the employee identified by EMP#, and the foreign key specification is shorthand for a CONSTRAINT statement of the form:

```
CONSTRAINT ... EMP { MGR# } ‖≤‖ EMP { EMP# } RENAME ( EMP# AS MGR# ) ;
```

Note the need to do some attribute renaming in this constraint.

Special-casing such as the foregoing does at least provide explicit syntax for a pragmatically important concept, *foreign key,* that is not otherwise mentioned in the *Manifesto* (or in **Tutorial D,** come to that). It also provides a place to attach declarative specifications of certain "referential actions"—cascade delete, etc.—if such specifications are considered desirable, without necessarily having to get into the business of supporting triggered procedures in full generality. *Note:* The fact that we can update several relvars "simultaneously," using multiple assignment, implies that there is no logical need to support such referential actions. However, there are good usability and productivity arguments in favor of providing such support, and we certainly do not preclude it—though it would be remiss of us not to point out that (as noted, rather obliquely, in Chapter 3) it does have the potential to violate *The Assignment Principle*.

We close this section with a few miscellaneous observations:

- Note that we allow foreign keys to reference any candidate key, instead of—as historically—requiring them to reference a primary key specifically. In fact, for reasons explained in Chapters 2 and 6, we do not prescribe any explicit support at all for primary keys as such (though we do not prohibit them either).

- Referential constraints are usually thought of as applying to real relvars only. In the *Manifesto*, by contrast, we regard them as applying to virtual relvars as well.

- It is possible—though good design practice might militate against it—for two distinct relvars *R1* and *R2* each to involve a foreign key that references the other. Such a possibility suggests that we might need something akin to multiple assignment for data definition operations also (for otherwise it might not be possible to define *R1* until *R2* has been defined and vice versa).

RM VERY STRONG SUGGESTION 3: CANDIDATE KEY INFERENCE

Let RX *be a relational expression. By definition,* RX *can be thought of as designating a relvar,* R *say—either a user-defined relvar (if* RX *is just a relvar name) or a system-defined relvar (otherwise). It is desirable, though not always entirely feasible, for the system to be able to* **infer the candidate keys** *of* R, *such that (among other things):*

a. *If* RX *constitutes the defining expression for some virtual relvar* R', *then those inferred candidate keys can be checked for consistency with the candidate keys explicitly defined for* R' *and—assuming no conflict—become candidate keys for* R'.

b. *Those inferred candidate keys can be included in the information about* R *that is made available (in response to a "metaquery") to a user of* D.

D *should provide such functionality, but without any guarantee (a) that such inferred candidate keys are not proper supersets of actual candidate keys or (b) that such an inferred candidate key is discovered for every actual candidate key.*

If *K* is a candidate key for relvar *R*, it follows from the definitions of *candidate key* and *functional dependency* (see Chapter 2) that:

- Because of the *uniqueness* property, the functional dependence (FD) $K \rightarrow A$ holds for every attribute *A* of *R*.

- Because of the *irreducibility* property, there is no proper subset *K'* of *K* such that the FD $K' \rightarrow A$ holds for every attribute *A* of *R*.

By way of example, let *R* be the shipments relvar SP and *K* its sole key {S#,P#}. Then:

- It is the case that every attribute of SP is functionally dependent on the combination of attributes {S#,P#}.

- It is not the case that every attribute of SP is functionally dependent on some proper subset of that combination of attributes; to be specific, QTY is not. (By contrast, S# and P# both are, trivially, thanks to the trivial FDs {S#} → {S#} and {P#} → {P#}. An FD is *trivial* if the right side is a subset of the left side.)

It follows from the foregoing that if we know the FDs that hold for a given relvar, we can determine the keys for that relvar—they are, precisely, those irreducible combinations K of attributes such that the FD $K \rightarrow A$ holds for every attribute A of the relvar in question. Hence, in order to determine the keys for the result of some relational expression *RX*, we need to determine the corresponding FDs. In other words, we need an *FD inference mechanism,* which—assuming we know the FDs that hold in the "base" or real relvars—will let us infer the FDs that hold in the result of evaluating an arbitrary expression involving those real relvars. (And, of course, we do know the FDs that hold in the real relvars, because they will have been defined as constraints on the relvars in question.) Such an inference mechanism is presented in reference [28]. See also reference [108].

We remark that key inference is in fact a special case of constraint inference in general, support for which is required by RM Prescription 23. We mention keys explicitly here because of their pragmatic importance, and also because it might be desirable to use the special-case inferencing mechanism described in reference [28] instead of a more general mechanism that works for all constraints. As noted in our discussion of RM Prescription 23 in Chapter 6, however, there are known to be intrinsic limits on the degree to which such inferencing might be feasible in practice, which is why we allow for both of the following possibilities:

- The inference mechanism might in fact find *proper superkeys* rather than true candidate keys. (Recall from Chapter 2 that a superkey is a superset of a key; in other words, a superkey satisfies the uniqueness property but not necessarily the irreducibility property. A *proper* superkey is a superkey that definitely does not satisfy the irreducibility property.)

- Also, the inference mechanism might fail to discover certain keys entirely.

Implementations can thus compete with one another over their degree of success at inferring keys.

RM VERY STRONG SUGGESTION 4: TRANSITION CONSTRAINTS

D should support **transition constraints**—*i.e., constraints on the transitions that a given database can make from one value to another.*

Here is an example ("no supplier's status must ever decrease"):

```
CONSTRAINT TRC1 IS_EMPTY
   ( ( ( S' { S#, STATUS } RENAME ( STATUS AS STATUS' ) )
       JOIN
       ( S { S#, STATUS } ) )
     WHERE STATUS' > STATUS ) ;
```

Explanation: We introduce the convention that a primed relvar name, such as S' in the example, is understood to refer to the corresponding relvar as it was *prior to the update under consideration.* The constraint in the example can thus be understood as follows: If (a) we join together (over supplier numbers) the relation that is the value of relvar S before the update and the relation that is the value afterwards, and (b) we pick out the tuples in that join for which the old status value is greater than the new one, then (c) the final result must be empty. (Since the join is over supplier numbers, any tuple in the result of the join for which the old status value is greater than the new one would correspond to a supplier whose status had decreased.)

Now, constraint TRC1 is a transition constraint that applies to just a single relvar: namely, the suppliers relvar S. Here by contrast is an example of a transition constraint that applies to two relvars taken in combination ("the total quantity of any given part, taken over all suppliers, can never decrease"):

```
CONSTRAINT TRC2 IS_EMPTY (
    ( ( SUMMARIZE SP' PER ( S'{ S# } ) ADD ( SUM ( QTY ) AS SQ' ) )
    JOIN
    ( SUMMARIZE SP  PER ( S { S# } ) ADD ( SUM ( QTY ) AS SQ  ) ) )
    WHERE SQ' > SQ ) ;
```

Like the database constraints required by RM Prescription 23, transition constraints are checked at statement boundaries. *Note:* The database constraints of RM Prescription 23 are sometimes referred to as *state* constraints, because they refer to valid "states" of the database rather than valid transitions from one such "state" to another.

RM VERY STRONG SUGGESTION 5: QUOTA QUERIES

*D should provide some shorthand for expressing **quota queries**. It should not be necessary to convert the relation concerned into (e.g.) an array in order to formulate such a query.*

———— ♦ ♦ ♦ ♦ ♦ ————

A *quota query* is a query that specifies a desired limit, or **quota,** on the cardinality of the result: for example, the query "Get the three heaviest parts," for which the specified quota is three. (Note, however, that the actual result cardinality might be either more or less than the specified quota, as we will soon see.) Here is a possible **Tutorial D** formulation of this example:

```
WITH ( P RENAME ( WEIGHT AS WT ) ) AS T1 ,
     ( EXTEND P ADD ( COUNT ( T1 WHERE WT > WEIGHT ) AS #_HEAVIER ) AS T2 ,
     ( T2 WHERE #_HEAVIER < 3 ) AS T3 :
T3 { P#, PNAME, WEIGHT, COLOR, CITY }
```

Given our usual sample data, the result consists of parts P2, P3, and P6.

Quota queries are quite common in practice. Now, such queries can be formulated in terms of our usual relational operators, as we have just seen, but such formulations do tend to be rather roundabout and cumbersome. It therefore seems worthwhile to consider the possibility of providing some more user-friendly way of expressing them; hence RM Very Strong Suggestion 5. To be specific, we propose introducing a new relational operator of the following form:

```
<rank>
    ::=   RANK <relation exp> BY ( <order item commalist> AS <attribute name> )
```

The < *relation exp* > must not be a < *monadic or dyadic other built-in relation op inv* > . We remind you of the syntax of < *order item* > (repeated from Chapter 5):

```
<order item>
    ::=   <direction> <attribute ref>

<direction>
    ::=   ASC | DESC
```

Here is a more or less self-explanatory example of the use of RANK:

```
RANK P BY ( DESC WEIGHT AS WEIGHT_RANK )
```

Given our usual sample data, the result of this operation is as shown in Fig. 10.2 (we assume that attribute WEIGHT_RANK in that result is of type INTEGER). The effect of the operation is thus to "rank" part tuples in order of descending weight (of course, there is no implication that the system must perform a physical sort in order to obtain the desired result). The original quota query "Get the three heaviest parts" is now straightforward:

```
( r WHERE WEIGHT_RANK ≤ 3 ) { ALL BUT WEIGHT_RANK }
```

where *r* denotes the result of the RANK operation. *Note:* Given our usual sample data, this expression does indeed yield a result relation of exactly three tuples. However, if (say) part P4 had weight 18 instead of 14, it would yield four tuples, not three; and if there were currently only two parts altogether instead of six, it would necessarily yield only two tuples. See reference [56] for further analysis of such matters.

P#	PNAME	COLOR	WEIGHT	CITY	WEIGHT_RANK
P1	Nut	Red	12	London	5
P2	Bolt	Green	17	Paris	2
P3	Screw	Blue	17	Rome	2
P4	Screw	Red	14	London	4
P5	Cam	Blue	12	Paris	5
P6	Cog	Red	19	London	1

Fig. 10.2: RANK example (result)

RANK is just shorthand, of course[1]—the example just shown is equivalent to the following:

```
WITH ( P RENAME ( WEIGHT AS WT ) ) AS T1 :
EXTEND P ADD ( COUNT ( T1 WHERE WT > WEIGHT ) + 1 AS WEIGHT_RANK )
```

Here is another example:

---

1. Despite the fact that we claimed the opposite in reference [83] (and therefore proposed a different solution to the problem of quota queries in that reference, one that we now explicitly disavow).

```
S JOIN ( ( RANK S BY ( ASC STATUS AS SR ) ) WHERE SR ≤ 2 ) { STATUS }
```

("Get all suppliers whose status is one of the two smallest"; given our usual sample data, the two smallest status values are 10 and 20, and so the result consists of suppliers S1, S2, and S4). The second operand to the join is an expression denoting a relation with one attribute, called STATUS, that contains the two smallest status values. The join then yields a relation containing exactly those suppliers having one of those two status values.

The < *rank* > shorthand facilitates the formulation of many kinds of "statistical" queries. We give just one more example here:

```
( ( RANK S BY ( DESC STATUS AS SR ) ) WHERE SR ≤ ( COUNT ( S ) / 10 ) ) { ALL BUT SR }
```

("Get the top ten percent of suppliers," where by "the top ten percent" we mean those suppliers whose status is greater than that of the other 90 percent, loosely speaking).

RM VERY STRONG SUGGESTION 6: GENERALIZED TRANSITIVE CLOSURE

*D should provide some shorthand for expressing the **generalized transitive closure** operation, including the ability to specify generalized* concatenate *and* aggregate *operations.*

———— ♦ ♦ ♦ ♦ ————

Tutorial D already includes support for the transitive closure operator TCLOSE; unfortunately, however, TCLOSE by itself is not adequate for dealing with all possible recursive queries, as we now explain.

It is convenient to begin by repeating, and amplifying, some of the remarks on transitive closure from the discussion of RM Prescription 19 in Chapter 6. Consider the bill-of-materials relation MMQ shown in Fig. 10.3 (an extended version of Fig. 6.1 from Chapter 6). As explained in Chapter 6, we can refer to that relation as a *digraph relation,* because it can be represented as a directed graph of nodes and directed arcs; the nodes are named and possibly labeled (see later), the arcs are directed and (again) possibly labeled. For example, in the particular case of the graph for relation MMQ (refer to Fig. 10.4):

MMQ	MAJOR_P# : P#	MINOR_P# : P#	QTY : QTY
	P1	P2	5
	P1	P3	3
	P2	P3	2
	P2	P4	7
	P3	P5	4
	P4	P6	8

Fig. 10.3: Relation MMQ

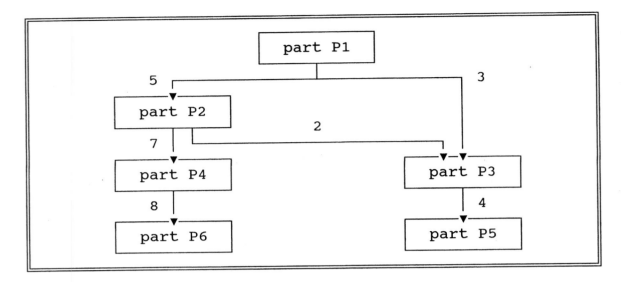

Fig. 10.4: Graph of relation MMQ

- Each node is named for a particular part.

- There is an arc from node *Pi* to node *Pj* if and only if part *Pi* contains part *Pj* as an immediate component.

- Each arc is labeled with the corresponding quantity.

- The nodes are unlabeled.

As noted in Chapter 6, it is often convenient to replace a directed graph such as that of Fig. 10.4 by a pure hierarchy with possibly repeated nodes, as in Fig. 10.5.

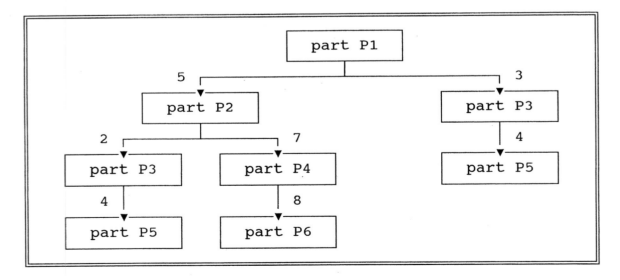

Fig. 10.5: Graph of relation MMQ as a hierarchy

Now, in Chapter 6 we explained how TCLOSE could be applied to what was effectively the projection of relation MMQ over MAJOR_P# and MINOR_P#; Fig. 10.6 (a repeat of Fig. 6.4) shows the result. And we claimed that TCLOSE was important in connection with the *part explosion* problem—i.e., the problem of finding all components, at all levels, of some specified part. For example, consider the problem of "exploding" part P2. Here is a **Tutorial D** formulation of this query:

```
( ( TCLOSE ( MM { MAJOR_P#, MINOR_P# } ) ) WHERE MAJOR_P# = P#('P2') ) { MINOR_P# }
```

MAJOR_P# : P#	MINOR_P# : P#
P1	P2
P1	P3
P2	P3
P2	P4
P3	P5
P4	P6
P1	P4
P1	P5
P1	P6
P2	P5
P2	P6

Fig. 10.6: Transitive closure of MMQ { MAJOR_P#, MINOR_P# }

The trouble is, what we really need is something rather more general than just TCLOSE per se. Consider the query "What is the total quantity of part P5 that is needed to make part P1?" Inspection of either Fig. 10.4 or Fig. 10.5 will quickly show that the answer is 52:

- For each path from node P1 to node P5, we multiply the quantities that are the arc labels along that path.

- Then we add together all the products so obtained.

Refer to Fig. 10.7.

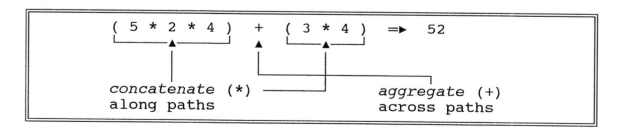

Fig. 10.7: Total quantity of part P5 in part P1

In practice, it turns out that what is often wanted is not just a simple part explosion as such but, rather, a *gross requirement*—which is, loosely speaking, a combination of the "part explosion" and "total quantity" queries. In other words, we want a listing of all the parts that go to make up a given part, together with the corresponding total quantities. Following reference [93], therefore, we suggest a generalized version of the transitive closure operation that is intended to address problems of this general nature. The operator takes four operands:

1.   A relation of nodes and node labels (see below)

2.   A relation of directed arcs and arc labels

3.   A *concatenate* operator

4.   An *aggregate* operator

In our example, operand 1 is the parts relation (not explicitly mentioned in the foregoing discussion); operand 2 is relation MMQ; operand 3 is "*"; and operand 4 is "+". The operation returns a ternary relation with heading

        ⟨ X T, Y T, Z C ⟩

where *X* and *Y* are "node" attributes and are as in operand 2 (note that they both have the same type *T*), *Z* represents the computed value obtained by following all paths from node *X* to node *Y* and applying the *concatenate* and *aggregate* operators appropriately, and *C* is the type of that computed value. The body of the result contains a tuple for every path, direct or indirect, in the operand 2 graph.

Note: As it happens, there are no node labels in the bill-of-materials example, but such is not always the case. For example, consider an airline schedule. Here the nodes denote cities, the node labels are minimum connection times, the arcs denote flights, and the arc labels are departure and arrival times. Note moreover that the bill-of-materials graph is *acyclic,* but the airline schedule graph is not. If there can be cycles in the graph, the *concatenate* operator must be defined to take care of them somehow; for example, in the airline schedule example, it must reject routes that visit the same city twice.

RM VERY STRONG SUGGESTION 7: USER-DEFINED GENERIC OPERATORS

*D should provide some means for users to define their own generic **operators,** including in particular generic **relational** operators.*

For simplicity, the discussion that follows concentrates on relational operators specifically. The points are all applicable to other generic operators as well, of course, mutatis mutandis.

Recall from earlier chapters that the built-in relational operators are all generic, in the sense that they work for all relations (loosely speaking). The operator JOIN, for example, applies to any pair of relations whatsoever; there is no question of the relations in question having to conform to certain specific relation types (except of course that attributes with the same name must be of the same type). Moreover, those operators are generic precisely because they are associated with a type generator—namely, RELATION—instead of with some specific relation type; they therefore apply to every specific relation type that is defined by means of that type generator.[1]

---

1. As mentioned in passing in Chapter 6, generic operators thus constitute another kind of polymorphism (we considered overloading polymorphism in Chapter 6, and we will be discussing inclusion polymorphism at length in Chapter 14).

RM Very Strong Suggestion 7 suggests that it would be advantageous for users to be able to define generic operators of their own. By way of example, suppose **Tutorial D** did not include direct support for the Great Divide. Then, if the suggestion under discussion were implemented, it would be possible for users to define a generic Great Divide operator of their own. User-defined aggregate operators provide another example (the built-in aggregate operators—SUM, MAX, and so on—are also generic in the foregoing sense); for instance, it might be possible to define a MEDIAN operator in this way.

We have no concrete suggestions to offer regarding user-defined generic operators at this time, because we believe the issue requires further study.

Note: The foregoing discussion raises another possibility—namely, that it would be nice if users could also define their own *type generators*. We do not go so far as to make this possibility a concrete part of RM Very Strong Suggestion 7, however, since we believe it requires further study (over and above the further study already mentioned in the previous paragraph).

RM VERY STRONG SUGGESTION 8: SQL MIGRATION

*SQL should be implementable in **D**—not because such implementation is desirable in itself, but so that a painless migration route might be available for current SQL users. To this same end, existing SQL databases should be convertible to a form that **D** programs can operate on without error.*

———— ♦ ♦ ♦ ♦ ————

We reject SQL as a long-term foundation for the future. However, we are not so naïve as to think that SQL will ever disappear; rather, it is our hope that some **D** will be sufficiently superior to SQL that it will become the database language of choice, by a process of natural selection, and SQL will become "the database language of last resort." In fact, we see a parallel with the world of programming languages, where COBOL has never disappeared (and never will); but COBOL has become "the programming language of last resort" for developing applications, because preferable alternatives exist. We see SQL as a kind of database COBOL, and we would like some **D** to become a preferable alternative to it.

To repeat something we said in Chapter 1, however, we do realize that SQL databases and applications are going to be with us for a long time—to think otherwise would be quite unrealistic—and so we do have to pay some attention to the question of what to do about today's SQL legacy. Hence the present "very strong suggestion."

Please note immediately that the suggestion in question does not mean that **D** needs to be a proper superset of SQL. Rather, it means that it should be possible to write a "front end"—i.e., a layer of **D** code on top of the true relational functionality of **D**—that (a) will accept SQL operations against converted SQL data and (b) will give the results that those SQL operations would have given if they had been executed against the original unconverted SQL data. We believe it should be possible to construct such a front end without contravening any of the prescriptions and proscriptions laid down in the *Manifesto*. (An analogous remark applies to the recommendation that SQL databases be convertible to **D** form, of course.) In fact—noting that **D** is computationally complete, and noting too that SQL front ends already exist for many nonSQL systems—we see no reason to doubt the feasibility of producing a front end such as the one under consideration.

Of course, we would not want a **D** database, even one that is really just a converted SQL database, to be accessible only via SQL; rather, we would like it to be available for use in "native **D** mode" as well. To that end, it is important for anyone involved in the development of such a front end to bear the following goals in mind:

- First of all (to repeat), users must be able to make direct use of **D** for ad hoc queries and for developing new applications on the **D** version of the database.

- That **D** database should not be encumbered with material placed there solely to support the SQL front end. Such material, having no obvious bearing on the enterprise the database is intended to serve, might cause undue confusion for **D** users.

- SQL users should not be deprived of the benefits of the **D** optimizer. Such deprivation would arise, for example, if the SQL front end used **D** as a mere access method, instead of mapping high-level SQL expressions into equally high-level **D** expressions.

We should add that it will almost certainly not be possible to achieve these goals 100 percent, though we do think they should be strongly striven for. The fact is, there are certain features in SQL that (as far as we can see) could only be fully supported in an SQL front end if **D** in turn contained analogous features of its own—and the features in question are either ones we explicitly proscribe or ones that would constitute blatant violations of **D**'s conceptual integrity (and such violations are implicitly proscribed by RM Prescription 26). We hope and believe that the SQL features in question are so pathological that uses of them will be few and far between, sufficiently so for it to be acceptable for such uses to be worked around on a case-by-case basis.[1] Examples that come to mind are

- View updating where the effects prescribed by SQL are logically incorrect (in particular, view updating when WITH CASCADED CHECK OPTION is not specified)

- The SQL statement SET CONSTRAINTS (all constraints are "immediate" in **D**, and there is no notion of dynamically switching them on and off)

- SQL expressions that select the same column twice without performing any kind of column renaming (e.g., the SQL expression SELECT A, A FROM T)

and so on.

To return to the main thread of the discussion: We now proceed to offer a few practical suggestions for implementing the desired SQL front end. Of course, it goes without saying that our suggestions are nowhere near being a complete design—they are only "notes toward" such a design—but they do address certain questions that come to mind almost immediately when our RM Proscriptions in particular are considered in such a context.

First of all, we assume that the process of converting an SQL database to a **D** analog is reasonably "direct," in the sense that (a) every SQL base table maps to a **D** real relvar, and (b) every column in such a base table maps to an attribute in the corresponding relvar. Under that assumption, of course, we are immediately confronted with the possibility that the base table in question might contain duplicate rows or nulls or both. Direct support for these features is expressly prohibited in **D** by RM Proscriptions 3 and 4, so what is to be done? This question is the topic of the two subsections immediately following.

Duplicate Rows

An SQL base table permits duplicate rows if and only if no key is declared for it via either PRIMARY KEY or UNIQUE. Given such a base table *T*, then, the **D** relvar *R* corresponding to *T* will have to have an extra attribute (i.e., one not corresponding to any column in *T*) to provide the necessary key functionality. That attribute can be declared with default SERIAL ()—meaning it constitutes a "system key"—if **D** supports RM Very Strong Suggestion 1 as discussed earlier in this chapter. The SQL front

---

1. In fact, we are somewhat skeptical as to whether the features in question are supported in existing SQL front ends either (or even in SQL DBMSs, in some cases).

end can now support certain SQL INSERT operations by mapping them directly into **D** INSERTs; since values for the extra attribute are provided by the system, no corresponding attribute is needed in the relation to be inserted, and of course there *is* no corresponding column in the SQL table to be inserted into.

Unfortunately, if *T* permits duplicate rows, it follows that any table *t* to be inserted into *T* might contain duplicate rows as well. Let *r* be the **D** relation corresponding to *t*. Like *R,* therefore, *r* will need an extra attribute (i.e., one over and above those corresponding to the columns of *t*). Our suggested TAG relational operator can be used to provide that extra attribute; if we are not careful, however, we could now be faced with a situation in which each of *r* and *R* has an attribute that has no counterpart in the other. And even if we *are* careful to ensure the extra attributes do correspond (i.e., they have the same name—*X,* say—and the same type in both *r* and *R*), there is still the problem that, in general, the *X* values provided for *r* by TAG will clash with the *X* values already present in *R*. *Note:* We are assuming here that TAG generates *X* values that start again from one every time it is invoked; the clash occurs because {*X*} is supposed to be a key for *R*. One solution to this problem is to extend TAG to allow the user to specify a different starting value on different invocations, a possibility mentioned under RM Very Strong Suggestion 1.

We also need to address the problem of *naming* the systematically generated attributes that have no corresponding SQL columns. Happily, SQL expressly prohibits column names that begin with an underscore; assuming **D** has no such prohibition, therefore, we have here the basis of an obvious way to avoid naming clashes. What is more, the same approach could also simplify the task of the SQL front end in hiding the extra attributes from its users.

Next, we need to consider the question of duplicate rows that are *dynamically generated*—i.e., the question of those SQL operators that can generate duplicate rows at run time. The operators in question are (a) SELECT without DISTINCT, (b) VALUES, and (c) UNION ALL:

- SELECT without DISTINCT and VALUES can both be implemented by using our suggested TAG operator and having the front end discard attributes generated by TAG on presentation of final results.

- The same treatment is not suitable for UNION ALL, but here an easy solution lies in merely adding a constant attribute to the **D** relations corresponding to the SQL tables that are the operands of the UNION ALL. For example, the SQL expression

```
SELECT * FROM T1
UNION CORRESPONDING ALL
SELECT * FROM T2
```

can be mapped to the **Tutorial D** expression

```
( EXTEND T1 ADD ( 1 AS _EXTRA ) )
UNION
( EXTEND T2 ADD ( 2 AS _EXTRA ) )
```

Again, of course, the front end would have to discard the extra attribute on presentation of the final result.

Nulls

Nulls in SQL are hard to explain. There are many reasons for this state of affairs, but one important one is that, despite the fact that in SQL circles they are often explicitly called null *values,* SQL nulls are not really values at all but "marks" [23]. However (and regardless of whether or not you agree with this position), the fact is that nulls will have to map to values in **D**, because in **D** every expression—be it an operator invocation, a simple literal, an attribute reference, a parameter reference, a variable reference, or whatever—always denotes a value specifically. With this point in mind, therefore, we offer the following observations:

- The built-in SQL type INTEGER is not the same as the built-in type of that name typically found in conventional programming languages (and a similar observation applies to all of the other built-in types in SQL). The reason is that, as the SQL standard puts it, "[every] data type includes a special value, called the null value" [99].

- The *Manifesto* prescribes support for the built-in type **boolean.** The SQL standard does support a type it calls BOOLEAN, but that type is not the same as the prescribed type for at least the reasons explained in Appendix H, q.v. In any case, most SQL implementations do not explicitly support type BOOLEAN (though they do support expressions—e.g., in WHERE clauses—that return truth values, as the SQL standard requires).

- The SQL equality comparison operator is not the same as that found in conventional languages. In particular, it is not the same as the equality comparison operator required in **D**.

- The other scalar operators of SQL, where they have apparent counterparts in conventional languages, are not the same as those apparent counterparts. For example, the SQL operators "+" and "||" (concatenate) are not the usual "+" and "||" operators. Indeed, the types of the operands of those operators are not the usual types, as already noted above.

These four points, we suggest, crystallize the problems (or, at least, the major problems) arising from nulls that confront the implementer of an SQL front end. Now we make some observations regarding **D** that might point to ways of addressing those problems:

- As noted in the introduction to this part of the book, the *Manifesto* is intended to be open ended; i.e., anything not explicitly prescribed is permitted, unless of course it leads to a violation of something explicitly prescribed or proscribed. In particular, therefore, there are no proscribed types, and there are no proscribed operators (generally speaking). Nor do we have any prescriptions or proscriptions concerning concrete syntax, *modulo* RM Prescription 26.

- As a consequence of the foregoing point, **D** is at least theoretically permitted to have (e.g.) an operator called "+" that is not the normal operator of that name. A similar remark applies to "=". That said, however, we venture to suggest that to use such names for SQL-like perversions of the operators they normally stand for would be counter to the spirit of **D**. A similar remark applies to the names of built-in types such as INTEGER and BOOLEAN (as well as all of the other familiar ones—CHAR, DATE, TIME, and so on).

- But if **D** had a built-in type called INTEGER that *was* the same as the type of that name found in conventional languages, it could certainly also have another type (built in or otherwise), perhaps called SQL_INTEGER, with properties analogous to those of the SQL type called INTEGER. A similar remark applies to other built-in types.

- Likewise, if **D** had "=" as its operator for equality comparison, it could also have another operator (perhaps "sql=") for the corresponding but different SQL operator. A similar remark applies to other SQL scalar operators.

In other words, we would expect **D** to have first claim on the usual names for the most familiar types and operators, but to provide counterparts (or allow the user to define counterparts) to all of the corresponding but different SQL types and operators, with names that are different from those of SQL for those counterparts.

Now suppose SQL base table *T* has a column *I* of (SQL) type INTEGER. Suppose too that when base table *T* is mapped to **D** relvar *T*, column *I* becomes attribute *I*, of type SQL_INTEGER. We now point out certain consequences of the foregoing observations (using **Tutorial D** syntax specifically, as and where appropriate):

- The SQL expression

  ```
  SELECT * FROM T WHERE I < 10
  ```

  maps to the **Tutorial D** expression

  ```
  T WHERE ( I sql< 10 ) = SQL_BOOLEAN ( 'TRUE' )
  ```

  We explain this mapping as follows. First of all, the SQL "<" operator maps to a **Tutorial D** analog of that operator ("sql<"). Since this latter operator does not yield values of the **Tutorial D** type BOOLEAN, we must operate on its result with some operator that does—namely, the **Tutorial D** equality comparison operator ("="). Let the **Tutorial D** type corresponding to operators such as "sql<" (and, in particular, "sql=") be SQL_BOOLEAN, with values SQL_BOOLEAN ('TRUE'), SQL_BOOLEAN ('FALSE'), and SQL_BOOLEAN ('UNKNOWN'). In the example, then, the right comparand in the WHERE clause is specified as an invocation of the selector corresponding to that type. In general, in fact, the SQL WHERE clause "WHERE *cond*" will map to the **D** WHERE clause "WHERE (*SQL_cond*) = SQL_BOOLEAN ('TRUE')" (where *SQL_cond* is the mapped version of *cond*, of course).

- The SQL expression

  ```
  SELECT DISTINCT I, J, ..., K FROM T
  ```

  can be mapped more directly into just

  ```
  T { I, J, ..., K }
  ```

  This straightforward mapping is possible because SQL reverts to the normal treatment of equality in places where its usual treatment is impossible to apply in any sensible or meaningful way.

- The SQL front end will certainly require SQL_INTEGER to be an ordinal type, because the INTEGER type of SQL is such a type. Thus, the **Tutorial D** expression

  ```
  T WHERE I < SQL_INTEGER ('20')
  ```

  might be valid. Whether the result of that expression includes those tuples of T for which the I value is SQL_INTEGER ('NULL') will depend, of course, on how the operator "<" is defined for type SQL_INTEGER.

- The result of the **Tutorial D** expression

  ```
  T WHERE I ≠ SQL_INTEGER ('20')
  ```

  certainly does include those tuples of T for which the I value is SQL_INTEGER ('NULL'), unlike its SQL counterpart

```
SELECT * FROM T WHERE I <> 20
```

(the symbol "<>" here is SQL syntax for "≠"). We venture to suggest that—at least in some cases—**D** expressions involving tables derived from SQL databases with nulls will give results that are more intuitively acceptable than those of SQL expressions.

The foregoing proposals, it has to be said, might make it difficult to meet our goal of making the converted SQL database usable "in native **D** mode." At the same time, we are aware that some SQL database administrators today already implement a null-free policy (at least insofar as it is in fact possible to steer clear of nulls in SQL), and it would be a shame for users of such databases to have to put up with any inconvenience arising from a migration strategy that takes nulls into account. For databases that have been implemented under a null-free policy, therefore, we believe it should be possible to map the built-in types and operators of SQL directly to their obvious counterparts in **D** and deal manually with any SQL expressions that make use of operators that generate nulls dynamically (e.g., outer joins and aggregations over empty sets).

We now turn to certain other SQL features and idiosyncrasies that will require special attention in the SQL front end. *Note:* Most of the subsections that follow have to do with features introduced into SQL with SQL:1999, and tutorial descriptions of those features can be found in references [41] and [116-117]. There do not seem to be any tutorials available on SQL:2003 at the time of writing.

SQL Column Names vs. D Attribute Names

The following SQL peculiarities will need to be addressed:

- There is more than one way of referring to a column in SQL expressions. For example, the SQL expression

```
SELECT T1.C FROM T AS T1
```

is equivalent to the SQL expression

```
SELECT C FROM T AS T1
```

As a consequence, the result of the first expression yields a table whose sole column is named C and not T1.C. Hence, the following expression (for example) is not valid in SQL:

```
SELECT T2.T1.C FROM ( SELECT T1.C FROM T AS T1 ) AS T2
```

It follows that if **D** adopts the simple approach to attribute naming and referencing used in **Tutorial D** (an approach we would certainly recommend for consideration by other **D** designers), then the mapping of SQL FROM clauses will be nontrivial. However, the **Tutorial D** support for systematic renaming of all attributes could be useful in this connection. For example, the SQL FROM clause

```
FROM T1, T2
```

could be mapped to

```
( T1 RENAME ( PREFIX '' AS 'T1_' ) )
JOIN
( T2 RENAME ( PREFIX '' AS 'T2_' ) )
```

This mapping would avoid the problem that arises when T1 and T2 have columns of the same name. Of course, there would be obvious implications for mapping other parts of the overall SQL expression that contained the FROM clause in question.

■ The SQL expression

```
SELECT A + B FROM T
```

yields a table with an "anonymous column." The SQL standard actually requires such columns to acquire unpredictable column names, so the SQL front end to **D** could perhaps simply follow the standard's prescription in this respect (so long as it also takes the precaution of ensuring that no two columns in the same table have the same name). Our previous suggestion concerning attribute names beginning with underscores could be of help here.

■ The SQL expression

```
SELECT * FROM T1
UNION
SELECT * FROM T2
```

cannot in general be mapped to

```
T1 UNION T2
```

(why not?). Thus, it might be necessary to rename attributes so that corresponding attributes in the operands of the union have the same name. Unfortunately, this fact implies that the SQL-to-**D** database conversion process will have to keep some record of SQL left-to-right column order, because there will (of course) be no analogous attribute ordering in **D**. (In fact, such a record will be needed for several other reasons anyway—e.g., supporting SELECT * or INSERT when no column names are specified.)

Character String Comparisons

As noted in Chapter 6 (under RM Prescription 8), it is possible in SQL for the character strings

```
'AB'
```

and

```
'AB '
```

to be treated as equal; to be specific, they are treated as equal if and only if PAD SPACE applies to the applicable *collation* [41]. In effect, PAD SPACE means that trailing space characters are implicitly trimmed before the comparison is done. That implicit trimming will have to be made explicit in **D**.

Cursors

Cursor operations can be implemented as follows:

■ OPEN causes the relation to be iterated over to be copied into an array (probably with some appropriate locking), as in the *<relation get>* operation of **Tutorial D** (see Chapter 5).

- If "the cursor is updatable" [41], then each row in that array will have to include, either explicitly or implicitly, some key value for the corresponding row from the underlying real relvar.

- FETCH is straightforward.

- DELETE or UPDATE WHERE CURRENT—in some respects the most questionable of all SQL operators—can be simulated by means of a **D** DELETE or UPDATE WHERE on the underlying table, using the appropriate key value (which will have to be retrieved in response to the corresponding FETCH, regardless of whether the key columns are "columns of the cursor"). If the cursor is a scroll cursor, however, there are some tricky decisions to be made:

  - *DELETE:* Suppose the cursor is positioned on the third row of a four-row result (i.e., that row is the DELETE target). In some implementations the DELETE closes the gap, so that FETCH ABSOLUTE 4 will now fail and FETCH ABSOLUTE 3 will fetch the original fourth row; in others, the DELETE just marks the row as deleted and does not close the gap, so that FETCH ABSOLUTE 3 will now fail and FETCH ABSOLUTE 4 will succeed. The standard allows either behavior.

  - *UPDATE:* Here the standard specifies that the current row of the cursor is to be updated as well as the corresponding base table row. However, it appears to overlook the fact that elsewhere it states that the UPDATE target column names refer to columns of the underlying base table, not columns of the cursor! For example, let table T have columns X, Y, and Z, and let cursor CR1 be defined on SELECT X AS Y FROM T. Then the effect of, e.g., UPDATE T SET X = 1, Y = 2, Z = 3 WHERE CURRENT OF CR1 is unclear. Presumably at most one of the three assignments can affect the sole column of the cursor, and presumably the assignment to Z cannot be the one in question. It would seem logical for the cursor column to be assigned the value 1, to keep it as a copy of T.X, but the standard does not actually say as much. The front end might like to take guidance from whichever SQL implementation it would most like to emulate.

ARRAY Types

The Third Manifesto does not prohibit **D** from including support for "collection" type generators, so **D** could legitimately support an ARRAY type generator, and we would certainly expect such support to include everything needed in connection with SQL's array types. (Of course, if such an ARRAY type generator were indeed supported, it would presumably replace or subsume the limited array support described in Chapter 5. Note, however, that it would still be the case that array variables would not be allowed in the database, thanks to *The Information Principle*. See RM Prescription 16.)

MULTISET Types

D could support a MULTISET type generator as a direct counterpart to SQL:2003's new MULTISET type constructor (though with the proviso that multiset variables would not be allowed in the database).

ROW Types

Everything needed in connection with SQL's row types can easily be simulated in **D** by means of the tuple type support required by RM Prescriptions 6 and 9.

XML Data

D could support an XML type as a direct counterpart to SQL:2003's type of that name (see reference [76] for a tutorial discussion of that new type). **D**'s support would necessarily include support for equality comparison (and all of the SQL constructs that depend on it, such as SELECT DISTINCT, NATURAL JOIN, FOREIGN KEY, and so on), over and above the XML facilities defined in the SQL standard.

User-Defined Types

SQL divides user-defined types into two kinds, "structured types" and "DISTINCT types." However, the difference between the two appears to be artificial and without good justification; we would not expect **D** to embrace it, therefore, even if it does not directly contravene any of our prescriptions or proscriptions. (The terminology is bad, too, inasmuch as all user-defined types, even the so-called structured ones, are still best thought of as scalar types in our terms.)

Representations: The most immediately obvious difference between structured and DISTINCT types is in the way their representations are specified. For a structured type, the representation is specified as a commalist of components called *attributes* (each consisting of an attribute-name/type-name pair); for a DISTINCT type, the representation is specified as a single type name, and furthermore the specified type must be built in (e.g., INTEGER, REAL, BLOB). Both of these styles of specification are easily mappable to a **D** possrep, with just a single component in the case of a DISTINCT type.

Unfortunately, however, there is no notion in SQL of each "possrep" automatically having an associated selector operator (see below), and so there cannot be any notion of every value of the type in question being produced by some invocation of such a selector. This fact could give rise to some difficulty in connection with inheritance (see Part IV of this book). For example, suppose type POINT has the usual cartesian coordinates representation, with components X and Y. Then SQL will allow us to define a subtype of POINT—COLORED_POINT, say—whose values cannot be represented by X and Y components! (By X and Y components alone, that is. The representation for colored points would presumably involve *three* components—X, Y, and COLOR.) By contrast, a **D** version of this example might involve three types, not two: a dummy type corresponding to both uncolored and colored points, and two subtypes of that dummy type, POINT and COLORED_POINT, corresponding to uncolored and colored points, respectively. (See Chapter 14 for an explanation of dummy types, and Appendix G for an extended discussion of examples of this same general nature.)

Operators implied by representations: RM Prescriptions 4 and 5 require each declared possrep to cause automatic provision of a corresponding selector operator and certain operators for exposing the possrep in question (THE_ operators, in **Tutorial D**). We have already observed that SQL has no counterpart to our selector; however, it does require each declared representation to cause automatic provision of certain *observer* and *mutator methods*. The "observer" methods correspond exactly to the read-only operators required by RM Prescription 5. The "mutator" methods do not correspond exactly to the update operators required by RM Prescription 5, however, because they are not update operators!—they do not operate on a variable specifically, and they do return a value. In fact, an SQL mutator method invocation is logically equivalent to a certain *selector* invocation (and hence can easily be implemented in the proposed front end). See Appendix H for further explanation.

Lack of selector operators: The fact that SQL does not automatically provide selectors makes it likely that SQL type implementations will explicitly include user-defined analogs of those operators. But those analogs will be redundant with **D**'s selectors and might well conflict in name with them.

Constructor functions: Let *T* be an SQL structured type; then *T* has an associated niladic *constructor function* that, when invoked, returns that value of type *T* whose every attribute has the default value defined for that attribute. While we would not expect **D** to provide direct analogs of such constructors, it should be clear that the SQL front end can easily do so.

We remark that certain other automatically provided SQL operators might also have no direct analogs in **D**, in which case they can be handled in like manner. Alternatively, **D** might include certain operators for the specific purpose of aiding SQL migration in this regard, operators that are not prescribed, nor even suggested, in the *Manifesto* as such. However, implementers considering such operators should watch out for possible violations of conceptual integrity; in particular, they should make sure that any advantage for migrators from SQL is not outweighed by *dis*advantages conferred on direct users of **D**.

Methods: SQL's "methods" are SQL functions (i.e., read-only operators) of a certain special kind. In particular, they are bundled with certain types—that is, the definition of any given method is actually part of the definition of some user-defined type—and they therefore contravene OO Very Strong Suggestion 2. But that bundling can surely be confined to the SQL front end (i.e., it need not be supported in **D** itself). Similarly, SQL's special method invocation syntax can be mapped to **D**'s own read-only operator invocation syntax.

A possible problem arises here in connection with inheritance, however. The problem is that in our inheritance model (again, see Part IV of this book), we suggest that the process of "run-time binding" be done on the basis of the types of all arguments; however, the analogous process for SQL's methods is done on the basis of the type of the argument corresponding to what SQL calls the "subject parameter" only. Care might thus be needed to ensure that an SQL method invocation, when mapped to some **D** read-only operator invocation, really does have exactly the desired effect.

NOT INSTANTIABLE types: The SQL concept of a NOT INSTANTIABLE type makes sense only if the type in question has subtypes. It maps directly to our "union type" concept (once again, see Part IV).

FINAL types: SQL allows a type to be specified as FINAL, prohibiting the subsequent definition of subtypes of that type. Support for FINAL could be provided directly in **D** if desired—in particular, if desired for SQL migration purposes—without contravening any aspect of the *Manifesto*. Without such support, FINAL types might constitute a small migration problem, but not one we believe to be particularly significant.

Further remarks on type inheritance: Overall, SQL's provisions for inheritance fall a long way short of conforming to our own inheritance model (see Appendix H for more details). So far as we are aware, however, all of the deviations are errors of omission, not commission (major examples include SQL's notable lack of support for type constraints and consequent lack of support for specialization by constraint, also its lack of proper support for multiple inheritance). Such errors thus present no problem insofar as mapping to **D** is concerned, with one major exception—the lack of support for selectors (and we have already discussed some of the consequences of this particular failure earlier in this section).

SQL Routines

SQL's user-defined procedures and functions (excluding methods) should be readily convertible to **D** update and read-only operators, respectively. User-defined methods will probably require some kind of special treatment as already discussed. Note that **D** would not contravene any of our prescriptions or proscriptions if it included special constructs to assist with support for SQL's "user-defined casts and transforms" [99].

REF Types

A strong case can be made that SQL's REF ("reference") types violate OO Proscription 2. Even if you do not agree with this position, it is certainly true that a "D" that included any such support would be in violation of RM Prescription 26, with respect to conceptual integrity in particular. Thus, **D** will in fact not include any such support. Assuming **D** does support system keys, however, along the lines described under RM Very Strong Suggestion 1 earlier in this chapter, all SQL operators on REF values are certainly implementable, because the operators in question are all defined as shorthands for SQL expressions whose implementation in the SQL front end we have already discussed.

Typed Tables

For the purposes of this subsection and the next, we take the term *typed table* to mean an SQL base table or view whose definition is specified in part by reference to some structured type. Column names and types for a typed table "of (structured) type *T*" are taken from the attribute definitions that constitute the specified representation of *T*. Clearly, this particular aspect of typed tables could be supported in the SQL front end without requiring any analogous support in **D** itself. (Indeed, we would not expect any analogous support in **D** itself, since such support would come dangerously close to contravening OO Proscription 1.)

In addition to the columns implied by the definition of its associated type *T*, an SQL typed table has a column of type REF(*T*), the REF type implied by the existence of *T*. Such a column is called a "self-referencing column" and is required to have the uniqueness property. Moreover, it is possible for the values of such a column to be system generated. We see no great difficulty for the SQL front end here (see the remarks in the previous subsection regarding RM Very Strong Suggestion 1).

Subtables and Supertables

If "typed tables" *TT1* and *TT2* are "of" types *T1* and *T2,* respectively, and if *T2* is a subtype of *T1*,[1] then SQL allows table *TT2* to be specified as a *subtable* of *supertable TT1*. For reasons explained at length in Appendix G, this notion is one we find especially suspect, and direct support for it in **D** is clearly out of the question. Indeed, we show in that same appendix how the problems that subtables and supertables are supposed to solve can easily be solved by conventional relational mechanisms, without the need for any new concepts at all. Those mechanisms should thus provide a basis for workarounds (probably manual ones) that might be needed in the case of applications that "take advantage of" this very dubious SQL feature.

Triggered Procedures

As noted in Chapter 1, *The Third Manifesto* is deliberately silent on the subject of triggered procedures. SQL's CREATE TRIGGER could perhaps be supported by some direct counterpart in **D** without violating any of our prescriptions or proscriptions, unless it led to violations of *The Assignment Principle* (note in particular in this connection that SQL's BEFORE triggers are explicitly permitted to override source values).

---

1. We stress the fact that the statement "*T2* is a subtype of *T1*" here is to be interpreted in accordance with the SQL specifications, *not* in accordance with our own inheritance model.

CUBE and ROLLUP, etc.

The extensions to GROUP BY that came into the standard with SQL:1999, such as CUBE and ROLLUP, are all specified as shorthands for certain SQL:1992 expressions. They should therefore present no great problem for our SQL front end—despite the fact that provision of direct counterparts in **D** would represent a violation of conceptual integrity (because the operators in question effectively involve unions of relations of different types).

WINDOW Clauses

SQL:2003's new WINDOW clauses do not violate any of our Prescriptions or Proscriptions, so direct counterparts could be provided in **D**.

Identity and System-Generated Columns

SQL:2003's new "identity column" and "system-generated column" features do not violate any of our prescriptions or proscriptions, so direct counterparts could be provided in **D**. (In the case of identity columns, that direct counterpart would effectively constitute an adoption of RM Very Strong Suggestion 1.)

Sequence Generators

SQL:2003's new sequence generators violate RM Prescription 16, for they are SQL database objects that are not even tables, let alone relvars. However, front end support for sequence generators should be a simple matter if RM Very Strong Suggestion 1 is adopted to support identity columns. In SQL, identity columns are defined in terms of sequence generators. In an SQL front end to **D**, it could be the other way around; for example, NEXT VALUE FOR ... could be implemented by inserting a tuple into a relvar with a system-generated key and returning the cardinality of that relvar after the insert.

EXERCISES

1. Consider any SQL product that might be available to you. Does that product support anything resembling the features discussed under RM Very Strong Suggestion 1?

2. What is a superkey?

3. Consider the "referential actions" (cascade delete, etc.) mentioned briefly under RM Very Strong Suggestion 2. Do such actions violate *The Assignment Principle?* Justify your answer.

4. It has been suggested that CASCADE might be supported as an option on DELETE and UPDATE instead of including it in a declarative foreign key specification; for example, DELETE S WHERE S# = S#('S1') CASCADE would delete the S tuple for supplier S1 and all of the SP tuples that referred to it. Evaluate this suggestion.

5. We said under RM Very Strong Suggestion 2 that there were good usability and productivity arguments in favor of supporting referential actions. What are those arguments?

6. The relational model as originally defined required a foreign key to reference not just some candidate key but, rather, a *primary* key specifically. What are the advantages of such a requirement? What are the disadvantages?

7.   Design an extension to the FOREIGN KEY syntax suggested in this chapter that would allow us to specify that every tuple of a specified relvar *R* has a value for a specified set of attributes that appears as a value of a specified key in (a) exactly one, (b) at least one, (c) all, of some specified set of relvars *R1*, *R2*, ..., *Rn* (*n* > 0).

8.   With reference to the usual suppliers-and-parts database, write an expression using RANK to get all parts whose weight is exactly the third smallest.

9.   Using the syntax sketched under RM Very Strong Suggestion 4, write transition constraints for the following "business rules" on the suppliers-and-parts database:

   a.   Suppliers in Athens can move only to London or Paris, and suppliers in London can move only to Paris.

   b.   The total shipment quantity for a given part cannot be reduced in a single update to less than half its current value.

   (What do you think the qualification "in a single update" means here? Why is it important? *Is* it important?)

10. Define a **Tutorial D** operator for the "gross requirement" problem (see RM Very Strong Suggestion 6).

Chapter 11

O O   V e r y   S t r o n g   S u g g e s t i o n s

OO VERY STRONG SUGGESTION 1: TYPE INHERITANCE

Some level of type inheritance should be supported (in which case, see OO Prescription 2).

———— ♦ ♦ ♦ ♦ ————

As explained in the discussion of OO Prescription 2 in Chapter 8, we do not include inheritance support as a mandatory component of our *Manifesto;* we merely require that **if** inheritance is supported at all, **then** that support shall be based on the model described in Part IV of this book. Note, however, that we would very much like to include such support!—especially since (as we will argue in the next chapter) we see our inheritance model in large part as a logical consequence of our type theory. For that reason, we have tried not to prescribe, proscribe, or even strongly suggest anything now that might preclude our ability to include such support later.

OO VERY STRONG SUGGESTION 2: TYPES AND OPERATORS UNBUNDLED

*Operator definitions should be **logically distinct** from the definitions of the types of their parameters and results, not "bundled in" with those latter definitions (though the operators required by RM Prescriptions 4, 5, 8, and 21 might be exceptions in this regard).*

———— ♦ ♦ ♦ ♦ ————

In object systems, operators ("methods") are typically bundled in with types ("classes"), meaning that the definition of any given operator is made part of the definition of some type. In the discussion of RM Prescription 3 in Chapter 6, for example, we might have included the definition of the read-only operator REFLECT—which, you will recall, takes a point with cartesian coordinates (x,y) and returns the "inverse" point with cartesian coordinates $(-x,-y)$—as part of the definition of the type POINT. But suppose we were to define an operator PERP_DIST that computes the perpendicular distance of some point from some line. Should PERP_DIST be bundled with type POINT or type LINE? Whichever it is, why? What are the implications?

As another example, consider the operator "*", which might be used (among other things) to multiply a speed by a time to give a distance. Which type does "*" belong to? SPEED? TIME? Perhaps DISTANCE? Surely the only sensible answer is "None of the above."

We see, therefore, that the idea of an operator being bundled in with some type works just fine so long as the operator in question takes exactly one operand, as REFLECT does. But as soon as it takes two or more, as PERP_DIST and "*" do, a degree of arbitrariness, artificiality, asymmetry, and awkwardness inevitably creeps in.

So let us step back for a moment. Why are operators bundled in with types anyway, in object systems? One answer to this question seems to be that those operators need (or might need) *privileged access:* access, that is, to the *physical representation* of instances of the type in question. In other words, those operators need (or might need) to invoke what we called *protected operators* in Chapter 3. *Note: We are using the fuzzy term "instances" here as a convenient shorthand for "values and/or variables."*

But we already have a mechanism for dealing with privileged access: viz., the *security* mechanism.[1] Would it not be better, therefore, to unbundle operators from types, and instead use the security mechanism—whatever that mechanism might be—to control, directly or indirectly, which operators are allowed access to which types (more accurately, access to the physical representation of instances of those types)? We believe it would. To be specific, we believe this approach has the advantages that:

- Operators can be permitted access to the physical representations of instances of as many types as desired, instead of being limited to just one.

- The arbitrariness, artificiality, asymmetry, and awkwardness inherent in the bundling scheme are all eliminated.

Further advantages are discussed under IM Prescription 17 in Chapter 14. What is more, adopting this approach implies that:

- **D** does not need to support the concept, found in some object systems, that operators have a *distinguished* or *receiver* or *target* operand. (In a typical object system, if operator *Op* is bundled with type *T,* then *Op* is invoked by "sending a message" to a specific *target operand:* namely, an instance of type *T.* That target operand is, typically, given special treatment, both syntactic and semantic, a fact that can have a variety of undesirable consequences. But if the present suggestion is implemented, all operands can be treated uniformly. Again, see Chapter 14 for further discussion.)

- **D** also does not need to support either the concept of *protected instance variables* or the concept of *friends.* (See reference [90] for an explanation of these concepts. Basically, they are both ad hoc techniques for getting around the limitation that one operator is permitted privileged access to instances of only one type.)

To repeat, we believe the problem all such notions are intended to address is better solved by judicious application of the system's security mechanism. As already noted, in fact, the problem in question degenerates to nothing more than that of deciding which operator definitions shall be allowed to make use of which protected operators. *Note:* We will go on in Chapter 14 to suggest that use of those protected operators should be limited to just a very small, well-defined set of operators: selectors, THE_ operators, and one or two others. And even there we believe the operator definitions in question can be system generated in many cases, though not all.

OO VERY STRONG SUGGESTION 3: SINGLE-LEVEL STORE

D should support the concept of **single-level storage.**

The concept of a single-level storage model was proposed—under the name of *direct reference*—by one of the present authors as far back as 1976 [42], and it is supported by most object systems today (though

---

1. Of course, we are talking about *database* systems specifically here. Programming systems typically do not have a security mechanism, and this lack perhaps accounts for the approach typically taken by object systems. Of course, we do not actually prescribe a security mechanism for **D** either, for reasons explained in Chapters 1 and 3, but we do assume that any industrial strength **D** will include some security support.

(though not by the "object/relational" DBMSs that became available from several vendors in the 1990s, because those DBMSs are based on SQL). The general idea is simply that there should be no unnecessary differences between access to data in the database and access to data not in the database; all such access should look the same to the user. And in **Tutorial D,** of course, it does. For example, a **Tutorial D** scalar expression can reference an attribute value within some tuple within some relation, and it makes no difference whether the relation in question is in the database or "in main memory." Note in particular, therefore, that there is no notion in **Tutorial D** of database data having to be "copied into main memory" before it can be processed. The net effect is that it makes no logical difference whether a given piece of data resides in main memory,[1] online secondary storage, tertiary backup storage, etc. What is important is whether it is persistent or not.

EXERCISES

1. *(For discussion.)* Under OO Very Strong Suggestion 1, we said the *Manifesto* tries not to prescribe, proscribe, or even strongly suggest anything that might preclude its ability to include inheritance support later. Do you think it succeeds in this respect?

2. Under OO Very Strong Suggestion 2, we said that **D** does not need to support the concept, found in some object systems, that operators have a *distinguished* or *receiver* or *target* operand. Such operators are sometimes known as *selfish methods,* because they have to access that special operand by means of a special parameter that is often called SELF. What are the advantages and disadvantages of selfish methods?

3. What are the advantages of a "single-level store"? What are the disadvantages?

---

1. It is relevant to observe here that main-memory DBMSs have been commercially available for some time; indeed, they are becoming increasingly important, for a variety of pragmatic reasons.

Part IV:

SUBTYPING AND INHERITANCE

Essentially, this part of the book does for our model of subtyping and inheritance what Parts I-III do for *The Third Manifesto*. Thus, Chapter 12 corresponds to Part I (it contains an overall introduction to the topic); Chapter 13 corresponds to Part II (it contains formal definitions); and Chapters 14, 15, and 16 correspond to Part III (they contain extended but informal explanations and discussions of those formal definitions). More specifically:

- Chapter 14 discusses single inheritance and scalar types only.

- Chapter 15 elaborates on the ideas discussed in Chapter 14 to deal with multiple inheritance as well.

- Finally, Chapter 16 goes on to take tuple and relation types into account too.

Chapter 12

P r e l i m i n a r i e s

As noted under OO Prescription 2 in Chapter 8, there is currently no consensus (at least in the data management literature) on a formal, rigorous, and abstract type inheritance model, and we have therefore been more or less forced to develop such a model of our own. In this part of the book, we describe that model in depth.

We should say immediately that we would like this effort on our part *not* to be seen as just an academic exercise. Rather, we would like our proposal to be considered by the community at large as a serious contender for filling the gap alluded to above (i.e., as a candidate for the role that *is* "formal, rigorous, and abstract" and can be generally agreed upon by that "community at large"). We offer it here in that spirit.

We begin by raising the question of why this topic might be worth investigating in the first place. There are at least two possible answers to this question:

■ First, the ideas of subtyping and inheritance do seem to arise naturally in the real world. That is, it is not at all unusual to encounter situations in which (more or less by definition) all values of a given type have certain properties in common, while some of those values have additional properties of their own. For example, all ellipses have an area, while some ellipses—namely, those that happen to be circles—have a radius as well; thus, we might say that type ELLIPSE has a *subtype* CIRCLE, and further that the subtype *inherits* the property of having an area from its *supertype* ELLIPSE (but circles also have certain properties of their own that ellipses in general do not). Thus, subtyping and inheritance look as if they might be useful tools for "modeling reality."

■ Second, if we can recognize such general patterns—patterns of subtyping and inheritance, that is—and build intelligence regarding them into our application and system software, we might be able to achieve certain practical economies. For example, a program that works for ellipses might work for circles too, even if it was originally written with no thought for circles at all (perhaps type CIRCLE had not even been defined at the time the program was written).

We remark that much of the existing literature seems to be concerned more with the second of these points than the first—that is, it seems to be principally interested in inheritance as a mechanism for designing, building, and using (and reusing) *programs.* Our own focus, by contrast, is more on the first point than the second; we are interested in inheritance more as a conceptual tool for designing, building, and using (and reusing) *data structures.* In other words, we are seeking an inheritance model that can be used to "model reality" (or, at least, certain aspects of reality), in the same kind of way that the relational model can be used to model certain aspects of reality. To put it yet another way, we are interested as always in the possibility of constructing *an abstract model,* not in matters of implementation merely. (As in earlier chapters, however, the discussions and explanations in what follows do sometimes touch on implementation matters for purposes of clarification.)

Caveat: Before going any further, we should warn you that this whole topic is considerably more complex than you might expect. The trouble is, although "the basic idea of inheritance is quite simple" [131], the devil is in the details: You have to study the topic in its entirety (and, we might add, extremely closely and carefully) in order to come properly to grips with it—in particular, to appreciate the fact that it is not at all as straightforward as it might seem at first sight. All of which goes some way, perhaps, to justify the possibly rather surprising length of this part of the book (especially Chapter 14).

There is another point we need to warn you of, too. The fact is, there is not even consensus in the literature on the meaning of such basic terms as *subtype* and *inheritance,* let alone on an entire inheritance model. Here also, therefore, we have been more or less forced to introduce our own definitions; and while we have naturally done our best to define terms and concepts in a manner that makes sense to us, you need to be aware that different definitions can be found elsewhere.[1] We defend our definitions—and our entire model, come to that—on the grounds that, among other things, they are mostly just a logical consequence of our type theory as described in earlier parts of this book. In other words, we think it would be inconsistent to agree with the *Manifesto*'s approach to types in general but not to agree with the proposed inheritance model. But you must be the judge of this claim, of course.

One last introductory point: The subject of type inheritance has a lot to do with data in general, of course, but not much to do with persistent or database data in particular (there is little or nothing about inheritance that applies to persistent data *only*). For simplicity, therefore—and despite our remarks in Chapter 1 regarding the general focus in this book on database management specifically—most of the examples in this part of the book are expressed in terms of local data instead of database data.

TOWARD A TYPE INHERITANCE MODEL

To repeat, we use the term *inheritance* to refer to that phenomenon according to which we can sensibly say, for example, that every circle is an ellipse, and hence that all properties that apply to ellipses in general apply to—i.e., are **inherited by**—circles in particular. For example, every ellipse has an area, and therefore every circle has an area too. More formally, we say we have two types, ELLIPSE and CIRCLE, such that ELLIPSE is a **supertype** of CIRCLE and CIRCLE is a **subtype** of ELLIPSE; we also say, somewhat loosely, that all properties that apply to the supertype necessarily apply to the subtype as well. Of course, the converse is not true: The subtype will have properties of its own that do not apply to the supertype (again speaking somewhat loosely). For example, circles have a radius, but ellipses in general do not.

Incidentally, a point arises here that beginners sometimes find a little confusing: namely, that a subtype has a subset of the values but a superset of the properties. For example, the subtype CIRCLE contains a subset of the values of the supertype ELLIPSE, but an individual circle has all of the properties of an ellipse and more besides. *Note:* For exactly such reasons, some writers prefer to avoid the "sub and super" terminology and talk of *descendants* and *ancestors* instead (see, e.g, reference [100]); however, we think this latter nomenclature has problems of its own, and therefore choose to stay (mostly) with the "sub and super" terminology.

By the way, it should be understood that *constraints* are properties too, of a kind, and are therefore inherited too—where by the term "constraints" we mean type constraints specifically, a convention we will adhere to throughout this part of the book (barring explicit statements to the contrary). Thus, e.g., any constraint that applies to ellipses in general also applies, necessarily, to circles in particular (for if it did not, then some circles would not be ellipses). For example, if ellipses are subject to the constraint that the length of their major semiaxis a is greater than or equal to that of their minor semiaxis b, then this same constraint must be satisfied by circles also. (For circles, of course, a and b coincide in the radius r, and this particular constraint is therefore satisfied trivially.)

Now, it is important in this context—as in all others!—to distinguish very carefully between *values* and *variables*. When we say that every circle is an ellipse, what we mean, more precisely, is that every circle *value* is an ellipse *value*. We certainly do not mean that every circle *variable* is an ellipse *variable:* i.e., that a variable of declared type CIRCLE is a variable of declared type ELLIPSE, and hence can contain a value that is an ellipse and not a circle. In other words, and speaking somewhat loosely once again, **inheritance applies to values, not variables** (although naturally there are

---

1. In fact, it has been suggested—see references [2], [19], [118], and [137], among others—that there are many *kinds* of inheritance, and hence many sets of concepts and many definitions of terms, that are all distinct from one another and yet overlap in various ways.

implications for variables too, as will be seen). We conjecture that much of the confusion we observe in this field—and there is a lot of it—is due precisely to a failure to distinguish properly between values and variables.

SINGLE VS. MULTIPLE INHERITANCE

As explained in Chapter 8, there are two broad "flavors" of type inheritance, single and multiple. Loosely speaking, single inheritance means each subtype has just one supertype and inherits properties from just that one type, while multiple inheritance means a subtype can have any number of supertypes and inherits properties from all of them. Obviously, the former is a special case of the latter.

Now, we do believe that support for multiple inheritance is desirable; in fact, as noted under OO Prescription 2 in Chapter 8, we believe that if inheritance is supported at all, it *must* be multiple. Despite this fact, our strategy in investigating this topic has been (a) to construct a sound model of single inheritance first, and then (b) to extend that model to incorporate multiple inheritance subsequently. Our reason for adopting this perhaps rather conservative approach is that even single inheritance raises numerous tricky questions; it therefore seemed reasonable to try to find good answers to those questions first, before having to concern ourselves too much about the additional complexities of multiple inheritance. Of course, we did try not to build anything into our model for single inheritance that might have precluded later extensions to deal with multiple inheritance, and it is a measure of our cautious optimism regarding our single-inheritance model that it does seem (at least to us) to extend gracefully to the multiple-inheritance case.

Be that as it may, the structure of Chapters 14 and 15 reflects this history:

- Chapter 14 discusses and illustrates a series of detailed prescriptions (**"IM Prescriptions"**) that together constitute a basis for the kind of robust inheritance model we are seeking, at least for the case of single inheritance only.

- Chapter 15 then goes on to extend the model discussed in Chapter 14 to incorporate multiple inheritance as well.

SCALARS, TUPLES, AND RELATIONS

We said earlier that inheritance applies to values, not variables. We were, however, making a tacit assumption at that point that the term *values* meant scalar values specifically. As explained under RM Prescription 1 in Chapter 6, of course, such values can have an arbitrarily complex internal structure or physical representation, but that internal structure is part of the implementation, not the model, and it is hidden from the user. Thus, for example, ellipses and circles can have a complicated internal structure and yet still be regarded as scalar values (as we already know). More to the point, inheritance has implications for nonscalar values—in particular, tuple and relation values—too, since such nonscalar values are ultimately built out of scalar values. But we obviously cannot even begin to talk sensibly about those implications until we have pinned down what subtyping and inheritance mean for scalar values specifically.

Throughout Chapters 14 and 15, therefore, we take the unqualified term *value* to mean a scalar value specifically. By the same token, throughout those two chapters we take the unqualified terms *type, subtype,* and *supertype* to mean scalar types, subtypes, and supertypes specifically, and we take the unqualified terms *variable, operator, expression,* and *result* to mean scalar variables, operators, expressions, and results specifically.[1] Note, however, that *formal* statements in those chapters—the IM Prescriptions themselves in particular—are deliberately worded in such a way as to allow, e.g., the term *value* to be taken to mean a scalar value or a tuple value or a relation value, as the context demands. They are also deliberately worded in such a way as to be applicable to multiple inheritance as well as single, barring explicit statements to the contrary.

To repeat, scalar values have no user-visible structure. But they do have associated operators, of course, and it follows that when we talk as we did earlier of inheritance of "properties," what we mean, primarily, is inheritance of *operators*. (More precisely, we mean inheritance of *read-only* operators specifically, thanks to our recognition of the fact that inheritance applies to values, not variables—though once again, of course, there are implications for variables too.) For example, when we say that every circle has an area because every ellipse has an area, what we mean is that subtype CIRCLE *inherits a (read-only) operator,* AREA say, from supertype ELLIPSE. In other words, we are interested in what is sometimes called **behavioral** inheritance.

Note: Much of the literature contrasts behavioral inheritance with **structural** inheritance. This latter term refers to inheritance of physical representations;[2] as such, it is properly an implementation matter, not part of the model. Of course, we certainly do not preclude such inheritance, but, to repeat, it is not part of the model. We observe, however, that much of the literature, especially in the object world, does tend to assume that inheritance means—or at least includes—inheritance of physical representations; it further tends to assume that some operators, at least, depend on those physical representations. We regard this state of affairs as evidence of confusion over the distinction between model and implementation, and choose not to discuss it further here.

Turning now to tuple and relation types: As noted earlier, the notions of scalar subtyping and inheritance do have implications for tuples and relations, because tuples and relations are ultimately constructed out of scalar components. For example, a relation with an attribute of type ELLIPSE might include some tuples in which the value corresponding to that attribute is specifically a circle, not "just an ellipse." In Chapter 16, we consider the question of what is involved in extending our inheritance model for scalar types (for both single and multiple inheritance, as discussed in Chapters 14 and 15) to take tuple and relation types into account as well.

THE RUNNING EXAMPLE

We now introduce a running example that will serve as a basis for much of the discussion in subsequent chapters (and in Appendixes F and G as well). The example deliberately involves scalar types only and single inheritance only; as already indicated, our model does include support for nonscalar types and multiple inheritance, but we feel that scalar types and single inheritance suffice to illustrate most of the points we need to make at this stage. If we do need to say something that either (a) applies to scalar and not nonscalar types (or the other way around), or (b) applies to single and not multiple inheritance (or the other way around), we will clearly indicate that such is the case.

The running example is based on a collection of geometric types: PLANE_FIGURE, ELLIPSE, POLYGON, and so on (refer to Fig. 12.1). In accordance with RM Prescription 1, each of those types is a named set of values; for example, there is a set of values named ELLIPSE, and every value in that

---

1. By *operators* here we really mean read-only operators, since update operators have no type.

2. There are those who would dispute this claim (see the brief explanation of "the EXTENDS relationship" in the section "Concluding Remarks" at the end of the chapter). We stand by it, however, so long as the types under discussion are scalar types specifically. The true state of affairs is too complicated to deal with adequately here (part of the problem is precisely that the literature does not always distinguish properly between scalar and nonscalar types). See Appendix G for further discussion.

set is some specific ellipse.[1] The types are arranged into what is called a **type hierarchy**.

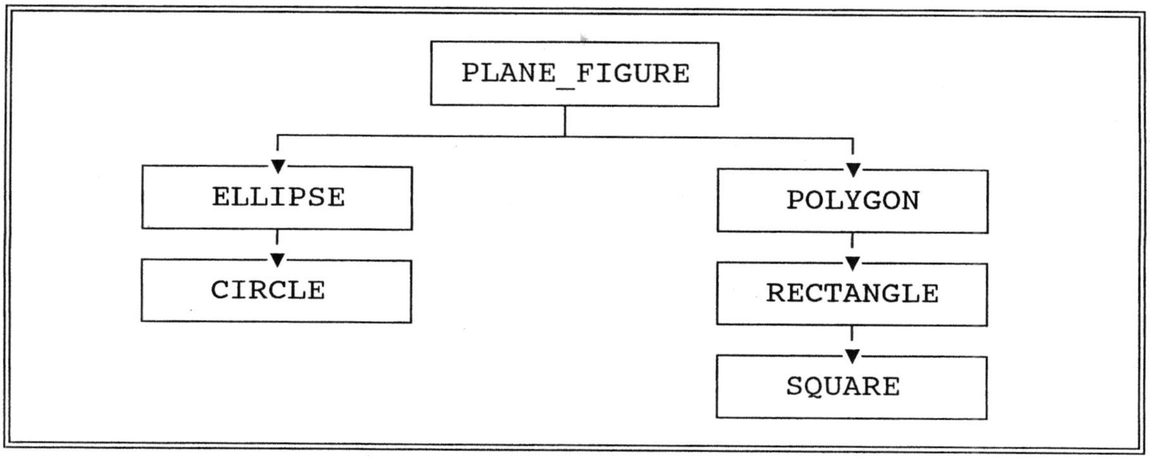

Fig. 12.1: Example of a type hierarchy

We should say immediately that our choice of a slightly academic example is deliberate. While it might be objected that geometric figures are not the kind of thing we expect to find in a typical database, in fact there are several advantages to such an example, the main one being that the semantics of the various types involved are or should be crystal clear to everyone. We can therefore avoid the kind of unproductive debates that tend to arise when "fuzzier" examples are chosen. For instance, suppose we had chosen an example involving a type BOOK. Are two copies of the same book two instances of that type or only one? What if the two copies are of different editions? What if one is a translation of the other? Is a journal a book? Is a magazine? And so on.

We also observe that type hierarchies as such will certainly be inadequate when we get to multiple inheritance (when we will have to replace them by more general type *graphs*). However, they are sufficient for the purposes of the present chapter.

To revert to Fig. 12.1: The type hierarchy in that figure should be more or less self-explanatory, of course; it shows, for example, that type RECTANGLE is a subtype of supertype POLYGON, which means that all rectangles are polygons, but the converse is not true (some polygons are not rectangles). As a consequence, all properties that apply to polygons in general apply to—i.e., are inherited by—rectangles in particular, but the converse is not true (rectangles have properties of their own that do not apply to polygons in general). *Note:* Recall that "properties" here essentially means *operators and constraints;* thus, operators and constraints that apply to polygons apply to rectangles too (because a rectangle *is* a polygon), but some operators and constraints that apply to rectangles do not apply to mere polygons.

Now, **Tutorial D** as defined in Chapter 5 did not include any support for inheritance. However, we do need a way of telling the system which types are subtypes of which (in other words, a way of defining type hierarchies). So let us extend **Tutorial D** to support a new syntactic category, *<user scalar nonroot type def>*, as an alternative form of *<user scalar type def>* (the existing form, as you will recall from Chapter 5, being *<user scalar root type def>*). A *<user scalar nonroot type def>* in turn includes an *<is def>* ("IS definition"), thereby enabling us to write type definitions like these:

---

1. More precisely, it is an ellipse *at some specific position in two-dimensional euclidean space*. We assume for the sake of the example that geometric figures that occupy different positions in that space but are otherwise identical are distinct.

```
TYPE ELLIPSE
     IS { PLANE_FIGURE
          POSSREP { A LENGTH, B LENGTH, CTR POINT
                    CONSTRAINT A ≥ B } } ;


TYPE CIRCLE
     IS { ELLIPSE
          CONSTRAINT THE_A ( ELLIPSE ) = THE_B ( ELLIPSE )
          POSSREP { R   = THE_A   ( ELLIPSE ) ,
                    CTR = THE_CTR ( ELLIPSE ) } } ;
```

Now the system knows that CIRCLE is a subtype of ELLIPSE (loosely, every circle "is a" ellipse), and hence that operators and constraints that apply to ellipses in general apply to circles in particular.

Let us take a closer look at these type definitions. First of all, we assume as we did in Chapter 6 that ellipses are always oriented such that their major axis is horizontal and their minor axis vertical. Thus, ellipses might indeed have a possrep[1] consisting of their semiaxes a and b (and their center). By contrast, circles might have a possrep consisting of their radius r (and their center). Observe now that:

- For type ELLIPSE, we have specified that every ellipse "is a" plane figure. We have also specified the $\{a,b,ctr\}$ possrep in the usual way, with what in Chapter 5 we called a *<possrep constraint>* to the effect that $a \geq b$ (as in Chapter 6).

- For type CIRCLE, by contrast, we have specified that every circle "is a" ellipse. We have also specified an additional constraint to the effect that $a = b$. (That constraint is not, however, a possrep constraint; in fact, type CIRCLE has no possrep constraint.) Along with that constraint, moreover, we have specified the $\{r,ctr\}$ possrep for circles, and we have indicated how that possrep is derived from that for ellipses. Observe the use of the supertype name ELLIPSE within the constraint—also within the derived possrep definition—to denote an arbitrary value of the supertype in question (i.e., an arbitrary ellipse).

Note, therefore, that the type constraint for a given type is specified by means of either a *<possrep def>* or an *<is def>*, depending on which is included in the type definition. (Note too that the first of these alternatives is the only one available in the absence of inheritance support.)

A Note on Possible Representations

It should be clear that every possrep for ellipses is necessarily, albeit implicitly, a possrep for circles as well, because circles *are* ellipses. (Of course, the converse is not true—a possrep for circles is not necessarily a possrep for ellipses.) Thus, we might regard possreps as further "properties" that are inherited by subtypes from supertypes. However, we do not regard that inherited possrep as a *declared* one in the sense of RM Prescription 4, because to do so would lead to a contradiction between IM Prescription 19, q.v., and RM Prescription 5. Thus, to say that type CIRCLE inherits a possrep from type ELLIPSE is only a *façon de parler*—it does not carry any formal weight.

To pursue the point a moment longer: Let type T' be a subtype of type T. Then it will often be the case in practice that T' does have a possrep—a *declared* possrep, that is—that is similar (possibly identical) to some possrep for T. This fact suggests that it might be convenient in practice to have some

---

1. We remind you that we take the unqualified term *possible representation*, or the abbreviated form *possrep*, to refer to a *declared* possrep specifically, barring explicit statements to the contrary.

syntactic shorthand for declaring a possrep for T', perhaps along the lines of "same as possrep *PR* for T but subtracting component(s) x and adding component(s) y." However, we see this issue as a purely syntactic one and secondary to our main purpose.

By the way, it is certainly possible for T and T' to have possreps that differ from each other quite markedly. For example, let T and T' be PENTAGON and REGULAR_PENTAGON, respectively. Then T could have a possrep consisting of five points (the five vertices), while T' has one consisting of just two points (the center and one vertex). However, it is always the case—in fact, it *must* always be the case—that each possrep for the subtype is expressible in terms of, and thus derivable from, each possrep for the supertype.

Terminology

We now introduce a number of further terms and concepts, most of them fairly self-explanatory (in any case, they are all amplified in later chapters):

- A supertype of a supertype is itself a supertype (e.g., POLYGON is a supertype of SQUARE).

- Every type is a supertype of itself (e.g., ELLIPSE is a supertype of ELLIPSE).

- If T is a supertype of T' and T and T' are distinct, then T is a **proper** supertype of T' (e.g., POLYGON is a proper supertype of SQUARE).

Analogous remarks apply to subtypes, of course. Thus:

- A subtype of a subtype is itself a subtype (e.g., SQUARE is a subtype of POLYGON).

- Every type is a subtype of itself (e.g., ELLIPSE is a subtype of ELLIPSE).

- If T' is a subtype of T and T' and T are distinct, then T' is a **proper** subtype of T (e.g., SQUARE is a proper subtype of POLYGON).

Moreover:

- If T is a proper supertype of T' and there is no type that is both a proper subtype of T and a proper supertype of T', then T is an **immediate** supertype of T' and T' is an **immediate** subtype of T (e.g., RECTANGLE is an immediate supertype of SQUARE, and SQUARE is an immediate subtype of RECTANGLE).

- A **root** type is a type with no proper supertype (e.g., PLANE_FIGURE is a root type); a **leaf** type is a type with no proper subtype (e.g., SQUARE is a leaf type). *Note:* Strictly speaking, a given type can be said to be a root or leaf type only in the context of some specific type hierarchy or type graph. For example, type RECTANGLE is a leaf type in the hierarchy that results from by deleting type SQUARE from the hierarchy of Fig. 12.1. Informally, however, we usually take the context as understood.

Incidentally, we can now give a precise characterization of single inheritance: Single inheritance means, precisely, that *every proper subtype has exactly one immediate supertype.*

The Disjointness Assumption

It is convenient for tutorial purposes to adopt the following simplifying assumption:

- If types *T1* and *T2* are such that neither is a subtype of the other, then they are **disjoint**—i.e., no value is of both type *T1* and type *T2*. For example, no value is both an ellipse and a polygon.

Now, this assumption, which we call *the disjointness assumption,* is certainly valid as long as we limit our attention to single inheritance only; in that context, in fact, it is implied (perhaps not very obviously) by IM Prescription 8, q.v. It will cease to be valid when we get to multiple inheritance; as already noted, however, we are emphasizing single inheritance in this preliminary chapter, and so we will take it as valid until further notice. Here are some immediate consequences of the assumption:

- Distinct root types are disjoint, and hence distinct type hierarchies are disjoint also (no value is of two distinct types *T1* and *T2* such that *T1* and *T2* are part of two distinct type hierarchies).

- Distinct subtypes of the same supertype are disjoint unless one is a subtype of the other. In particular, distinct leaf types are disjoint.

- *(Important!)* Every value has exactly one **most specific type**. For example, a given value might be "just an ellipse" and not a circle, meaning its most specific type is ELLIPSE (in the real world, some ellipses are not circles).

- In fact, following on from the previous point, if value *v* is of most specific type *T,* then the set of types possessed by *v* is, precisely, the set consisting of all supertypes of *T* (a set that includes *T* itself, of course). In other words, *v* is of every type that is a supertype of *T* and is of no other type.

One reason the disjointness assumption is desirable is that it avoids certain ambiguities that might otherwise occur. For suppose, contrariwise, that some value *v* could be of two distinct types *T1* and *T2*, neither of which was a subtype of the other. Suppose further that an operator named *Op* has been defined for type *T1* and another operator with the same name *Op* has been defined for type *T2*.[1] Then an invocation of *Op* with argument *v* would be ambiguous.

We note in passing that analogous ambiguities do not arise over constraints. For if type *T1* is subject to constraint *C1* and type *T2* is subject to constraint *C2,* and if constraints *C1* and *C2* conflict, then it simply means that types *T1* and *T2* are disjoint (because no value *v* can possibly satisfy both *C1* and *C2*). Loosely speaking, in fact, it is **necessary** and **sufficient** that *C1* and *C2* conflict in order for *T1* and *T2* to be disjoint.

Finally, we have said that the disjointness assumption applies to single inheritance only; however, there are situations even with multiple inheritance in which certain types are required to be disjoint. Unfortunately, it is always possible that the type designer could make a mistake and specify types that are supposed to be disjoint but in fact are not. For example, the designer might specify types RECTANGLE and RHOMBUS as subtypes of type PARALLELOGRAM and forget that some parallelograms are both a rectangle and a rhombus. The consequences of such violations will be unpredictable, in general. Although this fact need not concern us from the point of view of the model—a violation is simply a violation, and there is no need *within the model* to spell out what the consequences might be—in practice, we would hope that some kind of mechanical aid would be available to help the designer avoid such errors.

---

1. In other words, *Op* is *polymorphic.* What is more, the kind of polymorphism involved could be either *overloading* or *inclusion* polymorphism. See IM Prescription 9 in Chapter 14 for further explanation.

Substitutability

By definition, if *T'* is a subtype of *T*, then all operators that apply to values of type *T* apply to values of type *T'* too. For example, if AREA(*e*) is valid, where *e* is an ellipse, then AREA(*c*), where *c* is a circle, must be valid too. In other words, wherever the system expects a value of type ELLIPSE, we can always substitute a value of type CIRCLE (because, to say it again, circles *are* ellipses).

Now, this matter of **substitutability** is in many ways the whole point of inheritance. We claimed earlier that one reason for wanting to support inheritance in the first place is that (for example) a program that works for ellipses might work for circles too, even if it was originally written with no thought for circles. Well, it should be clear now that it is substitutability that makes such an objective attainable.

Observe, incidentally, that there is another logical difference here that we need to be very careful over: viz., that between the **parameters** in terms of which an operator is defined, with their *declared* types, and the corresponding **arguments** to some invocation of that operator, with their *actual*—i.e., *most specific*—types. In the AREA example, for instance, the operator is presumably defined in terms of a parameter of declared type ELLIPSE, but the most specific type of the argument *c* in the invocation AREA(*c*) is CIRCLE. (Indeed, the *declared* type of the expression denoting that argument might be CIRCLE too.)

A Note on Physical Representations

Although we are primarily concerned with a *model* of inheritance, not with implementation issues, there are certain implementation issues that do need to be understood if the overall concept of inheritance is to be properly understood in turn—and now we come to one such (which will turn out to be important at several points in subsequent chapters):

■   The fact that *T'* is a proper subtype of *T* does not imply that the physical representation of *T'* values is the same as that of *T* values.

For example, ellipses and circles might be physically represented by their center and semiaxes and their center and radius, respectively (though we know from Chapter 3 that there is no need, in general, for a physical representation to be the same as any declared possrep). As another example, it might be that the built-in type INTEGER is a proper subtype of the built-in type RATIONAL, but they are implemented internally in 32-bit two's-complement notation and IEEE 64-bit floating-point notation, respectively. *Note:* In fact, we already know from Chapters 1 and 6 that there is no logical reason why all values of the *same* type need have the same physical representation. For example, some points might be physically represented in cartesian coordinates and others in polar; some temperatures might be physically represented in Celsius and others in Fahrenheit; some integers might be physically represented in decimal and others in binary; and so on.

More on Type Hierarchies

Here now is a precise definition of the term *type hierarchy*. Basically, a **type hierarchy** *TH* is a special kind of graph. The graph consists of a finite set *N* of **nodes** and a finite set *DA* of **directed arcs** and satisfies the following properties:

a.   *TH* is **empty** if *N* is empty (in which case *DA* is necessarily empty too), otherwise it is **nonempty**.

b.   Each node is given the name of a type. No two nodes have the same name.

c.   Each arc connects exactly two distinct nodes and represents a directed path from one of those two nodes (the *parent*) to the other (the *child*). There is a directed arc from parent *T* to child *T'* if and only if type *T* is an immediate supertype of type *T'*.

d.   Each parent is connected to one or more children. Each child is connected to exactly one parent.

e.   Node *Y* is a *descendant* of node *X* if it is a child of *X* or a child of a descendant of *X*. No node is a descendant of itself. (Also, node *X* is an *ancestor* of node *Y* if and only if node *Y* is a descendant of node *X*. No node is an ancestor of itself.)

f.   A node connected to no parent is a **root** node. Types corresponding to root nodes are called **root** types. *Note:* If *TH* is nonempty, it has exactly one root node, otherwise it has no root node at all.

g.   A node connected to no children is a **leaf** node. Types corresponding to leaf nodes are called **leaf** types.

We remark that type hierarchies per se are not part of our inheritance model as such—they are merely an intuitively convenient way of depicting supertype/subtype relationships, which are. Indeed, type hierarchies play a role in our inheritance model analogous to that played by *tables* in the relational model: Tables per se are not part of the relational model as such, they are merely an intuitively convenient way of depicting relations, which are.

We also remark that type hierarchies are known by a variety of different names, the following among them:

■   *Class hierarchies* (on the grounds that types are sometimes called *classes,* especially in the object world)

■   *Generalization hierarchies* (on the grounds that, e.g., an ellipse is a generalization of a circle)

■   *Specialization hierarchies* (on the grounds that, e.g., a circle is a specialization of an ellipse)

■   *Inheritance hierarchies* (on the grounds that, e.g., circles inherit properties from ellipses)

■   *Is-a hierarchies* (on the grounds that, e.g., every circle "is a" ellipse)

and so on (this is not an exhaustive list).

Syntax

Here for purposes of reference is a summary (covering both single and multiple inheritance) of our proposal for extending the **Tutorial D** syntax for *<user scalar type def>*. Detailed explanations are given in Chapters 14 and 15. *Note:* The syntax of *<is def>*, q.v., has changed slightly from that given in reference [83]; to be specific, everything following the keyword IS is now enclosed in braces.

```
<user scalar type def>
    ::=    <user scalar root type def>
         | <user scalar nonroot type def>

<user scalar root type def>
    ::=    TYPE <user scalar type name> [ ORDINAL ] [ UNION ] <possrep def list>
```

UNION must be specified if and only if the root type being defined is a union type. The *<possrep def list>* must be empty if and only if the root type being defined is a dummy type. *Note:* Every dummy type is necessarily a union type. A type that is not a dummy type is a regular type.

```
<user scalar nonroot type def>
    ::=   TYPE <user scalar type name> [ ORDINAL ] [ UNION ] <is def>
```

UNION must be specified if and only if the nonroot type being defined is a union type.

```
<is def>
    ::=   <single inheritance is def> | <multiple inheritance is def>
```

```
<single inheritance is def>
    ::=   IS { <scalar type name> <possrep or specialization details> }
```

```
<possrep or specialization details>
    ::=   <possrep def list>
        | <additional constraint def> [ <derived possrep def list> ]
```

Let the immediate supertype of the nonroot type being defined be *IST*. The *<possrep def list>* must be specified if *IST* is a dummy type; however, it must be empty if (and only if) the nonroot type being defined is a dummy type. The *<additional constraint def>* must be specified if *IST* is not a dummy type. The *<derived possrep def list>* must be specified (and must not be empty) unless *IST* is either a dummy type or a system-defined type without a possrep.

```
<additional constraint def>
    ::=   CONSTRAINT <bool exp>
```

The *<bool exp>* must not mention any variables, but the name of the immediate supertype of the nonroot type being defined can (and in fact must) be used to denote an arbitrary value of the supertype in question.

```
<derived possrep def>
    ::=   POSSREP [ <possrep name> ] { <derived possrep component def commalist> }
```

```
<derived possrep component def>
    ::=   <possrep component name> = <exp>
```

The *<exp>* must not mention any variables, but the name of an immediate supertype of the nonroot type being defined can (and in fact must) be used to denote an arbitrary value of the supertype in question.

```
<multiple inheritance is def>
    ::=   IS { <scalar type name commalist> <derived possrep def list> }
```

The *<scalar type name commalist>* must contain at least two *<scalar type name>*s. The *<derived possrep def list>* must be empty if and only if the nonroot type being defined is a dummy type.

Recursively Defined Types and Headings

We noted in Chapter 6 that (a) the concept of a *recursively defined type* and (b) the concept of a *recursively defined heading* both require some extension if type inheritance is supported. Just to remind you, Chapter 6 said:

- Scalar type T is recursively defined if there exists some n ($n > 0$) such that T is a member of a certain set $S(n)$, where sets $S(1)$, $S(2)$, etc., form a certain sequence of sets of types.

- Likewise, heading $\{H\}$ is recursively defined if there exists some n ($n > 0$) such that TUPLE$\{H\}$ or RELATION$\{H\}$ is a member of a certain set $S(n)$, where again sets $S(1)$, $S(2)$, etc., form a certain sequence of sets of types.

The required extension is as follows: In the first bullet item, replace "such that T is a member" by "such that **some subtype or supertype of** T is a member"; in the second, replace "such that TUPLE$\{H\}$ or RELATION$\{H\}$ is a member" by "such that **some subtype or supertype of** TUPLE$\{H\}$ or RELATION$\{H\}$ is a member" (see Chapter 16). For the purposes of the present book, however, we continue to follow *The Principle of Cautious Design* [46] and assume, where it makes any difference, that recursively defined types and headings are not permitted.

Practical Problems

In closing this section, it would be remiss of us not to point out that type inheritance does give rise to some thorny practical problems. Given the type hierarchy of Fig. 12.1, for example, what should happen if we try to drop type ELLIPSE? Should there be a way to "alter" or rename type ELLIPSE without dropping it? Should we be able to introduce a new type as an immediate supertype of an existing type? What if that existing type is system defined? And so on. Such questions must clearly be answered in any real implementation, but we do not regard them as issues that affect the model per se, and we have little to say about them in this book.

CONCLUDING REMARKS

We have presented an introduction to some of the basic ideas of our inheritance model. As noted near the beginning of the chapter, however, many other approaches to inheritance are discussed in the literature. We briefly mention two significant ones here:

- Reference [17] among others discusses what it calls *the EXTENDS relationship*, which it defines as "a single inheritance relationship between two classes whereby the subordinate class inherits all of the [structure, also called *state*] and all of the behavior of the class that it extends." It gives an example in which class *EmployeePerson* extends class *Person* by adding "attributes" *hireDate* and *payRate* to the ones (*name* and *birthDate*) it inherits from class *Person*. Appendix G discusses this idea in more detail. *Note:* C++ [90], Java [94], and the SQL standard [99] all support the EXTENDS relationship.

- Reference [129] among others advocates support for *subtables and supertables* (not by that name, however). This concept might be thought of as an application of "the EXTENDS relationship" to tables specifically. (We do not say *relations* or *relvars* here because the tables in question do not have to be properly relational.) Reference [129] gives an example in which a STUDENT table inherits all of the columns of a PERSON table but adds a GPA column ("grade point average"). Appendix G discusses this idea in more detail as well. *Note:* The SQL standard [99] supports this one, too.

Finally, for purposes of reference, and also to give some idea of the scope of our inheritance model, we close this chapter by giving opposite a mnemonic list of the 25 IM Prescriptions. Note that the first 20 take care of scalar types; the last five are needed to take care of tuple and relation types as well.

IM Prescriptions

1. Types are sets	14. TREAT
2. Subtypes are subsets	15. Type testing
3. "Subtype of" is reflexive	16. Read-only operator inheritance and value substtutability
4. Proper subtypes	17. Operator signatures
5. "Subtype of" is transitive	18. Read-only parameters to update operators
6. Immediate subtypes	19. Update operator inheritance and variable substitutability
7. Root types disjoint	20. Union, dummy, and maximal and minimal types
8. Scalar values with inheritance	21. Tuple/relation subtypes and supertypes
9. Scalar variables with inheritance	22. Tuple/relation values with inheritance
10. Specialization by constraint	23. Maximal and minimal tuple/relation types
11. Assignment with inheritance	24. Tuple/relation most specific types
12. Equality etc. with inheritance	25. Tuple/relation variables with inheritance
13. Join etc. with inheritance	

EXERCISES

1. Explain the concepts of *type inheritance* and *subtype* in your own words.

2. Distinguish between immediate and proper subtypes.

3. What do you understand by the term *most specific type?*

4. What do you understand by the term *substitutability?*

5. With reference to the type hierarchy of Fig. 12.1, consider a value *e* of type ELLIPSE. The most specific type of *e* is either ELLIPSE or CIRCLE. What is the *least* specific type of *e?*

6. Define the terms *root type* and *leaf type.*

7. State the disjointness assumption. What are some of the implications of that assumption? What do you think should replace that assumption if multiple inheritance is supported? *Note:* The latter question was not answered in the body of the chapter; the point of the question is simply to get you thinking about the issue, should you feel so inclined, before we get to the detailed discussions in Chapter 15.

8. Give as precise a definition as you can of the term *type hierarchy.* (You might like to try giving a *recursive* definition, different from the nonrecursive one given in the body of the chapter.) Why are type hierarchies strictly not part of the inheritance model?

9. Are possreps inherited? If not, why not?

10. Use the syntax sketched in this chapter to give definitions for types RECTANGLE and SQUARE from Fig. 12.1. Assume for simplicity that all rectangles are centered on the origin, but do not assume that all sides are either vertical or horizontal. What about types POLYGON and PLANE_FIGURE?

11. Given your answer to Exercise 10, define an operator to rotate a specified rectangle through 90° about its center.

12. *(This exercise will probably take longer to read than to answer!)* Let *TH* be a type hierarchy. Then:

    ■ Any graph *G* derived from *TH* by choosing the node corresponding to some type *T* and deleting (a) all nodes not corresponding to some subtype *T'* of *T*, and (b) all arcs emanating from those nodes, is also a type hierarchy, with *T* as its root.

    ■ Any graph derived by deleting a node from the graph *G* just defined is also a type hierarchy (again with *T* as its root, unless node *T* was the one deleted), provided that deletion of a node is always accompanied by deletion of (a) the arc entering into that node and (b) each corresponding immediate subtype node.

    By contrast, if (a) *TH* is a type hierarchy with root *T*, and (b) type *T* is an immediate supertype of type *T'* and type *T'* is an immediate supertype of type *T''* (and we assume for simplicity that type *T'* is an immediate supertype of no types other than type *T''*), and (c) *G* is the graph derived from *TH* by deleting node *T'* and coalescing the arc connecting nodes *T* and *T'* and the arc connecting nodes *T'* and *T''* into a single arc connecting nodes *T* and *T''*, then (d) *G* is *not* a type hierarchy (at least, not one that can be derived from *TH*), because it causes *T''* to lose some of its inheritance (as it were). For example, the graph that contains just nodes POLYGON and SQUARE from Fig. 12.1 (with a single connecting arc) is not a type hierarchy that can be derived from the one in that figure.

    Given the foregoing definitions, how many distinct type hierarchies can be derived from that of Fig. 12.1?

13. In the body of the chapter we said that if inheritance is supported at all, it must be multiple. Why do you think this is? *Note:* As with the second question in Exercise 7, this question was not answered in this chapter; again, the point of the question is simply to get you thinking about the issue.

Chapter 13

The Inheritance Model

In this chapter, we simply state the various IM Prescriptions that go to make up our model of subtyping and inheritance, with no attempt at discussion or further explanation. The material is provided primarily for reference; you probably should not even attempt to read it straight through (at least, not on a first reading).

A note on terminology: Throughout what follows, we assume that all of the types under discussion are members of some given set of types S; in particular, the definitions of the terms *root type* and *leaf type* are to be interpreted in the context of that set S. Also, we use the symbols T and T' generically to refer to a pair of types such that T' is a subtype of T (equivalently, such that T is a supertype of T'). You might find it helpful to think of T and T' as ELLIPSE and CIRCLE, respectively. Keep in mind, however, the fact that they are *not* limited to being scalar types specifically, barring explicit statements to the contrary.

IM PRESCRIPTIONS

1. T and T' shall indeed both be types; i.e., each shall be a named set of values.

2. Every value in T' shall be a value in T; i.e., the set of values constituting T' shall be a subset of the set of values constituting T (in other words, if a value is of type T', it shall also be of type T). Moreover, if T and T' are distinct (see IM Prescriptions 3 and 4), then there shall exist at least one value of type T that is not of type T'.

3. T and T' shall not necessarily be distinct; i.e., every type shall be both a subtype and a supertype of itself.

4. If and only if types T and T' are distinct, T' shall be a **proper** subtype of T, and T shall be a **proper** supertype of T'.

5. Every subtype of T' shall be a subtype of T. Every supertype of T shall be a supertype of T'.

6. If and only if T' is a proper subtype of T and there is no type that is both a proper supertype of T' and a proper subtype of T, then T' shall be an **immediate** subtype of T, and T shall be an **immediate** supertype of T'. A type that is not an immediate subtype of any type shall be a **root** type. A type that is not an immediate supertype of any type shall be a **leaf** type.

7. If $T1$ and $T2$ are distinct root types, then they shall be disjoint; i.e., no value shall be of both type $T1$ and type $T2$.

8. Every set of types $T1, T2, \ldots, Tn$ shall have a common subtype T' such that a given value is of each of the types $T1, T2, \ldots, Tn$ if and only if it is of type T'.

9. Let scalar variable V be of declared type T. Because of value substitutability (see IM Prescription 16), the value v assigned to V at any given time can have any subtype T' of type T as its most specific type. We can therefore model V as a named ordered triple of the form $<DT,MST,v>$, where:

a.   The name of the triple is the name of the variable, *V*.

b.   *DT* is the name of the declared type for variable *V*.

c.   *MST* is the name of the **most specific type**—also known as the **current** most specific type—for, or of, variable *V*.

d.   *v* is a value of most specific type *MST*—the **current value** for, or of, variable *V*.

We use the notation *DT*(*V*), *MST*(*V*), *v*(*V*) to refer to the *DT*, *MST*, *v* components, respectively, of this model of scalar variable *V*.

Now let *X* be a scalar expression. By definition, *X* specifies an invocation of some scalar operator *Op* (where the arguments, if any, to that invocation of *Op* are specified as expressions in turn). Thus, the notation *DT*(*V*), *MST*(*V*), *v*(*V*) just introduced can be extended in an obvious way to refer to the declared type *DT*(*X*), the current most specific type *MST*(*X*), and the current value *v*(*X*), respectively, of *X*—where *DT*(*X*) is *DT*(*Op*) and is known at compile time, and *MST*(*X*) and *v*(*X*) refer to the result of evaluating *X* and are therefore not known until run time (in general).

10.   Let *T* be a regular proper supertype (see IM Prescription 20), and let *T'* be an immediate subtype of *T*. Then the definition of *T'* shall specify a **specialization constraint SC**, formulated in terms of *T*, such that a value shall be of type *T'* if and only if it is of type *T* and it satisfies constraint *SC*. There shall exist at least one value of type *T* that does not satisfy constraint *SC*.

11.   Consider the assignment

```
V := X
```

(where *V* is a variable and *X* is an expression). *DT*(*X*) shall be a subtype of *DT*(*V*). The assignment shall set *MST*(*V*) equal to *MST*(*X*) and *v*(*V*) equal to *v*(*X*).

12.   Consider the equality comparison

```
Y = X
```

(where *Y* and *X* are expressions). *DT*(*X*) and *DT*(*Y*) shall have a nonempty common subtype. The comparison shall return TRUE if *MST*(*Y*) is equal to *MST*(*X*) and *v*(*Y*) is equal to *v*(*X*), FALSE otherwise.

13.   Let *rx* and *ry* be relations with a common attribute *A*, and let the declared types of *A* in *rx* and *ry* be *DTx*(*A*) and *DTy*(*A*), respectively. Consider the join of *rx* and *ry* (necessarily over *A*, at least in part). *DTx*(*A*) and *DTy*(*A*) shall have a nonempty common subtype and hence shall also have a most specific common supertype, *T* say. Then the declared type of *A* in the result of the join shall be *T*.

Analogous remarks apply to union, intersection, and difference operators. That is, in each case:

a.   Corresponding attributes of the operands shall be such that their declared types have a nonempty common subtype.

b.   The declared type of the corresponding attribute of the result shall be the corresponding most specific common supertype.

14. Let *X* be an expression, let *T* be a type, and let *DT(X)* and *T* have a nonempty common subtype. Then an operator of the form

    ```
    TREAT_AS_T ( X )
    ```

    (or logical equivalent thereof) shall be supported. We refer to such operators generically as "TREAT" or "TREAT AS" operators; their semantics are as follows. First, if *MST(X)* is not a subtype of *T*, then a type error shall occur. Otherwise:

    a. If the TREAT invocation appears in a "source" position (for example, on the right side of an assignment), then the declared type of that invocation shall be *T*, and the invocation shall yield a result, *r* say, with *MST(r)* equal to *MST(X)* and *v(r)* equal to *v(X)*.

    b. If the TREAT invocation appears in a "target" position (for example, on the left side of an assignment), then that invocation shall act as a pseudovariable reference, which means it shall actually *designate* its argument *X* (more precisely, it shall designate a version of *X* for which *DT(X)* is equal to *T* but *MST(X)* and *v(X)* are unchanged).

15. Let *X* be an expression, let *T* be a type, and let *DT(X)* and *T* have a nonempty common subtype. Then a logical operator of the form

    ```
    IS_T ( X )
    ```

    (or logical equivalent thereof) shall be supported. The operator shall return TRUE if *v(X)* is of type *T*, FALSE otherwise.

16. Let *Op* be a read-only operator, let *P* be a parameter to *Op*, and let *T* be the declared type of *P*. Then the declared type (and therefore, necessarily, the most specific type) of the argument *A* corresponding to *P* in an invocation of *Op* shall be allowed to be **any subtype** *T'* of *T*. In other words, the read-only operator *Op* applies to values of type *T* and therefore, necessarily, to values of type *T'*—*The Principle of (Read-Only) Operator Inheritance*. It follows that such operators are *polymorphic,* since they apply to values of several different types—*The Principle of (Read-Only) Operator Polymorphism*. It further follows that wherever a value of type *T* is permitted, a value of any subtype of *T* shall also be permitted—*The Principle of (Value) Substitutability*.

17. Any given operator *Op* shall have exactly one **specification signature,** a nonempty set of **version signatures,** and a nonempty set of **invocation signatures.** For definiteness, assume the parameters of *Op* and the arguments appearing in any given invocation of *Op* each constitute an ordered list of *n* elements (*n* ≥ 0), such that the *i*th argument corresponds to the *i*th parameter. Then:

    a. The specification signature shall denote *Op* as perceived by potential users. It shall consist of the operator name *Op*, the declared types (in order) of the parameters to *Op*, and the declared type of the result, if any, of executing *Op*. No two distinct operators shall have specification signatures that differ only in the declared types of their results (if any). Moreover, let *S* be a set of types with a nonempty common subtype. Then no two distinct operators shall have specification signatures that differ only in that, for some *i, j, ..., k*, the declared types of their *i*th parameters are distinct members of *S*, the declared types of their *j*th parameters are distinct members of *S*, ..., and the declared types of their *k*th parameters are distinct members of *S*.

    b. There shall be one version signature for each implementation version *V* of *Op*. Each such signature shall consist of the operator name *Op* (and possibly the version name *V*), the declared types (in order) of the parameters to *V*, and the declared type of the result, if any, of executing *V*.

    c.   There shall be one invocation signature for each possible combination of most specific argument types to an invocation of *Op*. Each such signature shall consist of the operator name *Op* and the pertinent combination of most specific argument types (in order). *Note:* The invocation signatures for *Op* can easily be derived from the corresponding specification signature, but the concepts are logically distinct.

Every version of *Op* shall implement the same semantics.

18.   Let *Op* be an update operator and let *P* be a parameter to *Op* that is not subject to update. Then *Op* shall behave as a *read-only* operator as far as *P* is concerned, and all relevant aspects of IM Prescription 16 shall therefore apply, mutatis mutandis.

19.   Let *Op* be an update operator, let *P* be a parameter to *Op* that is subject to update, and let *T* be the declared type of *P*. Then it might or might not be the case that the declared type (and therefore, necessarily, the current most specific type) of the argument *A* corresponding to *P* in an invocation of *Op* shall be allowed to be a proper subtype of type *T*. It follows that for each such update operator *Op* and for each parameter *P* to *Op* that is subject to update, it shall be necessary to state explicitly for which proper subtypes of the declared type *T* of parameter *P* operator *Op* shall be inherited—*The Principle of **(Update) Operator Inheritance**. (And if update operator *Op* is not inherited in this way by type *T'*, it shall not be inherited by any proper subtype of type *T'* either.) Update operators shall thus be only conditionally polymorphic—*The Principle of **(Update) Operator Polymorphism**. If *Op* is an update operator and *P* is a parameter to *Op* that is subject to update and *T'* is a proper subtype of the declared type *T* of *P* for which *Op* is inherited, then by definition it shall be possible to invoke *Op* with an argument corresponding to parameter *P* that is of declared type *T'*—*The Principle of **(Variable) Substitutability**.

20.   A **union type** is a type *T* such that there exists no value that is of type *T* and not of some immediate subtype of *T* (i.e., there is no value *v* such that *MST(v)* is *T*). A **dummy type** is a union type that has no declared possible representation (and hence no selector); a given union type shall be permitted to be a dummy type if and only if it is empty or it has no regular immediate supertype (where a **regular type** is a type that is not a dummy type). Moreover:

    a.   Conceptually, there is a special scalar dummy type, *alpha*, that contains all scalar values. Type *alpha* is **the maximal type** with respect to every scalar type; by definition, it has no declared possible representation and no immediate supertypes.

    b.   Conceptually, there is a special scalar dummy type, *omega*, that contains no values at all. Type *omega* is **the minimal type** with respect to every scalar type; by definition, it has no declared possible representation and no immediate subtypes.

21.   Let types *T* and *T'* be both tuple types or both relation types, with headings

```
{ <A1,T1>,  <A2,T2>,  ...,  <An,Tn> }
```

```
{ <A1,T1'>,  <A2,T2'>,  ...,  <An,Tn'> }
```

respectively. Then type *T'* is a **subtype** of type *T* (equivalently, type *T* is a **supertype** of type *T'*) if and only if, for all *i* (*i* = 1, 2, ..., *n*), type *Ti'* is a subtype of type *Ti* (equivalently, type *Ti* is a supertype of type *Ti '*).

22.   Let {*H*} be a heading defined as follows:

```
{ <A1,T1>, <A2,T2>, ..., <An,Tn> }
```

Then:

a.   *t* is a tuple that **conforms** to heading {*H*} if and only if *t* is of the form

```
{ <A1,T1',v1>, <A2,T2',v2>, ..., <An,Tn',vn> }
```

where, for all *i* (*i* = 1, 2, ..., *n*), type *Ti '* is a subtype of type *Ti* and *vi* is a value of type *Ti '*.

b.   *r* is a relation that **conforms** to heading {*H*} if and only if *r* consists of a heading and a body, where:

- The heading of *r* is of the form

```
{ <A1,T1'>, <A2,T2'>, ..., <An,Tn'> }
```

where, for all *i* (*i* = 1, 2, ..., *n*), type *Ti '* is a subtype of type *Ti*.

- The body of *r* is a set of tuples, all of which conform to the heading of *r*.

23.   Let types *T, T_alpha,* and *T_omega* be all tuple types or all relation types, with headings

```
{ <A1,T1>,        <A2,T2>,        ..., <An,Tn>       }

{ <A1,T1_alpha>, <A2,T2_alpha>, ..., <An,Tn_alpha> }

{ <A1,T1_omega>, <A2,T2_omega>, ..., <An,Tn_omega> }
```

respectively. Then types *T_alpha* and *T_omega* are **the maximal type with respect to type *T*** and **the minimal type with respect to type *T*,** respectively, if and only if, for all *i* (*i* = 1, 2, ..., *n*), type *Ti_alpha* is the maximal type with respect to type *Ti* and type *Ti_omega* is the minimal type with respect to type *Ti*.

24.   Let {*H*} be a heading defined as follows:

```
{ <A1,T1>, <A2,T2>, ..., <An,Tn> }
```

Then:

a.   If *t* is a tuple that conforms to *H*—meaning *t* is of the form

```
{ <A1,T1',v1>, <A2,T2',v2>, ..., <An,Tn',vn> }
```

where, for all *i* (*i* = 1, 2, ..., *n*), type *Ti '* is a subtype of type *Ti* and *vi* is a value of type *Ti '*—then the **most specific** type of *t* is

```
TUPLE { <A1,MST1>, <A2,MST2>, ..., <An,MSTn> }
```

where, for all i ($i = 1, 2, ..., n$), type $MSTi$ is the most specific type of value vi.

b.   If r is a relation that conforms to H—meaning the body of r is a set of tuples, each of which has as its most specific type a type that is a subtype of the type TUPLE$\{H\}$, and meaning further that each such tuple can be regarded without loss of generality as being of the form

```
{ <A1,T1',v1>, <A2,T2',v2>, ..., <An,Tn',vn> }
```

where, for all i ($i = 1, 2, ..., n$), type Ti' is a subtype of type Ti and is the most specific type of value vi (note that distinct tuples in the body of r will be of distinct most specific types, in general; thus, type Ti' varies over the tuples in the body of r)—then the **most specific** type of r is

```
RELATION { <A1,MST1>, <A2,MST2>, ..., <An,MSTn> }
```

where, for all i ($i = 1, 2, ..., n$), type $MSTi$ is the most specific common supertype of those most specific types Ti', taken over all tuples in the body of r.

25.   Let tuple or relation variable V be of declared type T, and let the heading of T have attributes $A1$, $A2, ..., An$. Then we can model V as a named set of named ordered triples of the form $<DTi,MSTi,vi>$, where:

a.   The name of the set is the name of the variable (V in the example).

b.   The name of each triple is the name of the corresponding attribute.

c. DTi is the name of the declared type of attribute Ai.

d. $MSTi$ is the name of the **most specific type**—also known as the **current** most specific type—for, or of, attribute Ai. (If V is a relation variable, then the most specific type of Ai is the most specific common supertype of the most specific types of the m values in vi—see the explanation of vi below.)

e.   If V is a tuple variable, vi is a value of most specific type $MSTi$—the **current value** for, or of, attribute Ai. If V is a relation variable, then let the body of the current value of V consist of m tuples; label those tuples (in some arbitrary sequence) "tuple 1," "tuple 2," ..., "tuple m"; then vi is a sequence of m values (not necessarily all distinct), being the Ai values from tuple 1, tuple 2, ..., tuple m (in that order); note that all of those values are of type $MSTi$.

We use the notation $DT(Ai)$, $MST(Ai)$, $v(Ai)$ to refer to the DTi, $MSTi$, vi components, respectively, of attribute Ai of this model of tuple or relation variable V. We also use the notation $DT(V)$, $MST(V)$, $v(V)$ to refer to the overall declared type, overall current most specific type, and overall current value, respectively, of this model of tuple or relation variable V.

Now let X be a tuple or relation expression. By definition, X specifies an invocation of some tuple or relation operator Op (where the arguments, if any, to that invocation of Op are specified as expressions in turn). Thus, the notation $DTi(V)$, $MSTi(V)$, $vi(V)$ just introduced can be extended in an obvious way to refer to the declared type $DTi(X)$, the current most specific type $MSTi(X)$, and the current value $vi(X)$, respectively, of the DTi, $MSTi$, vi components, respectively, of attribute Ai of tuple or relation expression X—where $DTi(X)$ is known at compile time, and $MSTi(X)$ and $vi(X)$ refer to the result of evaluating X and are therefore not known until run time (in general).

RECENT INHERITANCE MODEL CHANGES

There are a few differences between the inheritance model as defined in the present chapter and the version documented in this book's predecessor (reference [83]). For the benefit of readers who might be familiar with that earlier version, we summarize the main differences here.

- The root and leaf type concepts are no longer regarded as absolutes but are instead defined relative to some given set of types (which can be thought of, informally, as a type hierarchy or type graph). This change primarily affects IM Prescriptions 6 and 7.

- The wording of several prescriptions has been changed to cover (a) both single and multiple inheritance and (b) both scalar and tuple/relation types. These changes—which are not intended to affect the model as such—apply primarily to IM Prescriptions 7 and 8.

- In IM Prescription 12, the requirement that $DT(X)$ and $DT(Y)$ shall have a common supertype has been replaced by the stronger requirement that $DT(X)$ and $DT(Y)$ shall have a nonempty common subtype. (The fact that the new requirement is stronger than the old one might not be obvious but is proved in Chapter 15.)

- Analogously, in IM Prescription 13, the requirement that $DTx(A)$ and $DTy(A)$ shall have a common supertype has been replaced by the stronger requirement that $DTx(A)$ and $DTy(A)$ shall have a nonempty common subtype.

- In IM Prescription 14, TREAT DOWN has been renamed TREAT AS, referred to more usually as just TREAT.

- IM Prescriptions 14 and 15 have been generalized slightly (previously we required T to be a subtype of $DT(X)$; now we require only that they have a nonempty common subtype).

- IM Prescription 17 has been amplified to make the rules regarding specification signatures more explicit.

- IM Prescription 20 has been corrected slightly (previously it required a dummy type to have no regular immediate supertypes, but this rule overlooked the possibility that a dummy type might be empty).

In addition to all of the foregoing, almost all of the prescriptions have been reworded somewhat. However, those revisions in themselves are not intended to induce any changes in what is being described.

Chapter 14

Single Inheritance with Scalar Types

In this chapter, we elaborate on the first 20 of our IM Prescriptions, using the type hierarchy of Fig. 12.1 from Chapter 12 as a basis for most examples. We remind you that until further notice we take the unqualified terms *type, subtype,* and *supertype* to mean scalar types, subtypes, and supertypes specifically and the unqualified terms *value, variable, (read-only) operator, expression,* and *result* to mean scalar values, variables, operators, expressions, and results specifically.[1] In addition, we take the unqualified term *inheritance* to mean single inheritance specifically and the unqualified term *constraint* to mean a type constraint specifically. We assume that all of the types under consideration are members of some given set of types *S* (and all references to root or leaf types are to be understood in the context of that set *S*). Finally, we use the symbols T and T' to refer generically to a pair of types such that T' is a subtype of T—equivalently, such that T is a supertype of T'. As noted in Chapter 13, you might find it helpful to think of T and T' as ELLIPSE and CIRCLE, respectively, except where otherwise indicated.

IM PRESCRIPTION 1: TYPES ARE SETS

T *and* T' *shall indeed both be types; i.e., each shall be a named set of values.*

IM Prescription 1 simply asserts that supertypes and subtypes are indeed types, in the full sense of that term as required by *The Third Manifesto*. One consequence is that **subtypes can have lower-level subtypes of their own** (and supertypes can have higher-level supertypes of their own), as we already know.

IM PRESCRIPTION 2: SUBTYPES ARE SUBSETS

Every value in T' *shall be a value in* T; *i.e., the set of values constituting* T' *shall be a subset of the set of values constituting* T *(in other words, if a value is of type* T', *it shall also be of type* T*). Moreover, if* T *and* T' *are distinct (see IM Prescriptions 3 and 4), then there shall exist at least one value of type* T *that is not of type* T'.

In general, to say that value v is of type T does not preclude the possibility that v is also of type T'. For example, to say that e is an ellipse does not preclude the possibility that e is also a circle. In fact, to say that v is of type T means, precisely, that the *most specific* type of v (see IM Prescription 8) is *some subtype* of T (see IM Prescriptions 3-5). It follows that if v is of type T', the operators that apply to v include (by definition) all of the operators that apply to values of type T', and those operators include (by

---

1. To repeat from Chapter 12, however, *formal* statements—the IM Prescriptions themselves in particular—are deliberately worded in such a way as to allow, e.g., the term *value* to be taken to mean a scalar value or a tuple value or a relation value as the context demands. They are also deliberately worded in such a way as to apply to multiple inheritance as well as single, barring explicit statements to the contrary.

definition) all of the operators that apply to values of type *T*. For example, if AREA is an operator that applies to values of type ELLIPSE, then AREA is also an operator that applies to values of type CIRCLE. In other words (loosely): **Operators associated with type *T* are inherited by type *T'*.**

Here in outline are some of the operators that (we will assume) apply to values of type ELLIPSE and hence to values of type CIRCLE also. *Note:* As we will see later, some of these operators might need to be *reimplemented* for type CIRCLE, implying that two **implementation versions** of the operator in question, an ELLIPSE version and a CIRCLE version, might exist under the covers. See IM Prescription 9 for further discussion.

```
OPERATOR THE_A ( E ELLIPSE ) RETURNS LENGTH ;
   /* "the a semiaxis of" */ ... ;
END OPERATOR ;

OPERATOR THE_B ( E ELLIPSE ) RETURNS LENGTH ;
   /* "the b semiaxis of" */ ... ;
END OPERATOR ;

OPERATOR THE_CTR ( E ELLIPSE ) RETURNS POINT ;
   /* "the center of" */ ... ;
END OPERATOR ;

OPERATOR AREA ( E ELLIPSE ) RETURNS AREA ;
   /* "area of"; note that AREA is both the name of the  */
   /* operator and the name of the type of the result    */
   /* (meaning it is probably the name of the            */
   /* corresponding selector too); such punning might or */
   /* might not be valid in a real D (?)                  */
   ... ;
END OPERATOR ;
```

And here is an operator that applies to values of type CIRCLE but not to values of type ELLIPSE:

```
OPERATOR THE_R ( C CIRCLE ) RETURNS LENGTH ;
   /* "the radius of" */ ... ;
END OPERATOR ;
```

Of course, the operators THE_A, THE_B, and THE_CTR (for type ELLIPSE) and THE_R and THE_CTR (for type CIRCLE) are in fact required by RM Prescription 5, and they are provided "automatically." (As we saw in Chapter 3, "automatically" here might or might not mean *automated,* in the sense that the implementation is provided by the system.) In the case of THE_CTR for type CIRCLE in particular, it is precisely *inheritance from type ELLIPSE* that serves as the required "automatic" provision of that operator (though, to repeat, it is possible that the operator might need to be reimplemented for type CIRCLE). As for THE_A and THE_B for type CIRCLE, these operators are required, not by RM Prescription 5, but rather by the very notion of inheritance (though once again it is possible that they might need to be reimplemented for type CIRCLE).

It follows from all of the above that if *v* is of type *T'*, then *v* must satisfy all of the constraints that apply to values of type *T* (as well as all of the constraints that apply to values of type *T'* specifically). To repeat an example from Chapter 12, if *c* is a circle (and hence an ellipse), and if ellipses are subject to the constraint that the length of their major semiaxis *a* must be greater than or equal to that of their minor semiaxis *b*, then that same constraint must be satisfied by *c*—as indeed it is, trivially, because in the case of a circle the semiaxes *a* and *b* coincide in the radius *r*. In other words (loosely): **Constraints associated with type *T* are inherited by type *T'*.**

Now, in Chapter 3 we said that if *v* is a scalar value, it can be thought of as carrying around with it a kind of flag that announces "I am an integer" or "I am a supplier number" or "I am a geometric point" (and so on). Now we see that, conceptually speaking, it might have to carry around several distinct flags—e.g., "I am an ellipse" *and* "I am a circle." (Of course, a flag that announces just the most specific type is all that is logically required. See IM Prescription 8.)

We also said in Chapter 6 that distinct types are disjoint "except possibly if type inheritance is supported." Now we see that two types are definitely not disjoint if one is a subtype of the other. We will encounter some further cases of nondisjointness in Chapters 15 and 16.

We now observe that our informal characterization of IM Prescription 2 ("subtypes are subsets") can more accurately be stated as follows: *Proper* subtypes are *proper* subsets (see IM Prescription 4). **This stronger characterization follows from the requirement that if *T* and *T'* are distinct, then there must exist at least one value of type *T* that is not of type *T'*—a requirement we now proceed to justify. Suppose it were not satisfied; i.e., suppose every value of type *T* were in fact a value of type *T'*. Then:

- Any operator that applied to values of type *T'* would apply to all values of type *T*.

- Any constraint that applied to values of type *T'* would apply to all values of type *T*.

In other words, *T'* and *T* would effectively be identical except for their names, and there would be no logical reason to distinguish between them.

Incidentally, it follows immediately from the foregoing that **the most specific type of a given value is not necessarily a leaf type.** It also follows that **type hierarchies cannot contain any cycles** (i.e., they are indeed hierarchies). For suppose, contrariwise, that there existed some sequence of types *T1, T2, T3, ..., Tn* such that *T1* was an immediate supertype of *T2*, *T2* was an immediate supertype of *T3*, ..., and *Tn* was an immediate supertype of *T1*. Then every one of these types *T1, T2, T3, ..., Tn* would be a proper supertype, and hence a proper superset, of itself!

One last point: It is an obvious corollary of IM Prescription 2 that there cannot be more values of type *T'* than there are of type *T*. This apparently trivial observation can be very helpful in pinpointing errors and clearing up confusions. For example, it would be an error according to our model to define COLORED_CIRCLE as a subtype of type CIRCLE (a state of affairs that might come as a surprise, if you are familiar with object systems). Assuming circles were originally seen as "plain" or uncolored, then there are clearly more colored circles than there are just plain circles. Moreover, there is clearly no CIRCLE selector invocation that could possibly yield a value of type COLORED_CIRCLE. (We are assuming here that, e.g., a red circle and a blue circle of the same size and at the same location are different colored circles.) And so the proposed supertype/subtype relationship, as such, does not in fact exist. *Note:* We will have quite a lot more to say regarding this particular example in Appendix G.

IM PRESCRIPTION 3: "SUBTYPE OF" IS REFLEXIVE

T *and* T' *shall not necessarily be distinct; i.e., every type shall be both a subtype and a supertype of itself.*

This prescription and the next five all have to do with matters of terminology (they elaborate on certain of the terms and concepts introduced in the section "The Running Example" in Chapter 12). The current prescription in particular recognizes that it is convenient to regard any given type *T* as both a subtype and a supertype of itself. This convention has the effect of simplifying the formulation of many of the prescriptions that we will be discussing later. Thus, for example, "ELLIPSE is a subtype of ELLIPSE" is a true statement, and so is "ELLIPSE is a supertype of ELLIPSE."

Note: To say that a given dyadic logical operator *Op* is **reflexive** merely means that *x Op x* evaluates to TRUE for all *x*. Thus, e.g., "=" is reflexive, and so is "is a subtype of." By contrast, "<" and ">" are not.

IM PRESCRIPTION 4: PROPER SUBTYPES

If and only if types T *and* T' *are distinct,* T' *shall be a **proper** subtype of* T, *and* T *shall be a **proper** supertype of* T'.

This prescription introduces some terminology for talking about subtypes and supertypes when the types in question are distinct. In terms of our running example, we can say that, e.g., CIRCLE is a proper subtype of ELLIPSE. (By virtue of IM Prescription 5, q.v., it is also a proper subtype of PLANE_FIGURE.) It is also a subtype of CIRCLE, but not a proper one. Likewise, PLANE_FIGURE is a proper supertype of both ELLIPSE and CIRCLE; it is also a supertype of PLANE_FIGURE, but not a proper one.

We remind you from Chapter 12 that if *T'* is a proper subtype of *T*, there is no requirement that (a) physical representations of appearances of values of type *T'*, and (b) physical representations of appearances of values of type *T*, be of the same form. Of course, there is no requirement that they be different, either.

IM PRESCRIPTION 5: "SUBTYPE OF" IS TRANSITIVE

Every subtype of T' *shall be a subtype of* T. *Every supertype of* T *shall be a supertype of* T'.

This prescription simply says that a subtype of a subtype is a subtype and a supertype of a supertype is a supertype. Thus, for example, RECTANGLE is a subtype of PLANE_FIGURE, and PLANE_FIGURE is a supertype of RECTANGLE.

Note: To say that a given dyadic logical operator *Op* is **transitive** merely means that, for all *x, y,* and *z,* if *x Op y* and *y Op z* both evaluate to TRUE, then so does *x Op z.* Thus, e.g., "=" is transitive, and so is "is a subtype of." By contrast, "≠" and "is disjoint from" are not.

IM PRESCRIPTION 6: IMMEDIATE SUBTYPES

If and only if T' *is a proper subtype of* T *and there is no type that is both a proper supertype of* T' *and a proper subtype of* T, *then* T' *shall be an **immediate** subtype of* T, *and* T *shall be an **immediate** supertype of* T'. *A type that is not an immediate subtype of any type shall be a **root** type. A type that is not an immediate supertype of any type shall be a **leaf** type.*

In terms of our running example, this prescription says that, e.g., CIRCLE is an immediate subtype of ELLIPSE, and ELLIPSE is an immediate supertype of CIRCLE. CIRCLE is also a subtype of PLANE_FIGURE, but not an immediate one; equivalently, PLANE_FIGURE is a supertype of CIRCLE, but not an immediate one. PLANE_FIGURE is a root type. CIRCLE and SQUARE are leaf types.

IM PRESCRIPTION 7: ROOT TYPES DISJOINT

If T1 *and* T2 *are distinct root types, then they shall be disjoint; i.e., no value shall be of both type* T1 *and type* T2.

This prescription is in fact a logical consequence of IM Prescription 8. We state it explicitly for emphasis but defer detailed discussion to the next section.

IM PRESCRIPTION 8: SCALAR VALUES WITH INHERITANCE

Every set of types T1, T2, ..., Tn *shall have a common subtype* T' *such that a given value is of each of the types* T1, T2, ..., Tn *if and only if it is of type* T'.

The definition of **scalar value** needs some extension if type inheritance is supported—basically because such a value can now be of more than one type. The present prescription addresses this issue, but in a rather roundabout way, as we now show.

First of all, we need to introduce the special scalar type *omega*. Type *omega* is empty, meaning it contains no values at all (no scalar values in particular). We will have more to say about *omega* under IM Prescription 20; for now, it is sufficient to observe that such a type does exist, at least conceptually, and it can be regarded as being a subtype of every scalar type[1] (since the empty set is a subset of every set).

Observe next that the prescription refers to a common subtype *T'* of a set of *n* types *T1, T2, ..., Tn*. Consider the case $n = 2$, meaning we are dealing with precisely two types *T1* and *T2;* moreover, we can assume that *T1* and *T2* are distinct (for otherwise we are dealing with the case $n = 1$). Now, if *T1* and *T2* have *omega* as their only common subtype, they are certainly disjoint; in fact, the only way *T1* and *T2* can have a nonempty common subtype—under our assumption of single inheritance—is if one is a (necessarily proper) subtype of the other. Assume without loss of generality that *T2* is a proper subtype of *T1*. Then the requirements of IM Prescription 8 are satisfied with $T' = T2$.

It should be clear without going into detail that the foregoing argument can be extended to the case of arbitrary $n > 2$. So what about the remaining possibilities, $n = 1$ and $n = 0$? For $n = 1$, the requirements of IM Prescription 8 are satisfied trivially with $T' = T1$. For $n = 0$, they are satisfied even more trivially, as it were, since in this case there simply *is* no value that is "of each of the types *T1, T2, ..., Tn,*" and the requirements of IM Prescription 8 are satisfied trivially with $T' = omega$.

By the way, note carefully that we have said that type *omega* exists "at least conceptually." What this means is that we do not require or expect it to be explicitly defined; indeed, we believe it would usually not be. (Note that if it is, it will necessarily be the only leaf type.) In what follows, we will assume it is *not* explicitly defined, barring explicit statements to the contrary.

An immediate logical consequence of IM Prescription 8 is *the disjointness assumption* (already discussed in Chapter 12 but repeated for convenience here):

---

1. It follows that we are moving here into the realm of multiple inheritance, albeit in a very limited kind of way. Nevertheless, we continue to assume throughout most of this chapter that it makes sense to talk in terms of single inheritance only. Note in particular that the fact that *omega* is a subtype of every scalar type does not in itself violate the disjointness assumption (!).

■ If types *T1* and *T2* are such that neither is a subtype of the other, then they are **disjoint**—i.e., no value is of both type *T1* and type *T2*.

To repeat from Chapter 12, this assumption is valid as long as we limit our attention to single inheritance only.[1] And it has a number of important implications, the following among them:

■ Distinct root types are disjoint (IM Prescription 7).

■ Distinct type hierarchies are disjoint. That is, if *TH1* and *TH2* are type hierarchies with distinct root types *RT1* and *RT2*, respectively, and if types *T1* and *T2* belong to *TH1* and *TH2*, respectively, then *T1* and *T2* are disjoint. For example, if we deleted type PLANE_FIGURE (only) from Fig. 12.1, we would be left with two type hierarchies, one rooted at type ELLIPSE and one at type POLYGON, that are necessarily disjoint (there is no value that is both an ellipse and a polygon).

■ Distinct immediate subtypes of the same supertype are disjoint.

■ Distinct leaf types are disjoint.

■ Every value has exactly one **most specific type** (and this is the real point of IM Prescription 8, in the context of single inheritance). For example, a given value might have types PLANE_FIGURE, POLYGON, and RECTANGLE, but not SQUARE, in which case the most specific type would be, precisely, RECTANGLE. In fact, as noted in Chapter 12, if value *v* is of most specific type *T,* then the set of types possessed by *v* is, precisely, the set consisting of all supertypes of *T* (a set that includes *T* itself, of course). In other words, *v* is of every type that is a supertype of *T* and is of no other type.

IM PRESCRIPTION 9: SCALAR VARIABLES WITH INHERITANCE

Let scalar variable V *be of declared type* T. *Because of value substitutability (see IM Prescription 16), the value* v *assigned to* V *at any given time can have any subtype* T' *of type* T *as its most specific type. We can therefore model* V *as a named ordered triple of the form* < DT,MST,v > , *where:*

a. *The name of the triple is the name of the variable,* V.

b. DT *is the name of the declared type for variable* V.

c. MST *is the name of the **most specific type**—also known as the **current** most specific type—for, or of, variable* V.

d. v *is a value of most specific type* MST—*the **current value** for, or of, variable* V.

We use the notation DT*(V)*, MST*(V)*, v*(V) to refer to the* DT, MST, v *components, respectively, of this model of scalar variable* V.

Now let X *be a scalar expression. By definition,* X *specifies an invocation of some scalar operator* Op *(where the arguments, if any, to that invocation of* Op *are specified as expressions in turn).*

---

1. It is also valid if we depart from single inheritance only in that we explicitly define type *omega*.

Thus, the notation DT(V), MST(V), v(V) just introduced can be extended in an obvious way to refer to the declared type DT(X), the current most specific type MST(X), and the current value v(X), respectively, of X—where DT(X) is DT(Op) and is known at compile time, and MST(X) and v(X) refer to the result of evaluating X and are therefore not known until run time (in general).

Like the definition of *scalar value,* the definition of **scalar variable** also needs some extension if type inheritance is supported—basically because such a variable is permitted to have a value that is of *any subtype of* the declared type of the variable in question. For example, let scalar variable E be defined as follows:

```
VAR E ELLIPSE ;
```

At run time, then, the current value of variable E can have any subtype of ELLIPSE (including ELLIPSE itself in particular) as its most specific type. Thus, the current value might be a circle instead of "just an ellipse" (such a possibility is intuitively reasonable, of course, since a circle *is* an ellipse). If it is, then we can say that:

- *DT*(E) is ELLIPSE.

- *MST*(E) is CIRCLE.

- *v*(E) is whatever circle happens to be the current value of E.

Observe, therefore, that (as noted in Chapter 12) we must now be careful over the logical difference between the two important types that apply to any given variable: the **declared** type, which does not change over time, vs. the **current most specific** type, which does (in general). Of course, the second of these must always be some subtype—not necessarily a proper subtype—of the first; nevertheless, there is a logical difference between the two concepts.

Observe further that if type *T* is the current most specific type of variable *V,* then every proper supertype of type *T* is also a "current type" of variable *V,* in a sense. However, the term "current type" is usually used, informally, to refer to the *most specific* current type of the variable in question.

Note: By virtue of IM Prescription 8, *MST*(*V*) is in fact implied by *v*(*V*), and is thus logically unnecessary as a component of the model of *V.* We include it for reasons of convenience and explicitness. Also, by virtue of RM Prescription 11, *DT*(*V*) can never be *omega.* (Nor can *MST*(*V*), of course, since there is no value of type *omega.*)

Now, it should be clear that—as IM Prescription 9 in fact states—the foregoing definitions can readily be extended to apply to arbitrary scalar expressions instead of just to scalar variables specifically. Let *X* be such an expression, and let *v*(*X*) be the result of evaluating that expression. Then:

- *X* has a *declared type, DT*(*X*): namely, the declared type of the operator *Op* that is invoked at the outermost level of *X*. *DT*(*X*) is known at compile time; in fact, it is determined by the *specification signature* for *Op,* as we will see under IM Prescription 17. Note in particular that *Op* might be a selector.

- *X* also has a *current most specific type, MST*(*X*): namely, the type that is the most specific type of *v*(*X*). *MST*(*X*) is not known until run time, in general.

We have now laid sufficient groundwork to be able to discuss an important concept that pervades the topic of type inheritance: **polymorphism.** (Of course, we have met this concept before, in Chapter 3 in particular, but there is a lot more to be said about it in the present context.) As we have seen, if *T'* is a subtype of *T,* then all operators that apply to values of type *T* apply to values of type *T'* as well. Thus (to repeat a by now familiar example), if AREA(*e*) is valid, where *e* is an ellipse, then AREA(*c*), where *c* is a circle, must be valid as well. It follows that the AREA operator is polymorphic: It can take arguments of different types on different invocations.

Recall now that ellipses and circles, at least as we defined them in Chapter 12, have different possreps:

```
TYPE ELLIPSE ... POSSREP ( A ..., B ..., CTR ... ) ;

TYPE CIRCLE  ... POSSREP ( R ..., CTR ... ) ... ;
```

It is conceivable, therefore, that two different versions of the AREA operator will exist under the covers, one that makes use of the ELLIPSE possrep and one that makes use of the CIRCLE possrep. To say it again, it is conceivable—but it is *not* absolutely necessary. So long as the code that implements AREA for type ELLIPSE is written in terms of the ELLIPSE possrep, that code will necessarily work for circles, because the ELLIPSE possrep is necessarily, albeit implicitly, a possrep for CIRCLE too (though, as explained in Chapter 12, not a *declared* one). To be more specific, the area of a general ellipse is πab, while that of a circle is πr^2. Thus, the code that implements the ellipse version of AREA will presumably invoke THE_A and THE_B, and that code will certainly work for a circle.

Note further that the implementer might want to provide distinct versions of some operator at the supertype and subtype levels anyway, even when there is no logical need to do so. Consider polygons and rectangles, for example. The algorithm that computes the area of a general polygon will certainly work for a rectangle; for rectangles, however, a much more efficient algorithm—multiply the height by the width—is available. Thus, it might be desirable to have two implementation versions of the operator for reasons of efficiency, if for no other reason.

To return to ellipses and circles: Observe now, however, that the ellipse AREA code will definitely not work for circles if it is written in terms of a *physical* representation instead of a possible one, and physical representations for types ELLIPSE and CIRCLE differ. The practice of implementing operators in terms of physical representations is thus clearly contraindicated. Code defensively! In fact, we would strongly recommend the following discipline: Access to physical representations should be limited to the following operators *and nothing else:*

- Selector operators

- THE_ operators

- IS_*T* operators (see IM Prescription 15)

We remind you that many of these operators (perhaps not all) will have system-provided implementations anyway.

Of course, it makes no logical difference to the user how many implementation versions of AREA exist under the covers; to the user there is just one AREA operator, which works for (say) ellipses and therefore works for circles too, by definition. To say it again, AREA is polymorphic.

Now, we have already seen many examples of polymorphic operators in earlier chapters: "=", ":=", "+", "||", SUM, and many others. But there is no inheritance, as such, involved in these examples—they are all instances of **overloading** polymorphism (also known as *general* polymorphism [137], ad hoc polymorphism [15], or just *overloading* for short). The kind of polymorphism exhibited by the AREA operator, by contrast, is known as **inclusion** polymorphism [15], on the grounds that the relationship between (e.g.) circles and ellipses is basically that of set inclusion.[1] For obvious reasons, we take the unqualified term *polymorphism* throughout this part of the book to mean inclusion polymorphism specifically, barring explicit statements to the contrary.

Now, a helpful way to characterize the logical difference between inclusion and overloading polymorphism is as follows:

- **Inclusion** polymorphism means there is just one operator, with several distinct implementation versions under the covers (but the user does not need to know that the versions in question are in fact distinct—to the user, to repeat, there is just one operator).

- **Overloading** polymorphism, by contrast, means there are several distinct operators with the same name (and the user does need to know that the operators in question are in fact distinct, with distinct—though preferably similar—semantics). *Note:* "Preferably similar" might be too strong here. For example, we use THE_A in this chapter to refer to an ellipse semiaxis, but in the next chapter we will use it to refer to a parallelogram vertex—so THE_A is definitely overloaded, and its meanings are quite different.

These matters are explained more fully later under IM Prescriptions 16-19, but we elaborate on them slightly here for purposes of reference (despite the fact that such elaboration might not make very much sense at this juncture). Briefly, for overloading polymorphism, each of the distinct operators will have its own distinct *specification signature* (because invocations of the operators in question would otherwise be ambiguous). For inclusion polymorphism, by contrast, the single operator will have just one specification signature, but each distinct under-the-covers implementation version of that operator will have its own distinct *version* signature. See IM Prescription 17 for further discussion.

The trouble is, as that further discussion will show, there can be no guarantee with inclusion polymorphism that the various versions under the covers do in fact all implement the same operator!—i.e., distinct versions might have distinct *semantics*. If they do, of course, we do not have true inclusion polymorphism any more, we have overloading polymorphism instead, and such a state of affairs is in violation of our model. But you should be aware that such violations are certainly possible in practice, and are even argued by some to be desirable. What is more, the situation is confused still further by the fact that, regrettably, much of the literature uses the term *overloading* to mean inclusion polymorphism anyway. Again, see IM Prescription 17 for further discussion.

Back to inclusion polymorphism specifically. What are the implications of this idea for the user? Consider the following example. Suppose we need to write a program to display some diagram, made up of squares, circles, ellipses, etc. Without polymorphism, the code for this task will look something like this:

```
FOR EACH x ∈ DIAGRAM
    CASE ;
        WHEN IS_SQUARE ( x ) THEN CALL DISPLAY_SQUARE ... ;
        WHEN IS_CIRCLE ( x ) THEN CALL DISPLAY_CIRCLE ... ;
        .....
    END CASE ;
```

(See IM Prescription 15 for an explanation of the operators IS_SQUARE, IS_CIRCLE, etc.) With polymorphism, by contrast, the code is much simpler and much more succinct:

---

1. The operators "=", ":=", "+", and so forth might *become* instances of inclusion polymorphism if inheritance is supported. For example, "=" might be inherited from type *alpha* (see IM Prescription 20).

```
FOR EACH x ∈ DIAGRAM CALL DISPLAY ( x ) ;
```

Explanation: DISPLAY here is a polymorphic operator. The version of DISPLAY that works for values of a given type will be defined (if necessary) when that type is defined—or possibly at some subsequent time—and will be made known to the system at that time. At run time, then, when the system encounters the DISPLAY invocation with argument x, it will determine the version of DISPLAY that is appropriate to the type of x and invoke that version: a process known as **run-time binding** (because the invocation in question is being "bound" to the appropriate implementation code at run time).[1] In other words, polymorphism effectively means that certain CASE expressions and CASE statements that would otherwise have had to appear in the user's source code are *moved under the covers*—the system performs those CASE operations in the user's behalf.

Note the implications of the foregoing for program maintenance in particular. For example, suppose that (a) a new type TRIANGLE is defined (another immediate subtype of POLYGON) and (b) a corresponding new version of DISPLAY is defined as well. Without polymorphism, we would have to examine every source code CASE expression and CASE statement of the form shown previously to see whether it needs to be modified to include the following:

```
WHEN IS_TRIANGLE ( x ) THEN CALL DISPLAY_TRIANGLE ... ;
```

With polymorphism, however, no such modifications are needed at all.

Because of examples like the foregoing, polymorphism is sometimes described, a little colorfully, as "old code invoking new code"; that is, a program P can effectively invoke some version of an operator Op that did not even exist (the version, that is) at the time P was written. Thus, we have, at least potentially, what is called **code reuse:** The very same program P might be usable on data that is of a type that had not even been defined at the time P was written. (Certainly the code of program P is being reused here. The code that implements operator Op under the covers might or might not be; for example, the code that implements the AREA operator for ellipses might or might not be reusable for circles, as we saw earlier.)

We now consider another example in order to make another point. Specifically, we consider the operators THE_A ("the a semiaxis of") and THE_R ("the radius of"). Assume first that ellipses and circles have the same physical representation and THE_A for type ELLIPSE is implemented in terms of that physical representation. Then that same implementation code can serve as the implementation of THE_A for type CIRCLE too, and THE_R can be implemented thus:

```
OPERATOR THE_R ( C CIRCLE ) RETURNS LENGTH ... ;
   RETURN ( THE_A ( C ) ) ;
END OPERATOR ;
```

Of course, it could also be implemented directly in terms of the physical representation if desired.

Now assume instead that ellipses and circles have different physical representations, but THE_A for type ELLIPSE is still implemented in terms of the ELLIPSE physical representation. Then THE_R

---

1. Two points. First, we will show under IM Prescription 17 that the system might in fact be able to do part or all of the binding at compile time instead of run time (an obvious performance benefit). Second, even if some run-time binding is required, it still might not involve as much overhead as you might think. As you probably noticed, we explained the run-time binding process in the example in terms of "the" type of x; well, we were being deliberately (and, we hope, uncharacteristically) vague here. Suppose types *T1, T2, T3, T4,* and *T5* are such that *T1, T2, T3,* and *T4* are immediate supertypes of *T2, T3, T4,* and *T5,* respectively; suppose operator Op has implementation versions for types *T1* and *T3* (only); finally, suppose the most specific type of x is *T5*. Then there is no need for the system to determine this latter fact; all it needs to do is ascertain that x is certainly of type *T3* and therefore invoke the *T3* version of Op.

might be implemented in terms of the CIRCLE physical representation, and THE_A for type CIRCLE could then be implemented thus:

```
OPERATOR THE_A ( C CIRCLE ) RETURNS LENGTH ... ;
    RETURN ( THE_R ( C ) ) ;
END OPERATOR ;
```

Of course, it could also be implemented directly in terms of the CIRCLE physical representation if desired.

The net of the foregoing example is just this: For type CIRCLE, either of THE_A or THE_R might be implemented in terms of the other, depending on circumstances (physical representations in particular). Either way, of course, it should make no logical difference so far as the user is concerned.

Recall now the concept of **substitutability,** which we said in Chapter 12 was "in many ways the whole point of inheritance." Just to remind you, substitutability means that, e.g., wherever the system expects a value of type ELLIPSE, we can always substitute a value of type CIRCLE, because circles *are* ellipses. In particular:

■   If some relation *r* has an attribute *A* of declared type ELLIPSE, some of the *A* values in *r* might in fact be circles rather than "just ellipses."

■   If type *T* has a possrep with a component *X* of declared type ELLIPSE, then for some values *v* of type *T* the operator invocation THE_*X*(*v*) might return a circle instead of "just an ellipse."

More generally, wherever the system expects a value of type *T,* we can always substitute a value of type *T'*—*The Principle of (Value) Substitutability* (see IM Prescription 16). But it should be clear from our earlier discussions that substitutability is really just inclusion polymorphism in a different guise; we mention it here principally because it is widely recognized as the sine qua non of type inheritance, and no discussion of that topic would be complete without such a mention.

We close this section by pointing out that the notions of polymorphism and substitutability, important though they might be in practice, are both logically implied by the notion of type inheritance—they are not, logically speaking, completely separate concepts. In other words, if the system supports type inheritance, it *must* support polymorphism and substitutability as well (for if it did not, then it would not be supporting type inheritance, by definition).

IM PRESCRIPTION 10: SPECIALIZATION BY CONSTRAINT

Let T *be a regular proper supertype (see IM Prescription 20), and let* T' *be an immediate subtype of* T. *Then the definition of* T' *shall specify a **specialization constraint** SC, formulated in terms of* T, *such that a value shall be of type* T' *if and only if it is of type* T *and it satisfies constraint SC. There shall exist at least one value of type* T *that does not satisfy constraint SC.*

Controversy has raged for years in the literature (especially the object literature) over the question of whether the system should be aware of the fact that, e.g., an ellipse whose semiaxes *a* and *b* are equal is really a circle. Clearly, if it is so aware, then updating a variable of declared type ELLIPSE could have the effect of changing the most specific type of that variable "down" from ELLIPSE to CIRCLE. We refer to such an effect as **specialization by constraint,** or *S by C* for short (though we should warn you that other writers use an almost identical term to mean something rather different, as we will see in Appendix F).

At first sight, it would seem obvious that a good model of inheritance must include S by C; "the more knowledge the system has, the better" is always a good general principle. After all, an ellipse with equal semiaxes certainly is a circle in the real world, and a model that does not understand this fact can hardly be said to be a good model of reality. However, we did not include S by C in the first version of our model [82]. Our reasons for adopting that position are not worth repeating here—well, not in detail, at any rate, but we should at least say that one of them was the fact that most other attempts at defining an inheritance model seemed to have done the same thing (see, e.g., reference [123]). Be that as it may, we did also say in reference [82] that we were "actively investigating the possibility of revising our model ... to include [S by C]." We are happy to be able to report that those investigations were successful, and our model—unlike just about every other proposal we have seen in this connection—does now include S by C, as we now proceed to explain. (In fact, it is our claim now that an inheritance model can be said to be good only if it does include S by C. See Appendix F for further discussion of this point.)

We begin by repeating from Chapter 12 the type definitions for types ELLIPSE and CIRCLE:

```
TYPE ELLIPSE
    IS { PLANE_FIGURE
        POSSREP { A LENGTH, B LENGTH, CTR POINT
                CONSTRAINT A ≥ B } } ;

TYPE CIRCLE
    IS { ELLIPSE
        CONSTRAINT THE_A ( ELLIPSE ) = THE_B ( ELLIPSE )
        POSSREP { R   = THE_A   ( ELLIPSE ) ,
                CTR = THE_CTR ( ELLIPSE ) } } ;
```

Now we focus on the "IS definition"—the $<is\ def>$, in **Tutorial D** terms—for type CIRCLE, which specifies three things:

1. *The name of the immediate supertype* (ELLIPSE)

2. *An additional constraint,* to the effect that the semiaxes a and b must be equal for the ellipse to be a circle

3. *A derived possrep* (i.e., a possrep for circles that is derived from one for ellipses)

Items 1 and 2 together constitute the required **specialization constraint** for type CIRCLE. Note that (as required by IM Prescription 10) it is formulated in terms of type ELLIPSE; note further that it is, precisely, the type constraint for type CIRCLE. In other words, it can be interpreted as follows. In order for some value c to be of type CIRCLE, the following boolean expression must evaluate to TRUE:

```
IS_ELLIPSE ( c ) AND THE_A ( c ) = THE_B ( c )
```

By way of example, consider the following ELLIPSE selector invocation:

```
ELLIPSE ( LENGTH ( 5.0 ), LENGTH ( 5.0 ), POINT ( 0.0, 0.0 ) )
```

This expression returns a value of most specific type CIRCLE, not ELLIPSE, because the value in question does indeed cause the boolean expression just shown to evaluate to TRUE; in other words, S by C occurs. In fact, the selector invocation in question, even though it names type ELLIPSE, is logically equivalent to a certain selector invocation for type *CIRCLE*[1]—viz.:

```
CIRCLE ( LENGTH ( 5.0 ), POINT ( 0.0, 0.0 ) )
```

Thus we see that S by C fundamentally implies that *certain selector invocations will produce results whose most specific type is **some proper subtype** of the designated target type.* Incidentally, it is worth pointing out explicitly that this fact does not constitute a violation of, or even an extension to, RM Prescription 4 as stated in Chapter 4.

Now suppose type CIRCLE has a proper subtype O_CIRCLE (where an "O-circle" is a circle with center the origin):

```
TYPE O_CIRCLE
    IS { CIRCLE
         CONSTRAINT THE_CTR ( CIRCLE ) = POINT ( 0.0, 0.0 )
         POSSREP { R = THE_R ( CIRCLE ) } } ;
```

Then the ELLIPSE selector invocation previously discussed now returns a value of most specific type O_CIRCLE, not CIRCLE, because the value in question satisfies the constraint for type O_CIRCLE as well. In other words, S by C implies that a given selector invocation will return a value that—in accordance with the specified constraints—is of *the most specific type possible.*

Recall now from Chapter 6 that, ultimately, the only way *any* expression can yield a value, of any type, is via some selector invocation. It follows that S by C can usefully be thought of as being implemented *inside selector implementation code,* using a procedure ("FIND_MST") along the following lines:[2]

```
OPERATOR FIND_MST ( v value, t type ) RETURNS type ;
    let t1, t2, ..., tn be all of the immediate subtypes of t in some arbitrary order ;
    let the corresponding specialization constraints be IC1, IC2, ..., ICn, respectively ;
    DO i := 1 TO n ;
        IF v satisfies ICi THEN RETURN ( FIND_MST ( v, ti ) ) ; END IF ;
    END DO ;
    RETURN ( t ) ;
END OPERATOR ;
```

The procedure is initially invoked with the selected value and the selector declared type. For example, in the case of the ELLIPSE selector invocation discussed earlier—

```
ELLIPSE ( LENGTH ( 5.0 ), LENGTH ( 5.0 ), POINT ( 0.0, 0.0 ) )
```

—the initial arguments are the indicated ellipse value and the type ELLIPSE.

So much for the basic idea of S by C. But there is much, much more to be said on this topic: so much, in fact, that it seemed better not to include it all in the body of the chapter—even though it does logically belong here—but instead to relegate most of it to Appendix F. (Note, however, that we do examine one particularly important aspect in the next section.) For the present, therefore, we content

---

1. Observe too that the system knows exactly *which* selector invocation for type CIRCLE it is equivalent to, thanks to the derived possrep specification.

2. Note carefully that we say "can be thought of" here. In practice, we envisage a much more efficient implementation of S by C than this conceptual discussion might suggest (see Appendix F).

ourselves with a few miscellaneous observations:

- All nonroot types have an associated IS definition; no root type does (but note that all types are root types in the absence of inheritance support).

- IM Prescription 10 states that "there shall exist at least one value of type *T* that does not satisfy constraint *SC*." This statement is just a more precise version of the requirement of IM Prescription 2, as it applies to the case where *T* is a regular type (see IM Prescription 20), that there shall exist at least one value that is of type *T* and not of type *T'*. As we said earlier, proper subtypes are proper subsets.

- Finally, we show for interest an example involving a user-defined subtype (EVEN_INTEGER) of a system-defined supertype (INTEGER):

```
TYPE EVEN_INTEGER ORDINAL IS { INTEGER CONSTRAINT MOD ( INTEGER, 2 ) = 0 } ;
```

We are assuming the availability of an operator called MOD ("modulo") that takes two numeric arguments and returns the remainder that results after dividing the first by the second. Since type INTEGER is a system-defined type with no declared possrep, type EVEN_INTEGER has no declared possrep either. One consequence of this state of affairs is that in order to assign the value 4 (say) to a variable EI of type EVEN_INTEGER, we will have to use a statement of the form:

```
EI := TREAT_AS_EVEN_INTEGER ( 4 ) ;
```

(See IM Prescription 14 for an explanation of TREAT.)

IM PRESCRIPTION 11: ASSIGNMENT WITH INHERITANCE

Consider the assignment

```
V := X
```

(where V is a variable and X is an expression). DT(X) shall be a subtype of DT(V). The assignment shall set MST(V) equal to MST(X) and v(V) equal to v(X).

The model of a scalar variable introduced in IM Prescription 9 is useful in pinning down the precise semantics of various operations, including assignment operations in particular. Consider the following example:

```
VAR E ELLIPSE ;
VAR C CIRCLE ;

C := CIRCLE ( ... ) ;
E := C ;
```

The first assignment here assigns some circle value to variable C (the expression on the right side of that assignment is a CIRCLE selector invocation). The second assignment then copies that circle value from variable C to variable E. (Of course, we could have simply assigned the result of the

CIRCLE selector invocation to variable E directly, without involving variable C at all.) After that second assignment, then, the current most specific type of E will be CIRCLE, not ELLIPSE (the declared type, of course, will still be ELLIPSE). Thus, whereas assignment without inheritance[1] requires the same type on both sides, assignment with inheritance means—thanks to substitutability—that:

- The declared type $DT(X)$ of the expression on the right side can be any subtype of the declared type $DT(V)$ of the variable on the left side (this is a compile-time check).

- The most specific type $MST(X)$ of the value denoted by the expression on the right side can be any subtype of the declared type $DT(V)$ of the variable on the left side. (In fact, of course, it must be some subtype of the declared type $DT(X)$ of the expression on the right side, and so it is necessarily some subtype of $DT(V)$.)

- The variable V on the left side acquires its new most specific type, as well as its new value, from the value denoted by the expression X on the right side. *Note:* As pointed out earlier in this chapter, the most specific type of any value, and hence the most specific type of any variable that currently contains that value, is in fact implied by the value in question. It follows that the assignment *must* have the effect of setting $MST(V)$ equal to $MST(X)$, as well as setting $v(V)$ equal to $v(X)$, and there is no need to say as much in so many words; we do so only for explicitness.

Observe, therefore, that what does *not* happen is that the value of the expression on the right side gets "converted up" to the declared type of the variable on the left side. For if such a conversion did occur, *the value would lose its most specific properties* (loosely speaking). In the case at hand, for example, we would not be able to ask for the radius of E—more precisely, the radius of the circle that is now the current value of E—because the circle would have been converted to "just an ellipse,"[2] and ellipses that are "just ellipses" do not have a radius.

By the way, you might possibly see a problem here, and indeed there is one. To be specific, the operator THE_R ("the radius of") cannot validly be applied to a variable such as E whose declared type is only ELLIPSE, not CIRCLE. IM Prescription 14 addresses this issue.

Suppose we now continue the example as follows:

```
VAR A AREA ;

A := AREA ( E ) ;
```

What happens now is the following:

- First, the system performs a compile-time type check on the expression AREA(E), as required by OO Prescription 1; the check succeeds, because E is of declared type ELLIPSE and the single parameter to AREA is of declared type ELLIPSE also (see the outline definition of the AREA operator as shown earlier under IM Prescription 2).

---

1. And, in accordance with our discussion of this topic in Chapter 3, without coercions.

2. In fact, IM Prescriptions 8 and 10 both imply that such a conversion is logically impossible. For if it were possible, it would mean that the very same value could have most specific type CIRCLE *and* most specific type ELLIPSE, thereby violating IM Prescription 8; it would also mean that, after the assignment, the target variable would contain an ellipse that could be "S by C'd" to a circle but has not been, thereby violating IM Prescription 10.

- Second, the system notes that—let us assume—a version of AREA exists that applies to circles.[1] (More generally, it will note *all* of the versions that apply to values of some proper subtype of type ELLIPSE, but in our example only one such subtype exists.)

- Third, the system discovers at run time that the current value of E is of type CIRCLE. Since it already knows that CIRCLE is the most specific subtype of type ELLIPSE for which a distinct implementation version of AREA exists, it then invokes that version (i.e., it performs the run-time binding process mentioned in our discussion of IM Prescription 9).

The fact that it is the circle version of AREA that is invoked might or might not be relevant to the user; it might be, if the declared type of the result of the operation varies depending on whether it is the circle version or the ellipse version that is invoked (it does not, in the case at hand). Note, however, that this state of affairs—i.e., the fact that the user might like to know which version of AREA is invoked—does not undermine our earlier claim to the effect that, so far as the user is concerned, there is really just one AREA operator. See IM Prescriptions 16 and 17 for further discussion of this issue.

We now consider another example in order to make another important point:

```
VAR E ELLIPSE ;

E := ELLIPSE ( LENGTH ( 6.0 ), LENGTH ( 5.0 ), POINT ( ... ) ) ;
THE_A ( E ) := LENGTH ( 5.0 ) ;
```

After the first assignment, *MST*(E) is ELLIPSE, of course. After the second, however, it is CIRCLE, thanks to S by C. To be more precise, the assignment to THE_A(E)—as we know from Chapter 6—is really shorthand for the following:

```
E := ELLIPSE ( LENGTH ( 5.0 ), THE_B ( E ), THE_CTR ( E ) ) ;
```

The selector invocation on the right side here returns a circle, because it yields a result with $a = b = 5.0$.

Now suppose we execute another assignment on E:

```
THE_A ( E ) := LENGTH ( 8.0 ) ;
```

It should be clear that *MST*(E) is now ELLIPSE again (because THE_A(E) is now greater than THE_B(E)). We refer to this effect as **generalization by constraint** (*G by C* for short). Indeed, it should be obvious that support for S by C implies support for G by C as well. (What is more, the algorithm given under IM Prescription 10 for implementing S by C in fact implements G by C as well, as should also be obvious. Though we should perhaps add that, unlike S by C, which occurs on the invocation of some selector, G by C occurs on the execution of some assignment.)

We now observe that assignment, with S by C and G by C, is the key to the problem of changing the current most specific type of some variable *V* from *T1* to *T2* (say), where the declared type of *V* is some common supertype *T* of *T1* and *T2*. For example, suppose we extend our running example to include another type NONCIRCLE (an immediate subtype of ELLIPSE, like CIRCLE), with the obvious

---

1. This step can be done at compile time or run time. Doing it at compile time means the run-time overhead of searching for versions is avoided, but programs might need to be recompiled when new implementation versions are defined. Doing it at run time means the possibly varying declared type of the result cannot be taken into account (and perhaps taken advantage of) at compile time.

semantics,[1] and suppose once again that E is a variable of declared type ELLIPSE. Suppose further that
MST(E) is NONCIRCLE (implying that THE_A(E) > THE_B(E); along with the fact that every
noncircle is an ellipse, this condition is basically the type constraint for type NONCIRCLE). Let
THE_A(E) and THE_B(E) be eight and five, respectively. Now consider the following assignment:

```
THE_A ( E ) := LENGTH ( 5.0 ) ;
```

After this assignment, E satisfies the condition THE_A(E) = THE_B(E), of course, and so
MST(E) is now CIRCLE instead of NONCIRCLE. In other words, we have changed the most specific
type of E "sideways," as it were. Thus, S by C and G by C together take care of the problem of
changing types not only "upward" and "downward," as we already know, but also "sideways" (apologies
for the sloppy manner of speaking here).

One last point: We have been assuming in accordance with our discussion of such matters in
Chapter 3 that the assignment operator has not been overloaded in such a way as to permit *DT*(X) not to
be a subtype of *DT*(V), thereby effectively requiring coercion of v(X) to the type, declared or current
most specific, of V.[2] Since IM Prescription 11 itself effectively assumes the same thing, it will clearly
need some revision if that assumption is jettisoned.

IM PRESCRIPTION 12: EQUALITY ETC. WITH INHERITANCE

Consider the equality comparison

```
Y = X
```

*(where Y and X are expressions). DT(X) and DT(Y) shall have a nonempty common subtype. The
comparison shall return TRUE if MST(Y) is equal to MST(X) and v(Y) is equal to v(X), FALSE
otherwise.*

Consider the following example:

```
VAR E ELLIPSE ;
VAR C CIRCLE ;

IF E = C THEN ... END IF ;
```

The comparison "E = C" here will evaluate to TRUE if and only if the current value of variable
E (a) is a circle—i.e., is of type CIRCLE—and (b) is in fact the same circle as the current value of
variable C. In general, the situation with respect to equality comparisons is analogous (though not
identical) to that with respect to assignments. To be more specific, whereas equality comparison without

1. ELLIPSE now becomes a *union type,* incidentally (see IM Prescription 20).

2. Such overloading might permit, e.g., the assignment of a U.K. sterling value to a variable of declared type U.S. dollars,
with implicit currency conversion from sterling to dollars. You might care to reflect on some of the complexities involved
in such an overloading, bearing in mind in particular the fact that currency conversion rates vary over time.

inheritance[1] requires the same type on both sides, equality comparison with inheritance means—thanks to substitutability again—that:

- The declared types $DT(X)$ and $DT(Y)$ of the expressions on the right and left side, respectively, must have some common supertype (this is a compile-time check). Note that this requirement is not explicitly stated in IM Prescription 12; however, we will show in the next chapter that it is in fact implied by the requirement—which *is* stated—that $DT(X)$ and $DT(Y)$ must have a nonempty common subtype.

- The comparison will definitely give FALSE if the current most specific types of the comparands are different (a difference in type is certainly a logical difference), but will give TRUE if those most specific types are the same *and* the values are the same too. *Note:* Again we remind you that the most specific type of any value is implied by the value in question. It follows that if $v(Y)$ and $v(X)$ are the same, then $MST(Y)$ and $MST(X)$ must be the same too, and there is no need to say as much in so many words; we do so only for explicitness.

- Under the disjointness assumption—which is to say, in the context of single inheritance—it should be clear that $DT(X)$ and $DT(Y)$ can have a nonempty common subtype only if one is a subtype of the other. If this condition is not satisfied, the comparison will fail on a compile-time type error. For example, if those declared types are ELLIPSE and RECTANGLE, respectively, then the comparison is not valid.

The comparison $Y \neq X$ is equivalent to NOT $(Y = X)$. The rules for "<" etc., in the cases where those operators apply, follow the same general pattern, though it might not be necessary to insist in those cases that the most specific types of the comparands be the same in order for the comparison to give TRUE. To repeat an example from Chapter 3, let 8 and 5 be values of most specific type EVEN_INTEGER and ODD_INTEGER, respectively, where EVEN_INTEGER and ODD_INTEGER have INTEGER as a common supertype. Then the comparison $8 > 5$ can surely (and reasonably) be defined in such a way as to give TRUE.

One last point: We have been assuming in accordance with our discussion of such matters in Chapter 3 that the equality comparison operator has not been overloaded in such a way as to permit the comparison to give TRUE even if the most specific types of X and Y are not the same (in effect requiring coercion of $v(Y)$ to the type, declared or current most specific, of X or the other way around).[2] Since IM Prescription 12 itself effectively assumes the same thing, it will clearly need some revision if that assumption is jettisoned.

IM PRESCRIPTION 13: JOIN ETC. WITH INHERITANCE

Let rx *and* ry *be relations with a common attribute* A, *and let the declared types of* A *in* rx *and* ry *be* DTx(A) *and* DTy(A), *respectively. Consider the join of* rx *and* ry *(necessarily over* A, *at least in part).* DTx(A) *and* DTy(A) *shall have a nonempty common subtype and hence shall also have a most specific common supertype,* T *say. Then the declared type of* A *in the result of the join shall be* T.

Analogous remarks apply to union, intersection, and difference operators. That is, in each case:

---

1. And, in accordance with our discussion of this topic in Chapter 3 once again, without coercions.

2. Such overloading might permit, e.g., a comparison to be performed between a U.K. sterling amount and a U.S. dollar amount, with implicit currency conversion either way. Again, you might care to meditate on some of the complexities involved in such an overloading.

   a.   *Corresponding attributes of the operands shall be such that their declared types have a nonempty common subtype.*

   b.   *The declared type of the corresponding attribute of the result shall be the corresponding most specific common supertype.*

This prescription should be easy enough to understand as stated,[1] but it is worth examining in detail because it might be felt to be slightly counterintuitive in one particular respect. Consider the relations RX and RY shown in Fig. 14.1; note that the sole attribute A in RX is of declared type ELLIPSE and its counterpart A in RY is of declared type CIRCLE. We adopt the convention that values in the figure of the form E*i* are ellipses that are not circles and values of the form C*i* are circles. Most specific types are shown in lowercase italics.

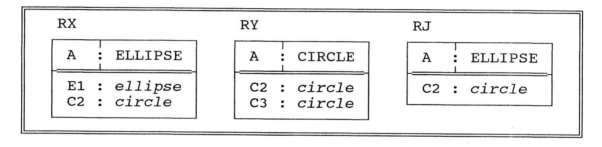

Fig. 14.1: Join with inheritance (example)

Now consider the join of RX and RY, RJ say (again, see Fig. 14.1). Clearly, every A value in RJ will necessarily be of type CIRCLE (because any A value in RX whose most specific type is merely ELLIPSE cannot possibly "compare equal" to any A value in RY). Thus, it might be thought that the declared type of attribute A in RJ should be CIRCLE, not ELLIPSE. But consider the following:

- Since RX and RY each have A as their sole attribute, RX JOIN RY reduces to RX INTERSECT RY, and so the rule regarding the declared type of the result attribute for JOIN must reduce to the analogous rule for INTERSECT.

- RX INTERSECT RY in turn is logically equivalent to RX MINUS (RX MINUS RY). Let the result of the second operand here—i.e., RX MINUS RY—be RZ. Then it is clear that:

  - RZ will include some A values of most specific type ELLIPSE, in general, and so the declared type of attribute A in RZ must be ELLIPSE.

  - The original expression thus reduces to RX MINUS RZ, where the declared type of attribute A in both RX and RZ is ELLIPSE, and hence yields a final result in which the declared type of attribute A must obviously be ELLIPSE once again.

---

1. Except perhaps for the fact that if *DTx(A)* and *DTy(A)* have a nonempty common subtype, they necessarily do have a most specific common supertype as well (see Chapter 15).

■ It follows that the declared type of the result attribute for INTERSECT, and therefore for JOIN too, must indeed be as stated.

The foregoing discussion takes care of RX MINUS RY, too. What about RY MINUS RX? Clearly, every A value in the result of this latter expression will be of type CIRCLE, and so again it might be thought that the declared type of A in that result should be CIRCLE, not ELLIPSE. However, noting that RX INTERSECT RY is also logically equivalent to RY MINUS (RY MINUS RX), we can quickly see that specifying the declared type of A in the result of RY MINUS RX to be CIRCLE would lead to a contradiction. It follows that the declared type of the result attribute for MINUS too must indeed be as stated.

Finally, consider RX UNION RY. Here it should be obvious that the result will include some A values of most specific type ELLIPSE, in general, and so the declared type of attribute A in that result must necessarily be ELLIPSE. Thus, the declared type of the result attribute for UNION too must be as stated (but in the case of UNION this situation can hardly be described as counterintuitive).

Further Discussion

As you might perhaps expect, IM Prescription 13 has been the subject of much discussion between the present authors; indeed, it has given rise to several comments and questions from readers of previous editions of this book. The following question captures the essence of the issue at hand:

Let RJ and RM be RX JOIN RY and RX MINUS (RX MINUS RY), respectively. Suppose that—IM Prescription 13 notwithstanding—the declared type of A FROM RJ is CIRCLE, while that of A FROM RM is ELLIPSE (because, let us assume, the system is unable to determine that RJ and RM are equivalent). What are the implications?

One is that RM is now not always substitutable for RJ. For example, if C is a variable of declared type CIRCLE, the assignment C := A FROM RJ is valid but the assignment C := A FROM RM is not. The consequences of such a state of affairs being unclear, we prefer to invoke *The Principle of Cautious Design* [46] and the mantra "Further research is needed." That way, if it proves possible to weaken IM Prescription 13 at a later time, existing applications will still work even though certain of their TREAT invocations might have become redundant (see IM Prescription 14).

That further research, by the way, is likely to involve research into expression analysis (of the kind used by optimizers, for example), in which case restriction conditions would perhaps need to be taken into account also. For example, consider the logically equivalent expressions RX WHERE FALSE and RX MINUS RX. As we will see in Chapter 16, the most specific type of attribute A in the (empty) relation denoted by each of these expressions is *omega*—but is it reasonable to expect that attribute to have that type as its *declared* type? And what if (for example) we replace that FALSE by some less obvious contradiction, such as the very slightly less obvious one NOT (A = A)? Consider also that for all relations *r*, *r* WHERE FALSE is equivalent to *r* JOIN TABLE_DUM.

It is worth noting in passing that the SQL standard [99] is in agreement with IM Prescription 13.

IM PRESCRIPTION 14: TREAT

Let X be an expression, let T be a type, and let DT(X) and T have a nonempty common subtype. Then an operator of the form

```
TREAT_AS_T ( X )
```

(or logical equivalent thereof) shall be supported. We refer to such operators generically as "TREAT" or "TREAT AS" operators; their semantics are as follows. First, if MST(X) is not a subtype of T, then a

type error shall occur. Otherwise:

a. *If the TREAT invocation appears in a "source" position (for example, on the right side of an assignment), then the declared type of that invocation shall be T, and the invocation shall yield a result, r say, with MST(r) equal to MST(X) and v(r) equal to v(X).*

b. *If the TREAT invocation appears in a "target" position (for example, on the left side of an assignment), then that invocation shall act as a pseudovariable reference, which means it shall* actually *designate its argument X (more precisely, it shall designate a version of X for which DT(X) is equal to T but MST(X) and v(X) are unchanged).*

Consider the following code fragment once again:

```
VAR E ELLIPSE ;
VAR C CIRCLE ;

C := CIRCLE ( ... ) ;
E := C ;
```

As explained under IM Prescription 11, what does not happen here is that the circle value of C gets converted to "just type ELLIPSE," because if such a conversion were to occur, then we would no longer be able to ask for the radius of the circle that is now the current value of E. Suppose now that we do want to ask for that radius. We might try:

```
VAR L LENGTH ;

L := THE_R ( E ) ;    /* invoke "the radius of" : TYPE ERROR! */
```

The right side of the assignment here gives a compile-time type error, because variable E is of declared type ELLIPSE and THE_R is defined in terms of a parameter of declared type CIRCLE (loosely, THE_R does not apply to ellipses). *Note:* If the compile-time type check were not done, we would get a *run-time* type error instead—which is worse—if the current value of E at run time were only an ellipse and not a circle. In the case at hand, of course, we know that the value at run time will be a circle; the trouble is, we know this, but the compiler does not.

TREAT is intended to address such situations. The correct way to obtain the radius in the example is as follows:

```
L := THE_R ( TREAT_AS_CIRCLE ( E ) ) ;
```

The expression TREAT_AS_CIRCLE(E) is defined to have declared type CIRCLE, so the compile-time type checking now succeeds. Then, at run time:

- If the current value of E is indeed of type CIRCLE, then the overall expression does correctly return the radius of that circle. More precisely, the TREAT invocation yields a result, Z say, with (a) *MST*(Z) equal to *MST*(E), which is CIRCLE in the example, and (b) *v*(Z) equal to *v*(E); then (c) the expression "THE_R(Z)" is evaluated, to give the desired radius (which can then be assigned to L).

- However, if the current value of E is only of type ELLIPSE, not CIRCLE, then the TREAT fails on a run-time type error.

In other words, the expression TREAT_AS_CIRCLE(E) is logically equivalent to an IF-THEN-ELSE expression along the following lines:

```
IF IS_CIRCLE ( E )
   THEN CIRCLE ( THE_A ( E ), THE_CTR ( E ) )
   ELSE type error
END IF
```

The broad intent of IM Prescription 14 is to ensure that run-time type errors can occur only in the context of a TREAT invocation.

Suppose now, as in our discussion of IM Prescription 10, that CIRCLE in turn has a proper subtype, O_CIRCLE say, where an "O-circle" is a circle that is centered on the origin. Then the current value of variable E at some given time might be of most specific type O_CIRCLE instead of just CIRCLE. If it is, then the invocation

```
TREAT_AS_CIRCLE ( E )
```

will succeed, and will yield a result, Z say, with $MST(Z)$ equal to O_CIRCLE, because O_CIRCLE is the most specific type of E, and $v(Z)$ equal to $v(E)$. (The *declared* type is, of course, CIRCLE, because of the "..._AS_CIRCLE" specification.) In other words (loosely): TREAT always leaves the most specific type alone, it never "pushes it up" to make it less specific than it was before.

Here now is an example of the use of TREAT in a pseudovariable context. Let the current value of variable E, of declared type ELLIPSE, be of type CIRCLE (i.e., let $MST(E)$ be some subtype of CIRCLE). Now consider the following assignment:

```
THE_R ( TREAT_AS_CIRCLE ( E ) ) := LENGTH ( 5.0 ) ;
```

Observe that the argument to THE_R on the left side is of declared type CIRCLE. Assume for the moment that $MST(E)$ is exactly CIRCLE, not some proper subtype of CIRCLE. Then the assignment will set the value of E to be a circle with radius five (and with center unchanged, i.e., equal to THE_CTR(E) as it was prior to the assignment). $MST(E)$ will still be CIRCLE after the update.

Now assume again that CIRCLE has a proper subtype O_CIRCLE, and the current value of E is of most specific type O_CIRCLE instead of just CIRCLE. Then the assignment will set the value of E to be an O-circle with radius five ($MST(E)$ will still be O_CIRCLE after the update).

Of course, we already know that THE_ pseudovariables are logically unnecessary. For example, the assignment shown above is logically equivalent to the following:

```
TREAT_AS_CIRCLE ( E ) := CIRCLE ( LENGTH ( 5.0 ), THE_CTR ( E ) ) ;
```

And this assignment in turn is logically equivalent to the following (pseudocode):

```
E := IF IS_CIRCLE ( E )
        THEN CIRCLE ( LENGTH ( 5.0 ), THE_CTR ( E ) )
        ELSE type error
     END IF ;
```

By way of another example, assume again that the current value of E is of most specific type O_CIRCLE, and consider the following assignment:

```
THE_CTR ( TREAT_AS_CIRCLE ( E ) ) := POINT ( 1.0, 0.0 ) ;
```

This one is equivalent to:

```
TREAT_AS_CIRCLE ( E ) := CIRCLE ( THE_R ( E ), POINT ( 1.0, 0.0 ) ) ;
```

As a consequence, generalization by constraint occurs (see IM Prescription 11) and *MST*(E) ceases to be O_CIRCLE and becomes CIRCLE instead.

TREAT and Single Inheritance

Given the expression TREAT_AS_*T*(*X*), IM Prescription 14 requires only that *T* and *DT*(*X*) have a nonempty common subtype (this is a compile-time check). In all of our discussions thus far, however, *T* has actually been a proper subtype of *DT*(*X*)—in most cases, *T* has been CIRCLE and *DT*(*X*) has been ELLIPSE—and the nonempty common subtype in question has thus just been *T* itself (CIRCLE). And indeed *T* normally would be a proper subtype of *DT*(*X*) in practice; our discussions have been completely realistic in this respect. But there is no reason to insist on this state of affairs, and in fact it might be undesirable to do so if multiple inheritance is supported (see the next chapter). With single inheritance, however, to say that *T* and *DT*(*X*) have a nonempty common subtype is merely to say that one must be a nonempty subtype of the other (not necessarily a proper subtype, of course). In terms of our usual variables E and C, for example, the expression

```
TREAT_AS_CIRCLE ( E )
```

is syntactically valid, as we already know (though it might fail at run time). More to the point, the expression

```
TREAT_AS_ELLIPSE ( C )
```

is also syntactically valid (and it cannot possibly fail at run time).

    Note: We do not mean to claim that an expression of the form TREAT_AS_ELLIPSE(C) is particularly useful; we permit it mainly because there seems little reason not to—also because general-purpose applications have a tendency to come up with surprising requirements of this nature.

Syntactic Shorthands

Support for the following slightly more general form of TREAT (both operator and pseudovariable versions) would also be desirable in practice:

```
TREAT_AS_SAME_TYPE_AS ( Y, X )
```

Here *X* and *Y* are scalar expressions such that *DT*(*Y*) and *DT*(*X*) have a nonempty common subtype, and the overall expression is equivalent to the expression

```
TREAT_AS_T ( X )
```

where *T* is *DT*(*Y*). *Note:* Since *DT*(*Y*) is known at compile time, this more general form of TREAT is strictly unnecessary; we include it for reasons of user-friendliness, convenience, and consistency with the tuple- and relation-type versions of TREAT to be discussed in Chapter 16.

    Support for the following new relational operator[1] would also be convenient in practice:

---

1. And a tuple operator analog, too, and corresponding tuple and relational pseudovariables.

```
R TREAT_AS_T ( A )
```

Here *R* is a relational expression, *A* is an attribute of the relation denoted by that expression, and *T* is a type. The overall expression is defined to be equivalent to the following:

```
UPDATE R ( A := TREAT_AS_T ( A ) )
```

The obvious generalized form should be supported too:

```
R TREAT_AS_SAME_TYPE_AS ( Y, A )
```

IM PRESCRIPTION 15: TYPE TESTING

Let X *be an expression, let* T *be a type, and let* DT*(X) and* T *have a nonempty common subtype. Then a logical operator of the form*

```
IS_T ( X )
```

(or logical equivalent thereof) shall be supported. The operator shall return TRUE if v*(X) is of type* T, *FALSE otherwise.*

The general intent here is simply that defining a given type should cause "automatic" provision of an operator for testing values to see whether they are of the type in question. Note that the declared type of the argument and the type in question must have a nonempty common subtype (this is a compile-time check). Thus, for example, if E is of declared type ELLIPSE, the expression

```
IS_SQUARE ( E )
```

is invalid (it will fail on a compile-time type error).

IS_T *and Single Inheritance*

Given the expression IS_*T*(X), *T* would typically be a proper subtype of *DT*(X) in practice. But there is no reason to insist on this requirement, and in fact it might be undesirable to do so if multiple inheritance is supported (see the next chapter). With single inheritance, however, to say that *T* and *DT*(X) have a nonempty common subtype is merely to say that one must be a nonempty subtype of the other (not necessarily a proper subtype, of course). In terms of our usual variables E and C, for example, the expression

```
IS_CIRCLE ( E )
```

is clearly valid (though it might give FALSE). More to the point, the expression

```
IS_ELLIPSE ( C )
```

is also valid (and it cannot possibly give FALSE). *Note:* We do not mean to claim that an expression of the form IS_ELLIPSE(C) is particularly useful; we permit it for the same kinds of reasons we permit expressions like TREAT_AS_ELLIPSE(C).

Syntactic Shorthands

Support for the following slightly more general form of IS_*T* would be desirable in practice:

```
IS_SAME_TYPE_AS ( Y, X )
```

Here *X* and *Y* are scalar expressions such that *DT*(*Y*) and *DT*(*X*) have a nonempty common subtype, and the overall expression is equivalent to the expression

```
IS_T ( X )
```

where *T* is *DT*(*Y*). *Note:* Since *DT*(*Y*) is known at compile time, this more general form of IS_*T* is strictly unnecessary; we include it for reasons of user-friendliness, convenience, and consistency with the tuple- and relation-type versions of TREAT to be discussed in Chapter 16.

Support for the following new relational operator would also be convenient in practice:

```
R : IS_T ( A )
```

Here *R* is a relational expression and *A* is an attribute of the relation—*r*, say—denoted by that expression. *T* and the declared type *DT*(*A*) of *A* must have a nonempty common subtype. The value of the overall expression is a relation with:

a. A heading the same as that of *r*, except that the declared type of attribute *A* in that heading is *T*

b. A body consisting of those tuples of *r* in which attribute *A* contains a value of type *T*, except that the declared type of attribute *A* in each of those tuples is *T*

Consider the following example. Suppose relvar R includes an attribute A of declared type ELLIPSE. Then (assuming the obvious operator precedence) the expression

```
R : IS_CIRCLE ( A ) WHERE THE_R ( A ) > LENGTH ( 2.0 )
```

returns those tuples of R in which the A value is a circle with radius greater than two—or, more precisely, it returns a relation with (a) a heading the same as that of R, except that the declared type of attribute A in that result is CIRCLE instead of ELLIPSE, and (b) a body consisting of just those tuples from R in which the A value is of type CIRCLE and the radius for the circle in question is greater than two. By contrast, the expression

```
R WHERE THE_R ( A ) > LENGTH ( 2.0 )
```

is invalid—it fails on a compile-time type error—since THE_R is not defined for type ELLIPSE (ELLIPSE being the declared type of attribute A of relation R).

Note that the (valid) expression

```
R : IS_CIRCLE ( A ) WHERE THE_R ( A ) > LENGTH ( 2.0 )
```

is almost but not quite equivalent to the following (also valid) expression:

```
R WHERE CASE
          WHEN       IS_CIRCLE ( A )   THEN THE_R ( TREAT_AS_CIRCLE ( A ) ) > LENGTH ( 2.0 )
          WHEN NOT ( IS_CIRCLE ( A ) ) THEN FALSE
        END CASE
```

The difference is that this latter expression yields a relation with the same heading as R, rather than one in which the declared type of attribute A is CIRCLE instead of ELLIPSE.

More generally, however, the expression

```
R : IS_T ( A )
```

is equivalent to, and therefore shorthand for, the following expression:

```
( R WHERE IS_T ( A ) ) TREAT_AS_T ( A )
```

Moreover, this latter expression is itself shorthand for a longer one (see the previous section).

We observe that a slightly more general form of the "R:IS_T(A)" operator could also be useful:

```
R : IS_SAME_TYPE_AS ( Y, A )
```

Here Y is an expression such that $DT(A)$ and $DT(Y)$ have a nonempty common subtype, and the overall expression is equivalent to the expression

```
R : IS_T ( A )
```

where T is $DT(Y)$. *Note:* Once again, since $DT(Y)$ is known at compile time, this more general form of the operator is strictly unnecessary; we include it for reasons of user friendliness, convenience, and consistency with the tuple- and relation-type versions to be discussed in Chapter 16.

Finally, we remark that "most specific type" counterparts to all of the foregoing operators could also be provided if desired. For example, we could define the operator

```
IS_MS_T ( X )
```

to give TRUE if $MST(X)$ is T, FALSE otherwise. (It might help to observe that, e.g., whereas the operator IS_ELLIPSE is perhaps best rendered into natural language as "is an ellipse," the operator IS_MS_ELLIPSE is probably better rendered as "is *most specifically* an ellipse"). Other possible "most specific type" operators include the following (the semantics should be obvious in every case):

- ```
  IS_SAME_MS_TYPE_AS ( Y, X )
  ```

- ```
  R : IS_MS_T ( A )
  ```

- ```
  R : IS_SAME_MS_TYPE_AS ( Y, A )
  ```

However, we see no compelling need for any of these operators; in fact, it is easy to see that they are logically unnecessary (exercise for the reader).
  ```

IM PRESCRIPTION 16: READ-ONLY OPERATOR INHERITANCE AND VALUE SUBSTITUTABILITY

Let Op *be a read-only operator, let* P *be a parameter to* Op, *and let* T *be the declared type of* P. *Then the declared type (and therefore, necessarily, the most specific type) of the argument* A *corresponding to* P *in an invocation of* Op *shall be allowed to be **any subtype** T′ of* T. *In other words, the read-only operator* Op *applies to values of type* T *and therefore, necessarily, to values of type* T′—The Principle of **(Read-Only) Operator Inheritance**. *It follows that such operators are* polymorphic, *since they apply to values of several different types*—The Principle of **(Read-Only) Operator Polymorphism**. *It further follows that wherever a value of type* T *is permitted, a value of any subtype of* T *shall also be permitted*—The Principle of **(Value) Substitutability**.

As we have seen, subtyping implies that a reference to a variable of declared type T can in fact denote a value of any subtype of T. What we have not emphasized prior to this point is that it also implies that an invocation of a *read-only operator* with declared type T can likewise denote a value of any subtype of T.[1] This latter fact is an immediate consequence of *The Principle of Value Substitutability,* as can be seen from the following rather trivial example:

```
OPERATOR EORC ( B BOOLEAN ) RETURNS ELLIPSE ;
    RETURN ( IF B THEN ELLIPSE ( 5.0, 4.0, POINT ( 1.0, 2.0 ) )
                    ELSE CIRCLE ( 5.0, POINT ( 1.0, 2.0 ) )
             END IF ) ;
END OPERATOR ;
```

Note that we are within our rights here when we specify in the ELSE portion of the IF ... END IF expression that a circle be returned instead of "just an ellipse," thanks to value substitutability. Note too that the ELLIPSE selector invocation in the THEN portion does indeed return "just an ellipse" and not a circle. Thus, an invocation of the read-only operator EORC returns either a circle or just an ellipse, depending on the value of the argument corresponding to the BOOLEAN parameter B.

Here is a simpler example that illustrates much the same point:

```
OPERATOR COPY ( E ELLIPSE ) RETURNS ELLIPSE ;
    RETURN ( E ) ;
END OPERATOR ;
```

An invocation of COPY returns either a circle or just an ellipse, depending on the most specific type of the argument corresponding to its ELLIPSE parameter E.

Now, this property—that if *Op* is a read-only operator, then the most specific type of the value returned from an invocation of *Op* can be any subtype $T′$ of the declared type T of *Op*—is sometimes referred to as **result covariance**, although we dislike this term for several reasons and do not use it much ourselves. One reason we dislike it is this: The term is presumably meant to reflect the fact that the type of the result "covaries" with the type of the argument (which is indeed what happens in the COPY example). But there seems to be a tacit assumption that there is exactly one argument! In the case of the operator MOVE, for example (see later in this section), the result type covaries with the type of the first argument but not that of the second. Moreover, the result type can "covary" even if the argument type remains fixed (see the EORC example), or even if there are no explicit arguments at all (imagine an

---

1. Though we do know that this property applies to selectors in particular, thanks to S by C (see IM Prescription 10).

operator that returns a circle on weekdays but just an ellipse at weekends).

Be that as it may, note carefully that the "result covariance" phenomenon can occur even if either of the following is true:

- No separate implementation versions of *Op* have been defined as described under IM Prescription 17 (see EORC and COPY for examples)

- No argument has a most specific type that is a proper subtype of the declared type of the corresponding parameter (see EORC for an example)

Now we can explain the remark we made under IM Prescription 11 earlier to the effect that (a) the fact that the user might like to know which implementation version of a given polymorphic operator *Op* is invoked does not undermine (b) our claim that the user's perception is still that there is really just a single operator. The point is, the semantics of *Op* can—and should—be explained to the user in such a way as to take into account any variations in the most specific types of its arguments (if applicable). For example, the semantics of COPY are simply that it returns a copy of its argument; thus, if it is passed a circle, it returns a circle, and if it is passed "just an ellipse," it returns "just an ellipse." And the semantics of EORC are that it returns either a circle or "just an ellipse," depending on the value (FALSE or TRUE, respectively) of the argument corresponding to the parameter B.

Next, there is another concept, **argument contravariance,** that is also described in the literature and seems to be vaguely related to the concept of result covariance. We do not include this concept in our own inheritance model, however, because we believe it stems from (at best) a confusion over the model vs. implementation distinction, and quite possibly from a flawed definition of the very concept of *subtype* as well.[1] On the other hand, we do think it worth trying to explain what the concept *is,* in order to be able to explain exactly why we reject it. By way of example, then, suppose we have an operator MOVE with a specification signature (see IM Prescription 17) that looks like this:

```
MOVE ( ELLIPSE, SQUARE ) RETURNS ELLIPSE
```

The purpose of MOVE is, loosely, to "move" its first argument (an ellipse) so that it is centered on the center of the second (a square). More precisely, an invocation of MOVE returns a result that is just like its first argument except that it is "located somewhere else"—it is, to repeat, centered on the center of the second argument. The implementation code for (the most general version of) this operator might look like this:

```
OPERATOR MOVE ( E ELLIPSE, S SQUARE ) RETURNS ELLIPSE VERSION E_MOVE ;
    RETURN ( ELLIPSE ( THE_A ( E ), THE_B ( E ), CTR ( S ) ) ) ;
END OPERATOR ;
```

We have assumed that an operator CTR has been defined that returns the center of its argument (a square). Also, the VERSION specification in the second line introduces a distinguishing name, E_MOVE, for this particular *version* of MOVE (implementation versions are discussed under IM Prescription 17).

---

1. The definition in question is flawed because it is circular (not recursive!): "A type *T'* **is a subtype** of a type *T* if ... for each method *M* of *T* there is a corresponding method *M'* of *T'* such that ... the *i*th argument type of *M* **is a subtype** of the *i*th argument type of *M'* *(rule of contravariance in arguments)* ..." (paraphrased from reference [7], boldface added). In other words, the concept of some type being a subtype of another is defined in terms of the concept of some type being a subtype of another. Note too that the definition seems to be saying *T'* is a subtype of *T* if substitutability applies, whereas we say that substitutability applies if *T'* is a subtype of *T*.

Now let us assume that for some reason[1] another version of MOVE, C_MOVE say, has been defined that moves circles in particular instead of ellipses in general (see IM Prescription 17 once again):

```
OPERATOR MOVE ( C CIRCLE, S SQUARE ) RETURNS CIRCLE VERSION C_MOVE ;
   RETURN ( CIRCLE ( THE_R ( C ), CTR ( S ) ) ) ;
END OPERATOR ;
```

This version always returns a circle, whereas the previous version (E_MOVE) sometimes returns "just an ellipse."

Now let variables E and S be of declared types ELLIPSE and SQUARE, respectively, but suppose the current value of E is of type CIRCLE. Consider the MOVE invocation

```
MOVE ( E, S )
```

The system performs a compile-time type check on this expression; that check succeeds, of course. Then, at run time, it discovers that argument E is of type CIRCLE and argument S is of type SQUARE, and it therefore invokes the version of MOVE that applies to circles and squares (namely, C_MOVE). But it would also invoke C_MOVE if the *declared* type of the *parameter* corresponding to argument S in C_MOVE were some proper supertype of SQUARE (a proper supertype, that is, for which the concept of having a center makes sense). It might, for example, be RECTANGLE, as here:[2]

```
OPERATOR MOVE ( C CIRCLE, R RECTANGLE ) RETURNS CIRCLE VERSION C_MOVE ; /* revised */
    RETURN ( CIRCLE ( THE_R ( C ), CTR ( R ) ) ) ;
END OPERATOR ;
```

This property—that if the declared type of one parameter to operator *Op* (in some version of *Op*) is further specialized, then the declared type of another parameter (in that same version of *Op*) can be further generalized—is the *argument contravariance* property. Again, however, we dislike this term for several reasons and do not use it much ourselves. One reason we dislike it is this: The term is presumably meant to reflect the fact that the type of one argument "contravaries" with that of another. But it is really *parameters* that "contravary," not *arguments,* so at the very least the term ought to be *parameter* contravariance. And in any case there seems to be a tacit assumption that there are exactly two parameters! In the case of MOVE, there are indeed two parameters, which "contravary"; but what if there had been three?

Note further that "argument contravariance" differs from "result covariance" in that it *must* be made explicit (by explicitly defining appropriate implementation versions of the operator in question), because it refers to the declared types of parameters to such versions.

Anyway: Regardless of whether we accept or reject the term "argument contravariance," we frankly do not find the concept very useful, nor very helpful. Rather, it seems clearer to us to talk in terms of *argument-type combinations.* Consider the MOVE operator once again. Presumably the person responsible for defining that operator will tell the user that it takes two arguments, of types ELLIPSE and RECTANGLE respectively—please notice that *RECTANGLE,* not SQUARE as previously—and returns a result of type ELLIPSE. (After all, to the user there is just one MOVE operator, regardless of how

---

1. The exact reason is not important here—in fact, there might be no good reason at all. See IM Prescription 19 for further discussion.

2. Note that the revised version of C_MOVE shown here would not be valid in our model, however, because the version signature is incompatible with the specification signature as previously defined (RECTANGLE is not a subtype of SQUARE!) Once again, see IM Prescription 17 for a detailed discussion of signatures.

many implementation versions might exist under the covers.) Then, because of value substitutability, the user knows that:

- The arguments to any given MOVE invocation can be of *any subtypes* of ELLIPSE and RECTANGLE, respectively.

- The result can be of *any subtype* of ELLIPSE.

However, the user also has to know that *certain combinations of most specific argument types are not allowed.* To be precise:

- The combination ELLIPSE-SQUARE (which corresponds to the implementation version called E_MOVE and gives a result of most specific type ELLIPSE) is allowed.

- The combination CIRCLE-RECTANGLE (which corresponds to the version called C_MOVE and gives a result of most specific type CIRCLE) is allowed.

- However, the combination ELLIPSE-RECTANGLE is not allowed.

So the obvious question arises: *Why did the person who defined the operator impose such a strange restriction?* Does it not constitute a violation of value substitutability? (After all, ELLIPSE is a subtype of ELLIPSE and RECTANGLE is a subtype of RECTANGLE, so we should surely be able to invoke the operator and pass it an ellipse per se and a rectangle per se.) In fact, the restriction might be regarded as a violation of orthogonality too, because there is an unpleasant—and unexplained—interdependence between the two arguments to any given invocation.

We believe there is no good reason for imposing such strange restrictions. Therefore, IM Prescription 16 requires simply that read-only operators be defined in such a way as to allow the most specific type of any given argument to any given invocation of any given operator to be the same as the declared type of the corresponding parameter. Indeed, it seems perverse to us to do otherwise! And if this discipline is followed, then we can forget about the "argument contravariance" concept entirely.

Note: The foregoing paragraph needs a tiny refinement to take care of the possibility that a parameter might be declared to be of some *union* type. A union type cannot be the most specific type of anything, by definition (see IM Prescription 20). Hence, if parameter P has declared type T and T is a union type, the most specific type of any argument corresponding to P is limited to being some subtype of T', where T' is the least specific subtype of T that is not a union type. See IM Prescription 20 for further explanation.

IM PRESCRIPTION 17: OPERATOR SIGNATURES

Any given operator Op *shall have exactly one* **specification signature**, *a nonempty set of* **version signatures**, *and a nonempty set of* **invocation signatures**. *For definiteness, assume the parameters of* Op *and the arguments appearing in any given invocation of* Op *each constitute an ordered list of* n *elements* (n ≥ 0), *such that the ith argument corresponds to the ith parameter. Then:*

a.   *The specification signature shall denote* Op *as perceived by potential users. It shall consist of the operator name* Op, *the declared types (in order) of the parameters to* Op, *and the declared type of the result, if any, of executing* Op. *No two distinct operators shall have specification signatures that differ only in the declared types of their results (if any). Moreover, let* S *be a set of types with a nonempty common subtype. Then no two distinct operators shall have specification signatures that differ only in that, for some* i, j, ..., k, *the declared types of their ith parameters are distinct members of* S, *the declared types of their jth parameters are distinct members of* S, ..., *and the declared types of their kth parameters are distinct members of* S.

b. *There shall be one version signature for each implementation version* V *of* Op. *Each such signature shall consist of the operator name* Op *(and possibly the version name* V*), the declared types (in order) of the parameters to* V, *and the declared type of the result, if any, of executing* V.

c. *There shall be one invocation signature for each possible combination of most specific argument types to an invocation of* Op. *Each such signature shall consist of the operator name* Op *and the pertinent combination of most specific argument types (in order).* Note: *The invocation signatures for* Op *can easily be derived from the corresponding specification signature, but the concepts are logically distinct.*

Every version of Op *shall implement the same semantics.*

Although the point is not strictly part of our inheritance model per se, it is important to understand that if the code that implements a given operator needs access to some possible representation[1] of some argument value *v* that is available only if *v* is of type *T'* and not just of type *T,* then—as explained under IM Prescription 9—two distinct versions of that code will probably have to exist under the covers. As also explained under IM Prescription 9, distinct implementation versions might also be desirable, even if logically unnecessary, if improved efficiency can be achieved by such means. Moreover, it is never logically wrong to implement additional versions, regardless of whether they are actually necessary. *Note:* If distinct versions are not provided, then (as mentioned under IM Prescription 9 once again) we have **code reuse:** The very same implementation code can operate upon arguments of different types. Observe, however, that here we are talking about reuse of "under the covers" code, not reuse of some program that *invokes* that "under the covers" code.

As a consequence of the foregoing, it should be clear that we need to distinguish carefully between any given operator *Op* as perceived by the user, on the one hand, and implementation versions under the covers of that operator *Op* on the other. It should also be clear that we need to distinguish carefully between the operator *Op* together with its implementation versions, on the one hand, and various possible invocations of *Op* on the other. The concept of **signatures** is intended to help make these distinctions.

We can define the term *signature* (or *operator* signature, to be more specific), a little loosely, as the combination of the name of the operator in question and the types of the operands and result (if any) for that operator. As you have probably come to expect by now, however, we need to be very careful once again over certain logical differences—namely, those between:

- Arguments and parameters

- Declared types and most specific types

- Operators as seen by the user and operators as seen by the system (meaning, in this latter case, implementation versions of the operator under the covers)

In fact, we can distinguish three different kinds of signatures that apply to any given operator

---

1. Or (worse) some physical representation.

Op:[1]

- First, there is exactly one **specification signature,** consisting of the operator name *Op* together with the declared types, in order, of the parameters (and the declared type of the result, if any), as perceived by potential *Op* users. For example, the specification signature for the operator MOVE (see IM Prescription 16) might look like this:

```
MOVE ( ELLIPSE, RECTANGLE ) RETURNS ELLIPSE
```

The specification signature thus corresponds to the user's understanding of what the operator looks like. More precisely, it is necessary but not sufficient for such an understanding; it is not sufficient, because it fails to capture the "result covariance" property. Unfortunately, none of the signatures is sufficient in this sense, as consideration of operator EORC will easily show.
   Note: It would be possible to capture more (though still not all) of the "result covariance" property by including parameter names in the specification signature and then allowing the RETURNS specification to refer to those names accordingly. Under such a scheme, the specification signature for MOVE might look like this:

```
MOVE ( E ELLIPSE, R RECTANGLE ) RETURNS SAME_TYPE_AS ( E )
```

The intent here is that an invocation of MOVE returns a result of the same declared type as that of the argument corresponding to its first (ellipse) parameter.[2] However, it is easy to see that such a scheme is still inadequate, in general; for example, consider an operator that returns a square if invoked with a circle, but "just a rectangle" (not a square) if invoked with a noncircular ellipse.

- Second, there is one **version signature** for each implementation version of *Op,* each consisting of the operator name *Op* (and possibly a *version name*) together with the declared types, in order, of the parameters (and the declared type of the result, if any) as defined for that version. For example, the following version signatures might have been defined for MOVE (note the version

---

1. We should mention that different writers and different languages ascribe slightly different meanings to the term "signature" anyway; for example, it is sometimes taken to include operand *names* (we do not include such names ourselves because we are assuming for simplicity that argument/parameter matching is done on the basis of ordinal position, as in **Tutorial D**).

2. Suppose such syntax for specification signatures is in fact supported. Let variable C be of declared type CIRCLE. Then the user might be allowed to write, e.g.,

```
THE_R ( MOVE ( C, ... ) )
```

instead of what would otherwise be required, viz.:

```
THE_R ( TREAT_AS_CIRCLE ( MOVE ( C, ... ) ) )
```

Note that relaxing the rules (as it were) in this way would not depend on the existence of different implementation versions, because the SAME_TYPE_AS specification guarantees that the result is of the declared type of the indicated argument. Indeed, we would not consider the mere fact that different versions exist to be sufficient justification for allowing TREATs to be omitted in such a manner (we certainly do not want to expose the concept of implementation versions to the user). On the other hand, if it turns out that such TREATs cannot be omitted, then we might at least expect the implementation to optimize them away, since they will effectively be "no ops."

names):

```
MOVE ( ELLIPSE, RECTANGLE ) RETURNS ELLIPSE VERSION ER_MOVE

MOVE ( ELLIPSE, SQUARE ) RETURNS ELLIPSE VERSION ES_MOVE

MOVE ( CIRCLE, RECTANGLE ) RETURNS CIRCLE VERSION CR_MOVE

MOVE ( CIRCLE, SQUARE ) RETURNS CIRCLE VERSION CS_MOVE
```

The version signatures thus correspond to the various pieces of implementation code that implement the operator under the covers. We remark that the availability of version names implies among other things that it might be possible to destroy—i.e., drop—a specific version without having to destroy the corresponding operator in its entirety.

By the way, we deliberately show a distinct version signature in the foregoing example for each possible combination of most specific argument types (i.e., one version signature for each possible invocation signature—see the next bullet item below). In practice, however, it is unlikely that there will always be such a one-to-one match between version and invocation signatures. We will return to this point later in this section.

Note: If overloading is supported, it might be necessary for certain version signatures to include a reference to the specification signature for the operator they implement—perhaps like this:

```
MOVE ( CIRCLE, SQUARE ) RETURNS CIRCLE VERSION CS_MOVE FOR MOVE ( ELLIPSE, RECTANGLE )
```

(Clearly there is no need to include the RETURNS portion of the specification signature, however.)

■ Third, there is one **invocation signature** for each possible combination of most specific argument types to an invocation of *Op*, each consisting of the operator name *Op* together with the corresponding combination of most specific argument types, in order (the result type, if any, is obviously irrelevant here). These signatures correspond to various possible invocations of *Op*. For example, the invocation signatures that apply to MOVE are basically as follows:

```
MOVE ( ELLIPSE, RECTANGLE )

MOVE ( ELLIPSE, SQUARE )

MOVE ( CIRCLE, RECTANGLE )

MOVE ( CIRCLE, SQUARE )
```

Different invocation signatures involving the same operator thus correspond, at least potentially, to different implementation versions under the covers of the operator in question. Thus, if several versions of "the same" operator do in fact exist under the covers, then which version is invoked on any given occasion will depend on which version signature is the *best match* for the applicable invocation signature. The process of deciding that best match—i.e., the process of deciding which version to invoke—is known variously as *run-time binding* (our own preferred term) or *dynamic binding* or *dynamic dispatch* or *function resolution* or *subject routine determination* (this last is the SQL term).

Note: Actually, a certain amount of compile-time binding might be possible too, based on argument declared types (certainly known to the compiler) and version signatures (at least potentially known to the compiler). For example, if the user invokes MOVE with arguments of declared types CIRCLE and SQUARE, the compiler—rather than the run-time system—should be able to determine that the version CS_MOVE is the one to be invoked, since CIRCLE and SQUARE are both leaf types and no "lower" version of MOVE can possibly exist.

More on Run-Time Binding

Let *Op* be a polymorphic operator and let *OpI* be some invocation of *Op*. As we have seen, the specific version of *Op* to be invoked for *OpI* will be determined on the basis of consideration of the most specific types of the arguments to that invocation *OpI*. *We propose that every argument be able to participate equally in this process.* In other words (and as in fact previously indicated under OO Very Strong Suggestion 2 in Chapter 11), we do not much care for the notion, supported by certain object systems, that an operator might have a special "distinguished" or "receiver" or "target" parameter, such that the corresponding argument plays some special role in the run-time binding process. To elaborate briefly: Treating one argument as special has the obvious advantage that it makes the run-time binding process simpler—simpler for the *system,* that is—because that process involves determining the most specific type of just that one argument. But it has certain obvious disadvantages too, not the least of which is that it can make it harder for the *implementer* to write the implementation code. For example:

- Suppose the first MOVE argument (i.e., the ellipse-or-circle argument) is chosen as the special one. Then there could be at most two distinct implementation versions of MOVE, one for moving a circle and one for moving just an ellipse; in effect, versions ER_MOVE and ES_MOVE would be combined into a single version, E_MOVE say, and versions CR_MOVE and CS_MOVE would be combined into a single version, C_MOVE say.

- So if the implementer wanted different implementation code depending on whether the second argument is a square or just a rectangle, then he or she might have to include explicit type testing and flow-of-control operations within both E_MOVE and C_MOVE, as well as possibly having to include both the square and rectangle code within both of those versions.

- Alternatively, and probably preferably, E_MOVE and C_MOVE could both invoke a rectangle-or-square subroutine, and that routine in turn could have two distinct implementation versions, one for squares and one for nonsquare rectangles. But even with this preferred approach, the fact remains that the MOVE implementer has to do a certain amount of work that would and could be done much better by the system.

Incidentally, it follows from the foregoing that the question of whether operator definitions should be bundled in with type definitions (again, see OO Very Strong Suggestion 2) is not just a matter of syntax. As a matter of fact, there is another, more pragmatic, argument against bundling also. Bundling implies that adding a new operator will have to involve some kind of ALTER TYPE operation. But the person defining the new operator might not have the ability or the authority to alter an existing type (especially if the type in question is provided as part of some kind of off-the-shelf "type package" from some third party). As a consequence, there is likely to be a strong temptation to *hack* ... The hack in question consists in (a) defining a new subtype *T'* of the existing type *T* that specifies CONSTRAINT TRUE (not permitted in our model—see IM Prescription 10), so that every value of *T* is also a value of *T',* and then (b) bundling the new operator with that phony subtype *T'* instead of with the supertype *T* where it "belongs."

To repeat, therefore, we propose that every argument should be able to participate equally in the run-time binding process. However, there is a well-known practical (though not unsolvable) problem here. By way of example, suppose (a) operator *Op* has a specification signature involving two parameters, both of declared type ELLIPSE; (b) implementation versions are defined for the most specific argument type combinations ELLIPSE-ELLIPSE, ELLIPSE-CIRCLE, and CIRCLE-ELLIPSE (only); and (c) *Op* is invoked with the most specific argument type combination CIRCLE-CIRCLE. The invocation signature here obviously does not exactly match *any* of the corresponding version signatures. Clearly, therefore, rules are needed in order to determine which particular version should be invoked—i.e., rules that define what the term "best match" (between version and invocation signatures) really means. But we stress the point that such rules are an implementation issue; they have nothing to do with the model as such.[1]

Semantics Must Not Change

The fact that it is always at least possible to define several implementation versions for the same operator has one very important consequence: It opens up the possibility of *changing the semantics* of the operator in question. For example, consider the following sequence of events:

1. Type ELLIPSE and the corresponding operator AREA are defined, but type CIRCLE is not defined yet. Variable E, of declared type ELLIPSE, is assigned an ellipse value for which $a = b$. The operator AREA is invoked on E, giving a result *area1*, say.

2. Type CIRCLE is now defined as a subtype of type ELLIPSE and a new version of AREA is implemented for this new type. Variable E is assigned the same ellipse value as before, but S by C now comes into play and *MST*(E) becomes CIRCLE. The operator AREA is invoked on E, giving a result *area2*, say.

At this point we would surely like to be able to say that the comparison *area1* = *area2* must give TRUE. However, this would-be requirement is not enforceable! That is, there is little to stop AREA from being reimplemented for circles in such a way as to return, e.g., the circumference instead of the area. (Careful type design can alleviate this problem somewhat; for example, if operator AREA is defined to return a result of type AREA, obviously the implementation cannot return a result of type LENGTH instead. It can, however, still return the wrong area.)

Now, it has been claimed that "changing semantics" in the way just outlined can actually be desirable. The following is an example of a situation in which such a claim might be made:

1. A type called HIGHWAY is defined, together with an operator called TRAVEL_TIME that computes the time it takes to travel between two points *a* and *b* on a highway *h* using the formula *d/s*, where *d* = distance between *a* and *b* and *s* = speed. The highway value *h* is assigned to a variable H of declared type HIGHWAY, and TRAVEL_TIME is invoked on H (and points *a* and *b* on *h*) and returns a result, *tt1* say.

2. Type TOLL_HIGHWAY is now defined as a subtype of type HIGHWAY and a new implementation version of TRAVEL_TIME is defined for this new type using the formula *(d/s)+(n*t)*, where *n* = number of tollbooths, *t* = time spent at each tollbooth, and *d* and *s* are as before.

3. Variable H is assigned the same highway value *h* as before. Assume for the moment that *h* is not a toll highway. Then invoking TRAVEL_TIME on H with the same points *a* and *b* as before gives the same result *tt1* as before.

---

1. Except inasmuch as (as we will see in the subsection immediately following) the model does require that all versions implement the same semantics; in particular, therefore, it requires that distinct versions whose signatures are equally good matches for a given invocation signature have the same result type.

4.   But suppose now that *h* is in fact a toll highway. Then S by C comes into play, *MST*(H) becomes TOLL_HIGHWAY, and invoking TRAVEL_TIME on H with the same points *a* and *b* as before gives a different result *tt2*.

Now, of course it is true that the presence or absence of tollbooths does affect travel time. An advocate of the idea that changing semantics can be desirable might therefore claim that the foregoing state of affairs (in particular, the fact that *tt1* ≠ *tt2*) is reasonable. However, we disagree with this reasoning. We argue as follows:

■   If TOLL_HIGHWAY truly is a subtype of HIGHWAY, it means by definition that every individual toll highway is in fact a highway.

■   Thus, some highways (i.e., some values of type HIGHWAY) are indeed toll highways—they do indeed have tollbooths. So type HIGHWAY is not "highways without tollbooths," it is "highways with *n* tollbooths," where *n* might be zero (and type TOLL_HIGHWAY is "highways with *n* tollbooths" where *n* is greater than zero).

■   So the operator TRAVEL_TIME for type HIGHWAY is not "compute the travel time for a highway *without* tollbooths," it is "compute the travel time for a highway *ignoring* tollbooths" (another logical difference here).

■   The operator TRAVEL_TIME for type TOLL_HIGHWAY, by contrast, is "compute the travel time for a highway *not* ignoring tollbooths." So we have found yet another logical difference—the two TRAVEL_TIMEs are logically different operators. Confusion arises because those two different operators have been given the same name (in fact, the example is an example of overloading polymorphism, not inclusion polymorphism at all).

Thus, we reject the suggestion that changing operator semantics can ever be a good idea. We therefore define our model to say that if a change in semantics occurs, the implementation is in violation—i.e., it is not an implementation of the model, and the implications are unpredictable.[1] Indeed, it could be argued that the ability to change operator semantics (or, rather, the fact that some writers seem to regard that ability as a virtue) is—like the business of "argument contravariance" discussed earlier—a case of *the implementation tail wagging the model dog.*

Observe that our position here does mean that, regardless of how many implementation versions of operator *Op* are defined, the user perception remains the same: namely, that (a) there exists a read-only operator—a *single* read-only operator, that is—called *Op,* and (b) that operator *Op* applies to argument values of type *T* and hence, by definition, to argument values of any subtype of *T*.

More on Compile-Time Binding

We pointed out earlier that it might be possible to perform some binding at compile time. In fact, we now observe that it might be possible to perform *all* binding at compile time! Let *T* and *T'* be supertype and subtype, respectively (as usual), and let *Op* be an operator that applies to values of type *T* and therefore to values of type *T'* as well. Assume that *Op* does not apply to values of any proper supertype of *T*. Assume also that both of the following conditions are satisfied:

---

1. Of course, our model does not preclude support for genuine overloading polymorphism. In particular, if (a) *T1* and *T2* are distinct subtypes of some dummy type *T,* (b) neither is a subtype of the other, and (c) an operator is defined for *T1* and another with the same name is defined for *T2,* then (d) there is no requirement, nor can there be, that those two operators implement the same semantics.

■   Implementation versions of *Op* are provided for both type *T* and type *T'*, but they implement the same semantics (as indeed our model requires).

■   Either (a) the implementation version for type *T* involves no access to the physical representation of values that are "just of type *T*" or (b) the physical representation of values that are "just of type *T'*" is the same as that for values of type *T'*.

Then no logical harm is done if an invocation of *Op* on a value of type *T'* is bound—at compile time, potentially—to the version of *Op* that is defined for type *T*. (Performance might suffer, but performance is not a model consideration.)

Note: Of course, the foregoing argument does rely on an implementation version of *Op* being defined for type *T*. If *T* is a dummy type, however, such a version might not exist, even if the operator itself is indeed defined at the level of type *T*. In other words, the presence of dummy types implies that some binding, at least, will probably have to be done at run time after all. See IM Prescription 20 for further discussion.

We conclude this subsection, and this section, by remarking that many of the concepts we have been discussing at such length—*inclusion polymorphism, value substitutability, result covariance, argument contravariance, code reuse, implementation versions, version signatures, invocation signatures,* and *run-time vs. compile-time binding*—are not really features of the model, as such, at all (despite the fact that you do need to understand them somewhat in order to appreciate what inheritance and subtyping are really all about). The only thing that is truly relevant to the model is this: "To say that *T'* is a subtype of *T* means, by definition, that operators that apply to values of type *T* apply to values of type *T'* also"—and the rest logically follows.

IM PRESCRIPTION 18: READ-ONLY PARAMETERS TO UPDATE OPERATORS

Let Op *be an update operator and let* P *be a parameter to* Op *that is not subject to update. Then* Op *shall behave as a* read-only *operator as far as* P *is concerned, and all relevant aspects of IM Prescription 16 shall therefore apply, mutatis mutandis.*

This prescription does not seem to require any further explanation, except to say that the property of "result covariance" is obviously irrelevant (update operators do not return a result).

IM PRESCRIPTION 19:   UPDATE OPERATOR INHERITANCE AND VARIABLE SUBSTITUTABILITY

Let Op *be an update operator, let* P *be a parameter to* Op *that is subject to update, and let* T *be the declared type of* P. *Then it might or might not be the case that the declared type (and therefore, necessarily, the current most specific type) of the argument* A *corresponding to* P *in an invocation of* Op *shall be allowed to be a proper subtype of type* T. *It follows that for each such update operator* Op *and for each parameter* P *to* Op *that is subject to update, it shall be necessary to state explicitly for which proper subtypes of the declared type* T *of parameter* P *operator* Op *shall be inherited—The Principle of* **(Update) Operator Inheritance.** *(And if update operator* Op *is not inherited in this way by type* T', *it shall not be inherited by any proper subtype of type* T' *either.) Update operators shall thus be only conditionally polymorphic—The Principle of* **(Update) Operator Polymorphism.** *If* Op *is an update operator and* P *is a parameter to* Op *that is subject to update and* T' *is a proper subtype of the declared type* T *of* P *for which* Op *is inherited, then by definition it shall be possible to invoke* Op *with an* *argument corresponding to parameter* P *that is of declared type* T'—The Principle of (**Variable**) **Substitutability**.

First we explain why it does not make sense for update operators to be inherited unconditionally.[1] Let variables R and S have declared types RECTANGLE and SQUARE, respectively. Then—speaking *very loosely!*—it is possible to change the height of R without changing its width; more precisely, it is possible to update R so as to replace the current rectangle value *r1* by a new rectangle value *r2* that has the same width but a different height. However, it is certainly not possible to do the same thing to S, because squares must always have equal height and width. In other words, a certain update operator ("change height but not width") is effectively defined for type RECTANGLE but not type SQUARE.

For a more probing example, we return to the operator MOVE from our discussion of IM Prescription 16. Now, we previously made a tacit assumption that MOVE was a *read-only* operator specifically. Here is the implementation code (ER_MOVE version):

```
OPERATOR MOVE ( E ELLIPSE, R RECTANGLE ) RETURNS ELLIPSE VERSION ER_MOVE ;
    RETURN ( ELLIPSE ( THE_A ( E ), THE_B ( E ), CTR ( R ) ) ) ;
END OPERATOR ;
```

As an aside, we observe that if ER_MOVE is implemented as shown, then the versions ES_MOVE, CR_MOVE, and CS_MOVE are not needed—the ER_MOVE code works for those other cases too, thanks to specialization by constraint! And thanks to generalization by constraint, it would even work for "O-circles" too—where, just to remind you, an O-circle is a circle with center the origin. (We deliberately ignored these points in our previous discussions under IM Prescriptions 16 and 17.)

Since it is a read-only operator, MOVE returns a result, by definition. But suppose we made it an *update* operator instead, thus:

```
OPERATOR MOVE ( E ELLIPSE, R RECTANGLE ) UPDATES { E } VERSION ER_MOVE ;
    THE_CTR ( E ) := CTR ( R ) ;
END OPERATOR ;
```

Instead of "returning a result that is just like its first argument except that it is located somewhere else" (as we put it earlier), this revised operator actually *updates* its first argument. Of course, that argument must be specified as a variable specifically; but that variable can be of declared type CIRCLE or just declared type ELLIPSE. *Like the read-only ER_MOVE code, in other words, this update code works for circles as well as ellipses.* Note, however, that it does not work for O-circles, because updating a variable of declared type O_CIRCLE to change its center is clearly invalid (the center for such a variable must be the origin and cannot be changed). What is more, it is not just this particular code that does not work for O-circles; *no* code that attempts to update the center of a variable of declared type O_CIRCLE can possibly work (unless the update is in fact a "no op," perhaps).

It follows from the foregoing that, as already stated, update operator inheritance has to be conditional (as indeed it is in our model). Essentially, what this means is that **which update operators are inherited by which subtypes must be specified explicitly**. For example, we might specify the

---

1. Unlike read-only operators! In fact, the arguments presented under this prescription constitute an important reason why we continually stress the logical difference between read-only and update operators.

following:[1]

- The update operators that apply to variables of declared type ELLIPSE are:

  - Assignment to THE_A, THE_B, THE_CTR

  - MOVE (update form)

- The update operators that apply to variables of declared type CIRCLE are:

  - Assignment to THE_CTR and THE_R

  - MOVE (update form)

  Observe in particular, therefore, that pseudovariables THE_A and THE_B do not apply to variables of declared type CIRCLE. *Note:* In **Tutorial D,** in fact, we adopt the conservative position that pseudovariable THE_*X* applies to variables of declared type *T* *if and only if* either (a) *T* has a declared possrep with a component called *X* (this is the normal case)[2] or, possibly, (b) *T* is a dummy type and pseudovariable THE_*X* applies to variables of each of its immediate subtypes (see the section on IM Prescription 20, subsection "Dummy Types," later, for an explanation of this latter possibility).

- The only update operator that applies to variables of declared type O_CIRCLE is:

  - Assignment to THE_R

  MOVE (update form) and pseudovariable THE_CTR do not apply to variables of declared type O_CIRCLE.

We now consider some of the consequences of the foregoing. Suppose we have variables E, C, and O declared as follows:

```
VAR E ELLIPSE ;
VAR C CIRCLE ;
VAR O O_CIRCLE ;
```

Let the variables be initialized as follows:

```
E := ELLIPSE ( LENGTH ( 6.0 ), LENGTH ( 5.0 ), POINT ( 4.0, 3.0 ) ) ,
C := CIRCLE   ( LENGTH ( 5.0 ), POINT ( 4.0, 3.0 ) ) ,
O := O_CIRCLE ( LENGTH ( 5.0 ) ) ;
```

Now consider the following updates (for simplicity we limit our attention to updates that are

---

1. We are tacitly ignoring simple assignment in this example, since simple assignment is an update operator that applies to variables of every type.

2. Thus, if we were to declare an {*a,b,ctr*} possrep for type CIRCLE, then pseudovariables THE_A and THE_B would be available for variables of declared type CIRCLE after all. However, any attempt to use them will fail if it violates the constraint $a = b$.

assignments to pseudovariables specifically; we have numbered them for ease of subsequent reference).

1.   `THE_A ( E ) := LENGTH ( 5.0 ) ;`

     MST(E) is now CIRCLE, thanks to S by C. However, if we now try the following—

2.   `THE_R ( E ) := LENGTH ( 4.0 ) ;`

     —we will get a compile-time type error, because assignment to THE_R does not apply to variables of declared type ELLIPSE. (More precisely, the error occurs because no possrep for type ELLIPSE has an R component, and hence no THE_R operator or pseudovariable is defined for that type.) By contrast, the following *will* work:

3.   `THE_R ( TREAT_AS_CIRCLE ( E ) ) := LENGTH ( 4.0 ) ;`

     So will the following:

4.   `THE_A ( E ) := LENGTH ( 6.0 ) ;`

     MST(E) is now ELLIPSE again, thanks to G by C.

5.   `THE_CTR ( C ) := POINT ( 0.0, 0.0 ) ;`

     MST(C) is now O_CIRCLE. However, we *can* invoke the MOVE operator (update form) on it; the effect will be to set *MST*(C) back to CIRCLE again, thanks to G by C. By contrast, if we try to invoke the MOVE operator (update form) on the variable O, we will get a compile-time type error (we cannot "G by C" a variable to some proper supertype of its declared type, of course).

As these examples illustrate, if update operator *Op* does not apply to variables of declared type *T*, it certainly does not apply to variables of declared type any proper subtype of type *T*.

So much for the examples. For completeness, we now observe that (as noted under IM Prescription 18) the property of "result covariance" does not apply to update operators, since update operators do not return a result. The property of "argument contravariance" does apply, but we reject that concept anyway. The remarks regarding code reuse, implementation versions, signatures, and run-time binding under IM Prescriptions 16 and 17 apply to update operators also, mutatis mutandis.

We close this section by admitting that the question of update operator inheritance is one in which our thinking might be regarded as a little controversial (heretical, some might say). To be specific, some writers claim that update operators, like read-only operators, should be inherited *unconditionally,* whereas we want them to be inherited only where they make sense.[1] But it seems to us that those who want such unconditional inheritance run into a variety of logical problems and other undesirable consequences that our scheme avoids. For example:

■   They require update operators to return a value, thereby allowing retrieval operations to have the side effect of updating the database (as noted under RM Prescription 3 in Chapter 6).

---

1. Actually our position here is not as controversial as it might seem. Nobody wants ":=" to be inherited unconditionally; e.g., assignment of a value of most specific type ELLIPSE to a variable of declared type CIRCLE is never valid (at least, not in any scheme we are aware of). And assignment is the only update operator that is logically necessary! Thus, those who want update operators to be inherited unconditionally might be accused of a certain lack of consistency.

■   Or they allow (e.g.) a value of type SQUARE to have sides of different lengths, thereby violating its own "squareness," undermining the database "as a model of reality," and causing programs to produce nonsensical results such as "nonsquare squares" or "noncircular circles."

■   Or they do not support S by C or G by C.

■   Or they simply do not support type constraints at all (see Appendix F for a detailed discussion of this particular—and important—issue).

The common thread running through all such thinking is, it seems to us, **a failure to make a clear distinction between values and variables**. To us, by contrast, that distinction is both crucial and fundamental; indeed, as explained in Chapter 1, we regard it as one of the great logical differences—one that underlies and buttresses our thinking throughout both *The Third Manifesto* and the inheritance model currently under discussion.

IM PRESCRIPTION 20: UNION, DUMMY, AND MAXIMAL AND MINIMAL TYPES

*A **union type** is a type T such that there exists no value that is of type T and not of some immediate subtype of T (i.e., there is no value v such that MST(v) is T). A **dummy type** is a union type that has no declared possible representation (and hence no selector); a given union type shall be permitted to be a dummy type if and only if it is empty or it has no regular immediate supertype (where a **regular type** is a type that is not a dummy type). Moreover:*

a.   *Conceptually, there is a special scalar dummy type,* alpha, *that contains all scalar values. Type* alpha *is **the maximal type** with respect to every scalar type; by definition, it has no declared possible representation and no immediate supertypes.*

b.   *Conceptually, there is a special scalar dummy type,* omega, *that contains no values at all. Type* omega *is **the minimal type** with respect to every scalar type; by definition, it has no declared possible representation and no immediate subtypes.*

In our discussion of IM Prescription 11, we briefly considered the possibility of introducing an additional immediate subtype of type ELLIPSE called NONCIRCLE, with the obvious semantics. Let us examine that possibility a little more closely. Here first is the definition of NONCIRCLE:

```
TYPE NONCIRCLE
     IS { ELLIPSE
          CONSTRAINT THE_A ( ELLIPSE ) > THE_B ( ELLIPSE )
          POSSREP { A   = THE_A   ( ELLIPSE ) ,
                    B   = THE_B   ( ELLIPSE ) ,
                    CTR = THE_CTR ( ELLIPSE ) } } ;
```

Type ELLIPSE now becomes a **union type**: Every ellipse is either a circle or a noncircle (there is no value of type ELLIPSE that is not also a value of some immediate subtype of that type), and so type ELLIPSE is the union—in fact, the *disjoint* union—of types CIRCLE and NONCIRCLE. *Note: Union type* is the traditional term for the concept we have in mind here [19]. However, you should be aware that other terms are also found in the literature, including *abstract* types (we mentioned this one briefly in Chapter 3), *noninstantiable* types (on the grounds that the types in question have no "instances"), or sometimes just as *interfaces*. Types that are not union types are then referred to as *concrete* types, *instantiable* types, or just *types*, respectively. (We have changed our own terminology slightly, too; in reference [82], we called union types dummy types and all other types regular types.)

A union type is not the most specific type of any value at all. Thus, such a type must have immediate subtypes—unless it is empty, a possibility we ignore until further notice—and every value of the type must be a value of one of those immediate subtypes; the specialization constraints for those immediate subtypes (see IM Prescription 10) must be such as to guarantee that this requirement is met. Note that union types make sense only in an inheritance context, because they rely on the existence of proper (in fact, immediate) subtypes. Note too that a union type must have at least two immediate subtypes, thanks to IM Prescription 2.

Why might it be desirable to define a union type? The major reason is that such a definition provides a way of specifying operators that apply to values and variables of several different types, all of them proper subtypes of the union type in question. Appropriate implementation versions of the operator in question can then be defined, if necessary, at each of the applicable subtype levels. For example:

```
TYPE ELLIPSE UNION
     IS { PLANE_FIGURE
          POSSREP { A LENGTH, B LENGTH, CTR POINT
                   CONSTRAINT A ≥ B } } ;

TYPE CIRCLE
     IS { ELLIPSE
          CONSTRAINT THE_A ( ELLIPSE ) = THE_B ( ELLIPSE )
          POSSREP { R   = THE_A   ( ELLIPSE ) ,
                    CTR = THE_CTR ( ELLIPSE ) } } ;

TYPE NONCIRCLE
     IS { ELLIPSE
          CONSTRAINT THE_A ( ELLIPSE ) > THE_B ( ELLIPSE )
          POSSREP { A   = THE_A   ( ELLIPSE ) ,
                    B   = THE_B   ( ELLIPSE ) ,
                    CTR = THE_CTR ( ELLIPSE ) } } ;

OPERATOR AREA ( E ELLIPSE ) RETURNS AREA ;
     /* declared type of parameter E is a union type, */
     /* but the following implementation code works   */
     /* for both circles and noncircles:              */
     RETURN ( 3.14159 * THE_A ( E ) * THE_B ( E ) ) ;
END OPERATOR ;
```

Observe that:

- We require union types to be explicitly declared as such—see the UNION specification in the definition of type ELLIPSE. (In fact, PLANE_FIGURE, whose definition is deliberately not shown above, is a union type too. We will return to this point in the next subsection.)

- Type ELLIPSE does have a declared possrep and hence a selector, but invoking that selector will never return a value of most specific type ELLIPSE (because there *are* no values of most specific type ELLIPSE).

- A variable of declared type ELLIPSE will always have most specific type some proper subtype of ELLIPSE (because, again, there are no values of most specific type ELLIPSE).

- Operator AREA is defined at the ELLIPSE level, but it will never be invoked on a value that is of most specific type ELLIPSE. (To say it one more time, no such value exists.)

- The fact that ELLIPSE is now a union type does not prevent operators from having declared (result) type ELLIPSE. The specification signature for our MOVE operator, for example (read-only version), will still specify a declared result type of ELLIPSE—but, of course, no MOVE invocation will now return a result of most specific type ELLIPSE.

- We remark that the type constraint for type ELLIPSE in the example seems to be redundant. Given that the purpose of defining the union type in the first place was to reduce redundancy, in a sense, this state of affairs suggests that in practice we might not want to define too many union types with possreps. (Dummy types, which are union types without possreps, are another matter—see further discussion below.)

Now, a union type obviously cannot be a leaf type (again, unless it is empty, a possibility we continue to ignore until further notice). However, it would be possible to set up the type hierarchy in such a way that all types except leaf types are union types; in terms of our running example, introducing type NONCIRCLE as above, together with types NONRECTANGLE and NONSQUARE (as immediate subtypes of POLYGON and RECTANGLE, respectively) would have such an effect. "All most specific types must be leaf types" might thus be regarded as the extreme form of the idea of union types, and some writers have indeed advocated such a notion. Our model does not prohibit such an arrangement, but it does not insist on it, either; i.e., we allow values to exist whose most specific type is, e.g., ELLIPSE and not CIRCLE, as we already know.

Dummy Types

A *dummy* type is a union type that has no possrep (and therefore in particular no possrep constraint). A type that is not a dummy type is a *regular* type. By way of example, let us revise types ELLIPSE, CIRCLE, and NONCIRCLE from the preceding discussion to make ELLIPSE a dummy type, thus:

```
TYPE ELLIPSE UNION
    IS { PLANE_FIGURE } ;

TYPE CIRCLE
    IS { ELLIPSE
        POSSREP { R LENGTH, CTR POINT } } ;

TYPE NONCIRCLE
    IS { ELLIPSE
        POSSREP { A LENGTH, B LENGTH, CTR POINT
            CONSTRAINT A > B } } ;
```

Observe that:

- Type ELLIPSE is indeed now a dummy type: It has no possrep (and no possrep constraint) and no selector. Incidentally, it is worth pointing out explicitly that this fact does not constitute a violation of, or even an extension to, RM Prescription 4 as stated in Chapter 4.

- No "additional constraints"—see IM Prescription 10—have been specified for types CIRCLE and NONCIRCLE (since type ELLIPSE has no possrep in terms of which such constraints might be formulated). Thus, specialization by constraint now does not apply to those types; i.e., circles and noncircles are no longer obtained from ellipses via S by C.

- Type CIRCLE does have a possrep (though, for simplicity, no possrep constraint) and a selector. It also has certain THE_ operators (THE_R and THE_CTR). Note that THE_A and THE_B now do not apply to type CIRCLE (nor to type ELLIPSE, of course).

- Type NONCIRCLE also has a possrep and a selector (unlike type CIRCLE, it also has a possrep constraint). It also has certain THE_ operators (THE_A, THE_B, and THE_CTR).

- Operators THE_A, THE_B, and THE_R do not apply to variables of declared type ELLIPSE, since that type has no possrep. (By contrast, THE_CTR might apply—see later.)

- The ELLIPSE-level implementation version of the AREA operator that we showed earlier will no longer work (basically because of the lack of a possrep for type ELLIPSE).[1] Instead, we will—in effect—have to give just an appropriate specification signature at the ELLIPSE level and then provide appropriate implementation versions at the CIRCLE and NONCIRCLE levels, as follows:

```
OPERATOR AREA ( E ELLIPSE ) RETURNS AREA ;
   /* declared type of parameter E is a dummy type; */
   /* no implementation code provided at this level */
   END OPERATOR ;

OPERATOR AREA ( E CIRCLE ) RETURNS AREA VERSION C_AREA ;
   /* implementation version for type CIRCLE */
   RETURN ( 3.14159 * THE_R ( E ) ** 2 ) ;
END OPERATOR ;

OPERATOR AREA ( E NONCIRCLE ) RETURNS AREA VERSION NC_AREA ;
   /* implementation version for type NONCIRCLE */
   RETURN ( 3.14159 * THE_A ( E ) * THE_B ( A ) ) ;
END OPERATOR ;
```

Now, the foregoing example is not very realistic, because we have already seen that if we make ELLIPSE a regular union type (i.e., one with a possrep) instead of a dummy type, then we can define an implementation version of AREA at the ELLIPSE level after all that will work for both circles and noncircles. But consider type PLANE_FIGURE. That type would almost certainly be a true dummy type—it is hard to think of a possrep that will work for an arbitrary plane figure!—and it might well make sense to give a specification signature for AREA at the PLANE_FIGURE level and implementation versions at (say) the ELLIPSE and POLYGON levels.

Despite the foregoing, let us stay with the example of ELLIPSE as a dummy type, for simplicity. Observe now that the operator THE_CTR applies to values of type CIRCLE and values of type NONCIRCLE—i.e., values of every proper subtype of type ELLIPSE—and yet apparently not to values of type ELLIPSE itself! (We say "apparently," because type ELLIPSE has no possrep from which such an operator can be derived.) But such a state of affairs is clearly absurd; to say that every ellipse is either a circle or a noncircle, and circles and noncircles both have a center but ellipses do not, is an affront to common sense. After all, compare the situation with areas: Every ellipse has an area, because every ellipse is either a circle or a noncircle and circles and noncircles both have an area, and so we do allow the operator AREA to be applied to variables of declared type ELLIPSE. By analogy, therefore,

---

1. These remarks should not be construed to mean that we can never specify implementation code at a dummy type level. See the discussion of the DOUBLE_AREA example later in this subsection.

we should surely be allowed to do the same with the operator THE_CTR. (Indeed, if we did not do so, then THE_CTR would be a case of overloading rather than inclusion polymorphism.)

The foregoing anomaly is easily fixed, however: We simply allow the ELLIPSE type definer to assert that THE_CTR does apply at the ELLIPSE level after all (since implementation versions of that operator will certainly be provided at both the CIRCLE and NONCIRCLE levels).[1] Thus, for example, the assignment

```
P := THE_CTR ( E ) ;
```

(where P is of declared type POINT and E is of declared type ELLIPSE) is effectively shorthand for something like the following:

```
P := CASE
        WHEN IS_CIRCLE ( E )    THEN THE_CTR ( TREAT_AS_CIRCLE ( E ) )
        WHEN IS_NONCIRCLE ( E ) THEN THE_CTR ( TREAT_AS_NONCIRCLE ( E ) )
     END CASE ;
```

Likewise, the assignment

```
THE_CTR ( E ) := P ;
```

(where P and E are as before and THE_CTR is being used as a pseudovariable) is effectively shorthand for something like the following:

```
E := CASE
        WHEN IS_CIRCLE ( E )    THEN CIRCLE ( THE_R ( TREAT_AS_CIRCLE ( E ) ), P )
        WHEN IS_NONCIRCLE ( E ) THEN NONCIRCLE ( THE_A ( TREAT_AS_NONCIRCLE ( E ) ),
                                                 THE_B ( TREAT_AS_NONCIRCLE ( E ) ), P )
     END CASE ;
```

By the way, we do not mean to suggest by everything we have said in this subsection so far that implementation code for operators defined at some dummy-type level *must* be provided at the level of the pertinent supertypes. By way of a simple counterexample, we might define an operator called DOUBLE_AREA, with the obvious semantics, at the ELLIPSE level or even (more strikingly) at the PLANE_FIGURE level, thus:

```
OPERATOR DOUBLE_AREA ( PF PLANE_FIGURE ) RETURNS AREA ;
   RETURN ( 2 * AREA ( PF ) ) ;
END OPERATOR ;
```

We close this subsection with a few miscellaneous observations. First, note that it follows from IM Prescription 20 that if *T* is a nonempty dummy type, then all of its proper supertypes are nonempty dummy types too (because "a [nonempty] type shall be permitted to be a dummy type if and only if ... it

---

1. Note that THE_CTR here is indeed a THE_ operator in the usual sense (i.e., it has prescribed semantics, and those semantics must not be overridden). In particular, it can be used as a *pseudovariable*—a fact that suggests that simply providing a specification signature at the ELLIPSE level might not quite be adequate as a mechanism for "asserting that THE_CTR does apply" (since other operators defined in such a fashion are generally not usable as pseudovariables). Note also that the provision of THE_ operators for a dummy type does not constitute a violation of, or even an extension to, RM Prescription 5 as stated in Chapter 4.

has no regular immediate supertype").

Second, recall from RM Prescription 4 that certain system-defined types—and, as we saw under IM Prescription 10, proper subtypes thereof—are allowed to have no possrep; type INTEGER is a case in point. Such a type is not a dummy type, however, because (a) values do exist, in general, whose most specific type is the type in question and (b) the type is still required to have at least one associated selector that permits the specification of literals of the type in question.

Last, we remark that some systems use dummy types as a way of providing **type generator** functionality. For example, RELATION might be a dummy type in such a system (with generic operators JOIN, SUMMARIZE, and so forth), and every specific relation type would then be a proper subtype of that dummy type. We do not adopt such an approach in the *Manifesto,* however, because we certainly do not want our support for type generators to rely on support for inheritance. We note too that the approach seems to imply that specific implementation code must be provided for each specific join, each specific summarize, and so forth (instead of reusing generic, optimized, system-provided code): surely not a very desirable state of affairs! Finally, we observe also that the kind of "relation type inheritance" this approach to a RELATION type generator seems to entail is not the kind of relation type inheritance we think we need (in particular, it does not provide the kind of substitutability we think we need). See Chapter 16 for a detailed discussion of our own approach to relation type inheritance.

Alpha *and* Omega

We did not discuss the point in detail before, but it is an immediate consequence of IM Prescription 7 that there can be any number of distinct type hierarchies. If there is more than one, however, we can always invent some kind of "system" type that is an immediate supertype for the root types for all of those hierarchies, thereby effectively tying all of those hierarchies together into one. In fact, some object systems come ready equipped with such a type, often called OBJECT (on the grounds that "everything is an object").

In our model, we address this issue by introducing a special type that we call type *alpha* (mentioned in passing in a footnote under IM Prescription 9). *Alpha* is **the maximal scalar type:** It contains all scalar values and is a supertype of every scalar type; more precisely, it is a proper supertype of every scalar type except itself, and an immediate supertype of every scalar type that would otherwise be a root type.

Analogously, we introduce another type that we call type *omega* (previously discussed briefly under IM Prescription 8). *Omega* is **the minimal scalar type:** It contains no values at all and is a subtype of every scalar type; more precisely, it is a proper subtype of every scalar type except itself, and an immediate subtype of every scalar type that would otherwise be a leaf type.

Note: The remarks in the previous two paragraphs assume that types *alpha* and *omega* are explicitly defined and thus included in the type hierarchy (or type graph, rather, in the case of *omega*). In practice, however, we would not expect them to be explicitly defined. They are useful primarily from a conceptual point of view (though they do turn out to be important in connection with tuple and relation type inheritance—see Chapter 16). In what follows, we will assume they are not explicitly defined, barring explicit statements to the contrary.

Now for more specifics. First, type *alpha:*

- *Alpha* is indeed a dummy type—it has no possrep and hence no selector.

- The corresponding type constraint is just TRUE.[1]

---

1. *Alpha* and *omega* are exceptions to the general rule that dummy types, having no possrep, therefore have no type constraint.

- IS_*alpha*(X) always gives TRUE.

- TREAT_AS_*alpha* (…) always succeeds.

As for type *omega* (which, perhaps surprisingly, turns out to be more important than type *alpha* in certain respects, as we will see in the next two chapters):

- *Omega is also a dummy type*—it has no possrep and hence no selector. *Note:* Omega is truly a union type, as all dummy types must be, because by definition there is no value of type *omega* that is not of some immediate subtype of *omega*. (You might want to read that sentence again.)

- The corresponding type constraint is just FALSE.

- IS_*omega*(X) always gives FALSE.

- TREAT_AS_*omega* (…) always fails.

- No variable, no operator, and in fact no expression can have either declared type or most specific type *omega*.

- Type *omega* inherits all possible read-only operators, but vacuously so, since they can never be invoked on any value of the type.

Finally, we repeat the point that since it is a subtype of every scalar type, the introduction of type *omega* takes us, by definition, into the realm of multiple inheritance. (This is one reason why we believe it makes little logical sense to consider single inheritance only—despite the fact that we have been doing exactly that for most of this chapter! But we were doing so for pedagogical reasons, not logical ones.) Indeed, the introduction of *omega* into any given type "hierarchy" has the effect of converting that "hierarchy" into a *lattice*. See Chapter 15 for further discussion.

EXERCISES

1. A possrep constraint implies that certain selector invocations will fail; a specialization constraint implies that certain TREAT invocations will fail. Are these statements true or false?

2. Given your answer to Exercise 11 in Chapter 12—"Define an operator to rotate a specified rectangle through 90° about its center"—define a version of that operator for squares.

3. A conic section (*conic* for short) is a curve in (x,y)-space, defined by the equation $ax^2 - 2px + y^2 = 0$. If $a < 0$, the conic is a hyperbola; if $a = 0$, it is a parabola; if $a > 0$, it is an ellipse (and if $a = 1$, the ellipse is a circle). Define a corresponding set of types. *Note:* You will need some additional knowledge regarding conic sections in order to answer this exercise.

4. Write **Tutorial D** definitions for types HIGHWAY and TOLL_HIGHWAY (see IM Prescription 17). Also write the code for the TRAVEL_TIME operator(s).

5. If C is a variable of declared type CIRCLE, assignment to THE_A(C) and THE_B(C) is not supported. What is the *formal* reason for this state of affairs?

6. Let CHAR_n ($n \geq 0$) be a family of types such that a value v is a value of type CHAR_n if and only if it is a character string of no more than n significant characters (where a character is

significant if and only if it is not a trailing space). Do you agree that type CHAR_n' is a subtype of type CHAR_n if and only if $n' \le n$? Does value substitutability apply? Are there any operators that apply to values of type CHAR_n' and not to values of type CHAR_n? Does S by C apply? Is there a nonempty type that is a subtype of all possible types in the family?

7. Following on from the previous exercise, consider the character string literal 'ABC ' (note the trailing space). What is the declared type of this literal? What is the most specific type?

8. Let T' be a proper subtype of type T. It has been conjectured that if the only operators that apply to values and variables that are of type T' and not of type T are those that are provided "automatically"—THE_ operators, selectors, "=", ":=", TREAT_AS_T, and IS_T operators—then type T' was probably not worth defining in the first place. Discuss.

9. In the body of this chapter, we made repeated use of the polymorphic operator AREA. The polymorphism in question was *inclusion* polymorphism, of course. However, we did also suggest that AREA might be the name of a selector operator for type AREA, in which case AREA becomes *overloaded* too. Write an appropriate set of specification signatures for all of these various AREA operators.

10. Can the implementation of TREAT_AS_T and IS_T be automated? Do these operators apply to built-in types?

11. Let T' be an existing type. What is involved in introducing a new proper supertype T of T'? Does it make any difference if T' is built in, not user defined?

12. The **Tutorial D** syntax for defining a proper subtype (under single inheritance) includes a specification of the form IS { <*scalar type name*> ...}. Does it make sense for the specified <*scalar type name*> to be the name of a *generated* type?

13. Consider the following type definition. Can you see anything wrong with it?

```
TYPE BETA ... POSSREP { X alpha ... } ... ;
```

What about this one?

```
TYPE GAMMA ... POSSREP { X omega ... } ... ;
```

14. No variable can have declared type *omega;* but what about an attribute (within some tuple or relation type)?

16. Let types T1 and T2 be defined as follows:

```
TYPE T1 POSSREP { CONSTRAINT FALSE } ;
TYPE T2 POSSREP { CONSTRAINT FALSE } ;
```

Clearly, these types are both empty; yet they have different names. In accordance with RM Prescription 1, therefore, are they not different types? Discuss.

Incidentally, what would happen if we deleted the specification CONSTRAINT FALSE from both of the foregoing type definitions?

Chapter 15

Multiple Inheritance

with Scalar Types

In this chapter we consider what happens to our inheritance model when we take multiple inheritance into account. It will turn out that none of the 20 IM Prescriptions discussed in the previous chapter needs any extension or reformulation; however, a couple of them, IM Prescriptions 7 and (especially) 8, do merit a much closer look. But first things first.

To review briefly, multiple inheritance is the phenomenon according to which a given subtype can have more than one immediate supertype and can therefore inherit operators and constraints from more than one such supertype (a simple example is given in the section immediately following). As noted in Chapter 12 and elsewhere, it is our position that multiple inheritance support is not only desirable but logically required. As reference [131] says:

> Most modern ... systems allow [multiple inheritance] ... A generally accepted view is that a
> modern ... language should support [multiple inheritance], despite the fact that [it] introduces
> many conceptual and technical intricacies.

We will be examining some of those "conceptual and technical intricacies" in this chapter. *Note:* For simplicity, we continue to follow the convention that the unqualified terms *type, subtype,* and *supertype* refer to scalar types, subtypes, and supertypes specifically; the unqualified terms *value, variable, (read-only) operator, expression,* and *result* refer to scalar values, variables, operators, expressions, and results specifically; and the unqualified term *constraint* refers to a type constraint specifically. We also continue to assume that all of the types under discussion are members of some given set of types S and that the root and leaf type concepts in particular are to be understood in terms of that set S. Finally, we continue to use the symbols T and T' to refer generically to a pair of types such that T' is a subtype of T—equivalently, such that T is a supertype of T'.

AN INTRODUCTORY EXAMPLE

In order to introduce some of the basic concepts of multiple inheritance, we use a simple variation on our geometric example from Chapters 12 and 14, involving parallelograms, rectangles, rhombi, and squares. (Just to remind you, a rhombus is a parallelogram whose sides are all the same length.) Fig. 15.1 shows a graph—a *directed acyclic graph,* to be precise—of the subtype/supertype relationships in this example. Observe that type PARALLELOGRAM is a root type, type SQUARE is a leaf type, and type SQUARE has two immediate supertypes, RECTANGLE and RHOMBUS.

To see that the subtype/supertype relationships in the figure are indeed reasonable, consider the following:

- Every parallelogram has a "long" diagonal of length *ld* and a "short" one of length *sd*, where *ld* $\geq$ *sd*.

- Every parallelogram also has two "long" sides of length *ls* and two "short" ones of length *ss*, where *ls* $\geq$ *ss*.

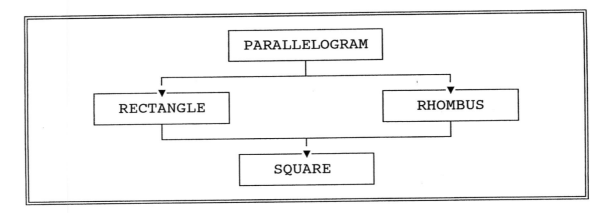

Fig. 15.1: A simple type graph

- A rectangle is a parallelogram for which *ld = sd.* Unlike parallelograms in general, every rectangle has a unique circumscribed circle (i.e., a circle that passes through each of the rectangle's four vertices); hence, every rectangle has a property, unique to rectangles alone among parallelograms, that is exactly that circumscribed circle.

- A rhombus is a parallelogram for which *ls = ss.* Unlike parallelograms in general, every rhombus has a unique inscribed circle (i.e., a circle that touches each of the rhombus's four sides); hence, every rhombus has a property, unique to rhombi alone among parallelograms, that is exactly that inscribed circle. (We remark in passing that a parallelogram that is not a rhombus is sometimes called a *rhomboid.*)

- A square is a parallelogram that is both a rectangle and a rhombus. Unlike rectangles and rhombi in general, every square has a unique associated *annulus* that is defined by the difference between the corresponding circumscribed and inscribed circles; hence, every square has a property, unique to squares alone among rectangles and rhombi, that is exactly that annulus. Moreover, every square has both (a) a unique *side,* which rectangles in general do not have, and (b) a unique *diagonal,* which rhombi in general do not have.

Possible Representations

It is instructive to consider the question of what possreps we might specify in this example. (You might want to sketch a parallelogram of your own in order to help you appreciate the points to be made in what follows.) Let *p* be a parallelogram with vertices (in clockwise sequence) A, B, C, D and center E. Then it should be clear that there are many different ways of "possibly representing" *p.* Here are some of them:

- We could use the four vertices A, B, C, and D. Of course, it is not the case that every set of four points defines a parallelogram; we would therefore have to impose an appropriate constraint on the points A, B, C, D. There are several different ways to state that constraint, too. For example, we could require that line segments AB and DC be parallel and line segments BC and AD be parallel also; or we could require that line segments AB and DC be of equal length and line segments BC and AD be of equal length also; or possibly other ways besides. Note too that A, B, C, and D must all be distinct!—and no three of them can be collinear.

- We could use any three of the vertices (A, B, and C, say). Here the only constraint we would have to impose is that the three points are not collinear (but note again that there are several different ways to state such a constraint). Of course, there are four possible choices for the set of three vertices.

- We could use any two adjacent vertices (A and B, say) and the center E. Here again the only constraint we would have to impose is that the three points are not collinear. There are four possible choices for the pair of adjacent vertices.

- We could use any two adjacent sides—AB and BC, say. Here we would have to impose the constraint that the line segments AB and BC do in fact meet at B (and A, B, and C are not collinear). There are four possible choices for the pair of adjacent sides.

- We could use a pair of opposite sides—AB and DC, say—with the constraint that those two sides are parallel and of equal length. There are two choices here.

- We could use the diagonals AC and BD, with the constraint that they bisect each other at E.

- We could use a pair of adjacent half-diagonals—EA and EB, say—with the constraint that the line segments do in fact meet at E (and E, A, and B are not collinear). Four choices here.

- We could use one vertex, an angle, and two lengths (for example, the point A, the angle DAB, and the lengths of the sides AB and AD). The angle must not be 180°. Four choices.

And so on, probably.

Type Definitions

Let us agree, somewhat arbitrarily, to specify just one possrep for type PARALLELOGRAM: viz., the one involving the four vertex points A, B, C, D.[1] Let us also agree to use that same possrep for each of the other three types as well. Of course, we already know that three vertices would suffice (in fact, just two—which two?—would suffice in the case of type SQUARE). We have chosen to specify all four, despite the redundancy, for reasons of symmetry; i.e., there does not seem to be any good argument in favor of any particular three over any other. Perhaps more study is required. Note in particular that our choice does mean that the components of the possrep are not mutually independent (see the discussion of such matters under RM Prescription 5 in Chapter 6). One possibly undesirable consequence of this state of affairs is discussed at the end of the present subsection.

Here then is a possible definition for the root type PARALLELOGRAM:

```
TYPE PARALLELOGRAM
    POSSREP { A POINT, B POINT, C POINT, D POINT
            CONSTRAINT DISTINCT ( A, B, C, D )
                   AND NOT ( COLLINEAR ( A, B, C ) )
                   AND NOT ( COLLINEAR ( B, C, D ) )
                   AND NOT ( COLLINEAR ( C, D, A ) )
                   AND NOT ( COLLINEAR ( D, A, B ) )
                   AND DIST ( A, B ) = DIST ( C, D )
                   AND DIST ( B, C ) = DIST ( D, A ) } ;
```

---

1. Some convention, left unspecified here, would be needed in practice to establish which point corresponds to which vertex, in order to ensure that references to (e.g.) angle DAB are unambiguous.

We are appealing here to:

- A presumably built-in operator called DISTINCT, which returns TRUE if and only if its arguments are all distinct

- An operator called COLLINEAR (code not given), which returns TRUE if and only if its three POINT arguments lie on a straight line

- The operator DIST from Chapter 3, which takes two points and returns the distance between them as a value of type LENGTH

Here next is a possible definition for type RECTANGLE:

```
TYPE RECTANGLE
      IS { PARALLELOGRAM CONSTRAINT
                        LD ( PARALLELOGRAM ) = SD ( PARALLELOGRAM )
                        POSSREP { A = THE_A ( PARALLELOGRAM ) ,
                                  B = THE_B ( PARALLELOGRAM ) ,
                                  C = THE_C ( PARALLELOGRAM ) ,
                                  D = THE_D ( PARALLELOGRAM ) } } ;
```

We have assumed the availability of two operators LD and SD (see the subsection "Operators" later), which return the length of the "long" and the "short" diagonal, respectively, of a given parallelogram. Incidentally, the POSSREP specification here lends weight to the suggestion from Chapter 12 that it might be convenient to have some syntactic shorthand for defining a subtype possrep that is similar or identical to some corresponding supertype possrep.

Next, type RHOMBUS:

```
TYPE RHOMBUS
      IS { PARALLELOGRAM CONSTRAINT
                        LS ( PARALLELOGRAM ) = SS ( PARALLELOGRAM )
                        POSSREP { A = THE_A ( PARALLELOGRAM ) ,
                                  B = THE_B ( PARALLELOGRAM ) ,
                                  C = THE_C ( PARALLELOGRAM ) ,
                                  D = THE_D ( PARALLELOGRAM ) } } ;
```

We have assumed the availability of two operators LS and SS (see the subsection "Operators" again), which return the length of the "long" and the "short" side, respectively, of a given parallelogram.

Finally, type SQUARE:

```
TYPE SQUARE
      IS { RECTANGLE, RHOMBUS
            POSSREP { A = THE_A ( RECTANGLE ) ,
                      B = THE_B ( RECTANGLE ) ,
                      C = THE_C ( RECTANGLE ) ,
                      D = THE_D ( RECTANGLE ) } } ;
```

The specialization constraint here states precisely that a given value *s* is of type SQUARE if and only if IS_RECTANGLE(*s*) and IS_RHOMBUS(*s*) both evaluate to TRUE. No additional CONSTRAINT specification is stated, or indeed permitted. In general, in fact, such an additional constraint is required if and only if (a) the subtype being defined has exactly one immediate supertype and (b) that supertype is regular. (Just to remind you, a type is regular if it is not a dummy type; in other

words, a regular type is a type with at least one possrep and hence at least one selector.)
A few further points arise in connection with the foregoing definitions:

- It seems we have to make an arbitrary decision in the POSSREP specification for type SQUARE. To be specific, we have to decide whether to define that possrep in terms of type RECTANGLE or in terms of type RHOMBUS. Purely for definiteness, we have defined it in terms of RECTANGLE, but we could equally well have defined it in terms of RHOMBUS instead (or even, perhaps, a mixture of the two!)—a situation that might be regarded as a little unsatisfactory. *Note:* The discussions in the final section of this chapter might have some bearing on this issue.

- As we have already seen, there are many distinct but logically equivalent candidate possreps that could have been used in this example. It follows that there are many distinct but logically equivalent ways of formulating the corresponding specialization constraints (at least for types RECTANGLE and RHOMBUS, though not for type SQUARE, of course).

- Our choice of possrep for type PARALLELOGRAM does have the advantage that operators THE_A, THE_B, THE_C, and THE_D are all available for parallelograms (and hence for rectangles, rhombi, and squares as well). What is more, corresponding pseudovariables are available for all four types too, by definition. However, any attempt to use those pseudovariables will fail if it violates some applicable constraint; in fact, any attempt to update just one vertex in isolation will necessarily fail (this state of affairs is a consequence of our decision to include some redundancy in the possreps). For example, consider what is involved in doubling the height of a rectangle (more precisely, updating a variable V of declared type RECTANGLE such that the values returned by AD(V) and BC(V)—see the operator definitions in the next subsection—are twice what they were before the update).

Operators

In this subsection we show definitions—the final few just in outline—for a set of operators that would surely prove useful in practice in connection with the foregoing example. (We will not actually be using these operators in the rest of the chapter; we show them here merely by way of illustration.)

```
OPERATOR AB ( P PARALLELOGRAM ) RETURNS LENGTH SYNONYMS { BA, CD, DC } ;
    /* "length of side AB"; note the SYNONYMS specification, which defines additional names */
    /* for the same operator                                                              */
    RETURN ( DIST ( THE_A ( P ), THE_B ( P ) ) ) ;
END OPERATOR ;

OPERATOR BC ( P PARALLELOGRAM ) RETURNS LENGTH SYNONYMS { CB, AD, DA } ;
    /* "length of side BC"; note the SYNONYMS specification, which defines additional names */
    /* for the same operator                                                              */
    RETURN ( DIST ( THE_B ( P ), THE_C ( P ) ) ) ;
END OPERATOR ;

OPERATOR AC ( P PARALLELOGRAM ) RETURNS LENGTH SYNONYMS { CA } ;
    /* "length of diagonal AC" */
    RETURN ( DIST ( THE_A ( P ), THE_C ( P ) ) ) ;
END OPERATOR ;
```

```
OPERATOR BD ( P PARALLELOGRAM ) RETURNS LENGTH SYNONYMS { DB } ;
   /* "length of diagonal BD" */
   RETURN ( DIST ( THE_B ( P ), THE_D ( P ) ) ) ;
END OPERATOR ;

OPERATOR DAB ( P PARALLELOGRAM ) RETURNS ANGLE SYNONYMS { BAD, BCD, DCB } ;
   /* "included angle at vertex A" */
   RETURN ( ARCCOS ( ( AB ( P ) ** 2 + AD ( P ) ** 2 - DB ( P ) ** 2 )
                 / ( 2 * AB ( P ) * AD ( P ) ) ) ) ;
END OPERATOR ;

OPERATOR ABC ( P PARALLELOGRAM ) RETURNS ANGLE SYNONYMS { CBA, ADC, CDA } ;
   /* "included angle at vertex B" */
   RETURN ( ARCCOS ( ( BA ( P ) ** 2 + BC ( P ) ** 2 - AC ( P ) ** 2 )
                 / ( 2 * BA ( P ) * BC ( P ) ) ) ) ;
END OPERATOR ;

OPERATOR LS ( P PARALLELOGRAM ) RETURNS LENGTH ;
   /* "length of long side of" */
   RETURN ( MAX { AB ( P ), BC ( P ) } ) ;
END OPERATOR ;

OPERATOR SS ( P PARALLELOGRAM ) RETURNS LENGTH ;
   /* "length of short side of" */
   RETURN ( MIN { AB ( P ), BC ( P ) } ) ;
END OPERATOR ;

OPERATOR LD ( P PARALLELOGRAM ) RETURNS LENGTH ;
   /* "length of long diagonal of" */
   RETURN ( MAX { AC ( P ), BD ( P ) } ) ;
END OPERATOR ;

OPERATOR SD ( P PARALLELOGRAM ) RETURNS LENGTH ;
   /* "length of short diagonal of" */
   RETURN ( MIN { AC ( P ), BD ( P ) } ) ;
END OPERATOR ;

OPERATOR AREA ( P PARALLELOGRAM ) RETURNS AREA ;
   /* "area of" */
   ... ;
END OPERATOR ;

OPERATOR CTR ( P PARALLELOGRAM ) RETURNS POINT ;
   /* "center of" */
   ... ;
END OPERATOR ;
```

All of the foregoing operators apply to parallelograms, and hence to rectangles and rhombi, and hence to squares as well. Note in particular that type SQUARE inherits these operators from both of its immediate supertypes RECTANGLE and RHOMBUS, a point we will return to in the final section of this chapter.

The following operators, by contrast, do not apply to parallelograms in general:

```
        OPERATOR CIR_CIRCLE ( RE RECTANGLE ) RETURNS CIRCLE ;
           /* "circumscribed circle of" */
           ... ;
        END OPERATOR ;


        OPERATOR IN_CIRCLE ( RH RHOMBUS ) RETURNS CIRCLE ;
           /* "inscribed circle of" */
           ... ;
        END OPERATOR ;


        OPERATOR ANNULUS ( S SQUARE ) RETURNS ANNULUS ;
           /* "annulus of" */
           ... ;
        END OPERATOR ;


        OPERATOR SIDE ( S SQUARE ) RETURNS LENGTH ;
           /* "side of" */
           ... ;
        END OPERATOR ;


        OPERATOR DIAG ( S SQUARE ) RETURNS LENGTH ;
           /* "diagonal of" */
           ... ;
        END OPERATOR ;
```

TYPE GRAPHS

As we saw in Chapter 12, single inheritance can be characterized as follows: *Every proper subtype has exactly one immediate supertype.* Multiple inheritance means, by contrast, that every proper subtype has *at least* one immediate supertype. In Fig. 15.1, for example, the proper subtypes RECTANGLE and RHOMBUS each have one immediate supertype, PARALLELOGRAM, and the proper subtype SQUARE has two, RECTANGLE and RHOMBUS. The obvious question arises: Could we additionally define PARALLELOGRAM as an immediate supertype of SQUARE? In terms of Fig. 15.1, such a definition would involve an additional directed arc from type PARALLELOGRAM to type SQUARE. Could we add such an arc?

Well, observe first of all that PARALLELOGRAM is not an immediate supertype of SQUARE as defined by IM Prescription 6, because there does exist a type that is both a proper supertype of SQUARE and a proper subtype of PARALLELOGRAM. (In fact, of course, there are two such types, RECTANGLE and RHOMBUS.) At the very least, therefore, we would have to revise IM Prescription 6 if we wished to permit the additional arc. So do we wish to permit it?

We answer this question in the negative. It seems to us that permitting such an additional arc does not lead to any useful additional functionality; to be specific, all of the operators and constraints that type SQUARE would then inherit "immediately" from type PARALLELOGRAM it already inherits anyway, transitively, via the intermediate types RECTANGLE and RHOMBUS. Furthermore, permitting such an extension to our understanding of the term *immediate supertype* certainly has the potential to complicate some of our later concepts and definitions unduly. We therefore reject such an extension. As already indicated, we do not need to change our model in any way to achieve this effect—IM Prescription 6 already takes care of matters for us.

Now, multiple inheritance clearly implies that we can no longer talk about type hierarchies as such; instead, we need to introduce the more general concept of a type *graph*. Here is a precise definition of this concept. A **type graph** is a directed acyclic graph of nodes and directed arcs from one node to another that satisfies the following properties:

a. Each node is given the name of a type. No two nodes have the same name.

b. There is a directed arc from node T to node T' if and only if type T is an immediate supertype of type T'.

c. If there is a directed arc from node T to node T', then node T' is not reachable from node T via any other path. *Note:* A **path** from node T to node T' is a sequence of n directed arcs $A1$ (from T to $T1$, say), $A2$ (from $T1$ to $T2$, say), ..., An (from $T(n-1)$, say, to T'), where $n \geq 0$, and $n = 0$ implies $T = T'$ (i.e., there is always a path from node T to itself). A node T' is **reachable** from a node T if and only if there is a path from node T to node T'.

d. If the graph includes any nodes at all, then—because it is directed and acyclic—it necessarily contains at least one node that has no immediate supertype node. Such a node is called a **root** node, and the type corresponding to that node is called a **root** type.

e. If the graph includes any nodes at all, then—because it is directed and acyclic—it necessarily contains at least one node that has no immediate subtype node. Such a node is called a **leaf** node, and the type corresponding to that node is called a **leaf** type.

f. If nodes $T1$ and $T2$ are distinct root nodes, then no node other than node *omega* (if such a node exists) is reachable from both $T1$ and $T2$.

g. If nodes $T1$, $T2$, T', and T'' are such that there exist paths from both $T1$ and $T2$ to both T' and T'', then there must exist a node T that is common to all of those paths.

Explanation:

- Points a. and b. are self-explanatory.

- Point c. simply reflects the fact that (as discussed earlier in this section) no type T can be both an immediate and a nonimmediate supertype of the same type T'.

- Points d. and e. are obvious generalizations of the corresponding portions of the "type hierarchy" definition for the single inheritance case. Note that a root can be regarded as an entry point into the overall type graph. As the definition indicates, we do not assume that there is exactly one root type; if there are two or more, however, we can always introduce some kind of "system" type—perhaps type *alpha*—that is an immediate supertype for all of them, and so there is no loss of generality in assuming just one.

- Point f. is discussed in the next section. As for point g., see Exercise 7 at the end of the chapter.

Of course, type graphs, like type hierarchies before them, are not really part of our model per se—they are just a convenient way of depicting subtype/supertype relationships, which are.

LEAST SPECIFIC TYPES UNIQUE

As noted at the beginning of the chapter, we do need to take a closer look at IM Prescriptions 7 and (especially) 8. We discuss IM Prescription 7 in this section and IM Prescription 8 in the next. We begin by repeating IM Prescription 7 ("root types disjoint") from the previous chapter:

7.   *If* T1 *and* T2 *are distinct root types, then they shall be disjoint; i.e., no value shall be of both type* T1 *and type* T2.

Now, with single inheritance, this prescription was tightly connected to the disjointness assumption ("If types *T1* and *T2* are such that neither is a subtype of the other, then they are disjoint"). With multiple inheritance, of course, that assumption no longer applies. For example, types RECTANGLE and RHOMBUS in Fig. 15.1 are certainly not disjoint, yet neither is a subtype of the other (because some rectangles are not rhombi and some rhombi are not rectangles). Of course, those values that are both rectangles and rhombi are, precisely, squares; note, however, that until such time as we actually introduce type SQUARE as a subtype of both type RECTANGLE and type RHOMBUS, we still do not have multiple inheritance as such. Thus, in order to support multiple inheritance, it is *necessary* but not *sufficient* that we relax the disjointness assumption. (More precisely, if we relax it for leaf types only, we do not have multiple inheritance; if we relax it for nonleaf types, we do.)

We do not have to relax that assumption completely, however, nor do we wish to. Rather, we proceed as follows. First, we introduce the concept of **least specific type:** If value *v* is of type *T* and not of any proper supertype of *T*, then we say that *T* is the *least specific* type of *v* (obviously *T* here must be a root type). Then we go on to insist that the least specific type of any value must be unique—which is what IM Prescription 7 says (at least, it is logically equivalent to what IM Prescription 7 says). As a consequence, a graph like the one shown in Fig. 15.2 is not a valid type graph, because it shows a proper subtype, SQUARE, with two distinct proper supertypes, RECTANGLE and RHOMBUS, that are both root types. *Note:* Our reasons for insisting on the uniqueness of least specific types will become clear in the next section.

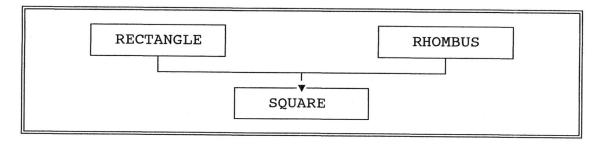

Fig. 15.2: A graph that is not a valid type graph

It follows from the foregoing that any given type graph can be divided into a set of **partitions,** one per root, such that:

- Within any given partition, every node is connected to every other. *Explanation:* When we say some node *T0* is **connected** to some node *Tn,* we mean that either (a) *T0 = Tn* (by definition, every node is connected to itself) or (b) there exists a sequence of *n* directed arcs *A0, A1, ... A(n-1),* say (where *n* ≥ 1), such that *A0* is from *T0* to *T1* or vice versa, *A1* is from *T1* to *T2* or vice versa, ..., and *An* is from *T(n-1)* to *Tn* or vice versa.

- No node in any given partition is connected to any node in any other partition (in other words, the partitions are disjoint)—unless the graph includes a node for type *omega;* by definition, such a node would be common to every partition. In this latter case, the *omega* node would be connected to every node, and those "partitions" would no longer truly be partitions as such. (But even then it would still be the case that no *value* is a value of two distinct types *T1* and *T2* such that *T1* and *T2* belong to distinct partitions.)

Observe that any given partition is always *fully connected,* in the sense that every node in that partition is connected to every other node in that partition. What is more, if we introduce type *omega* into the type graph, each of those partitions becomes (by definition) a **lattice** [8]; and if we introduce type *alpha* as well, the entire graph becomes a single partition (and a single lattice).

To close this discussion, here again is point f. from the definition of *type graph* in the previous section:

f.   If nodes *T1* and *T2* are distinct root nodes, then no node other than node *omega* (if such a node exists) is reachable from both *T1* and *T2*.

It should be obvious from the foregoing discussion that this point is an immediate consequence of IM Prescription 7.

MOST SPECIFIC TYPES UNIQUE

Now we turn to IM Prescription 8 ("scalar values with inheritance"):

8.   *Every set of types* T1, T2, ..., Tn *shall have a common subtype* T' *such that a given value is of each of the types* T1, T2, ..., Tn *if and only if it is of type* T'.

As we know from Chapter 14, with single inheritance this prescription leads to the important consequence that every value has a unique most specific type. Is the same true for multiple inheritance? In order to investigate this question, it is convenient to start from the other end, as it were. To be specific, we will begin with a simplified version of the prescription that is tailored for single inheritance as such:

Let value v *be of type* T. *If and only if no proper subtype* T' *of type* T *exists such that* v *is also of type* T', *then* T *is the **most specific type for (or of)*** v.

(This definition is indeed equivalent to the original in the absence of multiple inheritance, as you might like to confirm for yourself.) Now we consider the question of what needs to be added to this simplified definition—which, to avoid confusion, we will refer to henceforth as *IM Prescription 8S* ("S" for single)—in order to ensure that every value does still have exactly one most specific type.

Before we go any further, we should explain why we want this property to hold. In fact, the reason is easy to see. Suppose it did not hold; suppose that (e.g.) a given value *v* could be both a rectangle and a rhombus, and suppose further that type SQUARE has not yet been defined. Clearly, then, the expression "the most specific type of *v*" would be ambiguous. To repeat a point already made in Chapter 12, one undesirable consequence would be that if an operator named *Op* had been defined for rectangles and another operator with the same name *Op* had been defined for rhombi, an invocation of *Op* with argument *v* would be ambiguous. The (partial) solution to this problem is, of course, to insist that type SQUARE be defined after all. (The other part of the solution is discussed in the final section of this chapter.)

With the foregoing example as motivation, let us now consider the following possible replacement for IM Prescription 8S:

If two types T1 *and* T2 *overlap, then they shall have a common subtype* T' *such that a given value is of both types (i.e., T1 and T2) if and only if it is of type T'.*

Note: Two types **overlap** if and only if they are not disjoint. Moreover, to say that value *v* is of types *T1* and *T2* if and only if it is of type *T'* is to say, precisely, that the set of values constituting type *T'* is the **intersection** of the sets of values constituting types *T1* and *T2*. We can therefore refer to type *T'*, informally, as an **intersection type** (or intersection subtype).

Now, the point is perhaps not immediately obvious, but this revised version of IM Prescription 8S does in fact guarantee that most specific types are unique, as required. Before we can show that this is so, however, we need to dispose of a few degenerate cases:

- *Case 1: T1 = T2.*

  If types *T1* and *T2* are in fact the same type *T,* then *T* itself clearly serves as the required intersection subtype.

- *Case 2: T1* is a proper supertype of *T2.*

  In this case, *T2* is the required intersection subtype.

- *Case 3: T1* and *T2* are disjoint.

  The revised IM Prescription 8S can even take care of this case, if we include type *omega* in the type graph (type *omega* itself is the required intersection subtype in this case, of course). In other words, we can simplify IM Prescription 8S still further, thus:

  Any two types T1 *and* T2 *shall have a common subtype* T' *such that a given value is of both type* T1 *and type* T2 *if and only if it is of type* T'.

Having taken care of these three special cases, we assume for the remainder of this section (barring explicit statements to the contrary) that (a) *T1* and *T2* are distinct, (b) they overlap (i.e., they do have at least one value in common), and (c) neither is a subtype of the other. This combination is the most general and interesting case, of course.

By way of example, consider the type graph shown in Fig. 15.3 overleaf (type EQUILATERAL in that figure consists of polygons whose sides are all the same length). Note that, e.g., types QUADRILATERAL and EQUILATERAL satisfy the foregoing conditions: They are distinct, they overlap, and neither is a subtype of the other. But they do have a common subtype, RHOMBUS, such that it is indeed the case that a polygon that is both quadrilateral and equilateral must be, precisely, a rhombus. Thus, RHOMBUS is the intersection subtype for types QUADRILATERAL and EQUILATERAL.

Note: Just how our model allows the very same value to be of type QUADRILATERAL and type EQUILATERAL "at the same time," as it were, is explained in the discussion of the third "important logical consequence" in the subsection immediately following. Note too that SQUARE is also a common subtype for types QUADRILATERAL and EQUILATERAL, but it is not the intersection subtype per se (see the discussion of the fourth "important logical consequence" in the subsection immediately following).

For completeness, we give the intersection subtype for every pair of types in Fig. 15.3 that satisfy the pertinent conditions:

```
QUADRILATERAL   and  EQUILATERAL  :  RHOMBUS
PARALLELOGRAM   and  EQUILATERAL  :  RHOMBUS
RECTANGLE       and  EQUILATERAL  :  SQUARE
RECTANGLE       and  RHOMBUS      :  SQUARE
```

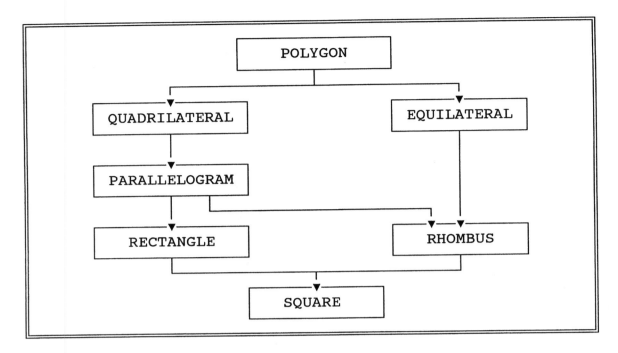

Fig. 15.3: Overlapping types must have an intersection subtype

Some Important Logical Consequences

Our revised version of IM Prescription 8S has several very important consequences, which we now proceed to explain.

Most specific types unique: The first point is that, as desired, it is indeed still the case that *every value has a well-defined, unique, most specific type.* For suppose, contrariwise, that there exists some value *v* that is of two distinct most specific types, *T1* and *T2* say, "at the same time." Observe that, by definition, neither of *T1* and *T2* is a subtype of the other (since they are both "most specific"). By our revised IM Prescription 8S, then, *v* must also be of some type *T'* that is a common subtype of *T1* and *T2*. Furthermore, *T'* must be a proper subtype of *T1* and *T2*, since neither of these latter two types is a subtype of the other. But to say that *v* is of some proper subtype of (e.g.) *T1* is to contradict the hypothesis that *T1* was a most specific type for *v* in the first place.

Of course, it is still the case, as it was with single inheritance, that not every value has to have a leaf type as its most specific type. For example, values can exist whose most specific type is RECTANGLE and not SQUARE.

Leaf types disjoint: It is also still the case that *leaf types are disjoint.* For suppose, contrariwise, that types *T1* and *T2* are distinct but overlapping leaf types. By our revised IM Prescription 8S, then, *T1* and *T2* must have a common subtype *T'*. Moreover, since *T1* and *T2* are distinct and are leaf types, neither is a subtype of the other, and hence *T'* must be a proper subtype of both. But if they have a proper subtype, then they are not leaf types after all.

Model of a scalar variable: It follows from the foregoing that our model of a scalar variable as defined in IM Prescription 9—i.e., as a named ordered triple of the form *<DT,MST,v>*—is still valid. It follows further that the FIND_*MST* algorithm we gave in our discussion of IM Prescription 10 ("specialization by constraint") in Chapter 14 for computing the most specific type of a given value still works. For example, suppose we are given a parallelogram *p* with AC = BD (so *p* is in fact a rectangle) and AB = BC (so *p* is a rhombus also). First, the algorithm will examine the type constraint for (say) type RECTANGLE, since RECTANGLE is a proper subtype of PARALLELOGRAM; it will discover that *p* satisfies that constraint, and so *p* is certainly of type RECTANGLE. Next, it will examine the type constraint for type SQUARE, since SQUARE is a proper subtype of RECTANGLE; it will then discover that *p* also satisfies the type constraint for type RHOMBUS, and hence the type constraint for type SQUARE as well. Hence, *p* is of all four types PARALLELOGRAM, RECTANGLE, RHOMBUS, and SQUARE, and *MST(p)* is SQUARE.

Least specific common subtypes unique: Next, observe that *the intersection subtype* T' *required by our revised IM Prescription 8S must be unique.* That is, given overlapping types *T1* and *T2*, there cannot exist two different types *T'* and *T''*, both of which are common subtypes of *T1* and *T2* and both of which satisfy the conditions of our revised IM Prescription 8S. For if they both satisfy those conditions, they are both, precisely, the intersection of *T1* and *T2;* hence they are identical. In other words, if *T1* and *T2* overlap, they have precisely one **least specific common subtype** (viz., the applicable intersection subtype)—and so, e.g., the situation shown in Fig. 15.4 makes no sense. (The arcs in that figure are broken in order to indicate that, e.g., *T'* and *T''* are not necessarily *immediate* subtypes of *T1* and *T2*.)

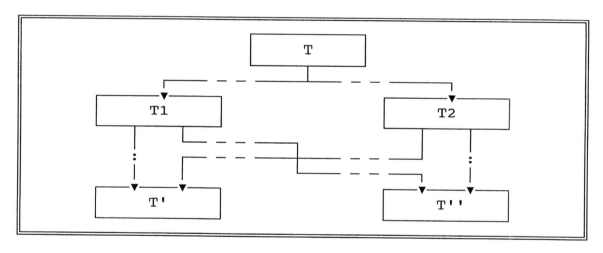

Fig. 15.4: Another graph that is not a valid type graph

Incidentally, note that "if and only if" in our revised IM Prescription 8S. In other words, loosely speaking, not only must two overlapping types have a nonempty common subtype, but if two types have a nonempty common subtype, then they must overlap. See Fig. 15.3 for several illustrations of this point.

Any number of overlapping types: Next, our revised IM Prescription 8S needs very little by way of extension in order to cater for the case where *n* types all overlap each other for some *n* > 2. For example, let types *T1, T2,* and *T3* be such that they overlap pairwise, and let the intersection subtypes required by IM Prescription 8S be *Ta* (for *T2* and *T3*), *Tb* (for *T3* and *T1*), and *Tc* (for *T1* and *T2*). Then types *Ta, Tb,* and *Tc* also overlap pairwise, in general; however, the three intersection subtypes required for these types *Ta, Tb,* and *Tc* taken pairwise are in fact all the same type, *T'* say. Proof of this fact and development of a concrete example to illustrate it are left as exercises for the reader.

Following on from the foregoing discussion, however, we must now point out that type *T'* is thus the intersection subtype for *three* immediate supertypes, *Ta, Tb,* and *Tc!* We will return to this point near the end of the present section.

Most specific common supertypes unique: Next, observe that not only do any given pair of overlapping types *T1* and *T2* have exactly one least specific common subtype (as already explained), they also have exactly one **most specific common supertype,** as we now show. (You might want to draw some diagrams as you work through the following explanation.) First of all, *T1* and *T2* certainly have at least one common supertype: viz., the (unique) applicable root type. Now suppose they have two distinct common supertypes *Ta* and *Tb,* say, neither of which is a subtype of the other. Note that *Ta* and *Tb* also overlap, since they have a common subtype (actually at least two common subtypes, *T1* and *T2*). Suppose further that *Ta* and *Tb* do not have a common proper subtype *T* that is a common proper supertype of *T1* and *T2* (i.e., *Ta* and *Tb* are both "most specific" common supertypes of *T1* and *T2,* loosely speaking). Now rename the types as follows: Rename *T1* and *T2* as *T'* and *T'',* respectively; rename *Ta* and *Tb* as *T1* and *T2,* respectively. Then we have exactly the invalid situation (excluding the root type *T*) previously shown in Fig. 15.4! It follows that the original supertypes *Ta* and *Tb* cannot be distinct after all—they must in fact be the same type. Hence, as stated, *T1* and *T2* have precisely one most specific common supertype.[1]

Overlapping regular types have a regular most specific common supertype: Suppose types *T1* and *T2* overlap and are regular types. Then *their most specific common supertype,* T *say, must be a regular type also.* For suppose not. Let *T1* and *T2* have possible representations *PR1* and *PR2,* respectively. Then, in general, each of *PR1* and *PR2* will be quite independent of the other (since there is no common source for them to be derived from, because *T* is a dummy type). Thus, for example, *PR1* might have a component *C1* not present in *PR2,* and *PR2* might have a component *C2* not present in *PR1.*

Now let *T'* be the (required) least specific common subtype for types *T1* and *T2* (*T'* is required because *T1* and *T2* overlap). Then there is no way, in general, for an invocation of the selector corresponding to *PR1* to return a value of type *T'* (equivalently, of type *T2*), because that selector has no argument corresponding to *C2.* (To put it another way, if that selector invocation returns the value *v,* the expression THE_C2(*v*) is undefined.) Equivalently, *specialization by constraint from type* T1 *to type* T' *does not work*—and likewise for S by C from type *T2* to type *T',* of course. In other words, allowing *T* to be a dummy type leads to a violation of IM Prescription 10.

Here is an example to illustrate the foregoing discussion. Consider the type graph of Fig. 15.1 once again. While type PARALLELOGRAM could possibly have a dummy type—say PLANE_FIGURE (not shown in Fig. 15.1)—as a proper supertype, type PARALLELOGRAM itself must be a regular type, because types RECTANGLE and RHOMBUS are overlapping regular types.

Equality comparisons: Recall from IM Prescription 12 that the comparison $X = Y$ requires the declared types of *X* and *Y* to have a common supertype. Thus, for example, the following code fragment is valid:

```
VAR RE RECTANGLE ;
VAR RH RHOMBUS ;

IF RE = RH THEN ... END IF ;
```

The comparison RE = RH here is valid because types RECTANGLE and RHOMBUS do have a common supertype; moreover, it will give TRUE if and only if the two variables both contain the same *square* (i.e., a value of the common *sub*type).

---

1. It might help to point out that while the least specific common subtype of *T1* and *T2* is certainly the *intersection* of *T1* and *T2* (loosely speaking), the most specific common supertype of *T1* and *T2* is not necessarily the *union* of *T1* and *T2;* for example, some parallelograms are neither rectangles nor rhombi. It might also help to point out that the very same type can be both an intersection type and a union type; such would be the case with type SQUARE, for example, if every square was either a SMALL_SQUARE or a LARGE_SQUARE.

TREAT: Recall from IM Prescription 14 that the TREAT invocation TREAT_AS_*T*(*X*) requires *T* and the declared type of *X* to have a nonempty common subtype. Thus, for example, the following code fragment is valid:

```
VAR RE RECTANGLE ;
VAR RH RHOMBUS ;

RH := TREAT_AS_RHOMBUS ( RE ) ;
```

The TREAT invocation here is valid because types RECTANGLE and RHOMBUS do have a nonempty common subtype; moreover, it will succeed if and only if the current value of variable RE is of type SQUARE (i.e., if and only if RE currently contains a value of that common subtype). In other words, the assignment shown is logically equivalent to—and could equally well have been expressed as—the following:

```
RH := TREAT_AS_SQUARE ( RE ) ;
```

Type testing: Recall from IM Prescription 15 that the type test IS_*T*(*X*) requires *T* and the declared type of *X* to have a nonempty common subtype. Thus, for example, the following code fragment is valid:

```
VAR RE RECTANGLE ;

IF IS_RHOMBUS ( RE ) THEN ... END IF ;
```

The type test here is valid because types RECTANGLE and RHOMBUS do have a nonempty common subtype; moreover, it will give TRUE if and only if the current value of variable RE is of type SQUARE (i.e., if and only if RE currently contains a value of that common subtype). In other words, the IF statement shown is logically equivalent to—and could equally well have been expressed as—the following:

```
IF IS_SQUARE ( RE ) THEN ... END IF ;
```

An Extended Example

It is our experience that the full implications of all of the foregoing points are far from obvious. We therefore present another example, rather more complicated than the one given in Fig. 15.3, that repays careful study. Refer to Fig. 15.5 overleaf. *Note:* We briefly remind you of the definitions of some of the possibly less familiar geometric terms mentioned in that figure:

- A trapezoid is a quadrilateral with at least one pair of opposite sides parallel. By the way, you might or might not be interested to learn that in researching this example we discovered that a quadrilateral with two parallel sides is called a *trapezoid* in the United States and a *trapezium* in the United Kingdom, while a quadrilateral with no parallel sides is called a *trapezium* in the United States and a *trapezoid* in the United Kingdom. But we digress.

- A kite is a quadrilateral with mirror symmetry about a diagonal, none of whose included angles is greater than 180° (if this latter condition is not satisfied, the quadrilateral is not a kite but a dart). If ABCD is a kite that is symmetric about diagonal AC, then AB = AD and CB = CD.

- A cyclic quadrilateral is a quadrilateral whose vertices lie on a circle. A quadrilateral is cyclic if and only if its opposite angles add up to 180°.

- An isosceles trapezoid is a trapezoid with mirror symmetry about the line that connects the midpoints of its parallel sides. If ABCD is an isosceles trapezoid with AB parallel to CD, then BC = AD and the included angles at A and B are equal, as are the included angles at C and D.

- A right kite is a kite in which the angles subtended by the diagonal of symmetry are right angles (if ABCD is a kite that is symmetric about diagonal AC, then the angles at B and D are right angles).

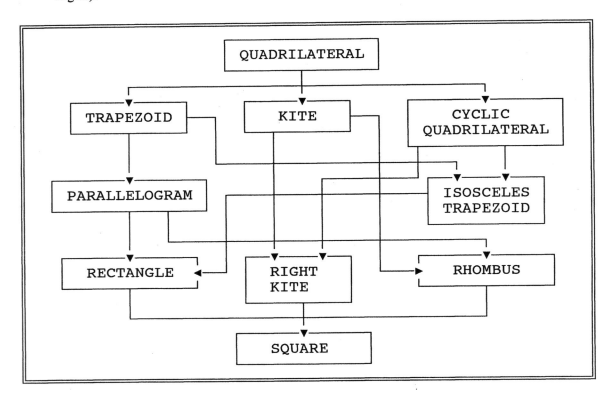

Fig. 15.5: Overlapping types must have a common subtype (a more complicated example)

"IM Prescription 8S" Revisited

We can now take care of a piece of unfinished business. In our discussion of the fifth "important logical consequence" in the previous subsection but one, we said that our revised IM Prescription 8S required very little extension to cater for the case of *n* mutually overlapping types where *n* > 2. However, our discussion of the issue quickly led to the need for a type *T'* that was the intersection subtype for *three* immediate supertypes *Ta, Tb,* and *Tc,* and so some extension is definitely needed. In fact, it should be clear, without having to go through a lot of detailed analysis, that all of the ideas we have been discussing do extend very straightforwardly to the case *n* > 2. Thus, we arrive at the following as the final and most general version of IM Prescription 8S:

> *Every set of types* T1, T2, ..., Tn *shall have a common subtype* T' *such that a given value is of each of the types* T1, T2, ..., Tn *if and only if it is of type* T'.

The value *n* here is an arbitrary nonnegative integer. Type *T'* is the unique intersection subtype—also known as the least specific common subtype—for types *T1, T2, ..., Tn.* Analogously, of course, types *T1, T2, ..., Tn* also have a unique most specific common supertype *T* (and *T* must be a regular type if *T1, T2, ..., Tn* are regular types and *T'* is nonempty).

Observe now that the formulation of "IM Prescription 8S" just given is in fact identical to the formulation we originally gave for IM Prescription 8 in Chapter 14! So we can drop our references to "IM Prescription 8S" as such from this point forward, and we will.

By way of an example to illustrate the foregoing, consider what happens if we delete types PARALLELOGRAM, ISOSCELES TRAPEZOID, RECTANGLE, RIGHT KITE, and RHOMBUS from the type graph of Fig. 15.5 (thus leaving QUADRILATERAL with three immediate subtypes, each of which is an immediate supertype of SQUARE).

One final point to close this section (repeated from Chapter 12): It should be clear that, sadly, it is always possible to make mistakes in setting up the type graph. For example, we might define the overlapping types RECTANGLE and RHOMBUS and forget to define the necessary intersection subtype SQUARE. The consequences of such mistakes will be unpredictable, in general; it is to be hoped that some kind of mechanical aid would be available in practice to help the person designing the type graph to avoid them.

REMARKS ON OPERATOR INHERITANCE

In this, the final section of the chapter, we turn our attention to two remaining issues. First, consider types RECTANGLE and RHOMBUS once again. Both of these types inherit the read-only operator AREA from type PARALLELOGRAM, and hence—as noted earlier in this chapter—type SQUARE inherits that operator from both of its immediate supertypes. What are the implications of this fact?

Well, if AREA is reimplemented for type SQUARE, there is no problem: An invocation AREA(*s*), where *s* is of most specific type SQUARE, will unambiguously refer to the version of AREA that has been defined for type SQUARE. But, of course, we would like to avoid such reimplementation as much as we reasonably can. Suppose, therefore, that AREA is not reimplemented for type SQUARE. Now there are two possibilities:

- If the semantics of the RECTANGLE and RHOMBUS versions of the AREA operator are the same—i.e., if the expression AREA(*s*) gives the same result, no matter whether the RECTANGLE version or the RHOMBUS version of AREA is invoked—then again there is no problem. (No problem so far as the model is concerned, that is. There will still have to be a way of telling the system which of the two versions is to be invoked. But this fact is of no concern to someone who is merely making use of type SQUARE; it is an implementation issue, not a model issue.)

- However, if the semantics of the RECTANGLE and RHOMBUS versions of the AREA operator differ, then it matters very much which version is inherited by type SQUARE. But now we face a logical absurdity! To say that SQUARE is a subtype of both RECTANGLE and RHOMBUS is to say that any given square is both a rectangle and a rhombus. But to go on and say that the area of that square depends on whether we think of it as a rectangle or as a rhombus is surely nonsense.

  As with our discussion of the TRAVEL_TIME operator in Chapter 14, therefore, we will set a stake in the ground here—as IM Prescription 17 in fact requires us to do—and insist that the semantics of the RECTANGLE and RHOMBUS versions of the AREA operator *must not* differ. (If they do, then the implementation is in violation; i.e., it is not an implementation of the model, and the implications are unpredictable.)

Now we turn to the second issue. Suppose some operator *Op* has been defined for rectangles and another operator with the same name *Op* has been defined for rhombi; suppose further that these operators are not inherited from parallelograms—i.e., there is no operator *Op* for type PARALLELOGRAM. Suppose also for simplicity that each of these operators takes just one parameter (of type RECTANGLE and type RHOMBUS, respectively). Suppose still further that the two operators named *Op* are really different operators (i.e., *Op* is overloaded). What do we do about the inheritance of *Op* by type SQUARE?

On the face of it, there *is* a problem here: By the very notion of type inheritance, both operators must indeed be inherited by type SQUARE, and an invocation *Op*(*s*), where *s* is of type SQUARE, would thus be ambiguous. Clearly, therefore, we must prohibit such a situation from arising in the first place. But that is exactly what the following rule (part of IM Prescription 17) does:

> Let *S* be a set of types with a nonempty common subtype. Then no two distinct operators shall have specification signatures that differ only in that, for some *i, j, ..., k,* the declared types of their *i*th parameters are distinct members of *S*, the declared types of their *j*th parameters are distinct members of *S*, ..., and the declared types of their *k*th parameters are distinct members of *S*.

Note: We do not expect this rule to cause significant hardship in practice, because the system should be able to detect violations as soon as they occur (i.e., at "operator definition time").

EXERCISES

1. Repeat Exercise 11 from Chapter 12—"Define an operator to rotate a specified rectangle through 90° about its center"—using the definition given for type RECTANGLE in this chapter.

2. Provide **Tutorial D** code for the operators AREA, CTR, CIR_CIRCLE, IN_CIRCLE, and ANNULUS from the section "An Introductory Example" (subsection "Operators") in the body of this chapter.

3. Identify all of the intersection types in Fig. 15.5.

4. Is type QUADRILATERAL in Fig. 15.5 a union type? If it is, do you think it should be a dummy type? Justify your answers.

5. How many possreps can you think of for type RIGHT KITE from Fig. 15.5? Write a **Tutorial D** definition for that type.

6. Give a concrete example of distinct types A, B, C, D, E such that A and B have C as a subtype and C has D and E as subtypes. *Note:* One such example was mentioned in passing in the body of the chapter (where?); you can give that example as your answer if you like, but we would prefer you to invent one of your own.

7. The definition of *type graph* in the body of the chapter includes the following: If nodes *T1, T2, T',* and *T''* are such that there exist paths from both *T1* and *T2* to both *T'* and *T''*, then there must exist a node *T* that is common to all of those paths. Show that this point is a logical consequence of IM Prescription 8.

8. *(Paraphrased from the body of the chapter.)* Let types *T1, T2,* and *T3* overlap pairwise, and let the corresponding intersection subtypes be *Ta* (for *T2* and *T3*), *Tb* (for *T3* and *T1*), and *Tc* (for *T1* and *T2*). Show that:

   ■ Types *Ta, Tb,* and *Tc* also overlap pairwise, in general.

   ■ The three intersection subtypes required for these types *Ta, Tb,* and *Tc* taken pairwise are in fact all the same type.

(Drawing a Venn diagram will help you visualize this situation and might suggest a proof.) Also give a concrete example to illustrate the foregoing possibility.

9. Let RATIONAL_p_q ($p \geq 1$, $q \geq 0$) be a family of types such that a value v is a value of type RATIONAL_p_q if and only if it is a number whose decimal representation takes the form *int.frac,* where:

    ■ *int* and *frac* are both sequences of decimal digits.

    ■ *int* involves no more than *p-q* digits (leading zeros are insignificant and can be dropped).

    ■ *frac* involves no more than *q* digits (trailing zeros are insignificant and can be dropped).

    Do you agree that type RATIONAL_p'_q' is a subtype of type RATIONAL_p_q if and only if $p' \leq p$ and $q' \leq q$? Do you agree that we have a case of multiple inheritance on our hands? What are the corresponding root types? Are those root types dummy types? Does value substitutability apply? Are there any operators that apply to values of type RATIONAL_p'_q' and not to values of type RATIONAL_p_q? Does S by C apply? Is there a nonempty type that is a subtype of all possible types in the family?

10. Following on from the previous exercise, consider the literal 0012.30. What is the declared type of this literal? What is the most specific type? What is the *least* specific type?

11. Again following on from Exercise 9, what is the relationship of type INTEGER to the RATIONAL_p_q family?

Chapter 16

Inheritance with

Tuple and Relation Types

In the previous two chapters we have presented, described, and illustrated a series of prescriptions for a model of subtyping and inheritance for scalar types. Now we turn our attention to the question of extending that model to take tuple and relation types into account as well—as indeed we really must, since we explicitly permit domains in the usual relational sense to be tuple or relation types in addition to the more traditional scalar types.

The style of presentation in what follows resembles that of Chapter 14; in other words, most of the sections consist of (a) a formal definition, followed by (b) an informal discussion (with examples) of the concepts involved in that definition. And once again we use the symbols T and T' generically to refer to a pair of types such that T' is a subtype of T (equivalently, such that T is a supertype of T')—but now, of course, those types might be tuple or relation types instead of just scalar types as previously.

One last introductory remark: It might have been thought better, at least from a pedagogic viewpoint, to treat tuple types exclusively first, and then to extend the treatment to include relation types subsequently. In practice, however, tuple and relation type inheritance are so intricately intertwined that it is virtually impossible to treat them separately. Indeed, it turns out that many of the concepts and definitions to be discussed:

- Come in pairs (a tuple version and a relation version), and

- Are both recursive (they refer to themselves) and mutually recursive (they refer to each other).

Indeed, this state of affairs is not really surprising, given that tuples can contain relation- and tuple-valued attributes and relations can contain tuple- and relation-valued attributes.

A small point of nomenclature: In what follows, we occasionally find it convenient, especially in section titles, to use the term *tuple/relation* as an abbreviation for either *tuple and relation* or *tuple or relation,* as the sense demands, when such terms are used as a qualifier (as in, e.g., the phrase "tuple and relation types," which we would thereby abbreviate to just *tuple/relation types*). The section title immediately following illustrates the point.

IM PRESCRIPTION 21: TUPLE/RELATION SUBTYPES AND SUPERTYPES

Let types T *and* T' *be both tuple types or both relation types, with headings*

    { <A1,T1>, <A2,T2>, ..., <An,Tn> }

    { <A1,T1'>, <A2,T2'>, ..., <An,Tn'> }

respectively. Then type T' *is a* **subtype** *of type* T *(equivalently, type* T *is a* **supertype** *of type* T' *) if and only if, for all* i *(i = 1, 2, ..., n), type* Ti' *is a subtype of type* Ti *(equivalently, type* Ti *is a supertype of type* Ti' *).*

———— ♦ ♦ ♦ ♦ ♦ ————

Consider the following variable definition:

```
VAR TV TUPLE { E ELLIPSE, R RECTANGLE } ;
```

TV here is a tuple variable, with declared type

```
TUPLE { E ELLIPSE, R RECTANGLE }
```

Values of this type are tuples with two attributes, one called E and ellipse valued, the other called R and rectangle valued.

Now, thanks to substitutability, a variable of declared type ELLIPSE can have a value that is a circle, because CIRCLE is a subtype of ELLIPSE; likewise, a variable of declared type RECTANGLE can have a value that is a square, because SQUARE is a subtype of RECTANGLE. In like fashion, the variable TV can have a value whose E value is a circle or whose R value is a square or both. What are the implications of this fact? Well, consider the following tuple types:

```
TUPLE { E ELLIPSE, R RECTANGLE }       /* tuple type "ER" */

TUPLE { E CIRCLE,  R RECTANGLE }       /* tuple type "CR" */

TUPLE { E ELLIPSE, R SQUARE    }       /* tuple type "ES" */

TUPLE { E CIRCLE,  R SQUARE    }       /* tuple type "CS" */
```

Let us refer to these types by the names ER, CR, ES, and CS, respectively, as the comments indicate. Note that they all have the same attribute names; clearly, then, tuples of any of these four types can all be values of the tuple variable TV. Note too that all four of these types are at least implicitly available, even though we have not explicitly defined any variables of types CR, ES, or CS. (Recall that, in **Tutorial D** at least, tuple types can simply be *used*—typically as part of the operation that defines a tuple variable, as in the case of tuple variable TV—without being separately defined. In fact, **Tutorial D** deliberately does not provide any kind of explicit "define tuple type" operator, for reasons explained in Chapters 3 and 6.)

Now let us concentrate for a moment on the two extreme cases, types ER and CS. Does it make sense to regard type CS as a "subtype" of "supertype" ER? Well, it should be clear that:

- Every type constraint that applies to values of type ER also applies to values of type CS, while the converse is not true, in general. (We remind you that the only type constraints, as such, that apply to tuple types in our model are constraints that are a logical consequence of the ones that apply to the scalar types in terms of which those tuple types are ultimately defined. Thus, there is no way tuple type ER could be subject to any type constraint that did not also apply to tuple type CS.)

- Hence, every value of type CS is certainly a value of type ER, while the converse is not true, in general.

- Every operator that applies to values of type ER also applies to values of type CS, while the converse is not true, in general. The operators that apply to values of type ER (and therefore to values of type CS) are (a) the built-in tuple operators of **D** (tuple comparisons, tuple rename, tuple join, and so on), together with (b) those user-defined tuple operators, if any, that have been defined for type ER. The operators that apply to values of type CS but not to values of type ER are (a) "compound" operators such as THE_R(E FROM ...) that rely on attribute E being of declared type CIRCLE or attribute R being of declared type SQUARE, together with (b) those user-defined tuple operators, if any, that have been defined for type CS specifically.

Now, all of these observations are in accord with our usual understanding of what it means for one type to be a subtype of another, so there does seem to be a prima facie case for regarding CS as a subtype of ER (equivalently, ER as a supertype of CS). But is it useful to do so? The answer, of course, is *yes*. In particular, the concept of *value substitutability* is applicable, meaning that wherever the system expects a tuple of type ER, we can always substitute a tuple of type CS instead. Among other things, therefore, we can assign a tuple of type CS to a variable of declared type ER, and we can test a variable of declared type CS and a variable of declared type ER for equality.

In a similar manner, we can say that types CR and ES are both subtypes of type ER and both supertypes of CS (note, however, that neither of CR and ES is a subtype of the other). And so CS is a subtype with two immediate supertypes, and we are dealing with multiple inheritance—which is one reason why we wanted to discuss multiple inheritance before considering tuple and relation type inheritance. It is also one reason[1] why we believe support for multiple inheritance is a logical requirement (assuming inheritance is supported at all, that is).

With the foregoing example by way of motivation, let us now try to define exactly what it means for tuple type *TT'* to be a subtype of tuple type *TT*. First of all, of course, *TT'* and *TT* must certainly have the same attribute names (for otherwise there is no way a value of type *TT'* could be a value of type *TT*). Thus, we might attempt a definition along the following lines:

- Let tuple types *TT* and *TT'* have headings

    ```
    { <A1,T1>,  <A2,T2>,  ..., <An,Tn>  }
    ```

    ```
    { <A1,T1'>, <A2,T2'>, ..., <An,Tn'> }
    ```

    respectively. Then tuple type *TT'* is a **subtype** of tuple type *TT* (equivalently, tuple type *TT* is a **supertype** of tuple type *TT'*) if and only if, for all *i* ($i = 1, 2, ..., n$), type *Ti'* is a subtype of type *Ti* (equivalently, type *Ti* is a supertype of type *Ti'*).

And this definition is perfectly acceptable, provided we understand that, for any given *i*, types *Ti* and *Ti'* might themselves be tuple or relation types in turn (because, of course, tuples can have tuple- and relation-valued attributes). In other words, our definition of what it means for one tuple type to be a subtype of another:

- Is recursive (a fact that should not cause any problems in itself, of course), but also

- Relies on a definition of what it means for one relation type to be a subtype of another—a possibility we have not yet considered.

So let us now turn our attention to this latter possibility. Suppose we have a relation variable (relvar) RV, say, defined thus:

```
VAR RV ... RELATION { E ELLIPSE, R RECTANGLE } ... ;
```

Then it should be clear that the current relation value of RV might include tuples of any mixture of the four tuple types ER, CR, ES, and CS discussed above. Thus, that current relation value might reasonably be of any of the following relation types:

---

1. The other has to do with type *omega,* as we saw in Chapter 14.

```
RELATION { E ELLIPSE, R RECTANGLE }     /* relation type "ER" */

RELATION { E CIRCLE,  R RECTANGLE }     /* relation type "CR" */

RELATION { E ELLIPSE, R SQUARE   }      /* relation type "ES" */

RELATION { E CIRCLE,  R SQUARE   }      /* relation type "CS" */
```

For example, if every tuple it contains is of tuple type CS, that relation will be of relation type CS.

Without going through the detailed analysis—it parallels that already given for the tuple case above—it should be clear that we can regard relation type CS as a subtype of relation type ER (equivalently, relation type ER as a supertype of relation type CS), and so on. Here then is a definition of what it means for relation type *RT'* to be a subtype of relation type *RT:*

- Let relation types *RT* and *RT'* have headings

  ```
  { <A1,T1>,  <A2,T2>,  ..., <An,Tn>  }
  ```

  ```
  { <A1,T1'>,  <A2,T2'>,  ..., <An,Tn'>  }
  ```

  respectively. Then relation type *RT'* is a **subtype** of relation type *RT* (equivalently, relation type *RT* is a **supertype** of relation type *RT'*) if and only if, for all *i* (*i* = 1, 2, ..., *n*), type *Ti'* is a subtype of type *Ti* (equivalently, type *Ti* is a supertype of type *Ti'*).

Again, however, it must be understood that, for any given *i*, types *Ti* and *Ti'* might themselves be tuple or relation types. In other words, our definition of what it means for one relation type to be a subtype of another:

- Is recursive, and also

- Relies on a definition of what it means for one tuple type to be a subtype of another (but this latter is a possibility we have already discussed).

To sum up, therefore: The definitions of *tuple subtype* and *relation subtype* are each both recursive (they refer to themselves) and mutually recursive (they refer to each other). Ultimately, however, they each rely on the notion of a *scalar* subtype, a notion that has already been defined in earlier chapters. And, of course—the point is obvious but is still worth stating explicitly—if tuple/relation type *T'* is a subtype of tuple/relation type *T* and *v* is a tuple or relation of type *T'*, then *v* is also a tuple or relation of type *T*.

Given the foregoing definitions, it turns out that all of the IM Prescriptions discussed in Chapters 14 and 15 apply essentially unchanged to tuples and relations as well, just so long as we are careful to interpret, e.g., the term *value* as now meaning a tuple or relation value instead of a scalar value. However:

- Certain of those existing prescriptions (primarily IM Prescriptions 11-15) do merit further attention.

- Four more prescriptions are also needed (IM Prescriptions 22-25), in addition to the one we have been discussing (IM Prescription 21). Those additional prescriptions all have to do with tuple and relation analogs of IM Prescriptions 8 and 9 ("scalar values and variables with inheritance").

These matters are discussed and explained in the sections that follow.

IM PRESCRIPTION 22: TUPLE/RELATION VALUES WITH INHERITANCE

Let {H} be a heading defined as follows:

```
{ <A1,T1>, <A2,T2>, ..., <An,Tn> }
```

Then:

a.   t *is a tuple that* **conforms** *to heading {H} if and only if* t *is of the form*

```
{ <A1,T1',v1>, <A2,T2',v2>, ..., <An,Tn',vn> }
```

where, for all i *(i = 1, 2, ..., n), type* Ti' *is a subtype of type* Ti *and* vi *is a value of type* Ti'.

b.   r *is a relation that* **conforms** *to heading {H} if and only if* r *consists of a heading and a body, where:*

- *The heading of* r *is of the form*

$$\{ <A1,T1'>, <A2,T2'>, ..., <An,Tn'> \}$$

   where, for all i *(i = 1, 2, ..., n), type* Ti' *is a subtype of type* Ti.

- *The body of* r *is a set of tuples, all of which conform to the heading of* r.

You might have noticed in the previous section that, although we explained what it meant for tuple/relation type *T'* to be a subtype of tuple/relation type *T*, we did not really pin down just what it meant for a given *value* to be of a given tuple/relation type; in fact, we deliberately ducked the issue in that section, because it is not quite as straightforward as might at first be thought (especially in the relational case). Now we turn our attention to that issue.

First, tuples. Let tuple type *T* have heading

```
{ <A1,T1>, <A2,T2>, ..., <An,Tn> }
```

Then we define *t* to be a tuple that **conforms** to the heading of type *T*—equivalently, we say that *t* is **of type** *T*—if and only if it is of the form

```
{ <A1,T1',v1>, <A2,T2',v2>, ..., <An,Tn',vn> }
```

where, for all *i* (*i* = 1, 2, ..., *n*), type *Ti'* is a subtype of type *Ti*—equivalently, type *Ti* is a supertype of type *Ti'*—and *vi* is a value of type *Ti'*.[1] And, of course, values of type *T* are precisely the tuples that are of type *T*.

_____

1. This definition is a compatible extension to the definition in RM Prescription 9 of what it means for a given tuple to conform to a given heading or to be of a given type. An analogous remark applies to relations too (see later).

Example: The tuple returned by the tuple selector invocation

```
TUPLE { E CIRCLE (...), R SQUARE (...) }
```

(note the CIRCLE and SQUARE selector invocations nested inside this tuple selector invocation) is of all four of the tuple types ER, CR, ES, CS discussed in the previous section.

Once again, of course, type Ti' in the foregoing definition might be a tuple or relation type in turn. Hence, that definition:

- Is recursive again (it relies on a definition of what it means for a value to be of a given tuple type), and also

- Relies on a definition of what it means for a value to be of a given *relation* type.

So let us now turn to this latter question. Let relation type T have heading

```
{ <A1,T1>, <A2,T2>, ..., <An,Tn> }
```

Then we define r to be a relation that **conforms** to the heading of type T—equivalently, we say that r is of type T—if and only if it consists of a heading and a body, where:

- The heading is of the form

```
{ <A1,T1'>, <A2,T2'>, ..., <An,Tn'> }
```

where, for all i ($i = 1, 2, ..., n$), type Ti' is a subtype of type Ti (equivalently, type Ti is a supertype of type Ti').

- The body is a set of tuples, all of which conform to the heading of r.

And, of course, values of type T are precisely the relations that are of type T.

Example: Consider the following relation type ("relation type ER") once again:

```
RELATION { E ELLIPSE, R RECTANGLE }    /* relation type "ER" */
```

Fig. 16.1 shows a few relations of this type. *Note:* We adopt the convention in that figure that values of the form Ei are ellipses that are not circles, values of the form Ri are rectangles that are not squares, values of the form Ci are circles, and values of the form Si are squares. The most specific types for all such values are shown in lowercase italics. (Perhaps we should elaborate briefly on the last example in particular. By definition, no scalar value is of type *omega* and no tuple value has an attribute of type *omega*. However, a relation value *can* have an attribute of type *omega*—though any such relation is necessarily empty.)

It follows from the foregoing definitions that:

- If tuple t is of type TT, it is also of all supertypes of TT.

- If relation r is of type RT, it is also of all supertypes of RT.

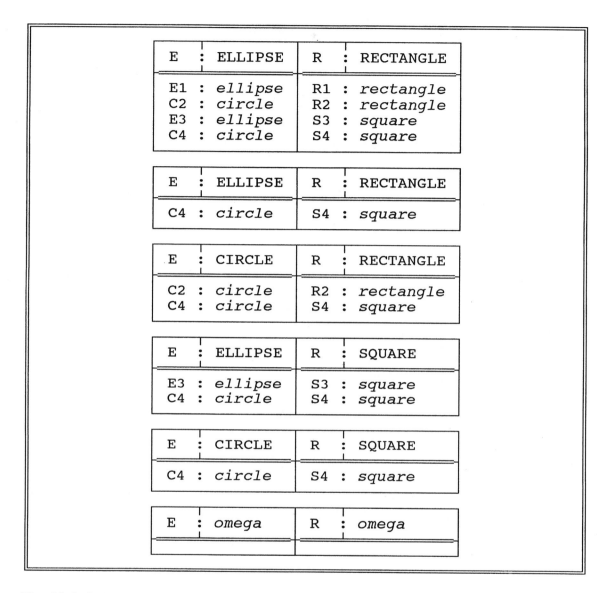

Fig. 16.1: Relations of type RELATION { E ELLIPSE, R RECTANGLE }

IM PRESCRIPTION 23: MAXIMAL AND MINIMAL TUPLE/RELATION TYPES

Let types T, T_alpha, *and* T_omega *be all tuple types or all relation types, with headings*

```
{ <A1,T1>,        <A2,T2>,        ..., <An,Tn>        }

{ <A1,T1_alpha>, <A2,T2_alpha>, ..., <An,Tn_alpha> }

{ <A1,T1_omega>, <A2,T2_omega>, ..., <An,Tn_omega> }
```

respectively. *Then types* T_alpha *and* T_omega *are **the maximal type with respect to type** T *and **the minimal type with respect to type** T, *respectively, if and only if, for all* i *(*i = 1, 2, ..., n*), type* Ti_alpha *is the maximal type with respect to type* Ti *and type* Ti_omega *is the minimal type with respect to type* Ti.

IM Prescription 20 introduced the special scalar—in fact, dummy—types *alpha* and *omega*. Just to review briefly:

■   *Alpha* is *the maximal scalar type;* it contains all scalar values (but no nonscalar values) and is a supertype of all scalar types. More precisely, it is a proper supertype of every scalar type except itself, and an immediate supertype of every scalar type except itself that would otherwise be a root type.

■   *Omega* is *the minimal scalar type;* it contains no scalar values at all (and no nonscalar values either!) and is a subtype of all scalar types. More precisely, it is a proper subtype of every scalar type except itself, and an immediate subtype of every scalar type except itself that would otherwise be a leaf type.

Note: We can and do refer to *alpha* and *omega,* a trifle more formally, as the maximal and minimal type, respectively, *with respect to any given scalar type.* This tiny matter of terminology will become significant in just a moment.

Now, analogs of *alpha* and *omega* do exist in connection with tuple and relation types, as you would surely expect, but the situation is a little more complicated than it is with scalar types, as you would probably also expect. We begin by considering the issue of maximal types. Here is a definition:

■   Let tuple types *TT* and *TT_alpha* have headings

```
{ <A1,T1>,       <A2,T2>,        ..., <An,Tn>       }

{ <A1,T1_alpha>, <A2,T2_alpha>, ..., <An,Tn_alpha> }
```

respectively. Then tuple type *TT_alpha* is **the maximal type with respect to type** *TT* if and only if, for all i ($i = 1, 2, ..., n$), type *Ti_alpha* is the maximal type with respect to type *Ti.*

Once again, of course, type *Ti* in the foregoing definition might be a tuple or relation type in turn. Hence, that definition:

■   Is recursive again, and also

■   Relies on a definition of what it means for a *relation* type to be a maximal type.

Let us therefore now turn to this latter question.

■   Let relation types *RT* and *RT_alpha* have headings

```
{ <A1,T1>,       <A2,T2>,        ..., <An,Tn>       }

{ <A1,T1_alpha>, <A2,T2_alpha>, ..., <An,Tn_alpha> }
```

respectively. Then relation type *RT_alpha* is **the maximal type with respect to type** *RT* if and only, if for all i ($i = 1, 2, ..., n$), type *Ti_alpha* is the maximal type with respect to type *Ti.*

Examples: The maximal type with respect to the tuple type

```
TUPLE { E ELLIPSE, R RECTANGLE }
```

is TUPLE { E *alpha*, R *alpha* }. Likewise, the maximal type with respect to the relation type

```
RELATION { E ELLIPSE, R RECTANGLE }
```

is RELATION { E *alpha*, R *alpha* }. Observe, therefore, that whereas with scalar types there is just one maximal type that applies to all possible scalar types, the same is not true for tuple and relation types. Rather, there is one tuple maximal type for each possible tuple type (loosely speaking), and one relation maximal type for each possible relation type (again, loosely speaking). More precisely, if and only if tuple types *TT1* and *TT2* have no common supertype, then the corresponding tuple maximal types are distinct (and analogously for relation types).

Another precise statement is the following: Tuple type *TT_alpha* contains all possible tuples of type some subtype or supertype of tuple type *TT*, and no other tuples (and analogously for relation type *RT_alpha*).

The definitions for minimal types parallel the foregoing definitions for maximal types, of course. To be specific:

■   Let tuple types *TT* and *TT_omega* have headings

```
{ <A1,T1>,        <A2,T2>,        ..., <An,Tn>        }

{ <A1,T1_omega>, <A2,T2_omega>, ..., <An,Tn_omega> }
```

respectively. Then tuple type *TT_omega* is **the minimal type with respect to type *TT*** if and only if, for all *i* ($i = 1, 2, ..., n$), type *Ti_omega* is the minimal type with respect to type *Ti*.

■   Let relation types *RT* and *RT_omega* have headings

```
{ <A1,T1>,        <A2,T2>,        ..., <An,Tn>        }

{ <A1,T1_omega>, <A2,T2_omega>, ..., <An,Tn_omega> }
```

respectively. Then tuple type *RT_omega* is **the minimal type with respect to type *RT*** if and only if, for all *i* ($i = 1, 2, ..., n$), type *Ti_omega* is the minimal type with respect to type *Ti*.

Examples: The minimal type with respect to the tuple type

```
TUPLE { E ELLIPSE, R RECTANGLE }
```

is TUPLE { E *omega*, R *omega* }. Likewise, the minimal type with respect to the relation type

```
RELATION { E ELLIPSE, R RECTANGLE }
```

is RELATION { E *omega*, R *omega* }. In general, the situation with respect to minimal types is analogous to that for maximal types; to be specific, there is one tuple minimal type for each possible tuple type (loosely speaking), and one relation minimal type for each possible relation type (again, loosely speaking). More precisely, if and only if tuple types *TT1* and *TT2* have no common subtype, then the corresponding tuple minimal types are distinct (and analogously for relation types). Also:

■   Unlike the scalar minimal type *omega*, the tuple minimal type *TT_omega* is not necessarily empty.

The particular example shown earlier—TUPLE { E *omega*, R *omega* }—is empty, of course (there are no tuples of this type). A conceptually important counterexample is as follows: Let *TT* be TUPLE{}. Then *TT_omega* is equal to *TT* (i.e., *TT* is its own minimal type), and it contains exactly one value: namely, the 0-tuple (i.e., the tuple with the empty set of attributes).

■ Moreover, the relation minimal type *RT_omega* is definitely not empty; as noted in Chapter 6, in fact, there is no such thing as an empty relation type (the very phrase is a contradiction in terms). The example shown earlier—RELATION { E *omega*, R *omega* }—contains exactly one value: namely, the empty relation of that type (which was illustrated in Fig. 16.1). Another conceptually important case is as follows: Let *RT* be RELATION{}. Then *RT_omega* is equal to *RT* (i.e., *RT* is its own minimal type), and it contains two values, TABLE_DEE and TABLE_DUM.

IM PRESCRIPTION 24: TUPLE/RELATION MOST SPECIFIC TYPES

Let {H} be a heading defined as follows:

```
{ <A1,T1>, <A2,T2>, ..., <An,Tn> }
```

Then:

a. *If* t *is a tuple that conforms to* H—*meaning* t *is of the form*

```
{ <A1,T1',v1>, <A2,T2',v2>, ..., <An,Tn',vn> }
```

where, for all i *(*i = 1, 2, ..., n)*, type* Ti' *is a subtype of type* Ti *and* vi *is a value of type* Ti'—*then the **most specific** type of* t *is*

```
TUPLE { <A1,MST1>, <A2,MST2>, ..., <An,MSTn> }
```

where, for all i *(*i = 1, 2, ..., n)*, type* MSTi *is the most specific type of value* vi.

b. *If* r *is a relation that conforms to* H—*meaning the body of* r *is a set of tuples, each of which has as its most specific type a type that is a subtype of the type* TUPLE{H}, *and meaning further that each such tuple can be regarded without loss of generality as being of the form*

```
{ <A1,T1',v1>, <A2,T2',v2>, ..., <An,Tn',vn> }
```

where, for all i *(*i = 1, 2, ..., n)*, type* Ti' *is a subtype of type* Ti *and is the most specific type of value* vi *(note that distinct tuples in the body of* r *will be of distinct most specific types, in general; thus, type* Ti' *varies over the tuples in the body of* r*)—then the **most specific** type of* r *is*

```
RELATION { <A1,MST1>, <A2,MST2>, ..., <An,MSTn> }
```

where, for all i *(*i = 1, 2, ..., n)*, type* MSTi *is the most specific common supertype of those most specific types* Ti', *taken over all tuples in the body of* r.

The concept of most specific type does apply to tuples and relations, though the situation is considerably more complicated than it is for scalars (at least in the case of relations, where the terminology of "most" specific type is arguably a trifle misleading; the tuple case is comparatively straightforward). As usual, it turns out that the definitions are both recursive and mutually recursive.

First of all, then, let t be a tuple of the form

```
{ <A1,T1,v1>, <A2,T2,v2>, ..., <An,Tn,vn> }
```

Then we define the **most specific** type of t to be that unique tuple type with heading

```
{ <A1,MST1>, <A2,MST2>, ..., <An,MSTn> }
```

where, for all i ($i = 1, 2, ..., n$), type $MSTi$ is the most specific type of value vi.

Example: Let t be the tuple

```
TUPLE { E EX, R RX }
```

and let the most specific types of EX and RX be CIRCLE and SQUARE, respectively. Then the most specific type of t is

```
TUPLE { E CIRCLE, R SQUARE }
```

("tuple type CS").

Now let r be a relation with heading

```
{ <A1,T1>, <A2,T2>, ..., <An,Tn> }
```

Then the body of r is a set of tuples, each of which has as its most specific type a type that is a subtype of the tuple type with the same heading as r. In other words, each such tuple can be regarded without loss of generality as being of the form

```
{ <A1,T1',v1>, <A2,T2',v2>, ..., <An,Tn',vn> }
```

where, for all i ($i = 1, 2, ..., n$), type Ti' is a subtype of type Ti, and is in fact the most specific type of value vi. Note that distinct tuples in the body of r will be of distinct most specific types, in general; thus, type Ti' varies over the tuples in the body of r. Then we define the **most specific** type of r to be that unique relation type with heading

```
{ <A1,MST1>, <A2,MST2>, ..., <An,MSTn> }
```

where, for all i ($i = 1, 2, ..., n$), type $MSTi$ is the most specific common supertype (note that "*super*type"!) of the types Ti', taken over all tuples in the body of r. See the explanation of "most specific common supertype" (for a set of types) immediately following.

Definition of *most specific common supertype:*[1] First, let T and T' be two scalar types. Then the most specific common supertype of T and T' is as defined in the previous chapter.

Second, let $T1, T2, ..., Tn$ and $T1', T2', ..., Tn'$ be two sets of types, where, for all i ($i = 1, 2, ..., n$), Ti and Ti' (a) are both scalar types or both tuple types or both relation types, and moreover (b)

---

1. The definitions that follow are a generalization of the definition given for scalar types in Chapter 15. Note that in these definitions we break for once with our convention that type T' is always a subtype of type T.

have a common supertype. Now:

- Consider tuple types T and T', with headings

  ```
  { <A1,T1>,  <A2,T2>,  ...,  <An,Tn> }
  ```

  ```
  { <A1,T1'>,  <A2,T2'>,  ...,  <An,Tn'> }
  ```

  respectively. Then we define the most specific common supertype of types T and T' to be the unique tuple type with heading

  ```
  { <A1,MSC1>,  <A2,MSC2>,  ...,  <An,MSCn> }
  ```

  where, for all i ($i = 1, 2, ..., n$), $MSCi$ is the most specific common supertype of Ti and Ti'.

- Consider relation types T and T', with headings

  ```
  { <A1,T1>,  <A2,T2>,  ...,  <An,Tn> }
  ```

  ```
  { <A1,T1'>,  <A2,T2'>,  ...,  <An,Tn'> }
  ```

  respectively. Then we define the most specific common supertype of types T and T' to be the unique relation type with heading

  ```
  { <A1,MSC1>,  <A2,MSC2>,  ...,  <An,MSCn> }
  ```

  where, for all i ($i = 1, 2, ..., n$), $MSCi$ is the most specific common supertype of Ti and Ti'.

The definition of most specific common supertype for a set of N types for $N > 2$, where the types are all scalar types or all tuple types or all relation types and all have a common supertype, follows by pairwise application of the foregoing definition to the set in question. But what about $N < 2$?

- The case $N = 1$ is straightforward—the set of types contains just one type, T say, and we can define the "most specific common supertype" for that set to be simply T itself.

- *However, we also need to address the case $N = 0$.* To be specific, what is the most specific common supertype for the (empty) set of types corresponding to the (empty) set of values of some attribute *within an empty relation?* You will probably not be surprised to learn that the answer to this question is the applicable minimal type. That is, if the declared type of the attribute in question is some scalar type, then the most specific common supertype is just *omega;*[1] if it is some tuple or relation type T, then the most specific common supertype is T_omega. *Note:* As an aside, we remark that the least specific common subtype of an empty set of types is, of course, the applicable maximal type.

Here then are some "most specific common supertype" examples. First, scalar types. The most specific common supertype of the set of types {POLYGON, RECTANGLE, SQUARE} is POLYGON;

---

1. This definition marks the first point in this book where we have encountered a practical use—a crucial practical use, in fact—for type *omega* (our previous discussions have all been primarily conceptual in nature). In an earlier paper [29], we said we were unable to find a use for the concept of an empty type; we are thus delighted to have found one here.

likewise, the most specific common supertype of the set of types {PLANE_FIGURE, RECTANGLE} is PLANE_FIGURE, and the most specific common supertype of the set of types {CIRCLE, SQUARE} is again PLANE_FIGURE. All of these examples are based on the type hierarchy in Fig. 12.1 from Chapter 12. Switching now to the type graph in Fig. 15.1 from Chapter 15, the most specific common supertype of the set of types {RECTANGLE, RHOMBUS} is PARALLELOGRAM; and the most specific common supertype of {}, where {} denotes the empty subset of the set of scalar types {RECTANGLE, RHOMBUS}, is simply *omega*.

Second, consider once again the tuple types

```
TUPLE { E ELLIPSE,  R RECTANGLE }        /* tuple type "ER" */

TUPLE { E CIRCLE,   R RECTANGLE }        /* tuple type "CR" */

TUPLE { E ELLIPSE,  R SQUARE    }        /* tuple type "ES" */

TUPLE { E CIRCLE,   R SQUARE    }        /* tuple type "CS" */
```

Then the most specific common supertype of CR and CS is CR; the most specific common supertype of ES and CS is ES; the most specific common supertype of CR and ES is ER; and the most specific common supertype of all four types is again ER.

Of course, we have only to replace these four tuple types by four analogous relation types to obtain a set of relation "most specific common supertype" examples.

Now we return to the real point of this section and consider the question of the most specific type of a given value. The scalar case has already been dealt with in Chapters 14 and 15, of course, and the tuple case is an obvious generalization of the scalar case—but the relation case is a little more complicated, as we now explain.

We begin by considering some examples. Take another look at the relations in Fig. 16.1. The most specific types of those relations are (from top to bottom) relation types ER, CS, CR, ES, CS again, and ER_*omega*, respectively (where by ER_*omega* we mean the type RELATION { E *omega*, R *omega* }, of course). Note further that, e.g., the top relation in that figure would still have relation type ER as its most specific type even if we deleted the only tuple—viz., the E1-R1 tuple—that is in fact of *tuple* type ER. (If we deleted the C2-R2 tuple as well, however, that relation would then have relation type ES as its most specific type.)

Now, you might feel something counterintuitive is going on here, and so it is, in a way. For example, look again at the top relation in Fig. 16.1 (call it *TopRel*). For relation *TopRel*, it almost seems as if we have defined the *most* specific type of that relation (viz., relation type ER) to be the *least* specific type of the tuples it contains!—and indeed so we have, in this particular example. Why then did we not define the most specific type of *TopRel* to be relation type CS (the other "extreme" type) instead? The answer is as follows:

- Suppose we had defined that most specific type to be CS instead of ER. Then certain of the attributes in certain of the tuples in *TopRel* would contain values that were not of the "right" type. The E1-R1 tuple, for example, contains a value of type ELLIPSE (not CIRCLE) and a value of type RECTANGLE (not SQUARE), and thus certainly is not of *tuple* type CS (in fact, it is of tuple type ER).

- But allowing a relation of relation type CS to contain a tuple of tuple type ER would be a contradiction in terms—it would mean, for example, that attribute E of that relation, of type CIRCLE, is allowed to include values that are "just ellipses" and not circles. Indeed, such a state of affairs would be just as bad as allowing a variable of declared type CIRCLE to have a value that is "just an ellipse."

It follows that we must define the most specific type for relation *r* in the way we have done: namely, in such a way that the type corresponding to attribute *A* is the most specific common supertype—and not, as might have been expected, the least specific common subtype—of the most specific types of all of the *A* values in *r*. As noted earlier, the terminology is perhaps a little misleading in the relational case.

In an attempt to help you understand better exactly what is going on here, we show in Fig. 16.2 below another set of relations, based on the type graph shown in Fig. 15.1 from Chapter 15. The most specific types of these relations (from top to bottom) are as follows:

- `RELATION { PX PARALLELOGRAM, PY RECTANGLE }`

- `RELATION { PX RHOMBUS,      PY RECTANGLE }`

- `RELATION { PX RECTANGLE,    PY SQUARE   }`

- `RELATION { PX SQUARE,       PY SQUARE   }`

- `RELATION { PX omega,        PY omega    }`

```
+-----------------------------+-----------------------------+
| PX : PARALLELOGRAM          | PY : PARALLELOGRAM          |
+-----------------------------+-----------------------------+
| X1 : rectangle              | Y1 : rectangle              |
| X2 : rhombus                | Y2 : rectangle              |
| X3 : rectangle              | Y3 : square                 |
| X4 : square                 | Y4 : square                 |
+-----------------------------+-----------------------------+

+-----------------------------+-----------------------------+
| PX : PARALLELOGRAM          | PY : PARALLELOGRAM          |
+-----------------------------+-----------------------------+
| X2 : rhombus                | Y2 : rectangle              |
| X4 : square                 | Y4 : square                 |
+-----------------------------+-----------------------------+

+-----------------------------+-----------------------------+
| PX : PARALLELOGRAM          | PY : PARALLELOGRAM          |
+-----------------------------+-----------------------------+
| X3 : rectangle              | Y3 : square                 |
| X4 : square                 | Y4 : square                 |
+-----------------------------+-----------------------------+

+-----------------------------+-----------------------------+
| PX : PARALLELOGRAM          | PY : PARALLELOGRAM          |
+-----------------------------+-----------------------------+
| X4 : square                 | Y4 : square                 |
+-----------------------------+-----------------------------+

+-----------------------------+-----------------------------+
| PX : PARALLELOGRAM          | PY : PARALLELOGRAM          |
+-----------------------------+-----------------------------+
|                             |                             |
+-----------------------------+-----------------------------+
```

Fig. 16.2: Relations of type RELATION { PX PARALLELOGRAM, PY PARALLELOGRAM }

By the way, you might find the last of these most specific types a little surprising (though it is in full accordance with all of our foregoing discussions). To be specific, you might have expected that type to be RELATION { PX *alpha*, PY *alpha* }. If it were, however, we would be faced with the unpalatable consequence that the relation in question could not be assigned to a relvar of type, say, RELATION { PX PARALLELOGRAM, PY PARALLELOGRAM }.

One further remark to close this section: Given the foregoing definition of the most specific type *MST(r)* of a relation *r*, we observe that computation of *MST(r)* might be too time consuming to be a practical proposition unless *r* is of low cardinality. One implication is that the implementer of an operator that has a parameter of some relation type might well want to avoid having special implementation versions of that operator to deal with proper subtypes of that relation type. For example, suppose we have an operator called AVG_AREA that computes the average area for the ellipses appearing in some attribute *A* of some relation *r*. Suppose further that two implementation versions of that operator exist, one for when *MST(A)* is ELLIPSE and one for when it is CIRCLE. Suppose finally that *r* contains a billion tuples, not one of which contains "just an ellipse" ... Clearly, then, the implementation will have to examine all billion tuples in order to perform the run-time binding process.

IM PRESCRIPTION 25: TUPLE/RELATION VARIABLES WITH INHERITANCE

Let tuple or relation variable V *be of declared type* T, *and let the heading of* T *have attributes* A1, A2, ..., An. *Then we can model* V *as a named set of named ordered triples of the form* <DTi,MSTi,vi>, *where:*

a.   *The name of the set is the name of the variable (*V *in the example).*

b.   *The name of each triple is the name of the corresponding attribute.*

c.   DTi *is the name of the declared type of attribute* Ai.

d.   MSTi *is the name of the **most specific type**—also known as the **current** most specific type—for, or of, attribute* Ai. *(If* V *is a relation variable, then the most specific type of* Ai *is the most specific common supertype of the most specific types of the* m *values in* vi—*see the explanation of* vi *below.)*

e.   *If* V *is a tuple variable,* vi *is a value of most specific type* MSTi—*the **current value** for, or of, attribute* Ai. *If* V *is a relation variable, then let the body of the current value of* V *consist of* m *tuples; label those tuples (in some arbitrary sequence) "tuple 1," "tuple 2," ..., "tuple m"; then* vi *is a sequence of* m *values (not necessarily all distinct), being the* Ai *values from tuple 1, tuple 2, ..., tuple m (in that order); note that all of those values are of type* MSTi.

We use the notation DT(Ai), MST(Ai), v(Ai) *to refer to the* DTi, MSTi, vi *components, respectively, of attribute* Ai *of this model of tuple or relation variable* V. *We also use the notation* DT(V), MST(V), v(V) *to refer to the overall declared type, overall current most specific type, and overall current value, respectively, of this model of tuple or relation variable* V.

Now let X *be a tuple or relation expression. By definition,* X *specifies an invocation of some tuple or relation operator* Op *(where the arguments, if any, to that invocation of* Op *are specified as expressions in turn). Thus, the notation* DTi(V), MSTi(V), vi(V) *just introduced can be extended in an obvious way to refer to the declared type* DTi(X), *the current most specific type* MSTi(X), *and the current value* vi(X), *respectively, of the* DTi, MSTi, vi *components, respectively, of attribute* Ai *of tuple or relation expression* X—*where* DTi(X) *is known at compile time, and* MSTi(X) *and* vi(X) *refer to the result of evaluating* X *and are therefore not known until run time (in general).*

Now (at last!) we are in a position to give the necessary extended definitions for *tuple variable* and *relation variable* (or relvar). Yet again, it turns out that the definitions are both recursive and mutually recursive.

Basically, of course, a **tuple variable of declared type** *TT* is a variable whose permitted values are tuples of type *TT*, and a **relation variable (relvar) of declared type** *RT* is a variable whose permitted values are relations of type *RT*. (In fact, these definitions are essentially the same as in Chapter 4—see RM Prescriptions 12 and 13—but the concept of a tuple or relation value being of a given type is now being given a considerably extended interpretation.)

We need to be a little more specific, however. In fact, what we really need is a model for tuple and relation variables, analogous to the model already described for scalar variables in Chapter 14. So let us examine this question. As usual, we consider tuples first.

Let tuple variable *V* be of declared type *T*, and let the heading of *T* have attributes *A1, A2, ..., An*. Then we can model *V* as a named set of named ordered triples of the form $<DTi,MSTi,vi>$, where:

- The name of the set is the name of the variable (*V* in the example).

- The name of each triple is the name of the corresponding attribute.

- *DTi* is the name of the declared type of attribute *Ai*.

- *MSTi* is the name of the **most specific type**—also known as the **current** most specific type—for, or of, attribute *Ai*.

- *vi* is a value of most specific type *MSTi*—the **current value** for, or of, attribute *Ai*.

We use the notation *DT(Ai)*, *MST(Ai)*, *v(Ai)* to refer to the *DTi*, *MSTi*, *vi* components, respectively, of attribute *Ai* of this model of tuple variable *V*. Of course, it must always be the case that *MST(Ai)* is some subtype—not necessarily a proper subtype—of *DT(Ai)*. Note also that *MST(Ai)* and *v(Ai)* change with time, in general; in other words, the phrase "most specific type of attribute *Ai*" refers to the most specific type of the value of *Ai* within the *current value* of tuple variable *V*, not to the most specific type that such *Ai* values are ever permitted to have. Note finally that *MST(Ai)* is in fact implied by *vi*.

We also use the notation *DT(V)*, *MST(V)*, *v(V)* to refer to the overall declared type, overall current most specific type, and overall current value (respectively), of tuple variable *V*. In other words (using **Tutorial D** notation):

- ```
  DT(V)  ≡ TUPLE { A1  DT1, A2  DT2, ..., An  DTn }
  ```

- ```
  MST(V) ≡ TUPLE { A1 MST1, A2 MST2, ..., An MSTn }
  ```

- ```
  v(V)   ≡ TUPLE { A1  v1, A2  v2, ..., An  vn }
  ```

DT(V)—and *MST(V)* and, for all *i*, *DTi* and *MSTi*—must not be empty.

Turning now to relation variables (i.e., relvars): Let relvar *V* be of declared type *T*, and let the heading of *T* have attributes *A1, A2, ..., An*. Let the body of the current value of *V* consist of *m* tuples; label those tuples (in some arbitrary sequence) "tuple 1," "tuple 2," ..., "tuple *m*." Then we can model *V* as a named set of named ordered triples of the form $<DTi,MSTi,vi>$, where:

- The name of the set is the name of the relvar (*V* in the example).
  ```

- The name of each triple is the name of the corresponding attribute.

- *DTi* is the name of the declared type of attribute *Ai*.

- *MSTi* is the name of the **most specific type**—also known as the **current** most specific type—for, or of, attribute *Ai* (it is in fact the most specific common supertype of the most specific types of the *m* values in *vi*—see below).

- *vi* is a sequence of *m* values (not necessarily all distinct), being the *Ai* values from tuple 1, tuple 2, ..., tuple *m* (in that order); all of those values are of type *MSTi*.

We use the notation *DT(Ai)*, *MST(Ai)*, *v(Ai)* to refer to the *DTi*, *MSTi*, *vi* components, respectively, of attribute *Ai* of this model of relvar *V*. Of course, it must always be the case that *MST(Ai)* is some subtype—not necessarily a proper subtype—of *DT(Ai)*. Note also that *MST(Ai)* and *v(Ai)* change with time, in general; in other words, the phrase "most specific type of attribute *Ai*" refers to the most specific common supertype of the most specific types of all of the *Ai* values within the *current value* of the relvar *V*, not to the most specific type that such *Ai* values are ever permitted to have. Note finally that *MST(Ai)* is in fact implied by *vi*.

We also use the notation *DT(V)*, *MST(V)*, *v(V)* to refer to the overall declared type, overall current most specific type, and overall current value (respectively), of relvar *V*. In other words (using **Tutorial D** notation):

- ```
  DT(V)   ≡  RELATION { A1 DT1, A2 DT2, ..., An DTn }
  ```

- ```
  MST(V)  ≡  RELATION { A1 MST1, A2 MST2, ..., An MSTn }
  ```

- ```
  v(V)    ≡  RELATION { TUPLE { A1 v11, A2 v12, ..., An v1n },
                        TUPLE { A1 v21, A2 v22, ..., An v2n },
                        ...............................
                        TUPLE { A1 vm1, A2 vm2, ..., An vmn } }
  ```

Here, of course, the symbol *vij* denotes the value of attribute *Aj* in tuple *i* ($i = 1, 2, ..., m; j = 1, 2, ..., n$).

SOME IMPLICATIONS OF IM PRESCRIPTIONS 21-25

As noted earlier in this chapter, the definitions in the four sections immediately preceding this one together constitute the tuple and relation analogs of IM Prescriptions 8 and 9 ("scalar values and variables with inheritance"). Now we turn to some important implications of those definitions.

Specialization by Constraint

IM Prescription 10 ("specialization by constraint") was formulated in Chapter 14 in terms of scalar types specifically—in part because tuple and relation types are not explicitly defined (at least in **Tutorial D**). If specialization by constraint is performed as prescribed for scalar types, however, it will happen "automatically" for tuple and relation types too, and nothing further needs to be said on the matter.
  ```

Union and Dummy Types

Remarks analogous to those in the preceding subsection apply to IM Prescription 20 (regarding union and dummy types) also, and effectively dispose of that issue as well. However, it is worth pointing out explicitly that a tuple type that includes an attribute of some union type will itself necessarily be a union type also (and likewise for dummy types, mutatis mutandis). By contrast, RELATION {A *omega*}, for example, is not a union type—why not?—even though its sole attribute is of a union, and in fact dummy, type.

Assignment

IM Prescription 11 ("assignment with inheritance") as discussed in Chapter 14 is sufficient to cover tuple and relation assignment too, provided we take the terms *variable* and *expression* in that prescription to refer to tuple or relation variables and expressions, as appropriate. Here is an example to illustrate tuple assignment:

```
VAR V1 TUPLE { P POINT, ER TUPLE { E ELLIPSE, R RECTANGLE } } ;
VAR V2 TUPLE { P POINT, ER TUPLE { E CIRCLE,  R SQUARE    } } ;

V2 := TUPLE { P POINT (...), ER TUPLE { E CIRCLE (...), R SQUARE (...) } } ;
V1 := V2 ;
```

After this latter assignment:

- *DT*(V1) is unchanged (it is the tuple type specified in the definition of V1, of course).

- *MST*(V1) is the same as *MST*(V2) (it is in fact the tuple type specified in the definition of V2, but only because that type happens to be the most specific type of the current value of V2).

- *v*(V1) is the same as *v*(V2).

Suppose now that V2 had been defined slightly differently:

```
VAR V2 TUPLE { Q POINT, ER TUPLE { E CIRCLE, R SQUARE } } ;
```

(the difference is that the point-valued attribute is now called Q instead of P). The assignment of V2 to V1 will now fail, because the declared type of V2 is no longer a subtype of that of V1 (this is a compile-time check). However, the following assignment is valid:

```
V1 := V2 RENAME ( Q AS P ) ;
```

It is only fair to point out a minor oddity here. Given *scalar* variables E and C of declared types ELLIPSE and CIRCLE, respectively, we can assign C to E. Yet if ET and CT are *tuple* variables, of tuple types TUPLE { E ELLIPSE } and TUPLE { C CIRCLE }, respectively, we cannot assign CT to ET; we have to assign CT RENAME (C AS E) to ET instead. The reason for this seeming anomaly is, of course, that tuple types have attributes, and the attribute names are part of the type; scalar types, by contrast, have no attributes, and so the question of the names of such attributes being somehow part of the type does not arise.

It should be clear that relational assignments obey the same general rules. We leave the provision of examples as an exercise for the reader.

Equality Comparisons

IM Prescription 12 ("equality etc. with inheritance") as discussed in Chapters 14 and 15 is sufficient to cover tuple and relation equality too, provided we take the term *expressions* to refer to tuple or relation expressions, as appropriate. Here is an example to illustrate tuple comparison:

```
VAR V1 TUPLE { E ELLIPSE, R SQUARE } ;     /* tuple type "ES" */
VAR V2 TUPLE { E CIRCLE,  R RECTANGLE } ; /* tuple type "CR" */

IF V1 = V2 THEN ... END IF ;
```

The comparison here is valid because tuple types ES and CR have a nonempty common subtype (tuple type CS). Further, it will give TRUE if (a) the current values of tuple variables V1 and V2 are of tuple type CS and (b) those current values are equal.

Relation comparison is analogous, of course. Further elaboration seems unnecessary, except to note that the rules regarding comparison operators other than equality ("is a subset of," etc.) can be derived in an obvious way from the rules for equality—though it is perhaps worth pointing out explicitly that relation *ry* can be a subset of relation *rx* only if *MST(ry)* is a subtype of *MST(rx)*.

As for IM Prescription 13 ("join etc. with inheritance"), that prescription applies to tuple and relation types essentially unchanged. For example, if the declared type of attribute *A* in relation *rx* is tuple type ES and the declared type of attribute *A* in relation *ry* is tuple type CR, then the declared type of attribute *A* in the join of *rx* and *ry* is tuple type ER.

TREAT

IM Prescription 14 ("TREAT") as previously defined is sufficient to cover tuple and relation TREAT too, provided we replace the reference in that prescription to an operator of the form

```
TREAT_AS_T ( X )
```

by a reference to one of the more general form

```
TREAT_AS_SAME_TYPE_AS ( Y, X )
```

(where *X* and *Y* are tuple or relation expressions, as applicable, and *DT(Y)* is *T*), and provided also that we interpret terms such as "expression" appropriately, of course. Consider the following example:

```
VAR V1 TUPLE { E ELLIPSE, R RECTANGLE } ;
VAR V2 TUPLE { E CIRCLE,  R SQUARE   } ;

V2 := TUPLE { E CIRCLE (...), R SQUARE (...) } ;
V1 := V2 ;
```

After the latter assignment, the current value of V1 consists of a circle and a square, not an ellipse and a rectangle (speaking very loosely!). Suppose now that we want to assign that value back to V2. Then the following assignment will *not* work:

```
V2 := V1 ;                    /* COMPILE-TIME TYPE ERROR !!! */
```

(it fails because the declared type of V1 is not a subtype of the declared type of V2). By contrast, the following will work:

```
V2 := TREAT_AS_SAME_TYPE_AS ( V2, V1 ) ;
```

The expression on the right side here is defined to have declared type the same as that of variable V2, so the compile-time type checking now succeeds. Then, at run time:

- If the current value of V1 is indeed of that type, then the expression yields a result, Z say, with (a) $MST(Z)$ equal to $MST(V1)$, which is the same as $DT(V2)$ in the example, and (b) $v(Z)$ equal to $v(V1)$.

- However, if the current value of V1 is only of the (declared) type of V1, not of V2, then the expression fails on a run-time type error.

In other words, the TREAT_AS_SAME_TYPE_AS operator as just discussed is indeed a tuple analog of TREAT as previously understood. (Note that we have to use the slightly more general "SAME TYPE AS" format because our tuple-type naming conventions do not lend themselves to the simpler format available in the scalar case.) *Note:* It is interesting to observe in passing that the particular TREAT invocation in the foregoing example is logically equivalent to the following tuple selector invocation:

```
TUPLE { TREAT_AS_CIRCLE ( E FROM V1 ) , TREAT_AS_SQUARE ( R FROM V1 ) }
```

Without going into further specifics, we hope it is clear that we can also support:

- A relation version of TREAT_AS_SAME_TYPE_AS

- Tuple/relation TREAT_AS_SAME_TYPE_AS pseudovariables

- Tuple/relation operators of the form

```
X TREAT_AS_SAME_TYPE_AS ( Y, A )
```

(where X is a tuple expression or a relational expression, A is a tuple- or relation-valued attribute of the tuple or relation denoted by X, and Y is an expression such that $DT(Y)$ is some proper subtype of $DT(A)$).

Together, these operators constitute a complete set of tuple/relation counterparts to the scalar facilities discussed under IM Prescription 14 in Chapter 14.

Type Testing

IM Prescription 15 ("type testing") as discussed in Chapters 14 and 15 is sufficient to cover tuple and relation type testing too, provided we replace the reference in that prescription to an operator of the form

```
IS_T ( X )
```

by a reference to one of the more general form

```
IS_SAME_TYPE_AS ( Y, X )
```

(where X and Y are tuple or relation expressions, as applicable, and $DT(Y)$ is T). Without going into further specifics, we hope it is clear that we can also support:

- Relation operators of the form

  ```
  X : IS_SAME_TYPE_AS ( Y, A )
  ```

  where X is a relation expression, A is an attribute of the relation denoted by X, and Y is an expression such that $DT(Y)$ is some subtype of $DT(A)$

- Type testing operators of the form

  ```
  IS_SAME_MS_TYPE_AS ( Y, X )
  ```

  (if desired)

- Relation operators of the form

  ```
  X : IS_SAME_MS_TYPE_AS ( Y, A )
  ```

  (if desired)

Together, these operators constitute a complete set of tuple/relation counterparts to the scalar facilities discussed under IM Prescription 15 in Chapters 14 and 15.

EXERCISES

1. How can a type be empty? List as many ways as you can think of.

2. Give an example, different from the one given in the body of the chapter, of a tuple type *TT* for which the corresponding minimal type *TT_omega* is nonempty.

3. Let *r* be a relation. Explain the most specific type of *r* in your own words. Give some examples.

4. Devise some examples to illustrate the general rules arising from IM Prescription 11 that govern relational assignment.

5. Our inheritance model as it applies to tuple and relation types has been criticized on the grounds that we cannot define, e.g., relation type *RT2* to be an explicitly constrained subtype of relation type *RT1* (i.e., all tuple and relation subtyping is implicit, being based as it is on the types of the pertinent attributes). Discuss.

6. *(Repeated from the body of the chapter.)* Why is RELATION {A *omega*} not a union type?

7. As the final exercise in the body of the book, go through the prescriptions and proscriptions of *The Third Manifesto* and demonstrate that the inheritance model as described in the past few chapters is fully consistent with them. *Note:* You might want to pay special attention to RM Prescriptions 1-5.

APPENDIXES

The appendixes that follow cover a mixed bag of topics:

- Appendix A presents an "almost minimal" relational algebra that we call **A**.

- Appendix B discusses a design issue or "dilemma" (?) that some have suggested might arise in a system that conforms to the prescriptions—especially the type prescriptions—laid down in *The Third Manifesto*.

- Appendix C presents some preliminary proposals for dealing with units (e.g., inches vs. centimeters or degrees Celsius vs. degrees Fahrenheit).

- Appendix D takes a closer look at the question of what exactly a database is.

- Appendix E investigates the problem of view updating.

- Appendix F goes into more detail on one extremely important aspect of our inheritance model, *specialization by constraint*.

- Appendix G elaborates on the question of structural inheritance and what is sometimes called "the EXTENDS relationship."

- Appendix H presents a detailed comparison of the SQL standard with the ideas of the *Manifesto*.

- Appendix I presents a **Tutorial D** syntax summary.

- Finally, Appendix J provides an annotated list of references and suggestions for further reading.

Appendix A

A New Relational Algebra

In this appendix, we describe a new relational algebra that we call **A**. The name **A** is a doubly recursive acronym: It stands for *ALGEBRA,* which in turn stands for *A Logical Genesis Explains Basic Relational Algebra.* As this expanded name suggests, **A** has been designed in such a way as to emphasize, perhaps more clearly than previous algebras have done, its close relationship to and solid foundation in the discipline of predicate logic. In addition, the abbreviated name **A** has pleasing connotations of beginning, basis, foundation, simplicity, and the like—not to mention that it is an obvious precursor to **D**.

The algebra **A** differs from Codd's original algebra [20-22] in four principal respects:

- Cartesian product (TIMES) is replaced by a natural join operator that, appealing to its counterpart in predicate logic, we call simply ◄AND►. The original TIMES becomes merely a special case of ◄AND►. *Note:* We adopt the convention of using solid arrowheads ◄ and ► to delimit **A** operator names, as in ◄AND►, in order to distinguish those operators from operators with the same name in predicate logic or **Tutorial D** or both. Also, in the case of ◄AND► in particular, do not be misled by the name: The ◄AND► operator of **A** is, of course, a relational operator (it operates on relations and returns a relation), whereas its predicate logic and Tutorial D counterparts are logical operators (they operate on propositions or, more generally, predicates and return a truth value). Analogous remarks apply to the **A** operators ◄OR► and ◄NOT► as well (see the next two bullet items).

- UNION is replaced by a more general ◄OR► operator that does not require its operands to be of the same type. The original UNION becomes merely a special case of ◄OR►.

- We include a relational complement operator, ◄NOT►. The availability of ◄NOT► allows us to drop the relational difference operator (MINUS), since that operator can easily be expressed in terms of ◄AND► and ◄NOT►.

- We are able to dispense with *restrict* (WHERE), EXTEND, and SUMMARIZE, since these operators all become further special cases of ◄AND►. *Note:* EXTEND and SUMMARIZE were not included in Codd's original algebra but were added subsequently [132].

In addition to ◄AND►, ◄OR►, and ◄NOT►, **A** includes three operators called ◄RENAME►, ◄REMOVE►, and ◄COMPOSE►, which are discussed in the next section but one. It also includes a transitive closure operator, ◄TCLOSE►; however, this operator is essentially identical to TCLOSE as discussed in Chapters 2 and 6, and we have little more to say about it in this appendix.

MOTIVATION AND JUSTIFICATION

In this section we explain our reasons for developing **A** and justify the departures from Codd's algebra identified in the previous section. Our explanations and notation are deliberately not too formal (formal definitions appear in a later section). In particular, we show tuples not as sets of $<A,T,V>$ triples, as the formal apparatus of Chapter 4 would require, but as simple commalists of values enclosed in angle brackets. For example, we use the expression $<EX,DX>$ to mean a 2-tuple in which EX denotes a certain employee and DX a certain department.

Since we often appeal in what follows to ideas from predicate logic, using natural language predicates as examples, a brief note on the terminology we use in that connection is in order:

- First, where our examples include operands that are relvar references, the predicates for the corresponding relvars are relvar predicates as described in Chapter 2. For example, the predicate "Employee E works in department D" might be the relvar predicate for a relvar called WORKS_IN.

- Second, we refer to the parameters of a predicate as its **free variables**.[1] For example, in the predicate "Employee E works in department D," E and D are free variables.

- Third, we use Greek derivatives involving the suffix *-adic* when referring to the number of free variables in a predicate, but Latin ones involving the suffix *-ary* when referring to the degree of a relation. For example, the predicate "Employee E works in department D" is dyadic, while a relation corresponding to that predicate is binary.

The algebra **A** has been motivated by certain general objectives, the following among them:

- For psychological reasons, we sought a collection of operators with immediate counterparts in logic and with less reliance on set theory in their nomenclature. We feel that relational theory is better taught and understood this way; indeed, we have been dismayed at the widespread lack of appreciation in the database community at large of the logical foundations of relational theory, and we think it likely that this lack has contributed to the deficiencies we observe in available relational (or would-be relational) technology.

- Previous algebras have had more than one operator corresponding to logical AND. We thought this apparent redundancy worth looking into, with a view to eliminating it.

- We wanted all of the relational operators of **Tutorial D** to be mappable to expressions in **A**, for convenience and also for our own satisfaction (and we would strongly recommend that the same be true for any industrial-strength **D** as well). Full details of the mappings in question are deferred to the final section of this appendix, but some idea of what is involved can be found in examples prior to that section.

We now proceed to justify the four principal respects in which **A** differs from previous algebras.

Dispensing with TIMES

In logic, when two predicates are connected by AND, attention must be paid to the names of the free variables. Any free variable name that appears in both predicates must be understood to stand for the same thing when it consequently appears more than once in the resulting predicate. For example, consider the natural language predicates "Employee E works in department D" and "Employee E works on project J." The AND of these two predicates yields a triadic predicate, not a tetradic one: namely, "Employee E works in department D and employee E works on project J." This latter predicate can perhaps be abbreviated to just "Employee E works in department D and on project J," to stress the fact that we cannot substitute some particular employee for the E that works in department D without at the same time substituting that very same employee for the E that works on project J. This observation regarding free variable names lies at the heart of the well-known natural join operator (the ◄AND► operator in **A**).

---

1. We apologize for this slight terminological inconsistency, but in fact—as we have discussed in detail elsewhere [78]—there seems to be almost no consensus on the use of terms in logic textbooks either.

As for the classical TIMES operator, it is of course just a special case of natural join (which hereinafter we abbreviate to simply *join*). More precisely, TIMES corresponds to the AND of two predicates that have no free variables in common—for example, "Employee E works in department D and project J has budget B." TIMES as such can thus be discarded.

We return for a moment to the predicate "Employee E works in department D and on project J" to make another point. As already noted, that formulation of the predicate is really an abbreviation. Now, it might be abbreviated still further, to just "Employee E works in department D on project J." However, that further abbreviation could lead to the erroneous conclusion that project J is somehow "in" department D. In reference [21], Codd characterized this kind of error as *the connection trap*, but it has since become known, at least in some circles, as the *join* trap instead—rather unfairly, we feel, since it is not unique to join in particular, nor to relational operators in general. In fact, it was precisely Codd's point in reference [21] that the error is more likely to arise in a nonrelational context than it is in a relational one.

Dispensing with UNION

We can combine natural language predicates with OR as well as AND. Thus, there is a ternary relation corresponding to the triadic predicate "Employee E works in department D or employee E works on project J." If employee EX works in department DX, then $<$EX,DX,$j>$ is a tuple in the body of this relation for all possible projects j, regardless of whether employee EX actually works on project j (and regardless of whether there is even a project j in the company at this time). Likewise, if employee EX works on project JX, then $<$EX,d,JX$>$ is a tuple in the body of this relation for all possible departments d, regardless of whether employee EX actually works in department d (and regardless of whether there is even a department d in the company at this time).

Just as we introduce ◄AND► as the **A** counterpart of AND, therefore, we introduce ◄OR► as the **A** counterpart of OR. As for the classical UNION operator, it is of course just a special case of ◄OR►. More precisely, UNION corresponds to the OR of two predicates that have exactly the same free variables—for example, "Employee E works in department D or employee E is on loan to department D." UNION as such can thus be discarded.

Note: We do not concern ourselves here with the computational difficulties that might arise from our generalization of Codd's UNION, because at this point we are only defining an algebra. Various safety mechanisms can be (and normally are) imposed in practice to circumvent such difficulties. For similar reasons, we also do not concern ourselves with the high degree of redundancy that most relations produced by ◄OR► will exhibit.

Dispensing with MINUS

Let WORKS_IN be a relation with attributes E and D, where E is an employee and D is a department, and let the corresponding predicate be "Employee E works in department D." Then the *logical complement* (◄NOT►) of this relation has a body that consists of all possible tuples of the form $<$E,D$>$ such that it is not the case that employee E works in department D. *Note:* Computational difficulties arise here as they did with ◄OR►, but again we need not concern ourselves with them at this juncture.

To see that MINUS can now be discarded, consider the following example. Let WORKS_IN be as above; let WORKS_ON be a relation with attributes E and J, where J is a project; and let the predicate corresponding to WORKS_ON be "Employee E works on project J." Now consider the unary relation corresponding to the monadic predicate "Employee E works in some department but works on no project at all." In Codd's algebra, we could obtain this relation by projecting both WORKS_IN and WORKS_ON over their E attributes and then taking the appropriate difference. In **A**, we first project WORKS_ON over E (see the next section for a discussion of projection), and then we take the ◄NOT► of that projection; the corresponding predicate is "There does not exist a project such that employee E works on that project." This relation can then be joined ("◄AND►ed") with WORKS_IN, and the result projected over E, to obtain the desired final result.

Dispensing with restrict *(WHERE)*, *EXTEND, and SUMMARIZE*

Restrict (WHERE), EXTEND, and SUMMARIZE all require certain operators to be invoked as part of their execution. In the case of *restrict,* the operators in question return values (truth values, to be precise) that are used to disqualify certain tuples from appearing in the result relation; in the case of EXTEND and SUMMARIZE, they return values that are used as the basis for defining certain attributes in the result relation.

It occurred to us that it made sense, and could possibly be useful, **to treat such operators as relations.** Consider an operator *Op* that is in fact a scalar function (a scalar function is an operator for which every valid invocation returns exactly one result and that result is a scalar value). Suppose *Op* has n parameters. Then *Op* can be treated as a relation with $n+1$ attributes, one for each parameter and one for the result. The attributes corresponding to the parameters clearly form a key for this relation;[1] however, that key is not necessarily the only one. For example, let PLUS be a relation with attributes X, Y, and Z, each of type INTEGER, corresponding to the scalar function "+" of integer arithmetic and to the predicate "X + Y = Z." Then each of {X,Y}, {Y,Z}, and {Z,X} is a key for relation PLUS; further, that relation contains exactly one 3-tuple $<x,y,z>$ for every possible combination of values x, y, and z that satisfies the predicate (i.e., such that $x + y = z$).

Note, incidentally, that the relation PLUS can be regarded as an example of what in Chapters 5 and 6 we referred to as a "relcon" or relation constant: It is named, like a relvar, but unlike a relvar it has a value that does not change over time. Of course, analogous remarks apply to the relational representation of any function; the keys discussed in the previous paragraph are thus keys for a "relcon," not a relvar.

Let us take a closer look at what is going on here. A scalar function is a special case of a relation, of course, as the PLUS example illustrates. In fact, any relation can always be regarded as an operator that maps from some subset of its attributes to the rest; and, if the mapping in question is a functional (i.e., many-to-one) mapping specifically, then the relation can be regarded as a function. In fact, since a set of n elements has 2^n subsets, a relation of degree n can be regarded as representing 2^n different operators, some of which will be functions and some not (in general). For example, PLUS can be regarded, among other things, as an operator that maps from Z to X and Y—but of course that particular mapping is not a functional one (the functional dependencies $Z \to X$ and $Z \to Y$ do not hold), and the corresponding operator is thus not a function.

We now claim that, given the fact that operators can be treated as relations, and given also the availability of the A operators ◄AND►, ◄REMOVE►, and ◄RENAME► (the latter two still to be discussed), it is indeed the case that we can dispense with *restrict,* EXTEND, and SUMMARIZE. We will justify this claim in the next section but one.

◄REMOVE►, ◄RENAME►, AND ◄COMPOSE►

◄REMOVE►

◄REMOVE► is the A counterpart to the existential quantifier of predicate logic. It corresponds to Codd's *project.* However, it differs from *project* in that it specifies, not an attribute (or attributes, plural) to be projected over, but rather an attribute to be "projected away"; it is equivalent to projecting the relation in question over all of its attributes except the one specified. Our motivation for this inversion, so to speak, with respect to Codd's *project* is a psychological one—projecting a relation with (say) attributes X and Y over attribute X is equivalent to existentially quantifying over attribute Y. For

---

1. Recall from Chapter 2 that it is possible to apply the "key" concept to relations as well as relvars.

example, the projection of WORKS_IN over E corresponds to the natural language predicate "There exists some department D such that employee E works in department D." We thus feel that ◄REMOVE► is psychologically closer to our foundation in logic than *project* is. *The Third Manifesto*, however, explicitly requires the language **D** not to arbitrate in this matter; rather, projection over specified attributes and projection over all except specified attributes are required to be equally easy to express.

◄*RENAME*►

The purpose of ◄RENAME► is, loosely, to rename some attribute of some relation. More precisely, the ◄RENAME► operator takes a given relation and returns another that is identical to the given one except that one of its attributes has a different name. Such an operator is required[1] in any concrete syntax for relational expressions in which attributes are distinguished by name, as they are in **A** (and **D**).

◄*COMPOSE*►

In addition to the operators discussed so far—◄AND►, ◄OR►, ◄NOT►, ◄REMOVE►, and ◄RENAME►—we have allowed ourselves the luxury (some might think) of including a "macro" operator called ◄COMPOSE►. ◄COMPOSE► is a combination of ◄AND► and ◄REMOVE►, in which attributes common to the "◄AND►ed" relations are subsequently "◄REMOVE►d." The name ◄COMPOSE► is meant to be suggestive of the fact that relational composition is a natural generalization of functional composition. (In case you are not familiar with this latter notion, the composition of two functions $f(...)$ and $g(...)$, in that order, is the function $f(g(...))$.) *Note:* Codd did in fact include a relational composition operator in his earliest papers [20-21] but for some reason subsequently discarded it; we find it useful in support of our desire to treat operators as relations. To be specific, it turns out that a certain degenerate form of composition can be used to simulate the expression of operator invocations, as will be seen in the next section.

Closing Remarks

It should be obvious that **A** is relationally complete [22]. Previous algebras have needed six operators for this purpose (typically RENAME, *restrict, project,* TIMES, UNION, and MINUS); we have reduced that number to five. Moreover, thanks to our observation that operators can be treated as relations, we have also avoided the need for EXTEND and SUMMARIZE; indeed, these operators might have been added needlessly in the past, simply for lack of that observation. Points arising:

- As a matter of fact **A** is "more than" relationally complete, in the sense that its unconstrained ◄OR► and ◄NOT► operators permit the definition of relations that cannot be defined in previous algebras. The point is purely academic, of course, since as already noted the ◄OR► and ◄NOT► operations will not be totally unconstrained in practice, in order to avoid certain computational problems that would otherwise arise.

- We do not actually need both ◄AND► and ◄OR► in order to achieve relational completeness, thanks to De Morgan's Laws. For example, *A* ◄AND► *B* is identically equal to ◄NOT►((◄NOT► *A*) ◄OR► (◄NOT► *B*)), so we could dispense with ◄AND► if we included both ◄NOT► and ◄OR►. We could even collapse ◄NOT► and ◄OR► into a single operator, ◄NOR► ("neither *A* nor *B*"; equivalently, "not *A* and not *B*"). Equally well, of course, we could dispense with ◄OR► and collapse ◄AND► and ◄NOT► into a single operator, ◄NAND► ("not

---

1. Or highly desirable, at any rate. As the next section shows, ◄RENAME► is in fact not a primitive operation.

A or not *B"*). Overall, therefore, we could if desired reduce our algebra to just three operators: ◄RENAME►, ◄REMOVE►, and either ◄NOR► or ◄NAND► (plus ◄TCLOSE►).

■ In fact, we will show in the next section that we do not really need ◄RENAME► either; thus, we could in fact reduce our algebra still further to just the two operators ◄REMOVE► and either ◄NOR► or ◄NAND► (plus ◄TCLOSE►).

Of course, we are not suggesting that all of the various operators that we claim can be dispensed with should in fact *be* dispensed with in the concrete syntax of **D**—they are useful and convenient shorthands, generally speaking, and as a matter of fact RM Prescription 18 of our *Manifesto* expressly requires that they ("or some logical equivalent thereof") all be supported. But we do suggest that such operators be explicitly defined *as* shorthands, for reasons of clarity and simplicity among others [31].

TREATING OPERATORS AS RELATIONS

In this section we elaborate on our idea of treating operators as relations. Consider the relation PLUS once again, with attributes X, Y, and Z, each of type INTEGER, corresponding to the predicate "X + Y = Z." Let TWO_AND_TWO be that relation whose body consists of just the single 2-tuple

```
{ < X, INTEGER, 2 >, < Y, INTEGER, 2 > }
```

(we now revert to something closer to the formal notation for tuples—i.e., as sets of $<A,T,v>$ triples—introduced in Chapter 2). Then the expression

```
TWO_AND_TWO ◄COMPOSE► PLUS
```

yields a relation whose body consists of the single 1-tuple

```
{ < Z, INTEGER, 4 > }
```

Observe, therefore, that we have effectively invoked the "+" operator with arguments X = 2 and Y = 2 and obtained the result Z = 4.[1] Of course, that result is still embedded as an attribute value inside a tuple inside a relation (like all **A** operators, ◄COMPOSE► returns a relation); if we want to extract that result as a pure scalar value, we will have to go beyond **A** per se and make use of the operators (required by RM Prescriptions 7 and 6, respectively) for (a) extracting a specified tuple from a specified relation (necessarily of cardinality one) and then (b) extracting a specified attribute value from a specified tuple. In **Tutorial D** terms, for example, these extractions can be performed as follows:

```
Z FROM ( TUPLE FROM ( result ) )
```

where *result* denotes the result of evaluating the **A** expression TWO_AND_TWO ◄COMPOSE► PLUS.

In other words, while it is certainly true that any given operator can be treated as a relation, it will still be necessary to step outside the confines of the algebra per se in order to obtain the actual result of some invocation of that operator. For present purposes, however, we are interested only in treating operators as relations *within a pure relational context;* such a treatment allows us to explain the classical relational operation EXTEND, for example, in a purely relational way (i.e., without having to leave the relational context at all), as we now proceed to demonstrate.

---

1. Note that the result has a name, Z. We are still considering the implications of this fact for the language **D**.

Consider the expression

```
TWO_AND_TWO ◄AND► PLUS
```

(this expression is the same as before, except that we have replaced ◄COMPOSE► by ◄AND►). The result is a relation whose body consists of just the single 3-tuple

```
{ < X, INTEGER, 2 >, < Y, INTEGER, 2 >, < Z, INTEGER, 4 > }
```

It should be clear, therefore, that the original **A** expression is logically equivalent to the following **Tutorial D** *extension:*

```
EXTEND TWO_AND_TWO ADD ( X + Y AS Z )
```

This example should thus be sufficient to suggest how we can indeed dispense with EXTEND, as claimed.

Moreover, that very same expression TWO_AND_TWO ◄AND► PLUS is logically equivalent to the following **Tutorial D** *restriction:*

```
PLUS WHERE X = 2 AND Y = 2
```

This same example should thus also be sufficient to suggest how we can dispense with *restrict*, again as claimed.

As an aside, we remark that if we were to rename attributes X and Z of PLUS as Z and X, respectively, then the expression TWO_AND_TWO ◄AND► PLUS would yield a relation whose body consists of just the single 3-tuple

```
{ < Z, INTEGER, 2 >, < Y, INTEGER, 2 >, < X, INTEGER, 0 > }
```

In other words, MINUS would be just a good a name for our "relcon" as PLUS is, psychologically speaking.

As for SUMMARIZE, it is well known that any given summarization can be expressed in terms of EXTEND instead of SUMMARIZE per se (though the details are a little complicated and we omit them here; see the final section of this appendix for further explanation). It follows that we can dispense with SUMMARIZE as well.

Now consider the following **Tutorial D** expression:

```
R RENAME ( X AS Y )
```

(we assume here that R denotes a relation with an attribute called X and no attribute called Y). Then the **Tutorial D** expression

```
( EXTEND R ADD ( X AS Y ) ) { ALL BUT X }
```

is semantically equivalent to the original RENAME expression. Thus, it should be clear that ◄RENAME► can be expressed in terms of EXTEND (which as we already know is basically just ◄AND►) and ◄REMOVE►, and hence is not primitive.

Before we leave this section, we would like to stress the point that it is not just operators that are scalar functions specifically that can be treated as relations. Consider the following examples:

■ An example of an operator that is scalar but not a function is SQRT—"square root"—which, given a positive numeric argument, returns two scalar results (at least, we will assume so for the sake of this discussion). For example, SQRT(4.0) returns both +2.0 and -2.0.

■   An example of an operator that is a function but not scalar is ADDR_OF ("address of"), which, given an employee E, returns the address of that employee as a collection—more precisely, a tuple—involving four scalar values (STREET, CITY, STATE, and ZIP).

Again we take a closer look. First, SQRT. SQRT can obviously be treated as a relation with attributes X and Y, say, each of type RATIONAL ($X \geq 0$). However, that relation is not a function because the functional dependency X → Y does not hold: for example, the tuples (4.0, +2.0) and (4.0,-2.0) both appear. (By contrast, the functional dependency Y → X does hold; SQRT can be regarded as a function if it is looked at in the inverse—i.e., "square of"—direction.) Observe that the relation contains:

■   For $x = 0$, exactly one tuple with X = x

■   For $x > 0$, exactly two tuples with X = x

■   For $x < 0$, no tuples at all with X = x

It follows from the foregoing that the expression

```
SQRT ◄COMPOSE► { { < X, RATIONAL, 4.0 > } }
```

effectively represents an invocation of the SQRT operator, but—in contrast to the situation in conventional programming languages—the invocation in question returns two results. More precisely, it produces a (unary) relation with the following body:

```
{ { < Y, RATIONAL, +2.0 > }, { < Y, RATIONAL, -2.0 > } }
```

(If desired, we could now go on to extract the individual scalar values +2.0 and -2.0 from this relation.) One implication of this example is that a relational language such as **D** might reasonably include an extended form of EXTEND that—unlike the traditional EXTEND—is not necessarily limited to producing exactly one output tuple from each input tuple.
By way of another example, consider the expression

```
SQRT ◄COMPOSE► { { < X, RATIONAL, -4.0 > } }
```

This expression also represents an invocation of the SQRT operator, but—again in contrast to the situation in conventional programming languages—the invocation in question returns no result (more precisely, it produces a relation with heading {Y RATIONAL} and body empty). In conventional programming languages the invocation SQRT(-4.0) would give rise to a run-time exception.
Now we turn to ADDR_OF. This operator too can obviously be treated as a relation, this one having attributes E, STREET, CITY, STATE, and ZIP, where {E} is a key. *Note:* The other four attributes might form a key as well, if no two employees ever live at the same address (in which case the ADDR_OF relation would correspond to the inverse function that also happened to apply). Of course, the name ADDR_OF would be a little questionable if such were the case; EMP_AT might be just as appropriate, EMP_ADDR perhaps more so. The issue is merely psychological, of course.[1]

---

1. Actually, analogous remarks apply to the SQRT example, where the name is again not very appropriate if the relation is looked at in the inverse ("square of") direction.

It follows from the foregoing that the expression

```
{ { < E, EMPLOYEE, e > } } ◄COMPOSE► ADDR_OF
```

(where *e* denotes some employee) effectively represents an invocation of the ADDR_OF operator, but—in contrast to the situation in conventional programming languages—the invocation in question returns *a nonscalar result*. One implication of this example is that a relational language such as **D** might reasonably include an extended form of EXTEND that (unlike the traditional EXTEND) is not necessarily limited to producing just one additional attribute.[1]

FORMAL DEFINITIONS

We now proceed to give formal definitions for the **A** operators discussed up to this point.[2] First we explain our notation (which is based on that introduced in Chapter 2, of course, and—unlike that of previous sections—is now meant to be completely precise). Let *r* be a relation, let *A* be the name of an attribute of *r*, let *T* be the name of the corresponding type (i.e., the type of attribute *A*), and let *v* be a value of type *T*. Then:

- The heading H*r* of *r* is a set of attributes (i.e., ordered pairs of the form $<A,T>$). By definition, no two attributes in that set contain the same attribute name *A*.

- Let *tr* be a tuple that conforms to H*r*; i.e., *tr* is a set of ordered triples of the form $<A,T,v>$, one such triple for each attribute in H*r*.

- The body B*r* of *r* is a set of such tuples *tr*. Note that (in general) there will be some such tuples *tr* that conform to H*r* but do not appear in B*r*.

The rest of our notation is meant to be self-explanatory.

Observe that a heading is a set, a body is a set, and a tuple is a set (and we remind you from Chapter 2 that every subset of a heading is a heading, every subset of a body is a body, and every subset of a tuple is a tuple). A member of a heading is an attribute (i.e., an ordered pair of the form $<A,T>$); a member of a body is a tuple; and a member of a tuple is an ordered triple of the form $<A,T,v>$.

Now we can define the operators per se. Each of the definitions that follow consists of (a) a formal specification of the rules, if any, that apply to the operands of the operator in question, (b) a formal specification of the heading of the result of that operator, and (c) a formal specification of the body of that result, followed by (d) an informal discussion of the formal specifications.

- Let *s* be ◄NOT► *r*.

  Hs = Hr

  Bs = { ts : exists tr (tr ∉ Br and ts = tr) }

  The ◄NOT► operator yields the complement *s* of a given relation *r*. The heading of *s* is the

---

1. **Tutorial D** does support such an operator. What is more, the additional attributes can be scalar, tuple, or relation valued, or any combination.

2. Greaves [97] gives definitions of all of the operators of **A** in terms of the formal specification language Z.

heading of *r*. The body of *s* contains every tuple with that heading that is not in the body of *r*.

■ Let *s* be *r* ◄REMOVE► *A*. It is required that there exist some type *T* such that $<A,T> \epsilon$ H*r*.

```
Hs = Hr minus { <A,T> }

Bs = { ts : exists tr exists v ( tr ε Br and v ε T and <A,T,v> ε tr and
                                 ts = tr minus { <A,T,v> } ) }
```

The ◄REMOVE► operator yields a relation *s* formed by removing a given attribute *A* from a given relation *r*. The operation is equivalent to taking the projection of *r* over all of its attributes except *A*. The heading of *s* is the heading of *r* minus the ordered pair $<A,T>$. The body of *s* contains every tuple that conforms to the heading of *s* and is a subset of some tuple of *r*.

■ Let *s* be *r* ◄RENAME► (*A,B*). It is required that there exist some type *T* such that $<A,T> \epsilon$ H*r* and that there exist no type *T* such that $<B,T> \epsilon$ H*r*.

```
Hs = ( Hr minus { <A,T> } ) union { <B,T> }

Bs = { ts : exists tr exists v ( tr ε Br and v ε T and <A,T,v> ε tr and
                                 ts = ( tr minus { <A,T,v> } ) union { <B,T,v> } ) }
```

The ◄RENAME► operator yields a relation *s* that differs from a given relation *r* only in the name of one of its attributes, which is changed from *A* to *B*. The heading of *s* is the heading of *r* except that the ordered pair $<A,T>$ is replaced by the ordered pair $<B,T>$. The body of *s* consists of every tuple of the body of *r*, except that in each such tuple the triple $<A,T,v>$ is replaced by the triple $<B,T,v>$.

■ Let *s* be *r1* ◄AND► *r2*. It is required that if $<A,T1> \epsilon$ H*r1* and $<A,T2> \epsilon$ H*r2*, then *T1* = *T2*.

```
Hs = Hr1 union Hr2

Bs = { ts : exists tr1 exists tr2 ( ( tr1 ε Br1 and tr2 ε Br2 ) and ts = tr1 union tr2 ) }
```

The ◄AND► operator is relational *conjunction*, yielding a relation *s* that in previous literature has been referred to as the (natural) join of the two given relations *r1* and *r2*. The heading of *s* is the union of the headings of *r1* and *r2*. The body of *s* contains every tuple that conforms to the heading of *s* and is a superset of both some tuple in the body of *r1* and some tuple in the body of *r2*. We remark that the ◄AND► operator might logically be called the *conjoin*.

■ Let *s* be *r1* ◄OR► *r2*. It is required that if $<A,T1> \epsilon$ H*r1* and $<A,T2> \epsilon$ H*r2*, then *T1* = *T2*.

```
Hs = Hr1 union Hr2

Bs = { ts : exists tr1 exists tr2 ( ( tr1 ε Br1 or tr2 ε Br2 ) and ts = tr1 union tr2 ) }
```

The ◄OR► operator is relational *disjunction*, being a generalization of what in previous literature has been referred to as union (in the special case where the given relations *r1* and *r2* have the same heading, the result *s* is in fact the union of those two relations in the traditional sense). The heading of *s* is the union of the headings of *r1* and *r2*. The body of *s* contains every tuple that conforms to the heading of *s* and is a superset of either some tuple in the body of *r1* or some tuple in the body of *r2*. We remark that the ◄OR► operator might logically be called the *disjoin*.

We also define the "macro" operator ◄COMPOSE►. Let *s* be *r1* ◄COMPOSE► *r2* (where *r1* and *r2* are as for ◄AND►). Let the attributes common to *r1* and *r2* be *A1, A2, ..., An* ($n \geq 0$). Then *s* is the result of the expression

```
( r1 ◄AND► r2 ) ◄REMOVE► An ... ◄REMOVE► A2 ◄REMOVE► A1
```

Note that when $n = 0$, *r1* ◄COMPOSE► *r2* is the same as *r1* ◄AND► *r2*, which is in turn the same as *r1* TIMES *r2* in Codd's algebra.

Finally, we remind you that the **A** operator ◄TCLOSE► is essentially identical to the TCLOSE operator already discussed in Chapters 2 and 6.

HOW Tutorial D BUILDS ON A

As noted in the body of the book, many—in fact, almost all—of the built-in relational operators in **Tutorial D** are really just shorthands. In this section we justify this remark by showing how the operators in question[1] map to those of the relational algebra **A** defined in earlier sections. The notation is intended to be self-explanatory, for the most part.

Transitive Closure: The **Tutorial D** *<tclose>*

```
TCLOSE r
```

is semantically equivalent to the **A** expression

```
◄TCLOSE► r
```

Rename: The **Tutorial D** *<rename>*

```
r RENAME ( A AS B )
```

is semantically equivalent to the **A** expression

```
r ◄RENAME► (A,B)
```

Other **Tutorial D** *<rename>* formats are just shorthand for repeated application of the format shown above.

Project: The **Tutorial D** *<project>*

```
r { ALL BUT A }
```

is semantically equivalent to the **A** expression

```
r ◄REMOVE► A
```

---

1. Or most of them, at any rate; for simplicity, we ignore operators like *<n-adic join>* that are clearly equivalent to certain combinations of other operators.

Other **Tutorial D** <*project*> formats are readily defined in terms of the format shown above.

Join: The **Tutorial D** <*dyadic join*>

    r1 JOIN r2

is semantically equivalent to the **A** expression

    r1 ◄AND► r2

The **Tutorial D** <*dyadic intersect*> *r1* INTERSECT *r2* is just that special case of *r1* JOIN *r2* in which *r1* and *r2* have the same heading, so the ◄AND► operator of **A** takes care of INTERSECT as well.

Compose: The **Tutorial D** <*compose*>

    r1 COMPOSE r2

is semantically equivalent to the **A** expression

    r1 ◄COMPOSE► r2

Union: The **Tutorial D** <*dyadic union*>

    r1 UNION r2

(where *r1* and *r2* have the same heading) is semantically equivalent to the **A** expression

    r1 ◄OR► r2

Minus: The **Tutorial D** <*minus*>

    r1 MINUS r2

(where *r1* and *r2* have the same heading) is semantically equivalent to the **A** expression

    r1 ◄AND► (◄NOT► r2)

Semijoin: The **Tutorial D** <*semijoin*>

    r1 SEMIJOIN r2   *or*   r1 MATCHING r2

is semantically equivalent to the **Tutorial D** expression

    (r1 JOIN r2) { A, B, ..., C }

(where *A, B, ..., C* are all of the attributes of *r1*), and can therefore be expressed in **A**. Since this latter expression involves only operators that have already been shown to be expressible in **A**, it follows that semijoin can also be expressed in **A**. *Note:* A remark similar to the foregoing sentence applies to many of the operators still to be discussed. We will let that one sentence do duty for all.

Semidifference: The **Tutorial D** $<semiminus>$

    `r1 SEMIMINUS r2`   *or*   `r1 NOT MATCHING r2`

is semantically equivalent to the **Tutorial D** expression

    `r1 MINUS ( r1 SEMIJOIN r2 )`

Divide: The **Tutorial D** $<divide>$

    `r1 DIVIDEBY r2 PER ( r3 )`

(a Small Divide) is shorthand for the **Tutorial D** expression

    `r1 { A1 } MINUS ( ( r1 { A1 } JOIN r2 { A2 } ) MINUS r3 { A1, A2 } ) { A1 }`

(where *A1* is the set of attributes common to *r1* and *r3* and *A2* is the set of attributes common to *r2* and *r3*), and can therefore be expressed in **A**. Likewise, the **Tutorial D** $<divide>$

    `r1 DIVIDEBY r2 PER ( r3, r4 )`

(a Great Divide) is shorthand for the **Tutorial D** expression

    `( r1 { A1 } JOIN r2 { A2 } ) MINUS ( ( r1 { A1 } JOIN r4 { A2, A3 } ) MINUS ( r3 { A1, A3 }`
    `JOIN r4 { A2, A3 } ) ) { A1, A2 }`

(where *A1* is the set of attributes common to *r1* and *r3*, *A2* is the set of attributes common to *r2* and *r4*, and *A3* is the set of attributes common to *r3* and *r4*), and can therefore be expressed in **A**.

Extend: Let PLUS be a relation constant with heading

    `{ X INTEGER, Y INTEGER, Z INTEGER }`

and with body consisting of all tuples such that the Z value is equal to the sum of the X and Y values. Then the **Tutorial D** $<extend>$

    `EXTEND r ADD ( A + B AS C )`

(where we assume without loss of generality that *A* and *B* are attributes of r^1 of type INTEGER) is semantically equivalent to the **Tutorial D** expression

    `r JOIN ( PLUS RENAME ( X AS A, Y AS B, Z AS C ) )`

and can therefore be expressed in **A**. Analogous equivalents can be provided for all other forms of $<extend>$ (including forms in which the $<exp>$ in the $<extend\ add>$ is tuple or relation valued). For example, the **Tutorial D** expression

---

1. If they are not, we can effectively make them so by means of appropriate joins. An analogous remark applies to many of our examples; for brevity, we will not make it every time.

```
    EXTEND r ADD ( TUPLE { A A, B B } AS C )
```

is semantically equivalent to the **Tutorial D** expression

```
    r JOIN s
```

where *s* is a relation with heading

```
    { A TA, B TB, C TUPLE { A TA, B TB } }
```

containing exactly one tuple for each possible combination of *A* and *B* values, in which the *C* value is exactly the corresponding <*A,B*> tuple (*TA* and *TB* here being the types of attributes *A* and *B*, respectively).

Restrict: Let ONE be a relation constant with heading

```
    { X INTEGER }
```

and with body consisting of a single tuple, with X value one. Then the **Tutorial D** <*where*>

```
    r WHERE A = 1
```

(where *A* is an attribute of *r* of type INTEGER) is semantically equivalent to the **Tutorial D** expression

```
    r JOIN ( ONE RENAME ( X AS A ) )
```

and can therefore be expressed in **A**.

Now let GT be a relation constant with heading

```
    { X INTEGER, Y INTEGER }
```

and with body consisting of all tuples such that the X value is greater than the Y value. Then the **Tutorial D** <*where*>

```
    r WHERE A > B
```

(where *A* and *B* are attributes of *r* of type INTEGER) is semantically equivalent to the **Tutorial D** expression

```
    r JOIN ( GT RENAME ( X AS A, Y AS B ) )
```

and can therefore be expressed in **A**.

More generally, consider the **Tutorial D** <*where*> *r* WHERE *x*, where *x* is an arbitrarily complex <*bool exp*>. Let *A*, *B*, ... , *C* be all of the attributes of *r* mentioned in *x*. Let *rx* be a relation whose body consists of all tuples of the form <*A,B,...,C*> that satisfy *x*. Then *r* WHERE *x* is equivalent to *r* JOIN *rx*.

Summarize: The **Tutorial D** <*summarize*>

SUMMARIZE *r1* PER (*r2*) ADD (*ss* (*exp*) AS Z)

(where *r2* has attributes *A*, *B*, ... , *C*; *r1* has the same attributes and possibly more; and *ss* is any

<*summary spec*> except COUNT, EXACTLY, or EXACTLYD) is semantically equivalent to the **Tutorial D** expression

```
( EXTEND r2 ADD ( r1 JOIN RELATION { TUPLE { A A, B B, ..., C C } } AS Y,
                  agg ( ( EXTEND Y ADD ( exp AS X ) ) { X }, X ) AS Z ) )
{ ALL BUT Y }
```

(where *agg* is identical to *ss* unless *ss* is COUNTD, SUMD, or AVGD, in which case *agg* is COUNT, SUM, or AVG, respectively, and where the projection over *X* in the third line is included only if *ss* is COUNTD, SUMD, or AVGD), and can therefore be expressed in **A**.

Similarly,

```
SUMMARIZE r1 PER ( r2 ) ADD ( ss ( exp1, exp2 ) AS Z )
```

(where *ss* is therefore EXACTLY or EXACTLYD) is semantically equivalent to the **Tutorial D** expression

```
( EXTEND r2 ADD ( r1 JOIN RELATION { TUPLE { A A, B B, ..., C C } } AS Y,
                  EXACTLY ( exp1, ( EXTEND Y ADD ( exp2 AS X ) ) { X }, X ) AS Z ) )
{ ALL BUT Y }
```

(where the projection over *X* in the third line is included only if *ss* is EXACTLYD), and can therefore be expressed in **A**.

Similarly,

```
SUMMARIZE r1 PER ( r2 ) ADD ( COUNT ( ) AS Z )
```

is semantically equivalent to the **Tutorial D** expression

```
( EXTEND r2 ADD ( r1 JOIN RELATION { TUPLE { A A, B B, ..., C C } } AS Y,
                  COUNT ( Y ) AS Z ) )
{ ALL BUT Y }
```

and can therefore be expressed in **A**.

Note: Each of the foregoing SUMMARIZE expansions involves an invocation of some aggregate operator (COUNT, for example, in the third case). But we have already seen, in the section "Treating Operators as Relations," that read-only operators can be implemented in **A**, and our conclusion that SUMMARIZE can also be expressed in **A** is thus not undermined by our reliance on those aggregate operators in the expansions.

Wrap and Unwrap: The **Tutorial D** <*wrap*>

```
r WRAP ( { A, B, ..., C } AS X )
```

is shorthand for the **Tutorial D** expression

```
( EXTEND r ADD ( TUPLE { A A, B B, ..., C C } AS X ) ) { ALL BUT A, B, ..., C }
```

and can therefore be expressed in **A**. Likewise, the **Tutorial D** <*unwrap*>

```
r UNWRAP ( X )
```

is shorthand for the **Tutorial D** expression

```
( EXTEND r ADD ( A FROM X AS A,
                 B FROM X AS B,
                 ......
                 C FROM X AS C ) ) ( ALL BUT X )
```

(where *A*, *B*, ..., *C* are all the attributes of *X*), and can therefore also be expressed in **A**.

Group and Ungroup: Let relation *r* have attributes *A*, *B*, ..., *C*, *D*, *E*, ..., *F*. Then the **Tutorial D** *<group>*

```
r GROUP ( { D, E, ..., F } AS X )
```

is shorthand for the **Tutorial D** expression

```
( EXTEND r ADD ( r AS RR ,
                 RELATION { TUPLE { A A, B B, ..., C C } } AS TX ,
                 RR COMPOSE TX AS X ) )
{ A, B, ..., C, X }
```

(where *RR* and *TX* are attribute names not already appearing in *r*), and can therefore be expressed in **A**. Likewise, the **Tutorial D** *<ungroup>*

```
r UNGROUP ( X )
```

(where *r* has attributes *A*, *B*, ..., *C*, and *X*, and *X* in turn is a relation-valued attribute with attributes *D*, *E*, ..., *F*) is shorthand for the **Tutorial D** expression

```
( EXTEND ( r COMPOSE s ) ADD ( A FROM Y AS A, B FROM Y AS B, ..., C FROM Y AS C ) )
{ A, B, ..., C, D, E, ..., F }
```

where *s* is a relation with heading

```
{ X RELATION { D, E, ..., F }, Y TUPLE { D, E, ..., F } }
```

and with body containing every possible tuple such that the *Y* value (a tuple) is a member of the body of the *X* value (a relation). It follows that the original *<ungroup>* can be expressed in **A**.

Appendix B

A Design Dilemma

It is sometimes suggested that to consider relational domains as fully fledged data types, as *The Third Manifesto* does, is to introduce a design dilemma. For example, suppose we need to deal with employees, where every employee has an employee number (EMP#), a name (ENAME), a department number (DEPT#), and a salary (SALARY). Consider the following **Tutorial D** definitions (constraints deliberately omitted until further notice, for simplicity):

```
TYPE EMP
POSSREP { EMP# CHAR, ENAME CHAR, DEPT# CHAR, SALARY MONEY ... } ;      /* "Design T" */

VAR EMP REAL
RELATION { EMP# CHAR, ENAME CHAR, DEPT# CHAR, SALARY MONEY } ... ;      /* "Design R" */
```

Clearly, we could define an EMP *type* ("Design T") or an EMP *relvar* ("Design R"). The question we address in this appendix is: Which approach is better? What grounds are there for choosing one over the other?

ENCAPSULATION

One immediate difference between Design T and Design R is that the EMP type is **encapsulated**, while the EMP relvar is not. Now, *encapsulation* is a term much used in the object world, and you might already be familiar with it. However, you might also have noticed that we have not used it at all in this book prior to this point—mainly because we do not find much need for it; in fact, we believe it is the source of some confusion [64]. Be that as it may, we now explain it.

Briefly, to say some object is encapsulated is simply to say the object in question has *no user-visible components,* no matter how complex its physical representation—i.e., its internal encoding—might be. (We are using the term *object* here in its generic sense, not its special object-oriented sense.) Observe immediately, therefore, that all scalar values and variables are encapsulated by definition. Tuple and relation values and variables, by contrast, are not encapsulated in this sense, because they involve a set of user-visible attributes. In fact, **an object is encapsulated if and only if it is scalar;** that is, *encapsulated* and *scalar* mean exactly the same thing. And this fact explains why we find little use for the term: After all, it really just means users do not need to worry about what they *should* not need to worry about: namely, internal encodings. Indeed, the idea that scalar values and variables must be encapsulated is a logical consequence of the distinctions we draw between model and implementation in general, and between type and representation in particular.

Getting back to the example, the fact that the EMP type in Design T is encapsulated means that values and variables of type EMP are scalar (they have no internal structure so far as the user is concerned). Of course, we do have a set of operators available to us—THE_EMP#, THE_SALARY, etc., in **Tutorial D**—that allow us to "get and set" certain employee properties, but the availability of those operators says nothing about any internal structure employees might possess, as we have explained at several places in the body of this book already.

By contrast, the EMP relvar in Design R is definitely not encapsulated; that is, the user definitely does know with Design R that employees have a component that is the EMP# attribute, a component that is the SALARY attribute, and so on. Furthermore, of course, access to those components is not by means of "THE_ operators" or anything of that nature but is more direct (or what might be thought of as more direct, at any rate).

DISCUSSION

We now proceed to argue that, at least in the particular case under discussion, the "choice" is really no choice at all. Observe first that Design T gives us no way to hire and fire!—thus, that design is clearly insufficient as it stands. The reason is that type EMP is the set of *all possible employees*,[1] and there is simply no way to insert new employees into that set or delete existing ones. To put it another way, the set in question contains *all possible* values of the form EMP(*e#,en,d#,sal*), where *e#*, *en*, *d#*, and *sal* are values of types CHAR, CHAR, CHAR, and MONEY, respectively, regardless of whether any employee actually exists with the indicated properties. In other words (loosely): *Types are static.* Again, if you are having difficulty with this idea, consider the simpler example of type INTEGER. This type is the set of *all possible* integers, and it is clearly not possible to insert new ones or delete existing ones. (Indeed, to pursue the point a moment longer, suppose it *were* possible to "insert a new integer." Where would that "new integer" come from?)

It follows from the foregoing that Design T additionally requires an accompanying relvar, perhaps looking like this:

```
VAR EMP1 REAL RELATION { EMP EMP } KEY { EMP } ;
```

Relvar EMP1—"1" because it has just one attribute—contains a tuple for every employee currently of interest (meaning, presumably, every employee who currently works for the company), and now of course we do have a way to hire new employees and fire existing ones. Note carefully, however, that relvar EMP1 does indeed have just one attribute, not four, thanks to encapsulation. Note too that the KEY specification is almost a "no op"; in particular, it does *not* say that employee numbers are unique.

One implication of the Design T approach is thus that it tends to suggest that the database will wind up containing a large number of single-attribute relvars: a fact that should perhaps give us some pause (see later).

Anyway, note that now not only can we "hire and fire employees," we can also perform operations analogous—though not identical—to the usual relational operations that we would have performed on the relvar EMP if we had opted for Design R. Here are a couple of examples:

"Restriction": Get employees with salary greater than $50,000.

```
EMP1 WHERE THE_SALARY ( EMP ) > MONEY ( 50000 )
```

"Projection": Get all employee-name/employee-salary pairs.

```
( EXTEND EMP1 ADD ( THE_ENAME ( EMP ) AS ENAME, THE_SALARY ( EMP ) AS SALARY ) )
                                                          { ENAME, SALARY }
```

As you can see, however, the result in this second example has two attributes, not one! Thus, it should be clear that:

- Given the single-attribute relvar EMP1 required by Design T, we can create the four-attribute relvar EMP required by Design R (as a "view," perhaps).

---

1. More accurately, the set of all possible employee *surrogates* or *representatives*. The type EMP does not contain actual employees, of course, but rather *symbols*—symbols that can be used as surrogates or representatives (inside a database, for example) that stand for employees per se.

- Furthermore, we would probably want to do exactly that in practice, because—for a variety of reasons—the four-attribute relvar is considerably more convenient than the single-attribute one.

Here to spell it out is a definition for that four-attribute "view" (let us call it EMP4):

```
VAR EMP4 VIRTUAL ( ( EXTEND EMP1 ADD ( THE_EMP#   ( EMP ) AS EMP#,
                                       THE_ENAME  ( EMP ) AS ENAME,
                                       THE_DEPT#  ( EMP ) AS DEPT#,
                                       THE_SALARY ( EMP ) AS SALARY ) )
          { EMP#, ENAME, DEPT#, SALARY } ) KEY { EMP# } ;
```

Note in particular that the KEY specification for EMP4 does state that employee numbers are unique. In other words, we can start off with Design T, the type design, if we like, which means we also need an associated single-attribute relvar—but we quickly find that, in effect, we have created Design R (the relvar design) as well. So Design T implies that we wind up with everything in Design R, plus the type EMP, plus the single-attribute relvar EMP1 as well. So what was the point of opting for Design T in the first place? And what purpose is served, exactly, in Design T by the type EMP and the single-attribute relvar EMP1?

FURTHER CONSIDERATIONS

What then is the criterion for making something a type and not a relvar? (We must have some types, of course, if only for the obvious reason that relvars cannot be defined without them.) In our opinion, this question is still somewhat open. However, we offer the following points for consideration.

- In conventional design terms, types correspond—loosely speaking—to *properties* and relvars to *entities* (or sets of properties and sets of entities, rather). Hence, if something is "only" a property, it should map to a type and not a relvar.

  The trouble with this idea, of course, is that "one person's property is another person's entity." For example, consider colors. We would usually tend to think of (say) the color red as a property,[1] not an entity, and we would therefore usually tend to map colors into a type. But some users might be very interested in the color red as an entity, with further properties of its own (shade, for example, or intensity)—in which case we might want to map colors into a relvar. Perhaps this is an example of a situation where we need both a type and a relvar.

- Another important general point is that if "hire and fire" (or something analogous to "hire and fire") is a requirement, then we are definitely talking about entities rather than properties, and we should definitely be aiming for a relvar design.

  Given this state of affairs, incidentally, it is odd that so many articles and presentations on object systems use employees, departments, and so forth as examples of object classes. An object class is a type, of course, and so those presentations are typically forced to go on to define a "collection" for those employees, a "collection" for those departments, and so on. What is more, those "collections" are collections of encapsulated objects, and they therefore effectively omit the all-important user-visible attribute names. As a consequence, they do not lend themselves very well to the formulation of ad hoc queries, declarative integrity constraints, and so forth—a fact that advocates of the approach themselves often admit, apparently without being aware that it is

---

1. As a property of some entity, that is. The concept of a property in isolation makes no sense.

precisely the lack of user-visible attribute names (in effect, the encapsulation) that causes the difficulties.[1] As a trivial example, consider the class (i.e., type) INTEGER and some corresponding collection of "currently interesting" integers. Does that collection have a name for its sole attribute? Probably not. And if not, we cannot (e.g.) join it to any other collection.

■ The following conjecture (previously articulated in the exercises in Chapter 14) is relevant to the issue too: If the only operators that apply to some given type are the ones that are provided "automatically"—THE_ operators, selectors, "=", ":=", and so on—then the type was probably not worth defining in the first place.

Overall, we believe the most appropriate design will emerge if careful consideration is given to the distinction between (a) declarative sentences in natural language, on the one hand, and (b) the vocabulary used in the construction of such sentences on the other. As we showed in Chapter 2 (but simplifying slightly here), it is *unencapsulated tuples in relations* that stand for those sentences, and it is *encapsulated domain values in attributes in those tuples* that stand for particular elements—typically nouns—in that vocabulary. To say it slightly differently (and to repeat what we said in Chapter 2, albeit in different words): Domains, or types, give us values that represent things we might wish to make statements about; relations give us ways of making those statements.

Consider once again the EMP relvar of Design R. Suppose that relvar includes the tuple

```
TUPLE { EMP# 'E7', ENAME 'Amy', DEPT# 'D5', SALARY MONEY ( 60000 ) }
```

The existence of this tuple in the relvar means, by definition, that the database includes something that asserts that the following declarative sentence (statement) is true:

Employee E7, named Amy, is assigned to department D5 and earns a salary of $60,000.

By contrast, consider the EMP type of Design T. Where the relvar of Design R allowed us to insert the tuple just shown (loosely speaking), with the interpretation just explained, the type of Design T allows us instead to execute the following *selector invocation:*

```
EMP ( 'E7', 'Amy', 'D5', MONEY ( 60000 ) )
```

This invocation does not of itself assert or deny the truth of anything at all. Rather, it constitutes nothing more than a certain rather heavy-duty noun, something like "an E7-numbered, Amy-named, D5-assigned, $60,000-earning employee." Now, we can if we like form a 1-tuple containing just that noun—i.e., that EMP value—and then effectively insert that 1-tuple into the single-attribute relvar EMP1 that Design T additionally requires; to do so, however, is effectively just to place a "There exists" in front of that noun, to make a declarative sentence, the truth of which is thereby asserted.

Of course, the "true fact" asserted by the 4-tuple in Design R is exactly the same as the "true fact" asserted in different words (as it were) by the 1-tuple in Design T. However, designers might profitably reflect on which of the two ways of asserting that fact is the more economical, the more communicative, and the more tractable to further reasoning.

---

1. In fact, object systems typically support ad hoc queries, etc., by breaking encapsulation and exposing physical representations! To quote reference [107]: "All object DBMS products currently require that [object components] referenced in ... queries be public [i.e., visible to the user]." Likewise, reference [7] says: "Query management ... is one situation where violating encapsulation is almost obligatory."

Appendix C

Types and Units

We mentioned the fact a few times in earlier chapters (especially Chapter 6) that certain types—WEIGHT, LENGTH, ANGLE, TEMPERATURE, and many others—raise the question of how we ought to deal with units (e.g., inches vs. centimeters, in the case of lengths). In this appendix we examine this question more carefully. For definiteness, we focus for the most part on type LENGTH specifically.

Now, values of type LENGTH are lengths, of course—but what exactly does this statement mean? What exactly is a length? Clearly, it is a measure: a measure that has to be understood as being expressed in certain units in order for it to have a sensible interpretation. For example, we cannot meaningfully say that a certain length is "24" (say); rather, we have to say that it is, specifically, "24 inches" (say). Furthermore, of course, we could equally well say that the length in question is not "24 inches" but rather "2 feet" or "60.96 centimeters"; all three of these expressions denote the same value.

How can we deal with such matters in a formal computer system? What follows is one proposal, perhaps not very ambitious.

TYPE DEFINITION

The basic idea underlying our proposal is that there should be one declared possrep for each relevant unit of measure for the type in question (note the importance, therefore, of being able to declare two or more possreps for the same type). Consider type LENGTH, for example. In Chapter 6, we defined this type as follows:

```
TYPE LENGTH ORDINAL POSSREP { M RATIONAL CONSTRAINT M ≥ 0.0 } ;
```

("M" here stands for measure, as you will recall.) Now, however, we propose defining the type like this:

```
TYPE LENGTH ORDINAL
     POSSREP LENGTH_IN_INCHES { NO_OF_INCHES RATIONAL CONSTRAINT NO_OF_INCHES ≥ 0.0 }
     POSSREP LENGTH_IN_FEET   { NO_OF_FEET   RATIONAL CONSTRAINT NO_OF_FEET   ≥ 0.0 }
     POSSREP LENGTH_IN_CM     { NO_OF_CM     RATIONAL CONSTRAINT NO_OF_CM     ≥ 0.0 } ;
```

The possrep LENGTH_IN_INCHES, for example, corresponds to lengths measured in inches, and the single component of that possrep, which is called NO_OF_INCHES, denotes the corresponding measure (i.e., the applicable number of inches). Hence, e.g., the following code fragment will have the effect of setting the variable L to contain the length "six inches":

```
VAR L LENGTH ;

L := LENGTH_IN_INCHES ( 6.0 ) ;
```

Note: We deliberately give each possrep a distinct and explicit name in the foregoing example, instead of relying on the **Tutorial D** system of defaults as described in Chapters 3 and 5. It is our experience that using the default system can make it harder to see what is really going on (in the context under discussion, at any rate). Thus, for example, observe in the assignment to L that the selector invoked on the right side is specifically called LENGTH_IN_INCHES, not just LENGTH. (It might be more user-friendly in practice to give each possrep the same name as its sole component, but we deliberately do not do so here.)

SELECTORS

Suppose the physical representation of lengths is indeed in terms of inches (though as usual there is no need for the physical representation to be the same as any of the declared possreps, in general). Let the "highly protected operators not part of **D**" that provide access to physical representations be denoted by lowercase pseudocode, as in Chapter 3. Here then is the implementation code for the LENGTH_IN_INCHES selector:

```
OPERATOR LENGTH_IN_INCHES ( N RATIONAL ) RETURNS LENGTH ;
   BEGIN ;
      VAR L LENGTH ;
      I component of physical representation of L := N ;
      RETURN ( L ) ;
   END ;
END OPERATOR ;
```

We are assuming that the physical representation of a length involves a single component, of type RATIONAL, called I (for inches).

The LENGTH_IN_FEET and LENGTH_IN_CM selectors could and probably should be implemented analogously, as follows:

```
OPERATOR LENGTH_IN_FEET ( N RATIONAL ) RETURNS LENGTH ;
   BEGIN ;
      VAR L LENGTH ;
      I component of physical representation of L := N * 12 ;
      RETURN ( L ) ;
   END ;
END OPERATOR ;

OPERATOR LENGTH_IN_CM ( N RATIONAL ) RETURNS LENGTH ;
   BEGIN ;
      VAR L LENGTH ;
      I component of physical representation of L := N / 2.54 ;
      RETURN ( L ) ;
   END ;
END OPERATOR ;
```

Alternatively, they could be implemented in terms of the LENGTH_IN_INCHES selector, as follows (and what follows is genuine **Tutorial D** code, not pseudocode):

```
OPERATOR LENGTH_IN_FEET ( N RATIONAL ) RETURNS LENGTH ;
   RETURN ( LENGTH_IN_INCHES ( N * 12 ) ) ;
END OPERATOR ;

OPERATOR LENGTH_IN_CM ( N RATIONAL ) RETURNS LENGTH ;
   RETURN ( LENGTH_IN_INCHES ( N / 2.54 ) ) ;
END OPERATOR ;
```

Here is a code fragment showing some sample invocations of these selectors:

```
VAR L LENGTH ;

L := LENGTH_IN_INCHES (  6.0  ) ;
L := LENGTH_IN_FEET   (  0.5  ) ;
L := LENGTH_IN_CM     ( 15.24 ) ;
```

These three assignments all have the same effect.

THE_ OPERATORS

The operator THE_NO_OF_INCHES could be implemented as follows (pseudocode again):

```
OPERATOR THE_NO_OF_INCHES ( L LENGTH ) RETURNS RATIONAL ;
   RETURN ( I component of physical representation of L ) ;
END OPERATOR ;
```

The operators THE_NO_OF_FEET and THE_NO_OF_CM could be implemented analogously:

```
OPERATOR THE_NO_OF_FEET ( L LENGTH ) RETURNS RATIONAL ;
   RETURN ( ( I component of physical representation of L ) / 12 ) ;
END OPERATOR ;

OPERATOR THE_NO_OF_CM ( L LENGTH ) RETURNS RATIONAL ;
   RETURN ( ( I component of physical representation of L ) * 2.54 ) ;
END OPERATOR ;
```

Or they could be implemented in terms of THE_NO_OF_INCHES, as here (and this is valid **Tutorial D** code again):

```
OPERATOR THE_NO_OF_FEET ( L LENGTH ) RETURNS RATIONAL ;
   RETURN ( THE_NO_OF_INCHES ( L ) / 12 ) ;
END OPERATOR ;

OPERATOR THE_NO_OF_CM ( L LENGTH ) RETURNS RATIONAL ;
   RETURN ( THE_NO_OF_INCHES ( L ) * 2.54 ) ;
END OPERATOR ;
```

Here is a code fragment showing some sample invocations of these THE_ operators:

```
VAR N RATIONAL ;

N := THE_NO_OF_INCHES ( L ) ;
N := THE_NO_OF_FEET ( L ) ;
N := THE_NO_OF_CM ( L ) ;
```

If the current value of L is "six inches," these three assignments have the effect of setting N to 6.0, 0.5, and 15.24, respectively. And here are examples of the use of the same three THE_ operators as pseudovariables:

```
THE_NO_OF_INCHES ( L ) :=  6.0  ;
THE_NO_OF_FEET ( L )    :=  0.5  ;
THE_NO_OF_CM ( L )      := 15.24 ;
```

Again these three assignments all have the same effect; in fact, they are logically equivalent to—i.e., shorthand for—the three assignments shown at the end of the previous section (the ones with L on the left side and selector invocations on the right side).

COMPUTATIONAL OPERATORS

We clearly need to be able to perform various kinds of computations involving lengths. Here first is an operator that allows two lengths to be added to yield another:

```
OPERATOR ADD_LENGTHS ( L1 LENGTH, L2 LENGTH ) RETURNS LENGTH ;
   RETURN ( LENGTH_IN_INCHES ( THE_NO_OF_INCHES ( L1 ) + THE_NO_OF_INCHES ( L2 ) ) ) ;
END OPERATOR ;
```

Points to note:

- The ADD_LENGTHS implementation makes use of the "+" operator for rational numbers. It would be nice to be able to use the same syntax—in other words, to overload the "+" operator—for invoking ADD_LENGTHS, thereby writing (e.g.) L1+L2 instead of ADD_LENGTHS (L1,L2). For simplicity, therefore, we will assume for the rest of this appendix that the usual infix notation "+" can indeed be used for lengths. We omit the details of how that infix notation might be specified in practice, since it is basically just a syntax issue (but see the next bullet item). *Note:* We could have implemented "+" for lengths in terms of feet or centimeters instead of inches without making any logical difference, just so long as we are careful to use the same units throughout the code. (For efficiency, however, we might want the possrep involved to be the same as, or close to, the physical representation.)

- Of course, the foregoing implementation of "+" for lengths effectively just says: "Addition for lengths is done by invoking the regular addition operator on a certain component of a certain possrep for lengths." In other words, we are talking about a mechanism known as **operator delegation**—the responsibility for implementing "+" for type LENGTH is "delegated" to the type, RATIONAL, of a certain component of one of its possreps. *Note:* We will have more to say about delegation in Appendix G. In practice it might be desirable to provide some shorthand syntax for it, instead of requiring operator definitions to be written out in longhand as in our example.

- As you can see, units are definitely a consideration in the *implementation* of the "+" operator for lengths. However, they are not a consideration in the *use* of that operator. For example, given variables L1 and L2 as follows—

```
VAR L1 LENGTH ;
VAR L2 LENGTH ;
```

—we can write an expression such as L1+L2 without having to worry about whether the lengths are measured in inches or centimeters or whatever.

- In practice, it would be desirable to be able to inform the system (e.g., for optimization purposes) that "+" for lengths is commutative—i.e., L1+L2 = L2+L1 for all possible lengths L1 and L2.

Analogously, it would be desirable to be able to inform the system that the operator is also associative—i.e., L1+(L2+L3) = (L1+L2)+L3 for all possible lengths L1, L2, and L3. We have no concrete suggestions to offer in this connection, however, other than to note that the shorthand syntax for delegation mentioned under the second bullet item above might be sufficient to take care of the issue.

Here are some other computational operators that we would probably want for type LENGTH (we omit the implementation code for brevity):

- An operator to subtract one length from another to return a length. We will use the infix notation "-" for this operator.

- An operator to multiply a length by an integer or a rational to return a length. We will use the infix notation "*" for this operator. In practice, we would like to be able to let the system know that the operator is both commutative and associative (again, the shorthand delegation syntax might suffice).

- An operator to multiply two lengths to return an area (i.e., we assume the existence of another type, AREA, to which analogous units considerations also apply). We will use the infix notation "*" for this operator too, thereby overloading it even further. We would like to be able to tell the system that this new operator is commutative and associative, too.[1]

- An operator to allow a length to be divided by a rational or an integer to return a length. We will use the infix notation "/" for this operator.

And so on.

Here are some examples to illustrate the use of some of these computational operators:

```
VAR L  LENGTH ;
VAR L1 LENGTH ;
VAR L2 LENGTH ;
VAR A  AREA ;

L := L1 + L2 ;
L := 2.0 * ( L1 - L2 ) ;
A := 2 * L1 * L2 ;
```

Note that (to repeat) units are not a consideration in any of these examples.

DISPLAY OPERATORS

Assume the existence of a DISPLAY operator that returns a character string representation of its argument value, which we take for present purposes to be a length specifically. Now, it could certainly be argued that displaying a length without some indication of the corresponding units makes little sense. Thus, for example, the following assignment might be prohibited:

---

1. In connection with associativity, however, note that while the expression L1*L2*L3 (where L1, L2, and L3 are all lengths) is certainly valid, the value denoted by that expression is a volume, not an area.

```
N := DISPLAY ( L ) ;                              /* invalid ??? */
```

Instead, we might have to say something like this:

```
N := DISPLAY ( THE_NO_OF_INCHES ( L ) ) ;
```

In other words, the DISPLAY operator is perhaps best defined to take a parameter of type RATIONAL, not one of type LENGTH. Alternatively, we might define a version of DISPLAY that does take a parameter of type LENGTH and returns a character string such as, say, '6.00 inches', in which certain *default* units are made explicit.

TYPE CONSTRAINTS

The definition for type LENGTH shown earlier in this appendix constrained lengths (not unreasonably) to be nonnegative. In practice, however, we would probably want to constrain them to be less than some maximum, too. Suppose for the sake of the example that the maximum length we ever want to deal with is one mile. Then the type definition might look like this:[1]

```
TYPE LENGTH ORDINAL
     POSSREP LENGTH_IN_INCHES  { NO_OF_INCHES RATIONAL CONSTRAINT NO_OF_INCHES ≥ 0.0
                                                     AND NO_OF_INCHES ≤ 63360.0 }
     POSSREP LENGTH_IN_FEET    { NO_OF_FEET   RATIONAL CONSTRAINT NO_OF_FEET   ≥ 0.0
                                                     AND NO_OF_FEET   ≤ 5280.00 }
     POSSREP LENGTH_IN_CM      { NO_OF_CM     RATIONAL CONSTRAINT NO_OF_CM     ≥ 0.0
                                                     AND NO_OF_CM     ≤ 160934.40 } ;
```

Observe that, given the foregoing constraints, an attempt to add one length to—or subtract one length from—another might lead to a type constraint violation. (We mention this possibility in connection with ADD_LENGTHS specifically because ADD_LENGTHS was the one operator we gave a definition for in the section "Computational Operators." However, a similar remark is likely to apply to other operators as well. In the case of ADD_LENGTHS specifically, the type constraint violation will occur if the argument to the LENGTH_IN_INCHES selector invocation is out of range.)

A MORE COMPLEX EXAMPLE

We conclude this appendix with a slightly more complicated example, in order to show how some of the ideas we have been discussing might fit together in practice. Suppose we have the following types (the semantics are meant to be obvious):

```
TYPE DURATION ORDINAL
     POSSREP MILLISECONDS { NO_OF_MSECS RATIONAL ... }
     POSSREP SECONDS      { NO_OF_SECS  RATIONAL ... }
     POSSREP MINUTES      { NO_OF_MINS  RATIONAL ... } ;
```

---

1. The various CONSTRAINT specifications in this example are all equivalent (as indeed they must be, as noted in the discussion of type POINT under RM Prescription 23 in Chapter 6), and thus clearly involve some redundancy—a fact that raises the question of whether there might be some better way of stating them. Further study is required.

```
TYPE SPEED ORDINAL
     POSSREP FEET_PER_SEC { NO_OF_FPS RATIONAL ... } ;

TYPE ACCELERATION ORDINAL
     POSSREP FEET_PER_SEC_SQD { NO_OF_FPS_SQD RATIONAL ... } ;
```

Here then is a possible implementation of the well-known formula $s = ut + \frac{1}{2}ft^2$ (s = distance, u = initial speed, t = time, f = acceleration):

```
OPERATOR S ( U SPEED, T DURATION, F ACCELERATION ) RETURNS LENGTH ;
   RETURN ( LENGTH_IN_FEET ( THE_NO_OF_FPS ( U ) * THE_NO_OF_SECS ( T )
                          + 0.5 * THE_NO_OF_FPS_SQD ( F ) * ( THE_NO_OF_SECS ( T ) ** 2 ) ) ) ;
END OPERATOR ;
```

Appendix D

What Is a Database?

This book's predecessor [83] included text along the following lines:

> The first version of the *Manifesto* drew a distinction between database values and database variables, analogous to that between relation values and relation variables. It also introduced the term *dbvar* as shorthand for *database variable*. While we still believe this distinction to be a valid one, we found it had little direct relevance to other aspects of the *Manifesto*. We therefore decided, in the interests of familiarity, to revert to more traditional terminology.

And we have continued to use the term *database* in the traditional way in the present book, of course. However, reference [85] quotes the foregoing text and then adds:

> Now this bad decision has come home to roost! With hindsight, it would have been much better to "bite the bullet" and adopt the more logically correct terms *database value* and *database variable* (or dbvar), despite their lack of familiarity.

That same reference gives arguments in support of this position, but those arguments need not concern us here; the simple fact is, a database *is* a variable (its value changes over time), regardless of whether we call it a "dbvar" or just a database. As William Shakespeare would agree, differences in terminology (only) are not logical differences.

UPDATING THE DATABASE

It follows from the foregoing that when we update a database relvar, what we are really doing is updating the dbvar that contains that relvar (for clarity, we adopt the term *dbvar* for the remainder of this discussion). For example, the **Tutorial D** *<relation delete>*—

```
DELETE SP WHERE QTY < QTY(150)
```

—updates the shipments relvar SP and thus "really" updates the entire suppliers-and-parts dbvar (the "new" database value for that dbvar being the same as the "old" one except that certain shipment tuples have been removed).

Recall now, however, that in Chapter 6 (under RM Prescription 13) we said this:

> Do not make the mistake of thinking that a relation variable is a set of tuple variables. A relation variable is a variable whose permitted values are relation values; updating a relation variable replaces the current relation value of that variable by another such value. There is no notion, nor can there be any notion, that "updating a relation variable" really means updating some tuple variable(s) within the relation variable in question.

This idea—i.e., that it makes no sense to regard, e.g., a relation variable as a collection of tuple variables—is considered at more length in reference [79]. But if it makes no sense to regard a relvar as a collection of tuple variables or "tuplevars," how can it make sense to regard a dbvar as a collection of relvars? Are we not being inconsistent here?

A point of clarification: Before we try to answer these questions, we need to make it clear that when we say the database is a variable, we are speaking *conceptually*. The *Manifesto* includes no prescription regarding the ability to define such variables or the ability to operate on them (other than indirectly, via database relvars); it does not even have anything to say regarding the names of such variables. And **Tutorial D** has nothing to say about such matters either. To quote Chapter 5: "[Neither] databases nor catalogs are explicitly mentioned anywhere in the syntax of **Tutorial D**."

DATABASES VS. TUPLES

We now claim there is no inconsistency in our position after all. (Were you surprised?) While we might say, informally, that a dbvar is a variable that contains other variables (viz., relvars), we stress the fact that such a characterization is indeed only informal. We claim further that there is a more formal and more accurate way to describe the situation—viz.:

A dbvar is a tuplevar.

The tuplevar in question has one attribute for each real relvar[1] in the dbvar (and no other attributes), and each of those attributes is relation valued. In the case of suppliers and parts, for example, we can think of the entire dbvar as a tuplevar of the following tuple type:

```
TUPLE { S  RELATION { S# S#, SNAME NAME, STATUS INTEGER, CITY CHAR },
        P  RELATION { P# P#, PNAME NAME, COLOR COLOR, WEIGHT WEIGHT, CITY CHAR }
        SP RELATION { S# S#, P# P#, QTY QTY } }
```

Suppose we call the tuplevar in question SPDB. Then the DELETE example from the previous section might be regarded as shorthand for the following < *tuple update* >:

```
UPDATE SPDB ( SP := SP WHERE NOT ( QTY < QTY(150) ) )
```

And this < *tuple update* > in turn is shorthand for the following < *tuple assign* >:

```
SPDB := UPDATE SPDB ( SP := SP WHERE NOT ( QTY < QTY(150) ) )
```

This < *tuple assign* > expands to:

```
SPDB := ( ( EXTEND SPDB
              ADD ( SP WHERE NOT ( QTY < QTY(150) )
              AS NEWSP ) ) { ALL BUT SP } )
          RENAME ( NEWSP AS SP )
```

Or equivalently to:

```
SPDB := TUPLE { S  (  S  FROM SPDB ) ,
                P  (  P  FROM SPDB ) ,
                SP ( ( SP FROM SPDB ) WHERE NOT ( QTY < QTY(150) ) ) }
```

In sum: A dbvar is a tuplevar, and a database (i.e., the value of some given dbvar at some given time) is a tuple. What is more, given a < *relation assign* > of the form

---

1. We ignore virtual relvars in this appendix, for simplicity.

```
R := r
```

(where R is a *<relation target>* and r is a *<relation exp>*), we can say that the expression R appearing on the left side is really a pseudovariable reference!—the *<relation assign>* is shorthand for an assignment that "zaps" one component of the corresponding dbvar (or tuplevar).

We close this section (and this appendix) by noting that Exercise 1 in Chapter 1 asked for a precise definition of the term *database*. This appendix provides such a definition—one that is possibly rather different from what you might have expected.

Appendix E

View Updating

Every scientific discipline has its share of unsolved problems. In mathematics, for example, nobody has succeeded in over 100 years in either proving or disproving the Riemann Hypothesis; in computer science, the "P = NP" question is still open after some 35 years; in physics and cosmology, the long search for a "theory of everything" remains just that, a search (some might dispute this last claim). Thus, no book that addresses the frontiers of some field of scientific endeavor can claim to have all the answers, as it were. In this appendix, we examine an aspect of the database field, view updating, where there are certainly still some unresolved issues. Of course, we do not mean to suggest that the problem of view updating is in the same league as the Riemann Hypothesis or the "P = NP" issue or some hypothetical "theory of everything"—but we do believe it merits attention as a matter of considerable practical and theoretical interest, and we continue to work on it. This appendix is a progress report on that activity.

In the interests of full disclosure, we must now explain that view updating is an area where, unusually, the authors of this book are not yet in full agreement. Given the importance of the subject matter, however, we decided to go ahead and set our thoughts down in writing anyway, with the hope of at least getting some debate going among those who are interested in such matters. We also decided to present Date's opinions first and Darwen's, as an alternative perspective, second. For obvious reasons, we also decided, again unusually, to write in the first person singular where appropriate.

All opinions expressed in what follows, up to the section "Darwen's Approach," are thus Date's specifically.

DATE'S APPROACH

I claim that *constraints*—specifically, database constraints—are the key to the view updating problem, and I therefore propose to take a closer look at such constraints in this appendix. In fact, I need to cover quite a lot of preliminary material before I can get to view updating as such. I should say too that I have been down numerous blind alleys in this investigation! It would be much too tedious to document all of those blind alleys here, but it would be dishonest not to admit that my previous writings on this topic have suffered from a good deal of error and confusion. And there are still, to repeat, some unresolved issues (appropriately flagged in what follows). But I feel enough issues have been resolved to make me cautiously optimistic about the remainder. Despite its incompleteness, therefore, I explicitly regard what follows as superseding all of my previous writings on this subject.

Of course, a great deal of work has been done on view updating by other researchers. I do not claim to be familiar with all of that prior work, but I have not seen a treatment in the literature that is the same as, or even close to, the one that follows—with the exception of that by David McGoveran and myself in reference [88], which as I have already indicated I see the treatment that follows as superseding (or extending and superseding, rather). *Note:* McGoveran's proposals in his patent application [114] are broadly consistent with what follows, but some of the details seem to be different, and I will certainly be going into more specifics than reference [114] does.

ASSUMPTIONS AND NOTATION

For simplicity I adopt a number of assumptions and notational abbreviations in what follows. To be specific:

- As you might have noticed already, I (usually) use the term *view* instead of the *Manifesto* term *virtual relvar*—though I retain the *Manifesto* term *real relvar* for a relvar that is not a view, and I continue to use the generic term *relvar* to mean a real relvar or a view or both, as the context demands.

- I use uppercase italic letters for generic relvar names (among other things) and corresponding lowercase italic letters for corresponding relvar values. Thus, for example, relvar R has current value r.

- I take the unqualified term *constraint* to mean, specifically, what Chapter 2 called a *total relvar constraint*, barring explicit statements to the contrary.

- I use RC to denote the constraint for relvar R. I also use RX and RY to denote what I will be calling the X constraint for R and the Y constraint for R, respectively (see the section "A Closer Look at Constraints" for an explanation of these latter terms).

- I use the symbol "$\equiv$" to mean "is equivalent to" or "is defined as" or "be defined as" or "can be defined as" or just "defined as," as the context demands.

  I also abbreviate several **Tutorial D** keywords and syntactic constructs:

- I use the symbols "∩", "∪", and "-" to denote INTERSECT, UNION, and MINUS, respectively.

- I usually, though not exclusively, use the symbols "&", "|", and "¬" to denote AND, OR, and NOT, respectively.

- I use the symbol "ϕ" to denote an empty relation.

- I use the symbol "=▶" to denote logical implication, thereby writing, e.g., "p =▶ q" instead of "IF p THEN q END IF" (the **Tutorial D** analog).

- I use dot qualification to denote the operation of extracting an attribute value from a tuple, thereby writing, e.g., "$t.A$" instead of "A FROM t" (the **Tutorial D** analog).

- As elsewhere in this book, I use a simplified syntax for tuples—more precisely, tuple selector invocations—thereby writing, e.g., <S1,P1,300> instead of

  ```
  TUPLE { S# S#('S1'), P# P#('P1'), QTY QTY(300) }
  ```

  (the **Tutorial D** analog).

- I use a syntax for constraints that is directly based on that of predicate logic, instead of the more algebraic style used in the body of the book. I also introduce some shorthands. To be specific, I use the expression

  ```
  FORALL t ∈ R ( p )
  ```

("all tuples *t* in *R* are such that *p*") as shorthand for

```
FORALL t ( ( t ∈ R ) ⟹ ( p ) )
```

Analogously, I use the expression

```
EXISTS t ∈ R ( p )
```

("there exists a tuple in *R* such that *p*") as shorthand for

```
EXISTS t ( ( t ∈ R ) & ( p ) )
```

Note: The expressions FORALL *t* ∈ *R* and EXISTS *t* ∈ *R* in these shorthands are examples of what reference [22] calls *range-coupled quantifiers*.

A CLOSER LOOK AT RELATIONAL ASSIGNMENT

Note: This section is based on ideas first suggested by David McGoveran.

To say that *V* is a variable is to say that *V* is assignable to (i.e., updatable).[1] As stated in Chapter 3, moreover, after assignment of value *v* to variable *V*, the comparison *v* = *V* is required to evaluate to TRUE (*The Assignment Principle*), otherwise the assignment fails ("is undone") and *V* retains its previous value.

Now, the foregoing remarks are true of variables in general and therefore of relvars in particular. That is, the way we update a relvar *R* is precisely by means of a relational assignment in which the target is *R*:

```
R := exp
```

R here is a *relvar reference* (denoting relvar *R*, of course) and *exp* is an expression that denotes some relation *x* that is to be assigned to that relvar *R*. After the assignment, *R* = *x* must evaluate to TRUE; also, the constraint *RC* must be satisfied (**The Golden Rule**). If either of these requirements is violated, the update is undone and *R* retains its previous value. *Note:* Strictly speaking, **The Golden Rule** applies to the database in its entirety. Here I am appealing to what Chapter 2 called a weaker form of that rule (a logical consequence of the more general version), which states that no assignment statement can ever leave any *relvar* in a state that violates its own constraint.

From this point forward, I take the term *assignment* to mean a relational assignment specifically.

Next I remind you that INSERT, DELETE, and UPDATE are really just shorthands for certain assignments. Again consider the assignment:

```
R := exp
```

It is intuitively obvious that the expression *exp* is logically equivalent to, and can therefore be replaced by, an expression of the form

```
r - d ∪ i
```

---

1. In this connection, I remind you that, as noted in Chapter 6, if some relvar (in particular, some view) turns out to be intrinsically nonupdatable—as opposed to being nonupdatable simply because of, e.g., some constraint violation—then it is hardly appropriate to call it a "relvar" (i.e., a variable) in the first place.

where:

- r is the value of R before the assignment, d is a set of tuples to be deleted from R, and i is a set of tuples to be inserted into R after that deletion has been done. (More precisely, d and i, like r, are really relations, and the "sets of tuples" I am talking about are really the bodies of those relations. I will ignore this detail in what follows.)

- d is a subset of r (i.e., $d\text{-}r = \phi$), because deleting a tuple that was not there in the first place has no logical effect; in other words, there is no point in making d any bigger than it need be.

- r and i are disjoint (i.e., $r \cap i = \phi$), because inserting a tuple that was already there has no logical effect; in other words, there is no point in making i any bigger than it need be.

- d and i are disjoint (i.e., $d \cap i = \phi$), because there is no point in deleting a tuple and then inserting it again all as part of the same assignment.

I now show that, for a given assignment $R := r\text{-}d\cup i$ and a given initial value r of R, d and i are unique. Suppose, contrariwise, that

```
r - d1 U i1 = r - d2 U i2
```

for some $d1 \neq d2$ and/or some $i1 \neq i2$, where (in accordance with the conditions spelled out above), $d1\text{-}r = d2\text{-}r = r \cap i1 = r \cap i2 = d1 \cap i1 = d2 \cap i2 = \phi$. Then:

- Let $t \in d1\text{-}d2$. Since $d1\text{-}r = \phi$, $t \in r\text{-}d2$ and $t \notin r\text{-}d1$. Hence $t \in r\text{-}d2\cup i2$; therefore $t \in r\text{-}d1\cup i1$. Since $t \notin r\text{-}d1$, $t \in i1$. But then $d1 \cap i1 \neq \phi$, which is a contradiction; hence no such t exists and $d1\text{-}d2 = \phi$ (i.e., $d1$ is a subset of $d2$). A similar argument shows that $d2$ is a subset of $d1$. Hence $d1 = d2$.

- We thus have $r\text{-}d1 = r\text{-}d2 = z$, say. Then $z\cup i1 = z\cup i2$. But $r \cap i1 = \phi$, so $(r\text{-}d1) \cap i1 = \phi$, so $z \cap i1 = \phi$. A similar argument shows that $z \cap i2 = \phi$. Hence, since $z\cup i1 = z\cup i2$, $i1 = i2$.

It follows from the foregoing that if x is the relation to be assigned to R, then x can be expressed as either $r\text{-}d\cup i$ or $r\cup i\text{-}d$ (i.e., it makes no difference whether we do the delete first or the insert). It further follows that, given r and x, we have:

```
d = r - x
i = x - r
```

I can now define the operations INSERT and DELETE: An INSERT is an assignment for which $d = \phi$, a DELETE is an assignment for which $i = \phi$ (and an UPDATE is a DELETE followed by an INSERT). In other words:

- ```
  INSERT i INTO R  ≡  R := R U i   /* syntax    */
                   ≡  R := r U i   /* semantics */
  ```

- ```
  DELETE d FROM R  ≡  R := R - d   /* syntax    */
                   ≡  R := r - d   /* semantics */
  ```

where $i \cap r = d\text{-}r = \phi$. Moreover:

- After INSERT, the comparison $R = r \cup i$ and the constraint RC must both evaluate to TRUE.

- After DELETE, the comparison $R = r\text{-}d$ and the constraint RC must both evaluate to TRUE.

Note: I deliberately do not use **Tutorial D** INSERT and DELETE syntax here. Also, note that in Chapter 6 we did not legislate on whether it was an error to try to insert a tuple that was already present or delete one that was not, but here I do (because I require that $i \cap r = d\text{-}r = \phi$). In the case of DELETE, however, I observe that in practice the operation will usually be expressed in the form DELETE R WHERE p, in which case d is necessarily a subset of r, and we have:

- ```
  DELETE R WHERE p  ≡  R := R WHERE ¬ ( p )  /* syntax */
                    ≡  R := r WHERE ¬ ( p )  /* semantics */
  ```

It follows from all of the above that it would be sufficient to investigate INSERT and DELETE operations specifically rather than general assignment, and for a long time I tried to do exactly that (I felt it was a good idea because INSERT and DELETE are, at least arguably, intuitively easier to understand than assignment in general). But this idea turned out to be one of the blind alleys I mentioned earlier. One reason it was a blind alley had to do with "nested updates"; I will be discussing that topic in detail in a later section, but the point should be intuitively understandable even without that detailed discussion (though no harm is done if not). Consider an update of the form INSERT i INTO R, where $R \equiv A \cap B$. It should be clear that this update might involve the "insertion" of a tuple t into A (say) that in fact already exists in A, thereby violating the precondition for INSERT. Likewise, a request of the form DELETE d FROM R where $R \equiv A \cup B$ might involve the "deletion" of a tuple t from B (say) that in fact does not exist in B, thereby violating the precondition for DELETE. In other words, it turned out to be useful to talk in terms of both:

- *INSERT-type assignments* of the form $R := r \cup i$ where $i \cap r$ is not necessarily equal to ϕ[1]

- *DELETE-type assignments* of the form $R := r\text{-}d$ where $d\text{-}r$ is not necessarily equal to ϕ

In what follows, therefore, I will talk mostly in terms of INSERT- and DELETE-type assignments instead of INSERTs and DELETEs as such (note that I do still find it helpful to consider the two cases separately). In other words, I will be discussing view updating in terms of assignment after all. Observe, however, that the assignments in question will be multiple assignments, in general; for example, updating $R \equiv A \cap B$ will usually involve updating both A and B (a double assignment). Observe too that UPDATE in particular can be thought of as a double assignment—to be specific, an UPDATE on R can be thought of as an assignment of the form $R := R\text{-}d$, $R := R \cup i$. (Though this double assignment in fact reduces to the single assignment $R := $ WITH $R\text{-}d$ AS R: $R \cup i$, as explained in Chapter 6.)

---

1. Footnote 1 on page 154 raises the possibility of supporting two distinct "insert" operators—INSERT, which does not treat an attempt to insert an existing tuple as an error, and D_INSERT, which does. If this suggestion is adopted, all references to "INSERT" and "INSERT-type assignment" in my portions of this appendix could be replaced by references to D_INSERT and INSERT, respectively.
  ```

A MODEL OF UPDATING

Consider the assignment

```
R := x
```

where R is a real relvar. Clearly, the semantics of this assignment can be explained in terms of the following conceptual algorithm:

1.   Assign x to R.

2.   (Check *The Assignment Principle*.) If $R = x$ evaluates to FALSE, undo the assignment.

3.   (Check **The Golden Rule**.) If RC evaluates to FALSE, undo the assignment.

I remark in passing that conceptual algorithms along the foregoing lines appear at several points in what follows. In some cases, some of the steps can safely be omitted (for example, it might sometimes be impossible for *The Assignment Principle* to be violated); however, I will usually show all steps for explicitness.

Now recall *The Principle of Interchangeability,* which was mentioned briefly under RM Prescription 14 in Chapter 6: *There must be no arbitrary and unnecessary distinctions between views and real relvars* (emphasis on *arbitrary and unnecessary*). It follows that updates on views in particular must behave as far as possible as if those views were real relvars. By way of example, let $R \equiv A \cap B$, and consider the update INSERT i INTO R. R is supposed to "look and feel" as far as possible just like a real relvar, and so it follows that the semantics of the INSERT must be as defined by the following conceptual algorithm:[1]

1.   (Materialize R.) Create a temporary real relvar R' with initial value r ($= a \cap b$, where a and b are the current values of A and B, respectively).

2.   (Update R'.) INSERT i INTO R'.

3.   (Recompute R.) Given the new value $r \cup i$ of R', assign the new values $a' = (a-b) \cup (r \cup i)$ and $b' = (b-a) \cup (r \cup i)$ to A and B, respectively, and thereby obtain the new value $a' \cap b'$ for R.

4.   Check *The Assignment Principle* for R ($a' \cap b'$ should be equal to $r \cup i = (a \cap b) \cup i$).

5.   Check **The Golden Rule** for A and B (a' and b' should satisfy constraints AC and BC, respectively). Note that if a' and b' do satisfy AC and BC, respectively, then $r' = a' \cap b'$ will necessarily satisfy RC. *Note:* I assume here and throughout this paper that any constraints expressed directly in terms of a view R are replaced, at least conceptually, by equivalent constraints expressed in terms of the relvar(s) in terms of which R is defined; in effect, therefore, I assume that constraints refer to real relvars only. This simplifying assumption does not prevent us from talking in terms of "the constraint RC for a view R" when we need to do so, of course.

6.   Discard R'.

---

1. Note that the definitional trick used in this algorithm—that of introducing a temporary target—could be used as the basis for an alternative definition of multiple assignment, one that might be simpler than that given in Chapter 4.

The algorithm for DELETE *d* FROM *R* is analogous.

Algorithms such as those outlined above constitute a model for how updating is supposed to work, and that model at least implicitly underpins everything I have to say in the rest of this appendix. Of course, I do not mean the DBMS actually has to execute those algorithms as such; rather, it is free to perform updates in whatever way it likes, just so long as whatever it does do is guaranteed to give the result prescribed by the model. Indeed, in what follows I usually give what might be seen as implementation algorithms (albeit ones that are far from optimal) instead of relying on the conceptual algorithms of the model as such. For example, the DBMS might—and often will, as I will show in the next section—be able to tell "ahead of time" that some tuple presented for insertion would cause the target relvar to violate its own constraint; thus, it (the DBMS) might be able to "undo" the update by simply not performing it in the first place. These remarks apply to both real relvars and views.

A CLOSER LOOK AT CONSTRAINTS

Now I turn to the promised closer look at constraints. I begin with some definitions. Let *DBC* be the total database constraint for some database *DB*. Without loss of generality, we can assume *DBC* takes the following form—

```
( DBC1 ) & ( DBC2 ) & ... & ( DBCn ) & TRUE
```

—where (a) each *DBCi* ($i = 1, 2, ..., n$) in turn takes the form[1]

```
( Pi1 ) | ( Pi2 ) | ... | ( Pim )
```

and (b) each *Pij* ($j = 1, 2, ..., m$) is a nonnegated proposition of one of the following forms:

```
FORALL t ∈ R ( RQij )
```

or

```
EXISTS t ∈ R ( RQij )
```

Here *R* is some relvar *R* in database *DB* and *RQij* is a predicate with sole parameter *t* (and I rely on the fact that leading NOTs can be eliminated, thanks to the equivalence ¬(EXISTS *x*(*p*)) ≡ FORALL *x*(¬(*p*))). *Note:* As previously stated, I assume for simplicity that every *DBCi* is formulated in terms of real relvars only; in fact, I assume until further notice that all relvars are real ones.

Now set to TRUE each *DBCi* in *DBC* for which none of the constituent propositions *Pij* mentions relvar *R* at any level of nesting. Next, for each *DBCi* in *DBC*, set to FALSE each *Pij* in *DBCi* that fails to mention relvar *R* at any level of nesting. What results is **the total relvar constraint, *RC*,** for relvar *R*.

I now conjecture[2] that, in general, *RC* is logically equivalent to an expression of the form (*RZ*)&(*RY*), where:

- *RZ* is either simply TRUE or it takes the form

---

1. It might help to think of each *DBCi*, informally, as being a database constraint as explicitly declared in concrete syntax (loosely, the total database constraint is the AND of all such explicitly declared constraints).

2. Throughout this appendix I use the term *conjecture* in connection with issues that might need further investigation.

```
FORALL t ∈ R ( RX )
```

where *RX* is quantifier free and thus has the property that, given any tuple *t* with the same heading as *R*, it can be evaluated for that tuple *t* by examining just that tuple *t* in isolation.

- *RY* (which also might be simply TRUE) has the property that, given any relation *r* assignable to *R*, it can be evaluated for that relation *r*, albeit not without examining other relvars referenced in *RY*.

I assume that if *R* is a real relvar, then *RX* and *RY* are known (I will consider the case of a virtual relvar later), and I will refer to them in what follows as "the *X* and *Y* constraints" for *R*. *Note:* In practice it would probably be desirable for *RY* to include no nontrivial "subconstraint," as it were, with the same properties as *RZ*—in other words, it would be desirable for *RZ* to be the *maximal* subconstraint of *RC* to possess the properties in question—but I do not rely on *RZ* being maximal in this (or any other) sense. But no harm is done, logically speaking, if we replace *RZ* by TRUE and *RY* by *RC* throughout; my aim in splitting *RC* into *RZ* and *RY* is merely (a) to make certain explanations intuitively easier to understand, (b) to provide a basis for certain simple optimizations, and (c) to mirror, in certain respects, the way we define constraints in practice.[1]

I now illustrate these ideas with a series of examples. For simplicity I assume in each case that the particular constraint under discussion is the total relvar constraint, barring explicit statements to the contrary.

1. Supplier status is greater than zero. Formal expression:

```
FORALL t ∈ S ( t.STATUS > 0 )
```

For this example, the *X* and *Y* constraints *SX* and *SY* are *t*.STATUS > 0 and TRUE, respectively. Overall, the constraint says: If we insert some tuple into S, then after that INSERT every tuple in S must have status greater than zero; likewise, if we delete some tuple from S, then after that DELETE every tuple in S must have status greater than zero. Two obvious optimizations are possible:

- If we attempt to insert some tuple *t*, the DBMS can reject the attempt "ahead of time" (i.e., before doing the INSERT) if that tuple violates the *X* constraint for S—i.e., if *t*.STATUS ≤ 0.

- If we attempt to delete some tuple *t*, the DBMS need not check the constraint at all, since DELETE cannot possibly cause it to be violated.

2. Suppliers in London have status 20:

```
FORALL t ∈ S ( t.CITY = 'London' ⇒ t.STATUS = 20 )
```

Here *SX* is *t*.CITY = 'London' ⇒ *t*.STATUS = 20 and *SY* is TRUE. Thus, if we attempt to insert the tuple <S8,Finzi,30,London>, the DBMS does not need to perform the actual insertion because it can tell ahead of time that it will fail.

---

1. In fact, we could if we liked simply regard the total database constraint *DBC* as the *relvar* constraint for each and every individual relvar; after all, subconstraints within *DBC* that fail to mention relvar *R* are simply irrelevant so far as *R* is concerned.

3. Supplier numbers are unique:

```
FORALL t ∈ S ( FORALL u ∈ S ( u.S# = t.S# ═► u = t ) )
```

In this example, *SX* is just TRUE and *SY* is the whole of *SC*—and indeed it is intuitively obvious that if a tuple is presented for insertion into S, we cannot tell ahead of time whether that tuple causes the uniqueness constraint to be violated without examining other tuples, in general. *Note:* Another obvious shorthand would allow the foregoing expression to be simplified to just:

```
FORALL t,u ∈ S ( u.S# = t.S# ═► u = t )
```

I will make use of this further shorthand from time to time in what follows.

4. No supplier with status less than 20 can supply part P6:

```
FORALL t ∈ S ( t.STATUS < 20 ═► FORALL u ∈ SP ( u.S# = t.S# ═► u.P# ≠ P#('P6') ) )
```

Again *SX* is just TRUE and *SY* is the whole of *SC*,[1] but the interesting point about this example is that it mentions relvar SP as well as relvar S. The constraint is thus a constraint on SP as well, as the following alternative but equivalent formulation makes clear:

```
FORALL u ∈ SP ( u.P# = P#('P6') ═► FORALL t ∈ S ( t.S# = u.S# ═► t.STATUS ≥ 20 ) ) )
```

Here we can say *SPX* ≡ TRUE and *SPY* ≡ *SPC*.

5. Every shipment involves an existing supplier:

```
FORALL t ∈ SP ( EXISTS u ∈ S ( u.S# = t.S# ) )
```

Again this constraint is a constraint for both S and SP. We have *SX* ≡ *SPX* ≡ TRUE, *SY* ≡ *SPY* ≡ *SC* ≡ *SPC*. Note that inserting a tuple into S or deleting one from SP cannot possibly violate the constraint.

6. Let relvar SPJ, with heading {S#,P#,J#}, be subject to the *join dependency*[2]

```
* { SP, PJ, JS }
```

where SP denotes the projection of SPJ on attributes S# and P#, and similarly for PJ and JS. This join dependency is logically equivalent to the following:

```
FORALL x,y,z ∈ SPJ ( x.S# = y.S# & y.P# = z.P# & z.J# = x.J#
                 ═► EXISTS u ∈ SPJ ( u.S# = x.S# & u.P# = y.P# & u.J# = z.J# ) )
```

---

1. Though at least we know that an attempt to insert a supplier tuple with STATUS ≥ 20 cannot violate the constraint.

2. See reference [76] for some background to this example. It might help to explain that the intended interpretation (i.e., the relvar predicate) for SPJ is: *Supplier S# supplies part P# to project J#.* The join dependency means, loosely, that if (a) supplier S# supplies part P# and (b) part P# is supplied to project J# and (c) project J# is supplied by supplier S#, then (d) supplier S# supplies part P# to project J#.

We have *SPJX* ≡ TRUE, *SPJY* ≡ *SPJC*. If we attempt to insert or delete some tuple into or from relvar *SPJ*, constraint *SPJY* will be evaluated after that insertion or deletion has (tentatively) taken place.

7. There must always be at least one supplier:

```
EXISTS t є S ( TRUE )
```

Once again we have *SX* ≡ TRUE, *SY* ≡ *SC*. Inserting a tuple cannot violate this constraint, but deleting a tuple might.

8. All parts are either blue or green and there exists at least one part:

```
FORALL t є P ( t.COLOR = 'Blue' OR t.COLOR = 'Green' ) AND EXISTS t є P ( TRUE )
```

Here *PX* ≡ *t*.COLOR = 'Blue' OR *t*.COLOR = 'Green'; *PY* ≡ EXISTS *t* є P (TRUE).

9. All parts are either blue or green, or there exists at least one red part:

```
FORALL t є P ( t.COLOR = 'Blue' OR t.COLOR = 'Green' ) OR EXISTS t є P ( t.COLOR = 'Red' )
```

Here *PX* ≡ TRUE, *PY* ≡ *PC*.

Now I turn my attention to views. Let view *R* be defined, possibly via several levels of indirection, in terms of real relvars *R1*, *R2*, ..., *Rn*. Then we can say that view *R* has a relvar constraint *RC*, which we define to be satisfied by *R* if and only if *R1C*, *R2C*, ..., *RnC* are satisfied by *R1*, *R2*, ..., *Rn*, respectively. Furthermore, I conjecture that, in general, *RC* is logically equivalent to an expression of the form

```
( FORALL t є R ( RX ) ) & ( RY )
```

(as previously), where *RX* in turn can easily be defined in terms of *R1X*, *R2X*, ..., *RnX*. By way of example, let view *R* be defined as a restriction of relvar *A:*

```
R ≡ A WHERE p
```

Recall from Chapter 2 that *p* here is a quantifier-free predicate. Then *RC* ≡ (*AZ*)&(*p*), and we define *RX* ≡ (*AX*)&(*p*) and *RY* ≡ *AY*. For example, let *R* ≡ S WHERE STATUS > 20 and let *SY* be

```
FORALL t є S ( FORALL u є S ( u.S# = t.S# ⟹ u = t ) )
```

("supplier numbers are unique"). Then *RC* is:

```
FORALL t є R ( ( SX ) & ( t.STATUS > 20 ) ) &
    FORALL t є S ( FORALL u є S ( u.S# = t.S# ⟹ u = t ) )
```

So we can define *RX* as (*SX*) & (*t*.STATUS > 20) and *RY* as *SY*. Note that *RY* is basically a constraint on *S*, not *R*.

As another simple example, let *R* ≡ *A* RENAME (*F* AS *G*). Then *RC*, *RX*, and *RY* are identical to *AC*, *AX*, and *AY*, respectively, except that all references to *F* are replaced by references to *G*.

I conclude this section with a refined version of the conceptual update algorithm from the end of the section "A Model of Updating." Consider the assignment

```
R := r U i - d
```

where *R* is a relvar, possibly virtual. The semantics are as follows:

1. Every tuple in *i* must satisfy *RX*, otherwise the assignment fails.

2. Create a temporary real relvar *R'* with initial value *r*U*i*-*d*.

3. From *R'*, compute the new values for all real relvars *R1*, *R2*, ..., *Rn* involved in the definition of *R* and assign those values to those relvars, and thereby obtain the new value for *R*. (Details of this step are spelled out, at least implicitly, in subsequent sections.)

4. If *The Assignment Principle* is violated for *R*, the assignment fails.

5. If **The Golden Rule** is violated for any of *R1*, *R2*, ..., *Rn*, the assignment fails.

6. Discard *R'*.

Note that *RX* (a) can be used to check ahead of time that INSERTs are valid and (b) cannot be violated by DELETEs; *RX* can be thought of, informally, as "the tuple-level constraint" for *R*. *RY* cannot be checked until after the update has (tentatively) been done; in general, it can be violated by both INSERTs and DELETEs.

UPDATING RESTRICTIONS

In this section I investigate the question of updating restriction views specifically. I treat restrictions first because in a sense they are "the easy case," and also because several later sections rely on the discussions in this section. I will present the rules first, then show some examples.

Let $R \equiv A$ WHERE *p*; then *RC*, *RX*, and *RY* are as given in the previous section (in particular, $RX \equiv (AX)\&(p)$). Consider the INSERT-type assignment:

```
R := R U i
```

Every tuple in *i* must satisfy *RX*. The given assignment expands[1] into:

```
A := A U i
```

After this assignment, *R* must have the value *r*U*i* and *a*U*i* must satisfy *AY* (where, to remind you, *r* and *a* are the original values of *R* and *A*, respectively), otherwise the update is undone.

Consider now the DELETE-type assignment:

```
R := R - d
```

This assignment expands into:

```
A := A - d
```

---

1. "Expands" is perhaps not the mot juste in this simple case but becomes so in more complex cases.

After this assignment, *R* must have the value *r-d* and *a-d* must satisfy *AY,* otherwise the update is undone.

By way of example, consider the usual suppliers relvar S, with its usual sample value (repeated in Fig. E.1 for convenience). Let the constraint *SC* for suppliers be such that *SX* is just TRUE and *SY* is just "supplier numbers are unique." Let $R \equiv$ S WHERE STATUS > 20; then $RX \equiv$ TRUE & *t*.STATUS > 20 (which reduces to just *t*.STATUS > 20, of course) and $RY \equiv SY$. Now consider the following updates on *R:*

S	S#	SNAME	STATUS	CITY
	S1	Smith	20	London
	S2	Jones	10	Paris
	S3	Blake	30	Paris
	S4	Clark	20	London
	S5	Adams	30	Athens

Fig. E.1: The suppliers relvar S—sample value

1.   INSERT < S6,Lopez,30,Madrid > INTO *R:* The specified tuple satisfies *RX,* so it is tentatively inserted into S (and therefore appears in *R,* so *The Assignment Principle* is satisfied for *R*). After that insertion, *SY* is satisfied, and so the update succeeds.

2.   INSERT < S6,Lopez,20,Madrid > INTO *R:* The specified tuple violates *RX,* so the update fails.

3.   INSERT < S1,Lopez,30,Madrid > INTO *R:* The specified tuple satisfies *RX,* so it is tentatively inserted into S (and therefore appears in *R,* so *The Assignment Principle* is satisfied for *R*). After that insertion, however, *SY* is violated, and so the update is undone.

4.   DELETE < S5,Adams,30,Athens > FROM *R:* The specified tuple is tentatively deleted from S (and therefore no longer appears in *R,* so *The Assignment Principle* is satisfied for *R*). After that deletion, *SY* is satisfied, and so the update succeeds.

As a basis for certain future examples, I now define a series of additional restriction views over relvar *S:*

■   RI ≡ S WHERE (STATUS > 20) & (CITY = 'Paris')

■   RU ≡ S WHERE (STATUS > 20) | (CITY = 'Paris')

■   RD ≡ S WHERE (STATUS > 20) & (¬ (CITY = 'Paris'))

■   RQ ≡ S WHERE (STATUS > 20) & (¬ ((STATUS > 20) & (¬ (CITY = 'Paris'))))

Assume again that *SX* is just TRUE and *SY* is just "supplier numbers are unique." Then, using *p* and *q* to denote the expressions (*t*.STATUS > 20) and (*t*.CITY = 'Paris'), respectively, we have *X* constraints as follows:

- RIX ≡ p&q

- RUX ≡ p|q

- RDX ≡ p&(¬q)

- RQX ≡ p&(¬(p&(¬q))) ≡ p&q ≡ RIX

UPDATING INTERSECTIONS

In this section and the next two, I consider what is involved in updating intersection, union, and difference views, respectively. First of all, then, let $R \equiv A \cap B$ (so $r = a \cap b$); then $RC \equiv (AC)\&(BC)$, and in particular $RX \equiv (AX)\&(BX)$. Now consider the INSERT-type assignment:

```
R := R U i
```

Every tuple in i must satisfy RX. The given assignment expands into:

```
A := A U i , B := B U i
```

After these assignments, (a) R must have the value $r \cup i$ and (b) $a \cup i$ must satisfy AY and $b \cup i$ must satisfy BY, otherwise the update is undone.
Consider now the DELETE-type assignment:

```
R := R - d
```

This assignment expands into:

```
A := A - d , B := B - d
```

After these assignments, (a) R must have the value $r-d$ and (b) $a-d$ must satisfy AY and $b-d$ must satisfy BY, otherwise the update is undone. *Discussion:* The specified assignment means "The tuples of d are to be deleted from $A \cap B$"; so every tuple of d must clearly be deleted from at least one of A and B. However, there is no good reason for deleting from A and not B or vice versa; moreover, if we did delete from just one, it is likely that deleting d from $A \cap B$ and deleting d from $B \cap A$ would have different effects. Symmetry therefore strongly suggests that we delete from both. Moreover, deleting from both has the advantage that the rule is not just symmetric in itself, it is symmetric with the insert rule also.

Examples

Let real relvars A and B have just one attribute each, of type nonnegative integer, and let their constraints and initial values be as follows:

```
A : AX ≡ n ≤ 7 : initial value a = 0 4 5 7
    AY ≡ TRUE

B : BX ≡ n ≥ 2 : initial value b = 3 4 6 7 8
    BY ≡ TRUE
```

Points arising:

- As the form in which I have stated these constraints and initial values suggests, I talk for simplicity as if A and B contained sets of nonnegative integers as such, instead of (as would be more correct) tuples containing such integers.

- For clarity I show sets of integers as simple lists with adjacent integers separated by a blank, thereby writing, e.g., 0 4 5 7 instead of the more conventional {0,4,5,7}.

- I assume the same initial values for each example.

- The examples all involve attempts to insert or delete sets of integers of cardinality one, and so we can speak, loosely, of inserting or deleting individual integers per se.

- I have already explained that, e.g., an INSERT-type assignment is not the same thing as an INSERT as such; in the examples in this section, however (also in the next two), I will ensure that the preconditions for INSERT and DELETE are always satisfied (barring explicit statements to the contrary), and I will therefore feel free to use the more user-friendly terms INSERT and DELETE per se in those examples.

Now consider the following updates on $R \equiv A \cap B$:

```
INSERT 2    INSERT 5    DELETE 7
```

Observe that:

- RX $\equiv$ (AX)&(BX) $\equiv$ (n $\leq$ 7) & (n $\geq$ 2).

- 2 appears in neither a nor b.

- 5 appears in a but not b.

- 7 appears in both a and b.

Here now are the results of the three updates. *Note:* I use the symbol "::" from this point forward to mean "gives" or "yields" or "produces."

```
INSERT 2 :: A = 0 2 4 5 7
            B = 2 3 4 6 7 8
INSERT 5 :: A unchanged
            B = 3 4 5 6 7 8
DELETE 7 :: A = 0 4 5
            B = 3 4 6 8
```

For each of these examples, let us also consider what happens if we immediately follow the specified operation by its inverse:

```
INSERT 2 / DELETE 2 :: A and B both unchanged
INSERT 5 / DELETE 5 :: A = 0 4 7, B unchanged
DELETE 7 / INSERT 7 :: A and B both unchanged
```

As you can see, the sequence INSERT 5 / DELETE 5 fails to preserve the status quo, and the INSERT and DELETE in question are thus not really inverses after all. I will revisit this issue—i.e., the question of whether INSERT and DELETE should be inverses—in the section "Some Remarks on

Orthogonality," later.

Now I return to the usual suppliers relvar S. Let *RI* be defined as follows:

```
RI ≡ ( S WHERE STATUS > 20 ) ∩ ( S WHERE CITY = 'Paris' )
```

Observe that this view is semantically identical to the view of the same name from the previous section. Its *X* constraint *RIX* is

```
( t.STATUS > 20 ) & ( t.CITY = 'Paris' )
```

which is clearly identical to the constraint of the same name from the previous section. Now consider the following updates on *RI:*

1. INSERT < S7,Jones,25,Paris > INTO *RI:* Let *i* be the relation containing just the specified tuple. Then the expansion is:

    ```
    A := A U i , B := B U i
    ```

    where $A \equiv$ S WHERE STATUS > 20 and $B \equiv$ S WHERE CITY = 'Paris', respectively. The rules for updating through a restriction thus come into play, and the foregoing expansion expands again, into:

    ```
    S := S U i , S := S U i
    ```

    As explained in Chapter 6, this latter multiple assignment in turn is equivalent to the following:

    ```
    S := WITH S U i AS S : S U i
    ```

    If we think of this expansion as a *sequence* of assignments

    ```
    S := S U i ;
    S := S U i ;
    ```

    then it should be clear that the second has no effect. But that is not the point; rather, the point is the collection of the two assignments into one,[1] which guarantees that just one assignment to S is actually performed. Thus, the net effect is that the new tuple is successfully inserted into S, and hence into both *A* and *B,* and hence into *RI. The Assignment Principle* is thus satisfied, and so is **The Golden Rule.**

2. INSERT < S6,Lopez,30,Madrid > INTO *RI:* Here the tuple presented for insertion satisfies the constraint *AX* but not the constraint *BX* (where *A* and *B* are as in the previous example). The update therefore fails.

It should be clear from these examples that, at least as far as INSERTs are concerned, the intersection view *RI* exhibits behavior identical to that of the restriction view *RI* from the section "Updating Restrictions." An analogous remark applies to DELETEs also (exercise for the reader). This

---

1. Note, however, that the second assignment in the example violates the preconditions for INSERT. This is one reason why I need to talk in terms of INSERT- and DELETE-type assignments instead of INSERTs and DELETEs per se. Other reasons will emerge as we proceed.

state of affairs is highly gratifying, of course, given that the view definitions are semantically equivalent; indeed, reference [76] asserts it as a principle, or at least an objective, that "view updatability is a semantic issue, not a syntactic one—i.e., it must not depend on the particular syntactic form in which the view definition in question happens to be stated." Part of my aim in this appendix is to see whether this objective can be achieved.

Suppose now that *A* ("suppliers with status greater than 20") and *B* ("suppliers in Paris") are two distinct *real* relvars, and we attempt the same two INSERTs on *RI* ≡ *A*∩*B*. The second INSERT still fails. The first, however, has the effect of inserting the new tuple into both of those real relvars, as you will easily see for yourself if you work through the expansions. I will revisit this example also in the section "Some Remarks on Orthogonality."

I close this section by remarking that (as is well known) intersection is a special case of join. It follows that the rules for updating intersections must be a special case of those for updating joins, and so indeed they are. However, I defer detailed discussion of the question of updating joins to a later section.

UPDATING UNIONS

Let *R* ≡ *A*∪*B* (so *r* = *a*∪*b*); then *RC* ≡ (*AC*)|(*BC*), and we can define *RX* as (*AX*)|(*BX*).[1] Now consider the INSERT-type assignment:

```
R := R U i
```

Let *ia* be the tuples of *i* that satisfy *AX* and let *ib* be the tuples of *i* that satisfy *BX*, respectively. Then the given assignment expands into the double assignment:

```
A := A U ia , B := B U ib
```

After these assignments, (a) *R* must have the value *r*∪*i* and (b) *a*∪*ia* must satisfy *AY* and *b*∪*ib* must satisfy *BY*, otherwise the update is undone. *Discussion:* The given assignment means "The tuples of *i* are to be inserted into *A*∪*B*"; so every tuple of *i* must clearly be inserted into *A* or *B* or both. But how do we decide which ones go where? The intuitively obvious (and symmetric) answer is: For each tuple *t* of *i*, insert *t* into *A* if and only if it satisfies *AX* and into *B* if and only if it satisfies *BX*. Note clearly, however, that the overall operation will still fail if either *AY* or *BY* is violated after those insertions have been done; as usual, therefore, those insertions are only tentative, in a sense.

Consider now the DELETE-type assignment:

```
R := R - d
```

This assignment expands into:

```
A := A - d , B := B - d
```

After these assignments, (a) *R* must have the value *r-d* and (b) *a-d* must satisfy *AY* and *b-d* must satisfy *BY*, otherwise the update is undone.

---

1. Defining *RX* as (*AX*)|(*BX*) guarantees that if *RX* is not satisfied, then certainly *RC* is not satisfied—though if *RX* is satisfied, it does not follow that *RC* is satisfied.

Examples

First let me return to the "nonnegative integer" relvars *A* and *B* from the examples in the previous section:

```
A : AX ≡ n ≤ 7 : initial value a = 0 4 5 7
    AY ≡ TRUE

B : BX ≡ n ≥ 2 : initial value b = 3 4 6 7 8
    BY ≡ TRUE
```

Now consider the following updates on $R \equiv A \cup B$:

```
INSERT 1     INSERT 2     DELETE 0     DELETE 3     DELETE 4
```

Observe that:

■ `RX ≡ (AX)|(BX) ≡ (n ≤ 7) | (n ≥ 2).`

■ 1 appears in neither *a* nor *b* and satisfies *AX* but not *BX*.

■ 2 appears in neither *a* nor *b* and satisfies both *AX* and *BX*.

■ 0 appears in *a* but not *b*.

■ 3 appears in *b* but not *a*.

■ 4 appears in both *a* and *b*.

Here now are the results of the five updates:

```
INSERT 1 :: A = 0 1 4 5 7
            B unchanged
INSERT 2 :: A = 0 2 4 5 7
            B = 2 3 4 6 7 8
DELETE 0 :: A = 4 5 7
            B unchanged
DELETE 3 :: A unchanged
            B = 4 6 7 8
DELETE 4 :: A = 0 5 7
            B = 3 6 7 8
```

Let us also consider in each case what happens if we immediately follow the specified operation by its inverse:

```
INSERT 1 / DELETE 1 :: A and B both unchanged
INSERT 2 / DELETE 2 :: A and B both unchanged
DELETE 0 / INSERT 0 :: A and B both unchanged
DELETE 3 / INSERT 3 :: B unchanged, A = 0 3 4 5 7
DELETE 4 / INSERT 4 :: A and B both unchanged
```

As you can see, the only sequence that fails to preserve the status quo is DELETE 3 / INSERT 3.

Again, I will revisit this issue in the section "Some Remarks on Orthogonality."
Now let us switch to the suppliers example. Let *RU* be defined as follows:

```
RU ≡ ( S WHERE STATUS > 20 ) U ( S WHERE CITY = 'Paris' )
```

Observe that this view is semantically identical to the view of the same name from the section "Updating Restrictions." Its *X* constraint *RUX* is

```
( t.STATUS > 20 ) | ( t.CITY = 'Paris' )
```

which is clearly identical to the constraint of the same name from the section "Updating Restrictions." I leave it as an exercise to show that view *RU* exhibits the same behavior with respect to INSERTs and DELETEs, regardless of which way it is defined.

UPDATING DIFFERENCES

Let $R \equiv A\text{-}B$ (so $r = a\text{-}b$); then $RC \equiv (AC)$ & (FORALL $t \in R$ $(t \notin B)$), and we can define *RX* as simply *AX*. Consider the INSERT-type assignment:

```
R := R U i
```

Every tuple in *i* must satisfy *RX*. The given assignment expands into:

```
A := A U i
```

After this assignment, (a) *R* must have the value $r \cup i$ and (b) $a \cup i$ must satisfy *AY*, otherwise the update is undone.
Consider now the DELETE-type assignment:

```
R := R - d
```

This assignment expands into:

```
A := A - d
```

After this assignment, (a) *R* must have the value $r\text{-}d$ and (b) $a\text{-}d$ must satisfy *AY*, otherwise the update is undone. *Exercise:* What happens if we try to delete a tuple from (or insert a tuple into) the view $R \equiv A\text{-}A$?

Examples

Again I return to the "nonnegative integer" relvars *A* and *B:*

```
A : AX ≡ n ≤ 7 : initial value a = 0 4 5 7
    AY ≡ TRUE

B : BX ≡ n ≥ 2 : initial value b = 3 4 6 7 8
    BY ≡ TRUE
```

Consider the following updates on $R \equiv A\text{-}B$:

```
INSERT 1      DELETE 0
```

I leave it to you to figure out why I choose exactly these examples; however, I note that $RX \equiv n \leq 7$. Results:

```
INSERT 1 :: A = 0 1 4 5 7
               B unchanged
DELETE 0 :: A = 4 5 7
               B unchanged
```

Let us also consider in each case what happens if we immediately follow the specified operation by its inverse:

```
INSERT 1 / DELETE 1 :: A and B both unchanged
DELETE 0 / INSERT 0 :: A and B both unchanged
```

Now consider the suppliers example once again. Let *RD* be defined as follows:

```
RD ≡ ( S WHERE STATUS > 20 ) - ( S WHERE CITY = 'Paris' )
```

Observe that this view is semantically identical to the view of the same name from the section "Updating Restrictions." Its *X* constraint *RDX* is

```
t.STATUS > 20
```

which is *not* identical to the constraint of the same name from the section "Updating Restrictions." It is nevertheless still the case that view *RD* exhibits the same behavior with respect to INSERTs and DELETEs, regardless of which way it is defined (another exercise for the reader).

I close this section by remarking that difference is in fact a special case of *semi*difference (to use **Tutorial D** syntax, *A* SEMIMINUS *B*—equivalently, *A* NOT MATCHING *B*—reduces to *A* MINUS *B* if *A* and *B* are of the same type).[1] It follows that the rules for updating differences must be a special case of those for updating semidifferences, and so they are. For purposes of reference, let me explicitly state the rules for semidifference here. Let *R* ≡ *A* NOT MATCHING *B* (so *r* = *a* NOT MATCHING *b*). Then *RC* is:

```
FORALL t ∈ R ( ( AX ) & ¬ ( EXISTS u ( BX ( u ∪ t ) ) ) ) & ( AY )
```

where *u* is a tuple whose heading consists of the attributes of *B* that are not also attributes of *A;* I use the notation *BX(u∪t)* to stress the point that it is the (tuple) union of *u* and *t* that is required to satisfy *BX*. Thus, *RX* ≡ *AX*. Consider the INSERT-type assignment:

```
R := R U i
```

Every tuple in *i* must satisfy *RX*. The given assignment expands into:

```
A := A U i
```

---

1. By contrast, join is not a special case of semijoin—in fact, the opposite is at least partly true. To be specific, *A* SEMIJOIN *B* (equivalently, *A* MATCHING *B*) reduces to *A* JOIN *B* if the heading of *B* is a subset of that of *A*.

After this assignment, (a) *R* must have the value *r*∪*i* and (b) *a*∪*i* must satisfy *AY*, otherwise the update is undone.

Consider now the DELETE-type assignment:

```
R := R - d
```

This assignment expands into:

```
A := A - d
```

After this assignment, (a) *R* must have the value *r-d* and (b) *a-d* must satisfy *AY*, otherwise the update is undone.

By way of example, let *R* ≡ S NOT MATCHING SP, and let relvars S and SP have their usual sample values and be subject to the usual constraints (in particular, the usual key and foreign key constraints). Then:

1. INSERT < S7,Jones,25,Paris > INTO *R:* Succeeds.

2. INSERT < S1,Lopez,30,Madrid > INTO *R:* Fails on a violation of constraint *SY* (supplier number not unique).

3. DELETE < S5,Adams,30,Athens > FROM *R:* Succeeds.

4. DELETE < S4,Clark,20,London > FROM *R:* Fails on a violation of constraint *SY* (referential integrity violation).

NESTED UPDATES

Before going on to consider the rules for updating through other relational operators, I need to elaborate somewhat on the issue of nested updates (e.g., updating *R* ≡ *A*∩*B* where *A* and *B* are not just simple relvar references but more general relational expressions). Of course, I did touch on this issue in the last three sections when I discussed the views *RI, RU,* and *RD,* all of which were defined (in one of their incarnations) in terms of restrictions; however, now I can take a closer look.

Once again I use "nonnegative integer" relvars as a basis for my examples. Assume we have three such relvars *A, B,* and *C,* with constraints *AC, BC, CC* all just TRUE, for simplicity, and initial values as follows:

```
A : initial value a = 0 4 5 7 10
B : initial value b = 3 4 6 7 8 11
C : initial value c = 0 1 2 7 8 9 12
```

Again I assume the same initial values for each example, barring explicit statements to the contrary. I also assume the set of integers we want to insert is *i* = 1 2 3 9 (again, the same for each example; for reasons I will get to in a little while, the examples all involve INSERT-type assignments specifically).

Example 1

Let *R* ≡ *A*∪(*B*∩*C*), and consider the INSERT-type assignment *R* := *R*∪*i*. We can represent this operation by means of the following tree structure. *Note:* I have taken a slight syntactic liberty in that tree by including assignments at some of the nodes in which the target is not a simple variable reference but, rather, a more general operational expression—a pseudovariable reference, in fact. (As noted in Chapter 5, **Tutorial D** does not currently support such pseudovariables.)

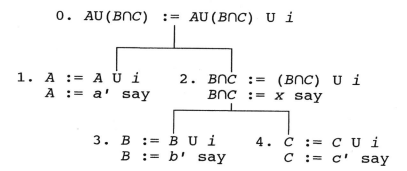

Explanation: The root of the tree (Node 0) represents the original update. We apply the rule for updating through union to obtain updates to A and $B \cap C$, respectively (Nodes 1 and 2); a' and x are the values denoted by the assignment sources at Nodes 1 and 2, respectively. Observe that a' and x are immediately computable from a, b, c, and i. Next, we apply the rule for updating through intersection to obtain updates to B and C, respectively (Nodes 3 and 4); b' and c' are the values denoted by the assignment sources at Nodes 3 and 4, respectively. Observe that b' and c' are immediately computable from b, c, and i (x is not directly needed; effectively, x is just the value of some temporary variable that is used internally during the execution of the overall update but is never exposed to the user).

Given the specified values for a, b, c, and i, we obtain:

```
a' = aUi = 0 1 2 3 4 5 7 9 10
b' = bUi = 1 2 3 4 6 7 8 9 11
c' = cUi = 0 1 2 3 7 8 9 12
```

We also have:

```
x  = (bnc)Ui = 1 2 3 7 8 9 = b'nc'
```

Observe that:

- The initial value of $A \cup (B \cap C) = a \cup (b \cap c) = 0\ 4\ 5\ 7\ 8\ 10$ and the final value $= a' \cup (b' \cap c') = 0\ 1\ 2\ 3\ 4\ 5\ 7\ 8\ 9\ 10$, and the overall update thus satisfies *The Assignment Principle.*

- Nodes 3 and 4 considered together also satisfy *The Assignment Principle,* because $b' \cap c' = x$. So do Nodes 1 and 2, of course, as we effectively saw in the previous bullet item.

- Nodes 3 and 4 both involve an assignment of the form $R := R \cup i$ in which i and r are not disjoint (and the assignment is thus not a valid INSERT, though it is "INSERT-type").

Now, immediately following the INSERT-type assignment of the foregoing example by the DELETE-type assignment $R := R - i$ does not preserve the status quo (though it does work satisfactorily in other respects); yet again, I refer you to the section "Some Remarks on Orthogonality" for further discussion. Apart from such considerations, it should be intuitively clear from this example that updates via an arbitrarily complex relational expression will certainly work[1] if both of the following conditions are satisfied:

- *Condition 1:* The expression involves intersections and unions only—because INSERT-type assignments via such an expression ultimately expand to an INSERT-type assignment on every real relvar involved and DELETE-type assignments via such an expression ultimately expand to a DELETE-type assignment on every real relvar involved. (This is why I do not bother to show any examples in this section involving DELETE-type assignments.)

- *Condition 2:* The expansion does not involve two or more assignments to the same real relvar.

Examples 2-6 therefore examine the question of what happens if these conditions are violated. To be specific, Examples 2 and 6 consider the effect of violating Condition 1 only; Example 3 considers the effect of violating Condition 2 only; and Examples 4 and 5 consider the effect of violating both.

Example 2

Let $R \equiv A \cap (B\text{-}C)$, and consider $R := R \cup i$. Here is the tree:

```
    0.  A∩(B-C)  :=  A∩(B-C)  U  i
                        |
           ┌────────────┴────────────┐
           |                          |
    1.  A  :=  A  U  i       2.  B-C  :=  (B-C)  U  i
        A  :=  a' say            B-C  :=  x say
                                     |
                              3.  B  :=  B  U  i
                                  B  :=  b' say
```

Now, no integer in *B-C* can appear in *C*, by definition. Given the specified values for *c* and *i*, therefore, the foregoing update will necessarily fail on a violation of *The Assignment Principle*—so let me change the initial value *c* to just 0 12. Then we obtain:

```
a' = aUi      = 0 1 2 3 4 5 7 9 10
b' = bUi      = 1 2 3 4 6 7 8 9 11
c' = c        = 0 12 (C is not updated at all)
x  = (b-c)Ui  = 1 2 3 4 6 7 8 9 11 = b'-c'
```

Observe that the initial value of $A \cap (B\text{-}C) = a \cap (b\text{-}c) = 4\ 7$ and the final value $= a' \cap (b'\text{-}c') = 1\ 2\ 3\ 4\ 7\ 9$, and the update thus satisfies *The Assignment Principle*.

Without going into further details, it should be intuitively clear that updates via an expression involving any combination of intersections, unions, and differences will work satisfactorily so long as Condition 2 is satisfied. So what happens if we violate Condition 2?

---

1. The term "work" here (and in similar contexts elsewhere) is intended to include the case in which the update fails on a violation of either *The Assignment Principle* or **The Golden Rule**.

Example 3

Let $R \equiv A \cup (A \cap B)$, and consider $R := R \cup i$ (this example is effectively the same as Example 1, except that I have replaced C by A). Here is the tree:

```
0.  AU(A∩B)  :=  AU(A∩B) U i
                    |
      ┌─────────────┴─────────────┐
1. A := A U i        2. A∩B := (A∩B) U i
   A := a' say          A∩B := x say
                          |
              ┌───────────┴───────────┐
        3. A := A U i          4. B := B U i
           A := a'' say           B := b' say
```

The significant thing about this tree is that it includes two distinct assignments (at Nodes 1 and 3) to the same target A; in other words, Condition 2 has been violated. As a consequence, it might seem that the order in which individual assignments are performed could affect the overall result. Let us take a closer look.

It should be clear that, although trees are (of course) constructed from the top down, they need to be processed from the bottom up. Thus, the tree in the example can be regarded as representing the following multiple assignment:

```
A := A U i , B := B U i , A := A U i
```

(corresponding to Nodes 3, 4, and 1, in that order). The two assignments to A are then collected together, yielding:

```
B := B U i , A := WITH A U i AS A : A U i
```

Evaluating, we obtain:

```
b' = bUi     = 1 2 3 4 6 7 8 9 11
a' = aUi     = 0 1 2 3 4 5 7 9 10 = a''
x  = (a∩b)Ui = 1 2 3 4 7 9 = a'∩b'
```

Once again, then, the overall update works (the final value of R is 0 1 2 3 4 5 7 9 10 = $a' \cup (a' \cap b')$). But the example is weak, in a way, precisely because $a'' = a'$ (the order in which we execute the assignments to A thus clearly makes no difference in this particular example). Now, the reason why $a'' = a'$ is that the constraints AC and BC are both just TRUE. Even if this were not the case, however, it would still be the case that the order in which we execute those assignments to A would make no difference to the overall result. Why? Because (as we have already seen) those assignments will be either all INSERT-type assignments or all DELETE-type assignments, not a mixture, and the assignments

```
A := WITH A U j AS A : A U k
```

and

```
A := WITH A U k AS A : A U j
```

are logically equivalent, as are the assignments

```
A := WITH A - j AS A : A - k
```

and

```
A := WITH A - k AS A : A - j
```

The foregoing example raises another issue, however. As we have seen, the example involves assignment of a new value b' to relvar B. **But why does it?** Given that $A \cup (A \cap B)$ is identically equal to A, why does B get updated at all? Why is updating $A \cup (A \cap B)$ not equivalent to updating just A? I will return to this question in the section "Some Remarks on Orthogonality"; for now, I simply note that this example does appear to violate the principle, articulated earlier, that view updating is or should be a matter of semantics, not syntax.

Example 4

Let $R \equiv A-(A-A)$, and consider $R := R \cup i$. The tree in this case is very simple:

```
0. A-(A-A)  :=  A-(A-A) U i
                   |
                   |
                   |
          1. A := A U i
             A := a' say
```

Further discussion seems superfluous.

Example 5

Let $R \equiv (A \cup B)-(A \cap B)$, and consider $R := R \cup i$. Here is the tree:

```
0. (AUB)-(A∩B)  :=  (AUB)-(A∩B) U i
                        |
                        |
                        |
            1. AUB := (AUB) U i
               AUB := x say
              ┌─────────┴─────────┐
              |                   |
   2. A := A U i          3. B := B U i
      A := a' say            B := b' say
```

This update necessarily fails, because (thanks to the semantics of "-") no integer appearing in $(A \cup B)-(A \cap B)$ is allowed to appear in $A \cap B$, a state of affairs that is logically impossible unless $a \cap b = i = \phi$. (In fact, $(A \cup B)-(A \cap B)$ is equivalent to $(A-B) \cup (B-A)$—the "symmetric difference" of A and B—and it is intuitively obvious that inserting anything into the view is impossible.)

Example 6

For the final example in this section, I return to suppliers once again. Let RQ be defined as follows:

```
RQ ≡ ( S WHERE STATUS > 20 ) - ( ( S WHERE STATUS > 20 ) - ( S WHERE CITY = 'Paris' ) )
```

Observe that this view is semantically identical to the view of the same name from the section "Updating Restrictions." Its *X* constraint *RQX* is

```
t.STATUS > 20
```

which is not identical to the constraint of the same name from the section "Updating Restrictions." It is nevertheless still the case that view *RQ* exhibits the same behavior with respect to INSERTs and DELETEs, regardless of which way it is defined (another exercise for the reader).

UPDATING EXTENSIONS

I now turn my attention to some of the other relational operators. This section deals with EXTEND; the next two deal with joins and projections, respectively.

Let $R \equiv$ EXTEND A ADD (z AS Z); then $RC \equiv (AC)$ & (FORALL $t \in R$ ($t.Z = z$)), and we can define *RX* as

```
( AX(u) ) & ( t.Z = z )
```

Here $u \equiv t\{$ALL BUT $Z\}$; I use the notation $AX(u)$ to stress the point that it is u, not t, that is required to satisfy *AX*. Now consider the INSERT-type assignment:

```
R := R U i
```

Every tuple in i must satisfy *RX*. The given assignment expands into:

```
A := A U ( i { ALL BUT Z } )
```

After this assignment, (a) *R* must have the value $r \cup i$ and (b) the new value of *A* must satisfy *AY*, otherwise the update is undone.

Consider now the DELETE-type assignment:

```
R := R - d
```

This assignment expands into:

```
A := A - ( d { ALL BUT Z } )
```

After this assignment, (a) *R* must have the value *r-d* and (b) the new value of *A* must satisfy *AY*, otherwise the update is undone.

Note: Every EXTEND invocation is equivalent to a certain join invocation, and the update rules just outlined are consistent with this fact.

By way of example, let *R* be defined thus:

```
R ≡ EXTEND P ADD ( WEIGHT * 454 AS GMWT )
```

Then:

1. INSERT <P7,Cog,Red,12,Paris,5448.0> INTO *R:* Succeeds (the projection of this tuple over all but GMWT is inserted into P).

2.   INSERT <P7,Cog,Red,12,Paris,5449.0> INTO *R:* Fails.

3.   DELETE <P1,Nut,Red,12,London,5448.0> FROM *R:* Succeeds (the tuple for part P1 is deleted from P).

UPDATING JOINS

To what extent join views might or might not be updatable has been the subject of controversy for many years. Partly for that reason, I proceed a little differently in this section—instead of simply stating a set of rules and then showing examples to illustrate them, I want to consider a series of examples first and use those examples as a basis from which to extrapolate a suitable set of rules. The examples are all based on the usual suppliers-and-parts database (with its usual constraints) and the usual sample values (see Fig. E.2).

S

S#	SNAME	STATUS	CITY
S1	Smith	20	London
S2	Jones	10	Paris
S3	Blake	30	Paris
S4	Clark	20	London
S5	Adams	30	Athens

P

P#	PNAME	COLOR	WEIGHT	CITY
P1	Nut	Red	12.0	London
P2	Bolt	Green	17.0	Paris
P3	Screw	Blue	17.0	Oslo
P4	Screw	Red	14.0	London
P5	Cam	Blue	12.0	Paris
P6	Cog	Red	19.0	London

SP

S#	P#	QTY
S1	P1	300
S1	P2	200
S1	P3	400
S1	P4	200
S1	P5	100
S1	P6	100
S2	P1	300
S2	P2	400
S3	P2	200
S4	P2	200
S4	P4	300
S4	P5	400

Fig. E.2: The suppliers-and-parts database—sample values

First of all, let $R \equiv A$ JOIN B (so $r = a$ JOIN b); then $RC \equiv (AC)\&(BC)$, and in particular RX is:

```
( AX(a) ) & ( BX(b) )
```

Here a and b are the projections of t on the attributes of A and B, respectively (t being the tuple that is supposed to satisfy RX, of course); I use the notation $AX(a)$ to stress the point that it is a, not t, that is required to satisfy AX, and similarly for $BX(b)$. *Note:* If A and B are of the same type, A JOIN B degenerates to A INTERSECT B, and the constraint degenerates to that for intersection; if A and B have no common attribute names, A JOIN B degenerates to the cartesian product of A and B, and the constraint degenerates to that for cartesian product.

The usual requirements regarding *The Assignment Principle* and **The Golden Rule** apply. I omit further details (or most of them, at any rate) in the discussions that follow.

Example 1

For my first example, I consider suppliers only. In Fig. E.2, suppliers are represented by a single real relvar that looks like this:

```
S { S#, STATUS, CITY }
```

(I ignore supplier names for simplicity). Thus, we might define projection views as follows:

```
ST ≡ S { S#, STATUS }
SC ≡ S { S#, CITY }
```

In accordance with *The Principle of Interchangeability,* however, we could come up with a different design in which ST and SC are real and S is a join view, thus:

```
S ≡ ST JOIN SC
```

This join is key-to-key and therefore one-to-one. Moreover, every S# value appearing in ST also appears in SC and vice versa—i.e., this constraint is effectively part of the relvar constraint for each of S and ST and SC (and S in particular is not in sixth normal form, 6NF,[1] regardless of whether it is real or virtual)—for otherwise the two designs would not be equivalent.

For this revised design, it is obvious that

```
INSERT i INTO S
```

expands into

```
INSERT i { S#, STATUS } INTO ST , INSERT i { S#, CITY } INTO SC
```

and

```
DELETE d FROM S
```

expands into

```
DELETE d { S#, STATUS } FROM ST , DELETE d { S#, CITY } FROM SC
```

As this first example suggests, therefore, updating a one-to-one join is straightforward. Also, I noted earlier that intersection is a special case of join; more precisely, it is a special case of one-to-one join specifically, and the update rules just outlined are consistent with this fact.

Note: For clarity, I abbreviate the terms "INSERT-type assignment" and "DELETE-type assignment," both in this section and the next, to just INSERT and DELETE, respectively (and I show expansions in terms of INSERT and DELETE specifically). These simplifications are legitimate, for the

---

1. Loosely, a relvar is in 6NF if and only if it cannot be nonloss-decomposed into two or more projections. See reference [76] for an explanation of nonloss decomposition and a tutorial on all the normal forms mentioned in this appendix.

most part, because I will usually make no attempt either to insert a tuple that is already present or to delete one that is not. When the expansions do violate either of these preconditions, I will note the fact explicitly. Observe in particular that the expansions shown in connection with the foregoing example do not violate them.

Now let me revise the foregoing example slightly. To be specific, suppose some suppliers have a status but no city and vice versa (in other words, ST and SC are real relvars and some suppliers are represented in just one of the two). Then deleting a tuple from ST JOIN SC could be implemented by deleting a tuple from just one of ST and SC without violating either *The Assignment Principle* or **The Golden Rule**. But deleting from both has the advantage of symmetry—see the discussion of updating intersections, earlier—as well as the advantage that we have just one rule, universally applied. Of course, we can avoid deleting from both, if we want to, by not deleting from S in the first place: in particular, by not giving the user DELETE rights over that view.

Example 2

For my next example, I consider both suppliers and parts. In Fig. E.2, suppliers and parts are represented by two real relvars that look like this:

```
S { S#, CITY }
P { P#, CITY }
```

(I ignore other attributes for simplicity). Thus, we might define a join view as follows:

```
SCP ≡ S JOIN P
```

In accordance with *The Principle of Interchangeability,* however, we could come up with a different design in which SCP is real and S and P are projection views, thus:

```
S ≡ SCP { S#, CITY }
P ≡ SCP { P#, CITY }
```

Again we have SCP ≡ S JOIN P, of course—and the join is many-to-many, regardless of whether SCP is real or virtual. What is more, if tuples $<s,c,p>$ and $<s',c,p'>$ appear in SCP, then tuples $<s',c,p>$ and $<s,c,p'>$ must appear in SCP also—i.e., this constraint is effectively part of the relvar constraint for each of S and P and SCP (and SCP in particular is not in fourth normal form, 4NF, regardless of whether it is real or virtual)—for otherwise the designs would not be equivalent. It follows that even if SCP is real, the updates

```
INSERT <S9,London,P8> INTO SCP
```

and

```
DELETE <S1,London,P1> FROM SCP
```

both fail, because they violate that constraint. The following INSERT, by contrast, succeeds—

```
INSERT i INTO SCP
```

—if *i* contains exactly the tuples

```
<S9,London,P1>   <S9,London,P8>
<S9,London,P4>   <S1,London,P8>
<S9,London,P6>   <S4,London,P8>
```

Observe in particular that this INSERT has the effect of inserting $<$S9,London$>$ into S $\equiv$ SCP{S#,CITY} and $<$P8,London$>$ into P $\equiv$ SCP{P#,CITY}.

In similar fashion, the following DELETE also succeeds—

```
DELETE d FROM SCP
```

—if *d* contains exactly the tuples

```
<S1,London,P1>   <S4,London,P1>
<S1,London,P4>   <S4,London,P4>
<S1,London,P6>   <S4,London,P6>
```

This DELETE has the effect of deleting $<$S1,London$>$ and $<$S4,London$>$ from S $\equiv$ SCP{S#,CITY} and $<$P1,London$>$, $<$P4,London$>$, and $<$P6,London$>$ from P $\equiv$ SCP{P#,CITY}.

So if SCP is in fact a join view, it should be clear that

```
INSERT i INTO SCP
```

expands into

```
INSERT i { S#, CITY } INTO S , INSERT i { P#, CITY } INTO P
```

and

```
DELETE d FROM SCP
```

into

```
DELETE d { S#, CITY } FROM S , DELETE d { P#, CITY } FROM P
```

As this example suggests, updating a many-to-many join is also straightforward; in fact, the expansions are the same as for the one-to-one case, though specific INSERTs and DELETEs are more likely to fail in the many-to-many case on violations of **The Golden Rule**. Also, I noted earlier that cartesian product is a special case of join; more precisely, it is a special case of many-to-many join specifically, and the update rules just outlined are consistent with this fact—in other words, they apply directly to updating cartesian products.

Example 3

For my last example, I consider suppliers and shipments. In Fig. E.2, suppliers and shipments are represented by two real relvars that look like this:

```
S  { S#, CITY }
SP { S#, P#, QTY }
```

(I ignore other attributes for simplicity). Thus, we might define a join view as follows:

```
SSP ≡ S JOIN SP
```

In accordance with *The Principle of Interchangeability,* however, we could come up with a different design in which SSP is real and S and SP are projection views, thus:

```
S  ≡ SSP { S#, CITY }
SP ≡ SSP { S#, P#, QTY }
```

Again we have SSP ≡ S JOIN SP, of course—and the join is a key-to-matching-foreign-key join[1] and therefore one-to-many, regardless of whether SSP is real or virtual. What is more, if tuples $<s,c,p,q>$ and $<s,c',p',q'>$ both appear in SSP, then $c = c'$—i.e., this constraint is effectively part of the relvar constraint for each of S and SP and SSP (and SSP in particular is not in third normal form, 3NF, regardless of whether it is real or virtual)—for otherwise the designs would not be equivalent. It follows that even if SSP is real, the update

```
INSERT <S4,Athens,P1,100> INTO SSP
```

fails, because it violates that constraint. The following updates, by contrast, both succeed:

```
INSERT <S4,London,P1,100> INTO SSP
```

```
INSERT <S9,London,P1,100> INTO SSP
```

The first has the effect of inserting $<S4,P1,100>$ into SP ≡ SSP{S#,P#,QTY} (only, because the tuple $<S4,London>$ is already present in S ≡ SSP{S#,CITY}); the second has the effect of inserting $<S9,London>$ into S ≡ SSP{S#,CITY} and $<S9,P1,100>$ into SP ≡ SSP{S#,P#,QTY}.

So if SSP is in fact a join view, it should be clear that

```
INSERT i INTO SSP
```

expands into

```
INSERT i { S#, CITY } INTO S , INSERT i { S#, P#, QTY } INTO SP
```

(though the "INSERT" into S, at least, is really an "INSERT-type assignment," since it might be "inserting" some tuples that already exist). This expansion is as for the one-to-one and many-to-many cases.

What about DELETE? On the face of it, there seems to be a problem here. The "obvious" expansion for

```
DELETE d FROM SSP
```

is

```
DELETE d { S#, CITY } FROM S , DELETE d { S#, P#, QTY } FROM SP
```

This expansion is as for the one-to-one and many-to-many cases and is symmetric with the expansion for INSERT. But consider the following example:

---

1. Even if S and SP are both views!—that is, the fact that every S# value appearing in view SP also appears in view S constitutes a foreign key constraint from one view to another.

```
DELETE <S1,London,P1,300> FROM SSP
```

If SSP is a real relvar, this DELETE succeeds; but if it is a join view, it fails (given the foregoing expansion) on a referential integrity violation, because it leaves some tuples for supplier S1 in SP but no such tuple in S, and we have therefore violated both **The Golden Rule** and *The Principle of Interchangeability*. *Note:* Reference [76] would allow *triggered actions* such as cascade delete to occur at this point, the effect of which is not to violate **The Golden Rule** after all but to violate *The Assignment Principle* instead. I do not pursue this possibility here for obvious reasons.

Precisely because of the state of affairs just explained, many writers have suggested that DELETE on a one-to-many join view should delete from the "many" side only—that is, the expansion for

```
DELETE d FROM SSP
```

should be just

```
DELETE d { S#, P#, QTY } FROM SP
```

This approach means the example previously discussed—

```
DELETE <S1,London,P1,300> FROM SSP
```

—has the effect of deleting < S1,P1,300 > from SP (only); thus, the DELETE succeeds, and *The Principle of Interchangeability, The Assignment Principle,* and **The Golden Rule** are all preserved. However, the approach has its disadvantages too:

- The INSERT and DELETE rules are asymmetric.

- INSERT and DELETE are not necessarily inverse operations.

- The DELETE rule (unlike the INSERT rule) for one-to-many joins is different from that for one-to-one and many-to-many joins.

On the third hand ... To continue to talk in terms of the SSP example specifically for definiteness, the INSERT rule can be characterized, informally, as "insert S tuples if they do not exist, plus insert matching SP tuples." Thus, we might consider extending the DELETE rule accordingly, along the lines of "delete SP tuples if they exist, plus delete S tuples if they now have no matching SP tuples." We might even make the argument that the DELETE rule in the one-to-one and many-to-many cases behaves in essentially the same way, implying that this revised approach overcomes all three of the objections identified above. In fact, I do make this argument!—that is, I do argue that the DELETE rule is really the same in all three cases. My argument is based on an appeal to first principles[1] (see the earlier section "A Model of Updating"). To be specific, the semantics of the update

```
DELETE <S1,London,P1,300> FROM SSP
```

are given by the following algorithm:

1.   Materialize SSP; call the result T.

---

1. Of course, all previous discussions were based on those principles as well, but implicitly so.

2.   `DELETE <S1,London,P1,300> FROM T.`

3.   `S  := S  - SSP { S#, CITY }    U T { S#, CITY },`
     `SP := SP - SSP { S#, P#, QTY } U T { S#, P#, QTY }.`

4.   Check *The Assignment Principle* for SSP ≡ S JOIN SP.

5.   Check **The Golden Rule** for S and SP (though the particular constraint that every S# value appearing in SP also appears in S will necessarily be satisfied).

6.   Discard T.

Note that the foregoing algorithm works even if SSP is real (except that in that case we would need to check **The Golden Rule** for SSP instead of S and SP). And if SSP is a view, the algorithm has the effect of deleting the specified tuple from SP *and*, if and only if that tuple is the sole tuple for supplier S1 in SSP, deleting the tuple for supplier S1 from S as well.

UPDATING PROJECTIONS

The structure of this section resembles, somewhat, that of the previous section on updating joins: Again I proceed by considering a series of examples and extrapolating a suitable set of rules from them.

First of all, let $R \equiv A\{ALL\ BUT\ Z\}$ (so $r = a\{ALL\ BUT\ Z\}$); then *RC* is:

`FORALL t ε R ( EXISTS u ( ( t = u { ALL BUT Z } ) & ( AC ( u ) ) ) )`

We can define *RX* as follows. Recall first that *X* constraints are quantifier free; without loss of generality, therefore, we can assume that *AX* is in conjunctive normal form. Now replace every conjunct in *AX* that mentions *Z* by TRUE. What results is *RX*.

In the previous section, I showed three examples. In this section, I show essentially the same three examples, but I look at them from the opposite point of view, as it were—i.e., I assume the joins are real relvars and the projections are views. Note in particular, therefore, that the projections I will be discussing in connection with those three examples are all the result of some nonloss decomposition.

The usual requirements regarding *The Assignment Principle* and **The Golden Rule** apply; I omit the details (mostly) in the discussions that follow.

Example 1

Let S{S#,STATUS,CITY} be a real relvar. Define projection views ST and SC thus:

`ST ≡ S { S#, STATUS }`
`SC ≡ S { S#, CITY }`

These views satisfy the constraint that every S# value appearing in ST also appears in SC and vice versa; following *The Principle of Interchangeability,* therefore, the same would have to be true if ST and SC were real relvars and S was a join view. This fact strongly suggests that ST and SC will often have to be updated "simultaneously," via some user-visible multiple assignment (where by *user-visible* I mean the multiple assignment in question must be explicitly specified as such by the user). For example, if ST and SC were real relvars, the following would clearly be a valid update:

`INSERT <S9,20> INTO ST , INSERT <S9,London> INTO SC`

It follows that the same must be true if ST and SC are views. In order to explain the semantics of this update in the view case, I again appeal to first principles. Here is the algorithm:

1. Materialize ST and SC; call the results ST' and SC', respectively.

2. `INSERT <S9,20> INTO ST'`, `INSERT <S9,London> INTO SC'`.

3. `S := ST' JOIN SC'`.

4. Check *The Assignment Principle* for ST ≡ S{S#,STATUS} and SC ≡ S{S#,CITY}.

5. Check **The Golden Rule** for S.

6. Discard ST' and SC'.

The foregoing algorithm also works if ST and SC are real, not views (except that in that case we would need to check **The Golden Rule** for ST and SC instead of S).

Of course, to repeat a point from the section "A Model of Updating," there is no requirement that the foregoing sequence of steps actually be executed in order to achieve the desired result. To be more specific, we have seen that, e.g., inserting the tuple $<S9,20>$ into ST requires a "complementary" tuple $<S9,c>$ to be inserted into SC for some CITY value c; but there is nothing to prevent the DBMS from treating some specified CITY value c as a "default" and performing that complementary INSERT automatically. In other words, I have no objection to the possibility of building some kind of default scheme—so long as it is *systematic*—on top of what I am proposing here. What I do not want to do, however, is to make any such scheme an integral part of my proposal, because existing default schemes, at least, are notoriously ad hoc and suffer from numerous well-known problems. I ignore defaults for the rest of this appendix.[1]

Now consider the following "simpler" INSERT example:

`INSERT <S9,20> INTO ST`

Here is the conceptual algorithm (with apologies for the mixture of tuple- and relation-level notation in Step 2):

1. Materialize ST and SC; call the results ST' and SC', respectively.

2. `INSERT <S9,20> INTO ST'`, `INSERT φ INTO SC'`.

3. `S := ST' JOIN SC'`.

4. Check *The Assignment Principle* for ST ≡ S{S#,STATUS} and SC ≡ S{S#,CITY}.

5. Check **The Golden Rule** for S.

---

1. Except to observe that the idea of an attribute having just one default to be used in all contexts is certainly too rigid. For example, consider a view defined as the projection over all but STATUS of S WHERE STATUS = 20, for which a default STATUS value of 20 clearly makes sense, vs. a view defined as the projection over all but STATUS of S WHERE STATUS ≠ 20, for which a default STATUS value of 20 clearly does not. Consider also the fact that the projection over all but Z of EXTEND A ADD (z AS Z) is identically equal to A. Further investigation is obviously needed.

6. Discard ST' and SC'.

It follows that:

■ If ST and SC are views (as I am assuming), the INSERT violates *The Assignment Principle,* because the tuple for S9 disappears when S, and therefore ST, is recomputed.

■ If they are real—in which case Step 5 applies to ST and SC instead of to S—it violates **The Golden Rule** instead, because it causes a tuple for S9 to appear in ST and not SC.[1]

Either way, therefore, if user *U* "sees" just ST and not SC, then *user U should not be given INSERT rights over ST,* because such INSERTs will always fail (unless they are "no ops"—or unless as previously suggested the DBMS has some mechanism for automatically performing the necessary complementary INSERT into SC; I will not mention this latter possibility again).

Turning now to DELETE, the update

```
DELETE <S1,20> FROM ST , DELETE <S1,London> FROM SC
```

succeeds regardless of whether ST and SC are real or virtual. By contrast, the update

```
DELETE <S1,20> FROM ST
```

fails—if ST and SC are views, it violates *The Assignment Principle* for SC; if they are real, it violates **The Golden Rule,** because it causes a tuple for S1 to appear in SC and not ST. Either way, therefore, if user *U* "sees" just ST and not SC, then *user U should not be given DELETE rights over ST,* because such DELETEs will always fail (unless they are "no ops").

A remark on UPDATE: An UPDATE is basically just a DELETE followed by an INSERT, and for that reason I have had little to say about UPDATE as such in this appendix. However, there is one point worth making in connection with UPDATE specifically in the present context. Consider an attempt to replace the tuple $<S1,20>$ in ST by the tuple $<S1,25>$ ("update the status for supplier S1 from 20 to 25"). This UPDATE is shorthand for the multiple assignment:

```
DELETE <S1,20> FROM ST , INSERT <S1,25> INTO ST
```

This multiple assignment in turn is shorthand for the following:

1. Materialize ST and SC; call the results ST' and SC', respectively.

2. ```
DELETE <S1,20> FROM ST', DELETE φ FROM SC',
INSERT <S1,25> INTO ST', INSERT φ INTO SC'.
```

3. ```
S := ST' JOIN SC'.
```

4. Check *The Assignment Principle.*

5. Check **The Golden Rule.**

---

1. Incidentally, note the implication that if user-visible relvars are always in 6NF, user-visible multiple assignments are likely to be quite common.

6.   Discard ST' and SC'.

And this algorithm produces exactly the desired effect, regardless of whether ST and SC are real relvars or views. Approaches that rely on default values, by contrast, have to treat UPDATE as a special case in order that (e.g.) updating the status for supplier S1 does not have the side effect of setting the city for supplier S1 to some default value, instead of leaving it unchanged.

Example 2

Let SCP{S#,CITY,P#} be a real relvar. Define projection views S and P thus:

```
S ≡ SCP { S#, CITY }
P ≡ SCP { P#, CITY }
```

These views satisfy the constraint that every CITY value appearing in S also appears in P and vice versa. Analysis similar to that under Example 1 thus shows—in general, and without going into too much detail—that inserting into or deleting from just one of the two views will always fail (unless the INSERT or DELETE is a "no op"), while inserting into or deleting from both at the same time will sometimes succeed.

Example 3

Let SSP{S#,CITY,P#,QTY} be a real relvar. Define projection views S and SP thus:

```
S  ≡ SSP { S#, CITY }
SP ≡ SSP { S#, P#, QTY }
```

These views satisfy the constraint that every S# value appearing in S also appears in SP and vice versa. Again, therefore, analysis similar to that under Example 1 thus shows—in general, and without going into too much detail—that:

▪   Inserting into or deleting from just S fails (unless the INSERT or DELETE is a "no op").

▪   Inserting into just SP succeeds so long as the specified S# values already appear in SP (the "INSERT" into S in the expansion is really an "INSERT-type assignment" in this case, since it is "inserting" some tuples that already exist).

▪   Deleting from just SP succeeds so long as the specified S# values still appear in SP.

▪   Inserting into or deleting from both S and SP at the same time sometimes succeeds.

Example 4

So far all of the projections I have considered have been the result of some nonloss decomposition. What happens otherwise? For example, let V ≡ SP{S#,QTY}. Then INSERTs on V clearly fail, in general, because (appealing once again to the conceptual implementation algorithm) there is no way to compute SP from V; that is, inserting the tuple $<s,q>$ into V is virtually certain to violate either *The Assignment Principle* or **The Golden Rule**. As for DELETEs, it might be argued that deleting a tuple of the form $<s,q>$ from V could be supported by deleting all tuples of the form $<s,p,q>$ from SP, but even there violations of *The Assignment Principle* would be likely in practice.

Note: Given that in principle V could be a real relvar (in which case it would presumably be updatable), it might be thought that the foregoing state of affairs constitutes a violation of *The Principle of Interchangeability*. It does not, however, because such a real relvar V and the view V discussed above are not interchangeable; in particular, they have different constraints. To be specific, the constraint for the real relvar is—let us agree for the sake of the example—just:

```
FORALL t ε V ( TRUE )
```

But the constraint for the view is:

```
FORALL t ε V ( EXISTS p ( ( SPX(u) ) & ( SPY ) )
```

where $u \equiv$ EXTEND t ADD (p AS QTY).

SOME REMARKS ON ORTHOGONALITY

In earlier sections, I identified three possible problems with the view updating approach I espouse. To review briefly, the problems in question are as follows:

a. INSERT can sometimes have the effect of inserting into two or more distinct real relvars. Likewise, DELETE can sometimes have the effect of deleting from two or more distinct real relvars.

b. INSERT and DELETE are sometimes not inverses of each other.

c. Updating $A \cup (A \cap B)$ (for example) is sometimes not equivalent to updating just A.

In this section, I want to show how *The Principle of Orthogonal Design* (also known as "the orthogonality principle," or just *orthogonality* for short) can help in avoiding such problems. This principle was first documented in a paper by McGoveran and myself titled "A New Database Design Principle" (the first of the papers listed under reference [87]). Like the principles of further normalization, it is concerned with reducing data redundancy in database designs. And the simplest version of the principle, which is all I want to consider here, is quite straightforward and can be stated informally as follows:[1]

Let A and B be distinct relvars. Then the constraints for A and B should not be such as to require the same tuple to appear in both.

Now, certainly no tuple can be required to appear in both A and B if no tuple can satisfy both of the associated X constraints AX and BX; enforcing this latter condition thus has the effect of enforcing what might be regarded as a strong form of orthogonality. In what follows, I limit my attention to this strong form.

By way of illustration, consider once again the "nonnegative integer" relvars A and B from the earlier examples of updating intersections, unions, and differences, with constraints and initial values as follows:

---

1. It would be more accurate to refer to this "simplest version" as a *logical consequence* of the principle in its general form. Indeed, there is much more to be said about orthogonality in general, but this appendix is not the place; a detailed discussion can be found in the papers listed under reference [87].

```
A : AX ≡ n ≤ 7 : initial value a = 0 4 5 7
    AY ≡ TRUE


B : BX ≡ n ≥ 2 : initial value b = 3 4 6 7 8
    BY ≡ TRUE
```

Here it is clearly possible for the very same integer *n* to satisfy both *AX* and *BX* (take *n* = 4, for example). And we know from our earlier discussions that (a) some updates (e.g., INSERTs on *A∪B*) will affect both *A* and *B*—possibly causing the very same integer (or tuple, rather) to be inserted into both relvars—and (b) INSERTs and DELETEs will sometimes not be inverses of each other. So let us examine an example that is similar to the foregoing, except that it is impossible for the same integer to satisfy both *AX* and *BX*. To be specific, let *A* and *B* be relvars with constraints and initial values as follows:

```
A : AX ≡ n ≤ 4 : initial value a = 0 3 4
    AY ≡ TRUE


B : BX ≡ n ≥ 5 : initial value b = 5 6 8 9
    BY ≡ TRUE
```

Observe that:

```
a∩b = φ                 /* necessarily empty          */
a∪b = 0 3 4 5 6 8 9     /* necessarily disjoint union */
a-b = 0 3 4             /* necessarily equal to a     */
```

Then, ignoring "no ops" for simplicity, it is easy to see that:

- **Intersection:** INSERT *n* INTO *A∩B* always fails. DELETE *n* FROM *A∩B* always fails. Thus, both INSERT *n* INTO *A∩B* followed by DELETE *n* FROM *A∩B* and DELETE *n* FROM *A∩B* followed by INSERT *n* INTO *A∩B* always preserve the status quo, albeit trivially.

- **Union:** INSERT *n* INTO *A∪B* never affects both *A* and *B*. DELETE *n* FROM *A∪B* never affects both *A* and *B*. INSERT *n* INTO *A∪B* followed by DELETE *n* FROM *A∪B* always preserves the status quo (recall that we must have *n* ∉ *a∪b* for the INSERT to be valid). DELETE *n* FROM *A∪B* followed by INSERT *n* INTO *A∪B* always preserves the status quo (recall that we must have *n* ∈ *a∪b* for the DELETE to be valid).

- **Difference:** Both INSERT *n* INTO *A-B* followed by DELETE *n* FROM *A-B* and DELETE *n* FROM *A-B* followed by INSERT *n* INTO *A-B* always preserve the status quo (recall that we must have *n* ∉ *a* for the INSERT to be valid and *n* ∈ *a* for the DELETE to be valid).

I leave examples to illustrate the foregoing as an exercise, if you feel they are necessary.

Recall now Example 1 from the section "Nested Updates." Just to remind you, we had *R* ≡ *A∪(B∩C)*, and we considered the INSERT-type assignment *R* := *R∪i*. The initial values were:

```
a = 0 4 5 7 10
b = 3 4 6 7 8 11
c = 0 1 2 7 8 9 12

i = 1 2 3 9
```

And the values after the update were:

```
A = 0 1 2 3 4 5 7 9 10
B = 1 2 3 4 6 7 8 9 11
C = 0 1 2 3 7 8 9 12
```

And I pointed out that following this INSERT-type assignment with the DELETE-type assignment $R := R-i$ would not restore the status quo. But the problem, again, is the fact that the very same integer (e.g., 7) can appear in any two or even all three of A, B, C (recall that the constraints AC, BC, CC are all just TRUE). So let us consider an example that is similar to the previous one but does not permit the same integer to appear in more than one of A, B, C:

```
AX ≡ 0 ≤ n ≤ 4 : initial value a = 0 3 4
AY ≡ TRUE

BX = 9 ≤ n     : initial value b = 10 11 12
BY ≡ TRUE

CX ≡ 5 ≤ n ≤ 8 : initial value c = 6 7 8
CY ≡ TRUE
```

Then the X constraint RX for $R \equiv A\cup(B\cap C)$ is $(AX)\,|\,((BX)\&(CX))$, which reduces to $AX\,|\,$FALSE, or in other words to just AX. Now take i to be the set of integers 1 2. Then it is easy to see that $R := R\cup i$ gives $A = 0\ 1\ 2\ 3\ 4$ and leaves B and C unchanged. Moreover, deleting i from the result now clearly does restore the status quo.

Consider also the case of updating $R \equiv A\cup(A\cap B)$ (Example 3 from the section "Nested Updates"). Recall that previously we had the result that inserting into R could affect the value of B, even though $A\cup(A\cap B)$ is (or should be?) identically equal to A. However, if AX and BX are such that no value can satisfy them both, then the constraint $RX \equiv (AX)\,|\,((AX)\&(BX))$, which again reduces to just AX. In the update $R := R\cup i$, then, no value in i can satisfy BX, the overall update reduces to just $A := A\cup i$, and B remains unchanged—and the principle that view updating is a matter of semantics, not syntax, is upheld.

One consequence of all of the above is the following. Let x be a relational expression. If x appears in a "read-only" position, then the implementation is free to transform it (typically for optimization purposes) into any logically equivalent expression. But if x appears in an "update" position, the implementation is *not* free to perform such a transformation unless it can be sure it is safe to do so. Adherence to the strong form of orthogonality discussed in this section is a sufficient condition for ensuring such safety.

A REMARK ON MULTIPLE ASSIGNMENT

Note: Thanks to Hugh Darwen for alerting me to the issue addressed in this section.

Consider the following example (a modified version of one from the previous section). Let the "nonnegative integer" relvars A and B have constraints and initial values as follows:

```
A : AX ≡ n < 5 : initial value a = 0 3
    AY ≡ TRUE

B : BX ≡ n > 5 : initial value b = 6 8 9
    BY ≡ TRUE
```

Now let $R \equiv A \cup B$ and consider the following multiple assignment:

```
INSERT 5 INTO R , UPDATE R WHERE n = 5 ( n := 7 ) ;
```

It should be clear that if we expand the constituent assignments separately, the overall operation will fail; more precisely, the INSERT will fail, because the value 5 does not satisfy the constraint $RX \equiv (n < 5) | (n > 5)$. Yet the overall operation would clearly succeed if R were real, not virtual. What is to be done about this situation? One possible solution would be to add another step to the multiple assignment algorithm—see RM Prescription 21—according to which distinct assignments to the same virtual relvar are "collected" before Step a. (the syntactic expansion step) is performed; in the example, this approach would cause the two assignments to be collapsed into one, and the final result would be A unchanged, $B = 6\ 7\ 8\ 9$, and $R = 0\ 3\ 6\ 7\ 8\ 9$. But note the implication that we *still* might not have the semantics of multiple assignment quite right … More study is required.

SUMMARY

In the foregoing sections, I have identified or at least touched on a number of principles, or objectives, that I believe any systematic approach to the view updating problem needs to satisfy. I summarize those principles here for purposes of future reference. (The summary that follows is based on a similar but less extensive one given in reference [76], but differs from that earlier one in several details.)

1. *Relations only:* I am interested in a *relational* mechanism specifically; in particular, I have no interest in trying to extend my view updating scheme to support "relations" that contain either nulls or duplicate tuples. Moreover, I would resist any attempt to do so, too, if it meant compromising on any of the other objectives.

2. *The Assignment Principle:* After assignment of x to relvar R, the comparison $R = x$ must evaluate to TRUE, otherwise the assignment fails.

3. **The Golden Rule:** After assignment of x to relvar R, R must satisfy its constraint RC, otherwise the assignment fails. (If R is virtual, it is sufficient, in order to ensure that R satisfies RC, to ensure that the relvars $R1, R2, …, Rn$ in terms of which R is defined satisfy their constraints $R1C$, $R2C, …, RnC$, respectively.)

4. *INSERT- and DELETE-type assignments only:* Any relational assignment can be expressed in the form $R := R\text{-}d \cup i$; thus, all such assignments can be expressed as a suitable combination of INSERT- and DELETE-type assignments. UPDATE in particular is shorthand for an assignment of the form $R := $ WITH $R\text{-}d$ AS R: $R \cup i$.

5. *Relvar constraints* (this one is a conjecture on my part, but it is easy to see that the conjecture is at least trivially true): Relvar constraints can always be expressed in the form (FORALL $t \in R\ (RX)$) & (RY), where RX is a quantifier-free predicate with at most one parameter—namely, t—and RY is a proposition, in general not quantifier free.

6. *Semantics not syntax:* The semantics of view updating should not depend on the particular syntactic form in which the view definition in question happens to be stated.

7. *The Principle of Interchangeability:* The rules must work for real relvars too.

8. *Symmetry:* Operands to symmetric operations should be treated symmetrically. (This principle fundamentally applies to unions and joins; the other symmetric operators intersect and cartesian

product are just special cases of join.)

9.   *All updates supported:* Every relvar should support all three of INSERT / DELETE / UPDATE.

10.   *Inverse operations:* INSERT and DELETE should be inverses of each other.

11.   *Recursion:* The rules must be capable of recursive application (i.e., "nested updates" should work satisfactorily).

12.   *Database design:* The rules cannot assume the database is well designed (though they might occasionally produce results that some might find counterintuitive if it is not).

I have presented an approach to view updating that, I believe, goes a long way toward meeting the foregoing objectives. The approach in question is based on ideas originally articulated in references [88] and [114], but I have found it necessary to dot a lot of *i*'s and cross a lot of *t*'s in order to get it into the shape described herein—which, let me be the first to say, doubtless still needs a considerable amount of polishing in order to make it anywhere close to watertight. As noted previously, however, I feel cautiously optimistic about the approach, for the following reasons among others:

- No views are inherently nonupdatable (though certain specific updates will fail on violations of either *The Assignment Principle* or **The Golden Rule**).

- Join views in particular are always updatable (again, modulo violations of *The Assignment Principle* or **The Golden Rule**); it is not a matter of whether the join in question is one-to-one, one-to-many, or many-to-many.

- The approach gives a predictable result in every case.

- Moreover, it gives the intuitively expected and useful result in most cases (possibly not all).

- If *The Principle of Orthogonal Design* is followed, the number of cases (it is tempting to call them pathological) in which the result might be "unexpected" is further reduced.

DARWEN'S APPROACH

This final section describes Darwen's objections to Date's approach and sketches one that he might support—one that is more conservative in some respects and more ambitious in others. For the remainder of this appendix, therefore, the first person singular refers to Darwen.

My objection to Date's approach is simply that the rules for inserting through union and deleting through join require the system sometimes to make an arbitrary interpretation of an ambiguous request. I maintain instead that ambiguous requests should be rejected.

As a basis for the discussions to follow, I now introduce some notation, of my own personal preference (the notation in question was mentioned in Chapter 2 but not much used elsewhere in this book). Let R be a relvar. Then I define the expression $R(t)$ to be equivalent to the truth-valued expression $t \in R$. The notation appeals to my perception of a relvar as representing a time-varying truth-valued function—the extension of the relvar predicate varies over time (though the intension of course does not). Thus, the expression $R(t)$ can be thought of as denoting an invocation of that function.

Objections to Date's Proposals for Updating Unions and Joins

In order to illustrate my objections here, I consider the simplest database imaginable that is sufficient for the purpose at hand: one consisting of just two relvars, both of degree zero. (I deliberately violate the strong form of *The Principle of Orthogonal Design* here. That strong form is a principle I certainly do not hold with at all, a point I will return to later.) To give my example a semblance of realism, imagine the enterprise to be a shop. At all times the shop is either open for business or closed. The shop is equipped with a burglar alarm. At all times the alarm is either set or not set. The purpose of the database is to record (a) whether or not the shop is open and (b) whether or not the alarm is set. Assume until further notice that the two variables are not subject to any constraint, even though it might seem a little peculiar to allow the alarm to be set while the shop is open. Here is the **Tutorial D** definition:

```
VAR THE_SHOP_IS_OPEN REAL RELATION { } KEY { } ;

VAR THE_ALARM_IS_SET REAL RELATION { } KEY { } ;
```

Either of the following statements will suffice to record the fact that the shop is open:

```
THE_SHOP_IS_OPEN := TABLE_DEE ;

INSERT THE_SHOP_IS_OPEN TABLE_DEE ;
```

Likewise, either of the following will suffice to record the fact that the alarm is not set:

```
THE_ALARM_IS_SET := TABLE_DUM ;

DELETE THE_ALARM_IS_SET ;
```

Just to remind you, TABLE_DEE is shorthand for RELATION{TUPLE{}}, the relation with no attributes and just one tuple (the 0-tuple), and TABLE_DUM is shorthand for RELATION{}{}, the relation with no attributes and no tuples at all.

Observe now that, using my $R(t)$ notation, the expression

```
THE_SHOP_IS_OPEN ( TUPLE { } )
```

is a formal assertion of the truth of the proposition "The shop is open." I will abbreviate it from this point forward to just

```
THE_SHOP_IS_OPEN ( )
```

And I will define the expression

```
THE_ALARM_IS_SET ( )
```

("The alarm is set") analogously.

In accordance with certain ideas previously articulated in reference [85], I would also like to introduce some new notation for updating the database. In *The Third Manifesto,* we regard relational assignment as the fundamental update operator, and of course I have no problem with that position. For present purposes, however (and possibly others), I prefer to think of *expressing belief in a single "atomic" proposition* as being even more fundamental than relational assignment. To "insert a tuple" into a relvar is to express belief in the truth of the proposition represented by the appearance of that tuple in that relvar; to "delete a tuple" from a relvar is to express the corresponding disbelief (i.e., belief in the truth of the negation of that proposition). In keeping with that perception, I will use imperatives of the following deliberately verbose form—

```
IT IS [ NOT ] THE CASE THAT R ( [ t ] )
```

—where the 0-tuple is implicit if *t* is omitted. So IT IS THE CASE THAT $R(t)$ is equivalent to $R := R$ UNION RELATION$\{t\}$ and also to INSERT R RELATION$\{t\}$; likewise, IT IS NOT THE CASE THAT $R(t)$ is equivalent to $R := R$ MINUS RELATION$\{t\}$ and also to some DELETE statement. Thus, for example, to record the opening of the shop for business and the simultaneous turning off of the alarm, I can write:

```
IT IS THE CASE THAT THE_SHOP_IS_OPEN ( ) , IT IS NOT THE CASE THAT THE_ALARM_IS_SET ( ) ;
```

(a multiple assignment).

Now let me introduce a couple of views:

```
VAR THE_SHOP_IS_OPEN_OR_THE_ALARM_IS_SET VIRTUAL
  ( THE_SHOP_IS_OPEN UNION THE_ALARM_IS_SET ) ;

VAR THE_SHOP_IS_OPEN_AND_THE_ALARM_IS_SET VIRTUAL
  ( THE_SHOP_IS_OPEN JOIN THE_ALARM_IS_SET ) ;
```

Under Date's proposals the following updates would both be legal:

```
IT IS THE CASE THAT THE_SHOP_IS_OPEN_OR_THE_ALARM_IS_SET ( ) ;

IT IS NOT THE CASE THAT THE_SHOP_IS_OPEN_AND_THE_ALARM_IS_SET ( ) ;
```

Under the semantics of UNION and JOIN, those two update statements both mean exactly what they say, and therefore they are both ambiguous—indeterminate—as far as the required effect on the database is concerned. The first can be implemented by assigning TABLE_DEE to either THE_SHOP_IS_OPEN or THE_ALARM_IS_SET, or both. Date proposes that the DBMS be required to choose the third possibility, advancing an observation regarding symmetry as justification. Similarly, the second can be implemented by assigning TABLE_DUM to either THE_SHOP_IS_OPEN or THE_ALARM_IS_SET, or both, and again Date's proposal requires the DBMS to choose the third possibility and again the observation regarding symmetry is advanced as justification. I remark that this justification could also be used to allow an expression of the form $x+y$ (or a name standing for that expression, to make the analogy with views a little closer) to be the target of an assignment: If z is the value to be assigned, just assign $z/2$ to both x and y.

In my opinion, however, both updates should be rejected. The reader who thinks that position harsh should perhaps consider what advantages database users might gain from the proposals that I am rejecting. The ability to insert through union? Well, if I, the designer of THE_SHOP_IS_OPEN and THE_ALARM_IS_SET, really want my users to be able to insert into their union, I would resort to the following artifice in the view definition:

```
VAR THE_SHOP_IS_OPEN_OR_THE_ALARM_IS_SET VIRTUAL
    WITH RELATION ( TUPLE ( STATUS 'open'   ) ) AS OPEN,
         RELATION ( TUPLE ( STATUS 'alarmed' ) ) AS ALARMED :
      ( THE_SHOP_IS_OPEN JOIN OPEN ) UNION ( THE_ALARM_IS_SET JOIN ALARMED ) ;
```

Here it is clear that the operands of the UNION are disjoint. Now, for example, the opening of the shop can be expressed as:

```
IT IS THE CASE THAT THE_SHOP_IS_OPEN_OR_THE_ALARM_IS_SET ( TUPLE { STATUS 'open' } )
```

Similarly, the turning off of the alarm can be expressed as:

```
IT IS NOT THE CASE THAT THE_SHOP_IS_OPEN_OR_THE_ALARM_IS_SET ( TUPLE { STATUS 'alarmed' } )
```

I assume here that the two joins and the union mentioned in the view definition would indeed be updatable, under both Date's proposal and the proper subset of that proposal that I believe I would not object to. (I use JOIN rather than EXTEND in the view definition just to float the idea that a dyadic operator invocation might be updatable even if only one of its operands is a variable.)

Now let me get back to the original view definitions:

```
VAR THE_SHOP_IS_OPEN_OR_THE_ALARM_IS_SET VIRTUAL
  ( THE_SHOP_IS_OPEN UNION THE_ALARM_IS_SET ) ;

VAR THE_SHOP_IS_OPEN_AND_THE_ALARM_IS_SET VIRTUAL
  ( THE_SHOP_IS_OPEN JOIN THE_ALARM_IS_SET ) ;
```

I note in passing, incidentally, that if these two views are the only relvars ever used as targets of update operations, then under Date's approach they will always be equal in value in spite of the stark logical difference (OR vs. AND) in the predicates they represent. Be that as it may, here again are the two updates previously discussed on the foregoing views:

```
IT IS THE CASE THAT THE_SHOP_IS_OPEN_OR_THE_ALARM_IS_SET ( )

IT IS NOT THE CASE THAT THE_SHOP_IS_OPEN_AND_THE_ALARM_IS_SET ( )
```

I have shown that these updates are indeterminate. However, I agree that if those indeterminacies can be resolved by the existence of an appropriate constraint, then the update in question might be permitted. For example, suppose the shop sensibly decides that it is not a good idea ever to set the alarm when it is open for business:

```
CONSTRAINT NOT_ALARMED_WHEN_OPEN IS_EMPTY ( THE_SHOP_IS_OPEN JOIN THE_ALARM_IS_SET ) ;
```

But this particular constraint does not resolve the indeterminacies. For the first update, the DBMS knows that just one of the two underlying real relvars is to be assigned TABLE_DEE, but it does not know which. For the second, all three possibilities satisfy the constraint.

Date also advances, in connection with his position on insert through union, a certain "strong form" of *The Principle of Orthogonal Design,* observing that results such as the one I object to are avoided if that strong form of the principle is followed. (I remark that there does not seem to be a counterpart to this observation that could apply to delete through join, except in the special case where the join degenerates to intersection.) I do not hold with this strong form of the principle at all. I see no advantage, ever—and sometimes positive disadvantage—in choosing a design that adheres to it over one that does not, as I now explain.

Objections to Invoking "the Strong Form of Orthogonality"

Date gives the following informal definition of (a certain logical consequence of) *The Principle of Orthogonal Design:*

Let *A* and *B* be distinct relvars. Then the constraints for *A* and *B* should not be such as to require the same tuple to appear in both.

I cannot dispute that any violation of this principle, as far as it goes, would lead to redundancy, but I remark that it does not go very far. There are many ways in which redundancy can occur without the same tuple appearing in two relvars. For example, let relvars *A* and *B* have the same heading except that one attribute of *B* has a different name (say *Y* instead of *X*) from its counterpart in *A*. Further, let there be a constraint in effect that requires *A* to be equal at all times to *B* RENAME (*Y* AS *X*). This case is perhaps the simplest of the many that are not covered by the principle as stated. (Date does not disagree with this observation; in fact, he and I have worked together on the more general definition of the principle, as given in the last of the papers listed under reference [87].)

But Date continues:

> Now, certainly no tuple can be required to appear in both *A* and *B* if no tuple can satisfy both of the associated *X* constraints *AX* and *BX*; enforcing this latter condition thus has the effect of enforcing what might be regarded as a strong form of orthogonality. In what follows, I limit my attention to this strong form.

And he goes on to show that adherence to this "strong form" will avoid the undesired effects that sometimes arise in his approach to the updating of unions and joins.

I perceive a tacit suggestion here that adherence to the strong form of orthogonality is a good database design principle to follow, especially if undesired effects of update operations are to be avoided. I disagree on two counts:

1. I disagree with the tacit suggestion, because (a) as I have already explained, even the weak form given in Date's informal definition only scratches the surface of redundancy, and (b) the strong form does not appear to address any cases of redundancy that the weak form misses and, worse, rules out many designs that do not entail redundancy at all.

2. I disagree with the idea that a database should be designed "correctly" or "appropriately" in order to ensure that operators never have undesired effects—in particular, effects that represent unsafe conclusions from the premises that are represented by invocations of update operators (under our agreed interpretation).

As applied to 2-tuples, for example, the strong form of orthogonality seems to be saying that the database should not permit the same two things to be related to each other in two or more different ways—or, at least, should not permit such facts to be represented in the most obvious way (by allowing the same 2-tuple to appear in several relvars). This state of affairs strikes me as being a violation of orthogonality! (in a possibly different sense of that term). Moreover, my characterization is not entirely accurate either (hence "seems"), because for two 2-tuples to be identical their headings need to consist of the same set of attributes (and hence involve the same set of attribute names in particular). Therefore, if I want to be able to record, for example, that a pair of cousins happen also to be a married couple, I can do so without violating the strong form of the principle by choosing different attribute names for the two relvars: MARRIED{A,B} and COUSINS{A,C}, for example. But to place a restriction on my freedom of choice of attribute names strikes me also as a violation of orthogonality.

As applied to 1-tuples, the strong form of orthogonality is effectively saying that the database should not permit the same thing to have more than one "property" (a term used by some logicians to characterize monadic predicates). Consider, for example, the predicates "Employee E is on vacation" and "Employee E is awaiting phone number allocation." What more natural way is there of representing those than defining two unary relvars with those very predicates? What problems are solved by adopting a different approach? (I see none of any significance.) What problems arise in that different approach? (For the different approaches I find myself able to imagine, apart from the simple one of choosing different attribute names for those two E's, I see significant problems arising.)

I turn now to Date's claim that orthogonal design "is concerned with reducing data redundancy." I have already mentioned that his informal definition does not really go very far toward addressing the redundancy question. This issue is dealt with in the papers (excluding the first such) listed under reference [87]. However, those papers also question whether redundancy really can or must always be avoided; they even show that there might be cases where redundancy is positively desirable (though in such cases it should at least be properly controlled).

So we have:

1. A desire, arising frequently but possibly not always, to avoid redundancy in database designs

2. A design principle, *The Principle of Orthogonal Design,* adherence to which goes some way toward avoiding redundancy

3. One stated consequence of that principle, covering just the special case where redundancy involves having more than one appearance of the very same tuple

4. A "strong form" of that consequence whereby the cases covered by it can be addressed without knowledge of the declared constraints, by avoiding altogether the possibility of having more than one appearance of the very same tuple, regardless of whether such appearances would represent redundancy

5. An observation that adherence to that strong form eliminates the undesired effects that can otherwise result from certain update operations

I accept points 1 and 2. I see no real value in mentioning point 3 in connection with the issue of redundancy. It follows that I see no real value in point 4, in spite of the slight relief from burden offered to the database designer who would like to be sure of adhering to point 3 regardless of what constraints are declared. Besides, to compensate for the burden it avoids, it introduces a new burden to which I strongly object. It further follows, from my rejection of point 4 and from the fact noted in point 1 that we do not always want to avoid redundancy, that point 5 does nothing to address my objections to Date's proposals for updating views.

This concludes my objections to Date's proposals. The question now arises, to what extent do *I* think views might be updatable? And what general principles underlie *my* position? I address the second question first.

Principles

I accept **The Golden Rule** without question.

I accept *The Assignment Principle* without question but not without comment. Of course, any update operator invocation is equivalent to some assignment (possibly multiple). What assignment it is equivalent to depends on the definition of the operator being invoked. For example, we have given what we think are reasonable, useful, and intuitive definitions for the familiar INSERT, DELETE, and UPDATE operators in terms of relational assignment. It follows that every INSERT, DELETE, or UPDATE invocation should have the same effect on its target relvar as the assignment to which it is equivalent; for if not, *The Assignment Principle* is violated. My comment is that it might be possible to subvert the intent of *The Assignment Principle* by defining perverse update operators (a possibility I actually consider in my notes on UPDATE through extension and UPDATE through join).

As already noted, I reject the strong form of *The Principle of Orthogonal Design.*

I propose the following two additional principles:

- *The Principle of No Ambiguity:* If relation *r* is to be assigned to view *R*, then there must exist exactly one corresponding set of assignments to the real relvars on which *R* is defined such that

The Golden Rule and *The Assignment Principle* are adhered to; otherwise, the assignment is rejected.

■   *The Principle of View and Pseudovariable Equivalence:* Every permitted assignment to view *R* is also permitted, with exactly the same effect, to the expression *x* on which *R* is defined. (That expression *x*, when appearing as a target, is therefore acting as a pseudovariable.)

Note: I state the second of these principles only because Date does not do so explicitly himself. We are not in disagreement here. Indeed, we mentioned the possibility of using relational expressions as pseudovariables in Chapter 5, and Date referred to it also in the section of this appendix titled "Nested Updates."

In the remaining subsections, I provide some notes on each relational algebra operator through which I see some reasonable opportunity for updatability. I have put these notes together with more haste than usual, as a result of the lateness of our decision to include this appendix. The serious student should scrutinize them carefully and perhaps with a certain amount of suspicion.

Rename

If view *V* is defined on some invocation of RENAME on relvar *R1*, then all update operations on *V* are permitted and are effected by transforming them into operations on *R1* merely by replacing references to attributes of *V* by references to the corresponding attributes of *R1*.

Projection

If view *V* is defined on some projection of relvar *R1*, then deletions from *V* are permitted but insertions, in general, are not.

The relvar predicate, *P* say, for *V* is

```
EXISTS x ( R1 ( x U y ) )
```

where *x* is a tuple whose heading consists of the attributes of *R1* that are excluded by the projection and *y* is a tuple consisting of the remaining attributes of *R1*.

To delete tuple *y* from *V* is to deny that there exists such an *x* (i.e., to assert that NOT *P*). The only way of achieving that effect is to delete all tuples of the form *x*U*y* from *R1*.

To insert tuple *y* into *V* is to assert that there does exist such an *x*. In general, there are many equally reasonable ways of achieving that effect and to choose one of those ways would be arbitrary. Now, some writers have proposed to treat as special the case where all of the attributes of the heading of *x* have default values defined for them. My objection to that proposal is that we cannot safely conclude, given that there exists at least one *x* that makes *R1*(*x*U*y*) evaluate to TRUE, that there exists *exactly* one such *x*; hence, to insert exactly one tuple into *R1* would be arbitrary. However, it has been proposed (and this proposal has been implemented in more than one product) to make a special case of projections whose attributes include a key of *R1*, simply because of the existence of an explicit constraint to the effect that there cannot now exist more than one such *x*, so to insert a single tuple is not arbitrary after all.

A further thought: It might be possible to allow *V* to appear as the target of an UPDATE without the foregoing INSERT limitation (to the effect that the attributes of *V* must include a key of *R1*). For example, if *V* is defined as EMP {SALARY}, we could give everybody a 10% salary increase as follows:

```
UPDATE V ( SALARY := SALARY * 1.1 )
```

Is it really so important for UPDATE to be shorthand for DELETE followed by INSERT? I suppose we can keep it that way with a bit of sleight of hand, by defining it as DELETE-but-remember-the-deleted-tuples, then apply the updates to the remembered tuples, then INSERT. For UPDATE through projection we would have to propagate those three steps to the underlying relvar.

Restriction

If *V* is defined on some conjunction *R1* AND *p* and *p* is quantifier free, then *V* is either a restriction or an extension of *R1*. If it is a restriction, then all update operations are permitted on *V* and are effected by transforming them into operations on *R1*. An attempt to insert tuple *t* is rejected if *p(t)* is false (because "*p(t)* false" contradicts *V(t)*). To delete *t* from *V* is to deny *R1(t)*, because the truth of *p(t)* is not subject to change, so the deletion can safely be effected by deleting *t* from *R1*.

Extension

Following on from the previous subsection, if *V* is an extension of *R1*, then all deletions are permitted, and are effected by transforming them into deletions from *R1* in an obvious manner (the details are tedious but straightforward). The justification for permitting deletions is analogous to the justification already given in connection with restrictions. Insertions are permitted with a proviso analogous to that already given in connection with restrictions.

UPDATE through extension is a case where *The Assignment Principle* might be seen as an annoyance. Intuitively it seems not unreasonable (and possibly desirable) to permit UPDATE invocations that affect only those attributes of *V* that are inherited from R1, with the additional attributes of *V* being recomputed. This treatment might be acceptable if some agreeable extension to the definition of UPDATE can be formulated such that *The Assignment Principle* is not violated under it.

Join

If *V* is defined on some conjunction *R1* AND *R2*, then *V* is the join of *R1* and *R2* (with *R1* INTERSECT *R2* and, if the heading of *R2* is a subset of that of *R1*, *R1* MATCHING *R2* as degenerate but not special cases). Insertions into *V* are permitted; for IT IS THE CASE THAT *V(t)* is equivalent to *R1(u)* AND *R2(v)*, where *u* is the projection of *t* over the attributes of *R1* and *v* is the projection of *t* over the attributes of *R2*. (I assume that inserting a tuple that already exists in the target relvar is a "no op.") However, deletions from *V* are not permitted, in general, for IT IS NOT THE CASE THAT *V(t)* can be effected by any of the following logically distinct statements:

1.   `IT IS NOT THE CASE THAT R1(u) ;`

2.   `IT IS NOT THE CASE THAT R2(v) ;`

3.   `IT IS NOT THE CASE THAT R1(u) , IT IS NOT THE CASE THAT R2(v) ;`

(No. 3 is a multiple assignment.) Because *R1* and *R2* are both subject to change, it is not possible to identify exactly one of these invocations to effect deletion of *t* from *V*.

Note: I would relax the foregoing general prohibition in cases where exactly one of the choices satisfies both **The Golden Rule** and *The Assignment Principle*. I would also consider relaxing the prohibition in the specific case where the common attributes of *R1* and *R2* include a key of *R2*. Some people advocate supporting deletion (and therefore UPDATE) in such cases by propagating the operation to *R1* only. The justification for this position is that each tuple being deleted from *V* has exactly one matching tuple in *R1*, as a consequence of which *The Assignment Principle* is guaranteed to hold. In the case where the matching tuple in *R2* is matched by no other tuples in *R1*, *The Assignment Principle* also holds if that matching tuple is deleted from *R2*, but it seems reasonable to resolve the ambiguity by applying the same treatment as in the more general case. Unfortunately, this relaxation for many-to-one joins would appear to have to permit deletion from both operands in the one-to-one case where the common attributes include a key of *R1* as well as a key of *R2*. If you think this treatment of DELETE seems a bit suspect (as it does to me, at least), I remark that it does seem utterly reasonable to permit UPDATE in these cases, noting that if common attributes are affected then we would have a possible violation of *The Assignment Principle* on our hands (and again I very tentatively wonder about the possibility of extending the definition of UPDATE to avoid such violation).

Union

If *V* is defined on some disjunction *R1* OR *p*, then we are talking about *R1* UNION *R2* (for other kinds of disjunction where *R1* is one of the disjuncts are not permitted). The situation is the inverse of what applies in the conjunction cases. Inserting into *V* is prohibited, because IT IS THE CASE THAT *V(t)* can be effected by any of the following logically distinct statements:

1.   `IT IS THE CASE THAT R1(u) ;`

2.   `IT IS THE CASE THAT R2(v) ;`

3.   `IT IS THE CASE THAT R1(u) , IT IS THE CASE THAT R2(v) ;`

(where, as it happens, $u = v = t$). There is no justification for choosing exactly one of these three possibilities over the other two. However, all deletions are permitted. Deleting *t* from *V* is effected by deleting *u* from *R1* and *v* from *R2* (i.e., deleting *t* from both *R1* and *R2*).

The prohibition on insertion might be relaxed when there is a constraint to the effect that *R1* and *R2* be at all times disjoint, provided that the constraint in question can be used to determine to which unique operand a given tuple, proffered for insertion, must belong. For example, the constraint NOT_ALARMED_WHEN_OPEN given in the subsection "Objection to *The Principle of Orthogonal Design*" cannot be used for the purpose at hand. However, a constraint such as the following (expressed for convenience in logic notation)—

   `FORALL t ( R1(t) ⟹ t.A > 5 & R2(t) ⟹ t.A ≤ 5 )`

—could perhaps be used. For any given tuple *t* the system needs only to evaluate the expression $t.A > 5$ to determine whether *t* is to be inserted into *R1* or *R2* (not both). A common shorthand for constraints such as these allows one to write something like CHECK A > 5 inside the relvar definition; use of such syntax might make it comparatively easy for the system to determine at compile time whether the constraint can be used to disambiguate inserts into unions.

Semidifference

If *V* is defined on *R1* AND NOT (*p*), then either *p* is not subject to change, in which case the rules for restriction apply, or we are talking about *R1* NOT MATCHING *R2* (with *R1* MINUS *R2* as a degenerate but I hope not special case).

Insertion into *V* might be permitted. IT IS THE CASE THAT *V(t)* is equivalent to:

   `IT IS THE CASE THAT R1(u) , IT IS NOT THE CASE THAT EXISTS w (R2(v ∪ w)) ;`

(where $u = t$, *v* is the projection of *t* over the common attributes, and *w* is a tuple whose heading consists of the remaining attributes of *R2*). One approach would be to adopt the same rules as for restriction (i.e., treating *R2* as immutable via inserts into *V*). Another approach would be to effect the insertion of *t* into *V* by inserting *u* into *R1* and deleting *v* from the projection of *R2* over the common attributes.

Deletion might also be permitted, for the only reasonable way in general of effecting the deletion of *t* from *V* is to delete it from *R1* and do nothing to *R2*. However, I remark that in the special case of *R1* MINUS *R2,* inserting *t* into *R2* appears to have just as much merit as deleting it from *R1*—and I have already said I do not want to treat *R1* MINUS *R2* as a special case.

Appendix F

A Closer Look at

Specialization by Constraint

Our inheritance model requires support for specialization by constraint (S by C). You might recall, however, that after we had explained the basic idea of S by C in Chapter 14, we said this:

> But there is much, much more to be said on this topic: so much, in fact, that it seemed better not to include it all in the body of the chapter [but] instead to relegate most of it to [this appendix].

We also said the topic was controversial; in fact, we excluded it from our original model [82], basically because everyone else seemed to have done the same thing (not a very good reason!). Why, then, is there this broad sentiment against S by C? The answer seems to do with performance; there seems to be a widespread belief that S by C is difficult to implement efficiently and must perform badly. Now, performance by definition is not a model concern—we would always rather get the model right first and worry about the implementation afterward—but we do have some thoughts on the performance issue, which we will discuss later. First, however, we would like to take a closer look at S by C from the perspective of the model, and that is the primary purpose of this appendix.

The discussion is structured as follows. Following these introductory remarks, the next two sections offer a brief historical review. The following sections then summarize the benefits of S by C and suggest that the reason it has typically not been supported in the past is because most work on inheritance has been done in an object setting. The final section offers some thoughts on implementation and performance. *Note:* To keep the appendix shorter than it might be, we assume—where it makes any difference (actually in very few places)—that we are dealing with single inheritance only and scalar types only.

THE 3 OUT OF 4 "RULE"

It is instructive to begin by taking a look at a historical issue that is directly related to the S by C controversy. The issue in question is known as "the 3 out of 4 rule,"[1] and it turns out that S by C—or, rather, generalization by constraint (G by C), which is part of the same overall phenomenon, of course—is the key to resolving it.

We have said that S by C is controversial. Just to remind you, S by C means the system should be aware that, e.g., if an ellipse has equal semiaxes, it is really a circle. Now, we have assumed throughout this book, tacitly, that the inverse notion—i.e., that the system should be aware that, e.g., if an ellipse is really a circle, its semiaxes must be equal—is not controversial at all; in fact, of course, it is just a type constraint on circles, and we have tacitly assumed that type constraints are *obviously* desirable. Indeed, without type constraints we do not even have a way of specifying the values that go to make up a given type.

Not everyone agrees with us on this point, however (in other words, our position on type constraints is controversial as well). Consider the following lightly edited extract from reference [137]:

---

1. We call your attention to the deliberately different positioning of the quotation marks in the title to this section.

We can list four features of a subtyping mechanism that all seem to be desirable, yet ... it is not possible to combine them in a single type system. The four features are:

- Substitutability
- Static type checking
- Mutability
- Type constraints

[*We break in here to explain a couple of matters. First, the term "mutability" just means* updatability; *as mentioned in Chapter 6,* mutator *is the object term for what we call an update* operator *(the object term for a read-only operator, you will recall, being* observer). *Second, reference [137] identifies the last feature in the list not as type constraints but rather as* specialization via constraints. *But it does not mean by that term quite what we mean by S by C. Rather, it refers to the more fundamental notion—of which S by C is a logical consequence—that type* T' *might be defined as a "constrained" form of type* T; *in other words, it really is talking about type constraints. To continue:*]

All four of these properties seem to be desirable ... We submit, however, that it is impossible to have all four of them in the same type system. This conflict can be illustrated with the following example. [*We have replaced the example given in reference [137] by one that is essentially similar but conforms to our own notation and our own running example. Also, for consistency with the body of the book, we use LENGTH as a selector, despite the fact that we have argued in Appendix C that, e.g., LENGTH_IN_INCHES would be preferable.*]

```
VAR E ELLIPSE ;
VAR C CIRCLE ;

C := CIRCLE ( LENGTH ( 3.0 ), ... ) ;
E := C ;
THE_A ( E ) := LENGTH ( 4.0 ) ;
```

[The first assignment initializes C to a circle of radius three.] The [second] assignment must be allowed ... if we have substitutability and mutability ... The [third assignment] would type-check at compile time ... Of course, [that assignment] ... will fail [at run time] even though the compile-time check determined that it was all right.

[*And the extract concludes:*]

We observe that any three of the four features seem to work just fine. No one of them is obviously the one that must be discarded, but in any type system, at least one of them must be sacrificed to achieve consistency with the others.

Now, perhaps you can see right away what is wrong with this argument. To be specific, in our model, G by C would occur on the third assignment, *MST*(E) would become ELLIPSE again, and everything would indeed "work just fine." However, reference [137] does not consider the possibility of G by C, so let us suspend disbelief for a while and see where the foregoing argument takes us. We begin by taking a closer look at the four features and seeing how each relates to the example at hand:

- *Substitutability:* As explained in Chapter 14, type inheritance implies substitutability (value substitutability, at any rate), so this feature cannot possibly be discarded. The second assignment in the example appeals to value substitutability.

- *Static type checking:* Reference [137] defines static type checking to mean that "there is no need to insert expensive run-time [type] checks [into the compiled] code, and also the coder can be assured that [run-time type] errors can never occur." In our inheritance model, by contrast, run-time type errors certainly can occur in the context of TREAT (though nowhere else), even if static type checking is performed. So perhaps it can be claimed that static type checking—full static type checking, that is, in the sense of reference [137]—is the feature we have discarded.

  However, we would argue that to insist that everything be fully type-checkable at compile time is to throw the baby out with the bathwater. For example, consider the following code fragment:

```
VAR L LENGTH ;

E := C ;
L := THE_R ( E ) ;
```

  The expression THE_R(E) will fail on a compile-time type check, of course. So now we have no way to obtain the radius of the circle that is the current value of E (we cannot use TREAT, because TREAT *intrinsically* cannot be fully type-checked at compile time). So there is really no point in saying that the current value of E is of type CIRCLE; we might as well have converted that circle to make it "just an ellipse" when we assigned C to E. So we have lost substitutability!—and therefore the whole idea of type inheritance, in fact.

- *Mutability:* As noted earlier, mutability just means updatability. Updatability in turn implies support for variables and assignment (and the example does involve variables and assignment, obviously). Now, we did say in Chapter 1 that a functional-style language would not need variables or assignment as such, so we might be persuaded that mutability could be discarded (though we doubt whether this interpretation is what the authors of reference [137] had in mind). And even if the language is imperative in style, as **Tutorial D** is, and therefore does require variables and assignment, we could certainly be persuaded—indeed, it is obvious—that assignment is the only update operator (or "mutator") that is logically necessary. But that still leaves us with mutability as a sine qua non.

  Note: It is possible that what reference [137] means by the term "mutability" is not assignment as such, but rather the idea that certain "mutator" operators work in such a way as to assign to *some component of* their target while leaving other components unchanged (as in the assignment to THE_A(E) in the example). If so, then we have already argued under RM Prescription 5 in Chapter 6 that such operators are very desirable in practice, despite the fact that in the final analysis they are also logically unnecessary.

- *Type constraints:* As already indicated, reference [137] does not consider the possibility of G by C. As a consequence, it observes that if type constraint checking is done, then the assignment to THE_A(E) will fail at run time. To be more specific, it fails because the most specific type of the target is CIRCLE, and assignment to THE_A for a circle will, in general, violate the constraint on circles that $a = b$.[1] It follows that, if we want the assignment not to fail at run time, **the system must not be informed of the constraint**. But this conclusion is surely unacceptable; surely, the more constraints the system is aware of and can enforce, the better (we surely want our data to be as correct as possible at all times).

---

1. We do not agree with this argument, of course—we are just doing our best to explain the point of view of reference [137].

Now, in reference [111], Mattos and DeMichiel examine the foregoing claims and conclude that type constraint checking (and enforcement) is indeed the feature that must be discarded. Their analysis goes somewhat as follows:

- *Can we discard substitutability?* Well, no: As we have already seen, substitutability—value substitutability, that is—cannot possibly be thrown away without undermining the whole idea (and point) of type inheritance.

- *Can we discard static type checking?* Well, no: Discarding static type checking is highly undesirable, of course, and in any case it solves nothing—in the example, the assignment to THE_A(E) will still fail at run time.

- *Can we discard mutability?* Well, no: We must have assignment, at least (assuming the language is imperative in style), and component-level update operators are highly desirable too in practice. (We note in passing that in fact reference [111] does assume that the term *mutability* refers specifically to the idea of component-level updating, not just to assignment in general.)

Reference [111] thus concludes that "the most appropriate [solution] is to not permit specialization via constraints" (meaning, to say it again, that they advocate not enforcing, or even declaring, type constraints). They claim that to do otherwise would mean "[forcing] the overloading of all [operators] defined on supertypes." We should immediately explain that by "overloading" here, they really mean *defining new implementation versions,* to use the terminology of Chapter 14;[1] in terms of our example, that is, they are claiming that assignment to THE_A would have to be "overloaded" for a circle in such a way as to have the side effect of assignment to THE_B too, so that the circle still satisfies the constraint *a* = *b* after the update. And they go on to say:

> This option [i.e., of forcing "overloading"] seems to be unacceptable because we believe that ... users are not likely to define type hierarchies themselves, but to buy them as class libraries from third-party vendors. It is an important requirement that users be able to define ... subtypes of these type hierarchies [*sic*] ... If we force all operators to be overloaded, users will have to redefine every [operator] provided by the class libraries whenever they need to [define such a subtype].

We agree that forcing such "overloading" is unacceptable. In fact, we would argue that the semantics of assignment to THE_A in particular are (for good reasons) prescribed by our model and *must not* be "overloaded" in the manner suggested. And even if those semantics were not prescribed by the model, we would still argue that (a) changing the semantics of an operator in arbitrary ways is a bad idea in general, and (b) changing the semantics of an operator in such a way as to cause arbitrary side effects is an even worse one; it is a good general principle to insist that operators have exactly the requested effect, no more and no less.[2] Furthermore, we observe that the option of changing the semantics in the manner suggested is not always available, anyway. For example, let type ELLIPSE have another immediate subtype NONCIRCLE, with the obvious semantics; let the constraint *a* > *b* apply to noncircles; and consider an assignment to THE_A for a noncircle that, if accepted, would set *a* equal to *b*. What would be an appropriate "overloading" for that assignment? Exactly what side effect would be

---

1. Note in particular, therefore, that they are not using the term "overloading" as we did in Chapters 6 and 14 to mean something that is properly part of the model; rather, they are using it to mean something that is of concern to the implementation merely.

2. In fact it might be regarded as a strong form of *The Assignment Principle*.

appropriate?

On the face of it, then, the conclusion of reference [111] that type constraints should be rejected does seem inescapable. But observe the following implications of adopting that position:

- As already explained, assignment to THE_A is not reimplemented ("overloaded") for circles.

- The fact that the current value of E in the example is a circle does not cause the assignment to THE_A to fail.

- The result is thus that after that assignment, variable E contains a "noncircular circle"—that is, it contains a value of type CIRCLE for which $a > b$. (The type is still CIRCLE because, according to reference [111], we have done nothing to change it.)

- Even worse, the fact that assignment to THE_A is supported (without any type checking) for a variable of declared type ELLIPSE but current most specific type CIRCLE strongly suggests that assignment to THE_A should be supported (again without any type checking) for a variable of *declared* type CIRCLE.

- So let C be such a variable. After such an assignment, then, variable C will (in general) contain a "noncircular circle"—that is, a value of type CIRCLE for which $a > b$.

- So the constraint $a = b$ is not being enforced for type CIRCLE, and there is therefore no point in even stating it.

- More generally, type constraints cannot be enforced—and therefore are not worth even stating—**even if inheritance is currently not supported at all,** just in case such support might be added at some future time.

To us, these implications, the last one in particular, seem even more unacceptable than the option of "forcing overloading." (We note in passing, however, that SQL behaves in exactly the manner just outlined! See Appendix H.)

So what is to be done? Well, let us step back a moment and take stock. It seems to us that the system should indeed support all of the four features (substitutability, static type checking, mutability, and type constraints). More precisely, it seems to us that:

- The system should support *The Principle of Value Substitutability* 100 percent.

- The system should support static type checking to the maximum extent possible (the only place where run-time type checking is needed is in the context of TREAT).

- The system should support mutability—meaning not only that it should support assignment per se, but also that it should support component-level update operators as a shorthand.

- The system should support type constraints—meaning it should be aware of the fact that circles are subject to the constraint that $a = b$, and meaning further that assignment to THE_A(C) fails at compile time if the declared type of C is CIRCLE.

- *But the system should additionally support S by C and G by C!* In particular, if the declared type of E is ELLIPSE, then it should always permit assignment to THE_A(E), and it should be prepared for *MST*(E) to change on such an assignment, either "down" from ELLIPSE to CIRCLE ("S by C") or "up" from CIRCLE to ELLIPSE ("G by C"), as and when appropriate.

In other words, S by C and G by C are the solution to "the 3 out of 4 problem." In fact, we now see that the 3 out of 4 "rule" is not really a rule at all, so long as S by C and G by C are supported—as we claim they should be.

WHAT DOES INHERITANCE REALLY MEAN?

We are now in a position to take care of a piece of business that we tacitly (but of course deliberately) left unfinished in Chapter 14. Recall IM Prescription 19 ("update operator inheritance and variable substitutability"), which states among other things that update operators are inherited only conditionally; thus, for example, assignment to THE_A is not inherited by type CIRCLE, as we saw at the end of the previous section. But this position raises a major issue—namely, what does inheritance really *mean?* Does a sensible model even exist? If assignment to THE_A does not apply to variables of type CIRCLE, is it reasonable to regard type CIRCLE as a subtype of type ELLIPSE? After all, to say that type CIRCLE is a subtype of type ELLIPSE means that all operators that apply to type ELLIPSE apply to type CIRCLE too, does it not?

Well, no, it does not. To repeat from Chapter 12:

[It] is important in this context—as in all others!—to distinguish very carefully between *values* and *variables*. When we say that every circle is an ellipse, what we mean, more precisely, is that every circle *value* is an ellipse *value*. We certainly do not mean that every circle *variable* is an ellipse *variable:* i.e., that a variable of declared type CIRCLE is a variable of declared type ELLIPSE, and hence can contain a value that is an ellipse and not a circle. In other words ... **inheritance applies to values, not variables.**

Thus, it seems to us that the key to the problem is to recognize:

- The logical difference between values and variables, and hence

- The logical difference between read-only and update operators, and hence

- The logical difference between *The Principle of Value Substitutability* and *The Principle of Variable Substitutability*

(and, of course, to act appropriately upon such recognition).

It further seems to us that the positions argued in references [111] and [137] (and a host of similar writings) stem from a failure to make these crucial distinctions. And it seems still further that such failures are at least partly responsible for the lack of consensus, noted several times earlier in this book, on a formal, rigorous, and abstract inheritance model. For example:

- The Object-Oriented Database System Manifesto [2] states that "[there] are at least four types of inheritance: *substitution* inheritance, *inclusion* inheritance, *constraint* inheritance, and *specialization* inheritance ... Various degrees of these four types of inheritance are provided by existing systems and prototypes, and we do not prescribe a specific style of inheritance."

- Reference [19] states that "[inheritance can be] based on [a variety of] different criteria and there is no commonly accepted standard definition"—and proceeds to give eight (!) possible interpretations. (Reference [118] gives twelve.)

- Reference [4] states that "[a given language merely] provides a set of [inheritance] mechanisms. While these mechanisms certainly restrict what one can do in that language and what views of inheritance can be implemented [in that language], they do not by themselves validate some view of inheritance or other. [Types,] specializations, generalizations, and inheritance are only concepts, and ... they do not have a universal objective meaning ... This [fact] implies that how inheritance is to be incorporated into a specific system is up to the designers of [that] system, and it constitutes a policy decision that must be implemented with the available mechanisms." In other words, there simply is no model.

It is, however, relevant to mention that the authors of reference [4] draw their conclusion after analysis of an example that is essentially isomorphic to the example discussed in the previous section of assignment to THE_A for a variable of declared type ELLIPSE but current most specific type CIRCLE—and their analysis is essentially isomorphic to that of reference [111], too. For such reasons, we reject their conclusion.

Our own position, by contrast, is as follows: We do believe there is such a thing as a good inheritance model; we believe further that any such model must pay careful attention to the logical differences (values vs. variables and the rest) articulated in this book; and we believe still further that any such model must support S by C and G by C. And yes, we do believe a circle is an ellipse!—see the section immediately following.

BENEFITS OF S BY C

We have seen that one advantage of S by C and G by C is that they solve the 3 out of 4 "problem." But there are, of course, many other advantages that accrue from S by C and G by C, and those advantages are the principal subject of this section.

First, however, we should see whether there are any *dis*advantages. The obvious one is as follows. Recall from Chapter 14 that S by C has the fundamental consequence that—at least as far as the model is concerned—a selector invocation might return a value of some proper subtype of the designated target type; for example, the selector invocation

```
ELLIPSE ( LENGTH (...), LENGTH (...), POINT (...) )
```

will return a value of type CIRCLE, not ELLIPSE, if the two LENGTH invocations happen to return the same value. As explained in Chapter 14, it follows that—at least conceptually—S by C must be implemented inside selector implementation code. Note carefully, however, that we say "at least conceptually." In fact, we will argue later, in the section "Implementation Considerations," that it is not actually necessary to compute the most specific type of the result of a selector invocation—at least, not at the time of that invocation. For the record, however, we consider in the paragraph immediately following what would be involved if S by C did indeed have to be implemented inside selector implementation code.

Assume for the moment, therefore, that the implementation does have to determine the most specific type of the result of a selector invocation as soon as that result is computed. Every time we define a new proper subtype *T'*, then, the selector(s) for the immediate supertype(s) *T* of *T'* will need to be reimplemented, or at least revised, because they might now return values of that new type *T'* as their most specific type. But those revisions can clearly be automated! In the case of ellipses and circles, for example, the system knows exactly *when* an ellipse is in fact a circle, and furthermore it knows exactly *which* circle the ellipse in question is. (Note in particular, therefore, that what we do not have to do—*pace* the claim, noted two sections back, in reference [111]—is "redefine every [operator] provided by the class libraries whenever [we] need to [define a subtype].") In other words, the possible need to revise certain selectors (which, we stress, is the only disadvantage to the S by C idea as far as we can see) is perhaps a minor burden on the system, but it is no burden at all on any human user.[1]

Now we turn to the advantages. We have numbered the points that follow for convenience.

1.   The first is simply the overriding point that S by C obviously means the model is a better model of reality. As we put it in Chapter 14, "the more knowledge the system has, the better" is always a good general principle.

2.   It is a direct consequence of S by C that values of most specific type ELLIPSE correspond to ellipses that are definitely not circles in the real world. In other models—including the original version of our own [82]—values of most specific type ELLIPSE can have $a = b$ and can thus correspond to circles in the real world. Hence, defining CIRCLE as a subtype of ELLIPSE in such a model partitions the set of ellipses, not into circles vs. noncircles, but rather into circles vs. "maybe-circles"—intuitively not a very satisfactory state of affairs.

3.   It is also a direct consequence of S by C that values of most specific type CIRCLE correspond to ellipses that are definitely circles in the real world. In other words, "noncircular circles" and similar nonsenses cannot occur. (Nor could they in our previous model, but for a different reason. More to the point, perhaps, they *can* occur in SQL, as already noted, since SQL does not support type constraints. See Appendix H.)

4.   More compile-time type checking can be done and fewer run-time type errors can occur; in fact, run-time type errors can occur solely on an attempt to TREAT a value as being of a type it does not possess. (In our original model, by contrast, additional run-time type errors could occur—for example, on an attempt to assign to THE_A of a variable of declared type ELLIPSE but current most specific type CIRCLE.)

5.   Assignments are logically simpler (especially assignments to THE_ pseudovariables, which in our original model involved a complicated CASE expression on the right side in their expansion). In particular, changing types "up" or "down" is easy. That is, given variable E of declared type ELLIPSE, in order to change the most specific type of E from ELLIPSE to CIRCLE or the other way around, it is sufficient just to update E appropriately.

6.   Changing types "sideways" is also easy. That is, given (say) types ELLIPSE, CIRCLE, and NONCIRCLE, in order to change the most specific type of variable E (of declared type ELLIPSE) from CIRCLE to NONCIRCLE or the other way around, it is sufficient just to update E appropriately. (In our original model, by contrast, changing types "sideways" in such a manner was a considerably more complex process, involving a "TREAT UP" operation on E—see points 7 and 8 below—to force it to be "just an ellipse" first, followed by an assignment with a complicated CASE expression on its right side second. What is more, the overall process did not work properly anyway if ELLIPSE was a union type, as in fact it is in the example. All of these complications go away with S by C.)

7.   Equality comparisons are easy. For example, given our usual variables E and C of declared types ELLIPSE and CIRCLE, respectively, we can test them for equality as follows:

```
E = C
```

In our original model, by contrast, we would have had to have written something like this:

---

1. Not even a performance burden, in our opinion. Again, see the section "Implementation Considerations," later.

```
TREAT_UP_AS_ELLIPSE ( E ) = TREAT_UP_AS_ELLIPSE ( C )
```

("treat both comparands as just ellipses and then compare the two ellipses").

8. In fact, the TREAT UP operator, which as we have seen was included in our original model for a variety of reasons, is completely unnecessary with S by C and G by C, and so can be dropped. (Actually it was only shorthand anyway, but any simplification is generally to be desired.) *Note:* Perhaps we should point out that our model does still support "treating up" as well as "treating down," but only in a harmless kind of way. Given our usual variable C, for example, the expression TREAT_AS_ELLIPSE(C) is valid, but it can never fail; in fact, it is a "no op."

9. With S by C and G by C, the rules regarding conditional inheritance of update operators apply to declared types. In our original model, by contrast, they applied to most specific types instead, a fact that made them harder to understand and harder to implement and led to more run-time type checking and more run-time type errors.

10. More code reuse is achievable, and programs are more immune to the introduction of new subtypes. For example, a program that assigns to THE_A(E) will still work after type CIRCLE is introduced (as it might not have done under our original model).

11. There is never any logical need to CAST—i.e., convert—a value of type ELLIPSE to type CIRCLE, because an ellipse that can be "converted to" type CIRCLE will in fact be of type CIRCLE already, under S by C. The operator itself thus becomes unnecessary (as it was not, under our previous model).

12. S by C can also have the effect of making certain implementation versions of certain operators logically unnecessary. For example, the update version of MOVE discussed in Chapter 14 for ellipses and rectangles will work for any combination of most specific argument types—ELLIPSE or CIRCLE for the first argument and RECTANGLE or SQUARE for the second argument—whereas such was not the case with our original model.

In fact, we would now like to go further and argue that **S by C is the** *only* **conceptually valid way of defining subtypes!**—so long as the supertype is a regular type, at any rate (S by C from a dummy type makes no sense). We justify this strong claim as follows. Let type T' be a subtype of (regular) type T. Then:

- T and T' are both *sets* (sets of values), and T' is a subset of T.

- Therefore T and T' both have *membership predicates*—predicates, that is, such that a given value is of the type in question if and only if it satisfies the corresponding predicate. Let those predicates be P and P', respectively.

- Since we are dealing with finite sets only, we can for simplicity regard predicates P and P' as effectively just enumerating the values of types T and T', respectively.

- Note in particular that since every value of type T' is also a value of type T, predicate P' can be formulated in terms of values of type T (not T') only.

- And that predicate P', formulated in terms of values of type T, is precisely the constraint that values of type T have to satisfy in order to be values of type T'. In other words, a value of type T is specialized to type T' precisely if it satisfies the constraint P'. *Note:* P' is what IM

Prescription 10 calls *the specialization constraint* for T'. In **Tutorial D,** it is specified by means of an $< is\ def >$ on the definition of that type T'.

Thus, to repeat, we see S by C as the only conceptually valid way of defining subtypes. In particular, therefore (see reference [71] for a detailed discussion of this particular issue), our answer to the notorious question "Is a circle an ellipse?" is a very firm *yes*.

WHAT ABOUT OBJECTS?

We have now laid sufficient groundwork to be able to explain a claim we made in Chapter 9, in our discussion of OO Proscription 2 ("no object IDs"). The claim in question was basically this: *Object IDs undermine inheritance.* (What we actually said was that "pointers ... can lead to a serious problem if type inheritance is also supported.") In this section, we take a closer look at this issue.

First of all, we remind you that (unlike **D**) object languages make heavy use of *object IDs,* or in other words *pointers,* and variables in such languages typically contain such pointers instead of regular nonpointer values. Thus, for example, the analog of our usual variables E and C in such a language would typically be variables—call them XE and XC—that contain pointers to ellipses and circles instead of ellipses and circles as such. Furthermore, when we say pointers to ellipses and circles, we really mean pointers to ellipse and circle *variables,*[1] because by definition it is variables, not values, that have addresses.

Next, we remind you from Chapter 9 that languages that support pointers also typically support two operators called *referencing* and *dereferencing,* respectively:

- *Referencing:* Given a variable V, the referencing operator applied to V returns a pointer to V.

- *Dereferencing:* Given a variable P of type pointer, the dereferencing operator applied to P returns the variable that P currently points to.

Note: Referencing and dereferencing operations are often implicit in practice. However, we show them explicitly in the examples that follow, because we have found that implicitness in this context can unnecessarily obscure some of the points we want to make.

With these preliminaries out of the way, we now present our first code fragment:

```
VAR E  ELLIPSE ;
VAR XE PTR_TO_ELLIPSE ;

E  := CIRCLE ( LENGTH ( 5.0 ), POINT ( 0.0, 0.0 ) ) ;
XE := PTR_TO ( E ) ;
```

Explanation: We are making use of two hypothetical extensions to **Tutorial D:**

- First, if T is a type, then PTR_TO_T is a type too, and its values are pointers to, or object IDs of, variables of type T. In other words, PTR_TO_ is a type generator (a scalar type generator, in fact).

- Second, if V is a variable of type T, then the operator invocation PTR_TO (V) returns a pointer to V. In other words, PTR_TO is the referencing operator mentioned above.

---

1. Object languages would say they are pointers to ellipse and circle *objects*.

The effect of the code fragment is thus (a) to set the variable E to contain a circle of radius five—note the appeal to substitutability—and (b) to set the variable XE to contain a pointer to E. Now we introduce another variable:

```
VAR XC PTR_TO_CIRCLE ;
```

We assume that—as is in fact typically the case in object languages—type PTR_TO_CIRCLE is a proper subtype of type PTR_TO_ELLIPSE. Thus, we can legitimately perform the following assignment:

```
XC := TREAT_AS_PTR_TO_CIRCLE ( XE ) ;
```

Now XC also contains a pointer to E—in fact, it contains the same pointer value as XE does. Finally, we attempt the following assignment (let us call it Assignment Z):

```
THE_A ( DEREF ( XE ) ) := LENGTH ( 6.0 ) ;
```

Explanation: We are assuming the existence of a dereferencing operator, DEREF, which takes a variable of some pointer type and returns the variable that pointer variable currently points to. (In the example, we are actually using DEREF as a pseudovariable,[1] since it appears on the left side of the assignment.) Thus, the intent of Assignment Z is, loosely speaking, to update the length of the *a* semiaxis of the ellipse variable that XE currently points to, setting it to six. So what happens?

Well, it seems there are three possibilities, all of them bad. We consider each in turn.

- *Case 1:* Assignment Z fails on a run-time type error, because *MST*(E) is CIRCLE and assignment to THE_A is not supported for type CIRCLE. In this case, **the model is bad** because (a) it leads to run-time type errors in a context other than TREAT, and (b) more important, it does not support G by C, and so is not "a good model of reality."

- *Case 2:* Assignment Z "succeeds" (i.e., there is no run-time type error and the update is done), but G by C does not occur. In this case, **the model is bad** because (a) it fails to support G by C (and so is not "a good model of reality"); (b) variable XC now points to a "noncircular circle"; (c) more generally, *type constraints cannot be supported.* (As pointed out earlier, this case corresponds to the way SQL works.)

- *Case 3:* Assignment Z "succeeds" (i.e., there is no run-time type error and the update is done), and G by C does occur. In this case, **the model is bad** because (a) variable XC, of declared type PTR_TO_CIRCLE, now points to a variable of current most specific type ELLIPSE; (b) hence, *type constraints cannot be supported. Note:* In practice, this option is probably a nonstarter, precisely because of point (a); thus, G by C probably does *not* occur, and we are back with Case 2.

Conclusion: Whichever option we choose, the model is bad. And the culprit (in this particular example) is the concept of "shared variables": Pointer variables XE and XC "share" the ellipse variable

---

1. This observation is not strictly accurate, because the overall assignment is not just shorthand for something else. In other words, support for pointers implies that we need to extend our definition (both syntactic and semantic) of the assignment operator. We omit the details here, since the whole aim of the discussion is to bolster the argument that pointers should not be supported in the first place.

E. Furthermore, it is pointers (i.e., object IDs) that permit that sharing in the first place. It follows that *object IDs*—at least if they permit shared variables—*and a good model of inheritance are incompatible.*

As a matter of fact, we do not even need to invoke the concept of shared variables in order to illustrate the problem. Consider the following simpler version of the example:

```
VAR E  ELLIPSE ;
VAR XC PTR_TO_CIRCLE ;

E := CIRCLE ( LENGTH ( 5.0 ), POINT ( 0.0, 0.0 ) ) ;
XC := TREAT_AS_PTR_TO_CIRCLE ( PTR_TO ( E ) ) ;
THE_A ( E ) := LENGTH ( 6.0 ) ;
```

Explanation: The first assignment sets E to contain a circle of radius five. The second sets XC to point to E. The third ("Assignment Z") attempts to update the length of the *a* semiaxis of the ellipse variable E to six. What happens? Without going into details, it should be clear that there are the same three possibilities as before, again all bad, and the overall conclusion is the same as before as well: *Object IDs and a good model of inheritance are incompatible.*

For a third and final example, we consider the following still simpler code fragment:

```
VAR C  CIRCLE ;
VAR XE PTR_TO_ELLIPSE ;

C  := CIRCLE ( LENGTH ( 5.0 ), POINT ( 0.0, 0.0 ) ) ;
XE := PTR_TO ( C ) ;
THE_A ( DEREF ( XE ) ) := LENGTH ( 6.0 ) ;
```

Here S by C and G by C have no part to play (variable C can never have most specific type ELLIPSE), but the final assignment still either raises a run-time type error or produces a noncircular circle. Once again, therefore, we conclude that object IDs and a good model of inheritance are incompatible.

We conjecture that the foregoing conclusion goes some way toward explaining why (so far as we know) there have been no good inheritance models in the past. To be specific, all of the prior work on inheritance that we are aware of has been done in an object setting specifically, and the object world generally seems to take it as a sine qua non that object IDs must be supported. As we have now seen, however, object IDs imply that the model must be bad. In other words, (a) objects imply object IDs; (b) object IDs and a good model of inheritance are incompatible; (c) hence, objects per se and a good model of inheritance are incompatible!

What is more, since it is clearly an assumption underlying the claims of reference [137] regarding "the 3 out of 4 rule" that object support is a desideratum, it is tempting to suggest that we should really have been talking all along about "a 4 out of 5 rule" instead, where the fifth element—and clearly the one to be discarded—was *objects themselves.*

One last point on this topic: Nothing we have said in this section has anything to do with databases specifically. In other words, the problems we have been discussing apply equally well to the use of pointers or object IDs for purely local data as well as for database data per se. (This observation does not necessarily mean there should be no pointer support in the nondatabase portions of **D**, but it does mean that such support, if it exists, should be treated with all due caution.)

Why the Problems Do Not Arise with Foreign Keys

It is interesting to observe that problems analogous to those we have been discussing do not arise with foreign keys (which are sometimes claimed to be the relational world's counterpart to pointers or object IDs). By way of illustration, consider this example once again (the second of those previously discussed):

```
VAR E  ELLIPSE ;
VAR XC PTR_TO_CIRCLE ;

E := CIRCLE ( LENGTH ( 5.0 ), POINT ( 0.0, 0.0 ) ) ;
XC := TREAT_AS_PTR_TO_CIRCLE ( PTR_TO ( E ) ) ;
THE_A ( E ) := LENGTH ( 6.0 ) ;
```

Ignoring irrelevancies, a relational analog of this example might involve relvars looking something like this:

```
VAR R1 ... RELATION { K ELLIPSE ... } KEY { K } ;

VAR R2 ... RELATION { K CIRCLE ... } FOREIGN KEY { K } REFERENCES R1 ;
```

For simplicity, we assume no "referential actions"—cascade update, etc.—are specified (this simplifying assumption does not materially affect the argument in any way). Both relvars are initially empty.

Observe now that every value of K in relvar R1 that "matches" some value of K in relvar R2 must be of type CIRCLE, not just of type ELLIPSE. So let us insert a tuple into each of the two relvars:

```
INSERT R1 ... TUPLE { K CIRCLE ( LENGTH ( 5.0 ), POINT ( 0.0, 0.0 ) ) } ... ;

INSERT R2 ... TUPLE { K CIRCLE ( LENGTH ( 5.0 ), POINT ( 0.0, 0.0 ) ) } ... ;
```

Finally, let us try to "update the tuple" in R1:

```
UPDATE R1 WHERE K = CIRCLE ( LENGTH ( 5.0 ), POINT ( 0.0, 0.0 ) )
          ( THE_A ( K ) := LENGTH ( 6.0 ) ) ;
```

This UPDATE attempts to "G by C" the circle in the single tuple in R1 to type ELLIPSE. That attempt fails, however (and the overall UPDATE fails), on a referential integrity violation. So we do get a run-time error. But the error in question is a run-time integrity violation, not a run-time type error (run-time integrity violations are *always* possible, of course). What we do not get is a noncircular circle, nor a failure of G by C. Overall, in fact, we have a system in which noncircular circles cannot occur, type constraints can be supported, and in particular S by C and G by C are supported too.

IMPLEMENTATION CONSIDERATIONS

As we have seen, S by C (including G by C) is an area in which our inheritance model differs significantly from that usually found in object languages. The following quote from a paper by Rumbaugh [123] illustrates the point:

> Is SQUARE a subclass of RECTANGLE? ... Stretching the *x*-dimension of a rectangle is a perfectly reasonable thing to do. But if you do it to a square, then the object is no longer a square. This is not necessarily a bad thing conceptually. When you stretch a square you *do* get a rectangle ... But ... most object-oriented languages do not want objects to change class ... [This] suggests [a] design principle for classification systems: *A subclass should not be defined by constraining a superclass.*

Observe that Rumbaugh's conclusion—i.e., his "design principle for classification systems"—is the diametric opposite of our own, which is that S by C is the only conceptually valid way of defining a subclass (or subtype, in our terms). Note too, however, that Rumbaugh takes the position he does, at least in part, because "[object] languages do not want objects to change class." Our own model, by contrast, was deliberately not constrained by existing languages or implementations;[1] we wanted to define the abstract model first and leave implementation concerns till later. In particular, as explained earlier in this appendix, we included S by C in that model because we think it is useful. But we would certainly remove it if it turned out to be impossible to implement or impossible to implement efficiently.

So can S by C be implemented efficiently? Well, it is relevant to observe that Rumbaugh buttresses his conclusion with the following claim:

> It would be computationally infeasible to support a rule-based, intensional definition of class membership, because you would have to check the rules after each operation that affects an object.

(The phrase *rule-based, intensional definition of class membership* refers to S by C and G by C; it means, for example, that a given ellipse is a member of the class of circles if it satisfies the rule that $a = b$.)

However, we reject the foregoing claim; we believe the computational aspects of S by C can be handled both simply and efficiently. To be more specific, we reject both (a) the suggestion that S by C is "computationally infeasible" (i.e., that it imposes intolerable computational overhead) and (b) the suggestion that the most specific type has to be (re)computed "after each operation that affects an object." We now proceed to elaborate on these points.

Let X be an expression. Then the first and most important point is that it is *never* necessary to compute the current most specific type $MST(X)$, as such, of that expression X; it is necessary only to determine in certain contexts whether the current value $v(X)$ of X is of some particular type—to be more precise, whether it is of some specific proper subtype of the declared type $DT(X)$ of X. By way of example, consider the simple type graph shown in Fig. F.1 (a repeat of Fig. 15.1 from Chapter 15). Let $DT(X)$ and $MST(X)$ be PARALLELOGRAM and SQUARE, respectively, and consider the expression TREAT_AS_RECTANGLE(X). In order to evaluate that expression, we clearly do not need to compute $MST(X)$—all we need to do is ascertain whether X is indeed of type RECTANGLE.

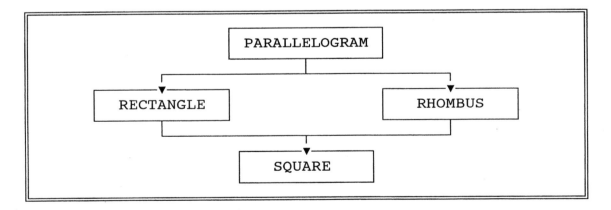

Fig. F.1: A simple type graph

---

1. Though the original version was!

Next, we observe that the remarks of the foregoing paragraph apply if X is a selector invocation in particular. To revert for a moment to our usual example of ellipses and circles: As we know, the selector invocation

```
ELLIPSE ( LENGTH ( 5.0 ), LENGTH ( 5.0 ), POINT ( 0.0, 0.0 ) )
```

is defined by the model to return a value of most specific type CIRCLE, not ELLIPSE ("in other words, S by C occurs," as we put it in Chapter 14 when we first discussed this example). But there is no need for the implementation to perform S by C as such at this time; to repeat, all it has to do is be able to ascertain subsequently that the value in question is indeed a circle, if and when some operation—e.g., TREAT_AS_CIRCLE(X)—is executed that depends in some way on that fact.

As the basis for a more searching discussion, we return to the type graph of Fig. F.1. Suppose again that $DT(X)$ is PARALLELOGRAM and we need to determine whether $v(X)$ is of type SQUARE. Now, there are two paths in the graph from PARALLELOGRAM to SQUARE, via RECTANGLE and RHOMBUS respectively, and the system needs to choose one in order to make that determination. Suppose it chooses the one via RHOMBUS. If $v(X)$ fails to satisfy the constraint for RHOMBUS, then it is certainly not of type SQUARE; but if it does satisfy the constraint for RHOMBUS, then it needs to be tested against the constraint for SQUARE. On the face of it, therefore, it seems that no more than two nodes of the graph need be visited in order to discover whether $v(X)$ is a square: two if it is a rhombus, otherwise just one.

Recall from Chapter 15, however, that the type constraint for type SQUARE takes the form:

```
IS { RECTANGLE, RHOMBUS }
```

(we omit the POSSREP specification for simplicity). Thus, it looks as if it might be necessary to traverse the path from PARALLELOGRAM to RECTANGLE as well as the one from PARALLELOGRAM to RHOMBUS, in order to determine whether $v(X)$ is of type RECTANGLE as well as of type RHOMBUS. However, we can avoid this apparent need to visit additional nodes by labeling the arc from RHOMBUS to SQUARE with the constraint that determines whether a given parallelogram is a rectangle.[1] Then, if the implementation discovers that $v(X)$ is a rhombus, it can immediately check to see whether it is a rectangle (and hence a square) too, without having to visit any additional nodes.

Here then is an algorithm ("TEST_*s*"), embodying the foregoing ideas, for determining whether some specified value v of some known type t is of some specified type s:

```
OPERATOR TEST_s ( v value, t type, s type ) RETURNS BOOLEAN ;
   IF t = s THEN RETURN TRUE ;
   ELSE BEGIN ;
        let t' be some immediate subtype of t that is also a supertype of s ;
        let IC be the specialization constraint on the arc from t to t' ;
        IF v satisfies IC THEN RETURN ( TEST_s ( v, t', s ) ) ; ELSE RETURN FALSE ;
        END IF ;
      END ;
   END IF ;
END OPERATOR ;
```

---

1. If there were any intervening nodes between PARALLELOGRAM and RECTANGLE, the constraint in question would have to be the *conjunction* of all constraints on the path from PARALLELOGRAM to RECTANGLE. And if there were more than one such path, the system would have to choose one, just as it had to choose whether to follow the RECTANGLE or RHOMBUS path to SQUARE in our earlier discussion.

It should be clear that this algorithm of itself is certainly "computationally feasible" and does not impose intolerable overhead. Of course, we do need to consider how often it needs to be invoked; in particular, we need to consider whether it is invoked so frequently that those invocations do constitute an excessive performance burden. We will return to these matters at the end of this section. First, however, we need to pin down the contexts in which TEST_*s* needs to be invoked. Careful consideration of the inheritance model described in this book reveals that there are precisely three such contexts:

- *TREAT:* The expression TREAT_AS_*T*(*X*), where *T* is a proper subtype of *DT*(*X*), is evaluated by raising an exception if TEST_*s*(*X*,*DT*(*X*),*T*) returns FALSE.

- *Type testing:* The expression IS_*T*(*X*), where *T* is a proper subtype of *DT*(*X*), is logically equivalent to TEST_*s*(*X*,*DT*(*X*),*T*).

- *Operator version selection ("binding"):* As explained under IM Prescription 17, operators are allowed to have several implementation versions, each with a different version signature; moreover, the system is generally expected to "bind" a given invocation, somehow, to the version whose signature best matches the corresponding invocation signature—though as noted in Chapter 14 there is actually no requirement in the model per se that it do so. Let *Op* be an operator, then, and let *OpI* be some invocation of *Op*. If the most specific types of all arguments to *OpI* are known, then the binding problem reduces to one that has already been solved in existing languages. However, determining those most specific types under S by C clearly does involve overhead, so let us concentrate for the moment on the argument declared types instead (which are certainly known). If any of those types is a proper subtype of its corresponding parameter, and an implementation version for that proper subtype is available, then at least part of the binding process can be done at compile time. At run time, the system will need to know which implementation versions are available to suit the declared types of the arguments. If there are several such, and at least one has a parameter whose declared type is a proper subtype of that of the corresponding argument, then the system does have some type testing to do (i.e., it does need to invoke TEST_*s* at run time). We will have a little more to say in connection with this point in the very last sentence of this appendix.

We claim there is nothing else in our inheritance model that requires TEST_*s* to be invoked at run time.[1] In particular, equality comparisons do not require it. To be more specific, it is sufficient in order to evaluate the comparison *X* = *Y* (a) to determine the most specific common supertype of *DT*(*X*) and *DT*(*Y*) (which can be done at compile time) and then (b) to invoke the "=" operator for that common supertype. (Actually, any common supertype that is not a dummy type can be chosen for this purpose.)

We offer one further argument to justify our claim that S by C does not entail excessive overhead: Whenever the assignment *X* := *Y* is executed, either explicitly or implicitly, the system knows the declared type of *Y* and can thus flag *X* internally as being of that type. Such a flag could allow subsequent invocations of TEST_*s* on *X* to be performed on a smaller portion of the type graph, or even to be eliminated entirely in some cases. In the same kind of way, whenever *X* is specified as an argument to some operator invocation that requires run-time examination of the types of its arguments, the system can take the opportunity to "remember" any types it discovers.

---

1. Observe in particular that—unlike SQL (see Appendix H)—our model prescribes no operator for testing whether a given expression is of a given most specific type (see the remarks on this issue at the end of IM Prescription 15 in Chapter 14). If such an operator were supported nonetheless, the algorithm FIND_*MST* given in Chapter 14 could be used to implement it. In this connection, it is worth pointing out that FIND_*MST* does *not* necessarily entail visiting every node between the declared type and most specific type of its operand.

We turn now to the suggestion that the most specific type has to be (re)computed "after each operation that affects an object." In fact, of course, we have already seen that there is no need to compute the most specific type, as such, at all. In particular, if variable *V* is updated by some invocation of some update operator, there is no need to determine *MST*(*V*) after that invocation (at least, not at the time of the invocation). All we need is to be able to determine subsequently whether *V* is of some specified type—and we have already discussed that requirement at length.

Finally, we return as promised to the issue of how often TEST_*s* needs to be invoked and consider whether those invocations might constitute a serious performance burden. Suppose the system did not support inheritance and S by C at all, and suppose we have a user-defined type POLYGON. Then there are two possibilities—(a) we might want, on certain occasions, to execute different code depending on whether a given polygon is in fact a rectangle or "just a polygon," or (b) we might not. For example, suppose we want to implement an AREA operator for polygons. Then we might or might not want to check whether the argument to a given AREA invocation is in fact a rectangle (and use the simple "height times width" formula when it is):

- Suppose we do want to perform such a check. In effect, then, we will have to include our own implementation of the IS_RECTANGLE operator—in effect, of TEST_RECTANGLE—inside the AREA code. Clearly, support for inheritance with S by C would make our task a little easier in this case, because there would be no need for us to provide that implementation after all. Moreover, the effect on overall system performance is more or less the same either way; the main difference is just that the type checking is done by the system instead of the application, if S by C is supported.

- By contrast, suppose we do not want to perform such a check. In this case, support for S by C (and TEST_*s*) would clearly impose no overhead at all, because the type checking would simply not be done.

Analogous remarks apply to TREAT operations and the binding process (these being the other areas requiring invocation of TEST_*s*, if S by C is supported). We consider the binding process briefly. To continue with the AREA example, the question is: Would we include code in the AREA implementation, not only to check whether the argument to a given AREA invocation is a rectangle, but also to use the simple "height times width" formula when it is?

- Suppose we would include such code. In effect, then, we will be providing two separate versions of the AREA operator bundled together within the AREA implementation, as well as code to perform the run-time binding process. Again, direct support for inheritance with S by C would surely make our task a little easier, and the effect on overall system performance will be more or less the same either way.

- By contrast, suppose we would not include such code. In that case, support for S by C clearly imposes no overhead at all.

In conclusion, it is worth pointing out that (as the foregoing discussion suggests) what overhead S by C does impose is a function of the number of different implementation versions provided, not a function of the number of subtypes and constraints involved.

Appendix G

A Closer Look at

Structural Inheritance

The inheritance model described in Part IV of this book is concerned with behavioral inheritance, so called because what is inherited is "operational behavior." But there is another kind of inheritance, structural inheritance, where what is inherited is physical representations—at least, so we claimed in Chapter 12, though we did also say there were those who would dispute that claim, and we suggested there might be a connection with what is sometimes called "the EXTENDS relationship." In this appendix, we investigate these matters further.

The structure of the appendix is as follows. The section immediately following discusses a simple example, with a view to exposing the real issues underlying the concept of structural inheritance. The next section considers what might be involved in supporting that concept. The next two sections then respectively (a) examine a particular version of the concept ("subtables and supertables") in some depth and (b) offer some thoughts on examples of a certain common kind, of which "COLORED_CIRCLE is a subtype of CIRCLE" is a typical illustration. The final section shows how it might be possible to achieve the benefits of structural inheritance without departing from the prescriptions of our own inheritance model as laid down in the body of the book.

AN INTRODUCTORY EXAMPLE

The following example is typical of those commonly used to introduce the notion of structural inheritance. Consider entity types EMP ("employees") and PGMR ("programmers"). Assume that every programmer is an employee but some employees are not programmers. Clearly, this example parallels our familiar ellipses-and-circles example, where every circle is an ellipse but some ellipses are not circles, and it thus seems entirely reasonable from an intuitive point of view to say that "programmers are a subtype of employees." But does this point of view stand up to closer inspection?

Well, let us focus for a moment on employees alone and ignore programmers. Suppose every employee has an employee number (EMP#), a name (ENAME), a department number (DEPT#), and a salary (SALARY). Now, we saw in Appendix B that there are two ways we could represent this state of affairs: We could have an EMP type (scalar by definition) or an EMP relvar (nonscalar by definition). Suppose we choose the former. Then:

- The EMP type will be "encapsulated" (scalar), meaning it has no user-visible structure. *Note:* We deliberately use the object term "encapsulated" here because most of the work on structural inheritance has been done in an object context.

- That type will have a possrep with components EMP#, ENAME, DEPT#, and SALARY, and THE_ operators to access each of those components.

Now we can go on to define a scalar type PGMR as a proper subtype of the scalar type EMP, just as earlier in this book we defined type CIRCLE as a proper subtype of type ELLIPSE. The PGMR type will inherit all operators (all read-only operators, at least) that apply to employees, and will additionally have operators of its own—in particular, operators to access the particular language skill (LANG) for a given programmer.[1] *Note:* For simplicity, we assume each programmer has just one language in which he or she is proficient. This assumption is not very realistic, of course, but the point is not important for present purposes.

Given the foregoing design, it really would be the case that PGMR is a subtype of EMP in the sense of our inheritance model. However, the kind of inheritance involved here is, by definition, behavioral, not structural, and that kind of design is thus not what we want to talk about in the present appendix. Indeed, following the discussions in Appendix B, we would be more likely to represent employees and programmers not as types anyway but as relvars, perhaps as follows (in outline only, for simplicity):

```
EMP   { EMP#, ENAME, DEPT#, SALARY }
      KEY { EMP# }


PGMR  { EMP#, ENAME, DEPT#, SALARY, LANG }
      KEY { EMP# }


CONSTRAINT E_P_DISJOINT IS_EMPTY ( EMP { EMP# } JOIN PGMR )
```

Note the constraint: Employee *e* is represented in relvar PGMR if and only if *e* is a programmer, and in relvar EMP if and only if *e* is not a programmer.

Now, this design clearly involves two relation types, neither of which is a subtype of the other as far as our model is concerned (recall from Chapter 16 that relation type *RT'* can be a subtype of relation type *RT* in our model only if *RT'* and *RT* involve exactly the same attributes). Under structural inheritance, however, we might say that type PGMR *inherits the structure* of type EMP but "extends" that structure to include an additional attribute—and we *might* then to go on to say, under this very different notion of inheritance, that type PGMR is indeed a subtype of supertype EMP after all.

Now, in Chapter 12 we said we do not preclude such inheritance; however, we also said it had nothing to do with the model. Now we can elaborate on these remarks. With regard to whether it has anything to do with the model, then (we deliberately consider the second remark first): It is clear that if we limit our attention to scalar types, any structural inheritance that might apply is definitely an implementation issue,[2] because scalars have no (user-visible, model-level) structure to inherit. In the case of object systems, therefore, it follows that an object, if it is properly encapsulated, ought not to be subject to structural inheritance at all, at the model level. But the picture is muddied by the fact that—as mentioned in Appendix B—even "encapsulated" objects often do expose their structure to the user in object systems, in the form of what are called *instance variables*. For example, an EMP object might have user-visible instance variables EMP#, ENAME, DEPT#, and SALARY; as you can see, therefore, user-visible instance variables in object systems are analogous, somewhat, to tuple attributes in a relational system or record fields in a traditional file system. We think the only way to make sense of this state of affairs is to regard the user-visible structure of those "encapsulated" objects as the *physical* structure, and hence to regard the model and the implementation as (to say the least) inadequately distinguished. We further think that to say that structural inheritance applies to such objects is to mean that it is physical representations that are inherited, which is why we claim it has nothing to do with the

---

1. Observe, however, that the possrep for type EMP would have to include a LANG component, even though nonprogrammers have no such property. The specialization constraint for PGMR, required by IM Prescription 10, might then reasonably take the form LANG ≠ '' (say). But of course the simple fact that the LANG possrep component is effectively required even for nonprogrammers is enough to show that this approach is very unrealistic.

2. Unless the structure being inherited is only a *possible* representation, not a physical one. We briefly consider the question of inheriting possreps in the section "Scalar Types Revisited," later.

model. (It is also why we prefer to explain our own ideas in terms of constructs like tuples that are carefully and precisely defined. See the paragraph immediately following.)

Turning now to the question of precluding support: On the face of it, our model cannot handle the kind of inheritance illustrated by the example of employees and programmers (relvar version). Do we want it to? If we do, do we have to revise our model in some way, or can it somehow handle that kind of inheritance after all? We consider these questions in what follows. First, however, we spell out the obvious point that if we want to examine the possibility of inheriting user-visible structure, then by definition we are talking about tuple and/or relation types, because (by definition) those are the types that possess such structure. To be absolutely precise, therefore, the principal question we will be examining is this: Can we make sense of the idea of structural inheritance for tuple or relation types?

One final point to close this section: As we have said, it does seem intuitively reasonable to say, at least informally, that every programmer is an employee. But there is a better way to characterize the situation—a way, that is, that points up the logical difference between examples like employees and programmers vs. examples like ellipses and circles—and that is to say that a programmer is an employee who **has a** language skill. In other words, the crucial issue here is not the *is-a* relationship (a programmer "is a" employee) but, rather, the *has-a* relationship (a programmer "has a" language skill). Contrast the situation with ellipses and circles: Although we might say a circle "has a" property (the radius) that ellipses in general do not have, *that property is really just a degenerate form of a property (a semiaxis) that ellipses in general do have.* The situation is different with employees and programmers: A programmer's language skill does not correspond to *any* property of nonprogrammer employees.

We will have quite a lot more to say regarding the distinction between *is-a* and *has-a* in later sections of this appendix.

TUPLE TYPES, VALUES, AND VARIABLES

Until further notice, we limit our attention (for simplicity) to tuple types only. So the question we want to look at becomes: Can we make sense of structural inheritance for tuple types? Well, suppose we want to say that tuple type *TT'* "extends" tuple type *TT* by adding further attributes. For example (to invent some syntax on the fly):

```
TYPE EMP_TT  TUPLE { EMP# CHAR, ENAME CHAR, DEPT# CHAR, SALARY MONEY } ;

TYPE PGMR_TT TUPLE EXTEND EMP_TT ADD { LANG CHAR } ;
```

Observe that we immediately run into a syntax problem! In our *Manifesto,* tuple types are "unnamed"—meaning, more precisely, that they have no name other than the one of the form TUPLE{...} that is required by RM Prescription 6, and there is no separate "define tuple type" operator. There are good reasons for these rules, too, but we will have to overlook them for present purposes and assume that the foregoing syntax is valid after all.

Now we can define tuple variables (hereinafter "tuplevars") of these types.[1] For example:

```
VAR EMP_VAR  EMP_TT ;
VAR PGMR_VAR PGMR_TT ;
```

Values of variable EMP_VAR are tuples of four components (EMP#, ENAME, DEPT#, and SALARY); values of variable PGMR_VAR are tuples of five components (the same four, plus LANG).

---

1. We cannot include such variables in a relational database, of course, but as we know from Chapter 12 inheritance has little to do with database data as such anyway.

In other words, the set of values constituting type PGMR_TT is the join (in fact the cartesian product) of the set of all possible tuples of type

```
TUPLE { EMP# CHAR, ENAME CHAR, DEPT# CHAR, SALARY MONEY }
```

and the set of all possible tuples of type

```
TUPLE { LANG CHAR }
```

These Subtypes Are Not Subsets

In our usual ellipses-and-circles example:

- Every circle is an ellipse.

- Hence, the set of all possible circles (i.e., type CIRCLE) is a subset of the set of all possible ellipses (i.e., type ELLIPSE).

- Moreover, the set of all current circles is a subset of the set of all current ellipses—where by *the set of all current circles* we mean, precisely, the set of values of just those variables whose current most specific type is some subtype of CIRCLE, and similarly for ellipses.

The situation is very different with our tuple types EMP_TT and PGMR_TT, however:

- No value of type PGMR_TT is a value of type EMP_TT. Conversely, no value of type EMP_TT is a value of type PGMR_TT, either.

- It follows that the set of all possible values of type PGMR_TT is not a subset of the set of all possible values of type EMP_TT. Conversely, the set of all possible values of type EMP_TT is not a subset of the set of all possible values of type PGMR_TT, either.

- It also follows that the set of all current values of type PGMR_TT is not a subset of the set of all current values of type EMP_TT. Conversely, the set of all current values of type EMP_TT is not a subset of the set of all current values of type PGMR_TT, either.

Now, in the inheritance model described in Part IV of this book, to say that type T' is a subtype of type T is to say that T' is a *subset* of type T (IM Prescription 2). It follows that we cannot say that PGMR_TT is a subtype of type EMP_TT without doing considerable violence to the commonsense notion of subtype, and indeed to our inheritance model in general. Let us agree, therefore, not to use the terminology of subtyping in this connection; let us agree to say, rather, that (e.g.) PGMR_TT is an **extension** of EMP_TT—and let us agree to say analogously that EMP_TT is a **projection** of PGMR_TT, since it is obtained from PGMR_TT by projecting away an attribute. Then we can least say that the set of *projections* of all possible PGMR_TT tuples, over all but LANG, is a subset of—is in fact equal to—the set of all possible EMP_TT tuples.[1]

To pursue the point just a moment longer: Despite the foregoing, those who advocate the idea of

---

1. It is still not the case, however, that the set of projections of all *current* PGMR_TT tuples over all but LANG is a subset of the set of all current EMP_TT tuples; for that to be so, we would need a certain integrity constraint to be enforced. However, such considerations take us into the realm of structural inheritance as it applies to relvars, not tuplevars. See the section "Subtables and Supertables," later.

structural inheritance normally do refer to EMP_TT and PGMR_TT as supertype and subtype, respectively (see the subsection immediately following). But we now observe that the terminology is really bad—because the "*sub*tuples" (i.e., tuples of the "subtype") have a superset of the attributes of the "*super*tuples" (i.e., tuples of the "supertype")! A programmer tuple, for example, has all of the attributes of an employee tuple, plus one more (LANG).

Substitutability

Recall now that the whole point of inheritance is substitutability; for example, a program that works for ellipses can work for circles too, because we can always substitute a circle wherever the system expects an ellipse. So what about employees and programmers? Does substitutability apply?

Well, we have seen that no tuple of type PGMR_TT is a tuple of type EMP_TT (and vice versa). Thus, if *Op* is an operator that takes a parameter of type EMP_TT, it cannot validly be invoked with an argument of type PGMR_TT instead. In other words, inclusion polymorphism does not apply, and there is no value substitutability either. (Of course, we can validly invoke *Op* with an argument that is the projection over all but LANG of some tuple of type PGMR_TT. By definition, however, that argument is of type EMP_TT, and it hardly seems appropriate to dignify this rather trivial possibility with the grand name of substitutability.)

So what can we do? There would be little point in supporting structural inheritance in the first place if it turned out to provide no substitutability. How can we rescue the situation?

Well, one thing we could do is expand our notion of what it means for variable *V* to be of type *T*, such that the value of *V* at any time could be of any subtype of *T* **or any extension of** *T* (or any extension of any subtype of *T*, perhaps). Then it would be possible for variable EMP_VAR, of declared type EMP_TT, to contain a value of most specific type PGMR_TT, for example. It would also be possible to assign a value of most specific type PGMR_TT to a variable of declared type EMP_TT (and so on—all the things we expect to be able to do with behavioral inheritance would now be possible, in fact). Indeed, if we did not expand our notion in such a way of what it means to declare something to be of a certain type, we could not have (e.g.) a relation *r* with an attribute *A* of declared type EMP_TT, such that some tuples in *r* contain an *A* value of type PGMR_TT instead of EMP_TT. So it looks as if part of the solution, at any rate, to the problem of rescuing substitutability is going to have to involve the foregoing scheme.

However, one objection to that scheme is the pragmatic one that the implementation would not be able to tell ahead of time, in general, how much storage to allocate for any given variable. As a result, we might have to move to an implementation in which variables contain pointers to their corresponding allocated storage, instead of actual values as in our model. If so, then there is a possibility that this feature of the implementation will show through at the model level (as indeed it does in object systems)—and that consequence, if it is a consequence, is something we are adamantly opposed to, for reasons explained in Appendix F and elsewhere.

Another way we might attempt to rescue substitutability is to use *overloading polymorphism*. As a simple example, suppose we want to conduct a "what if" experiment to determine the total cost to the company of raising certain salaries by ten percent; so we want an operator to compute the hypothetical new salary for a given employee, regardless of whether that employee is a programmer or "just an employee." Then we might define two distinct operators, both called RAISE,[1] as follows:

---

1. Recall that "overloading" really means overloading operator names (to say that *Op* is overloaded really means there are two or more distinct operators with the same name *Op*). We note in passing that the particular kind of overloading polymorphism under discussion here is also referred to in the literature as *extension* polymorphism [137], for obvious reasons.

```
OPERATOR RAISE ( E EMP_TT ) RETURNS MONEY VERSION E_RAISE ;
   RETURN ( ( SALARY FROM E ) * 1.1 ) ;
END OPERATOR ;

OPERATOR RAISE ( P PGMR_TT ) RETURNS MONEY VERSION P_RAISE ;
   RETURN ( ( SALARY FROM P ) * 1.1 ) ;
END OPERATOR ;
```

Now, e.g., the expression RAISE (EMP_VAR) will cause the version of RAISE called E_RAISE to be invoked, while the expression RAISE (PGMR_VAR) will cause the version of RAISE called P_RAISE to be invoked instead. (We remark in passing on a slight awkwardness here, arising from the fact that tuple types are "named"—viz., the operators have to be defined in terms of an attribute, SALARY, that is not immediately visible as an attribute of the pertinent parameter.)

Of course, once we start down the overloading path, there is nothing to stop different versions of "the same" operator from implementing different semantics (and we remind you from Chapter 14 that some might even argue that this state of affairs is a good thing). For example, suppose the salary increase for a given employee is supposed to be 25 percent if the employee is a programmer but only 10 percent otherwise:

```
OPERATOR RAISE ( E EMP_TT ) RETURNS MONEY VERSION E_RAISE ;
   RETURN ( ( SALARY FROM E ) * 1.1 ) ;
END OPERATOR ;

OPERATOR RAISE ( P PGMR_TT ) RETURNS MONEY VERSION P_RAISE ;
   RETURN ( ( SALARY FROM P ) * 1.25 ) ;
END OPERATOR ;
```

Now the two RAISE operators are indeed different operators, not just different implementation versions of "the same" operator.

We modify the foregoing example in order to illustrate another point (the modified example is very contrived but is sufficient for our purpose). Suppose the intent of the operator is to compute the hypothetical new salary by increasing the original salary by 10 percent and then (for programmers only) doubling the result:

```
OPERATOR RAISE ( E EMP_TT ) RETURNS MONEY VERSION E_RAISE ;
   RETURN ( ( SALARY FROM E ) * 1.1 ) ;
END OPERATOR ;

OPERATOR RAISE ( P PGMR_TT ) RETURNS MONEY VERSION P_RAISE ;
   RETURN ( 2 * RAISE ( TREAT_AS_EMP_TT ( T ) ) ) ;
END OPERATOR ;
```

Version E_RAISE here is straightforward. Version P_RAISE, however, involves an invocation of TREAT, which, for the purposes of this discussion, we are assuming has been given somewhat revised semantics. To be specific, we assume that the expression TREAT_AS_EMP_TT (T) means "treat the argument T—which is actually of type PGMR_TT—as if it were of type EMP_TT instead." Thus, version P_RAISE computes its result by (a) invoking version E_RAISE to increase the salary by 10 percent and then (b) doubling that increased salary. In other words, we are talking here about the mechanism called **operator delegation** (see Appendix C)—the function of increasing the salary by 10 percent is not implemented explicitly for type PGMR_TT but is "delegated" to type EMP_TT instead.

Observe that delegation is not the same as inheritance; we cannot say the operator "increase salary by 10 percent" is *inherited* by programmers from employees, because PGMR_TT is not a subtype of

EMP_TT. It is true that, like inheritance, delegation might imply a certain amount of code reuse; unlike inheritance, however, we regard delegation more as an implementation issue (and perhaps an optimization issue) than it is a model issue. We note, however, that whereas the *is-a* relationship leads naturally to inclusion polymorphism (as we know from Part IV of this book), it seems that the *has-a* relationship—which, we remind you, is the fundamental issue here—seems to lead naturally to overloading polymorphism instead, which in turn seems to lead to delegation. We remark too that the automatic provision, discussed in Chapter 6, of implementation code for, say, the "<" operator for type QTY might be regarded as a form of delegation.

As an exercise, you might like to ponder the implications of the ideas discussed in this subsection for assignments and equality comparisons in particular.

SUBTABLES AND SUPERTABLES

In Part IV of this book, we proposed a detailed model for what in relational terms might be called *domain* inheritance. When approached regarding the possibility of inheritance in a relational context, however, many people—perhaps most—immediately jump to the conclusion that it is some kind of *table* inheritance that is the subject under discussion.[1] For example, we mentioned the fact in Chapter 12 that the SQL standard [99] includes something it calls "subtables and supertables," according to which some table *B* might inherit all of the columns of some other table *A* and then add some more of its own. An example is shown in Fig. G.1.

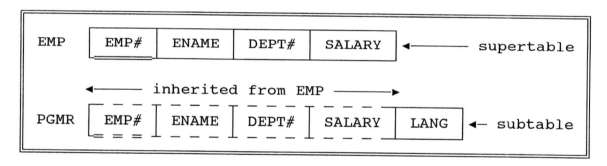

Fig. G.1: Subtable/supertable example

Here are the SQL definitions:

```
CREATE TYPE EMP_RT AS ( EMP# CHAR, ENAME CHAR, DEPT# CHAR, SALARY MONEY ) ... ;

CREATE TYPE PGMR_RT UNDER EMP_RT AS ( LANG ... ) ;

CREATE TABLE EMP OF EMP_RT ... PRIMARY KEY ( EMP# ) ... ;

CREATE TABLE PGMR OF PGMR_RT UNDER EMP ;
```

Explanation: EMP_RT and PGMR_RT are what SQL calls *structured types*—for present

---

1. We deliberately use the "fuzzy" terms *table, row,* and *column* in this section instead of our preferred terms *relation, relvar, tuple,* and *attribute,* because our examples and discussion are based on SQL, at least in part (though we have not hesitated to omit or simplify many SQL details that are irrelevant to our purpose).

purposes, you can think of them as relation or table types—and PGMR_RT is a "subtype" of "supertype" EMP_RT. (We prefer the terms *extension type* and *projection type,* however, for reasons explained in the previous section.) Tables EMP and PGMR are of types EMP_RT and PGMR_RT, respectively; EMP has four columns and PGMR only one (but it "inherits" the four columns of EMP as well). Nonprogrammers have a row in EMP only, while programmers have a row in both tables—so every row in PGMR has a counterpart in EMP, but the converse is not true.[1] However, the properties EMP#, ENAME, DEPT#, and SALARY are not recorded twice for programmers; rather, the PGMR table "inherits" those properties from the EMP table, as already indicated.

It should be clear already that subtables and supertables are basically just another example of structural inheritance (or "the EXTENDS relationship"), as it applies to the case of tables specifically. It follows that much of the discussion in the previous section applies more or less unchanged, and we will not bother to make the same points all over again. However, there are a few additional points arising that are worth calling out explicitly, and that is the purpose of the present section.

First, then, here are the implications of the design of Fig. G.1 on the usual SQL retrieval and update operations. *Note:* We caution you that different systems and different writers interpret the idea of subtables and supertable in different ways—see, e.g., the annotation to reference [124] in Appendix J. What follows is the way the SQL standard works, more or less.

- *SELECT:* Retrieval from EMP behaves normally. Retrieval from PGMR behaves as if PGMR actually contained the columns EMP#, ENAME, DEPT#, and SALARY (as well as LANG, of course).

- *INSERT:* INSERT into EMP behaves normally. INSERT into PGMR effectively causes new rows to appear in both EMP and PGMR.

- *DELETE:* DELETE from EMP causes rows to disappear from EMP and (if the rows in question happen to correspond to programmers) from PGMR too. DELETE from PGMR causes rows to disappear from both EMP and PGMR.

- *UPDATE:* Updating EMP# or ENAME or DEPT# or SALARY in EMP applies the same updates to any corresponding rows in PGMR. Updating those columns in PGMR applies the same updates to the corresponding rows in EMP. Updating LANG in PGMR updates PGMR only.

Note, incidentally, that the INSERT/DELETE behavior sketched above means we are not dealing with a conventional foreign-key-to-candidate-key relationship from PGMR to EMP, with conventional "referential actions"—for if we were, then, e.g., deleting a row from PGMR could not possibly cause deletion of a row from EMP. Note too that we have overlooked a couple of complicating factors in our brief explanations. For example:

- Suppose an existing nonprogrammer becomes a programmer. If we simply try to insert an appropriate row into PGMR, the system will attempt to insert a corresponding row into EMP as well—an attempt that will fail on a key uniqueness violation. Thus, it looks as if we will need an additional form of INSERT ("INSERT ONLY"?) that will let us insert a row into the subtable only.

- Conversely, suppose an existing programmer becomes a nonprogrammer. If we simply try to

---

1. It follows that the set of projections of all current programmer *rows* (speaking a little loosely) over all but LANG is a subset of the set of all current employee rows; in effect, there is an automatically enforced referential constraint from table PGMR to table EMP.

delete the appropriate row from PGMR, the system will delete the corresponding row from EMP as well—a side effect that will presumably not be desired. Thus, it looks as if we will need an additional form of DELETE ("DELETE ONLY"?) that will let us delete a row from the subtable only.

We remark in passing that SQL does not include support for any such INSERT ONLY and DELETE ONLY operators.

The obvious question now is: What if anything do the foregoing ideas have to do with inheritance? Well, it should be immediately clear that they have nothing to do with the prescriptions for relation types discussed in Chapter 16. According to those prescriptions, just to remind you, if RT' and RT are relation types such that RT' is a subtype of supertype RT, there is no notion that RT' somehow "inherits columns" from RT; rather, RT' and RT have the *same* columns, loosely speaking. So far as we are concerned, in fact, the subtype/supertype relationship is actually implied, in part, by the fact that types RT' and RT have the same columns (recall once again that we have no way of explicitly defining tuple and relation types outside of the statements that make use of them, and hence no way of explicitly stating that one such type is a subtype of another). To repeat, then: What do subtables and supertables have to do with inheritance?

Well, the fact that our model deals exclusively with type inheritance does not of itself rule out the possibility of some kind of table inheritance, of course. Indeed, it should be the case that our model provides a framework for understanding whether some sense might be made of such a notion; after all, that model is quite general and does necessarily address the implications of inheritance for values and variables in general—including relation values and variables in particular—and of course "tables" in the present context are really just relation variables (relvars), at least to a first approximation.

But herein lies a crucial point. "Tables" are indeed variables; thus, to talk of "subtables and supertables" is to talk of what might be called "subvariables and supervariables" ... whatever that might mean! (How can two distinct *variables* possibly be such that one is a "subvariable" of the other?) This observation immediately suggests that:

- First, whatever "subtables and supertables" might be all about, the one thing they are definitely not about is type inheritance; the tables in question are variables, and variables are not types.

- Second, the idea seems a little suspect right away. We explained in Part IV of this book that inheritance applies to values, not variables. (To paraphrase a remark from Chapter 12: "To say a circle is an ellipse is to say that every circle *value* is an ellipse *value,* not that every circle *variable* is an ellipse *variable.*") What then can it mean to say that relation *variable* PGMR is a "sub"-*anything* of relation *variable* EMP?

Thus, it might be possible to make some kind of sense out of "subtables and supertables," but (as we will show) it is a completely different phenomenon, one that has essentially nothing to do with type inheritance as such.

Next, when we talk of PGMR being a "subtable" of EMP (and inheriting columns from EMP), what we really mean is that each PGMR *row* inherits certain properties from the corresponding EMP *row*. In other words, we should really be talking about "subrows and superrows," not "subtables and supertables" at all. (And we pointed out in the previous section, in effect, that this latter terminology is very bad, because each "subrow" is a superset of the corresponding "superrow.")

Next, it follows that, whatever else they might be, "subtables and supertables" are not an application of our inheritance ideas in which the variables are relvars specifically. Nor are they an application of our inheritance ideas in which the variables are tuplevars (or "rowvars") specifically, because the only tuplevars we deal with in our model are "free-standing" ones—there is not, nor can there be, any notion of a tuplevar somehow being embedded within a relvar, as we have observed at several points in this book previously.

So why might subtables and supertables be a good idea? What are the advantages? Well, the only advantage we can see (and it is a pretty minor one) is this:

> Informing the system that, e.g., PGMR is a subtable of supertable EMP is shorthand for stating certain new kinds of referential actions declaratively.

To be specific, it allows:

- Insertion of a row into PGMR to cause automatic insertion of the corresponding row into EMP

- Deletion of a row from PGMR to cause automatic deletion of the corresponding row from EMP

But there is no need to pretend that certain columns are "inherited" by PGMR from EMP in order to achieve these effects! In fact, we could achieve these effects very simply by:[1]

a. Defining two base tables as follows (in outline):

```
EMP      ( EMP# ..., ENAME ..., DEPT# ..., SALARY ... )
EMP_LANG ( EMP# ..., LANG ... )
```

b. Defining PGMR as a view of these two base tables, thus:

```
PGMR = EMP JOIN EMP_LANG
```

This approach, which is described in detail in reference [76], provides all of the functionality described earlier for the subtable/supertable design; it also gets around the INSERT ONLY and DELETE ONLY problem (trivially so, in fact—the operators are simply no longer needed). What is more, the approach could serve as a basis for *implementing* subtables and supertables (if they are regarded as worth implementing at all, that is). *Note:* Actually, we suspect the whole idea derives from a confusion over model vs. implementation once again. To be more specific, we suspect that if table *B* and table *A* are a subtable and corresponding supertable, respectively, then the intent is that tables *B* and *A* should be physically implemented—for performance reasons—as one "stored table" on the disk, with nulls in the *B*-only columns in "stored rows" corresponding to *A* rows and not to *B* rows. But such implementation concerns should never show through to the model level! The relational model quite deliberately has nothing to say regarding physical storage matters.

In sum, it looks as if the whole business of a subtable inheriting columns from a supertable is nothing but a syntactic shorthand—not that there is anything wrong with syntactic shorthands in general, of course, but this particular shorthand does not seem very useful, and in any case it is already more than adequately supported by the conventional view mechanism.

One final point to close this section: It is worth noting that the terminology of subtables and supertables might more reasonably be applied "the other way around," as it were. Consider our usual suppliers-and-parts database, and suppose some parts have no color. Instead of using a null to represent the color of such a part—a notion we reject anyway—the following design might make more sense:

```
P   { P#, PNAME, COLOR, WEIGHT, CITY }    /* "supertable */

NCP { P#, PNAME, WEIGHT, CITY }           /* "subtable"  */
```

Here parts with no color are represented in NCP and other parts are represented in P. See

---

1. Thanks to Spencer Olson of State Street Bank, Boston, Mass., for these observations.

reference [33] for further discussion.

SCALAR TYPES REVISITED

In the present section we offer a few further thoughts regarding structural inheritance in connection with scalar types. First of all, we saw earlier in this book that if T' is a subtype of T, then every possrep for T is necessarily, albeit implicitly, a possrep for T' as well; for example, every possrep for ellipses is necessarily a possrep for circles as well, because circles *are* ellipses. As noted in Chapter 12, therefore, we might regard possreps as further "properties" that are inherited, albeit silently, by subtypes from supertypes. And we might go further and regard such inheritance as structural inheritance, of a kind. Note, however, that the possrep that is inherited in this way by type T' is identical to the corresponding possrep for type T; there is no notion, as there is with structural inheritance as usually understood, of the subtype "structure" having additional components, over and above those in the "structure" for the supertype.

Also, if T' is a subtype of T, then every declared possrep for T' is *derived* from some possrep for T,[1] and we might regard the derivation process as structural inheritance, of a kind. Here, however, the derived possrep not only has no additional components over and above those in the possrep for the supertype, it typically has fewer (think of ellipses and circles, for example). Again, therefore, this kind of inheritance is not structural inheritance as usually understood. Indeed, subtypes and supertypes as we have defined them make little sense as examples of structural inheritance as usually understood. For example, suppose we were to represent ellipses and circles not by scalar types as usual but by tuple types instead, thus:

```
TYPE ELLIPSE TUPLE { A LENGTH, B LENGTH, CTR POINT } ;

TYPE CIRCLE   TUPLE EXTEND ELLIPSE ADD { R LENGTH } ;
```

Now every circle will have three attributes (A, B, and R) whose values are always equal!—not a very sensible design, it might be thought (especially if those three attributes map directly to three physical "attributes" in storage).

We have now laid the groundwork for discussing another outstanding issue. Under IM Prescription 2 in Chapter 14, we said that examples along the following lines are often found in the literature: "Let type COLORED_CIRCLE be a subtype of type CIRCLE." And we said we would return to this particular example in the present appendix. Now read on ...

The example clearly suggests that colored circles are a special case of circles in general. But are they? We think not. By definition, surely, "colored circles" are *images* (on a display screen perhaps), whereas circles in general are not images but *geometric figures in two-dimensional space*. Thus, it seems to us more reasonable to regard COLORED_CIRCLE not as a subtype of CIRCLE but rather as a completely separate type. Now, that separate type might well have a possrep in which one component is of type CIRCLE and another is of type COLOR, thus—

```
TYPE COLORED_CIRCLE POSSREP { CIR CIRCLE, COL COLOR ... } ;
```

—but it is not, to repeat, a subtype of type CIRCLE, any more than it is a subtype of type COLOR.

Note: Another way of saying the same thing is to say that every colored circle *has* a circle property but *is not* a circle (just as it has a color property but is not a color). As with employees and programmers, therefore, what we are really talking about here is the *has-a* relationship, not the *is-a*

---

1. We assume here for simplicity that (a) we are dealing with single inheritance and (b) T is a regular type.

relationship that characterizes inheritance and subtyping as such.

We now proceed to present a series of arguments to bolster the foregoing conclusion. (Well, we say "a series of arguments," but perhaps we should admit up front that the arguments in question are really all just the same argument in different guises, as will soon be seen.)

We begin by reminding you of the following remark from Chapter 14:

> It is an obvious corollary of IM Prescription 2 that there cannot be more values of type T' than there are of type T. This apparently trivial observation can be very helpful in pinpointing errors and clearing up confusions.

In the case at hand, it is surely obvious—as in fact we pointed out in Chapter 14—that there are more colored circles than there are just plain circles. (We assume, reasonably enough, that two circles that differ in color but are otherwise identical are the same circle but different colored circles.) Thus, this simple test should be sufficient to show right away that type COLORED_CIRCLE is indeed not a subtype of type CIRCLE.

Second, recall RM Prescription 4, which says in part that if S is a selector for type T, then every value of type T must be produced by some invocation of S. But no invocation of the CIRCLE selector can possibly produce a value of type COLORED_CIRCLE, since the CIRCLE selector has no color parameter; hence, a value of type COLORED_CIRCLE is not a value of type CIRCLE, and type COLORED_CIRCLE is not a subtype of type CIRCLE.

Third, we pointed out earlier in this section that, informally, we might regard possreps as further "properties" that are inherited by subtypes from supertypes. Yet our CIRCLE possrep, with its radius and center components, is not a possrep for colored circles, because it has no color component. Once again, therefore, type COLORED_CIRCLE cannot be a subtype of type CIRCLE.

Last, we offer the important observation that *there is no way to obtain a colored circle from a circle via S by C*. That is, there is no constraint we can write for type COLORED_CIRCLE that, if satisfied by a given value of type CIRCLE, means the circle in question is really a colored circle. And the reason is, of course, again basically that the CIRCLE possible representation has no color component.

It should be clear, then, that CIRCLE and COLORED_CIRCLE are completely different types. As suggested earlier, however, it is probably true that type COLORED_CIRCLE has a possrep in which one component is of type CIRCLE. And it is probably also true that we would like to be able to say that, e.g., the operator CTR which returns the center of a given colored circle is basically just the THE_CTR operator that applies to the CIRCLE component CIR of the possrep for that colored circle. Once again, then, we are talking about the mechanism of *delegation*—the responsibility for implementing CTR for type COLORED_CIRCLE is delegated to the type, CIRCLE, of a certain component of (one of) its possrep(s).

STRUCTURAL INHERITANCE WITH FEWER TEARS

We have said that we do not preclude direct support for structural inheritance. However, we have now seen that such support might well be problematic for various reasons. In this section, therefore, we show how our own model can be used to achieve the effect of structural inheritance without having to support that concept directly.

It is convenient to begin by repeating something we said in Chapter 14. In our discussion of IM Prescription 17 in that chapter, we said this:

> [We] are still not convinced that changing operator semantics is ... a good idea. We therefore define our model to say that if a change in semantics occurs, then the implementation is in violation—i.e., it is not an implementation of the model, and the implications are unpredictable.

We are not without our critics on this issue, of course. The typical counterargument goes something like this:

One significant advantage that is often claimed for object orientation is *code reuse*. The idea is that some existing class might be "almost right" for a new application, and that much of it can be reused by a subclass that introduces some additions and changes. E.g., suppose a company has a class called EMPLOYEE, with various operators, including a PAYROLL operator that (among other things) computes the net pay for a given employee. Suppose the company now introduces a new kind of employee who is paid in a different way, perhaps at an hourly rate instead of monthly. The company might be able to reuse most of the PAYROLL code by creating a subclass, HOURLY_EMPLOYEE, with its own PAYROLL operator. The new subclass might not find the representation of the original class to be sufficient, so it will probably need to add new instance variables, such as HOURS_WORKED. Overloading the PAYROLL operator makes it possible to process a column of employees, some of whom are paid by the hour, without putting logic into the application to branch on employee type, using the principle called *polymorphism*. However, this example of code reuse and polymorphism will clearly not work under the constraint that the semantics of the PAYROLL operator must not change as we go from class EMPLOYEE to class HOURLY_EMPLOYEE. So a refusal to allow changes in semantics forfeits the advantage of code reuse, one of the principal advantages claimed for object orientation.

(The foregoing is based on one specific criticism [1], but we have revised the original considerably. In particular, we have replaced the example by one of our own. Of course, we have tried not to change the essential nature of the argument.)

So what is wrong with this criticism? The overriding point, it seems to us, is that *examples like the one quoted are not examples of subtyping*. If we say that employees have a monthly salary, and hourly employees are employees, then it follows as the night the day that hourly employees have a monthly salary!—for otherwise they are not employees in the first place. To put it another way, to say that hourly employees are *somewhat like* regular employees is not the same as saying that hourly employees are *a special case of* regular employees. A mechanism that allows us to say that hourly employees are "somewhat like" regular employees might possibly be useful—it might even allow a certain amount of code reuse—but, to repeat, that mechanism is not type inheritance as such. After all, if to say that type *B* is a subtype of type *A* just means that type *B* is "somewhat like" type *A* except that certain properties are added and/or dropped and/or altered, then **absolutely any type whatever could be regarded as a subtype of absolutely any type whatever!**

In fact, it seems to us that, once again, what we are really talking about here is a *has-a* relationship, not an *is-a* relationship at all: Hourly employees "have a" certain property that employees in general do not have, and likewise for monthly employees. Note in particular that, once again, S by C does not apply (at least, not directly).

A Possible Solution

Despite the foregoing analysis, it turns out that we can convert the monthly vs. hourly employees example into an application of true subtyping and inheritance if we want to. The key is to recognize that monthly and hourly employees can both be regarded as special cases of the abstract concept "employees in general." We proceed as follows.

First of all, in accordance with the arguments presented in Appendix B, we would probably have three real relvars looking something like this:

```
VAR EMP REAL RELATION          /* employees in general */
  { EMP# ... ,
    DEPT# ... }
    KEY { EMP# } ;
```

```
VAR MONTHLY_EMP REAL RELATION          /* monthly employees */
  { EMP# ... ,
    MONTHLY_RATE ... }
    KEY { EMP# }
    FOREIGN KEY { EMP# } REFERENCES EMP ;

VAR HOURLY_EMP REAL RELATION           /* hourly employees */
  { EMP# ... ,
    HOURS_WORKED ... ,
    HOURLY_RATE ... }
    KEY { EMP# }
    FOREIGN KEY { EMP# } REFERENCES EMP ;
```

Next, we introduce some constraints to ensure that every employee is either monthly or hourly and not both:

```
CONSTRAINT MONTHLY_AND_HOURLY_DISJOINT
   IS_EMPTY ( MONTHLY_EMP { EMP# } INTERSECT HOURLY_EMP { EMP# } ) ;

CONSTRAINT MONTHLY_AND_HOURLY_SPAN
  ( MONTHLY_EMP { EMP# } UNION HOURLY_EMP { EMP# } ) = EMP { EMP# } ;
```

We also define a couple of useful views (virtual relvars):

```
VAR MONTHLY_EMP_ALL_INFO VIRTUAL RELATION
  ( EMP JOIN MONTHLY_EMP )
    KEY { EMP# } ;

VAR HOURLY_EMP_ALL_INFO VIRTUAL RELATION
  ( EMP JOIN HOURLY_EMP )
    KEY { EMP# } ;
```

Now, the object of the exercise is to be able to "[overload] the PAYROLL operator [and thus make] it possible to process a column of employees, some of whom are paid by the hour, without putting logic into the application to branch on employee type." It follows that we are going to need a relvar that includes an attribute of some *scalar* "employee type," some of whose values correspond to monthly employees and some to hourly employees. (*Note:* The attribute cannot be of a tuple type, because the tuple types corresponding to EMP, MONTHLY_EMP, and HOURLY_EMP tuples are all different, and no two of them have a common supertype; hence, if the attribute in question were of any of those three types, it obviously could not take on values of either of the other two.) So let us define three scalar types, S_EMP, S_MONTHLY_EMP, and S_HOURLY_EMP (S_ for scalar), thus:

```
TYPE S_EMP UNION ;

TYPE S_MONTHLY_EMP
        IS { S_EMP POSSREP { EMP# ... , DEPT# ... , MONTHLY_RATE ... } } ;

TYPE S_HOURLY_EMP
        IS { S_EMP POSSREP { EMP# ... , DEPT# ... , HOURS_WORKED ... , HOURLY_RATE ... } } ;
```

Every value of type S_EMP is in fact a value of type S_MONTHLY_EMP or type

S_HOURLY_EMP—there are no values of most specific type S_EMP. However, there is no "S by C" from S_EMP to S_MONTHLY_EMP or S_HOURLY_EMP, because S_EMP is a dummy type. (Despite this fact, we would still expect THE_EMP# and THE_DEPT# operators and pseudovariables to be defined at the S_EMP level. Compare the analogous example in Chapter 14, under IM Prescription 20, in which THE_CTR is defined as applying at the ELLIPSE level even when ELLIPSE is a dummy type.)

Now we can define the PAYROLL operator. To be more precise, we can define *two* PAYROLL operators, one at the S_MONTHLY_EMP ("monthly employees") level and one at the S_HOURLY_EMP ("hourly employees") level. Note very carefully that those two PAYROLL operators really are different operators (though they might be able to share some implementation code):

```
OPERATOR PAYROLL ( E S_MONTHLY_EMP ) RETURNS MONEY ;
   /* compute on basis of monthly rate */
   ... ;
END OPERATOR ;

OPERATOR PAYROLL ( E S_HOURLY_EMP ) RETURNS MONEY ;
   /* compute on basis of hours worked and hourly rate */
   ... ;
END OPERATOR ;
```

We also need a PAYROLL specification signature at the S_EMP level:

```
OPERATOR PAYROLL ( E S_EMP ) RETURNS MONEY ;
   /* specification signature only */
END OPERATOR ;
```

Now we define a view that contains the desired attribute, EMP, of type S_EMP. Note the use of S_MONTHLY_EMP and S_HOURLY_EMP selectors and the appeal to IM Prescription 13 here!

```
VAR REQD_VIEW VIRTUAL RELATION
( ( EXTEND MONTHLY_EMP_ALL_INFO
    ADD ( S_MONTHLY_EMP ( EMP#, DEPT#, MONTHLY_RATE ) AS EMP ) ) { EMP }
    UNION
  ( EXTEND HOURLY_EMP_ALL_INFO
    ADD ( S_HOURLY_EMP ( EMP#, DEPT#, HOURS_WORKED, HOURLY_RATE ) AS EMP ) ) { EMP } ) ;
```

This view contains just one attribute, EMP, of declared type S_EMP.

Finally, "to process [the] column of employees, some of whom are paid by the hour, without putting logic into the application to branch on employee type":

```
EXTEND REQD_VIEW ADD ( PAYROLL ( EMP ) AS PAY )
```

Attribute PAY in the relation that results from this expression contains exactly what is required.

Another Example

In this subsection we sketch a similar (but different) solution to a similar (but different) problem. This problem involves multiple instead of single inheritance and inclusion instead of overloading polymorphism. However, the "objects" that participate in the inheritance relationships are again, for reasons explained in Appendix B, better represented—at least initially—by means of relvars, not types. The "objects" in question are again employees. This time, however, some employees are part-time and some are managers (and some are both), and the assumption is that we want to be able to treat part-time managers differently in some way from the way we treat full-time managers and part-time nonmanagers.

Our approach to this problem goes something like this. First of all, here is the relational design:

```
VAR EMP REAL RELATION
  { EMP# ... ,
    DEPT# ... }
    KEY { EMP# } ;

VAR PART_TIME_EMP REAL RELATION
  { EMP# ... ,
    DAY_OFF ... }
    KEY { EMP# }
    FOREIGN KEY { EMP# } REFERENCES EMP ;

VAR MANAGER_EMP REAL RELATION
  { EMP# ... ,
    BUDGET ... }
    FOREIGN KEY { EMP# } REFERENCES EMP ;

VAR PART_TIME_MANAGER_EMP REAL RELATION
  { EMP# ... ,
    SOMETHING_ELSE ... }
    FOREIGN KEY { EMP# } REFERENCES PART_TIME_EMP
    FOREIGN KEY { EMP# } REFERENCES MANAGER_EMP ;
```

From the foregoing relational design, we can, in a manner similar to that sketched in the previous section, define the following scalar types (shown here in outline only; the details are tedious but straightforward). Note in particular that type EMP includes two BOOLEAN components, PART_TIME and MANAGER, to indicate whether a given employee is part- or full-time and whether he or she is a manager.

```
TYPE EMP POSSREP { EMP# ... ,       DEPT# ... ,
                   PART_TIME ... , DAY_OFF ... ,
                   MANAGER ... ,    BUDGET ... ,
                   SOMETHING_ELSE ... } ;

/* If NOT ( THE_PART_TIME (e) ), then THE_DAY_OFF (e) and    */
/* THE_SOMETHING_ELSE (e) are both special "missing" values; */
/* if NOT ( THE_MANAGER (e) ), then THE_BUDGET (e) and       */
/* THE_SOMETHING_ELSE (e) are both special "missing" values. */
/* These constraints need to be stated formally, of course;  */
/* we omit the details here.                                  */


/* This is not a GOOD design!—but it's a possible one.       */


/* Note in particular that type EMP is a regular type (it     */
/* might or might not be a union type), and so subtyping      */
/* (e.g., to PART_TIME_EMP) can and must be done via S by C,  */
/* as here:                                                   */
```

```
TYPE PART_TIME_EMP
    IS ( EMP CONSTRAINT THE_PART_TIME ( EMP )
        POSSREP { EMP#            = THE_EMP# ( EMP ),
                 DEPT#            = THE_DEPT# ( EMP ),
                 DAY_OFF          = THE_DAY_OFF ( EMP ),
                 MANAGER          = THE_MANAGER ( EMP ),
                 BUDGET           = THE_BUDGET ( EMP ),
                 SOMETHING_ELSE = THE_SOMETHING_ELSE ( EMP ) } } ;


/* Type MANAGER_EMP is very similar ... As for type        */
/* PART_TIME_MANAGER_EMP, it looks something like this:     */

TYPE PART_TIME_MANAGER_EMP
    IS ( PART_TIME_EMP, MANAGER_EMP
        POSSREP { EMP# = ... /* etc., etc. */ } } ;
```

Now we can define operators that apply only at (say) the PART_TIME_MANAGER_EMP level, define relvars with attributes of type EMP that contain values of any of the four types, etc., etc.

As the comments above suggest, the foregoing is perhaps not a very elegant solution to the problem, but at least it gets the job done, and it abides 100 percent by the prescriptions of the *Manifesto* (including the inheritance prescriptions in particular).

Appendix H

A Comparison with SQL

Naturally we believe the ideas of *The Third Manifesto* are valuable in and of themselves. However, we also believe they can be useful as a yardstick or framework—i.e., as a basis against which (as noted in Chapter 1) alternative proposals, and indeed concrete implementations, can be carefully analyzed, criticized, evaluated, and perhaps judged. In this appendix, we use that framework to examine the SQL standard [99] in particular. Please note immediately, however, that we expressly do not want our ideas to be used in connection with any kind of "checklist" evaluation (neither of the SQL standard nor of anything else). We do think those ideas can serve as a convenient framework for structuring discussions, but they are not meant to serve as a basis for some kind of scoring scheme. We are not interested in scoring schemes.

Back to the SQL standard per se. As the formal name "SQL:2003" suggests, the current version of that standard was ratified in late 2003, when it replaced the previous version ("SQL:1999"). It consists of a series of separate documents, called *Parts;* most of the material that is relevant to this appendix is in Part 2, "SQL/Foundation" (see the annotation to reference [99] in Appendix J for further discussion). In principle, SQL:2003 includes the whole of SQL:1999—with a few comparatively minor exceptions—as a proper subset. In this appendix, however, we follow the usual convention of using the formal name "SQL:2003" only when we want to emphasize the point that we are discussing some aspect of the language that was not present in SQL:1999. Elsewhere, we adopt the convention that the unqualified name "SQL" refers to SQL:2003, the most recent version, specifically (where it makes any difference).

Before going any further, we need to acknowledge the fact that one of the present authors was actively involved in the production of SQL standards for several years (from 1988 to 2004, to be precise). Therefore—just in case any reader, possibly seeing some conflict of interest in that involvement, might think of raising an eyebrow at some of the stark differences to be observed between the SQL standard and our *Manifesto*—we would like to take a moment to point out some of the ways in which we as independent manifesto writers enjoy certain freedoms that SQL standardizers do not:

- First and foremost, we do not have to deal with *The Shackle of Compatibility* [27]. SQL standardizers at large might very well share our regrets over (e.g.) nulls and duplicate rows, but they are powerless to remove them from the standard, just as vendors are powerless to remove them from products already shipped and perhaps widely used.

- Second, the design and implementation of established products might have an adverse effect on the feasibility and cost-effectiveness of proposed SQL extensions.

- Third, an SQL standardizer whose participation is funded by an employer, say, might sometimes feel obliged to place the commercial interests of that employer above his or her own personal opinions, should there be any conflict.

- Fourth, an SQL standardizer has to make compromises within a large group of people with perhaps widely differing opinions and interests. By contrast, coauthors with closely shared opinions and interests have to make hardly any compromises at all, especially on matters considered by both to be very important.

It follows from the foregoing that the criticisms that follow are definitely not intended as, nor should they be taken as, criticisms of the individuals involved in the production of the SQL standard. Nor do we necessarily mean to suggest that we think the SQL standard could and should have been more closely aligned with *The Third Manifesto*. Indeed, it is our recognition of the inevitability of misalignment that makes us advocate serious consideration of something that might supersede SQL in the long term.

Comparison format: The bulk of this appendix consists of a series of point-by-point comparisons of pertinent features of SQL with the various prescriptions, proscriptions, and suggestions from the body of the book. The comparisons are presented mostly as bald statements of fact; for the most part, we do not restate opinions, give value judgments, or comment on the relative severity of various points. Also, we use the terms **conforms** and **fails,** in **boldface,** to indicate our general finding in connection with each point. Very often these terms have to be qualified, and sometimes both are used in connection with the same point. For example, SQL sometimes conforms to (say) a certain prescription in some respects but fails in others; sometimes it conforms as far as it goes but does not go far enough; sometimes it conforms **vacuously,** because none of the most widely used implementations actually includes the required feature; sometimes it fails not because of specifics of the feature at hand, but rather because that feature depends on some other feature on which it fails in turn. Such dependencies are appropriately indicated.

We now proceed with our point-by-point comparisons.

RM PRESCRIPTIONS

1. Scalar types

SQL **conforms,** sort of. User-defined scalar types can be defined and destroyed by means of appropriate CREATE TYPE and DROP TYPE statements (though there are some questions over the extent to which such types are truly scalar—see the next paragraph). Built-in scalar types (BOOLEAN, INTEGER, REAL, DECIMAL, CHARACTER, DATE, TIME, TIMESTAMP, XML, etc.) are also supported, of course. Each such type is a named set of scalar values and is distinct from all the rest.[1] Values and variables of such types can be operated upon solely by means of the operators defined for the type in question. (We remark in passing that SQL does not use the term "operator" in the same generic way as the *Manifesto* does, but reserves it for built-in functions like "+" and "-" that make use of some special notation—typically infix notation, though "+" and "-" can also be used as monadic prefix operators.)

Our reasons for saying "sort of" in the previous paragraph are as follows. First, user-defined scalar types in SQL fall into two broad categories, "DISTINCT types" and "structured types." As explained under RM Very Strong Suggestion 8 in Chapter 10, DISTINCT types are limited to having a representation that involves just one type, which must be built in (and hence scalar). By contrast, structured types can have a representation involving any number of types, and those types can be either built in or user defined (and they do not need to be scalar, either). What is more, there is at least one context in which a structured type—which is a scalar type, by definition, and usually behaves like one—nevertheless behaves as if it were not scalar: namely, when the type in question is used as a basis for creating a table that is "of" that type.

SQL also meets our requirement for operators whose purpose is to expose each declared possible representation for a given type. For user-defined types, it requires exactly one representation to be specified, and the implementation automatically provides appropriate operators for each component of that representation. For built-in types, it provides appropriate literals.

SQL **fails** in that it is possible for a user-defined type to have nothing corresponding to a selector operator; that is, no such operators are provided automatically, though it is always possible to provide a

---

1. Actually there is some confusion here. Certain pairs of built-in types—REAL and FLOAT, for example—seem to be regarded as both distinct and not distinct, depending on context. If they are distinct, they are certainly not disjoint as required by RM Prescription 1; if they are not distinct, they violate the requirement (again part of RM Prescription 1) that two types that are really the same type must have the same name.

user-defined one to serve the purpose. It is true that certain operators *are* provided automatically for user-defined types, including something called a *constructor function*. However, every invocation of such a function always returns the same value (specified, explicitly or implicitly, by the type definer). In other words, what such a function really does is *allocate storage* and initialize it to contain the "value" whose every immediate component is the applicable default value[1]—it does not support the selection of an arbitrary value of that type, as RM Prescription 1 requires.

SQL also fails in that it does not really meet our requirement for a built-in boolean type. To be specific, its BOOLEAN type, which might have been thought to fit the bill, suffers from certain anomalies arising from SQL's idiosyncratic concept of nulls and its foundation in three-valued logic. That type does include just the two values we prescribe, TRUE and FALSE—but we make that prescription precisely because we require **D** to be based on two-valued logic! We would naturally expect a language based on three-valued logic, as SQL is, to support three "boolean" values (TRUE, FALSE, and UNKNOWN), not two. But SQL represents the UNKNOWN truth value not by a value at all but by means of the SQL-style null. Null is not a value in SQL because it does not have all the properties of values.[2] In particular, it is not always treated as equal to itself and unequal to everything else, though it is sometimes so treated.

While we are on the subject of SQL's BOOLEAN type, we should mention that it suffers from certain further anomalies as well—anomalies that, while they might not violate RM Prescription 1 per se, certainly do violate other prescriptions (RM Prescription 26 and OO Prescription 6 in particular). For example, if B is a column of type BOOLEAN, a WHERE clause of the form WHERE B is invalid; and if B happens to be empty, the aggregate operators EVERY and ANY applied to B both return null (instead of the logically correct results, which are TRUE and FALSE, respectively).

In any case, SQL's support for BOOLEAN is somewhat **vacuous,** because in most implementations the type name is not available, as a consequence of which support for the type is subject to severe restrictions. Such an implementation does support certain boolean expressions (e.g., CITY = 'La Paz'), which can be used in certain contexts—for example, a constraint definition, a CASE expression, or the WHERE clause of a query (as in any SQL system). However, such an implementation does not permit BOOLEAN as such to be the explicit declared type of anything (e.g., a column). Furthermore, in the case of columns in particular, it cannot be the implicit declared type either, and so boolean expressions are not permitted as items in a SELECT clause. Furthermore, the aggregate functions EVERY and ANY are typically not supported at all and thus cannot even be invoked in a HAVING clause.

SQL does not support empty types.

2. Scalar values are typed

SQL **conforms** (except for the possible overlap among certain built-in types noted under RM Prescription 1).

3. Read-only vs. update operators

SQL **conforms** with respect to our prescribed user-defined update operator support, via its CREATE PROCEDURE statement. It also conforms with respect to our prescribed user-defined read-only operator support, in that the output parameters that can be declared in CREATE PROCEDURE statements are prohibited in CREATE FUNCTION and CREATE METHOD statements (though we note

1. We set "value" in quotes here because defaults are often defined to be null and null is not a value at all.

2. There are major logical differences, in fact, (a) between nulls and values in general, and (b) between null and "the third truth value"—i.e., UNKNOWN—in particular. See, e.g., reference [76] for further discussion.

that—unlike our read-only operators—SQL functions and methods are allowed to update the database, so long as their definition includes the option MODIFIES SQL DATA). SQL also conforms to our prescription regarding the ability to destroy user-defined operators, via certain DROP statements.

4. Physical vs. possible representations

SQL **conforms** in that it does permit a representation (at most one) to be specified for a given user-defined type, and such a specification does involve components as assumed in RM Prescription 4. It **fails** in that (as already noted) it does not automatically provide selector operators. It also fails because every representation must involve at least one component.

5. Expose possible representations

SQL **conforms,** subject to its shortcomings with respect to RM Prescription 4. To repeat some material from Chapter 10 (RM Very Strong Suggestion 8), the components of a representation are called *attributes*[1] (not to be confused with tuple and relation attributes as defined in the *Manifesto*), and each attribute definition automatically causes definition of one *observer* method and one *mutator* method. An SQL observer method is a read-only operator, of course, but an SQL mutator is not the corresponding update operator that might have been expected (and the term is thus being used in a somewhat unconventional manner). However, it is at least true that assignment of the result of invoking such a method back to the applicable variable can achieve the required "mutation" effect. For example, let T be a type, let V be a variable of type T, let C be a component of the representation of type T, let TC be the type of that component, and let X be an expression of type TC. Then the assignment

```
SET V = V.C ( X )    /* exp on right is a mutator invocation */
```

updates V such that its C component is set to the value of X and all other components remain unchanged. Further, a shorthand is available that permits the foregoing assignment to be abbreviated to just

```
SET V.C = X
```

$V.C$ here is thus SQL's counterpart to our THE_$C(V)$ pseudovariable.
   Nesting is supported on the left side, too, as in the following example:

```
SET LS.BEGIN.X = Z
```

(*cf.* the discussion of nested THE_ pseudovariables in Chapter 6).
   Note: Throughout our examples in this appendix we use semicolons as statement terminators, as in *direct SQL* [41,99].

6. Type generator TUPLE

SQL **conforms** to the following extent. First, it supports a ROW type constructor, which is the obvious analog of our TUPLE type generator (SQL uses the term *constructor* rather than our preferred *generator*). The components of a row type are called *fields;* thus, the SQL analog of our heading is an ordered list (not a set—see below) of ordered pairs of the form $<F,T>$, where F is a field name and T is the name of the corresponding type (which is not necessarily scalar). A row type can be used for all of

---

1. We are making a tacit assumption here that the type in question is a structured type specifically. The situation with DISTINCT types is slightly different, but the differences are not important for present purposes.

the purposes mentioned in RM Prescription 6.

SQL **fails** in that it assigns significance to the left-to-right order of $<F,T>$ pairs (in other words, those pairs form an ordered list, not a set, as already noted). Thus, for example, the row types

```
ROW ( F1 T1, F2 T2 )
```

and

```
ROW ( F2 T2, F1 T1 )
```

are different types in SQL.

SQL also fails because it has no counterpart—or sometimes no direct counterpart—to certain of our required tuple operators (WRAP, UNWRAP, tuple RENAME, tuple EXTEND, etc.).

SQL also fails because every row type must involve at least one field. Moreover, SQL's row type support has to be regarded as **vacuous,** as it is typically not included in actual implementations.

7. *Type generator RELATION*

SQL **fails,** having nothing that corresponds to our RELATION type generator.[1] It might be thought that the MULTISET type constructor (new in SQL:2003) could be made to serve the purpose, but it really cannot, even though a table is a multiset of rows and a row type can be the element type of a multiset type. For one thing, relations (or relation bodies, rather) are sets, not multisets. For another, an SQL row, in general, fails to conform to our definition of tuple. For a third, this support is **vacuous** because most implementations at the time of writing do not support either row types or multiset types. Also, the update operators INSERT, DELETE, UPDATE, and MERGE are not defined for variables whose declared type is of the form ROW (...) MULTISET.

SQL's use of structured types as "named table types" and various associated facilities together mean it also fails in connection with our requirement that relation types have names of a certain prescribed form.

SQL also fails because it has no direct counterpart to our required GROUP and UNGROUP operators.

8. *Equality*

SQL **fails.** For certain types, equality is not even defined! To be specific, equality for user-defined type *T* is—for some strange reason—defined only if an *ordering* is defined for *T,* and not all user-defined types are required to have an ordering. Equality is also undefined for the built-in type XML.

SQL also fails because (as we saw in Chapter 6) it is possible in SQL for, e.g., the comparison

```
'AB' = 'AB '
```

to give TRUE, while the comparison

```
CHAR_LENGTH ('AB') = CHAR_LENGTH ('AB ')
```

gives FALSE (the left comparand evaluates to two and the right one to three). *Note:* The example is an

---

1. Except for "created temporary tables," which are not tables at all but table type constructors of a very special and restricted kind [41,99]. (A TABLE type constructor was included in early drafts of SQL:1999, but it ran into difficulties, was shelved in the hope of speeding up the overall standardization process, and was not revived in SQL:2003.)

illustration of a more general phenomenon: namely, that SQL regards certain data values as "equal but distinguishable." For further discussion, see reference [41].

We further remark that it is possible in SQL for the expression $X = Y$ not to return TRUE and yet for X and Y to be otherwise indistinguishable. Such is the case, for example, when X IS NULL and Y IS NULL both give TRUE.

SQL also fails here, seriously, in connection with user-defined types; the definer of such a type can (and in fact must, if "=" is to be supported at all) specify the algorithm by which the system is to determine equality of values of the type, and there is no requirement, or even suggestion, that that algorithm abide by RM Prescription 8.

We remark finally that several of today's SQL DBMSs fail to support equality for the standard's CHARACTER LARGE OBJECT (CLOB) and BINARY LARGE OBJECT (BLOB) types.

9. Tuples

SQL **conforms** to the extent that its row concept is a counterpart to our tuple concept.

SQL **fails** by attaching significance to the ordinal positions of row components (i.e., field values). Also, we require tuple components to have names; row components in SQL have names only when those names can be, and are, provided by the context in which the row in question is used. In particular, SQL's *row value constructor* (its analog of our tuple selector) takes the form

```
[ ROW ] ( <exp commalist> )
```

and thus provides no way of specifying field names (also, it must be nonempty).

SQL further fails in that a field "value" can be null, which, as we have already observed in connection with RM Prescription 1, does not have all the properties required for it to qualify as a value.

10. Relations

SQL **conforms** to the extent that its table concept is a counterpart to our relation concept. An SQL table has:

- A counterpart to our heading, in the form of an ordered list of $<C,T>$ pairs, where C is a column name and T is the name of the corresponding type (which is not necessarily scalar)

- A counterpart to our body, in the form of a bag or multiset (sometimes a set) of rows

It narrowly escapes failure to conform to our requirement for every attribute or column to have a name—even though it does allow the user to write an expression that yields a table that contains columns for which no name is specified explicitly. It does so by requiring the system to *generate* a name for each such column. However, such names are not required to be unique, since SQL does in general permit distinct columns of the same table to have the same name!

The VALUES construct of SQL provides a counterpart to our prescribed relation selector, though of course it suffers from the failures we have already observed in connection with relations in general.

SQL **fails** in the following respects:

- Every table must have at least one column.

- Significance is attached to the left-to-right order of columns.

- Two or more distinct columns of the same table can have the same name.

- The collection of rows corresponding to our body is, in general, a bag, not a set.

■ There is no direct counterpart to our relation-valued attributes (loosely, table-valued columns are not supported, though, bizarrely, columns of type ROW (...) MULTISET are).

■ Rows do not fully conform to our prescription for tuples (as already noted under RM Prescription 9).

We observe too that, in its nomenclature at least, SQL does not adequately distinguish between table values and table variables.

11. Scalar variables

SQL **conforms** (apart from its support for nulls).

12. Tuple variables

SQL **conforms** insofar as it conforms to RM Prescriptions 6 and 9.

13. Relation variables (relvars)

SQL **conforms** (to a greater extent than that to which it conforms to RM Prescriptions 7 and 10), thanks to its support for base tables, views, and declared temporary tables, its counterpart to our real, virtual, and private relvars, respectively. As noted under RM Prescription 7, there is no counterpart in general to our RELATION type generator; however, a base or declared temporary table definition can make use of a construct that is somewhat analogous: namely, an ordered list of $<C,T>$ pairs, where C is a column name and T is the name of the corresponding type (which is not necessarily scalar). Further, no two columns of a given base or declared temporary table are permitted to have the same name. (This latter fact notwithstanding, SQL still attaches significance to the left-to-right order of the columns.)

SQL **fails** because it allows a base table to be "of" some structured type,[1] instead of in terms of an ordered list of $<C,T>$ pairs. Certain operators—in particular, certain *dereferencing* operators—and certain other properties apply to such base tables that do not apply to base tables defined in the more usual way. Thus, SQL effectively supports two different kinds of base tables, a fact we would certainly regard as violating the spirit, if not the letter, of RM Prescription 13. What is more, we would also regard this second kind of base table as contravening RM Prescription 26 (because they violate orthogonality, parsimony, and conceptual integrity); RM Proscription 6 (because they mix logical and physical issues); OO Proscription 2 (because of their support for dereferencing); and possibly other prescriptions and proscriptions as well.

SQL also **fails** inasmuch as, at any isolation level other than SERIALIZABLE, updating a base table is not logically equivalent to a simple relational assignment. The same is also likely to be true if any triggered procedures have been defined for the pertinent base table.

14. Kinds of relvars

SQL **conforms** insofar as it conforms to RM Prescription 13. It **fails** in that it provides no counterpart to our public relvars.

---

1. In order to prevent (or perhaps cause) confusion, it needs to be said that a table in SQL that is "of" type T is not in fact of type T. Rather, the type of such a table—just like that of any other table—is derived from the heading in the usual way.

15. Candidate keys

SQL **fails**. It permits but does not require keys for a base or declared temporary table, and does not even permit them for a view. In addition, SQL permits one key to be a proper superset of another, in which case it is blatantly not a key but a proper superkey.

16. Databases

Strictly speaking, there is no such thing as a database in SQL. Instead, there is something called *SQL-data*, which is "data described by SQL-schemas—data that is under the control of an SQL-implementation in an SQL-environment" [99]. However, some might say that SQL **conforms** to the general intent of RM Prescription 16, inasmuch as "SQL-data" really means database relvars, loosely speaking. Others might say it **fails,** because tables that are "of" some structured type carry certain extra baggage, causing them to violate the uniformity of structure and operators that was a prime objective of the relational model.

17. Transactions

SQL **conforms.**

18. Relational algebra

SQL **conforms** in that (a) all of the prescribed operators are directly or indirectly available, and (b) it is possible to ensure by judicious use of the language that the operands to invocations of these operators are effectively true relations (i.e., they are tables whose columns have distinct names, whose bodies are sets, and whose rows contain no nulls). However, it **fails** in some cases, notably MATCHING and NOT MATCHING, DIVIDEBY, SUMMARIZE, RENAME, and GROUP and UNGROUP, to provide these operators "without excessive circumlocution."

That said, we should note that at the time of writing:

- Many well-known SQL products have failed to implement NATURAL JOIN or JOIN with the USING option. As a result, the SQL analog of our own JOIN operation sometimes involves a very great deal of "excessive circumlocution" indeed (specifically, when tables of high degree are involved).

- Most well-known SQL products have failed to implement the CORRESPONDING versions of UNION, INTERSECT, and EXCEPT. As a result, there is often no direct SQL analog of our UNION, INTERSECT, and MINUS operators (which place no significance on left-to-right column ordering, of course).

- The most important feature of all so far as expressive completeness is concerned—namely, the ability to specify table expressions[1] of arbitrary complexity in the FROM clause—is still absent from some implementations.

19. Relvar names, relation selectors, and recursion

SQL **conforms** with respect to relation selector invocations and recursion. First, a VALUES invocation is a valid table expression. Second, the WITH clause permits a table expression to be given a name and

---

1. The standard SQL term is *query* expression.

for that very name to be referenced in that very expression, thereby supporting what are commonly known as "recursive queries" (which are also supported via CREATE VIEW).

SQL **fails** to permit a table name to be a valid table expression. The current value of a named table can be referenced by writing the word TABLE, or alternatively SELECT * FROM, in front of the name in question; however, we do not regard these features as satisfying this part of RM Prescription 19.

20. User-defined tuple and relation operators

SQL **conforms** to some extent, with its support for nonupdatable views. However, it **fails** in that its view definitions cannot be parameterized. *Note:* Most of the remarks under RM Prescription 7 regarding SQL's support for types of the form ROW (...) MULTISET apply here also, mutatis mutandis.

21. Assignments

SQL **conforms,** more or less, with respect to scalar and tuple assignment (apart from known violations of *The Assignment Principle* and other failures already noted in connection with tuples). It also supports assignment to targets of MULTISET types, including in particular those of types ROW (...) MULTISET. However, it **fails** with respect to relational assignment, because "relvars"—base tables and updatable views, in SQL terms—cannot be directly assigned to; they can only have their current values "modified" via INSERT, DELETE, UPDATE, and MERGE (and even there violations of *The Assignment Principle* can occur).

SQL's conformance includes support for multiple assignment in connection with scalar and tuple assignment, and also in connection with assignment to MULTISET targets. But, crucially, this support does not directly extend to its table update operators INSERT, DELETE, UPDATE, and MERGE.

We observe too that there is a certain anomaly in the SQL provisions for assignment, arising from its support for nulls. To be specific, it is not always the case that, immediately following the assignment SET $X = Y$, the comparison $X = Y$ gives TRUE (in other words, *The Assignment Principle* is violated again). Further, when this anomalous circumstance arises, it is not necessarily the case that Y is null. For example, Y could be a value of some user-defined type T such that $Y.C$ IS NULL gives TRUE for some component (attribute) C of Y, while Y IS NULL is FALSE.

22. Comparisons

SQL **conforms** to this prescription with respect to scalar comparisons. It also conforms with respect to tuple comparisons, subject to failures already noted in connection with tuples, and subject also to the failure that it expressly does support the "tuple"—or, rather, row—comparison operators "<", ">", etc. It also conforms to our prescription for an operator to test membership of a tuple in a relation, via that version of its IN operator that takes a row expression on the left side and a table expression on the right side.

SQL also **conforms** to this prescription with respect to relation comparisons, but only very circuitously (a fact that is slightly odd, since SQL does provide more direct support for multiset comparisons). For example, let tables *T1* and *T2* denote true relations of the same relation type (in *Manifesto* terms). Then an SQL analog of the relation comparison *T1* = *T2* can be expressed as follows:

```
NOT EXISTS ( SELECT * FROM T1 EXCEPT CORRESPONDING SELECT * FROM T2 )
AND
NOT EXISTS ( SELECT * FROM T2 EXCEPT CORRESPONDING SELECT * FROM T1 )
```

23. Integrity constraints

SQL **conforms** with respect to database constraints, insofar as it does permit the definition of such constraints of arbitrary complexity. It also supports a certain degree of constraint inference, via functional dependency analysis. However, it also **fails** on at least two counts: its support for *deferred* constraints, which are checked only when the user "switches on" the necessary checking (end-of-transaction at the latest) by means of SET CONSTRAINTS—all constraint checking is immediate in the *Manifesto*—and its support for updatable views that are specified without WITH CASCADED CHECK OPTION.

For reasons explained in detail in Appendix F, SQL **fails** completely with respect to type constraints. *Note:* Do not be misled by the fact that (as noted in passing in Chapter 3) SQL does include something it calls "domains," and those "domains" do have associated constraints. But those "domains" are not true types—they are nothing to do with true relational domains—and those "domain constraints" are not true type constraints; rather, they are database constraints, in *Manifesto* terms, that happen to have been specified in a rather unorthodox way.

24. Total database predicates

SQL **conforms** insofar as it conforms to RM Prescription 23.

25. Catalog

SQL **conforms** in that its catalogs are themselves collections of tables (meaning table variables, of course).

SQL **fails** to support assignment to those tables for two reasons. First, the tables in question are nonupdatable views (so they are not *really* table variables!); second, SQL in any case has deficient support for relation assignment, as already noted under RM Prescription 21.

26. Language design

SQL **fails** to some considerable extent by most, if not all, of the generally agreed yardsticks of good language design. More specifically, it fails with respect to at least the following measures: conceptual integrity, syntactic consistency, parsimony, and orthogonality.

- It fails with respect to *conceptual integrity* in its treatment of nulls, for example. The originally intended interpretation of nulls when they were first introduced into SQL was "value unknown," and this interpretation accounts for the behavior of nulls in (e.g.) comparisons. Yet SQL sometimes generates nulls in circumstances where such an interpretation is utterly inappropriate. The nulls that result from OUTER JOIN, for example, might perhaps signify "not applicable"; the null that results from attempting to compute the average of an empty set of numbers surely signifies "undefined"; and the null that results from an attempt to sum that same set is just a perverse way of indicating zero. We remind you too that null is also used in SQL to signify "the third truth value" (see the discussion of RM Prescription 1, earlier).

  On another front, SQL claims that its tables, in general, are bags (multisets) of rows; yet the normal union operator on bags is not directly provided, and considerable circumlocution is required to obtain its effect.

  In any case, SQL concepts are not agreeably few, and they include many that in our opinion are not agreeable at all—for example, nulls, three-valued logic, left-to-right column ordering, duplicate rows, anonymous columns, subtables and supertables (see Appendix G), and many others.

- SQL fails with respect to *syntactic consistency* in the various ways it uses AS to give a name to an expression. In some contexts, such as the SELECT and FROM clauses, the expression comes before the AS and the name after. In others, such as the CREATE VIEW statement and the WITH clause, the name comes before and the expression after. And in some cases the AS is optional, while in others it is required.

SQL also fails in this respect in that the keyword TABLE sometimes means any named table (as in the query expression TABLE *T*) and sometimes a base table specifically (as in CREATE TABLE *T*).

SQL also fails in this respect in that some options that are expressed using the keyword WITH have explicit converses using WITHOUT, while others do not. Cursor declarations can be WITH or WITHOUT both HOLD and RETURN. DESCRIBE can be WITH or WITHOUT NESTING. A view definition can be WITH CHECK OPTION but cannot be WITHOUT it. A privilege can be granted WITH GRANT OPTION but cannot be granted WITHOUT it.

By way of another example (based on one in reference [41]), consider the following expressions:

```
SELECT * FROM ( A NATURAL JOIN B ) AS T

SELECT * FROM ( A UNION B ) AS T

TABLE A UNION TABLE B

TABLE A NATURAL JOIN TABLE B

SELECT * FROM A UNION SELECT * FROM B

SELECT * FROM A NATURAL JOIN SELECT * FROM B

( TABLE A ) UNION ( TABLE B )

( TABLE A ) NATURAL JOIN ( TABLE B )

( TABLE A ) AS AA NATURAL JOIN ( TABLE B ) AS BB
```

Some of these expressions are syntactically valid and others not, and it is a nontrivial exercise to figure out or remember which are which.

■ SQL fails with respect to *parsimony* in the remarkable (and regrettable) degree of redundancy—the variety of different ways, that is, sometimes radically different ways, of achieving the same effect—that has been noted by the present authors among others (see, e.g. reference [62]). For example, the plugging of those "holes" in the original SQL language that rendered it relationally incomplete has made all of the following features logically redundant: GROUP BY, HAVING, subqueries, and correlation names. And of these, we venture to suggest that HAVING, at least, is positively undesirable.

■ With respect to *orthogonality,* SQL:1992 had already addressed many of the complaints that very early on made SQL quite notorious among computer languages. However, some violations remained and persist in SQL:2003, along with a few more that were introduced in SQL:1999 (e.g., restrictions on the use of ROW types). For example:

  ▪ The availability of the CASCADE option of DROP depends on the kind of object being dropped.

  ▪ It is not possible to define subtypes of built-in types or DISTINCT types.

  ▪ The VALUES ARE SYSTEM GENERATED feature in column definitions is available only for base tables that are "of" a user-defined type. At least on the face of it, it would appear that these two features, "of" and VALUES ARE SYSTEM GENERATED, should be orthogonal.

The foregoing list of criticisms is not exhaustive.

RM PROSCRIPTIONS

1. No attribute ordering

SQL **fails**. Examples of where SQL attaches significance to the left-to-right order of columns include:

- SELECT *

- UNION, INTERSECT, EXCEPT (without CORRESPONDING in each case)

- CREATE VIEW (if column names are specified)

- INSERT (if no column names are specified)

- Row comparisons and assignments

- IN (of rows and tables)

- VALUES

2. No tuple ordering

SQL **conforms**.

3. No duplicate tuples

SQL **fails**. Duplicate rows can arise in at least the following ways:

- SELECT without DISTINCT

- INSERT into a base table for which no candidate key is specified

- UNION ALL

- Specifying the same row more than once in an invocation of VALUES

4. No nulls

SQL **fails**.

5. No nullological mistakes

SQL **fails**. Examples:

- Requiring at least one column in every table

- Requiring at least one expression in the SELECT clause

- Requiring at least one column in every key

Note: RM Proscription 5 specifically addresses only tables and keys, but we note here for purposes of reference certain further nullological mistakes in SQL:

- Requiring at least one table reference in the FROM clause[1]

- Requiring at least one item in ORDER BY (though in this case the desired effect can be obtained by omitting the clause)

- Several errors in the handling of empty tables (for example, treating such a table as a null in the context of a scalar subquery)

6. No internal-level constructs

SQL **conforms**.

7. No tuple-level operations

SQL **fails**. Its FETCH operation (not to be confused with our TUPLE FROM operator) retrieves an individual row. Worse, its DELETE and UPDATE WHERE CURRENT OF CURSOR operations operate on individual rows.

8. No composite attributes

SQL **conforms**.

9. No domain check override

SQL **conforms**.

10. Not SQL

SQL **fails**. The language defined in the SQL specification is called SQL.

OO PRESCRIPTIONS

1. Compile-time type checking

SQL **conforms**.

2. Type inheritance (conditional)

SQL **fails** by definition here, because it does not abide by the inheritance model described in Part IV of this book. We can be more specific than this, however, and we will be under the various IM

---

1. Some implementations commendably do not adhere to this restriction.

Prescriptions later in this appendix.

3. Computational completeness

SQL **conforms** via its Persistent Stored Modules feature, SQL/PSM.

4. Explicit transaction boundaries

SQL **conforms,** almost, with respect to transaction termination, but **fails** with respect to transaction initiation, which is allowed (and in some implementations required) to be implicit. *Note:* The reason for that "almost" qualifier is explained in Chapter 8.

5. Nested transactions

SQL **fails.** It does provide some analogous and useful functionality by means of its *savepoint* feature, but establishing a savepoint is not the same as starting a transaction [96]. In any case, one of the purposes of being able to nest transactions is to allow a unit of work to be specified independently of whether that unit is to be executed as an outermost transaction or as part of some encompassing transaction. Starting a transaction and establishing a savepoint are distinct operations in SQL, and they use different syntax.

6. Aggregate operators and empty sets

SQL **fails,** because SUM, AVG, MAX, MIN, EVERY, and ANY all incorrectly return null if invoked on an empty argument. *Note:* For simplicity we ignore here the additional aggregate operators introduced with what was originally called "SQL/OLAP" (see reference [76]), which have since been folded into Part 2 of the standard, "SQL/Foundation."

OO PROSCRIPTIONS

1. Relvars are not domains

It might be argued that SQL **conforms,** despite its support for what we called "the second kind of base table" under RM Prescription 13 earlier in this appendix, because it turns out that rows in such tables are just rows and not values of the type that the table is declared to be "of." We prefer to say it **fails,** because there is no doubt that support for that second kind of base table was motivated by a desire to perceive object classes as analogous to relvars. For example, an operator is provided to derive a value of the "of" type from a given row, and the system-generated REF values in the "self-referencing column" of such a table are intended to be analogous to object IDs (they thus prevent SQL from supporting type inheritance according to the model proposed in this book).

2. No object IDs

Again it might be argued the SQL **conforms,** because even though (to repeat) its system-generated REF values do look very much like object IDs, they also manage not quite to violate the letter of OO Proscription 2. We prefer to say it **fails,** for the reason given in connection with OO Proscription 1.

RM VERY STRONG SUGGESTIONS

1. System keys

SQL **conforms,** via its "identity columns" feature (new in SQL:2003), and also to some extent via its VALUES ARE SYSTEM GENERATED feature which, as we have already observed under RM Prescription 26, is not as generally available as we feel it might be. It has no analog of our suggested TAG operator.

2. Foreign keys

SQL **conforms.**

3. Candidate key inference

SQL **conforms** insofar as it conforms to RM Prescription 15. *Note:* Although SQL does require candidate keys to be inferred for query results, it makes only limited use of the results of such inference. The details are beyond the scope of this appendix.

4. Transition constraints

SQL **fails.** *Note:* It might be possible to use CREATE TRIGGER to achieve some (not all) of the same functionality as a general declarative transition constraint, but CREATE TRIGGER is at least partly procedural in nature. In particular, it specifies when the triggered procedure is to be invoked (e.g., ON UPDATE). One consequence is that it might be possible—for example—to subvert an UPDATE triggered procedure by executing a DELETE followed by an INSERT instead of executing an UPDATE per se.

5. Quota queries

SQL **conforms** via its support for the functions RANK and DENSE_RANK.

6. Generalized transitive closure

SQL **conforms,** via its support for recursion in WITH clauses and view definitions.

7. User-defined generic operators

SQL **fails.**

8. SQL migration

Not applicable (SQL is not a valid **D**).

OO VERY STRONG SUGGESTIONS

1. Type inheritance

SQL necessarily **fails,** because it fails on OO Prescription 2.

2. Types and operators unbundled

SQL partly **conforms** and partly **fails**. Some operators (namely, those specifically designated as "methods") must be bundled, others must not.

3. Single-level store

SQL **conforms** to some extent, through its feature SQL/PSM, but **fails** when used as an "embedded data sublanguage."

IM PRESCRIPTIONS

1. Types are sets

SQL **conforms**.

2. Subtypes are subsets

SQL **conforms,** but in a rather peculiar way, inasmuch as the set of all values of type *T* is not fully known until all proper subtypes of *T* have been defined. *Note:* The requirement that proper subtypes be proper subsets is not really supported, however, since SQL does not support type constraints (as we saw under RM Prescription 23).

3. "Subtype of" is reflexive

SQL **conforms**.

4. Proper subtypes

SQL **conforms,** except as noted under IM Prescription 2.

5. "Subtype of" is transitive

SQL **conforms**.

6. Immediate subtypes

SQL **conforms** (but it uses the term "direct" in place of the more apt "immediate").

7. Root types disjoint

SQL **conforms** for single inheritance. It also conforms for multiple inheritance insofar as it supports multiple inheritance at all (which is not very far—see IM Prescription 22, later). *Note:* The SQL term for *root type* is "maximal supertype" (not to be confused with a maximal type in the sense of IM Prescription 20). Oddly, the SQL term for *leaf type* is not "minimal subtype" but "leaf type."

8. Scalar values with inheritance

SQL **conforms** for single inheritance. It also conforms for multiple inheritance, insofar as it supports multiple inheritance at all.

9. Scalar variables with inheritance

SQL **conforms**.

10. Specialization by constraint

SQL **fails** completely; in fact, as we saw earlier, it does not support type constraints at all.

11. Assignment with inheritance

SQL **conforms**.

12. Equality etc. with inheritance

SQL necessarily **fails,** owing to its failure on RM Prescription 8. What is more—in terms of our running example from Chapter 14—SQL would even allow a comparison between an ellipse and a polygon to give TRUE. In other words, there is no requirement that the most specific types be the same in order for the comparison to give TRUE.

13. Join etc. with inheritance

SQL **conforms** insofar as it conforms to IM Prescription 12.

14. TREAT

SQL **conforms** inasmuch as it does support a TREAT operator (in fact the operator in question is called TREAT). However, it **fails** to support a TREAT pseudovariable.

15. Type testing

SQL **conforms**. Here is the SQL analog of our IS_*T*(*X*):

```
TYPE ( X ) [ IS ] OF ( T )
```

The optional IS is a noiseword. The expression following OF is a parenthesized commalist of <*type specification*>s (possibly including specifications of the form TYPE (<*exp*>), so SQL also supports an analog of our IS_SAME_TYPE_AS (*Y*,*X*)). Analogous remarks apply to all of the other operators discussed in this subsection (see below).

   SQL also supports an analog of our relational operator *R*:IS_*T*(*A*). However, its support is clumsy. Let *R* denote a relation with attributes *A*, *B*, and *C*. Then the SQL analog of our *R*:IS_*T*(*A*) looks like this:

```
SELECT DISTINCT TREAT A AS T AS A, B, C
FROM    R
WHERE   TYPE ( A ) IS OF ( T )
```

Such expressions become increasingly cumbersome as the number of attributes increases.

   SQL also supports "most specific type" analogs of the foregoing operators. Here is the SQL analog of IS_MS_*T*(*X*):

```
TYPE ( X ) [ IS ] OF ( ONLY T )
```

(though we cannot help remarking that the keyword ONLY here is very misleading if *T* is not a root type). And—with the same assumptions as before—here is the SQL analog of *R*:IS_MS_*T*(*A*):

```
SELECT DISTINCT TREAT A AS T AS A, B, C
FROM   R
WHERE  TYPE ( A ) IS OF ( ONLY T )
```

SQL also provides an operator that returns the most specific type of its argument as a character string.

16. Read-only operator inheritance and value substitutability

SQL **conforms**.

17. Operator signatures

In our discussion of IM Prescription 17 in Chapter 14, we suggested that all arguments to a given operator invocation should participate equally in the run-time binding process. SQL nearly conformed to this suggestion when inheritance was first introduced (in SQL:1999) but was changed at the eleventh hour. The reason for the change was that Java and C++, the two most likely host languages for applications using the "object" portions of SQL, themselves do not conform to the suggestion; rather, they perform run-time binding on the basis of the first argument only. As a result, SQL now supports both (a) Java- and C++-style *methods* (sometimes called "selfish methods"), for which the binding process is performed at run time on the basis of the *most specific* type of the first argument only, and (b) "nonmethod" operators called *functions* and *procedures,* for which the binding process is performed at compile time on the basis (necessarily) of the *declared* types of all arguments. Thus, SQL **fails** on this part of IM Prescription (a) for methods (because of their "selfish" nature) and (b) for functions and procedures (because here there is no run-time binding at all).

With regard to the different kinds of signatures required by IM Prescription 17, SQL's methods **conform** fully, while its functions and procedures do so only partially (in effect, specification and version signatures are combined in the latter case).

SQL has no requirement that if several versions of a given operator exist under the covers, then those versions all implement the same semantics.

18. Read-only parameters to update operators

SQL **conforms**.

19. Update operator inheritance and variable substitutability

SQL **fails**. It requires update operators to be inherited unconditionally.

20. Union, dummy, and maximal and minimal types

Not clear. SQL does support both (a) INSTANTIABLE types and NOT INSTANTIABLE types and (b) types that have a declared representation and types that do not. An INSTANTIABLE type with a declared representation is the straightforward case, of course. A NOT INSTANTIABLE type might correspond to our union type (regular or dummy depending on whether it has a declared representation or not), though it is hard to be sure. An INSTANTIABLE type with no proper supertype and no declared representation seems to be a type with exactly one value, like a **Tutorial D** type with a *<possrep def>* that contains no *<possrep component def>*s. An INSTANTIABLE nonroot type that adds no attributes to its inherited representation appears to be the degenerate case of subtyping by extension whereby the subtype does not actually "extend" its supertype at all. Perhaps such a subtype might be used for cases where specialization by constraint would be appropriate, if only it were available. But the responsibility for avoiding nonsenses such as noncircular circles would then lie with the type user instead of the type definer.

21. Tuple/relation subtypes and supertypes

SQL **conforms** with respect to tuples. Having no relation type generator at all, it obviously **fails** with respect to relations. (We remark, however, that SQL does support array and multiset subtypes and supertypes, and these constructs are defined in a manner analogous to the way the *Manifesto* defines tuple and relation subtypes and supertypes. Thus, for example, the type T' MULTISET is a subtype of the type T MULTISET if and only if T' is a subtype of T.)

22. Tuple/relation values with inheritance

SQL **conforms** with respect to tuples, albeit **vacuously,** inasmuch as tuple parameters to user-defined operators are not supported[1] (in fact the support is vacuous anyway because most implementations at the time of writing do not support row types at all). Having no relation type generator at all, it obviously **fails** with respect to relations.

23. Maximal and minimal tuple/relation types

SQL **fails**.

24. Tuple/relation most specific types

SQL **conforms** with respect to tuples, vacuously. Having no relation type generator at all, it obviously **fails** with respect to relations.

25. Tuple/relation variables with inheritance

SQL **conforms** with respect to tuples. Having no relation type generator at all, it obviously **fails** with respect to relations.

---

1. This conformance corresponds to the only kind of multiple inheritance supported by SQL. (Actually, SQL is usually described as not supporting multiple inheritance at all; however, Chapter 16 of the present book shows that multiple inheritance is necessarily supported to some degree, even if only implicitly, if (a) single inheritance for scalar types, and (b) tuple and/or relation types, are both supported.)

Appendix I

A Grammar for Tutorial D

In this appendix we present the **Tutorial D** production rules in alphabetical order, for ease of reference. Extensions from Part IV to deal with inheritance are included. However, the following are not:

- Features defined (or merely hinted at, in some cases) in Chapter 5 in prose form instead of by means of formal production rules

- Features merely "suggested" in Chapter 10

- Rules regarding the use of an *<attribute ref>* in the inheritance extensions (e.g., in a *<scalar type test>*) wherever a *<selector inv>* is permitted

- Rules regarding the use of a TREAT invocation as a pseudovariable reference

In connection with the last of these, here for reference is a complete list of syntactic categories not explicitly defined in this appendix:

<array var name>	<possrep name>
<attribute assign>	<relation var name>
<attribute name>	<scalar selector inv>
<bool exp>	<scalar var name>
<character string literal>	<statement name>
<constraint name>	<THE_ op name>
<identifier>	<THE_ pv name>
<integer exp>	<tuple var name>
<introduced name>	<user op name>
<parameter name>	<user scalar type name>
<possrep component assign>	<version name>
<possrep component name>	

For an explanation of the conventions used in the metalanguage (e.g., its use of syntactic categories of the form <... *list*> and <... *commalist*>), see the introductory remarks in Chapter 5.

———— ◆◆◆◆◆ ————

```
<additional constraint def>
    ::=   CONSTRAINT <bool exp>

<agg op inv>
    ::=   <agg op name> ( [ <integer exp>, ] <relation exp> [, <attribute ref> ] )

<agg op name>
    ::=   COUNT | SUM | AVG | MAX | MIN
          | AND | OR | XOR | EXACTLY | UNION | D_UNION | INTERSECT
```

```
<application relation var def>
     ::=   VAR <relation var name> <private or public> <relation type or init value>
            <candidate key def list>

<argument>
     ::=   <exp>

<array cardinality>
     ::=   COUNT ( <array var ref> )

<array target>
     ::=   <array var ref>

<array var def>
     ::=   VAR <array var name> ARRAY <tuple type>

<array var ref>
     ::=   <array var name>

<assign>
     ::=   <scalar assign> | <tuple assign> | <relation assign>

<assignment>
     ::=   <assign commalist>

<attribute>
     ::=   <attribute name> <type>

<attribute extractor inv>
     ::=   <attribute ref> FROM <tuple exp>

<attribute ref>
     ::=   <attribute name>

<attribute target>
     ::=   <attribute ref> | <attribute THE_ pv ref>

<attribute THE_ pv ref>
     ::=   <THE_ pv name> ( <attribute target> )

<attribute treat>
     ::=   TREAT_AS_<scalar type name> ( <attribute ref> )
          | TREAT_AS_SAME_TYPE_AS ( <exp> , <attribute ref> )

<attribute type test>
     ::=   IS_<scalar type name> ( <attribute ref> )
          | IS_SAME_TYPE_AS ( <exp> , <attribute ref> )

<begin transaction>
     ::=   BEGIN TRANSACTION
```

```
<built-in relation op inv>
    ::=   <relation selector inv> | <THE_ op inv> | <attribute extractor inv> | <project>
          | <n-adic other built-in relation op inv>
          | <monadic or dyadic other built-in relation op inv>

<built-in scalar op inv>
    ::=   <scalar selector inv> | <THE_ op inv> | <attribute extractor inv> | <agg op inv>
          | <scalar type test> | <scalar treat>
          | ... plus the usual possibilities

<built-in scalar type name>
    ::=   INTEGER | RATIONAL | CHARACTER | CHAR | BOOLEAN

<built-in tuple op inv>
    ::=   <tuple selector inv> | <THE_ op inv> | <attribute extractor inv>
          | <tuple extractor inv> | <tuple project> | <n-adic other built-in tuple op inv>
          | <monadic or dyadic other built-in tuple op inv>

<call>
    ::=   CALL <user op inv>

<candidate key def>
    ::=   KEY { [ ALL BUT ] <attribute ref commalist> }

<case>
    ::=   CASE ; <when def list> [ ELSE <statement> ] END CASE

<commit>
    ::=   COMMIT

<compose>
    ::=   <relation exp> COMPOSE <relation exp>

<compound statement body>
    ::=   BEGIN ; <statement list> END

<constraint def>
    ::=   CONSTRAINT <constraint name> <bool exp>

<constraint drop>
    ::=   DROP CONSTRAINT <constraint name>

<database relation var def>
    ::=   <real relation var def> | <virtual relation var def>

<derived possrep component def>
    ::=   <possrep component name> = <exp>

<derived possrep def>
    ::=   POSSREP [ <possrep name> ] { <derived possrep component def commalist> }
```

```
<direction>
     ::=   ASC | DESC

<divide>
     ::=   <relation exp> DIVIDEBY <relation exp> <per>

<do>
     ::=   [ <statement name> : ] DO <scalar var ref> := <integer exp> TO <integer exp> ;
           <statement> END DO

<dyadic disjoint union>
     ::=   <relation exp> D_UNION <relation exp>

<dyadic intersect>
     ::=   <relation exp> INTERSECT <relation exp>

<dyadic join>
     ::=   <relation exp> JOIN <relation exp>

<dyadic other built-in relation op inv>
     ::=   <dyadic union> | <dyadic disjoint union> | <dyadic intersect> | <minus>
         | <dyadic join> | <compose> | <semijoin> | <semiminus> | <divide> | <summarize>

<dyadic other built-in tuple op inv>
     ::=   <dyadic tuple union> | <tuple compose>

<dyadic tuple union>
     ::=   <tuple exp> UNION <tuple exp>

<dyadic union>
     ::=   <relation exp> UNION <relation exp>

<exp>
     ::=   <scalar exp> | <nonscalar exp>

<extend>
     ::=   EXTEND <relation exp> ADD ( <extend add commalist> )

<extend add>
     ::=   <exp> AS <introduced name>

<filter and cast>
     ::=   <relation exp> : <attribute type test>

<group>
     ::=   <relation exp> GROUP ( <grouping commalist> )

<grouping>
     ::=   { [ ALL BUT ] <attribute ref commalist> } AS <introduced name>

<heading>
     ::=   { <attribute commalist> }
```

```
<if>
    ::=    IF <bool exp> THEN <statement> [ ELSE <statement> ] END IF

<is def>
    ::=    <single inheritance is def> | <multiple inheritance is def>

<leave>
    ::=    LEAVE <statement name>

<minus>
    ::=    <relation exp> MINUS <relation exp>

<monadic or dyadic other built-in relation op inv>
    ::=    <monadic other built-in relation op inv> | <dyadic other built-in relation op inv>

<monadic or dyadic other built-in tuple op inv>
    ::=    <monadic other built-in tuple op inv> | <dyadic other built-in tuple op inv>

<monadic other built-in relation op inv>
    ::=    <rename> | <where> | <extend> | <wrap> | <unwrap> | <group> | <ungroup>
           | <substitute> | <tclose> | <relation treat> | <filter and cast>

<monadic other built-in tuple op inv>
    ::=    <tuple rename> | <tuple extend> | <tuple wrap> | <tuple unwrap>
           | <tuple substitute> | <tuple treat>

<multiple inheritance is def>
    ::=    IS { <scalar type name commalist> <derived possrep def list> }

<n-adic disjoint union>
    ::=    D_UNION [ <heading> ] { <relation exp commalist> }

<n-adic intersect>
    ::=    INTERSECT [ <heading> ] { <relation exp commalist> }

<n-adic join>
    ::=    JOIN { <relation exp commalist> }

<n-adic other built-in relation op inv>
    ::=    <n-adic union> | <n-adic disjoint union> | <n-adic intersect> | <n-adic join>

<n-adic other built-in tuple op inv>
    ::=    <n-adic tuple union>

<n-adic tuple union>
    ::=    UNION { <tuple exp commalist> }

<n-adic union>
    ::=    UNION [ <heading> ] { <relation exp commalist> }
```

```
<name intro>
    ::=    <exp> AS <introduced name>

<no op>
    ::=    ... an empty string

<nonscalar exp>
    ::=    <tuple exp> | <relation exp>

<order item>
    ::=    <direction> <attribute ref>

<parameter def>
    ::=    <parameter name> <type>

<per>
    ::=    PER ( <relation exp> [, <relation exp> ] )

<per or by>
    ::=    <per> | BY { [ ALL BUT ] <attribute ref commalist> }

<possrep component def>
    ::=    <possrep component name> <type>

<possrep component ref>
    ::=    <possrep component name>

<possrep component target>
    ::=    <possrep component ref> | <possrep THE_ pv ref>

<possrep constraint def>
    ::=    CONSTRAINT <bool exp>

<possrep def>
    ::=    POSSREP [ <possrep name> ]
                { <possrep component def commalist> [ <possrep constraint def> ] }

<possrep or specialization details>
    ::=    <possrep def list>
         | <additional constraint def> [ <derived possrep def list> ]

<possrep THE_ pv ref>
    ::=    <THE_ pv name> ( <possrep component target> )

<previously defined statement body>
    ::=    <assignment>
         | <user op def> | <user op drop> | <user scalar type def> | <user scalar type drop>
         | <scalar var def> | <tuple var def> | <relation var def> | <relation var drop>
         | <constraint def> | <constraint drop>
         | <array var def> | <relation get> | <relation set>
```

```
<private or public>
    ::=   PRIVATE | PUBLIC

<project>
    ::=   <relation exp> { [ ALL BUT ] <attribute ref commalist> }

<real or base>
    ::=   REAL | BASE

<real relation var def>
    ::=   VAR <relation var name> <real or base> <relation type or init value>
            <candidate key def list>

<relation assign>
    ::=   <relation target> := <relation exp>
        | <relation insert> | <relation delete> | <relation update>

<relation comp>
    ::=   <relation exp> <relation comp op> <relation exp>

<relation comp op>
    ::=   = | ≠ | ‖<‖ | ‖≤‖ | ‖>‖ | ‖≥‖

<relation delete>
    ::=   DELETE <relation target> [ WHERE <bool exp> ]

<relation exp>
    ::=   <relation with exp> | <relation nonwith exp>

<relation get>
    ::=   LOAD <array target> FROM <relation exp> ORDER ( <order item commalist> )

<relation insert>
    ::=   INSERT <relation target> <relation exp>

<relation nonwith exp>
    ::=   <relation var ref> | <relation op inv> | ( <relation exp> )

<relation op inv>
    ::=   <user op inv> | <built-in relation op inv>

<relation selector inv>
    ::=   RELATION [ <heading> ] { <tuple exp commalist> } | TABLE_DEE | TABLE_DUM

<relation set>
    ::=   LOAD <relation target> FROM <array var ref>

<relation target>
    ::=   <relation var ref> | <relation THE_ pv ref>

<relation THE_ pv ref>
    ::=   <THE_ pv name> ( <scalar target> )
```

```
<relation treat>
    ::=   TREAT_AS_SAME_TYPE_AS ( <relation exp> , <relation exp> )
        | <relation exp> <attribute treat>

<relation type>
    ::=   <relation type name> | SAME_TYPE_AS ( <relation exp> )
        | RELATION SAME_HEADING_AS ( <nonscalar exp> )

<relation type name>
    ::=   RELATION <heading>

<relation type or init value>
    ::=   <relation type> | INIT ( <relation exp> ) | <relation type> INIT ( <relation exp> )

<relation update>
    ::=   UPDATE <relation target> [ WHERE <bool exp> ] ( <attribute assign commalist> )

<relation var def>
    ::=   <database relation var def> | <application relation var def>

<relation var drop>
    ::=   DROP VAR <relation var ref>

<relation var ref>
    ::=   <relation var name>

<relation with exp>
    ::=   WITH <name intro commalist> : <relation exp>

<rename>
    ::=   <relation exp> RENAME ( <renaming commalist> )

<renaming>
    ::=   <attribute ref> AS <introduced name>
        | PREFIX <character string literal> AS <character string literal>
        | SUFFIX <character string literal> AS <character string literal>

<return>
    ::=   RETURN [ <exp> ]

<rollback>
    ::=   ROLLBACK

<scalar assign>
    ::=   <scalar target> := <scalar exp> | <scalar update>

<scalar comp>
    ::=   <scalar exp> <scalar comp op> <scalar exp>

<scalar comp op>
    ::=   = | ≠ | < | ≤ | > | ≥
```

```
<scalar exp>
    ::=   <scalar with exp> | <scalar nonwith exp>

<scalar nonwith exp>
    ::=   <scalar var ref> | <scalar op inv> | ( <scalar exp> )

<scalar op inv>
    ::=   <user op inv> | <built-in scalar op inv>

<scalar target>
    ::=   <scalar var ref> | <scalar THE_ pv ref>

<scalar THE_ pv ref>
    ::=   <THE_ pv name> ( <scalar target> )

<scalar treat>
    ::=   TREAT_AS_<scalar type name> ( <scalar exp> )
        | TREAT_AS_SAME_TYPE_AS ( <scalar exp> , <scalar exp> )

<scalar type>
    ::=   <scalar type name> | SAME_TYPE_AS ( <scalar exp> )

<scalar type name>
    ::=   <user scalar type name> | <built-in scalar type name>

<scalar type or init value>
    ::=   <scalar type> | INIT ( <scalar exp> ) | <scalar type> INIT ( <scalar exp> )

<scalar type test>
    ::=   IS_<scalar type name> ( <scalar exp> ) | IS_SAME_TYPE_AS ( <exp> , <exp> )

<scalar update>
    ::=   UPDATE <scalar target> ( <possrep component assign commalist> )

<scalar var def>
    ::=   VAR <scalar var name> <scalar type or init value>

<scalar var ref>
    ::=   <scalar var name>

<scalar with exp>
    ::=   WITH <name intro commalist> : <scalar exp>

<selector inv>
    ::=   <scalar selector inv> | <tuple selector inv> | <relation selector inv>

<semijoin>
    ::=   <relation exp> SEMIJOIN <relation exp>
        | <relation exp> MATCHING <relation exp>
```

```
<semiminus>
    ::=   <relation exp> SEMIMINUS <relation exp>
        | <relation exp> NOT MATCHING <relation exp>

<single inheritance is def>
    ::=   IS { <scalar type name> <possrep or specialization details> }

<statement>
    ::=   <statement body> ;

<statement body>
    ::=   <previously defined statement body> | <begin transaction> | <commit> | <rollback>
        | <call> | <return> | <case> | <if> | <do> | <while> | <leave> | <no op>
        | <compound statement body>

<subscript>
    ::=   <integer exp>

<substitute>
    ::=   UPDATE <relation exp> ( <attribute assign commalist> )

<summarize>
    ::=   SUMMARIZE <relation exp> [ <per or by> ] ADD ( <summarize add commalist> )

<summarize add>
    ::=   <summary> AS <introduced name>

<summary>
    ::=   <summary spec> ( [ <integer exp>, ] [ <scalar exp> ] )

<summary spec>
    ::=   COUNT | COUNTD | SUM | SUMD | AVG | AVGD | MAX | MIN
        | AND | OR | XOR | EXACTLY | EXACTLYD | UNION | D_UNION | INTERSECT

<synonym def>
    ::=   SYNONYMS { <user op name commalist> }

<tclose>
    ::=   TCLOSE <relation exp>

<THE_ op inv>
    ::=   <THE_ op name> ( <scalar exp> )

<tuple assign>
    ::=   <tuple target> := <tuple exp> | <tuple update>

<tuple comp>
    ::=   <tuple exp> <tuple comp op> <tuple exp>
        | <tuple exp> ∈ <relation exp> | <tuple exp> ∉ <relation exp>

<tuple comp op>
    ::=   = | ≠
```

```
<tuple component>
    ::=    <attribute ref> <exp>

<tuple compose>
    ::=    <tuple exp> COMPOSE <tuple exp>

<tuple exp>
    ::=    <tuple with exp> | <tuple nonwith exp>
        | <array var ref> ( <subscript> )

<tuple extend>
    ::=    EXTEND <tuple exp> ADD ( <extend add commalist> )

<tuple extractor inv>
    ::=    TUPLE FROM <relation exp>

<tuple nonwith exp>
    ::=    <tuple var ref> | <tuple op inv> | ( <tuple exp> )

<tuple op inv>
    ::=    <user op inv> | <built-in tuple op inv>

<tuple project>
    ::=    <tuple exp> { [ ALL BUT ] <attribute ref commalist> }

<tuple rename>
    ::=    <tuple exp> RENAME ( <renaming commalist> )

<tuple selector inv>
    ::=    TUPLE { <tuple component commalist> }

<tuple substitute>
    ::=    UPDATE <tuple exp> ( <attribute assign commalist> )

<tuple target>
    ::=    <tuple var ref> | <tuple THE_ pv ref>

<tuple THE_ pv ref>
    ::=    <THE_ pv name> ( <scalar target> )

<tuple treat>
    ::=    TREAT_AS_SAME_TYPE_AS ( <tuple exp> , <tuple exp> )
        | <tuple exp> <attribute treat>

<tuple type>
    ::=    <tuple type name> | SAME_TYPE_AS ( <tuple exp> )
        | TUPLE SAME_HEADING_AS ( <nonscalar exp> )

<tuple type name>
    ::=    TUPLE <heading>
```

```
<tuple type or init value>
    ::=   <tuple type> | INIT ( <tuple exp> ) | <tuple type> INIT ( <tuple exp> )

<tuple unwrap>
    ::=   <tuple exp> UNWRAP ( <unwrapping commalist> )

<tuple update>
    ::=   UPDATE <tuple target> ( <attribute assign commalist> )

<tuple var def>
    ::=   VAR <tuple var name> <tuple type or init value>

<tuple var ref>
    ::=   <tuple var name>

<tuple with exp>
    ::=   WITH <name intro commalist> : <tuple exp>

<tuple wrap>
    ::=   <tuple exp> WRAP ( <wrapping commalist> )

<type>
    ::=   <scalar type> | <tuple type> | <relation type>

<ungroup>
    ::=   <relation exp> UNGROUP ( <ungrouping commalist> )

<ungrouping>
    ::=   <attribute ref>

<unwrap>
    ::=   <relation exp> UNWRAP ( <unwrapping commalist> )

<unwrapping>
    ::=   <attribute ref>

<user op def>
    ::=   <user update op def> | <user read-only op def>

<user op drop>
    ::=   DROP OPERATOR <user op name>

<user op inv>
    ::=   <user op name> ( <argument commalist> )

<user read-only op def>
    ::=   OPERATOR <user op name> ( <parameter def commalist> ) RETURNS <type>
          [ <synonym def> ] [ VERSION <version name> ] ;
          [ <statement> ]
        END OPERATOR
```

```
<user scalar nonroot type def>
    ::=   TYPE <user scalar type name> [ ORDINAL ] [ UNION ] <is def>

<user scalar root type def>
    ::=   TYPE <user scalar type name> [ ORDINAL ] [ UNION ] <possrep def list>

<user scalar type def>
    ::=   <user scalar root type def>
        | <user scalar nonroot type def>

<user scalar type drop>
    ::=   DROP TYPE <user scalar type name>

<user update op def>
    ::=   OPERATOR <user op name> ( <parameter def commalist> )
             UPDATES { [ ALL BUT ] <parameter name commalist> }
          [ <synonym def> ] [ VERSION <version name> ] ;
          [ <statement> ]
          END OPERATOR

<user scalar nonroot type def>
    ::=   TYPE <user scalar type name> [ ORDINAL ] [ UNION ] <is def>

<virtual relation var def>
    ::=   VAR <relation var name> VIRTUAL ( <relation exp> ) <candidate key def list>

<when def>
    ::=   WHEN <bool exp> THEN <statement>

<where>
    ::=   <relation exp> WHERE <bool exp>

<while>
    ::=   [ <statement name> : ] WHILE <bool exp> ; <statement> END WHILE

<wrap>
    ::=   <relation exp> WRAP ( <wrapping commalist> )

<wrapping>
    ::=   { [ ALL BUT ] <attribute ref commalist> } AS <introduced name>
```

Appendix J

R e f e r e n c e s   a n d   B i b l i o g r a p h y

This final appendix provides a consolidated and annotated list of references for the entire book. We should immediately admit that some of the annotation is rather opinionated, in that it includes commentary of a critical nature (sometimes positive and sometimes negative). We should also apologize for the embarrassingly large number of references to publications by ourselves; such a state of affairs is almost unavoidable, however, given the nature of the book and of our subject.

Note: In addition to the references explicitly mentioned in what follows, other relevant material can be found on the websites *www.thethirdmanifesto.com* and *www.dbdebunk.com*.

1.   Anon.: Private communication (March 1999).

This item is discussed in detail in Appendix G.

2.   Malcolm Atkinson, François Bancilhon, David DeWitt, Klaus Dittrich, David Maier, and Stanley Zdonik: "The Object-Oriented Database System Manifesto," Proc. 1st International Conference on Deductive and Object-Oriented Databases, Kyoto, Japan (1989). New York, N.Y.: Elsevier Science (1990).

Like our own *Manifesto,* this reference proposes a foundation for future DBMSs. As noted in Chapter 1, however, it virtually ignores the relational model; in fact, it does not seem to take the idea of a model, as such, very seriously at all. To quote: "With respect to the specification of the system, we are taking a Darwinian approach: We hope that, out of the set of experimental prototypes being built, a fit model will emerge. We also hope that viable implementation technology for that model will evolve simultaneously." In other words, the authors are suggesting that the code should be written first, and that a model might possibly be developed later by abstracting from that code. By contrast, we believe it would be better to develop the model first (which is what happened in the relational case, of course).

Be that as it may, the paper goes on to propose the following as *mandatory* features—i.e., features that, it suggests, must be supported if the DBMS in question is to deserve the label "object-oriented"):

1. Collections
2. Object IDs
3. Encapsulation
4. Types or classes
5. Inheritance
6. Late binding
7. Computational completeness

8. User-defined types
9. Persistence
10. Large databases
11. Concurrency
12. Recovery
13. Ad hoc query

It also discusses certain *optional* features, including multiple inheritance and compile-time type checking; certain *open* features, including "programming paradigm" ("we see no reason why we should impose one programming paradigm more than another: the logic programming style, the functional programming style, or the imperative programming style could all be chosen"); and certain features on which the authors could reach no consensus, including—a little surprisingly, considering their importance—views and integrity constraints.

Here in a nutshell are our own positions on the proposed mandatory features (only). Please note that our comments are based on the premise that the object of the exercise is to define features of a good, genuine, general-purpose DBMS. We do not deny that the features mentioned might be useful for a highly specialized DBMS that is tied to some specific application area such as CAD/CAM, with no need for (say) integrity constraint support—but then we would question whether such a system is truly a DBMS, as that term is usually understood (see the annotation to references [9] and [100]).

- We agree that Numbers 8 and (probably) 5 are important. Number 4 is implied by Number 8. Number 6 is more or less implied by Number 5 (and therefore probably important too), but it is really an implementation matter, not part of the model (it is what we called *run-time* binding in Chapter 14). We also agree with Number 7.

- We agree that Numbers 10-13 are important, but they are independent of whether the system is object-oriented, relational, or something else entirely. (The point is worth repeating from Chapter 6, however, that ad hoc query support in particular can be difficult to provide in a pure object system, because it clashes with the goal of encapsulation and the idea that all access has to be by means of predefined methods. We note too that providing many different data structures at the logical level, as object systems typically do, inevitably makes the query interface, if any, more complicated. See reference [17] for an illustration of this point and reference [57] for an elaboration of the argument.)

- With regard to Numbers 1 and 9, the only kind of "collection" we really want, and certainly the only kind of data construct we want to possess the property of "persistence," is, very specifically, the database relvar. This reference, by contrast, argues for the "persistence orthogonal to type" idea [3].

- We think the emphasis on encapsulation (Number 3) is slightly off base. What is important is to distinguish between type and representation (and hence, in database terms, to achieve data independence [86]). After all, unencapsulated relations can provide just as much data independence, in principle, as encapsulated objects can [76].

- We reject Number 2 outright [59-60].

We should add that—and it is to the credit of the authors that they recognize as much—their paper was never really intended to be more than a stake in the ground: "We have taken a position, not so much expecting it to be the final word as to erect a provisional landmark to orient further debate."

3. Malcolm P. Atkinson and O. Peter Buneman: "Types and Persistence in Database Programming Languages," *ACM Comp. Surv. 19,* No. 2 (June 1987).

One of the earliest papers, if not *the* earliest, to articulate the position that persistence should be orthogonal to type (see references [57] and [65] for counterarguments). This paper is a good starting point for reading in the area of database programming languages in general (database programming languages being perceived by many people as the sine qua non of object database systems; see, for example, reference [17]).

4. Kenneth Baclawski and Bipin Indurkhya: Technical Correspondence, *CACM 37,* No. 9 (September 1994).

This item is discussed in Appendix F.

5. Catriel Beeri and Philip A. Bernstein: "Computational Problems Related to the Design of Normal

Form Relational Schemas," *ACM TODS 4*, No. 1 (March 1979).

To quote from the abstract: "[It] is shown that most interesting algorithmic questions about ... keys are NP-complete and are therefore probably not amenable to fast algorithmic solutions."

6. Jon Bentley: "Little Languages," in *More Programming Pearls*. Reading, Mass.: Addison-Wesley (1988).

This paper illustrates and discusses the following "yardsticks of language design":

1. Orthogonality
2. Generality
3. Parsimony
4. Completeness
5. Similarity
6. Extensibility
7. Openness

Regarding orthogonality in particular, see reference [54]. The term *parsimony,* incidentally, is nicely defined in *Chambers Twentieth Century Dictionary* as "praiseworthy ... avoidance of excess." Parsimony is of course related to Occam's Razor ("entities should not be multiplied beyond necessity").

7. Elisa Bertino and Lorenzo Martino: *Object-Oriented Database Systems: Concepts and Architectures*. Reading, Mass.: Addison-Wesley (1993).

Many publications from the object world try to draw a distinction (as we do not) between type and class, and this reference is one such: "Object-oriented systems can be classified into two main categories—systems supporting the notion of *class* and those supporting the notion of *type* ... [Although] there are no clear lines of demarcation between them, the two concepts are fundamentally different [*sic*] ... Often the concepts type and class are used interchangeably. However, when both are present in the same language, the type is used to indicate the specification of the interface of a set of objects, while class is an implementational notion [*so why is it "in the language" at all?*]. Therefore ... a type is a set of objects which share the same behavior ... [and] a class is a set of objects which have exactly the same internal structure and therefore the same attributes and the same methods. [*But if all objects in a "class" have the same attributes and the same methods, is not that class a type, by the authors' own definition?*] The class defines the implementation of a set of objects, while a type describes how such objects can be used." (Contrast ODMG [17], which uses the terms *type* and *class* in almost exactly the opposite way.)

The authors then go on to say: "With inheritance, a class called a *subclass* can be defined on the basis of the definition of another class called a *superclass.*" Surely—in accordance with their own earlier definitions—they should be talking in terms of types here, not classes? And then they add: "The **specification hierarchy** (often called *subtype hierarchy*) expresses ... subtyping relationships which mean that an instance of the subtype can be used in every context in which an instance of the supertype can correctly appear (*substitutability*)." Observe that they do now speak of types, not classes. Observe too that we now have two new terms for the type hierarchy ... Finally, observe the failure to distinguish properly between values and variables (note the reference to "instances"), and the consequent failure to distinguish between value substitutability and variable substitutability.

8. Garrett Birkhoff: *Lattice Theory* (American Mathematical Society Colloquium Publications Volume 25). Providence, Rhode Island: American Mathematical Society (1967).

9. Michael Blaha and William Premerlani: *Object-Oriented Modeling and Design for Database*

Applications. Upper Saddle River, N.J.: Prentice-Hall (1998).

Blaha and Premerlani's book is not really concerned with the kinds of issues that are the principal concern of *The Third Manifesto;* rather, it is concerned with a particular design methodology called "Object Modeling Technique" (OMT for short). Nevertheless, we do have our reasons for mentioning it here, which we will get to in just a moment.

OMT is a variant of the well-known entity/relationship model; like most such, therefore, it relies extensively on the use of graphical symbols ("boxes and arrows" and so forth). The book consists primarily of an in-depth description of OMT, with emphasis on its relevance to the design of databases in particular.[1] An OMT database design does not, or at least should not, depend on the capabilities of any particular DBMS; Blaha and Premerlani therefore also offer a detailed discussion of how to map such a design to a design that *is* specific to a particular object or SQL DBMS.

One reason we mention OMT at all is because it provides a good example of a point we made in Chapter 1: namely, that even the term *object* itself has a variety of different meanings in the object world. In the present context, it clearly means what the database community would more usually call an *entity*—implying among other things that it is not encapsulated—whereas in object programming languages it generally means something that definitely is encapsulated. *Note:* These remarks are not meant to disparage Blaha and Premerlani's book, of course; we are only using it to illustrate a point.

Following on from this point, we now observe that, presumably because OMT objects are really entities, OMT maps them to tuples in relvars instead of to values in domains. (More precisely, it maps *classes* to *relvars* instead of to domains.) OMT is not alone in this regard, of course (many other design methodologies do exactly the same thing); however, we speculate—and this is the crux of the matter—that it is this state of affairs (i.e., that "object modeling" is really just "entity/relationship modeling" by another name) that is the source of the infamous "relvar = class" mistake that we discussed at some length in Chapter 9.

We note in passing that the book uses several other terms in addition to "object" and "class" in ways that are at odds with the way we use them in the *Manifesto.* For example, on page 46 we find: "Do not confuse a domain with a class." At this point the book is certainly using *class* to mean what we definitely would call a domain or—preferably—type (though elsewhere it seems to use it to mean a collection instead), so its use of *domain* does not accord with ours. And it uses *inheritance* to mean not *type* inheritance as discussed in Part IV of our own book, but instead something akin to the rather suspect "subtables and supertables" notion discussed in Appendix G. Polymorphism is mentioned only in passing, and substitutability not at all.

Finally, the book also contains an interesting observation regarding code reuse. Recall from Part IV that code reuse is one of the objectives of type inheritance. Of course, reuse does not imply inheritance, but the kinds of reuse that are not related to inheritance are not new. And in this connection, the book makes the following point regarding DBMS code specifically: "DBMSs are intended to provide generic functionality for a wide variety of applications ... *You are achieving reuse when you can use generic DBMS code, rather than custom-written application code*" (our italics). We agree, and observe that such reuse is supported very well by relational DBMSs, less well by object DBMSs.

---

1. The book says that OMT is "especially helpful with database applications"—but this remark is a little puzzling, because databases are generally supposed to be designed, as far as possible, in a way that is independent of the applications that will use them. However, it is possible, given OMT's object "look and feel," that it is principally meant to help with the design of *application-specific* databases (in this connection, see the annotation to references [2] and [57]).

10. George Boolos: *Logic, Logic, and Logic.* Cambridge, Mass.: Harvard University Press (1998).

Though not the primary reason we include this reference, we observe with some pleasure that the title of one of the essays in Boolos's book is "To Be Is to Be a Value of a Variable (or to Be Some Values of Some Variables)."

11. Walter Bright: "The D Programming Language" (title of a class advertised in the brochure for the Software Development Conference, Santa Clara, Calif., March 15th-19th, 2004).

We include this reference mainly so that we can make it clear that "The D Programming Language" mentioned is not our **D** (which we first described in print in early 1995 [35]). The following *verbatim* extract from the description of the subject class will serve to highlight some of the differences between **D** and D: "The D Programming Language retains the look and feel of C++, eliminates obsolete and error-prone features like the primitive preprocessor and replaces them with modern equivalents. D adds power programming features like nested functions, modules, try-catch-finally, garbage collection, delegates, dynamic closures, extending C arrays to be fully dynamic arrays, associative arrays, integrated Unicode support, versioning, inline assembler, strong typedefs, etc. With today's emphasis on delivering more reliable software in less time, D adds Design by Contract and Unit Testing smoothly integrated into the syntax. Guaranteed initialization, automatic memory management, improved reference types and optional array bounds checking prevent large swaths of common errors. The language is easy to parse and analyze, enabling code management tools to be quickly produced. Anyone familiar with C++ will have little difficulty upgrading to D. D has struck a responsive chord in the programming community and is experiencing explosive growth."

12. Frederick P. Brooks, Jr.: *The Mythical Man-Month* (20th anniversary edition). Reading, Mass.: Addison-Wesley (1995).

The source of the principle of conceptual integrity.

13. John P. Burgess and Gideon Rosen: *A Subject with No Object: Strategies for Nominalistic Interpretation of Mathematics* (Oxford University Press, 1997).

We include this reference on the strength of the following quote from an Oxford University Press brochure advertising it, which might be viewed as bolstering our philosophical position regarding the nature of values (see Chapter 1): "Numbers and other mathematical objects are exceptional in having no location in space or time or relations of cause and effect. This [fact] makes it difficult to account for the possibility of the knowledge of such objects, leading many philosophers to embrace nominalism, the doctrine that there are no such objects, and to embark on ambitious projects for interpreting mathematics so as to preserve the subject while eliminating the objects."

14. Luca Cardelli: "A Semantics of Multiple Inheritance," in reference [136].

After we had developed the inheritance model described in Part IV of the present book, we were interested to discover that this paper by Cardelli had previously proposed some of the same ideas (including analogs of our TREAT and IS_*T* operators and union types). It even mentions the possibility of *alpha* and *omega* (calling them "anything" and "nothing," respectively), though it goes on to reject them. It is significant to note, however, that all of this work was done in the context of "the EXTENDS relationship" (see Appendix G), not specialization by constraint.

15. Luca Cardelli and Peter Wegner: "On Understanding Types, Data Abstraction, and Polymorphism," *ACM Comp. Surv. 17,* No. 4 (December 1985).

A nice quote from this paper: "A major purpose of type systems is to avoid embarrassing questions about representations, and to forbid situations in which these questions might come up." Indeed, type vs. representation is one of the great logical differences, a point we have tried to make abundantly clear in the present book.

16. R. G. G. Cattell: *Object Data Management* (revised edition). Reading, Mass.: Addison-Wesley (1994).

The first book-length tutorial on the application of object technology to database management. (Reference [128] is another good, though much less extensive, tutorial on the same general subject.) The following edited extract suggests that the field was certainly a long way from any kind of consensus when the book was written: "Programming languages may need new syntax ... swizzling, replication, and new access methods also need further study ... new end-user and application development tools [are] required ... more powerful query-language features [must be] developed ... new research in concurrency control is needed ... timestamps and object-based concurrency semantics need more exploration ... performance models are needed ... new work in knowledge management needs to be integrated with object and data management capabilities ... this [will lead to] a complex optimization problem [and] few researchers have [the necessary] expertise ... federated [object] databases require more study."

17. R. G. G. Cattell and Douglas K. Barry (eds.): *The Object Data Standard: ODMG 3.0.* San Francisco, Calif.: Morgan Kaufmann (2000).

A detailed comparison between an earlier version of ODMG (Version 2.0) and the proposals of *The Third Manifesto* can be found at the website *www.thethirdmanifesto.com.*

18. Donald D. Chamberlin: "Relations and References—Another Point of View," *InfoDB 10,* No. 6 (April 1997).

See the annotation to reference [59].

19. J. Craig Cleaveland: *An Introduction to Data Types.* Reading, Mass.: Addison-Wesley (1986).

20. E. F. Codd: "Derivability, Redundancy, and Consistency of Relations Stored in Large Data Banks," IBM Research Report RJ599 (August 19th, 1969).

Codd's very first paper on what became the relational model of data (it is essentially a preliminary version of reference [21]).

21. E. F. Codd: "A Relational Model of Data for Large Shared Data Banks," *CACM 13,* No. 6 (June 1970). Republished in "Milestones of Research," *CACM 26,* No. 1 (January 1982).

The first widely available description of the original relational model, by its inventor (the first *published* description was reference [20]).

22. E. F. Codd: "Relational Completeness of Data Base Sublanguages," in Randall Rustin (ed.): *Data Base Systems:* Courant Computer Science Symposia 6. Englewood Cliffs, N.J.: Prentice-Hall (1972).

This is the paper in which Codd first formally defined the original algebraic operators (definitions did appear in references [20-21] also, but they were somewhat less formal, or at least less complete). *Note:* One slightly unfortunate aspect of the paper is that it assumes "for notational and expository convenience" that the attributes of a relation have a left-to-right ordering and hence can be identified by their ordinal position (though Codd does say that "names rather than position numbers [should] be used [in practice]"—and he had previously said much the same thing in reference [21]). The paper therefore does not mention an attribute RENAME operator, and it does not consider the question of result type inference. Possibly as a consequence of these omissions, the same criticisms can still be leveled today (a) at many discussions of the algebra in the literature, (b) at today's SQL products, and (c) to a slightly lesser extent, at the SQL standard as well.

23.   E. F. Codd: *The Relational Model for Database Management Version 2.* Reading, Mass.: Addison-Wesley (1990).

Codd spent much of the late 1980s revising and extending the original relational model ("the Relational Model Version 1" or RM/V1), and this book was the result. It describes "the Relational Model Version 2" or RM/V2. (We include this reference primarily in order to make it clear that the version of the relational model on which *The Third Manifesto* is based is *not* "RM/V2," nor indeed "RM/V1" as this reference defines it. Rather, it is, as noted in Chapter 1, the version described in references [47] and [76].)

24.   E. F. Codd and C. J. Date: "Interactive Support for Nonprogrammers: The Relational and Network Approaches," in reference [36].

The paper that introduced the concept of *essentiality,* a concept that is critical to a proper understanding of data models in general. The relational model basically has just one essential data construct, the relation itself. The object model, by contrast, has many: sets, bags, lists, arrays, and so forth (not to mention object IDs), though typically *not* relations. See references [48] and [61] for further explanation.

25.   O. J. Dahl and K. Nygaard: "SIMULA—An Algol-Based Simulation Language," *CACM 9,* No. 9 (September 1966).

As the name suggests, SIMULA was originally intended specifically for programming simulations (e.g., of mechanical systems). However, it is often cited as the very first object programming language.

26.   Hugh Darwen (writing as Andrew Warden): "TABLE_DEE and TABLE_DUM," in reference [37].

27.   Hugh Darwen: "The Askew Wall: A Personal Perspective," in reference [38].

28.   Hugh Darwen: "The Role of Functional Dependence in Query Decomposition," in reference [38].

29.   Hugh Darwen: "The Nullologist in Relationland; *or,* Nothing Really Matters," in reference [38].

30.   Hugh Darwen: "Outer Join with No Nulls and Fewer Tears," in reference [38].

31.   Hugh Darwen: "Valid Time and Transaction Time Proposals: Language Design Aspects," in Opher Etzion, Sushil Jajodia, and Suryanaryan Sripada (eds.): *Temporal Databases: Research and Practice.* New York, N.Y.: Springer Verlag (1998).

This paper includes and discusses a set of language design principles that are similar but not identical to those of reference [6]:

1. Precise specification
2. Encouragement of Good Practice
3. Generality
4. Semantic consistency
5. Syntactic consistency

6. Orthogonality
7. Parsimony
8. Syntactic substitution
9. Conceptual integrity

Regarding syntactic substitution in particular, the paper has this to say:

> A language definition should start with a few judiciously chosen primitive operators ... Subsequent development is, where possible, by defining new operators in terms of ... previously defined [ones]. Most importantly, syntactic substitution does not refer to an imprecise principle such as might be expressed as "*A* is something like, possibly very like, *B*," where *A* is some proposed new syntax and *B* is some expression using previously defined operators. If *A* is close in meaning to *B* but cannot be specified by true syntactic substitution, then we have a situation that is disagreeable and probably unacceptable, in stark contrast to true syntactic substitution, which can be very agreeable and acceptable indeed.

As should be clear from the body of the present book, we applied the principle of true syntactic substitution liberally in the design of **Tutorial D**.

32.   Hugh Darwen: "The Importance of Column Names" (presentation slides), *www.thethirdmanifesto.com* (October 1st, 2003).

33.   Hugh Darwen: "How to Handle Missing Information Without Using Nulls" (presentation slides), *www.thethirdmanifesto.com* (May 9th, 2003).

In Appendix G, we briefly touched on a technique for designing databases involving missing information according to which, e.g., parts with no color are moved out of the regular parts relvar into a separate relvar of their own. This presentation elaborates on this technique. See also reference [113].

34.   Hugh Darwen and C. J. Date: "Into the Great Divide," in reference [38].

35.   Hugh Darwen and C. J. Date: *The Third Manifesto*. *ACM SIGMOD Record 24*, No. 1 (March 1995).

The first "official" version of the *Manifesto*. The *Manifesto* as described in the present book consists of a considerably revised and extended (but by and large compatible) version.

36.   C. J. Date: *Relational Database: Selected Writings*. Reading, Mass.: Addison-Wesley (1986).

37.   C. J. Date: *Relational Database Writings 1985-1989*. Reading, Mass.: Addison-Wesley (1990).

38.   C. J. Date (with Hugh Darwen): *Relational Database Writings 1989-1991*. Reading, Mass.: Addison-Wesley (1992).

39.   C. J. Date: *Relational Database Writings 1991-1994*. Reading, Mass.: Addison-Wesley (1995).

40.   C. J. Date (with Hugh Darwen and David McGoveran): *Relational Database Writings 1994-1997*.

Reading, Mass.: Addison-Wesley (1998).

41.   C. J. Date (with Hugh Darwen): *A Guide to the SQL Standard* (4th edition). Reading, Mass.: Addison-Wesley (1997).

A complete tutorial reference and guide to the SQL:1992 standard as it had become by 1997 (it includes coverage of both SQL/CLI and SQL/PSM, which were added to the "1992" standard in 1995 and 1996, respectively). The book contains numerous examples of violations of good language design principles! In particular, it includes an appendix, Appendix D, that documents "many aspects of the standard that appear to be inadequately defined, or even incorrectly defined, at this time." Although SQL:1992 has since been formally superseded (first by SQL:1999 and then by the current standard SQL:2003 [99]), just about everything in this 1997 book—in Appendix D in particular—is still applicable today.

42.   C. J. Date: "An Architecture for High-Level Language Database Extensions," Proc. ACM SIGMOD International Conference on Management of Data, Washington, D.C. (June 1976). A revised version of this paper entitled "An Introduction to the Unified Database Language (UDL)" can be found in reference [36].

43.   C. J. Date: "Some Principles of Good Language Design," in reference [36].

44.   C. J. Date: "A Critique of the SQL Database Language," in reference [36].

45.   C. J. Date: "What's Wrong with SQL?", in reference [37].

46.   C. J. Date: "The Principle of Cautious Design," in reference [38].

To quote: "*The Principle of Cautious Design* says, in effect, that whenever we are faced with a design choice, say between alternative *A* and alternative *B* (where *A* is upward compatible with *B*), and the full implications of alternative *B* are not yet known, then the recommendation is to go with alternative *A*." Our decision to prohibit coercions in **Tutorial D** can be seen as an application of this principle. By contrast, the decision to permit duplicate rows in SQL can be seen as a case in which the principle was flouted.

47.   C. J. Date: "Notes Toward a Reconstituted Definition of the Relational Model Version 1 (RM/V1)," in reference [38].

48.   C. J. Date: "Essentiality," in reference [39].

49.   C. J. Date: "Nothing in Excess," in reference [39].

50.   C. J. Date: "Empty Bags and Identity Crises," in reference [39].

51.   C. J. Date: "How We Missed the Relational Boat," in reference [39].

52.   C. J. Date: "The Primacy of Primary Keys: An Investigation," in reference [39].

53.   C. J. Date: "We Don't Need Composite Columns," in reference [40].

54.   C. J. Date: "A Note on Orthogonality," in reference [40].

Orthogonality means independence; a language is said to display orthogonality if it provides (a) a comparatively small set of primitive constructs, together with a consistent set of rules for putting those constructs together, and (b) every possible combination of those constructs is both valid and meaningful (i.e., a deliberate attempt has been made to avoid arbitrary restrictions). Such orthogonality is desirable because the less orthogonal a language is, the more complicated it is and—paradoxically but simultaneously—the less powerful it is:

- The language is more complicated because of the additional rules needed to define and document the exceptions and special cases.

- The language is less powerful because the purpose of those additional rules is precisely to prohibit certain combinations of constructs and hence to reduce the language's functionality.

In a nutshell: "Orthogonal design maximizes expressive power while avoiding deleterious superfluities" (from the Algol 68 specifications).

55.   C. J. Date: "Objects and Relations: Forty-Seven Points of Light," in reference [40].

A blow-by-blow response to reference [103].

56.   C. J. Date: "Quota Queries" (in three parts), in reference [40].

57.   C. J. Date: "Why 'The Object Model' Is Not a Data Model," in reference [40].

This paper argues among other things that (a) "the object model" is really a storage model, not a data model, and that partly because of that fact (b) object and relational systems are more different than is usually realized. The following excerpt captures the essence of the argument:

Object databases grew out of a desire on the part of object application programmers—for a variety of application-specific reasons—to keep their application-specific objects in persistent memory. That persistent memory might perhaps be regarded as a database, but the important point is that it was indeed application specific; it was not a shared, general-purpose database, intended to be suitable for applications that might not have been foreseen at the time the database was defined. As a consequence, many features that database professionals regard as essential were simply not requirements in the object world, at least not originally. Thus, there was little perceived need for:

1. Data sharing across applications
2. Physical data independence
3. Ad hoc queries
4. Views and logical data independence
5. Application-independent, declarative integrity constraints
6. Data ownership and a flexible security mechanism
7. Concurrency control
8. A general-purpose catalog
9. Application-independent database design

These requirements all surfaced later, after the basic idea of storing objects in a database was first conceived, and thus all constitute add-on features to the original object model ... One important consequence of all of the foregoing is that there really is a difference in kind between an object DBMS and a relational DBMS. In fact, it could be argued that an object DBMS is not really a DBMS at all—at least, not in the same sense that a relational DBMS is a DBMS. For consider:

- A relational DBMS comes ready for use. In other words, as soon as the system is installed, users (application programmers and end users) can start building databases, writing applications, running queries, and so on.

- An object DBMS, by contrast, can be thought of as a kind of DBMS construction kit. When it is originally installed, it is not available for immediate use by application programmers and end users. Instead, it must first be tailored by suitably skilled technicians, who must define the necessary classes and methods, etc. (the system provides a set of building blocks—class library maintenance tools, method compilers, etc.—for this purpose). Only when that tailoring activity is complete will the system be available for use by application programmers and end users; in other words, the result of that tailoring will indeed more closely resemble a DBMS in the more familiar sense of the term.

- Note further that the resultant "tailored" DBMS will be application specific; it might, for example, be suitable for CAD/CAM applications, but be essentially useless for, e.g., medical applications. In other words, it will still not be a general-purpose DBMS, in the same sense that a relational DBMS is a general-purpose DBMS.

The paper also argues against the "persistence orthogonal to type" idea, as follows:

> The object model requires support for a full complement of type generators ... Examples include STRUCT (or TUPLE), LIST, ARRAY, SET, BAG, and so on. These generators can be combined in arbitrary ways; thus, for example, an array of lists of bags of arrays of [integers] might constitute a single object in suitable circumstances. Along with object IDs, the availability of these type generators essentially means that *any data structure that can be created in an application program can be created as an object in an object database*—and further that the structure of such objects is *visible to the user*. For example, consider the object, EX say, that is (or rather denotes) the collection of employees in a given department. Then EX might be implemented either as a linked list or as an array, and users will have to know which it is (because the access operators will differ accordingly).
>
> This "anything goes" approach to what can be stored in the database is a major point of difference between the object and relational models, of course, and it deserves a little further discussion here. In essence:

- The object model says we can store anything we like—any data structure we can create with the usual programming language mechanisms.

- The relational model effectively says the same thing, but then goes on to insist that whatever we do store be presented to the user in pure relational form.

> More precisely, the relational model—quite rightly—says nothing about what can be physically stored ... It therefore imposes no limits on what data structures are allowed at the physical level; the only requirement is that whatever structures are in fact physically stored must be mapped to relations at the logical level and hence be hidden from the user. Relational systems thus make a clear distinction between logical and physical (model vs. implementation), while object systems do not. One consequence is that—contrary to conventional wisdom—object systems might very well provide less data independence than

relational systems. For example, suppose the implementation in some object database of the object EX mentioned above (denoting the collection of employees in a given department) is changed from an array to a linked list. What are the implications for existing code that accesses that object EX?

58.   C. J. Date: "Faults and Defaults" (in five parts), in reference [40].

SQL addresses the problem of missing information by means of nulls, but nulls constitute a clear violation of the relational model (see RM Proscription 4). So what can we do about missing information? This paper describes one approach: the "default" or "special values" scheme. Another approach, not totally unrelated, is described in references [33] and [113]. See also reference [30].

59.   C. J. Date: "Don't Mix Pointers and Relations!" and "Don't Mix Pointers and Relations—*Please!*", both in reference [40].

The first of these two articles argues strongly against the idea that relational databases should be allowed to include pointers to data as well as data per se. (In particular, therefore, it attacks the SQL standard [99], which supports something very close if not identical to such an idea.) In reference [18], Chamberlin offers a rebuttal to some of the arguments of that first article. The second article was written as a direct response to Chamberlin's rebuttal.

60.   C. J. Date: "Object Identifiers vs. Relational Keys," in reference [40].

Presents detailed arguments in support of the position that object IDs are, first and foremost, a performance feature and should not be part of the model as seen by the user. To elaborate briefly, the paper argues that (a) object IDs do perform some of the same functions as relational keys, but they are certainly not just "keys pure and simple" (not even what are sometimes called surrogate keys)—they carry a lot of additional baggage with them; (b) the baggage in question is strongly motivated by performance considerations and does not belong in the model. *The Third Manifesto* proscribes object IDs in part (but only in part) because of that extra baggage.

61.   C. J. Date: "Relational Really Is Different," in reference [70].

62.   C. J. Date: "Grievous Bodily Harm" (in two parts), *DBP&D 11*, Nos. 5 and 6 (May-June 1998).

One criticism of SQL is that it is an extremely redundant language, in the sense that, for all but the most trivial of queries, it provides far too many different ways of formulating the query in question (and some of the differences between formulations are quite radical). Such redundancies do not make the language more general, they just make it more complicated—with significant negative consequences for documentation, teaching, learning, remembering, applying, and (last but not least) implementation. This paper describes some major SQL redundancies in detail (including the GROUP BY and HAVING constructs in particular) and discusses some of the consequences of such redundancies.

63.   C. J. Date: "Fifty Ways to Quote Your Query," *www.dbpd.com* (July 1998).

More on SQL redundancies.

64.   C. J. Date: "Encapsulation Is a Red Herring," *www.dbpd.com* (September 1998).

Encapsulation implies data independence. As noted in Appendix B, however, we would rather not use the term (preferring the more traditional term *scalar*). Part of the justification for our position here is that, in principle, "encapsulated objects" cannot provide any more data independence than unencapsulated relations can. For example, there is no fundamental reason why a relation representing points, with cartesian coordinate attributes X and Y, should not be physically stored in terms of polar coordinates R and THETA instead. Thus, encapsulation per se is really not the issue.

65. C. J. Date: "Persistence *Not* Orthogonal to Type," *www.dbpd.com* (October 1998).

66. C. J. Date: *WHAT Not HOW: The Business Rules Approach to Application Development.* Reading, Mass.: Addison-Wesley (2000).

67. C. J. Date: "What Do You Mean, 'Post-Relational'?", *www.dbdebunk.com* (June 2000); "Great News, The Relational Model Is Very Much Alive!", *www.dbdebunk.com* (August 2000); "There's Only One Relational Model!", *www.dbdebunk.com* (February 2001).

The relational model has been attacked and criticized (and misunderstood) from the moment it first appeared to this day. These articles are responses to three comparatively recent attacks.

68. C. J. Date: "Models, Models, Everywhere, Nor Any Time to Think," *www.dbdebunk.com* (November 2000).

The term *model* is one of the most overused (not to say abused) terms in the IT world, especially in the database sector. This article was written in an attempt to alert readers to some of the worst excesses in this regard.

69. C. J. Date: "Basic Concepts in UML: A Request for Clarification" (in two parts), *www.dbdebunk.com* (December 2000).

An attempt to make sense of the Unified Modeling Language, UML.

70. C. J. Date: *The Database Relational Model: A Retrospective Review and Analysis.* Reading, Mass.: Addison-Wesley (2001).

This short book (160 pages) is offered as a careful, unbiased, retrospective review and analysis of Codd's relational contribution as documented in his 1970s papers. It examines the following papers in detail (as well as touching on several others in passing):

- Derivability, Redundancy, and Consistency of Relations Stored in Large Data Banks [20]

- A Relational Model of Data for Large Shared Data Banks [21]

- Relational Completeness of Data Base Sublanguages [22]

- Interactive Support for Nonprogrammers: The Relational and Network Approaches [24]

- A Data Base Sublanguage Founded on the Relational Calculus

- Further Normalization of the Data Base Relational Model

- Extending the Database Relational Model to Capture More Meaning

(The last three are not referenced elsewhere in the present book.)

71. C. J. Date: "Is a Circle an Ellipse?", *www.dbdebunk.com* (July 2001).

As noted in Chapter 14, the question of whether a circle is an ellipse is a surprisingly controversial one, at least in the object world. Consider the following extract from the book *The C++ Programming Language* (3rd edition), by Bjarne Stroustrup [90]:

> [In] mathematics a circle is a kind of an ellipse, but in most programs a circle should not be derived from an ellipse or an ellipse derived from a circle. The often-heard arguments "because that's the way it is in mathematics" and "because the representation of a circle is a subset of that of an ellipse" are not conclusive and most often wrong. This is because for most programs, the key property of a circle is that it has a center and a fixed distance to its perimeter. All behavior of a circle (all operations) must maintain this property (invariant ...). On the other hand, an ellipse is characterized by two focal points that in many programs can be changed independently of each other. If those focal points coincide, the ellipse looks like a circle, but it is not a circle because its operations do not preserve the circle invariant. In most systems, this difference will be reflected by having a circle and an ellipse provide sets of operations that are not subsets of each other.

Reference [71] analyzes the foregoing extract in detail and presents arguments—based, of course, on our own inheritance model—to suggest that, *pace* Stroustrup, a circle is an ellipse after all.

72. C. J. Date: "Double Trouble, Double Trouble" (in two parts), *www.dbdebunk.com* (April 2002).

73. C. J. Date: "What Does Substitutability Really Mean?" (in three parts), *www.dbdebunk.com* (July 2002).

An investigation into substitutability and "the Liskov Substitution Principle," LSP. The first part examines a couple of tutorial descriptions of LSP and finds them to be deficient in several respects. That examination in turn paves the way for a detailed discussion, in the other two parts, of the research paper [106] in which, according to reference [123], the LSP concept originated.

74. C. J. Date: "What First Normal Form Really Means," *www.dbdebunk.com* (June 2003).

First normal form has been the subject of much misunderstanding over the years (on our own part as much as anybody else's, we hasten to add). This paper is an attempt to set the record straight—even to be definitive, as far as possible. The crux of the argument is that the concept of atomicity (in terms of which first normal form was originally defined) has no absolute meaning.

75. C. J. Date: "A Sweet Disorder," *www.dbdebunk.com* (August 2003).

Paraphrasing, RM Proscription 1 states that there shall be no left-to-right ordering to the attributes of a relation. As is well known, SQL violates this proscription. The present paper explores some of the consequences, which turn out to be less trivial than one might think.

76. C. J. Date: *An Introduction to Database Systems* (8th edition). Boston, Mass.: Addison-Wesley (2004).

This book includes an extensive tutorial on the relational model and a somewhat less extensive tutorial on the inheritance model described in Part IV of the present book. The following quote (slightly edited here) is germane to the overall theme of the *Manifesto:*

The term *data model* is used in the literature with two quite different meanings. [*The first is identical to that given for the term* model, *unqualified, in the subsection "Model vs. Implementation" in Chapter 1 of the present book.*] The second is as a model of the persistent data of *some particular enterprise* ... The difference between the two meanings can be characterized as follows:

- A data model in the first sense is like a programming language—albeit one that is somewhat abstract—whose constructs can be used to solve a wide variety of specific problems, but in and of themselves have no direct connection with any such specific problem.

- A data model in the second sense is like a specific program written in that language. In other words, a data model in the second sense takes the facilities provided by some model in the first sense and applies them to some specific problem. It can be regarded as a specific application of some model in the first sense.

It goes without saying that the term is used throughout the present book in the first of these two senses.

77.   C. J. Date: "Why We Need Type BOOLEAN," *www.BRCommunity.com* (May 2004).

78.   C. J. Date: "The Logic of Business Rules," *www.dbdebunk.com* (June 2004).

This paper is essentially a tutorial on elementary ideas from logic. To quote from the abstract: "[This paper] shows how certain key concepts from elementary logic can be used to simplify the task of formulating business rules whose interpretation is clear, precise, and unambiguous. The concepts in question are described and illustrated in tutorial fashion. No prior knowledge of logic is assumed."

79.   C. J. Date: "On the Notion of Logical Difference"; "On the Logical Difference Between Model and Implementation"; and "On the Logical Differences Between Types, Values, and Variables" (in two parts), *www.dbdebunk.com* (August 2004).

80.   C. J. Date: *Database in Depth: Relational Theory for Practitioners.* Sebastopol, Calif.: O'Reilly Media, Inc. (2005).

This book is an informal, but careful and detailed, treatment of the relational model and related matters for readers who already have some practical database experience but want to know more about the theory on which their experience is based.

81.   C. J. Date: *Go Faster! The TransRelational*ᵗᵐ *Approach to DBMS Implementation.* To appear.

This book is a detailed tutorial on a radically new approach to implementing the relational model. It is based on reference [134] but covers much more ground than that reference does. *Note:* A considerably abbreviated version of this material, covering read-only operations and main-memory data only, can be found in Appendix A of reference [76].

82.   C. J. Date and Hugh Darwen: *Foundation for Object/Relational Databases: The Third Manifesto.* Reading, Mass.: Addison-Wesley (1998).

83.   C. J. Date and Hugh Darwen: *Foundation for Future Database Systems: The Third Manifesto* (2nd

edition). Reading, Mass.: Addison-Wesley (2000).

84.   C. J. Date and Hugh Darwen: "Multiple Assignment," *www.dbdebunk.com* (February 2004).

85.   C. J. Date, Hugh Darwen, and Nikos A. Lorentzos: *Temporal Data and the Relational Model.* San Francisco, Calif.: Morgan Kaufmann (2003).

As the title indicates, this book is an examination into the application of the relational model to the problem of temporal database management specifically. One aspect of that problem is the issue of "granularity": that is, dealing with time measured in (say) months vs. days, or hours vs. seconds. It turns out that the inheritance model discussed in the present book can help with that issue.

86.   C. J. Date and P. Hopewell: "Storage Structures and Physical Data Independence" and "File Definition and Logical Data Independence," both in Proc. 1971 ACM SIGFIDET Workshop on Data Definition, Access, and Control, San Diego, California (November 1971).

87.   C. J. Date and David McGoveran: "A New Database Design Principle," in reference [39]. See also C. J. Date: "Data Redundancy and Database Design" (in two parts), *www.dbdebunk.com* (March/April 2005), and "Data Redundancy and Database Design: Further Thoughts Number One," *www.dbdebunk.com* (July 2005).

88.   C. J. Date and David McGoveran: "Updating Union, Intersection, and Difference Views" and "Updating Joins and Other Views," both in reference [39].

These two informal papers were the first to discuss the view updating mechanism proposed in reference [114] and elaborated in Appendix E.

89.   Andrew Eisenberg and Jim Melton: "SQL:1999, Formerly Known as SQL3," *ACM SIGMOD Record 28,* No. 1 (March 1999).

A tutorial overview of SQL:1999, which was the first version of the standard to include "object" support. *Note:* Observing that, while this article certainly described the "object" features of SQL:1999, it did nothing to justify them, the authors of the present book wrote to the then editor of *SIGMOD Record* as follows:

> With reference to [the subject article]—in particular, with reference to the sections entitled "Objects ... Finally" and "Using REF Types"—we have a question: What useful purpose is served by the features described in those sections? To be more specific, what useful functionality is provided that can't be obtained via features already found in SQL:1992?

Our letter was not published, however, and to this day our question remains unanswered.

90.   Margaret A. Ellis and Bjarne Stroustrup: *The Annotated C++ Reference Manual.* Reading, Mass.: Addison-Wesley (1990). See also Bjarne Stroustrup: *The Design and Evolution of C++,* Addison-Wesley (1994) and *The C++ Programming Language* (3rd edition), Addison-Wesley (1997).

91.   P. T. Geach: "History of the Corruptions of Logic," in *Logic Matters.* Oxford, UK: Basil Blackwell (1972).

The source of the maxim "All logical differences are big differences." The complete quote is: "As I once heard Wittgenstein say, all logical differences are big differences; in logic we are not making *subtle* distinctions, as it were between flavours that pass over into one another by delicate gradations. "

92. Adele Goldberg and David Robson: *Smalltalk-80: The Language and Its Implementation.* Reading, Mass.: Addison-Wesley (1983).

According to reference [125], object-oriented programming has its roots in Smalltalk, and "the phrase *object-oriented programming* originated with the development of the Smalltalk language" (though Smalltalk in turn was surely influenced by SIMULA [25]). And in this book on Smalltalk (by two of the researchers responsible for its design and development), Goldberg and Robson state categorically that "an object consists of some private memory and a set of operations ... An object's public properties are the messages that make up its interface ... An object's private properties are a set of *instance variables* that make up its private memory." In other words, it is indeed the case (as we claimed in Chapter 9 and elsewhere) that pure objects have no public instance variables, and further that many object systems are not pure.

93. Nathan Goodman: "Bill of Materials in Relational Database," *InfoDB 5,* No. 1 (Spring/Summer 1990).

94. James Gosling, Bill Joy, and Guy Steele: *The Java Language Specification.* Reading, Mass.: Addison-Wesley (1996).

95. Ian Graham, Julia Bischof, and Brian Henderson-Sellars: "Associations Considered a Bad Thing," *Journal of Object-Oriented Programming* (February 1997).

We include this paper in this appendix because we find it a good illustration of the gulf that sometimes seems to exist between the object and database worlds (or communities). First, however, we should explain what the paper is trying to achieve. The authors' thesis is that treating "associations" (or "relationships") either as "first-class objects" in their own right or as some totally different kind of construct (as in ODMG [17]) compromises encapsulation and reusability. They therefore propose, in effect, that, e.g., the association between suppliers and parts should not be represented not by means of "shipments" as such, but rather, redundantly, by a parts attribute within suppliers and a suppliers attribute within parts (the two attributes in question being explicitly declared to the system to be "inverses" of each other). And they then go on to propose a set of rules for maintaining referential integrity given such a design and for keeping the inverse attributes in synch with each other.

We do not want to comment on the foregoing proposals as such. What we do want to do is quote and offer some comments on some remarks from the paper that, we believe, illustrate the "gulf" we mentioned:

■ A study of the literature of semantic data modeling ... reveals that there are two fundamental ways to connect data structures or entity types [*sic*: *constructors* and *pointers* ... [In] the first approach, emphasis is placed on building structures using constructors such as the tuple or the set. In the second, the stress is on linking types using attributes. *Comment:* From the context, "building structures using constructors" seems to mean that connections between data structures—"or entity types" (?)—are represented by foreign keys, or something very like foreign keys, while "linking types using attributes" means those connections are represented by pointers instead. At the very least, therefore, there does seem to be a *terminological* gulf.

■ In the 1980s the former approach [*i.e., "building structures using constructors"*] was dominant, largely because of the popularity and widespread use of relational databases. In entity-relationship models there are two logical types: *entity-relationships* and *relationship-relationships*. Both are represented by sets of tuples and no links between them are stored; the run-time system of the DBMS must search for the linkages. *Comment:* Quite apart from (a) the fact that "entity-relationship models" have very little to do with relational databases anyway, and (b) the fact that the phrase "two logical types" is a little mysterious, the final sentence here betrays a serious lack of understanding of the relational model and relational implementation technology (which was well over 20 years old, incidentally, when this paper was published).

■ Attempts to enrich [*sic*] the relational model led quickly to systems with more than two relationship types. [*Do they mean more than* one?] This unsatisfactory situation soon led to suggestions to replace these arbitrary type systems with a single notion of classes reminiscent of object-oriented programming ... The pointer-based approach is far more natural to an OO thinker [*we agree!*], but one suspects that the popularity of methods such as OMT [is] because developers with a relational background find the approach familiar and anodyne. **The danger here is that object-oriented principles will be ignored and highly relational models produced instead of true object-oriented ones** [*boldface added*]. *Comment:* OMT is described in reference [9].

96. Jim Gray and Andreas Reuter: *Transaction Processing: Concepts and Techniques.* San Mateo, Calif.: Morgan Kaufmann (1993).

   The standard and definitive text on transaction management.

97. Mark Greaves: "From Z to **A**" (private communication, June 16th, 1999).

98. Patrick Hall, Peter Hitchcock, and Stephen Todd: "An Algebra of Relations for Machine Computation," Conf. Record of the 2nd ACM Symposium on Principles of Programming Languages, Palo Alto, Calif. (January 1975).

   This paper was the first to recognize the important role of attribute names in the operators of a relational algebra; it has significantly influenced the thinking and output over the years of the present authors, and many of its ideas find expression again in **Tutorial D**. See also references [120] and [133].

99. International Organization for Standardization (ISO): *Database Language SQL,* Document ISO/IEC 9075:2003.

   This reference is, of course, the official SQL standard (known to the cognoscenti as *ISO/IEC 9075,* or sometimes just *ISO 9075*). The standard is not a single document—it consists of an open-ended series of separate *Parts* (ISO 9075-1, -2, etc.), under the general title *Information Technology—Database Languages—SQL.* Parts are sometimes added to the current edition of the SQL standard, subsequent to its publication. The Parts of SQL:2003 at the time of publication of this book are:

   Part 1: Framework (SQL/Framework)
   Part 2: Foundation (SQL/Foundation)
   Part 3: Call-Level Interface (SQL/CLI)
   Part 4: Persistent Stored Modules (SQL/PSM)
   Part 5: *There is no Part 5*
   Part 6: *There is no Part 6*
   Part 7: *There is no Part 7*

Part 8: *There is no Part 8*
Part 9: Management of External Data (SQL/MED)
Part 10: Object Language Bindings (SQL/OLB)
Part 11: The Information and Definition Schemas (SQL/Schemata)
Part 12: *There is no Part 12*
Part 13: Java Routines and Types (SQL/JRT)
Part 14: XML-Related Specifications (SQL/XML)

The features of primary concern to the present book—see Appendix H—mostly belong in Part 2. *Note:* Reference [89] is a tutorial overview of the features that were new in the previous edition, SQL:1999; reference [41] is also relevant. Much other pertinent material, including in particular the draft of a Technical Corrigendum (begun before SQL:2003 was even ratified!), can be found at *ftp://sqlstandards.org/SC32/WG3*.

By the way, it is worth mentioning that, although SQL is widely recognized as the international "relational" database standard, the standard documents do not describe it as such; in fact, they never use the term "relation" at all! (Indeed, they do not use the term "database" either; instead, as noted in Appendix H, they talk about something called "SQL-data," which is "data described by SQL-schemas—data that is under the control of an SQL-implementation in an SQL-environment.")

100.   Ivar Jacobson (with Magnus Christerson, Patrik Jonsson, and Gunnar Övergaard): *Object-Oriented Software Engineering* (revised printing). Reading, Mass.: Addison-Wesley (1994).

A widely respected book on software engineering. It presents a methodology called OOSE (Object-Oriented Software Engineering), a simplified version of a more extensive approach called *Objectory*. From a database perspective, however, we do find it a little puzzling, especially with respect to encapsulation and type vs. class (in fact, with respect to model vs. implementation in general). For example: "The behavior and information are **encapsulated** in the object" (page 48, boldface in the original), but "each ... attribute [of the class] will become one column in the table" (page 277). Tables are not encapsulated. And: "A type is defined by the manipulations you can do with the type. A class is more than that. You can also look inside a class ... to see its information structure ... [A] class is [an] *implementation* of a type" (page 50, italics in the original). These statements are clear enough, of course, but the book then goes on to talk almost exclusively in terms of classes where types would seem more appropriate.

Many of the comments in the annotation to reference [9] apply here too, mutatis mutandis. In particular, as the previous paragraph suggests, OOSE objects, like OMT objects, seem to correspond for the most part to what the database community would call *entities*—and we remind you of our speculation that this state of affairs is the source of the "relvar = class" mistake.

One last quote: "Most of the methods used in the industry today, for both information and technical system development, are based on a functional and/or data-driven decomposition of the system. These approaches differ in many ways from the approach taken by object-oriented methods where data and functions are highly integrated." It seems to us that here the authors put their collective finger on a significant mismatch between object and database thinking. Databases are *meant* to be somewhat divorced from "functions"; as noted in a footnote under reference [9], databases are usually supposed to be designed separately from the applications that use them. Thus, it seems to us once again that the term "database" as used in the object community really means a database that is application specific, not (as is more usual in the database community) one that is general purpose.

101.   W. Kent: "Consequences of Assuming a Universal Relation," *ACM TODS 6,* No. 4 (December 1981).

102.   Won Kim: "Object-Oriented Database Systems: Promises, Reality, and the Future," Proc. 19th International Conference on Very Large Data Bases, Dublin, Ireland (August 24th-27th, 1993).

103.   Won Kim: "On Marrying Relations and Objects: Relation-Centric and Object-Centric Perspectives," *Data Base Newsletter 22*, No. 6 (November/December 1994).

Reference [55] is a detailed response to this paper.

104.   Won Kim: "Bringing Object/Relational Down to Earth," *DBP&D 10*, No. 7 (July 1997).

In this article, Kim claims that "confusion is sure to reign" in the marketplace for object/relational DBMSs because, first, "an inordinate weight has been placed on the role of data type extensibility" and, second, "the measure of a product's object/relational completeness ... is a potentially serious area of perplexity." He goes on to propose "a practical metric for object/relational completeness that can be used as a guideline for determining whether a product is truly [object/relational]"—an idea that inevitably invites comparison with the approach taken in reference [2] to the question of determining whether a DBMS is truly object-oriented.

Kim's scheme (*metric* is really not the mot juste, since there is nothing quantitative about it) involves the following criteria:

1. Data model
2. Query language
3. Mission-critical services
4. Computational model
5. Performance and scalability
6. Database tools
7. Harnessing the power

With respect to Criterion Number 1, Kim takes the position—very different from ours—that the data model must be "the Core Object Model defined by the Object Management Group" [127], which "comprises the relational data model as well as the core object-oriented modeling concepts of object-oriented programming languages." According to Kim, it thus includes all of the following concepts: *class* (Kim adds "or type"?), *instance, attribute, integrity constraints, object IDs, encapsulation, (multiple) class inheritance, (multiple) ADT inheritance, data of type reference, set-valued attributes, class attributes, class methods,* and more besides.

(By the way, note that relations—which of course we regard as both crucial and fundamental—are never explicitly mentioned. Kim claims that the OMG Core Object Model includes the entire relational model in addition to everything in the foregoing list of concepts, but in fact it does not [127].)

As for Criterion Number 2 ("query language"), Kim's position—again very different from ours, in at least two major ways—is that the language must be some kind of "Object SQL" (i.e., a version of SQL that has been extended to deal with all of the various constructs just listed).

Criteria Numbers 3-6 all have to do with the implementation rather than the model. In other words, they might be important in practice, but they cannot, by definition, make the difference between a system that is object/relational and one that is not. In other words, it is not clear exactly what Kim's metric is supposed to be measuring.

The final criterion ("harnessing the power") constitutes an interesting, and major, point of difference between Kim's position and ours. It is our opinion that user-defined types constitute *the* primary justification for object/relational systems, as explained in Chapter 1. Kim's opinion, by contrast, is that user-defined types are merely a secondary feature (indeed, they have been "oversold"), and they constitute just one aspect of "harnessing the power." (The other, he claims, is the ability of an object/relational DBMS to act as the basis for "heterogeneous database fusion"—i.e., to serve as a unified front end to a variety of disparate databases "including RDBs, OODBs, hierarchical databases, CODASYL databases, and even flat files." But such functionality is properly ascribed to what is more usually called *data access middleware,* not to object/relational DBMSs. See reference [76].)

105.   Donald E. Knuth: *The Art of Computer Programming, Volume 1: Fundamental Algorithms* (3rd edition). Reading, Mass.: Addison-Wesley (1997).

106.   Barbara Liskov and Jeannette Wing: "A Behavioral Notion of Subtyping," *ACM Transactions on Programming Languages and Systems 16,* No. 6 (November 1994).

What we have called *substitutability* in this book is called by some "the Liskov Substitution Principle" (LSP), and this paper is identified—e.g., by reference [123]—as the source of that principle. However, the nearest the paper seems to come to stating any such principle is the following sentence: "[Objects] of the subtype ought to behave the same as those of the supertype as far as anyone or any program using supertype objects can tell." If this statement is intended as a formal definition, it hardly seems very precise. (In any case, some degree of substitutability was included in SIMULA [25], which predated the present paper by nearly 30 years.) *Note:* Reference [73] is, in part, a detailed commentary on this paper.

107.   Mary E. S. Loomis: *Object Databases: The Essentials.* Reading, Mass.: Addison-Wesley (1995).

108.   Claudio L. Lucchesi and Sylvia L. Osborn: "Candidate Keys for Relations," *J. Comp. and Sys. Sciences 17,* No. 2 (1978).

This paper presents an efficient algorithm for inferring candidate keys from functional dependencies.

109.   David Maier: "Comments on the Third-Generation Database System Manifesto," Tech. Report No. CS/E 91-012, Oregon Graduate Center, Beaverton, Ore. (April 1991).

A review and analysis of the proposals of reference [130]. Maier is highly critical of just about everything in that latter document; we agree with some of his criticisms and disagree with others. However, we do find the following remarks interesting (they bear out our contention that objects involve just one good idea—namely, *proper data type support*):

> Many of us in the object-oriented database field have struggled to distill out the essence of "object-orientedness" for a database system ... My own thinking about ... the most important features of OODBs has changed over time. At first I thought [they were] inheritance and the message model. Later I came to think that object identity, support for complex state, and encapsulation of behavior were more important. Recently, after starting to hear from users of OODBMSs about what they most value about those systems, I think that *type extensibility* is the key. Identity, complex state, and encapsulation are still important, but [only] insomuch as they support the creation of new data types.

110.   James Martin and James J. Odell: *Object-Oriented Methods: A Foundation* (2nd edition). Englewood Cliffs, N.J.: Prentice-Hall (1997).

As explained in Appendix F, we believe strongly that specialization by constraint or S by C is the only conceptually valid way to define a subtype (from a regular supertype, at least). Thus, we allow a selector invocation to return a value of most specific type some proper subtype of the specified target type, and we allow an update to some component of a variable (loosely speaking) to have the side effect of changing the current most specific type of that variable up or down or even "sideways." However, we did also note in that appendix that we were at odds with most of the object world over such issues (see, e.g., reference [123]). This book by Martin and Odell (mostly Odell, actually) seems to be one of the few publications from the object world to support our position. Consider the following extracts:

- *Pages 29-30:* [The] collection of concepts that applies to an object can change over time—a phenomenon called *dynamic classification* ... Most OO programming languages [insist that] an object can be an instance of only one ... class for life ... However, in OO analysis, we are not modeling how computer languages and databases work, we are analyzing the enterprise world as people understand it. *Comment:* This extract seems to be agreeing with us that S by C is what is needed in the real world but object systems do not support it.

- *Page 29:* Specifying the method of ... classification changes [*i.e., changes in most specific type*] is a technique at the very heart of OO process specification.

- *Page 128:* A *classification* event is the classification of an existing object. For example, ... a PERSON object [might become] a member of the EMPLOYEE set ... A *declassification* event is the declassification of an existing object. [For example, ...] a PERSON object [might be removed from] ... the EMPLOYEE set—after which the object remains a PERSON, but is no longer an EMPLOYEE. *Comment:* Unfortunately, however, Martin and Odell nowhere address the question of how such "classifications and declassifications" might actually be effected in practice, whereas our model explains these aspects in detail (we even offer some remarks on how they might be implemented). Of course, since their book is really concerned with object analysis and design, not object application programming (database or otherwise), such lack of specificity might perhaps be justified.

Anyway, we are naturally pleased to find that Martin and Odell agree with us regarding S by C. That said, however, we have to say too that we find several other aspects of their book a little puzzling. Here are a few examples:

- *Page 26:* An object is anything to which a concept applies. It is an instance of a type. *Comment:* This definition would certainly seem to suggest that values and variables are both objects. However, the business of values vs. variables is never discussed, although examples of objects in the book certainly include both. *Value* is not in the glossary; *variable* is, but it is defined as "synonymous with *field,*" where a *field* in turn is defined as "an implementation of a property."

- *Page 143:* All operations ... require objects as variables.

- *Page 361:* [An] *argument* [is] ... any object that is a parameter.

- *Page 40:* A ... *relation* ... is a type whose instances are tuples. *Comment:* Quite apart from (a) the fact that a relation *has* a type but *is not* a type and (b) the fact that instances of a relation type are, by definition, relations, not tuples, it is clear that (c) "instances" here means values, whereas such is usually not the case at other places in the book.

- *Page 15 and elsewhere:* The *extension* [of a concept] is the set of all objects to which the concept applies. *Comment:* "All objects" here should probably be taken to mean "all *current* objects." Certainly it is clear that in many places in the book the term *extension* refers to a "time-varying" set (i.e., to a variable). For example (page 386): The extension of the concept MORTAL [is] the collection, or *set,* of things to which the definition applies ... The set of MORTAL objects, therefore is not a fixed collection.

- *Page 354:* [The term] *extension* [is] used interchangeably with *set*. *Page 27:* [A] *set* is a particular collection, or *class*, of objects.

- *Page 27: Class* is technically considered to be the correct word when referring to the collection of objects to which a concept applies ... Some [writers] argue that *set* and *class* mean the same thing. Since *class* has a different meaning in OO programming languages, the word *set* will be used to avoid confusion. It is worth noting, however, that the inspiration for using the term *class* in OO originally came from the centuries-old mathematical notion.

- *Pages 33-35:* [We use] the term *concept* ... to mean a notion or idea that we apply to objects in our awareness ... A recommended term for *concept* in the object-oriented analysis standards community is *type*. Therefore ... the name *type* will be used ... In [the Unified Modeling Language] UML, there is a basic concept called *class*. Here, classes used in analysis are called *types* and classes used for implementation purposes are called *implementation classes*. *Comment:* Regarding UML and (especially) UML terminology, see reference [69].

111. Nelson Mattos and Linda G. DeMichiel: "Recent Design Trade-Offs in SQL3," *ACM SIGMOD Record 23*, No. 4 (December 1994).

This paper is discussed in Appendix F.

112. James D. McCawley: *Everything that Linguists Have Always Wanted to Know about Logic (but were ashamed to ask)*. Chicago, Ill.: University of Chicago Press (1981). *Note:* A second edition of this book was published in 1993.

113. David McGoveran: "Nothing from Nothing" (in four parts), in reference [40].

Part I of this paper explains the crucial role of logic in database systems. Part II shows why that logic must be two-valued logic (2VL) specifically, and why attempts to use three-valued logic (3VL) are misguided. Part III examines the "missing information" problems that 3VL is supposed to solve. Part IV describes a set of pragmatic solutions to those problems that do not involve 3VL.

114. David O. McGoveran: "Accessing and Updating Views and Relations in a Relational Database," US Patent Application 10/114,609 (April 2nd, 2002).

115. Jim Melton: "A Shift in the Landscape (Assessing SQL3's New Object Direction)," *DBP&D 9*, No. 8 (August 1996).

116. Jim Melton: *Advanced SQL:1999—Understanding Object-Relational and Other Advanced Features*. San Francisco, Calif.: Morgan Kaufmann (2003).

117. Jim Melton and Alan R. Simon: *SQL:1999—Understanding Relational Components*. San Francisco, Calif.: Morgan Kaufmann (2002).

118. Bertrand Meyer: "The Many Faces of Inheritance: A Taxonomy of Taxonomy," *IEEE Computer 29*, No. 5 (May 1996).

119. R. Morrison: *S-Algol Reference Manual*, Internal Report CSR-80-81, Dept. of Computer Science,

University of Edinburgh (February 1981).

120.   M. G. Notley: "The Peterlee IS/1 System," IBM U.K. Scientific Centre Report UKSC-0018 (March 1972).

121.   Raymond Reiter: "Towards a Logical Reconstruction of Relational Database Theory," in Michael L. Brodie, John Mylopoulos, and Joachim W. Schmidt (eds.), *On Conceptual Modelling: Perspectives from Artificial Intelligence, Databases, and Programming Languages.* New York, N.Y.: Springer-Verlag (1984).

122.   Mark A. Roth, Henry F. Korth, and Abraham Silberschatz: "Extended Algebra and Calculus for Nested Relational Databases," *ACM TODS 13,* No. 4 (December 1988).

123.   James Rumbaugh: "A Matter of Intent: How to Define Subclasses," *Journal of Object-Oriented Programming* (September 1996).

This paper is briefly discussed in Appendix F, but we add one further comment here. The paper is among the many we have seen that fail to distinguish properly between values and variables. To quote: "Barbara Liskov is responsible for the Liskov Substitution Principle that an instance of a subclass must be substitutable and usable wherever a *variable* [*our italics*] of one of its ancestor classes is allowed. This principle has helped to avoid a lot of confusion in forming class hierarchies and affects most discussions of OO classification." As we saw in Chapter 14, however, there is a logical difference between value substitutability and variable substitutability; the former is applicable 100 percent, but the latter is not.

124.   Cynthia Maro Saracco: *Universal Database Management: A Guide to Object/Relational Technology.* San Francisco, Calif.: Morgan Kaufmann (1999).

A readable high-level overview of object/relational systems. However, we note that Saracco embraces (as does Stonebraker, incidentally, in reference [129], q.v.) a form of inheritance that is based on a version of "subtables and supertables"—a notion that, as explained in Appendix G, we are somewhat skeptical about anyway—that is different from the version espoused by the SQL standard. To be specific, suppose table PGMR ("programmers") is a subtable of supertable EMP ("employees"). Then Saracco and Stonebraker both regard EMP as containing rows only for employees who are not programmers, whereas SQL would regard it as containing rows for all employees.

125.   Robert W. Sebesta: *Concepts of Programming Languages* (6th edition). Boston, Mass.: Addison-Wesley (2004).

126.   Richard T. Snodgrass (ed.): *The TSQL2 Temporal Query Language.* Norwell, Mass.: Kluwer Academic Publishers (1995).

A detailed analysis of the TSQL2 proposals by the present authors can be found at the website *www.thethirdmanifesto.com.*

127.   Richard Mark Soley and William Kent: "The OMG Object Model," in Won Kim (ed.): *Modern Database Systems: The Object Model, Interoperability, and Beyond.* New York, N.Y.: ACM Press / Reading, Mass.: Addison-Wesley (1995).

The ODMG Object Model [17] is based on the "core object model" of the Object Management Group, OMG. OMG (like ODMG) is not a formal standards body, but it "is developing standards in the form of wholesale agreements among member companies" (of which there were "about 340" at the time this paper was written).

The OMG core object model is based on "a small number of basic concepts: objects, operations, types, and subtyping." Note that values and variables are not included in this list; however, the paper does also recognize something it calls *nonobjects,* and gives as examples of "nonobject types" such things as CHAR and BOOLEAN, suggesting that "nonobjects" might perhaps be values (or perhaps a "nonobject type" is just a primitive built-in type?). Moreover, objects are certainly variables, although the term *variable* is not used. But then the paper goes on to say that objects and nonobjects together "represent the set of denotable *values* in the core object model" (our italics).

Objects have object IDs, nonobjects do not. Further, objects have behavior and no user-visible structure: "In the core object model, operations are used to model the external interface to state" (*state* here meaning the object's current value). But the paper then adds, somewhat confusingly, that "*attributes* and *relationships* ... can be used to model the externally visible declarations of state more succinctly."

Another puzzle concerns the distinction between read-only vs. update operators (to use *Third Manifesto* terminology). OMG expressly does not make any such distinction; in fact, it "defines a pass-by-value argument passing semantics," implying that operators are always read-only. However, it clearly also allows operations that produce "side effects, manifested in changes of state." There seems to be a contradiction here.

OMG also draws a distinction between subtyping and inheritance: "*Subtyping* [can be intuitively defined thus:] ... one type is a subtype of another if the first is a specialization or refinement of the second ... if *S* is a subtype of *T*, an object of type *S* may be used wherever an object of type *T* may be used [*note that this definition seems (a) to propose variable substitutability, since it is clear that objects are variables, and (b) not to propose value substitutability, since values are apparently not objects*] ... *Inheritance* is a notational mechanism for defining a type *S* in terms of another type *T* ... Intuitively, *inherit* means that the operations defined for *T* are also defined for ... *S*." So far, the distinction does not seem very clear! Anyway, the paper continues: "Subtyping is a relationship between interfaces (types). Inheritance can apply to both interfaces and implementations; that is, both interfaces and implementations can be inherited. The core object model is concerned with ... interfaces, ... not ... implementations." So why is the distinction even mentioned?

The paper then goes on to say (on the face of it, rather startlingly): "Whether [the set of operations defined for *S*] is a superset of [the set of operations defined for *T*] or the two are disjoint sets is an implementation issue and does not affect the core object model semantics."

It has to be said too that the OMG model of subtyping and/or inheritance—like that of ODMG [17], q.v.—appears to be considerably underspecified. Many of the features of our own inheritance model (see Part IV of this book)—for example, TREAT, the semantics of assignments, the semantics of equality comparisons, notions such as "most specific common supertype," and numerous other aspects—seem to have no counterpart at all.

Finally, objects in OMG, even though they are variables, can never change their type; in particular, they cannot be further specialized, implying that (e.g.) an object of type *employee* can never subsequently acquire the more specific type *manager*. Such restrictions surely constitute grounds for rejecting the frequently heard claims to the effect that objects—at least, OMG-style objects—are "a good model of reality"; as noted by Martin and Odell [110], real-world objects certainly do acquire and lose types dynamically (for example, an employee can certainly become or cease to be a manager).

By the way, the singular nature of the book in which Soley and Kent's paper appears should not go unremarked. Its overall title is *Modern Database Systems*—yet it contains almost nothing on relational theory, which (in our opinion) is certainly relevant to "modern database systems," and will remain so for future ones, too, for as far out as anyone can see. The book in fact consists of two parts: "Next-Generation Database Technology" (512 pages) and "Technology for Interoperating Legacy Databases" (188 pages). Part I in turn consists entirely of a single subpart, "Object-Oriented Database" (Part Ia; there is no Part Ib). In other words, the book subscribes to the position—a position in stark contrast to our own—that object DBMSs are the "next generation"; it therefore also subscribes to the position that we need to deal with the problem of "legacy databases" (by which the book clearly means SQL databases specifically)—a position we might agree with, though we have a different interpretation of what it really means.

128.   Jacob Stein and David Maier: "Concepts in Object-Oriented Data Management," *DBP&D 1*, No. 4 (April 1988).

A good and still useful early tutorial on the basic concepts of object database systems.

129.   Michael Stonebraker and Paul Brown (with Dorothy Moore): *Object-Relational DBMSs: Tracking the Next Great Wave* (2nd edition). San Francisco, Calif.: Morgan Kaufmann (1999).

This book is a tutorial on object/relational systems. It is heavily—in fact, almost exclusively—based on the Universal Data Option of Informix's Dynamic Server product. That Universal Data Option was based on an earlier system called Illustra, a commercial product that Stonebraker himself was instrumental in developing. Regrettably, the book seems nowhere to come right out and agree with our position that (a) a true "object/relational" system would be nothing more nor less than a true relational system, nor that (b) today's "relational" systems are not true relational systems at all, but SQL systems merely.

The book claims that a "good" object/relational DBMS must possess the following four "cornerstone characteristics," with features as indicated:

1.   Base type extension

   - Dynamic linking of user-defined functions
   - Client or server activation of user-defined functions
   - Secure user-defined functions
   - Callback in user-defined functions
   - User-defined access methods
   - Arbitrary-length data types

2.   Complex objects

   - Type constructors
   - User-defined functions
   - Arbitrary-length data types
   - SQL support

3.   Inheritance

   - Data and function inheritance
   - Overloading
   - Inheritance of types, not tables
   - Multiple inheritance

4.   Rule system

- Events and actions are retrieves as well as updates
- Integration of rules with inheritance and type extension
- Rich execution semantics for rules
- No infinite loops

To elaborate:

1.   *Base type extension:* The book uses this term to mean that users must be able to define their own scalar types and operators (it uses the term "functions," however, reserving "operators" for functions like "+" that make use of some special notation; it also—very unfortunately, in our opinion—asserts that "a data type is both information and operations [whereas] the relational notion of a domain includes only the stored representation, and there is no behavior associated with a domain"[1]). *Dynamic linking* is self-explanatory. *Client or server activation* means it must be possible to execute user-defined functions in the same address space as the DBMS (at the server) and also in other address spaces (at the client); moreover, such executions must be *secure*—i.e., they must not be allowed to read or (worse) write anything that is supposed to be protected. (For obvious reasons, this problem is particularly severe if the execution occurs at the server.) *Callback* means that user-defined functions must be allowed to perform database operations. *User-defined access methods* means that type definers or implementers must be permitted to extend the system by introducing new storage structures and corresponding access code. *Arbitrary-length data types* should be self-explanatory.

    Note: The Third Manifesto suggests that function definitions and type definitions are better kept separate instead of being bundled together (OO Very Strong Suggestion 2). The book agrees with this position.

2.   *Complex objects:* The book uses this term to mean that certain type generators—it uses the term "type constructors"—must be supported. (A "complex object" is presumably either a value or a variable of such a generated type.) In particular, the following type generators "must" be supported:

- Composites (records)
- Sets
- References

    Composites correspond, more or less, to our TUPLE type generator (though there seems to be some confusion over whether or not values and variables of the generated type are encapsulated). *Sets* are perhaps self-explanatory (note, however, that the corresponding type generator is not the same as our RELATION type generator). As for *references,* here is a quote: "An object/relational DBMS allows a column in a table to contain ... a [pointer] to a [row] ... in another table ... [The] actual value stored ... is an [object identifier or] OID." Our *Manifesto* categorically prohibits such a state of affairs, of course (see OO Proscription 2, also reference [59]); in fact, we find here, regrettably, a certain amount of confusion over the values vs. variables distinction and the model vs. implementation distinction once again.

    The *user-defined functions* and *arbitrary-length data types* features just mean that

---

1. This claim cannot be correct (if taken literally, "no behavior" implies no operators at all, not even "=").

(of course) generated types are indeed types; hence, users must be able to define functions that operate on values and variables of such generated types, and there must not be any implementation restrictions on the physical size of (the internally encoded versions of) such values and variables.

Last, we agree with the *SQL support* feature, but only as an aid to migration (see the discussion of RM Very Strong Suggestion 8 in Chapter 10).

3.   *Inheritance:* We agree with the need for inheritance. Unfortunately, the book uses this term to refer not to type inheritance as we understand that term, but rather to the business of "subtables and supertables"—a very different notion, as we tried to explain in Appendix G. While we do not necessarily reject that notion, we do claim that it is not type inheritance, and it does not provide the functionality we feel is needed. We also note that the book does not really address the question of an abstract inheritance model, nor does it mention most of the intrinsic complexities that seem to arise with inheritance in general (see Part IV of this book).

For the record, however, we offer a few comments on the features the book lists under its inheritance heading. *Data and function inheritance* means the "subtable" inherits both columns and (user-defined) functions from the "supertable." *Overloading* means polymorphism (but it is indeed, as stated, overloading polymorphism, not inclusion polymorphism). *Inheritance of types, not tables* means—to use the terminology of *The Third Manifesto*—that relation type definitions and relvar definitions are kept separate, and hence that several relvars can be of the same separately and explicitly named relation type. (The *Manifesto* takes the exact opposite approach, for reasons explained in Chapter 3.) *Multiple inheritance* is self-explanatory (at least, the basic idea is—the consequences are not, as we tried to show in Chapter 15).

4.   *Rule system:* We agree that a rule system might well be desirable in practice, but rule systems are (at least arguably) independent of whether the system is object/relational or something else. We therefore choose not to discuss them here.

It is noteworthy that the book nowhere discusses the debate over the equations domain = class vs. relvar = class (see OO Proscription 1). Indeed, the examples tend to suggest that relvar = class is the right equation, though it never comes out to say as much explicitly, and Stonebraker is on record elsewhere as stating that the opposite is the case.

130.   Michael Stonebraker, Lawrence A. Rowe, Bruce G. Lindsay, James Gray, Michael Carey, Michael Brodie, Philip Bernstein, and David Beech: "Third-Generation Database System Manifesto," *ACM SIGMOD Record 19,* No. 3 (September 1990).

In part, this paper is a response to—i.e., counterproposal or rebuttal to—the proposals of reference [2]. We should explain the title. Basically, first-generation database systems are the old hierarchic and network (CODASYL) systems, such as IMS and IDMS; second-generation systems are relational (or at least SQL) systems; and third-generation systems are whatever comes next. A direct quote: "Second-generation systems made a major contribution in two areas, nonprocedural data access and data independence, and these advances must not be compromised by third-generation systems." (We would argue that relational systems made many more than two "major contributions"!) In other words, third-generation systems—whatever else they might do—must certainly support the relational model. Unfortunately, the authors then go on to say that supporting the relational model really means supporting *SQL* ...

The following features are claimed as essential requirements of a third-generation DBMS (we have paraphrased the original somewhat):

1.   Provide traditional database services plus richer object structures and rules

- Rich type system
- Inheritance
- Functions and encapsulation
- Optional system-assigned tuple IDs
- Rules (e.g., integrity rules), not tied to specific objects

2.   Subsume second-generation DBMSs

- Navigation only as a last resort
- Intensional and extensional set definitions (meaning collections that are maintained automatically by the system and collections that are maintained manually by the user, respectively)
- Updatable views
- Clustering, indexes, etc., hidden from the user

3.   Support open systems

- Multiple language support
- Persistence orthogonal to type
- SQL (characterized as "intergalactic dataspeak")
- Queries and results must be the lowest level of client/server communication

Again we offer our own comments and reactions:

1.   *Traditional database services and richer object structures and rules:* Of course we agree with "traditional database services." We also agree with "rich type system" and "inheritance," so long as it is understood that (a) *type* is just another word for *domain,* and (b) the sole use made of such types insofar as the database is concerned is as the domains over which database relvars are defined.[1] "Functions"—we prefer *operators*—are implied by "rich type system." Regarding "encapsulation," see Appendix B. Regarding "tuple IDs," there seems to be some confusion here between tuples and "objects," a point that might be the cause for some alarm; we reject object IDs, of course, but we support the idea of system keys, and such keys might possibly be thought of as (user-visible) "tuple IDs." As for rules: We certainly support integrity rules specifically, of course; further, we do not preclude support for other kinds of rules (though such support might be regarded as a secondary matter).

2.   *Subsume second-generation DBMSs:* If "subsume" here means that the relational model must be subsumed, then we reject the suggestion (but perhaps it does not mean that). "Navigation only as a last resort": We take a firmer stand and reject navigation entirely; we believe it is incumbent on anyone who thinks that navigation is ever necessary to show *first* that a nonnavigational (relational) solution is logically—or at least effectively—impossible. We also reject "extensional set definitions" (in the sense meant here), because the meaning of such a set is hidden in some application instead of being exposed in the database. We agree with support for updatable views. Finally, we also agree that access mechanisms—indexes and the like—should be hidden from the user (they are not always

---

1. And as the types of those database relvars themselves, of course, in the case of relation types.

542 *Appendixes*

hidden in certain object systems, but they were always supposed to be hidden in relational systems).

3. *Support open systems:* We agree with this objective in principle, but we reject the idea of "persistence orthogonal to type," and of course we also reject SQL (we are in this business for the long haul). We do agree with the general sense of "queries and results being the lowest level of client/server communication," but remark that this objective seems to be in conflict with the earlier objectives concerning "extensional set definition" and "navigation."

131. Andrew Taivalsaari: "On the Notion of Inheritance," *ACM Comp. Surv. 28*, No. 3 (September 1996).

132. S. J. P. Todd: "The Peterlee Relational Test Vehicle—A System Overview," *IBM Sys. J. 15*, No. 4 (1976).

The Peterlee Relational Test Vehicle PRTV was an experimental system developed at the IBM U.K. Scientific Centre in Peterlee, England. It was based on an earlier prototype—possibly the very first implementation of Codd's ideas—called IS/1 [120]. It supported an algebraic language called ISBL (Information System Base Language), which was based on proposals documented in reference [98]. The ideas in the *Manifesto* regarding relation type inference can be traced back to ISBL, as well as to the proposals of reference [98].

133. Stephen Todd: Private communication (1988).

134. U.S. Patent and Trademark Office: *Value-Instance-Connectivity Computer-Implemented Database.* U.S. Patent No. 6,009,432 (December 28th, 1999).

135. Andrew Wright: "On Sapphire and Type-Safe Languages," *CACM 46*, No. 4 (April 2003).

A quote from this paper:

> [A] language is said to be "type-safe" [if] its implementation ensures, via some combination of compile- and run-time checks, that the value a variable takes on or a function is passed always matches the language's notion of the variable's or function's type ... Type safety makes program development and debugging easier by making program behavior more understandable. More importantly, type safety prevents an adversary from turning a type violation into a security breach. While an adversary might be able to provide inputs that trigger a run-time check, memory corruption cannot occur. There is no way the adversary can cause a buffer to overflow and be reinterpreted as a sequence of machine instructions.

Comment: It seems a trifle odd to say a *language* is type-safe if its *implementation* has some property; if the language is defined in a way that prohibits type violations, an implementation that permits such violations is surely incorrect. But we certainly agree with the general sense of the extract quoted.

136. Stanley B. Zdonik and David Maier (eds.): *Readings in Object-Oriented Database Systems.* San Francisco, Calif.: Morgan Kaufmann (1990).

137. Stanley B. Zdonik and David Maier: "Fundamentals of Object-Oriented Databases," in reference [136].

INDEX

Index

For alphabetization purposes, (a) punctuation symbols—hyphens, underscores, parentheses, quotation marks, etc.—are ignored; (b) differences in fonts are also ignored; (c) lowercase precedes uppercase; (d) numerals precede letters; (e) blanks precede everything else.